"THE KGB IS THE WORLD'S GREATEST SPY MACHINE

. . . Whole sections of this book read like spy fiction, with secret agents, double agents, writings in invisible ink and parcels of foreign currency left attached to bridges by powerful magnets. Yet this is no fictionalised account of the KGB activity. Every fact has been checked and substantiated . . . Few of the KGB's secrets are left untold in John Barron's remarkable book."

—Noel Barber, **London Daily Mail**

"The most authoritative account of the KGB I have ever seen."

—Ray S. Cline, former Director,
Bureau of Intelligence and Research,
U.S. Department of State

KGB

The Secret Work
of
Soviet Secret Agents

JOHN BARRON

BANTAM BOOKS
TORONTO · NEW YORK · LONDON · SYDNEY

This low-priced Bantam Book
has been completely reset in a type face
designed for easy reading, and was printed
from new plates. It contains the complete
text of the original hard-cover edition.
NOT ONE WORD HAS BEEN OMITTED.

♛

KGB: THE SECRET WORK OF SOVIET SECRET AGENTS
*A Bantam Book / published by arrangement with
Reader's Digest Press*

PRINTING HISTORY
Reader's Digest edition published January 1974
2nd printing ...... January 1974   3rd printing ...... January 1974
4th printing .... April 1974
A selection of the Book-of-the-Month Club and
the Macmillan Book Club July 1974

Portions of this material have appeared in Reader's Digest
in slightly different form

Bantam edition / December 1974
2nd printing .. December 1974   7th printing ...... August 1975
3rd printing ...... January 1975   8th printing ...... August 1976
4th printing .... February 1975   9th printing .... May 1978
5th printing .... February 1975   10th printing .... June 1979
6th printing .... May 1975   11th printing .... June 1981

ISBN 0-553-20254-5

Bantam Books are published by Bantam Books, Inc. Its trademark, consisting of the words "Bantam Books" and the por-
trayal of a bantam, is Registered in U.S. Patent and Trademark
Office and in other countries. Marca Registrada. Bantam
Books, Inc., 666 Fifth Avenue, New York, New York 10103.

PRINTED IN THE UNITED STATES OF AMERICA

20 19 18 17 16 15 14

CONTENTS

INTRODUCTION

by
Robert Conquest

The author has produced a very remarkable book about a very remarkable organization. Much of it consists of a number of vividly told and carefully researched stories of particular KGB actions abroad. Some of these are disastrous failures, being brilliantly countered by the Western intelligence services. In others, extraordinary successes are shown to have been obtained—successes which are a chilling lesson to all citizens of the democratic world.

It is clear that the KGB's foreign operatives may be divided into two distinct classes. First, there are extremely well-trained and highly competent professionals, comparatively few in number. In addition to this corps d'élite, there are a vast mass of diplomats, foreign trade representatives, correspondents of the Soviet news agencies, and so forth—for the actual majority of which categories work for the KGB is the main and major employment. These men are often crude and clumsy. Their training is limited. They owe their positions, as often as not, to family and similar connections. Time and time again, they are caught red-handed and expelled from the country in which they are serving. Yet it must not be thought that their effort is totally unproductive. In the first place, their remarkable numbers may help to swamp the limited Western counterintelligence effort. And then, in the nature of things, they spread the KGB's area of operations over a much wider number of individuals in the target country. They may strike lucky themselves. But in general they should perhaps be regarded as a body of scouts who can draw the attention of more serious operators to the potential sources they discover. The lesson, in any case, is firstly that we should not be too complacent at the failures and the expulsions which can so evidently be chalked up against them. There is nothing in that to imply that more successful operations are not also proceeding. But, secondly, host countries should at least insist (as few do) on restricting the Soviet representation to the numbers required for its true activities— and not accept in Soviet embassies "diplomats" who have already been exposed elsewhere. It is an absurd reflection on the flabbiness of some Western countries that these two obvious points are by no means always observed.

With such measures in hand, we should still be faced by a smaller, but highly competent, set of opponents of our society. These are men not to be underestimated or despised. Granted that ingenuity and courage are qualities which may be used in the service of a bad cause, they may nevertheless extort from us a certain degree of admiration on their own level. The account in Chapter X of the way in which the KGB penetrated the basic secrets of American arms deployment in Europe leaves one, for a number of reasons, shocked and horrified. But viewed simply as an espionage coup, it can only be regarded as a brilliant achievement by the KGB. A weak and unreliable instrument, come more or less into their hands, was utilized to supreme advantage.

But even such coups as that at Orly, however skillfully organized, could not have succeeded but for American lapses of vigilance and failure, even in an extremely secret location, to observe to the letter and on all occasions the rules laid down. For those who guard the West's secrets, no relaxation is possible. For the ordinary citizen not personally involved, at least a realization of the need for these precautions, a rejection of any campaign against the necessities of the situation, are essential. We are in no position to fall in with those superficial arguments which would deny the state the right to guard its security, let alone relax the legal provisions against betraying it.

We read in this book not only about the KGB's espionage and terrorist activities in the noncommunist countries but also of its role at home as an organ of mass repression. The secret battle being waged continuously on our own territory, full of dramatic surprises and revelations, may strike us the more vividly —especially as the author has unearthed such extravagantly interesting tales from the men directly involved in this field. There is indeed an overlap between internal and external operations, in that the KGB works inside Russia to compromise foreigners, as is shown in Chapter VI, either in order to blackmail them into immediate espionage work or with the aim of using them (as "sleepers") to penetrate in later years high into the political and other systems of their home countries.

But it is worth remembering that the major part of the KGB's effort, the greater number of its employees, are used in the massive and continuous work against its own populations. All the same, fundamentally, these are not two separate matters. We in the West are affected every time a Soviet dissident goes to the labor camps. Affected, that is, not only in our principles, but also in our interests. Every blow against the free flow of ideas in and into the U.S.S.R. is in effect a blow against our own ways of thought. But above all, it is a blow against the principles of lasting peace. For, above and beyond all the various temporary causes of international friction, the basic reason for the dangerous and deplorable division of the world is that the Soviet Union conceives itself to be in a state of ideological siege. There can be no lasting peace while a large section of the world is governed on the principle that the mere discussion of heretical or of foreign ideas is a danger against which the huge and pervasive apparatus of the KGB must be deployed, with the aim of crushing it at all costs.

For the system which the KGB operations abroad are designed to strengthen, and in the long run to expand to its furthest limits, has as its most striking characteristic the fact that it is in principle engaged in a permanent struggle not only with the rest of the world but also with its own population. It is, in fact, a police state—in the sense not that the KGB itself dominates the political machinery, but that the basic principle of that political machinery itself is the suppression of all but the most orthodox views and aspirations among the Russians themselves, and among their subject nations. Positive indoctrination has not in more than half a century shown itself effective enough for the regime to admit a competition of ideas. So the element of coercion and repression is the major pillar of the state. The KGB operations abroad are only doing, in one sense, what the secret services of other countries seek to effect—though going a great deal further with actual subversion, guerrilla training, and so forth. But the system these foreign operatives work for is that in which their colleagues of the incomparably larger home branches of the KGB are engaged in preserving a narrow and backward state, where economic failure in the consumer fields is matched by vast overproduction in offensive armaments; where even the most rudimentary liberties are nonexistent; and which thrusts itself forward as a model for the rest of the world.

In giving us the story of the KGB, the author is presenting the activities of the storm troops of a system whose long-term aim is to extirpate our own. We have the power, as most of us have the desire, not to succumb to this intention. Indeed, the weaknesses of the communist system are obvious, and proper policies in the West may lead in the long run to the peaceful erosion of its offensive characteristics. But, both for our immediate defense and for eventual progress to a freer and more peaceable relationship, a vigilant and well-informed citizenry is necessary. This book gives much highly essential information and implies the need for continual vigilance. In fact, it performs an admirable public service, while at the same time being as exciting as a dozen thrillers.

AUTHOR'S PREFACE

Since the Bolshevik Revolution, the Soviet Union frequently has made tactical changes in both its domestic and foreign policies. But the Soviet Union always has been ruled and has sought to rule others in large part through a clandestine apparatus presently known as the Committee for State Security, the Komitet Gosudarstvennoy Bezopasnosti or the KGB. Soviet leaders today employ this clandestine force with less brutality and more sophistication than did Stalin. But the fundamental and extraordinary role of the apparatus in Soviet internal and foreign affairs has not diminished. There is little likelihood that it will diminish in the near future, despite continuing shifts in the currents of international relations.

The idea of publishing a book about the KGB originated with my colleague Kenneth Gilmore in the spring of 1967. He had encountered the KGB in a variety of journalistic assignments, and I had first witnessed its operations while serving as a naval intelligence officer in the 1950s. Both of us long have been fascinated by the unseen influence the KGB exerts upon world affairs. Our studies and assessments during the next twenty months ultimately persuaded us that it is impossible to understand the Soviet Union without understanding the KGB.

In January 1969 Hobart Lewis, then president and executive editor of the *Reader's Digest,* approved the book project we had outlined. He authorized me to travel anywhere, to invest as much time in research as

I judged necessary, and to take maximum advantage of the worldwide research resources of the *Digest*.

There were two primary sources of original data about the KGB: (1) former Soviet citizens who had been KGB officers or agents; (2) security services who know the most about the KGB as a consequence of daily combat with it. We felt we could not rely upon evidence proffered by any one KGB officer or security service in the absence of independent corroboration from other officers or services. Therefore, to acquire means of verifying data and to gain a balanced, multinational perspective, we began soliciting the assistance of security services throughout the noncommunist world. At the same time, we undertook to locate and enlist the cooperation of the former Soviet nationals who had fled to the West with personal knowledge of the KGB.

The late J. Edgar Hoover allowed the Federal Bureau of Investigation to answer many of our questions. Cartha DeLoach, then Assistant to the Director of the FBI, briefed us about significant KGB operations against the United States and permitted us to meet an important former Soviet agent, Kaarlo Tuomi. We also were able to talk to retired FBI agents involved in some of the cases narrated in the book.

The Central Intelligence Agency eventually fulfilled most of our requests for addresses through which we were able to write former KGB personnel and negotiate our own arrangements for interviews. We further profited from the expert counsel of two retired CIA officers, William King Harvey and Peer de Silva.

Thomas D. Fox, who at the time of our research was chief of the counterintelligence department of the U.S. Defense Intelligence Agency, gave us technical guidance and confirmed numerous facts. He additionally read, criticized, and corrected Chapter X.

However, by far the majority of our data has emanated from private individuals occupying no official position or from sources outside the United States. Not all of the foreign security services approached were willing or able to help. But most of them contributed in some measure, and the contributions of several have been immense.

We believe we have interviewed or had access to reports from all postwar KGB defectors except two. Fearful of provoking retaliation against relatives in the Soviet Union, several have insisted upon anonymity. Those who may be thanked publicly are identified in the Acknowledgments on page 587.

Two of the most important former KGB personnel now in the West came to us of their own initiative. One was Yuri Ivanovich Nosenko, a KGB major who escaped to the United States through Switzerland in 1964. Although Nosenko testified in secret before the Warren Commission investigating the assassination of President Kennedy, he subsequently declined to grant any press interviews, and his considerable revelations have remained unknown outside the Western intelligence community. But in May 1970 Nosenko walked unannounced into our Washington offices, stated he had read of our project in the *Reader's Digest,* and offered his assistance. (Later I was told that the KGB long has hunted Nosenko with the intention of killing him. By coming unguarded to our offices, less than four blocks from the Soviet embassy, he created consternation among American authorities responsible for his safety. Nevertheless, we were able to interview Nosenko extensively on numerous occasions.)

On February 1, 1972, I received an unsolicited letter from Vladimir Nikolaevich Sakharov, who identified himself as a former Soviet diplomat and KGB agent. He suggested that he possessed information of possible interest. His story, which is told in Chapter II, proved to be one of the most significant of all.

In most cases, we have succeeded in verifying from security services or other independent sources the essence of information acquired from former KGB personnel. In those cases where a defector is the sole source of given information, we so indicate in the Chapter Notes that explain the basis upon which each chapter is written.

At the outset of our research, we were fortunate enough to engage the services of Katharine Clark, who brought to the project journalistic and linguistic skills developed during a distinguished career as a foreign correspondent. She devised a complex filing system for the storage and retrieval of voluminous data forwarded by *Reader's Digest* offices around the world. Especially notable contributions were made by the European Editorial Office. The foreign offices of the magazine enabled us to monitor publications in thirteen languages and to exploit leads, reportage, and scholarly writings no author possibly could have assembled by himself. The files Mrs. Clark amassed and so skillfully maintained during four years doubtless constitute the largest and richest reservoir of information about the KGB outside of government agencies.

In hope of making the book meaningful and interesting to a lay audience as well as of use to those professionally concerned with the Soviet Union, we have included a number of narratives dramatizing diverse facets of the KGB. Generally the dialogue has been reconstructed from recollections of a participant in the conversations quoted. However, in some instances the dialogue derives from what a source was told of the conversation, and in others it has been extracted from police or security service records of interrogations.

While honoring confidences and protecting the anonymity of certain sources, we nevertheless have tried to state in the Chapter Notes the sources of each passage of the book. Rarely have we relied upon daily press accounts as the primary or sole source of information. However, we frequently have cited newspaper reports in an effort to offer external evidence that a given event did occur or that a given statement was made. I believe the documentation is sufficiently detailed to enable readers to assess the credibility of each section, and I hope it may assist others in future studies of the KGB, which fears nothing so much as illumination.

—JOHN BARRON

Falls Church, Virginia
September 8, 1973

1

INSTRUMENT OF POWER

The KGB is a unique phenomenon of this century. Having no true counterpart, either in history or the contemporary world, it cannot be fully comprehended through analogy with other organizations, or adequately defined by Western terminology. But something of the importance of the KGB can be seen in the void its disappearance would create in the life of the Soviet Union.

Were the KGB to vanish, with it would evaporate the basic means of regulating Soviet thought, speech, and behavior; of controlling the arts, science, religion, education, the press, police, and military. Gone too would be the most effective means of suppressing ethnic minorities, of preventing the flight of Soviet citizens, of keeping watch on individuals, of compelling the whole populace to subserve the interests of the Soviet rulers. The staffs of Soviet embassies all over the world would shrink drastically; in some capitals scarcely any Soviet representatives would remain. The Soviet Union would lose most of its capacity to commit espionage abroad —to subvert public officials; to plot sabotage and assassinations; to foment strikes, demonstrations, and riots; to nurture terrorism and guerrilla warfare; to clandestinely pollute public discourse with misinformation and calumny. It would be largely unable to seek surreptitiously what it has been unable to attain overtly.

Indeed, dismantlement of the KGB would remove the very foundation of Soviet society, a foundation laid by Lenin more than half a century ago. "The scientific concept of dictatorship," Lenin declared in 1920, "means neither more nor less than unlimited power resting directly on force, not limited by anything, nor restrained by any laws or any absolute rules. Nothing else but that." Today the KGB primarily constitutes the force Lenin envisioned: the principal force by which Communist Party chieftains sustain their dictatorship over the Soviet people and try to project it into other societies. Hence, every person affected by the actions of the Soviet Union is affected by the KGB. A few examples of recent KGB activity suggest some of the ways in which it reaches daily into the lives of individuals and nations.

The Serbsky Institute of Forensic Psychiatry in Moscow is housed in an old stone building protected by steel gates and armed sentries. Daniil R. Lunts often arrives at the Institute in the uniform of a KGB colonel, but upon removing his tunic and donning a white coat, he becomes Doctor Lunts.

Colonel-Doctor Lunts directs a "special diagnostic department" that treats Soviet citizens suffering from political nonconformity. To help victims of this malady correct their behavior, the Serbsky Institute, like other Soviet mental hospitals, employs drug therapy as well as more clinically tested medical techniques. Sometimes patients are tightly bound, much like mummies, in wet canvas. As the canvas dries, it slowly contracts and produces excruciating pressure.

Colonel-Doctor Lunts on November 19, 1969, confronted an important yet difficult patient, Major General Petr Grigorevich Grigorenko, holder of the Order of Lenin, two Orders of the Red Banner, the Order of the Red Star, and the Order of the Patriotic War. The general had been arrested on May 7, 1969, after protesting the beating of Crimean Tatars and urging withdrawal of Soviet troops from Czechoslovakia. Psychiatrists in Tashkent found him of sound mind. However, the more discerning Colonel-Doctor Lunts perceived that General Grigorenko suffered from "schizophrenia of the paranoid type." Transferred to the notorious prison mental hospital in Chernyakhovsk, Grigorenko on January 17, 1971, underwent another diagnostic examination.

"Petr Grigorevich, have you changed your convictions?" a Soviet psychiatrist asked.

"Convictions are not like gloves; one cannot easily change them," the general answered.

"The treatment will continue," the doctor announced.

The psychiatric examination having ended, General Grigorenko was led back to his cell in the political ward for further treatment.

At an intersection near the broad Paseo de la Reforma in Mexico City, on October 20, 1971, Oleg Andreevich Shevchenko watched for an American. Parked in a car half a block away, another Russian from the Soviet embassy scanned the intersection, ready to signal Shevchenko if he sensed any danger. But the American failed to appear, and after half an hour Shevchenko left. Doubtless he was disappointed because what the American usually brought was important.

Following a prearranged plan, Shevchenko returned the next afternoon. Again he waited in vain. Two days before, at the airport in Panama City, Florida, Air Force security officers had arrested Sergeant Walter T. Perkins as he started to board a flight to Mexico. Perkins worked in the intelligence section of the Air Defense Weapons Center at Tyndall Air Force Base in Florida, where he had access to top secret documents revealing United States plans for combating Soviet air attack. In his attaché case the security officers found some of these documents. The Air Force on October 22 announced the arrest of Perkins. That same afternoon Shevchenko fled to Cuba.

The KGB arrested Father Juozas Zdebskis in August 1971, accusing him of teaching the catechism to Catholic children in Prienai, Lithuania, in preparation for their first communion. Fearing demonstrations, the authorities tried to keep the date and place of his trial secret. But on the morning of the trial, November 11,

1971, some six hundred men, women, and children gathered before the People's Court in Kaunas, many carrying flowers. As police and KGB plainclothesmen dispersed them, one woman suffered a broken rib, another was knocked unconscious, and others were dragged by their heels to the vans. It was over quickly, although bloodstains and trampled flowers still had to be removed from the courthouse steps.

About ten children were interrogated as witnesses. "What did he teach you?" the procurator asked a girl little more than nine years old.

"Not to steal or break windows," she answered. Several children were too frightened to answer and simply cried.

The procurator summed up his case: "Children get all the teaching they need at school; there is no reason for them to go to church for more. We shall not allow children to be taught anywhere except at school." The sentence: one year in a corrective labor camp for Father Zdebskis. As he was led away, witnesses could see the effects of beatings on his face.

Boris Davidov, a KGB officer using the title of Second Secretary at the Soviet embassy in Washington, invited an American specialist in Sino-Soviet affairs to lunch with him in early August 1969. Although the KGB realized that the American could not be recruited, it still wished to keep in touch with him. For it knew that he was in a position to relay messages to the Secretary of State and, if need be, to the President himself.

That afternoon Davidov came with the kind of chilling question that the Soviet Union could not prudently ask the United States government officially. Broaching the subject of armed clashes along the Soviet-Chinese border, he remarked: "The situation is very serious. In fact, it is so serious that my government may be forced to take much stronger action."

"What kind of action do you envisage?" asked the American. "A preemptive strike?"

Davidov answered with deliberation: "Yes. A preemptive strike is being contemplated, and the use of nuclear weapons is not excluded." Then he put the question the KGB had sent him to relay: "What would be the attitude of the United States government if we made such a strike?"

As the KGB anticipated, the American specialist immediately reported the conversation, and the White House was informed. Analyzing the situation, President Nixon concluded that any answer indicating that the United States would remain aloof could only strengthen those in the Soviet Union advocating a surprise nuclear attack on China. Conversely, a suggestion that the United States might intervene in a war between the Soviet Union and China could be interpreted by others in the Kremlin as a threat and an argument against improved relations with the West. Any answer at all could be misrepresented to the Chinese as evidence that the United States was conniving with the Russians against them. Accordingly, President Nixon ordered that no response whatsoever be made to this or any similar subsequent Soviet inquiry.

Valeri Panov is a premier dancer whose performances with the Kirov Ballet Company in Leningrad have earned him state honors and international plaudits. Panov also is a Jew. On March 21, 1972, he expressed a desire to emigrate to Israel, and asked his ballet union for the character references that must accompany any emigration application. The state-controlled union eighteen days later denounced him as a traitor and ousted him from membership, thereby abrogating his right to dance for the Soviet public. The ballet company then demoted his wife, the beautiful young ballerina Galina Rogozina, and cut her salary.

Walking along the street on May 26, Panov was halted by two militiamen who accused him of spitting. Convicted of "hooliganism," he was taken to a Leningrad jail for political prisoners and locked in a cell crowded with amputees, cripples, and invalids on crutches. Panov understood the KGB message—he too could be crippled. He was released on June 5, but five days later two plainclothesmen and a militiaman trailed him along the street and again accused him of spitting. He was jailed for fifteen more days.

Money sent by artists in the West to help him was intercepted, and Panov was left destitute. Many former friends shun him and hang up when he telephones. Although the state, through the union, has barred Panov from pursuing the only profession he knows, the authorities have threatened to imprison him for being unemployed. One loyal friend wrote in a letter to the West: "The great dancer, the most highly decorated artist of the Soviet Union ever to ask to leave, is being transformed into a desperate, cornered animal."

Slowly trawling for salmon in the Baltic, some forty miles off the coast of Sweden, the Danish cutter *Windy Luck* on September 8, 1972, was overtaken by a motorboat. The lone occupant, a haggard and fearful middle-aged man, shouted alternately in broken English and German, pleading for assurances that the *Windy Luck* was not "communistic." Then he yelled that he was a Soviet defector.

The skippers of the cutter, Arne and Borge Larsen, together with their crew, helped the refugee aboard and took the motorboat in tow. The man was exhausted from exposure in the open sea, and they could not understand his name or all he said. But they gathered that he was a native of Lithuania or Estonia who, before Soviet seizure of these Baltic nations, had sailed with a Scandinavian shipping line. He evidently had long planned his escape, hoarding what he thought would be enough food and gasoline to reach Sweden. Because of headwinds and adverse seas, however, his food was gone, and he had only a few gallons of gas left when he spotted the *Windy Luck*. When the Danes assured him that land and freedom were only hours away, his face conveyed relief and gratitude.

Altering course for Sweden, the Larsens saw a warship bearing down on them at high speed. It flew a green ensign with a hammer and sickle, a flag denoting that it belonged to the KGB rather than the regular navy. The Soviet ship drew alongside, and an officer with a megaphone commanded the *Windy Luck* to heave to. Courageously the Danes ignored the order and sailed on until the warship brushed against the stern and Soviet sailors on deck manned machine guns. Although they were in international waters, far from Soviet jurisdiction, the Danes had no choice but to submit. Soviet officers with revolvers climbed aboard and demanded to search the ship. Arne Larsen tried to block entry to the cabin where the defector hid, but a Soviet officer shoved him aside, saying, "I give the orders here." The Larsens claimed that the defector was a member of their crew and that the drifting motorboat was empty when they picked it up. Then Soviet officers searching the motorboat discovered the defector's passport. As the Russians threw him into a boat, the captured man called out to the Danes, *"Auf Wiedersehen."*

Twenty-two days later at four in the afternoon, the Danish cutter *Thomas Moeller* lay off the Swedish island of Gotland, putting out salmon nets. The sun still shone brightly, and the sea was calm. Soon a large Soviet ship appeared in the distance and rapidly closed the *Thomas Moeller* on a collision course. The Danish captain sounded international warning signals and changed course. But the Soviet ship, with four officers standing impassively on the bridge, plowed onward and rammed the stern of the *Thomas Moeller*. The Danish craft shook and heeled over, miraculously sliding along the side of the attacking ship instead of breaking up. Without a word or signal, the Soviet ship ripped through the salmon nets and sailed away. The collision, members of a Danish court of inquiry later surmised, was a warning to Danish fishermen not to assist future defectors found at sea.

Lawyers and businessmen from many nations assembled at Cannes, France, on April 23, 1972. They belonged to the International Association for the Protection of Industrial Property, an organization dedicated to the preservation of patents and trademarks. The

Russian delegate to the convention was Yevgenni Petrovich Pitovranov, senior vice president of the Soviet Chamber of Commerce.

Western businessmen found Pitovranov an engaging companion. A tall, scholarly-looking man of fifty-seven, he was poised and at ease speaking to them in fluent English, French, or German. He raised exciting prospects of lucrative trade opportunities, and his manner tended to belie apprehensions about the difficulty of doing business with the Russians. A facile conversationalist, he flattered people with questions connoting a genuine interest in their ambitions, problems, families, and circumstances. The Westerners understandably were impressed by Pitovranov, and they undoubtedly would have been even more impressed had they known his real identity.

Educated as an engineer, Pitovranov joined the secret political police in 1938 and emerged from World War II as a highly decorated major general. He directed repressions against the Soviet people from 1946 until August 1951, when he was imprisoned as a consequence of Kremlin intrigues. Georgi Malenkov helped restore him to favor, and in 1952 he was placed in charge of clandestine Soviet operations against foreign countries. But his talents were so great that the KGB decided to employ him as a master troubleshooter, sending him wherever its needs were most acute. He supervised espionage and kidnappings out of East Berlin from 1953 to 1958, then served as KGB Resident* in Peking before becoming director of KGB schools. Contemplating the opportunities for subversion promised by increasing trade with the West, the Politburo in the late 1960s assigned him to the Chamber of Commerce. Ever since, he has shown up at trade fairs and conventions, such as that at Cannes.

General Pitovranov is a keen and merciless hunter. He once startled colleagues by proposing to hunt wild boar at night using rifles equipped with infrared sights. At Cannes, he had his eye on other game.

---

*The Soviet term is *Rezident*, which denotes the senior KGB officer in charge of operations in a given foreign city or area.

With a special radio monitor, a security officer was making a routine electronic check of the U.S. embassy in Bucharest one March morning in 1969 when he heard two familiar voices frankly talking business. To his consternation, he recognized that one of the voices being broadcast was that of a senior diplomat at the embassy. The security officer rushed into the diplomat's office and handed him a note: "Walk out of the office and keep talking, but watch what you say. You are on the air."

Even after they moved into another room, the diplomat's words continued to be broadcast. Now the security officer knew that a transmitter had been planted somewhere in his belongings or clothing. Yet a minute search yielded nothing, and everything the diplomat said still was being broadcast. Finally, the officer signaled him to take off his shoes. Weighing and examining them, he ripped apart the heel of the left shoe. There it was.

An embassy maid a few days before had taken the shoes for repair. During the "repairs," the heel was hollowed out and fitted with a powerful transmitter weighing less than two ounces. A tiny hole provided the necessary outlet for a microphone. An equally small hole contained a pin. By moving it, the maid was able to turn the transmitter off at night and back on in the morning.

Except for the routine check, the American diplomat would have gone about indefinitely, broadcasting everything he and others around him were saying.

These events in Moscow, Mexico City, Florida, Lithuania, Washington, Leningrad, on the Baltic, and at Cannes and Bucharest represent routine KGB operations that are duplicated, day in and day out, throughout the world. Some, of course, are more dramatic and produce far greater consequences. But all are undertaken for the same basic purpose. In everything it does, within the Soviet Union and without, the KGB thinks of itself as being the "Sword and Shield of the Party," and this is probably its best single definition. For the KGB serves not so much the Soviet state as the Communist

Party and, more particularly, the small coterie of men who control the Party. It is the sword by which Party rulers enforce their will, the shield that protects them from opposition. The characteristics of the KGB which distinguish it from other clandestine organizations, past and present, all derive from the inordinate dependency of the Party oligarchy on the force and protection it provides. Because preservation of their power depends so on the KGB, the Soviet leaders have vested it with resources, responsibilities, and authority never before concentrated in a single organization.

There are flickering signs that certain Soviet leaders may not be entirely pleased with the apparatus they have created. Certainly the KGB is bloated, overstaffed, overly centralized, overly bureaucratic, and frequently inefficient to a degree that would be intolerable in free nations. Should a Western intelligence service ever suffer defections and penetrations comparable to those sustained by the KGB in recent years, an outraged press and electorate doubtless would demand its dismemberment.

KGB blunders frequently have had consequences damaging to the Soviet Union or dangerous to the world. A vengeful KGB act in 1964 sabotaged an important Soviet diplomatic initiative and probably facilitated the ouster of Nikita S. Khrushchev. Realizing that he was in great political difficulty, Khrushchev hoped to rescue himself and the faltering Soviet economy by concluding a major trade agreement with West Germany. He made the necessary private overtures, and in early September the Russians let it be known that he was willing to visit Bonn.

That same week, a skilled German technician, Horst Schwirkmann, came to Moscow to cleanse the West German embassy of KGB microphones. Whenever he uncovered one, Schwirkmann impressed immense voltage into it, administering painful shocks to those listening. But he most angered the KGB by discovering an ingenious electronic device it secretly had attached to a special machine at the embassy. The machine automatically enciphered typed messages and transmitted them by teletype to Bonn, but the affixed device broadcast the messages as they were typed and before they were enciphered. Thus for some time, the KGB had been able to read sensitive communications from the embassy. More important, by comparing the unenciphered messages with the enciphered versions, which were easily intercepted from the teletype, the KGB was able to analyze and probably break whole cipher systems.

The KGB avenged its losses on Sunday morning, September 6. While admiring religious relics at the Zagorsk Monastery outside Moscow, Schwirkmann suddenly felt excruciating pain in his buttocks. Physicians at the American embassy determined he had been shot with a nitrogen mustard gas that was eating away his flesh. Although the physicians saved Schwirkmann's life, his recuperation was long and agonizing.

An outraged West German government announced there would be no invitation to Khrushchev until the Schwirkmann case was satisfactorily resolved. The Soviet apology tendered October 13 came too late. That very day, Khrushchev was called back from vacation to Moscow and dismissed by the oligarchy. Whether his projected journey to Bonn would have kept him in power is a matter of conjecture. It is clear, however, that the KGB atrocity destroyed whatever chances the Soviet Union had at that time of achieving much-needed commercial relations with West Germany.

Considerable evidence indicates that KGB mistakes may well have caused the 1967 Arab-Israeli war. In its estimates to the Politburo, the KGB grossly miscalculated the will and ability of Israel to fight once its existence was threatened. Believing that Israel would make humiliating concessions beneficial to Soviet prestige, the KGB urged a policy of belligerency upon the late Egyptian President Gamal Abdel Nasser. It circulated false reports that Israel was massing forces to attack Syria, which Egypt was bound to defend. Both directly and through agents, it persuaded Nasser that even should Israel fight, the Arabs could win a war of attrition. In addition, there are now substantial signs that the KGB may have learned in advance of the Israeli attack plans but withheld this supremely vital intelligence either deliberately or through bureaucratic sloth.*

Nevertheless, the Kremlin continues to rely upon the KGB because it has devised no alternative means of ruling the Soviet people, and it remains wedded to a foreign policy that must be pursued in large part through clandestine methods. Whenever Soviet ambitions are frustrated abroad, the leadership increases the range and tempo of KGB operations. Whenever substantial dissent arises at home, it intensifies KGB repressions of the Soviet people.

The fundamental attitude of the oligarchy toward the people is faithfully reflected in the continuing Soviet glorification of one Pavlik Morozov, who lost his life in 1932 at the age of fourteen. The Soviet Union erected a statue in 1965 to honor Pavlik. The Palace of Culture of the Red Pioneers in Moscow is named after him. Komsomol, the youth organization of the Communist Party, teaches Soviet youth that the life and deeds of Pavlik Morozov represent an ideal to which every worthy citizen should aspire.

Pavlik became a Hero of the Soviet Union during the collectivization and dispossession of some ten million peasants. The more prosperous peasants, derisively termed kulaks, were slaughtered or deported to concentration camps by the secret political police. In the village of Gerasimovka, Pavlik's father, an otherwise loyal communist, gave refuge to some fleeing kulaks. Pavlik, recognizing his duty to Soviet society, informed on his father, who was summarily shot. Enraged peasants thereupon lynched Pavlik.

Today the Soviet Union maintains the house where the son betrayed the father as a communist shrine, and the press refers to it as "sacred and dear." Wrote *Komsomolskaya Pravda:* "In this timbered house was held the court at which Pavlik unmasked his father who had sheltered the kulaks. Here are reliquaries dear to the heart of every inhabitant of Gerasimovka."

As enshrinement of a child who betrays his father suggests, Soviet rulers of the 1970s are as obsessed as

---

*See Chapter II, pages 69 and 73.

any of their predecessors with the necessity of watching and controlling all citizens. Accordingly, the KGB has constructed a vast informant network that reaches into every crevice of society, from the Red Army General Staff down to the most humble village. At every strategic juncture—in all functions of society critical to the Party oligarchy—there stands the KGB, watching and controlling.

KGB officers guard the persons, families, homes, and offices of Party rulers. KGB signal troops maintain and safeguard the special electronic and telephone circuits over which members of the oligarchy communicate with one another. Until the late 1960s, when the military finally persuaded the leadership that it would be impractical to use atomic weapons in a future internal struggle, the KGB even retained custody of nuclear warheads.

The KGB watches all 41,595 miles of the Soviet Union's land and sea frontiers. According to a training manual used at the Higher Border Guards School, KGB patrols in 1965 captured more than two thousand people attempting to escape. And various Soviet statutes make people caught in unlawful flight liable to penalties ranging from a year's imprisonment to death.

The KGB watches the economy, investigating economic crimes such as "incorrect planning," "disorganization of production," unauthorized private enterprise, black marketeering, and currency speculation. Economic criminals caught by the KGB are sometimes denounced as saboteurs and treated sternly. The director and the manager of the restaurant at the Sverdlovsk railroad station, for example, together invented a machine to fry meat and pies. It required less than the amount of fat officially stipulated, and for a while the two conspirators pocketed savings of about four hundred rubles a month. Their crime discovered, both were sentenced to death in 1963.*

---

*Between 1961 and 1964 the Soviet press revealed the shooting of at least three hundred people found guilty of economic crimes. Since 1964 the press generally has not announced such executions, but recent ominous warnings to the population suggest that they are continuing.

Through its informant network the KGB attempts to divine the private attitudes of the populace. On occasion its officers themselves sample public opinion to gauge reaction to significant events. Hours after the assassination of President Kennedy, the KGB sent hundreds of officers in Moscow out to question friends and acquaintances. One of these KGB pollsters, Yuri Loginov, who was arrested in 1967 while on an illegal mission through South Africa, recalled: "Everybody was excited, and the Party wasn't sure what line to give the people. . . . Well, all the people my friends and I talked to seemed to feel about the same. They were shocked and sorry Kennedy was killed, and that is what we reported." The author Andrei Amalrik, imprisoned in a Siberian concentration camp in 1970 for "disseminating falsehoods derogatory to the Soviet state and social system," has noted: "The KGB, of course, supplies the bureaucratic elite with information, gathered by its special means, about popular feelings in the country. This information obviously differs from the picture drawn daily in the newspapers. It is, incidentally, paradoxical that the regime should devote enormous effort to keep everyone from talking and then waste further effort to learn what people are talking about and what they want."

The KGB stations its officers in important positions throughout the Soviet bureaucracy and within the Party hierarchy itself. The KGB today probably has more officers and alumni in positions of power than at any time in Soviet history. Ultimate power in the Soviet Union is centralized in the Politburo and the Secretariat of the Party's Central Committee. KGB Chairman Yuri V. Andropov in April 1973 became the first state security chief since Lavrenti Beria to gain full membership in the Politburo. During the Stalin era, the Politburo usually included no more than one man with personal ties to the state security apparatus. But of the seventeen members who formed the Politburo in 1973, three—Andropov, Aleksandr N. Shelepin, and Arvid Y. Pelshe—have spent significant portions of their careers in the apparatus. A fourth Politburo member, Kirill T. Mazurov, directed partisan forces of the secret police during World War II.

Shelepin, KGB chairman from 1958 to 1961, additionally heads the Soviet trade-union organization, which exists to regiment workers at home and subvert labor movements abroad. Three of Andropov's KGB deputies belong to the Central Committee of the Communist Party of the Soviet Union, as does former KGB General Aleksandr Panyushkin. A former ambassador to the United States and China, Panyushkin helped plan KGB assassinations in the 1950s. He currently chairs the Central Committee panel that determines which Party members and scientists may travel abroad. Two judges of the Soviet Supreme Court, Sergei Bannikov and Nikolai Chestyakov, are former KGB generals well equipped to review the cases of people arrested by their KGB colleagues.

The director of the propaganda agency Novosti, Ivan Ivanovich Udaltsov, is a KGB officer who, as minister counselor in Prague, participated in preparations for the Soviet invasion of Czechoslovakia. An entire division of Novosti, known as the Tenth Section, is staffed with KGB men, one of whom is the noted British traitor Harold A. R. ("Kim") Philby. KGB personnel also permeate the Council for Affairs of Religious Sects, the State Scientific and Technical Committee, the Committee for Youth Organizations, and the Red Cross and Red Crescent Societies. Intourist is a virtual fiefdom of the KGB. The Ministry of Foreign Trade, the Chamber of Commerce, and all other agencies that deal extensively with foreigners in the Soviet Union are peopled with KGB agents.

Indeed, it is difficult for a foreigner in the Soviet Union ever to escape the shadow of the KGB. Although the outright xenophobia of Stalin's time has faded, the leadership still looks upon foreigners as carriers of contaminating ideas threatening to the regime. The KGB continuously spies upon foreigners visiting or living in the Soviet Union, endeavoring to deny them normal contacts with the people and often trying to compromise or suborn them. It also keeps the diplomatic community in Moscow under remorseless clandestine siege. Western security services now know that over the years the KGB, in one form or another, has penetrated every major embassy in Moscow. Professional KGB burglars have broken into many embassies. In each, technicians opened and photographed the contents of safes, sometimes using specially designed radioactive devices to reveal the combinations. Although the loot from all these raids cannot be precisely catalogued, it is known that one KGB foray yielded the Soviet Union Japan's diplomatic cipher systems. The KGB in the early 1960s also obtained Canadian ciphers from an embassy code clerk recruited by a seductress named Larissa Fedorovna Dubanova.

Many details of embassy burglaries were provided by KGB Major Yuri Ivanovich Nosenko after he fled to the United States through Switzerland in 1964. According to Nosenko, each raid required prior approval from the Party secretary; that is, each had to be personally authorized by Stalin or Khrushchev. Some entries were accomplished with relative ease through the assistance of embassy staff members recruited by the KGB. Others were difficult, risky operations usually planned over a period of months, with the precision of a military invasion. Nosenko cites the penetration of the Swedish embassy as an example of the more complicated type of operation.

It commenced with the seduction of an embassy watchman by a female agent who engaged him in regular evening trysts when he was supposed to be on duty. To neutralize a huge and ferocious watchdog, the KGB sent an officer to the embassy grounds two or three nights a week to feed him choice cuts of meat. The KGB scheduled the raid on a night when most of the embassy staff had been invited to a party. Surveillance teams and telephone monitors tracked the movements of all Swedes in Moscow starting that afternoon. Squads parked at street intersections surrounding the embassy under orders to ram any Swedish car that approached. While the female agent diverted the watchman and an officer plied the dog with meat, the KGB team of a dozen or so men unlocked the embassy door and headed for the safes. The locksmiths, photographers, and specialists in opening sealed documents emerged in about an hour, their work done and undetected. The dog caused the only slight difficulty. The officer feeding him kept calling for more meat, complaining, "This dog is eating by the kilo."

Nosenko pinpointed for the State Department the location of forty-four microphones built into the walls of the American embassy when it was constructed in 1952. They were outfitted with covers that shielded them from electronic sweeps periodically made by U.S. security officers. American diplomats, of course, were instructed to be guarded in their talk because of the possibility of undetected listening devices. Nevertheless, the everyday conversations the microphones relayed for twelve years told the KGB much about what the embassy was reporting to Washington as well as about U.S. interests, concerns, and reactions to international events.

While apprehensive about alien ideas that foreigners may introduce, the leadership also fears propagation of dissident ideas by Soviet intellectuals whose access to the people is not so easily interdicted. Accordingly, the KGB infests the arts and sciences with officers and informants in an effort to police thought and creativity among the intelligentsia. The secretary of the Soviet Writers' Union from 1946 to 1956, Aleksandr Aleksandrovich Fadeyev, was a notorious collaborator who consigned at least six hundred intellectuals to concentration camps. After Khrushchev confirmed Stalin's mass murder and enslavement of innocent people, some of Fadeyev's surviving victims were rehabilitated and appeared in Moscow. Haunted by the reincarnation of men he had doomed, Fadeyev shot himself in 1956. He stated in his suicide note that he no longer could bear life in the Soviet Union. In September 1972 the Central Committee announced the appointment of Aleksei V. Romanov as editor of *Soviet Culture,* the Party publication that tells intellectuals what they are supposed to think. Romanov is the informant who caused the imprisonment of the author Aleksandr Solzhenitsyn back in 1945. Other methods by which the KGB seeks to compel conformity among the intelligentsia can be seen by contrasting the fates of two Soviet writers, one an old ally of the secret political police, the other a passionate young idealist.

The old writer is Mikhail Sholokhov, the 1965 Nobel Prize laureate, presumed author* of *The Quiet Don* and the one Soviet author with an international reputation on whom the Party can always count. When no other literary figure of stature will denounce a Solzhenitsyn or dissident Soviet artists, Sholokhov steps forward to do the job. In 1966 he applauded the imprisonment of writers Yuli Daniel and Andrei Sinyavsky. "If these young people with black consciences had lived in the memorable 1920s," said Sholokhov, "when people were judged not in law courts but by revolutionary tribunals—oh, what a different punishment would have been handed the accused! Yet here they speak of severity of the sentence." The next year Sholokhov scorned Soviet authors asking for freedom of the press, calling them "uninvited cheerleaders, who include the CIA of the United States of America." Quoting Lenin, he added, "We laugh at pure democracy." Sholokhov, the defender of KGB repression, lives luxuriously in a Moscow apartment and country dacha, favored and protected by the KGB.

As Sholokhov continued the debasement of fellow writers, a young poet, Yuri Timofeevich Galanskov, dared to challenge him in a signed declaration: "Sholokhov is not interested in truth. It was necessary for him to accuse Sinyavsky and Daniel of treason and slander. Why? Probably because the State Prosecutor did not have the moral authority to do so. And thus having thrown on the scale the full weight of his authority, the Nobel Prize laureate delivered his shameful 'speech for the prosecution.' . . . You, Citizen Sholokhov, are no longer a writer. Once you were an average novelist, but you have long since ceased to be even that; now you are an ordinary political demagogue.

---

*The possibility that Sholokhov's reputation rested on plagiarism is discussed in Chapter V, pages 145–7.

. . . People like you have no support in society except the machinery of the state."

Shortly afterward the KGB arrested Galanskov for anti-Soviet activity, and in January 1968 he was sentenced to seven years at hard labor. His lawyer at the trial submitted medical evidence that he suffered seriously and painfully from an ulcer. His mother came to Potma Camp 17A with a jar of honey, and he told her he was in great pain. Confiscating the honey, a camp official said, "He's not sick." A camp doctor remarked: "He's just a hooligan who shirks his work. There is nothing the matter with him. He's a poet, and he thinks too much of himself." To each plea from the family for medical help, the authorities replied that Galanskov was perfectly well. Friends in Moscow beseeched the poet Yevgenni Yevtushenko to intercede to obtain medical care, but he was too busy preparing for a trip to Chile to help. Galanskov suffered a perforated ulcer, and on October 18, 1972, a fellow inmate, a doctor untrained in surgery, operated. Peritonitis resulted, yet the authorities rejected new pleas that Galanskov be transferred to a civilian hospital. He died in the camp on November 4, at the age of thirty-three.

While ideas of freedom cumulatively are dangerous to the dictatorship, the guns of the Soviet military, if ever misdirected, could be immediately fatal. The military does possess the physical wherewithal to depose the oligarchy and wrest control of the country. So it is the military that the KGB watches most intensely of all.

One of the largest and most vital components of the KGB is the Armed Forces Directorate. It is divided into twelve major departments that oversee the Ministry of Defense and General Staff, the GRU,* conventional

---

*The GRU, Glavnoye Razvedyvatelnoye Upravleniye, is the Chief Intelligence Directorate of the Soviet General Staff. Although a separate organization, the GRU, in the opinion of the writer, functions essentially as an appendage of the KGB. Its history, operations, and relationship to the KGB are discussed in Appendix B.

ground forces, naval forces, air forces, border troops (of the KGB), the militia and internal troops under the Ministry of Internal Affairs, missile forces, nuclear forces, civil aviation, and the Moscow military district. Officers from the Directorate are emplaced at every echelon of the Soviet armed forces down to the company level, in each military district, with every naval group, at each military front. Although they wear military uniforms, KGB officers report through their own chain of command to KGB headquarters and are exempt from military orders when they choose to be. Typically, the KGB officer directs a net of informants among the military personnel of the unit to which he is assigned and additionally enlists civilian informants in the vicinity of his base. Thus, the entire Soviet armed forces are honeycombed with KGB spies who continuously provide the Party with an ideological appraisal of individual officers as well as a political evaluation of individual units.

In a study prepared for a private research corporation, Colonel James T. Reitz, a retired U.S. Army intelligence officer, writes that much of the KGB's time "is spent in the eradication of real or imagined anti-Soviet activity or thought and behavior among Soviet military personnel. . . . Anti-Soviet activity or thought encompasses a wide range of activity from poor training, slovenly appearance, griping, poor supply practices, negligence, waste and shortages. . . . The innate suspicion is apparent in the situation of any luckless pilot who happens to crash or parachutes from an airplane and then undergoes interminable grilling to prove himself not guilty of sabotage. . . . No one who falls into their hands [the KGB's] receives any different treatment because of his rank, decorations or honorable service or any other reason."

The slightest evidence of ideological deviation among the military can provoke swift KGB retribution. KGB officers in 1968, for example, searched the apartment of Major Genrikh Altunyan, a decorated army officer who was an instructor at a military academy in Kharkov. They found typewritten copies of Solzhenitsyn's *Cancer Ward* and the *Chronicle of Current*

*Events.** Major Altunyan successively was ousted from the Party, dismissed from the army, and sentenced to three years in a labor camp for anti-Soviet activity.

In May 1969 three Soviet naval officers, Gennadi Vladimirovich Gavrilov, Georgi Konstantinovich Paramonov, and Aleksei Vasilevich Kosyrev, were arrested for founding a "Union to Struggle for Political Rights." Investigating them, the KGB uncovered copies of the United Nations declaration of Human Rights and two poems entitled "Dream on Freedom" and "On the Death of Kennedy." Gavrilov was sentenced to six years' imprisonment and Kosyrev to two years. Paramonov was sent to a KGB mental hospital.

During the summer of 1969, the KGB arrested thirty-one more naval personnel stationed in Estonia, possibly because they criticized the invasion of Czechoslovakia. During the invasion, some Soviet soldiers disobeyed orders after being influenced by face-to-face appeals from the Czechoslovakian citizenry. According to reports received by Western newsmen in Moscow, the KGB confined these recalcitrant troops to mental hospitals.

Military officers resented and continued to resent spies in their midst, and, according to Colonel Reitz, during World War II they sometimes murdered them as opportunity arose. However, short of a catastrophic war or comparable upheaval, there appears to be virtually no possibility that the Soviet military will assert itself against the KGB and the Party. Together they can almost certainly identify and purge incipient opposition within the military before it coalesces into a substantial threat.

The same may be said for all other institutions of Soviet society. Wherever opposition is discerned, the

---

*The *Chronicle of Current Events* was the most celebrated of the underground publications that have circulated in the Soviet Union in recent years. Between 1968 and November 1972, twenty-seven bimonthly issues appeared more or less on schedule. They were promulgated by *samizdat*, or self-publishing, wherein the recipient of a banned work types copies and passes them on to friends.

The *Chronicle* was distinguished by objectivity and efforts at accuracy. It reported, sometimes in surprising detail, activities of the civil-rights movement and various KGB oppressions.

Party oligarchy instinctively reacts to crush it. In obedience to a Party command, the KGB in 1970 organized a huge new division, the Fifth Chief Directorate, to annihilate intellectual dissent, stop the upsurge in religious faith, suppress nationalism among ethnic minorities, and silence the *Chronicle of Current Events*. In 1971 the KGB established a special Jewish Department at the Center and Jewish sections in some of the larger KGB field offices. The Central Committee specifically instructed the KGB to intensify infiltration of agents into Jewish circles, to discourage emigration of educated Jews, and to silence Jewish protests.

Viewing the resurgent KGB repression, Andrei Dmitrevich Sakharov, perhaps the Soviet Union's greatest nuclear physicist, in June 1972 wrote the Central Committee: "With hurt and alarm I am forced to note, in the wake of illusory liberalism, the growth of restrictions on ideological freedom, of striving to suppress information not controlled by the government, of persecution for political and ideological reasons, of an international exacerbation of national [minority] problems.

"The wave of political arrests in the first months of 1972 is particularly alarming. . . . The use of psychiatry for political purposes is extraordinarily dangerous in its consequences for society and completely intolerable. . . . The persecution and destruction of religion has been conducted with persistence and cruelty. . . ."

Those persecuted by the specific repressions Sakharov mentions, those tortured in the mental institutions and suffering in the concentration camps, are not the only or indeed the most numerous victims of the KGB. For its victims include all Soviet people, who must live in fear and mistrust of each other. No one has better summed up the effects of the KGB on daily Soviet life than the gifted Russian author Anatoli Kuznetsov. Upon fleeing to Great Britain in 1969, he wrote: "Everybody knows that the number of people murdered by the secret police runs into many millions. But when we come to reckon the number of people who are terrorized and deformed by them, then we have to include the whole population of the Soviet Union."

In Soviet dealings with the rest of the world, the KGB is, if possible, even more omnipresent than in Soviet domestic life. The Ministry of Foreign Affairs, the military, the press, and technical and economic aid programs all contribute to implementation of foreign policy formulated by the Politburo. But the KGB is the primary executor of foreign policy, and this primacy shows up starkly in virtually all Soviet representation abroad. It is particularly evident in Soviet embassies.

Officers of the KGB and its military subsidiary, the GRU, ordinarily occupy a majority of embassy posts, composing as much as eighty percent of the staff in some third-world countries. According to the FBI, in Washington the ratio of Soviet representatives with clandestine assignments remains above 50 percent, and it doubtless would be higher were not the KGB able to utilize New York and Mexico City as major bases of operations against the United States. Additionally, in any embassy, the KGB can commandeer the services of Ministry of Foreign Affairs personnel. Many men who leave Moscow as bona fide diplomats are forced once abroad to work almost full time for the KGB. These co-opted agents, as they are called, often become more important operatives than the average professional intelligence officer.

Even some Soviet ambassadors are KGB officers. Pavl Stepanovich Kuznetsov, who was appointed ambassador to Indonesia in 1972, is an undisguised veteran of espionage. The British expelled him from London in 1952 for spying. In the mid-1960s he directed a KGB network in Yugoslavia that planted microphones in Marshal Tito's office. KGB officer Nikolai Andreevich Belous, ousted from Argentina after he incited and participated in a street riot that caused the burning of twenty automobiles, subsequently served as Soviet ambassador to Colombia. The Soviet ambassador to Cuba from 1962 to 1968 was Aleksandr I. Shitov (alias Aleksandr I. Alekseev), who began his KGB career in 1946. Sergei Petrovich Kiktev, designated ambassador to Morocco in December 1972, has worked with Soviet agents and conspired with Arab terrorists in the Middle East for nearly two decades. Kiktev abruptly abandoned his post as ambassador to Afghanistan in September 1972 after a prominent anticommunist editor in Kabul was killed by assassins traveling in a Soviet jeep and firing Soviet weapons.

Because the KGB crowds so many of its officers into Soviet embassies, they are often staffed in numbers absurdly disproportionate to the needs of normal diplomacy. In 1971 there were five Mexicans with diplomatic immunity in Moscow and sixty Soviet representatives with diplomatic immunity in Mexico City. There were 108 Americans in Moscow and 189 Soviet representatives with diplomatic immunity in Washington. Similar comparisons during 1971 showed two Lebanese in Moscow and thirty-one Russians in Beirut; four Danes in Moscow and thirty-one Russians in Copenhagen; five Norwegians in Moscow and twenty-five Russians in Oslo; twenty West Germans in Moscow and fifty Russians in Bonn. In Moscow the total number of accredited diplomats from eighty-seven noncommunist countries was 809, while the Soviet Union had 1,769 accredited diplomats in the same countries.

A like pattern of KGB predominance appears in the Soviet delegation to the United Nations and among the 207 Soviet nationals employed by the U.N. Secretariat in New York. A fascinating top-secret textbook obtained by a Western intelligence service from the KGB's Higher Intelligence School 101 outside Moscow stresses the value of the United Nations as a clandestine base.* The KGB textbook, entitled *The Practice of Recruiting Americans in the U.S.A. and Third Countries,* states: "In the U.S., in addition to ordinary cover, we use various international organizations. The most important of these is the United Nations and its branch institutions."

During the past two decades, eighteen Soviet na-

---

*Most of the KGB text is reproduced verbatim in Appendix C of this book.

tionals at the United Nations have been arrested or publicly expelled for illegal acts ranging from espionage to kidnapping. Two KGB officers, Aleksandr K. Guryanov and Nikolai F. Turkin, were ousted in April 1956 after they duped five Russian seamen into returning to the Soviet Union. Testimony by neighbors indicated that two of the sailors were abducted forcibly. Although the Soviet ambassador assured the sailors in the presence of State Department officials that none would be punished, at least one is known to be imprisoned in a mental hospital, reportedly for life.

In October 1971 the New York *Times* exposed Vladimir P. Pavlichenko, Director of External Relations in the U.N. Public Information Office, as a senior KGB officer. The *Times* noted that he circulated among American intellectuals at the Pugwash Conferences sponsored by the Ohio industralist Cyrus Eaton. The Soviet Union immediately demanded that the United States government instigate "measures" to stop the American press from trying to "evoke anti-Soviet hysteria in the U.S. and in other Western countries by exaggerating notorious spy mania." Two days after the *Times* stated that Pavlichenko was a KGB officer, the United Nations renewed his employment contract for two more years at a salary of $27,000 per annum.

KGB officer Valeri Ivanovich Markelov, while employed as a U.N. translator, flagrantly attempted to subvert an American engineer knowledgeable about the Navy's new F-14 fighter. The FBI finally arrested Markelov in February 1972. One of the more sinister Soviet diplomats at the U.N. in recent years was Mikhail Mikhailovich Antipov, who left in February 1972 after three years as first secretary of the Soviet delegation. Antipov belongs to KGB Department V ("V" as in Victor), the division responsible for assassination and sabotage, described in Chapter XIII. The Soviet ambassador to the United Nations, Yakov Aleksandrovich Malik, himself is experienced in the work of the KGB. Malik was co-opted as an agent before World War II at the Soviet embassy in Tokyo, and after the war he acted for a while as deputy director of all Soviet clandestine operations abroad.

Former Secretary General U Thant for years had a personal adviser named Viktor Mechislavovich Lessiovsky, who, unbeknown to him, was a KGB officer. U Thant states that he first met Lessiovsky in the early 1950s when he was Burmese Minister of Information and the Russian was stationed at the Soviet embassy in Rangoon. The two became so well acquainted that U Thant gave Lessiovsky's baby daughter a Burmese name. Lessiovsky moved on to Bangkok, where in 1957 he successfully tried to bribe and recruit an Indonesian government official. Subsequently he worked at the Center in Moscow before being placed on the United Nations payroll in New York.

Custom requires that the staff of the Secretary General include one citizen each of the United States, the Soviet Union, the United Kingdom, France, and China. When U Thant assumed the position in 1961, Lessiovsky was the only Russian he knew in the U.N. Secretariat. So he appointed him to the post of Personal Assistant to the U.N. Secretary General. U Thant notes that he had no reason to be wary because no one had ever warned him that Lessiovsky was a KGB officer.

However, U Thant stresses that Lessiovsky affected none of his decisions: "He was always very proper. . . . He never urged on me any policy or action, nor did I do anything or take any step according to his counsel."

Though unable to influence the Secretary General, Lessiovsky was able until he left New York in 1973 to provide the KGB with advance authentic intelligence about inner workings of the Secretariat. He additionally occupied an excellent position from which to assess foreign diplomats in whom the KGB was especially interested. Using the U.N. cachet, he also toured American universities in behalf of the KGB.

As the KGB textbook indicates, the KGB also exploits the havens provided by special agencies of the United Nations. One of the more prominent Soviet veterans of clandestine operations, Sergei M. Kudryavtsev, in 1971 presented himself as the permanent Soviet delegate to UNESCO in Paris. As a "diplomat" in Canada, Kudryavtsev helped steal Anglo-American nuclear data during World War II; and as Soviet ambassador to Cuba, he participated in the secret installation of missiles in 1962. Switzerland has twice expelled KGB officers working for the U.N. Telecommunications Union, and in 1969 Denmark ousted the World Health Organization press officer in Copenhagen, also a KGB agent.

The KGB derives still another advantage from placing its officers on the United Nations payroll. Since the United States pays 25 percent of the entire U.N. operating budget, it pays 25 percent of the bountiful salaries granted KGB officers insinuated into U.N. jobs.* American taxpayers thus are compelled to finance KGB operations against themselves and the noncommunist world. Moreover, the Soviet Union requires its citizens paid by international organizations to rebate the greater part of their salaries to the government. Thus, it actually makes money each time it plants a KGB officer in the U.N.

While preempting diplomatic posts, the KGB also stations its men abroad in other guises. A sizable portion of the Soviet nationals posted abroad as staff members of Tass, Aeroflot, Novosti, Amtorg, and Soviet commercial delegations are KGB and GRU officers. In recent years the Soviet Union has also been willing to expend millions of dollars on dubious business ventures simply to create pretexts for keeping KGB personnel in foreign countries.

After NATO shifted its headquarters to Brussels in 1967, the Russians spent $2.5 million to build the Skaldia-Volga auto assembly plant nearby. They insisted on locating near NATO even though more economically advantageous sites were available a few miles away. A radio antenna sprouted from the roof

---

*Prior to 1972, when the U.N., over vehement Soviet opposition, lowered the American assessment to 25 percent, the United States paid 31.5 percent of the regular United Nations budget in contrast to the 12.4 percent assessed the Soviet Union. In 1972, the most recent year for which data are available, the United States voluntarily contributed 45.1 percent of the budget of eleven subsidiary U.N. agencies such as UNICEF, whereas the Soviet Union contributed 1.5 percent of their budget. The total United States payment to the United Nations in 1972 was $281.4 million; the total Soviet payment was $52.9 million.

of the new plant, and soon Soviet "salesmen" appeared offering Moskvich sedans for $1,100—a quarter of their price in the Soviet Union. There were few takers and many complaints. An official of a Belgian company that accepted Soviet cars and trucks in part payment for services to the Soviet embassy declared: "Everything's gone wrong. Engines, brakes, steering, carburetors." Joseph Beherman, a Belgian executive who quit Skaldia-Volga after his Soviet bosses pressured him to steal a U.S. Army vehicle, revealed that the enterprise loses between $3 and $4 million annually.

Belgian police in March 1970 arrested Skaldia-Volga "salesman" Boris Trofimovich Savich, who was carrying miniature cameras, film, a large bundle of money, and instructions for a clandestine rendezvous with an agent. Then in October 1971, a GRU electronic specialist, Anatoli Chebotarev, fled from Brussels to the United States. He identified thirty-two Soviet intelligence officers in Brussels, many employed by Skaldia-Volga, Aeroflot, and other firms in which the Soviet Union had an interest. Chebotarev also disclosed that some of these spies had monitored the telephone conversations of senior Western diplomats and generals assigned to NATO and SHAPE.

The Russians have wasted more money on an auto dealership in Sweden, Matreco Bil Ab, which has offices in four cities. The Stockholm newspaper *Dagens Nyheter* reported that the company managed to sell only 271 vehicles in all of Sweden in 1970 and lost nearly a million dollars. The newspaper further noted that Swedish police frequently have followed Soviet "car salesmen" to "mobilization centers, radio stations, and other sensitive defense installations." Swedish pilots complain that the radio transmissions originating from the "auto company" disrupt their communications. Swedish monitors have ascertained that some of the transmissions are beamed to Soviet warships in the Baltic.

In most nations the KGB also is present in a less visible form. At the cost of much time and talent, the KGB continuously trains Soviet citizens to enter other countries in disguise and blend inconspicuously into the society against which they are sent to work. Because such agents live abroad illegally, relying upon false identities, forged documents, and fictitious pasts, the KGB terms them "illegals." The training of Yuri Loginov, whom South Africa captured in 1967, illustrates the effort sometimes invested in an illegal.

A highly educated and privileged son of a Party functionary, Loginov devoted the better part of eight years preparing for a long-term mission in the United States. He mastered English and the American idiom almost perfectly, versed himself in American mores and customs, and studied United States history, geography, government, and business. The KGB taught him to be a welder, a bookkeeper, and a travel writer so that he could move in different areas of society. As part of his training, Loginov circulated among Americans in Moscow and also traveled to Cairo, where he practiced against both Americans and Egyptians. While in Johannesburg he gathered intelligence against South Africa, but he was mostly concerned with examining locales, scenes, and history that were to be part of the background the KGB had created for him.

The KGB expected Loginov to direct Americans already in its employ and possibly some lesser Soviet illegals previously sent to the United States. However, other illegals are deployed to form dormant nets that can be activated at a time of Kremlin choosing to commit sabotage and murder.

KGB resources abroad are significantly augmented by the clandestine services of Cuba, Czechoslovakia, East Germany, Poland, Hungary, and, to some extent, Romania. The Soviet Union dominates these services so completely that for practical purposes they are mere extensions of the KGB. Soviet dictates are imposed by three primary means: through directives issued by the Soviet Communist Party's Central Committee to the Central Committees of the satellite nations, through KGB officers placed in the headquarters of the satellite services, and through officers of the satellite services recruited as covert Soviet agents.

The East Europeans and Cubans are valuable auxiliaries largely because they often are not perceived in the West as Soviet servants. The KGB also employs them as its proxies in certain high-risk operations for which the Soviet Union wishes to avoid blame in case of failure. Additionally, the Cubans are popular among some radicals and youthful subcultures inaccessible to Russians or East Europeans.

Although the Cuban service once retained considerable independence, Fidel Castro surrendered it to the KGB in the summer of 1968, when he bowed to a series of Soviet demands. A Cuban intelligence officer, Gerardo Perazo Amerchazurra, who fled to the United States from London in December 1971, revealed that under KGB orders the Cubans have established secret relations with FLQ (Quebec Liberation Front) terrorists in Canada. At the KGB's behest, they also are training both Palestinian and Irish terrorists, and are conspiring with British communists to perpetuate the internecine strife in Northern Ireland. According to Perazo, the Cubans have begun training professional intelligence officers to enter the United States on both espionage and sabotage missions. Should these clandestine Cuban operations create problems for Western nations, the Soviet Union gains; should they be uncovered and enrage foreign opinion, Cuba, not the Soviet Union, loses.

As long as KGB personnel are deployed so massively abroad, Soviet foreign relations inevitably will be conducted in large part by clandestine means. These, after all, are the means KGB officers are trained to use. With few exceptions, they are not prepared, disposed, or authorized to negotiate compromises of international issues or otherwise engage in legitimate diplomacy. Their careers and personal well-being depend upon clandestine action, not diplomatic achievements.

The Soviet leadership does resort to traditional diplomatic methods when it wishes to reach specific accommodations with other nations. It also may damp down KGB operations in a given country during periods of negotiations or after an embarrassing KGB debacle. But the KGB officers staffing Soviet embassies and infiltrated into foreign societies invariably resume what they have been trained and deployed to do.

No one of the techniques the KGB employs in executing Soviet foreign policy is an end unto itself. All are part of the same continuum of attack. All are synchronized into an unremitting campaign by which the Soviet Union seeks surreptitiously to expand its own power while sapping the will and capacity of other nations to resist its ambitions.

The most familiar KGB technique, of course, is espionage. Over the years, the Russians have become so addicted to spying that they seem to distrust information unless it is procured by illicit means. They traditionally have regarded technological and industrial espionage as an indispensable component of their own scientific research and development. Knowledge of Western plans obtained through espionage at times has enabled them to initiate profitable actions they might not otherwise have risked.

During the Berlin crisis of 1961, the KGB received from Georges Paques, a French official highly placed in NATO, a copy of the Allied contingency plan for defense of the city. The document clearly conveyed Allied determination to defend the three Western sectors of Berlin by all means necessary. But it also showed that should the communists erect a "barrier" to seal off East Berlin, the Allies were not prepared to use force to stop them. Certain of how far it could go, the Soviet Union went just that far—and not a centimeter further —by letting the East Germans throw up the Berlin Wall. Now fortified, the Wall, with its barbed wire, machine guns, killer dogs, and minefields, is not an attractive symbol of the Soviet system. But it has halted the human exodus that threatened to collapse East Germany and thereby endanger the Soviet Union's East European empire. No longer able to escape, the East Germans have become the most productive and docile of all Soviet colonies.

Increasingly, the KGB tries to discredit individuals, institutions, governments, or policies of other nations through what it calls *Dezinformatsiya,* or disinformation. This Russian term embraces not only forgeries, literary hoaxes, and dissemination of false information but also the commission of physical acts such as sabotage and murder for psychological effect. A passage in the previously mentioned KGB textbook mirrors one concept of disinformation. It quotes "a directive of the leadership of the Committee for State Security" entitled *On Intensifying Intelligence Operations Against the U.S. in Third Countries:*

"It is the duty of the Residency* to study carefully the contradictions existing between the U.S. and other capitalist countries, to analyze the information received from the agent network, and to develop and implement active measures to exacerbate these contradictions and to compromise and undermine the prestige of individuals active in U.S. politics and government."

Some disinformation operations are designed to exploit legitimate popular concerns about world problems or issues. The U.S. Department of Defense, for example, has learned authoritatively that the KGB seriously considered leaking radioactive waste into waters around a base used by Polaris submarines. "Discovery" of the contamination would have been widely cited as proof that nuclear submarines menace the environment. Such "proof" in turn was to be used in a KGB propaganda campaign against construction of the new generation of Trident submarines, which will form the backbone of the Western nuclear deterrent in coming years. The KGB abandoned this particular operation as technically unfeasible. But it continues to survey other means of capitalizing on environmental apprehensions to obstruct Western military and technological programs inimical to Soviet interests.

Demonstrations, strikes, and riots organized to debilitate morale and discredit public policies also fall within the Soviet concept of disinformation. Richard Pipes, director of the Russian Research Center at Harvard University, wrote in an analysis of Soviet foreign policy: "Public demonstrations are particularly useful. These

---

*The KGB term is *Rezidentura*, which means the KGB complement operating in a given foreign capital or designated area abroad.

are never spontaneous, but they appear as such and always receive public notice. A well-organized demonstration can create a completely false impression of the actual state of opinion in a given country and sway fence-sitters. In October 1968, while a crowd of 6000 protested on Grosvenor Square against American intervention in Vietnam, only seven demonstrators showed up in front of the Soviet embassy to protest the invasion of Czechoslovakia. In Tokyo the masses roam the streets to protest the terms on which Okinawa is to be transferred to Japan; there is no news of demonstrations against Soviet refusal even to discuss the transfer of the Kurile Islands (seized from Japan at the end of World War II)."

Foreign Communist Parties perform one of their most valuable services to the Soviet Union by fomenting demonstrations, riots, and strikes in furtherance of KGB disinformation operations. International communism of course is no longer a monolithic movement. Some foreign parties are split into antagonistic pro-Soviet and pro-Chinese factions, with the degree of servitude to the Soviet Union varying from country to country. Nonetheless, the Soviet Union considers many of the parties such useful tools that it continues to subsidize them secretly, usually through the KGB.

The United States has been able to trace millions of dollars delivered from Moscow to parties in the Western Hemisphere and Western Europe. Mexican security agents observed a KGB officer pass what turned out to be $30,000 to a Party representative in the summer of 1968, when young communists were preparing for the riots that nearly forced cancellation of the Olympic Games. Brazilian authorities searched local Party leader Fued Saad when he landed on a flight from Moscow in August 1972 and found $80,000 in his luggage.

In December 1972 Adauto Dos Santos quit the Brazilian Party after serving as a secret member and one of its leading clandestine agents for twenty years. He revealed that the KGB had been supplying Saad with as much as $300,000 a year for clandestine activities. The KGB funneled even larger sums into a construction firm, Castelo Branco, which the Party established as a front. Dos Santos also reported that in 1970 the KGB gave $170,000 to the chauffeur of Party Chairman Luis Carlos Prestes, who has since fled to Moscow. Among KGB officers with whom Dos Santos personally worked in Brazil were Intourist representative Nikolai Blagushin, Arseni Fedorovich Orlov of the Soviet trade mission, and Orlov's successor, Viktor Pavlovich Yemelin.

In accord with the repeatedly proclaimed Soviet determination to support "wars of national liberation," the KGB also assists selected terrorist and guerrilla movements. The Russians long were skeptical or even hostile toward violent movements not amenable to complete Soviet control. Among themselves they expressed contempt for Che Guevara because he was unmanageable as well as ineffectual. For decades they rebuffed Irish Republican Army requests for help, laughing at the grandiose military ranks the IRA supplicants bestowed on themselves. They looked upon the Palestinian guerrillas as hopelessly fragmented, unpredictable, and dangerously fanatical. Since the late 1960s, however the Politburo has come to appreciate that even uncontrolled terrorism can contribute to the Soviet objective of debilitating foreign societies. It does so by diverting resources from constructive national pursuits, provoking official repression, providing a pretext for Soviet-sponsored slander, and inflicting physical damage. Hence the KGB now lends clandestine aid to some terrorist groups that are not under total Soviet domination.

Brian Crozier, director of the London-based Institute for the Study of Conflict,* states that "at any given moment several hundred Africans are undergoing [guerrilla] training in Soviet camps." Though most trainees apparently are targeted against South Africa, Rhodesia, and the Portuguese colonies, defectors report having seen natives of Nigeria, Kenya, and Tanzania in the camps around Odessa.

The United States learned, through a penetration of the KGB, that in 1968 the Central Committee reversed

---

*The Institute, founded in 1971, is composed of eminent British scholars.

the previous Soviet policy of shunning the Palestinians. Soviet assistance to them, in the form of training and arms, has increased as the Soviet position in Egypt has weakened. KGB Residents in the Middle East are now under orders to recruit specified numbers of young Palestinians for indoctrination in the Soviet Union. And the Soviet Union openly collaborates with Yasir Arafat, chief of Al Fatah.

In October 1971, Dutch authorities at Amsterdam airport intercepted a shipment of Czechoslovak arms destined for the IRA. They came from a state firm controlled by the Czechoslovakian clandestine service, which in turn is controlled by the KGB. The weapons were consigned not to the Marxist ("Official") but to the noncommunist ("Provisional") faction of the IRA. The Soviet Union did not care who used the guns so long as they were used in Ireland to the detriment of Great Britain.

The most insidious and sometimes most dangerous KGB intrigue involves exploitation of what the Russians call agents of influence. Through them the Soviet Union endeavors to develop its own disguised voices in foreign governmental, political, journalistic, business, labor, artistic, and academic circles. While agents of influence may incidentally transmit intelligence, their overriding mission is to alter opinion and policy in the interests of the Soviet Union. No activity of the KGB abroad has higher priority than its efforts to manipulate the thought and action of other nations by insinuating such agents into positions of power.

Sometimes a Soviet agent of influence makes little effort to camouflage his real sympathies and allegiance. A good example is poet Pablo Neruda, who received the Nobel Prize for Literature in 1971 and served as Chilean ambassador to France from 1971 to 1973. Back in 1936, Neruda acted as such a blatant communist partisan that the Chilean government removed him from a diplomatic post in Madrid. While consul at Mexico City, Neruda helped the painter David Alfaro Siqueiros, a Soviet agent, gain refuge in Chile after he had been arrested for attempting to murder Leon Trotsky in 1940. Italy refused to accept him as Chilean envoy in 1948, the same year he was impeached and ousted from the Chilean senate.

Having earned the Stalin Prize in 1953, Neruda wrote paeans to Stalin. When the Soviet line changed, so did Neruda, and Stalin became that "cruel man." To Neruda the American hydrogen bomb was "infamous," the Soviet hydrogen bomb "as grand as the sun." He judged John F. Kennedy mentally unbalanced, Marshal Tito "a traitor covered with blood," and France "a little country bowing to the cowboys of Washington." On the occasion of the Soviet invasion of Czechoslovakia he declaimed: "The Soviet Union is my mother." To Neruda, the wide protest over KGB persecution of Aleksandr Solzhenitsyn was "a big bore."

However, in the literary salons of Paris and New York and among his audience throughout Latin America, Neruda was viewed not as a Soviet lackey but as a great poet whose words merited respect. Neruda wrote a hateful anti-American diatribe in the New York *Times* of July 20, 1973, alleging that the CIA spied upon him and a friend while he was in Mexico during the early 1940s. "They had magnetic tapes or video tapes, and kilometric tapes that spied on us from all sides, from the railway station right into our underwear," he claimed. At the time, the CIA did not even exist (it was founded in 1948) and surveillance cameras capable of producing video tapes had not been invented. Yet Neruda's charges may have impressed some readers, for the editorial notation accompanying his article identified him only as a "Chilean poet and Nobel laureate, [who] was also in his country's diplomatic service for many years."

Of course it is possible by careful review of what Neruda said and did over the years to recognize him for what he was. Normally, however, the agent of influence conceals his true motivation and his servility toward the Soviet Union. He almost never steals documents or commits other acts that might permit legal evidence to be amassed against him. Often his work affords plausible reasons for meeting Soviet representatives more or less openly, so usually he cannot be trapped in clandestine contact with the KGB. Analysis

in retrospect may demonstrate that he has consistently advocated policies beneficial to the Soviet Union and
harmful to his own country. But there is rarely legal
proof that his counsel represented anything other than
his own honest judgment.

The KGB in 1959 began a painstaking operation in
hope of eventually developing an agent of influence in
American politics. Working out of the United Nations,
KGB officer Yuri A. Mishukov cultivated a New York
law student, Richard Flink, by paying him to write
trivial research reports. After Flink became a lawyer,
Mishukov continued paying him for minor services,
gradually enmeshing the American in a relationship
cemented by signed receipts that supplied the wherewithal for blackmail. Then, in 1962, Mishukov offered
to finance Flink's campaign as a Republican candidate
for the New York State Assembly. In return, he asked
that Flink insert into his speeches statements favoring
certain policies. From the outset, Flink had reported to
the FBI, which, following this offer, decided to terminate the KGB operation by exposing it. Had Flink not
been a loyal and honorable man, he might have entered
upon a political career secretly financed and otherwise
abetted by the KGB.

The scope of KGB assaults upon other nations has
steadily increased since the early 1960s. In a 1973
analysis, the Institute for the Study of Conflict states:
"That Soviet intelligence activities are in fact on the
increase emerges from a study of the growth of Soviet
official representation of all kinds during the past ten
years. Ten years ago the overall total for Western
Europe was 1485; it has now risen to 2146—an increase of about 50 percent. . . . In NATO countries,
of every four Soviet officials accredited as diplomats,
three are spies of one kind or another."

KGB operations abroad have intensified most dra-
matically since 1970. Mexico expelled five KGB officers in 1971, after determining that the KGB had
recruited Mexican students, had them trained in North
Korea, then sent them back to Mexico to engage in
guerrilla warfare. That same year the Sudanese government, regaining power after a pro-Soviet coup, banished

the Soviet ambassador, the first secretary, and scores of Soviet "technicians." It also hanged three civilian communists and shot eleven army officers who had conspired with the Russians. In Great Britain, authorities gathered volumes of evidence documenting a KGB campaign to suborn politicians, scientists, businessmen, and civil servants. The findings included proof that the KGB was laying plans to sabotage British cities, even in peacetime. The British government privately asked the Soviet Union to desist. After their civilized requests were contemptuously ignored, the British, in September 1971, publicly expelled 105 KGB and GRU officers.

The next month, the Belgian government ejected nine Soviet intelligence officers. West Germany announced that in 1971 there was a 22 percent increase in the number of citizens reporting subversive approaches by the KGB. In 1971 it prosecuted forty-seven people on charges of treason. Bolivia, in March 1972, expelled sixty-nine Soviet representatives for subversive activities. Colombia in August 1972 expelled three KGB officers for subversion. During the decade ending in 1970, forty-six nations expelled 226 Soviet representatives. Between 1970 and July 1973, twenty nations found it necessary to expel a total of 164 Soviet officials because of their illegal, clandestine actions.

Each disruption of an operation, each expulsion of an officer, represents a KGB defeat. But no individual defeat halts the underlying assault. And the Soviet leadership frankly and publicly vows that the campaign will continue.

On June 27, 1972, shortly after negotiations with President Nixon, Leonid Brezhnev emphatically asserted that the Soviet Union remains determined to support "all revolutionary forces of our time." The détente with the United States, he declared, "in no way signifies a possibility of weakening the ideological struggle" against the West. Lest anyone misunderstand, he concluded: "On the contrary, we should be prepared for an intensification of this struggle."

II

SECRETS FROM THE DESERT

The impact of the KGB upon world affairs sometimes best can be seen through the eyes of individuals who are drawn into the subterranean world it inhabits. The experiences of one such man, Vladimir Nikolaevich Sakharov, yield remarkable revelations about KGB influence upon one of the continuing crises of current history, the travail of the Middle East. Both Sakharov himself and the fate that befell him are unusual. But the life he led while perched amid privilege atop Soviet society and while stationed in Soviet diplomatic posts abroad typifies important realities that rarely can be glimpsed by anyone outside the KGB.

The story that follows is based primarily upon extensive interviews with Sakharov. Throughout the interviews he spoke of his experiences and emotions frankly, sometimes painfully so. There is, though, one phase of his life that he had pledged to keep hidden. Otherwise the story is told as he lived and felt it.

At twenty-two, Vladimir Nikolaevich Sakharov was a young man everyone envied. He stood six feet three inches tall, weighed a muscular 235 pounds, had wavy chestnut hair, hazel eyes, a handsome face, and a reputation for brilliance. His family was influential and by Soviet standards wealthy; his wife was graceful, blonde, and beautiful. Among his closest friends were Igor Andropov, son of the KGB chairman; Mikhail Tsvigun, son of a deputy KGB chairman; and Viktor Kudryavtsev, son of Sergei Kudryavtsev, the old master of subversion.

Sakharov had distinguished himself during five years of Arabic studies at the most prestigious school in the Soviet Union, the Institute of International Relations. Awaiting him was a diplomatic career that promised perquisites, immunities, and material benefits usually reserved for the elite of the New Class.*

In the spring of 1967, Sakharov said good-bye to his wife, who was expecting their first child, and left Moscow for six months of field training in the Middle East, preparatory to his graduation. He volunteered for duty as a probationary consular officer in the strategic Red Sea port of Hodeida in Yemen. When he arrived in April, the temperature was 128 degrees and the humidity 96 percent. In the next few days he learned that neither ever fell much lower.

The body perspired continuously, a fresh shirt became soaked in five minutes, and shoes, if worn regularly, soon deintegrated from moisture. The Russian colony, consisting of about six hundred diplomats and KGB officers, construction personnel, and wives and children, lived in dread of virulent native diseases for which their doctors had no cure. Most feared was a strain of bacteria that produced feverish death by consuming or, as Soviet doctors said, "burning up" the brain. The corpses of Russians it killed were hurriedly carted into the desert, drenched with gasoline, and cremated to prevent contamination. In the streets, the Russians winced at the sight of amputees who were victims of the ancient Yemeni practice of cutting off the hands of thieves. Suspected criminals still were caged and pilloried in the marketplace, where passersby could poke, stone, or spit upon them. The Yemeni openly relieved themselves on the streets, using stones

---

*"The New Class" is the term first applied by Yugoslav political philosopher Milovan Djilas to the small minority that rules and administers a communist nation. The ruling New Class created by the communists after the Revolution consists mainly of the oligarchy, political bureaucrats, and Party workers. Djilas notes that because this minority controls the disposition and use of national resources, by the Roman definition of property it owns the state.

in lieu of toilet paper, and a latrine stench permeated the air.

The dangers posed by volatile, unpredictable Yemeni tribesmen were real enough. But these were exaggerated in the minds of the Russians by rumors only partially founded on fact. According to the lore prevalent in the Soviet colony, tribesmen without warning or cause had gutted the U.S. embassy in Taiz with bazooka fire and burned down the West German embassy, killing several people. According to another rumor widely believed in the Soviet colony, desert marauders had beheaded two KGB officers the previous year, mistaking them for Americans lost near the Aden border.*

The Russians assigned to Hodeida huddled together in a cramped compound of apartments that lacked air conditioning and provided one kitchen for each two families. A wall separated the compound from the grounds of the Chinese consulate. Frequently, in the dead of night, Chinese mounted the wall and banged tin pans, blew bugles, and shouted curses at the Russians. Sometimes they augmented the racket by circling the compound in cars, chanting imprecations through portable loudspeakers. Awakened by the din, Russian babies cried, distraught mothers complained, and husbands cursed helplessly. Soviet policy prohibited any response.

Although the Russians had bought control of Yemeni President Abdullah al Sallal, he was afraid to consort with them openly in the capital. So the KGB acquired a house in Hodeida for secret meetings, and Soviet Ambassador Mirzo Rakhmatovich Rakhmatov periodically drove across the desert from Taiz to rendezvous

---

*Yemen moved its capital from Taiz to Sanaa after the 1962 revolution. However, many nations retained embassy buildings in Taiz because of a lack of facilities in Sanaa. The Russians and Chinese additionally opened consulates in Hodeida (pop. 40,000) which provided a springboard for subversion along the Red Sea coast and against nearby oil sheikdoms.
The West German embassy was burned in September 1964 and the American embassy building ransacked in May 1967, but no fatalities occurred during either attack. Whether two KGB officers actually were beheaded is not known.

with the President there. Arriving early one morning in late April, the ambassador stopped by the consulate and asked for Sakharov, whose uncle was one of his oldest friends. He announced without explanation that the regular consul in charge at Hodeida, Ivan Skarbovenko, would not return from the vacation he had just begun in Moscow.

"Young man, I congratulate you. You are now the acting consul," Rakhmatov said grandly, offering a hearty handshake. "Skarbovenko assured me you were quite capable of carrying on in his absence, and knowing your uncle, I have confidence you can do the job until a permanent replacement comes." Sakharov was too astounded to ask for a definition of his new duties, and the ambassador hurried off without offering him any guidance.

The consulate had no telephones at the time, so the Russians often communicated through hand-delivered notes. The morning after the ambassador's visit, Sakharov received a scribbed message saying, "Come see me, please." It was from Vladimir Ivchenkov, the KGB Resident who posed as chief engineer of the State Committee for Economic Relations. Ivchenko, a wiry blond in his late thirties, was a keen and aggressive professional charged with nervous energy. Consecrated to his clandestine calling, he had amassed an encyclopedic knowledge of Arab culture, and he approached all problems clinically. He did not indulge in contemptuous diatribes against the Arabs, but would often tell Soviet newcomers: "The Egyptians need a hundred years to master our ways, the Yemeni three hundred." Yet he was not expressing personal disdain, merely his dispassionate judgment.

Inviting Sakharov to make himself comfortable in an office cooled by a Westinghouse window air conditioner, Ivchenkov remarked, "I suppose you know who I really am." Sakharov nodded.

"Well, let me be frank and straightforward," said Ivchenkov, lighting another of the British cigarettes he chain-smoked. "It is of course expected that you work for me. Your youth and background can make you quite useful, and your Arabic is admirable. However, our first duty, yours and mine, is to look after our own people. I want a report about everybody who comes to you. I want to know who's seeing Arabs, who's speculating in currency, who's sleeping with whom, who's dissatisfied—everything that's going on. You understand?"

"Perfectly," answered Sakharov.

Pouring himself a heavy slug of King George IV Scotch, Ivchenkov asked, "Want some?" It was not yet 9 A.M., and Sakharov politely declined. "If you are to deal with Arabs, you must learn to control and exploit alcohol," Ivchenkov continued. "It turns them into absolute putty."

"We are taught that their religion forbids it," replied Sakharov.

"Just so," said Ivchenkov. "They covet the forbidden, and they cannot handle it." Fidgeting and pacing the office, he began to lecture. "Seat the Arab at a table lined with bottles. Give him soda and nuts, while you drink whisky and comment about how relaxing it is. After a while, suggest that occasions of state take precedence over social custom, so it is permissible for him to take whisky. Once the Arab starts, he cannot stop. When he's drunk enough, he'll agree to anything, sign anything.

"Shelenkov* won a commendation here. It was actually for stupefying the Foreign Minister and photographing everything in his briefcase."

While Ivchenkov retained the ultimate, hidden power over all Russians in Hodeida, Sakharov, as acting consul, became the man to whom they came for help in their personal lives, quarrels, and other troubles. Bored and crammed together in the tiny, torrid apartments, wives argued and even engaged in hair-pulling battles over use of the kitchen or bath or over even pettier issues. Ethnic rivalries led to brawls among construction workers recruited from different Soviet republics. Summoned one night to stop a fight between

---

*Ivchenkov referred to Aleksandr Ivanovich Shelenkov. Stationed in Taiz, Yemen, until 1966, Shelenkov in 1971 turned up as the KGB Resident in Amman, Jordan.

an Armenian and a Kazakh, Sakharov found one had a broken arm and the other a broken leg.

No one could have assuaged all the human vexations with which he had to contend. But he tried, with patience, wit, and sympathy. Before long, Volodiya, as admirers called him, came to be known in the colony as a fair and compassionate arbiter, a "good guy" too young to be encrusted with bureaucratic cynicism.

All the while, of course, Sakharov privately reported to Ivchenkov, who entrusted him with more substantive assignments—the identification of Yemeni sympathetic to the Chinese, the spotting of potential KGB recruits among Egyptian forces stationed in Yemen, and the noting of likely Arabs who could help penetrate into the oil-storage areas of Aden. The two conferred almost daily and, because they liked each other, often stayed up late into the night drinking together.

After the Arab-Israeli war in June, the Chinese intensified their propaganda, accusing the Russians in leaflets and over loudspeakers of having caused the Arab defeat. Sakharov was so occupied in KGB efforts to counter the Chinese campaign that he fell further and further behind in his administrative duties. The morning of July 10 he worked at the consulate alone, hoping to reduce a pile of paperwork. About 10 A.M. he heard an ominous babble in the street and from a window saw the approaching vanguard of a Chinese-incited mob. Had he fled, Sakharov probably could have escaped. Instead, he chose to protect the consulate by bolting the doors, locking the windows, and turning on all the lights to create an impression that others were present. By the time he finished, the building was surrounded by some 1,500 frenzied Yemeni shouting Chinese charges of Soviet perfidy. Stones pounded the building, and as splinters of glass from smashed windows showered down around him, Sakharov climbed to the roof. There he looked down on the shrieking crowd armed with their long, curved knives and old British Enfield rifles. Recalling the attacks on the American and German offices, he concluded that eventually somebody in the mob would think of setting the consulate afire.

Sakharov had accepted the fact that he might have to die unnaturally, perhaps even in disgrace. Though he feared such a possibility, he was prepared for it, provided that his death could have a meaning and serve a cause. But to die now, having accomplished nothing, burned up or dismembered by crazed men in a forsaken, miserable Arab town, would be meaningless and terrible. Beating his fist against the palm of his hand, he cursed himself for not having run away. At that moment he heard the sound of rifles being fired into the air and the rumble of trucks bringing Egyptian troops to rout the mob.

By the next day, Sakharov was a hero. His honest attempts to explain that he had done little were interpreted as the modesty becoming to authentic bravery. To everyone in the compound he was the valiant Russain who singlehandedly stood up for his country against the loathsome "yellows" and "subhumans"— and triumphed. The ambassador sent proud congratulations. Ivchenkov embraced and kissed him. The construction workers cheered him, and the children shouted "Volodiya! Volodiya! Volodiya!"

Through the summer, Sakharov yearned more and more to go home and see his baby daughter, Yekaterina, who had been born in May. The evening before his return to Moscow in September to conclude his studies at the Institute of International Relations, Ivchenkov gave a farewell dinner. As the other Russians started to leave, he insisted that Sakharov remain. "I want you to read something," said the Resident. It was the fitness report he had written assessing Sakharov's work in Yemen. Everything stated was factual, or almost so, but was so cleverly worded that the report as a whole exaggerated the magnitude of Sakharov's achievements. Anyone reading the evaluation would have concluded that Sakharov was an exceptionally gifted young man with all the native talents of a great intelligence officer. "Can you think of anything we should add?" asked Ivchenkov.

"It is far too good as it is," replied Sakharov.

"Well, I think you deserve it," said Ivchenkov. "In any case, it won't do you any harm in Moscow. Now let's celebrate."

By 4 A.M. both were quite drunk, and Ivchenkov announced they must refresh themselves with a swim in the Red Sea so they could drink more. Staggering toward the beach, he boasted of a newly acquired mastery of karate. British intelligence symbolized his professional ideal, and he had persuaded himself that all MI-6 officers were karate experts. He had recently ordered a karate book to make himself the equal of his cunning British adversaries. Once in the water, he tried to demonstrate his techniques on Sakharov, and the pair nearly drowned grappling in the hot sea. Suffused with the spirit of laughing, intoxicated camaraderie, Sakharov thought no one could have a finer friend.

Back in Moscow, after he recovered from a round of welcoming parties, Sakharov called upon Skarbovenko, the consul who strangely had not come back to Hodeida. His appearance shocked Sakharov, for he seemed to have aged a decade in a few months. Bitterly, Skarbovenko told what had happened.

His wife long had dreamed of a sea voyage, so he arranged passage on a ship sailing from Alexandria to Odessa. Never had his wife been happier. She anticipated each hour of the voyage and also planned to pick up enough fine Egyptian cotton to sew dresses for a lifetime. Intent upon realizing her every expectation, she bought dollars in Yemen for use in Egypt and aboard ship. She knew all Russians were forbidden to deal in foreign currency. Yet because so many of them flouted the regulations, she made little effort to conceal her purchase. Ivchenkov found out about it and inexplicably decided to report her to the Center. When Skarbovenko reached Moscow, he was summoned to the Ministry of Foreign Affairs, demoted, and barred from going abroad again.

"Ivchenkov did that!" Sakharov exclaimed.

"Ivchenkov did it," Skarbovenko said, shaking his head. "I thought he was my best friend. Remember, I told you last year that if you needed help, you could trust Ivchenkov."

"I can't believe it," Sakharov said.

"You'd better believe it," replied Skarbovenko. "It is too late for me, but for you there is still time. You must learn to guard yourself against the Chekists. They have the highest positions, but they are the lowest form of our society. They spend all their lives betraying people, selling people. They sell us in the MFA [Ministry of Foreign Affairs]; they sell Party members, they even sell each other. Then the sons-of-bitches defect to the Americans and sell the whole Soviet people.

"The Chekists eventually will call you; they will try to make you one of them. Heed me, Volodiya. Have nothing to do with them!"

But Sakharov, for secret reasons of his own, already had determined that if the Chekists did call, he would answer as they wished. Far from dissuading him, the story of Skarbovenko only fortified his resolve to become an officer of the KGB.

The call came in November. The personnel director of the Institute, himself a KGB officer, handed Sakharov a slip of paper and told him to telephone the number written on it. He did so, and received instructions to come at ten the next morning to an office on Neglinnaya Street, half a block from Dzerzhinsky Square, and to ask for "Vasili Ivanovich."

A sentry ushered Sakharov into a reception room furnished only with a wooden table and two chairs. Vasili Ivanovich, a plump, middle-aged officer with white hair and a paternal manner, greeted him politely. "You understand, of course, that I represent the most respected organization in the Soviet Union—the Committee of State Security of the Council of Ministers of the U.S.S.R.," he began.

"My purpose in talking to you is to explain some of the work of our organization and to invite you to become a member. We have observed you during the last year of your study. We know of your command of Arabic and English. You have been given the highest recommendation by the Institute, and your work in

Yemen was outstanding. In fact, I myself congratulate you. In these times we need gifted, educated young men to contribute to the success of our state in the international field."

The officer specified numerous benefits the KGB would provide, including immediate and permanent possession of a good apartment in Moscow and a new suit and a new pair of shoes each year. Without disparaging the Ministry of Foreign Affairs, he stressed that KGB officers abroad have much more influence, opportunity, and money than ordinary Soviet diplomats. "At the same time, you will have all the prestige and privileges of a diplomat, which is what everyone will think you are. And for a young man our work is far more interesting and challenging. I will not tell you that it is completely without hazards. But I can assure you that always the full might of the Soviet Union stands behind you."

The interview, which was really a briefing, continued about two hours. Sakharov understood that after specialized KGB training lasting a year or two, he probably would be assigned to the American Department of the First Chief Directorate and posted to Washington or New York. But he gathered that from time to time he might also make use of his training as an Arabist by working against the United States in Arab lands.

"You may discuss our conversation with your father, if you desire," said the officer. "However you are to mention it to no one else, not even your wife or mother. You can take a couple of days to think it over, but I would be happier if I could have your decision now."

"I am greatly honored by this opportunity to serve the Soviet people," Sakharov responded. "I accept your invitation and pledge that I will always strive to be worthy of it."

It was as simple as that. The KGB, through its staff officers and informants at the Institute, surely observed Sakharov. But there was no searching investigation of his background, no examination of his ideals and motivation, no attempt to divine what he really thought. The reason for this lapse was that the KGB considered Sakharov's family credentials overwhelming. His father was a Ministry of Foreign Affairs courier, a job far more important and prestigious in the Soviet Union than in the West. For twenty years he had efficiently ferried Soviet secrets around the globe, all the while performing myriad useful services for the KGB. As a consequence, he had influential KGB friends in Moscow and numerous foreign capitals. Moreover, Sakharov's uncle was deputy director of the Ministry of Foreign Affairs archives department; his grandfather was an honored Red Army colonel assigned to the Central Committee. His mother-in-law was a Kremlin psychiatrist, trusted to treat Party leaders; her father commanded a concentration camp for political prisoners, another position of prestige in the Soviet Union. The KGB also knew that Sakharov's closest friends were the sons of its highest-ranking officers. Everything about him was ideal—his breeding, background, academic record, and performance in the field. Indeed, he represented the quintessence of the New Class.

From his earliest childhood, Sakharov's family imbued him with the values and aims of that class— the acquisition and preservation of special privilege, material possessions, and social status. The family carefully supervised his choice of playmates to ensure that he associated with no one beneath him. Children of Party officials, KGB officers, and senior bureaucrats were acceptable; those of doctors, engineers, and workers were not. As a small boy, when meeting possible new playmates, Sakharov's first question invariably was, "Who is your father?" His family shamelessly indulged him with foreign products, the ultimate status symbol. His father, with a diplomatic passport and highly placed friends, had constant access to dollars and Western goods. The dollars he sold in Moscow yielded a fortune in rubles, while those he kept bought Western merchandise cheaply at the special restricted stores that accept only hard currency. Sakharov learned at an early age that foreign goods bought favors. Once he accompanied his father to a KGB laboratory hidden in an old house on Sadovoy Koltso to have an IBM tape recorder repaired. His father re-

warded the KGB technicians with Parker pens and
Ronson cigarette lighters.

Virtually everything in the commodious Sakharov
apartment near the American embassy came from
abroad. Most of the furniture was Scandinavian; the
refrigerator Finnish, the vacuum cleaner a Hoover, the
stereo a Philips, the television from RCA, the short-
wave radio a Grundig, the shower head from Sears,
Roebuck. The first coffee Sakharov ever tasted was
Nescafé; his first cigarette was a Winston and his first
whisky White Horse. His best suit came from Brooks
Brothers and his favorite tweed jacket from the English
Shop in Copenhagen. He boasted a collection of nearly
five hundred American records, the most prized being
those of Stan Kenton, Glenn Miller, Cannonball Ad-
derley, Frank Sinatra, Dave Brubeck, and Peggy Lee.

Along with such luxuries, Sakharov's father brought
wondrous tales of the West, especially of Washington,
which he loved. "There is where I would like to live
out my life," he told his son. "It is my city—quiet,
beautiful, friendly. The people live in their own cot-
tages. If they want to go somewhere, they just get in
their car and go." Returning from a trip to Washington
in 1960, he remarked: "America is the happiest country in the world. It is written on the faces of the people.
Whatever you may hear, I have seen it for myself."

While secretly admiring the United States, Sakharov's father bore no deep grievances against the
Soviet system under which he prospered. However, because Sakharov's mother herself traveled frequently
during the prolonged absences of his father, he lived
much of the year with his grandparents, and they, in
different ways, were virulently anti-Soviet.

Turkish ancestry endowed his grandmother with a
dark, gypsylike beauty and a defiant, indomitable spirit
that made her loathe everything Soviet. "Shit!" she
habitually exclaimed upon reading *Pravda*. "Everything the Soviet press prints is shit. Tonight we will
get the truth from the BBC." Sakharov often fell asleep
listening to the BBC or the Voice of America on an
American-made radio with unjammed frequencies.

Sakharov's grandfather was a model officer whose

military record and political reliability had brought him through purges and earned him a staff position with the Central Committee. As an idealistic young communist he had fought with the special Cheka troops during the Revolution and afterward helped destroy unsubdued anticommunists as well as marauding criminal bands plaguing the countryside. He received two decorations for his valor during the 1941 Battle of Moscow. However, the 1936–38 purges in which most of his army friends perished and the subsequent official confirmation of the mass murders under Stalin left him with nothing but scorn for the cause to which he had given much of his life. Beyond his own comfortable survival, he now cared only about the future of his grandson.

On Sakharov's twelfth birthday, his grandfather took him for a walk in the park and spoke to him earnestly, summarizing the philosophy under which Sakharov was to grow up. "Our society is controlled by a small group of men," the old man said. "You can achieve a worthwhile life only by becoming a member of that group. It is not enough to be on the perimeter; you must gain the inner circle, and that is not easy. But it can be done with hard work and study. If you will work and study, I will give you anything, buy you anything you want.

"As you make your way upward, you will see with young eyes cruelties and injustices. You cannot change them, and it is futile to worry about what you cannot change. Once you are secure with money and position, you will learn to close your eyes and live your own life."

The family concluded that the surest route to the inner circle lay through the Institute of International Relations, whose students were graduated into careers affording status and the opportunity to work abroad, and hence to make money. The Institute was almost exclusively the preserve of the New Class. Even so, there were about fifteen applicants with the right family credentials for each of the six hundred annual openings, and the competition for entry was fierce. Sakharov's family thus devoted his adolescence to preparations that would give him advantages in the competition.

He swam, boxed, wrestled, played tennis, and won third place in the Moscow rowing championships, because athletic accomplishments were a plus. He took private German and piano lessons, because knowledge of a foreign language and music would further set him apart from other youths. After Khrushchev decreed that university applicants who had worked at a job would receive preference over those who had not, Sakharov's uncle arranged a "job" at a high-school physics laboratory administered by a friend. He was paid during the next two years for ostensibly working from 8 A.M. to 5 P.M. while attending night school. Actually, he showed up only in the morning to do his homework and left in the early afternoon to work at sports. The Institute required that every applicant present a written endorsement from Komsomol, the youth branch of the Party. The more glowing the recommendation, the better an applicant's chances. Sakharov looked upon Komsomol as a plebeian absurdity, and though he paid dues to retain paper membership, he did not deign to attend meetings. But his father telephoned a friend who had a friend who was Komsomol chairman of the Moscow District. There was some discussion of a portable RCA television. The testimonial the Komsomol chairman supplied as a result portrayed Sakharov as a veritable latter-day Lenin, the ideal communist youth.

Sakharov took his five entrance examinations in June 1962. The first consisted of writing a political essay, which was graded subjectively. It served to eliminate all female applicants except the daughters of the highest Party officials. If the girls thus excluded were attractive, they wound up at the MFA school for typists and stenographers; if talented, they were sent to the Institute of Eastern Languages. Another exam consisted of a standard set of questions about geography, accompanied by queries arbitrarily chosen for each applicant. By putting hard questions to some and easy ones to others, the faculty weeded out applicants with insufficient family influence. Out of a possible twenty-five points, Sakharov scored twenty-four on his examinations, and his family celebrated an entire weekend.

By virtue of admission to the Institute, students entered an exalted caste, recognized by one and all as the source of future oligarchs. Adults deferred to them, youths from other schools envied them, and girls looked upon marriage to one of them as a ticket to security, affluence, and the good life. Among themselves, the students maintained a highly refined system of snobbery. The lowest stratum was made up of those relatively few youths of humble origins accepted by the Institute for show, or because they worked for the KGB. Without family influence and forced to exist on monthly stipends of about forty rubles (roughly the amount Sakharov spent each month on taxis to and from school), they willingly acted as informants in return for KGB patronage. The status of other students was largely determined by their fathers' station in the oligarchy. If a father suffered a career reversal, the son suffered socially. Dmitri Tarabrin was perhaps the most brilliant and popular of the young men at the Institute until his father was suddenly ousted from the American Department of the KGB. As knowledge of this disgrace spread among the students, Dmitri stopped receiving invitations to their private parties. His ostracism was complete after about a year, when he appeared in Russian clothes rather than the American ones he had worn previously. Igor Andropov, whose father soon was to become KGB chairman, was in a class all his own. He alone could skip school as he pleased. After a prolonged vacation in Hungary left him unprepared for his annual exams, professors obligingly visited him at his apartment to administer special tests in private.

Except for the courses explicitly devoted to political indoctrination, the curriculum at the Institute was generally free of propaganda. The instruction, particularly in languages, area studies, and military intelligence, was outstanding. In an atmosphere of semimilitary discipline, subtly enforced by KGB officers on the faculty, and the knowledge that their informants were everywhere, students applied themselves during the day. Outside of school, though, a majority, including those in

Sakharov's clique, lived a life bordering on the dissolute, and a goodly number drank as much as a bottle of vodka every evening. Weekends were given over to alcoholic and sexual orgies at apartments of students whose parents happened to be away. Igor Andropov hosted such an affair in the spring of 1964, at which Sakharov wound up sleeping with a girl in the bed of the man who now heads the KGB.

Conditioned from boyhood to be conscious of class and to shun social inferiors, Sakharov had no friends outside the Institute except for some intimates of the family. He shopped in special stores, closed to the common citizenry; vacationed at state spas off limits to the public, dined at restaurants only foreigners and the oligarchy could afford. He even took taxis to school rather than the subway to avoid the stigma of mingling with the herd. Not until 1964, when he was nineteen, did he ever have any real associations with ordinary people.

That spring he vacationed in Estonia, using money his grandfather had given him as a reward for high grades at the Institute. Although the Russians occupied the little Baltic nation in 1940 as part of a deal with Hitler, the Estonians have stubbornly striven to perpetuate their language and culture. Sakharov found it delightful. However, he was constantly aware of a sullen hostility which the Estonians communicated in every manner they safely could. Twice after requesting street directions, he was deliberately steered far from where he asked to go. In shops, clerks ignored him as long as another customer was present. One evening in a Tallinn hotel lobby, he met Aeroflot crew members who invited him to come along for a birthday celebration at a restaurant that had a jazz band. When the party was recognized as Russian, the band abruptly stopped in the midst of a jazz tune and started playing *"Deutschland über Alles."* Many diners joined in this insult to the Russians by rising and singing the old German anthem.

Once Sakharov saw a man buying a fishing rod in a store. He decided to purchase one.

"These are only for display, not for sale," said the clerk, a thin little man of about sixty.

"But I just saw you sell one," Sakharov persisted.

"For display only," repeated the unyielding Estonian.

"Look, what have you got against me?" exclaimed Sakharov in exasperation. "What do you want?"

"We want you to go away and leave us alone," replied the clerk.

Sakharov's next experience among ordinary people occurred in September of 1965. During a morning class at the Institute a Party secretary announced: "All students will devote six weeks to assisting our agricultural workers. We leave tomorrow to demonstrate our solidarity with our comrades at the kolkhoz. Be here with appropriate clothing by 0700 hours."

Though Sakharov and his friends had never seen a collective farm, they had read numerous official stories depicting the collectives as scenes of pastoral happiness born of wholesome toil. Bouncing in a bus along a rutty road toward the kolkhoz, some hundred miles north of Moscow, they looked forward to a diverting lark in the country. But their first twenty-four hours at the collective left them incredulous and mortified.

The inhabitants lived in clusters of one- and two-room log huts spaced along an arc through the potato fields. The huts had dirt floors and no plumbing or electricity. What little heat there was in any of them came from small wood-burning stoves. The kolkhoz contained one ramshackle store to sell bread, vodka, canned goods, and sundries, but its shelves were mostly empty. Years before, Moscow planners had allotted the store a piano and two motorcycles. They still were there, unsold and encrusted with the dried spittle of contemptuous people who could neither afford nor use them. The students' first three meals consisted solely of milk and potatoes. As it turned out, milk and potatoes were all they ate for the next six weeks except on the four days when bread was available.

Physically fit young men raised on the kolkhoz escaped by enlisting in the army, and the more attractive girls escaped through marriage. The older or crippled men who remained monopolized jobs involving farm machinery. No matter how idle they might be, because of overstaffing and broken-down machinery, they concocted excuses for not going into the fields. Younger women chained to the farm by their plainness fought viciously for jobs in the crude kolkhoz dairy. So the tilling of the fields—the digging of potatoes—was left mostly to old women and children, who labored from 8 A.M. to 6 P.M. six days a week.

For the adults, the kolkhoz was a world without hope; nothing relieved their days save the oblivion of alcohol. A river offered the only means of bathing, and its waters were so frigid from autumn through spring that baths were rarities. Deprived of facilities or incentive to maintain their appearance, stripped of individual dignity and self-respect, everyone spoke to each other with a venom and vileness of language that shocked Sakharov. They spoke even more hatefully to the students, whose status and prospects symbolized everything they would never attain.

Sakharov felt the most compassion for a woman who, with her daughter, was forced out of her hut to make room for himself and ten of his classmates. She had a dumpy, worn body with straight, stringy hair and a forlorn, creased face marked by dark moles. Each morning and evening she was required to come and cook potatoes for the students who had displaced her. Shamed by his contribution to her eviction and additional servitude, Sakharov tried to make friends with her, but his efforts were unavailing until he thought of giving her a bottle of vodka. For the first time, he saw her smile, and on subsequent evenings she sometimes stayed awhile to talk with him.

She longed to own a cow. Its milk, which she would sell or consume, would give her a tiny measure of liberty. Its mere possession would make her superior to her neighbors. The state formerly permitted each family on the kolkhoz to keep one cow and cultivate a small private plot. Khrushchev abolished this policy on the theory that people would be more productive if not distracted by private enterprises. However, many of the cows that were confiscated by the state perished because the kolkhoz was not supplied with added fodder. Moreover, because the people worked no harder in the fields, the quantity of food grown declined. Now the state once more allowed the private plots and cows. But the woman had no money to buy a new cow or seed.

Sakharov had brought some of his belongings to the kolkhoz in a blue KLM flight bag given to him by his father. Just before the students returned to Moscow in October, he handed the bag to the woman, saying, "I want you to have this as a present." She unzipped the bag to find it contained bottles of vodka and nearly a hundred rubles, all the cash Sakharov had with him. "For a cow," he said. Tears flowed down the woman's wrinkled face.

Heretofore, Sakharov's experiences had denied him any sense of identity with the Soviet people—or any concern for them. The influences of family, class, and schooling all taught him that the purpose of life was the pursuit of his own interests. But riding back to Moscow, thinking of the kolkhoz and Estonia, he began to wonder if perhaps there might not be another purpose.

That fall, at a weekend party, Sakharov spotted an eighteen-year-old girl with golden silken hair, green eyes, beautifully formed features, and an exquisitely contoured body that made men stare. Having plied her escort into alcoholic collapse, he gallantly offered to take her home in a taxi. Instead, he took her to his grandparents' apartment for the night.

The alluring girl, Natalia Palladina, was as brilliant as she was beautiful. Because of sheer native intelligence, she quickly and easily mastered whatever she undertook to learn, whether ballet or cooking, foreign languages or esoteric art, social graces or Marxist theory. But Natalia was an even more spoiled child of the New Class than Sakharov. Her psychiatrist mother was determined that she should be a future queen of the Soviet Union. She molded her daughter from infancy onward to fulfill the ordained role. The rigorously controlled upbringing endowed Natalia with sophistication and regal manners that enabled her to captivate adults. Yet beneath the beguiling veneer, her mother's ambitions and values made her selfish, willful, and materialistic.

Upon meeting Natalia, Sakharov's family was ecstatic. Nothing was more important to them than his choice of a wife. Since his early adolescence, they had tacitly encouraged him to bring girls home for the night, discouraging him only from forming emotional attachments. Not only did they want to inspect each girl; they wanted his normal drives gratified, so that sexual impulse would not influence his marriage. Natalia personified their ideal. In her they saw every qualification his career required. "This is the girl for you!" raved his father, who immediately set out to promote a marriage, showering Natalia with presents from New York, among them a fur jacket from Saks. Natalia's mother, equally enthralled with Sakharov and his career prospects, became just as ardent a proponent of marriage.

Physical attraction was the strongest bond Sakharov and Natalia shared. Under the influence of it and parental pressures, they married in November 1965. But their differences in personality, temperament, and outlook soon caused sharp conflict. Sated by the materialism of his upbringing, affected by his experiences in Estonia and on the collective farm, Sakharov no longer looked upon luxury, privilege, and status as ends unto themselves. In quest of other goals, he read underground literature and came to regard Solzhenitsyn as a sublime example of courage and Russian patriotism. He had not completely shed the biases and class snobbery taught to him since childhood. Yet he had developed a tolerance and compassion toward others that made him interested in matters beyond his own self-interest. Natalia wholeheartedly embraced the New Class materialism and aspirations he now rejected. She looked upon Solzhenitsyn as a fool for not bending his talents to service of the state and reaping rewards in return. And she treated the slightest frustration of her whims as cause for indignation or an outright tantrum. They argued frequently and tempestuously.

Sometimes after arguments, days passed without their speaking to each other. Had it not been for the birth of Yekaterina and awareness that divorce would preclude them from achieving their common goal of going overseas, they certainly would have separated.

As soon as Sakharov announced his readiness in November 1968 to join the KGB, Vasili Ivanovich consummated the recruitment by requiring him to sign the standard KGB secrecy oath. It did not occur to Sakharov that he first should consult his family. He assumed they would be proud. Though never discussing details, his father always left the impression that he served the KGB as much as the Ministry of Foreign Affairs. Once he boasted: "If I wanted, I could come home tomorrow in the uniform of a KGB colonel." Yet when Sakharov confided that he was joining the KGB, his father, for the first time in his life, shouted at him in rage.

"My son will not be a Chekist!" he yelled. "Never!" With unprecedented vehemence, he named friends fired from the KGB after the death of Stalin, after the discovery in 1962 that Colonel Oleg Penkovsky was a spy, and as a consequence of some unexplained convulsion in the mid-1960s. "One man makes a mistake, and ten innocent men are fired," he continued. "They discover one American or British spy, and a hundred are fired. And when the KGB fires you, your life is at an end. You can do nothing. No one will touch you!

"If you slip in the MFA, you can catch yourself. You are not ruined. There are other places to go. And the MFA does not take away your soul."

Overwhelmed, Vladimir asked in bewilderment: "Isn't it true that you yourself have worked for the KGB? Aren't many of your friends in the KGB?"

"I live as I must. You must live as you can," his father quickly answered. "There are good men in the KGB, and I have friends. That I do not deny, but we will not always be here to protect you.

"Now hear my warning. I cannot stop you. But if you join the KGB, I disown you. I will never help you again. You will get nothing from me, ever."

"Father, it is impossible," said Sakharov. "I have

signed the papers. Tomorrow I start the physical examinations. What can I do?"

"Do nothing. Just don't go near them again," his father ordered. "I will arrange everything."

At the Institute the next afternoon, the Personnel Department sent a note commanding Vladimir to telephone the KGB number he first called. He ignored it, and the messages that followed. On the third day, the KGB stopped calling. Seemingly, his father's influence had prevailed.

Earning twenty-three of a maximum twenty-five points on his final examinations, Sakharov was graduated from the Institute in January 1968 and assigned as an assistant attaché to the Soviet consulate in Alexandria. After weeks of briefings at the Ministry of Foreign Affairs, he, Natalia, and Yekaterina departed from Odessa in May by ship. Awating them at the pier in Alexandria was a Russian of about forty, with dark hair, a pleasant round face, and a paunch spilling over his belt. "I am Viktor Sbirunov, vice consul," he introduced himself. "I have a nice apartment for you right across the hall from mine. Come on, my wife has supper."

As they drank and talked, Sakharov perceived that Sbirunov knew virtually everything about him—his family's connections, his accomplishments at the Institute, his service in Yemen, even his aborted recruitment by the KGB. Obviously Sbirunov was the KGB Resident, a fact he privately acknowledged later in the evening.

Sbirunov was a tough, aggressive, effective officer, a genuine Chekist who already had attained in life more than he expected. His career started as a militia investigator in the Caucasus. He later worked his way into the KGB by acting as a local informant and by sheer tenacity ultimately gained a transfer to Moscow. He then took night courses at the university and, in the expansion of KGB foreign operations during the early 1960s, was shifted to the First Chief Directorate. His language was obscene, his jokes vulgar, his table manners messy. "I fought my way up from the village into the KGB and made myself what I am today," he liked to boast.

A small incident that evening demonstrated to Sakharov that Sbirunov was a true Chekist. Three Russian women, one crying and hysterical, came to the apartment as they finished supper. From what Sakharov overheard of their conversation in the hall, he gathered that the crying woman had just been the victim of an attempted rape. Now she vaguely sought some sort of redress, or at least consolation, from a Soviet official.

"You fool! What do you expect me to do?" Sbirunov snapped. "The Arabs are subhuman and act like animals. You are supposed to be civilized and have sense enough to know that. I have told you not to go to the marketplace at night. You are to blame, not the animal. Stop bawling and go home. If you make more trouble, I will send you back [to the Soviet Union]."

Returning to the table, Sbirunov shook his head. "The Egyptians are Arabs, and the Arabs are all just like niggers,"* he declared. "Subhuman, all of them. I tell you, though, sometimes I don't know who are worse, the subhumans or our stupid women." Natalia smiled as if she had just heard something very chic.

After the wives had retired to another room, Sbirunov referred to Sakharov's dealings with the KGB in Moscow. "You tried to run away from us," he said laughing. "No one gets away from us. You see, we have you now." Sakharov laughed also. He realized that to avoid the bother of contesting his father, the KGB had let him go in Moscow, fully intending to recover him in Egypt. Sbirunov didn't even ask him if he wanted to work for the KGB. From that evening on, Sbirunov and other KGB officers simply told him what to do and treated him as one of theirs.

Natalia and Sakharov were instantly popular in the Soviet colony. The Russians liked to show off such a strikingly handsome couple in diplomatic society, representing them as typical young Soviet emissaries. At-

---

*The word Sbirunov actually used was the plural of *"chernozhopy,"* the term by which Russians popularly refer to black people of all nationalities. Literally translated, it means "black ass."

tired in clothes Sakharov's father had bought for her on Fifth Avenue, Natalia was one of the more elegant women in Alexandria. She taught herself English, learned to prepare exotic Middle Eastern dishes, and charmed those Russians and foreigners who could help her husband. Though their private relations remained empty and often antagonistic, in every other way Natalia was precisely the asset Sakharov's family had sought for him. Sakharov, however, needed no help. The eagerness and ease with which he accomplished assignments, menial or complex, led the KGB to congratulate itself on its own perspicacity in co-opting him. Everyone considered him an inordinately gifted young man who realized that he still had much to learn and who was determined to learn so that he could better serve his country. His thoughtful questions impressed his superiors, and his habit of returning to the consulate to work alone two or three nights a week further testified to his devotion.

These were important and dramatic times to be with the KGB in the Middle East, where the Soviet Union had mounted its greatest subversive operation of the decade. Whereas the Czars yearned for warm-water ports on the Mediterranean, Soviet leaders coveted control of Middle East petroleum, which comprises about 60 percent of the earth's reserves. Already, Western Europe and Japan depend almost entirely upon the Middle East for the oil that fuels their economies. According to some projections, unless American domestic resources are better exploited, by 1990 the United States will have to buy fully half of its petroleum from the Middle East. Thus, Soviet strategists accurately equated the power to control or interrupt the flow of oil from the Middle East with the power to blackmail the West and Japan.

By the summer of 1968, the Soviet Union had progressed far toward converting Egypt into its principal base of subversion against the Arab world. In return for some $2.5 billion worth of arms and aid, President Nasser had mortgaged both the policies and economy of his country to the Russians. Soviet officers gave orders to the Egyptian military. Soviet engineers supervised

Egyptian workers in the construction of bases from which Arabs subsequently were barred. An extraordinary delegation from the Central Committee itself, along with some fifty KGB and GRU officers, stood watch in Cairo to ensure that Egyptian actions reflected Soviet interests. Among themselves, the Russians, only partially in jest, referred to Egypt as the "Soviet Egyptian Republic."

Nevertheless, Soviet dominance of Egypt was neither absolute nor completely secure. Certainly the Russians could not consider Egypt an integral part of their empire as they do East Germany, Poland, Czechoslovakia, and Hungary. In each of these Eastern European satellites, the Soviet Union has installed an indigenous New Class largely unsupported by the people. Because their rule rests solely upon Soviet power, these regimes must remain servile to Moscow. Nasser, however, commanded the allegiance of the Egyptian populace and thus retained at least an option of independent action. The Russians also worried about a quiescent minority of Western-oriented Eygptians who opposed subserviency to the Soviet Union. They also realized that an accommodation between the Arabs and Israel would diminish Egyptian need for Soviet arms and thus endanger their hold on Nasser.

Therefore, the KGB endeavored to build a hidden foundation for an enduring Soviet dominance. It recruited agents in the Egyptian military, the security services, the press, the universities, the governing Arab Socialist Union Party, and even among Nasser's personal advisers. Shortly before Sakharov arrived, it also started to penetrate those groups sympathetic to the West. The Russians relied on all these agents to reinforce covertly their influence over the existing Egyptian regime. And they counted on them to form the nucleus of an Egyptian New Class wholly beholden to the Soviet Union.

Sakharov in executing KGB assignments, reading secret dispatches, translating intelligence reports from Arabic, and listening to KGB shop talk, was able to watch the Soviet strategy unfolding. Sbirunov instructed him to cultivate selected Egyptians the KGB

considered vulnerable to subversive overtures. One was
Abdel Madsoud Fahmi Hasan, the young chief of an
intelligence unit assigned to protect and watch foreign
consulates in Alexandria. "It is normal for you as a
new officer to introduce yourself and state our desire
for good relations," Sbirunov told Sakharov. "Hasan
is a little man now. But never forget that little men
sometimes grow into big men."

Taking along a bottle of whisky, Sakharov visited
Hasan and subsequently invited him to dinners and
then to a diplomatic reception, where he presented
Sbirunov. Periodically Sakharov called on the Egyptian
with gifts, usually caviar or whisky, which he sometimes explained away as part of an "overshipment"
mistakenly sent to the consulate. After about three
months, Sbirunov ordered him to stop seeing Hasan.

"He may be offended," said Sakharov. "We have
become rather good friends."

"He understands," Sbirunov replied.

Sakharov never saw the Egyptian again. But later he
translated reports about Egyptian intelligence operations and foreigners in Alexandria that Hasan regularly
provided Sbirunov.

The Egyptian responsible for counterintelligence on
Russians in the Alexandria area was Major Abdel
Hadi el-Sayed. As part of a plan to suborn him, the
KGB arranged a scholarship for his brother to study
in the Soviet Union. Sakharov met the brother before
his departure for the Agricultural Institute in Tbilisi
and, using this tenuous social link, introduced himself
to the major. Thereafter, he followed the usual pattern
of development until Sbirunov interceded to take
charge of el-Sayed.

Sbirunov also encouraged Sakharov to strike up acquaintances with government officials and businessmen
on his own. Local communists were the only Egyptians
with whom contact was prohibited. Sakharov pitied
these idealistic Marxists. They had been persecuted for
years, first under King Farouk, then under Nasser, who,
as a sop to the anticommunist elements among his
people, periodically made a great show of jailing them.
Now the Russians scorned them as foolish, trouble-

making "amateur Marxists" or agents of the Chinese. "The trash of society," Sbirunov called them. The communist editor Mohammad Koreitim offered to devote an issue of his magazine to commemoration of Lenin's birth, asking only that the Russians promise to buy five hundred copies. The Russians turned him down, and after he kept pleading, evicted him from the consulate. Faithful to the cause, Koreitim published the commemorative edition anyway from his own sparse resources. Sbirunov merely laughed when Egyptian journalists subsequently accused Koreitim of taking a Soviet bribe.

Although Sakharov never revealed his KGB affiliation to anyone in the Ministry of Foreign Affairs, he assumed that his nominal boss, Consul General Oleg Shumilov, had been briefed about it. However, in June Shumilov asked him to his office and shut the door. "A very serious matter has arisen," he announced gravely. "I am informed that two nights ago you went to a nightclub with an Egyptian. Our rules are clear, and you violated them by failing to report this contact. What is your explanation?"

"I am seeing the Arab at Sbirunov's orders," Sakharov answered.

"Who do you think you are working for?" Shumilov exploded. "The KGB or the MFA?"

"I am working for the Soviet Union," replied Sakharov.

Shumilov misconstrued this as a calculated impertinence, and his face reddened. "Young man, I don't care who you are or who your father is!" he shouted. "The Ministry sent you here to work for me. If you do anything else without consulting me first, I will ask the ambassador to send you home."

Sakharov went directly to Sbirunov. The next afternoon a humiliated Shumilov offered him an awkward apology. "Neither one of us can control the circumstances," Sakharov said respectfully. "I still want to do my duty for the MFA. Ask anything of me. I will help in every way I can."

The incident left Sakharov with a kind of immunity and liberty rarely enjoyed by Russians abroad. Under the aegis of the KGB, he could circulate freely among foreigners, and Shumilov no longer dared inquire about his associations or whereabouts. Because he performed some consular duties, the KGB did not demand as full an accounting of his time and contacts as it did from its own staff officers or from regular diplomats. Thus, no one questioned him when he took long afternoon drives across the desert—where neither Russians nor Egyptians could follow him without being detected. If questioned, he was prepared to explain that because of his evening work he seldom could spend time with his daughter, Yekaterina, whom he was merely treating to a swim in the sea.

On one occasion while they were frolicking together in a gentle surf, an immense man, weighing at least 320 pounds, wallowed toward them like a fat walrus. He had a long black beard, coal-black hair and eyes, and an intelligent, raffish face. Delighted to encounter fellow Russians, he introduced himself in a booming bass voice as Anatoli Kaznovetsky, Archbishop of the Russian Orthodox Church for all Africa. The bishop, without doubt, was the most colorful KGB agent in the Middle East.

He and his tall, graceful wife soon became the Sakharovs' favorite friends in Alexandria. Kaznovetsky was interested in everything. Skilled in mechanics and addicted to gadgetry, he repaired his own car, distilled his own liqueurs, and built his own spearfishing gear. He listened to Bach and Beethoven by the hour and sometimes drank two bottles of vodka at a single sitting with no visible effects except a florid face. He was perfectly capable of administering religious sacraments one hour and writing reports for the KGB the next. Beyond their common relationship with KGB, Sakharov and Kaznovetsky shared many obliquely expressed perceptions of Soviet reality.

The bishop's principal KGB mission was to persuade clergymen of other faiths to adopt and propound the Soviet view on international issues such as Vietnam, the world peace movement, and the Arab-Israeli conflict. At the same time, he assisted in recruiting religious agents, particularly among the Copts, the Christian minority. His clerical position also permitted him to reconnoiter African regions and social circles to which official Soviet representatives were not easily admitted. At the Alexandria consulate, Kaznovetsky dealt exclusively with Sbirunov, delivering written reports and receiving instructions every week. He also traveled to Cairo about once a month to confer with the KGB Resident there, Pavl Nedosekin, a ruthless wartime terrorist feared by everybody, including Sakharov. Accompanying the bishop to Cairo on business of his own, Sakharov saw him emerge from the guarded Room No. 6, where the embassy disbursed funds for clandestine operations.

In time, Sakharov felt secure enough with the bishop to request a secret favor in behalf of himself and Natalia. "Do you think," he asked, "that Yekaterina could be baptized? I mean, without anyone knowing."

With a fatherly embrace, Kaznovetsky answered, "Of course, my son, of course."

Sakharov kept hidden in the bottom of his cufflink box a small golden cross given to him by his grandmother at the time of his own baptism. Taking it along, he searched Alexandria hoping to find a matching one for Yekaterina. The night of the baptism, the bishop arranged his living room to resemble, as nearly as possible, a sanctuary, even setting up an altar. He appeared in the magnificent vestments of the Russian Church, adorned with a miter and carrying a crosier. The solemn setting and the organ chorales from the bishop's stereo made Sakharov feel as if he were in church. After the baptismal ceremony, Kaznovetsky's wife, in the old Russian fashion, served a grand festive supper in celebration.

Saying good-night, the bishop whispered, "Do not worry, Volodiya, no one will know." Both recognized that the KGB would consider the baptism a mark against Sakharov. The interest in religion that it signified might be dismissed as a harmless aberration or youthful whimsy, but the record of the baptism would be permanent, and, should circumstances ever arouse official suspicions about Sakharov, it would weigh against him.

Yekaterina fell asleep after the dinner, clutching a little cross in her hand. She was a beautiful, angelic child with her mother's golden hair. After settling her in her crib, Sakharov and Natalia spontaneously embraced and went to bed together for the first time in months.

Half a year or so later, the bishop approached Sakharov with a personal problem. The foreign car he owned in Moscow had long been inoperable because it required replacement parts unobtainable in the Soviet Union. The bishop had managed to buy all the needed parts plus some spares in Egypt, but, as their importation was strictly illegal, he had no means of transporting them to Moscow. He wondered if Sakharov might, with the aid of his diplomatic passport, take them along on his next home leave. Aware of the dangers of smuggling contraband, Sakharov hesitated. "Of course," said the bishop, "I do not wish to involve you in trouble. It merely occurred to me that a clever young man such as yourself might know a way." Then he added, "By the way, how is your beautiful little Yekaterina? Every time I think of her, I feel comforted that she enjoys the blessing of our Lord."

It was sheer blackmail. Despite Natalia's fears, Sakharov shipped the crate along with their luggage when they left for a Moscow vacation in August 1969. As it happened, the customs inspector looked at his diplomatic passport and waved them on without examining their belongings.

While in Egypt, Sakharov journeyed to Cairo two or three times a month to discharge tasks for Sbirunov or attend to consular business. After stopping at the embassy, he customarily stayed overnight with friends. He talked most often with KGB officers Gennadi Yenikeev and Valentin Polyakov; MFA Referentura Chief Ivan Ignatchenko; and an accomplished Soviet Arabist, Sergei Arakelyan, whom Nasser idolized and employed as his personal interpreter. During these visits Sakharov learned must about what really was happening behind all the public bombast and posturing typical of Middle Eastern affairs. His friends confided that Soviet pilots, flying MIGs with Egyptian markings, were dying in aerial combat. Once while he was in Cairo, the bodies of two Russian pilots shot down by Israeli Phantom jets were brought in from the desert, and he saw their wives weeping on the caskets. Arakelyan also told him of secret trips Nasser made to Moscow and of his conversations at the Kremlin.

He learned the most, however, from Sbirunov, his KGB boss, neighbor, and drinking companion in Alexandria. Although generally discreet, the Resident at times did succumb to an impulse to impress people with his secret knowledge. Drinking Scotch with him late on a spring evening in 1969, Sakharov expressed surprise that the KGB had not detected Israeli preparations for the lighting attack in June 1967.

"Everyone knew Israel was prepared for war," Sbirunov said. "But the main task of any Soviet representative is to ascertain the exact date of war and just what the enemy plans are."

"Well, in Yemen we wondered why this was not done," Sakharov remarked.

"Oh, no!" Sbirunov interjected. "There was information, exact information. We learned the exact date of the attack and the hour of the attack. That was sent to the Center. We were astonished they did not tell the Arabs. Maybe they did not believe it or doubted the source. Maybe it was just a routine fault at the Center, or maybe it was planned. I don't know."

Sakharov, of course, was intrigued by this assertion that the KGB acquired and yet withheld momentous intelligence that might have spared the Arabs their military debacle. Less than a week later he was even more intrigued by a revelation Sbirunov casually made at a routine consulate staff meeting. Present were Consul General Shumilov; Sbirunov and Sakharov, representing the KGB; the GRU Resident; and the Central Committee representative. Sakharov asked whether the increasing influence in the Egyptian government of a comparatively moderate editor, Mohammed Hassanein Heikal, might augur difficulties for the Soviet Union.

"No, not so long as Sharaf stays where he is," answered Sbirunov.

"I never heard of him," said Shumilov.

"Sami Sharaf in reality is the foremost figure in the government. He is the intelligence adviser to the President, the man Nasser listens to most," declared Sbirunov. "From our standpoint, he is the most positive force in Egypt. He is the one we rely on."

Sbirunov spoke truthfully but not wisely. Sharaf was far too important to be exposed to those who had no real need to know about him. In fact, at the time, Sami Sharaf was one of the most important KGB agents in the world. He represented a case of a "little man" who grew into a "big man"; a vindication of the KGB practice of recruiting myriad agents in the hope that a few will succeed years hence, a classic illustration of how a single agent of influence can alter history.

Sharaf, barely five feet six inches tall, with his stooped, round shoulders, bulging stomach, bald head, dark, moony eyes, and drooping mustache, looked like a sad pear. His appearance belied his quick mind, natural talent for intrigue, tough, ambitious personality uninhibited by scruples, and seemingly inexhaustible capacity for work. Aside from treason, he had no personal vices. The chief indulgence he granted himself was an occasional evening at the movies with his wife.

KGB cultivation of Sharaf began in 1955, when he visited Moscow with one of the first Egyptian military missions seeking Soviet aid. Shortly thereafter the procommunist Ali Sabry, who then headed the Egyptian cabinet, appointed Sharaf his assistant. Whether he did so at Soviet prodding is unknown. Sharaf soon reorganized Sabry's office, in the process gathering more power into his own hands and gaining direct access to Nasser. He returned to Moscow in 1957 with another Egyptian delegation, and again the KGB assiduously courted him. Sharaf visited New York in 1958 and twice met secretly with Vladimir Suslev, a KGB officer posing as a counselor with the Soviet delegation to the U.N.

Even some former KGB officers knowledgeable about the Sharaf case are not sure precisely when he became a controlled agent. Evidence suggests that the year was 1958. For subsequent to 1958 Sharaf was not mentioned by his true name either at the Center in

Moscow or in enciphered KGB dispatches. Instead, the KGB referred to him by the type of code name reserved for controlled agents. His was Asad, the Arabic word meaning "lion."

Under the misleading title of Director of the President's Office of Information, Sharaf emerged in 1959 as de facto chief of Egyptian intelligence—the principal intelligence adviser to Nasser. He disassociated himself from Sabry and adopted the pose, carefully formulated by the KGB, of a fervent Arab nationalist. He argued that Egypt's overriding domestic goal should be realization of a social democracy, along with a dominant foreign policy objective of Arab unity leading to Israel's dismemberment. In every way possible, he impressed upon Nasser the view that because of domestic political considerations, the United States would ultimately support Israel. Therefore, Egypt would play East against West and extract all it could from the Russians without compromising its sovereignty.

With or without Nasser's knowledge, Sharaf consummated a secret deal providing for joint Egyptian-KGB operations and Soviet training of Egyptian intelligence officers. The arrangement permitted the Russians to further penetrate the Egyptian government through the officers they indoctrinated. It also provided Sharaf with a pretext to meet openly with his KGB case officer in Cairo, Vadim Kirpichenko.

By the early 1960s, Sharaf approved all foreign assignments of Egyptian personnel, supervised security investigations of government employees, and personally directed foreign intelligence operations of particular interest to Nasser. For this purpose he organized within the intelligence service a special network of officers reporting directly to him. More significantly, he determined which reports reached Nasser, as well as the content of his daily briefings. Thus, through Sharaf, the KGB controlled the intelligence that the Egyptian President relied on most to form his judgments and national policy.

Still another dimension of the elaborate web the KGB spun around the Egyptians has been revealed by Ladislav Bittman, former deputy director of the disinformation and action department of Czechoslovak intelligence. Bittman, who fled to the United States in 1968, disclosed that during the 1960s the Czechs dangled their own agents before Egyptian intelligence officers in Western Europe. As soon as the Egyptians recruited some of these Czech spies, the disinformation department supplied them with a stream of false but persuasive reports alleging French, British, and American perfidy against Egypt. To the Egyptians this fake intelligence was all the more convincing because it presumably resulted from their own enterprise. And Sharaf was able to cite it as documentation in support of the anti-Western arguments he urged upon Nasser.

Sharaf continually sought ways to erode Egyptian ties with the West. With KGB guidance, he planned the November 1964 mob demonstration that culminated in the burning of the United States Information Service library in Cairo.

As Nasser's most intimate confidant, Sharaf by 1967 attained power in Egypt second only to that of the President himself. It was Sharaf who relayed presidential orders to Egyptian cabinet ministers, becoming in effect their superior. But his greatest influence upon Egyptian affairs derived from his success in masking his true allegiance. Nasser realized that the Russian advice was self-serving and might not coincide with Egypt's interests. He also recognized that many of his associates, notably Vice President Ali Sabry, Interior Minister Sharawi Gomaa, and War Minister Mohammed Fawzi, were Soviet allies. But he had no reason to question his trusted and loyal intelligence chief, who, guided by the KGB, steadfastly maintained the posture of a patriot concerned only with what was best for Egypt. Sharaf, in fact, was the one man upon whom Nasser felt he could rely for objective counsel. And during the critical spring of 1967, when Nasser was making the decisions that would lead to war or peace, Sharaf presented him the picture of the world the KGB wanted him to see.

Like Consul General Shumilov, Sakharov had not heard of Sharaf until Sbirunov incautiously praised him. But the casual remarks of the Resident conveyed to him extraordinary meaning. And during the next year, the one subject about which he most tried to learn was Sami Sharaf.

In May 1970, Soviet Ambassador Sergei Vinogradov called Sakharov to Cairo. After flattering him with comments about his performance in Alexandria, he announced that "the neighbors"—an MFA term for the KGB—had requested that Sakharov be assigned to Cairo. If Sakharov agreed to the transfer, the ambassador could guarantee him an excellent apartment and a promotion. Sakharov accepted with alacrity. Cairo ranked as a major center of KGB operations, and he particularly wanted to be stationed there. Unfortunately, his plans were to be thwarted.

Three or four days later, Sakharov's mother telephoned him from Moscow. "Have you heard about your new assignment?" she asked.

"Yes," he replied. "I saw the ambassador last week."

"Oh, it's not the one you think," his mother said proudly. "You are going to the golden land. Your father has arranged it."

Sakharov muttered some words of thanks, disguising disgust. In the Ministry of Foreign Affairs the "golden land" meant Kuwait, the oil-rich Arabian emirate on the Persian Gulf. Years before, through some bureaucratic miscalculation, the Soviet government had authorized personnel stationed in Kuwait an unduly high cost-of-living allowance. With this extra money, Soviet personnel in Kuwait could buy duty-free Western products that commanded huge sums in Moscow and thereby accumulate a small fortune. Sakharov long since had ceased caring about money, but he did care about what he could learn in Cairo. Once more, though, his family had interceded to control and change his life. There was nothing to do but go to Kuwait.

The third day after he landed there, Sakharov unexpectedly met Stanislav Yeliseev, a young Soviet diplomat and friend of his student days. Over dinner, Sakharov deliberately mentioned that the KGB had advance intelligence on the surprise Israeli attack in 1967, knowing Yeliseev had been working in the Middle East section of the Ministry of Foreign Affairs in Moscow at the time of the Arab-Israeli war. "Yes, that is true," Yeliseev said. "Later it became known in the MFA that we were informed in advance but did not tell the Egyptians. The big question was, Why?" That was all Yeliseev could offer. Though Sakharov tried, he never learned anything more about the fascinating possibility that the KGB may have furthered the Arab defeat.

Yeliseev was far more talkative about the miserable morale of the Soviet colony in Kuwait. As Sakharov soon saw for himself, it was in a state of sullen, mutinous disarray created by the newly arrived ambassador, Nikolai Kuzmich Tupitsyn.

A mean, foolish, and autocratic functionary, Tupitsyn had received the ambassadorship in reward for years of slavish service as a Party secretary in the Ministry of Foreign Affairs. He was an aging, tyrannical bureaucrat who enjoyed flaunting authority. So he banned the sale of duty-free liquor, prohibited recreational use of the embassy motor launch, and forbade the traditional farewell parties. He himself drank steadily from mid-morning on, and often commandeered the launch for fishing. From Moscow, Tupitsyn imported four lackeys to develop his own informant network within the colony. Among them was his secretary and mistress, Rita Smolicheva, a redheaded shrew.

Normally, a KGB Resident would have warned the Center about such an ambassador. Yet the Resident in Kuwait, Lieutenant Colonel Vladislav Sergeevich Lobanov, wearily had retreated into himself after twenty-five years of subversion and espionage. He still did his job but without the old Chekist impulses.

Unless an offender was Jewish or obviously incorrigible, Lobanov no longer filed the derogatory reports that led to recall. "You know our system," he told a young GRU officer arrested for drunkenness. "If someone who doesn't like you found out about this, he could ruin you. Now, let's forget about it and not let it happen again." Once he remarked to Sakharov: "It is no wonder our young people are turning to religion. What else can we give them besides alcohol?" Sakharov felt that if Lobanov had been a younger man, he would have been a likely candidate for defection to the British or Americans, whom he admired. As it was, the Resident wanted merely to complete his tour without incident and retire to his dacha with his books, folk music, and garden. He was patronizing toward Tupitsyn, content to watch in amusement as the ambassador clumsily tried to enforce the security procedures that were the proper province of the KGB. If security collapsed, as it soon did, Lobanov could rationalize that the ambassador was to blame, as he largely was.

Conditions in Kuwait were radically different from those Sakharov knew in Egypt, where the Russians could do as they pleased. The Kuwaiti security service was vigilant, efficient, and devoid of any illusions about the Russians. Moreover, the Kuwaitis realized that so long as the Soviet Union wished to maintain diplomatic relations with them, they could maintain as tough a policy as they wanted toward KGB personnel. They rigidly restricted the number of Russians allowed in the country. While Sakharov was there, the whole colony seldom totaled more than thirty, including women and children. To Tupitsyn's blustering demands that the quota be increased, the Kuwaiti replied that there were quite enough Russians there already, perhaps even too many. In Western countries, KGB officers have swung at photographers, assaulted citizens, and staged kidnappings, yet remained physically untouched by local police. But a Kuwaiti policeman, after being slugged by a drunken GRU officer, knocked down the Russian, picked him up, and beat him. The police kept the Russian in jail for three days, then ordered the embassy to come and get him.

In this dismal working climate, Sakharov expected to see or learn little. But on Monday of his second week in Kuwait, Lobanov gave him an assignment for which he could not reasonably have hoped. A specialist in operations against Turkey, Lobanov knew no Arabic. Neither did the GRU Resident, Valentin Yakovlevich Zimin, who barely spoke English. A translator promised by the Center was long overdue, and a growing backlog of reports remained untranslated. Because of the KGB endorsements from Egypt that preceded his arrival, the Resident felt he could trust Sakharov to process them. To do so, though, Sakharov would require some preliminary briefings.

The agents' reports, the files and messages to and from the Center to which Sakharov now obtained access, were revealing. Sakharov learned much more as he was taken into the confidence of both the KGB and GRU Residents. In time, he was able to identify numerous agents, recognize embryonic penetrations, and discern the general outline of four major Soviet operations.

One was aimed at sabotaging the oilfields and eventually subverting the government of Saudi Arabia. The KGB there had established and was attempting to sustain a terrorist guerrilla organization calling itself the Front of Liberation of Saudi Arabia. Sakharov translated several reports from KGB agents planted among the terrorists, written in invisible ink and mailed to drops in Kuwait. Each contained some complaint about the extreme difficulty of operating against the government, and one bemoaned the quick execution of terrorists who were captured.

The KGB also had begun to build cells of terrorists in the oil sheikdoms south of Kuwait, along the Persian Gulf. Here again it sought to wrest control of another source of Middle East oil vital to Western Europe and Japan. To attract future terrorists, the KGB held out to youths of these sheikdoms the lure of scholarships in the Soviet Union, where the most apt could be observed, recruited, and trained. Sakharov noted that eighty young men from the sheikdom of Qatar alone had already been ferried clandestinely to Russia through Cairo.

A third operation, consisting of a brutal campaign of urban terrorism, kidnapping, and assassination directed against Turkey, was much more advanced and successful. It began in the early 1960s with a few agents recruited by KGB officers working out of the Soviet embassy in Ankara and trained in the Soviet Union. Back in Turkey, this cadre inducted more radicals into the terrorist movement, some of whom were slipped into adjoining Syria for training in camps supervised by the

Russians. The consequent violence, which produced martial law, curfews, and other social dislocations, starkly exemplifies how the KGB has perfected the techniques of convulsing a society at little cost or risk to the Soviet Union.

Finally, the KGB and GRU were joined in an extremely sensitive effort to penetrate, dominate, and exploit the Palestinian guerrillas. The Soviet purpose was to neutralize Chinese influence among the Palestinians and, ultimately, to harness the guerrillas as a force against those Arab leaders trying to stay independent of a Russian hegemony over the Middle East. To avoid antagonizing the many Arab rulers who already felt menaced by the mercurial, unpredictable Palestinians, the Russians denied them official recognition. When the Palestinian chieftain Yasir Arafat visited Moscow in 1970, for example, he was received by the Soviet Afro-Asian Solidarity Committee—a KGB front—rather than by any representatives of the Soviet government.

However, in the summer of 1970, the KGB began smuggling arms to the Palestinian Liberation Army through Egypt.* The GRU dispatched thirty Palestinians to the Soviet Union to convert them into controlled agents while training them in guerrilla warfare. It also developed an influential agent in Colonel Sha'ir, a Syrian Palestinian in the Liberation Army.

Sakharov discovered no evidence of Soviet complicity in the hijacking and destruction of commercial airplanes that the Palestinians undertook shortly after they were assured secret Russian support. But the Russians were alarmed by the possibility that their clandestine relations might be exposed and cause them to be blamed for the more reckless terrorism. The Central Committee on May 10, 1971, issued an urgent top-secret order forbidding all Soviet embassies from any further dealings with the Palestinians. Contacts there-

---

*The New York *Times* of September 18, 1972, quoted unnamed Palestine guerrilla sources as stating that the Soviet Union had begun to supply arms directly to the Al Fatah organization. The report came thirteen days after the Black September terrorist group, an element of Al Fatah, murdered eleven members of the Israeli Olympic delegation at Munich.

after were made by KGB and GRU officers in the field and by the Afro-Asian Solidarity Committee.

Though none of these major operations originated from Kuwait, the KGB and GRU Residencies there assisted in all of them. An annual quota system required both Lobanov and Zimin to recruit at least three Palestinians for indoctrination in the Soviet Union and subsequent infiltration into the guerrilla movement. In addition, the KGB in Kuwait sought to manipulate segments of the Palestinian Liberation Organization through one of its principal agents, Dr. Ahmad Khatib, a wealthy businessman driven by pathological hatred of the Kuwaiti royal family. Through influence Khatib exerted on Palestinians around Foreign Minister Sheik Jaber el-Ahmad, the KGB in 1970 promoted the Kuwaiti decision to suspend subsidies to independent Jordan. The information Sakharov obtained, of course, was often fragmentary. Lobanov confided, for example, that he was involved in the Turkish operation, without letting Sakharov know just how. But Sakharov did glean names of Armenian, Ceylonese, Indian, and British residents of Kuwait used by the KGB in the operations against the sheikdoms and Saudi Arabia.

In the same way he had succeeded with Sbirunov in Alexandria, Sakharov earned the confidence of Lobanov through his display of efficiency, enthusiasm, and diligence. And as in Egypt, he established a routine that allowed him time alone on deserted beaches and at the office. He ordinarily awakened about 6 A.M., fixed a breakfast of Nescafé and cornflakes, then drove to the beach, ostensibly for a swim. At 2 P.M., when the official tropical workday ended, he returned to his apartment, some eight miles from the embassy, ate lunch, and took a nap. After playing with Yekaterina, he often went back to the embassy around seven and worked alone until ten or eleven o'clock.

Like Referentura personnel the world over, the guards were not allowed off the grounds without an escort, and Sakharov volunteered to be their escort. He took their wives shopping, brought them snacks at night, and became their friend. Sakharov cultivated their friendship in hope that, in some future emergency or other special circumstances, he might prevail upon them to bend the rules and let him into the Referentura alone for a few minutes.

The morning of May 22, 1971, Sakharov called upon Lobanov, intending to suggest that he was now prepared to become a staff officer of the KGB. His words and actions had been planned precisely. He had been overseas three years. Soon he would be recalled for a tour of at least two years at the Ministry, where his access to information might be relatively limited. He now needed to join the KGB officially and permanently, no matter what his father thought. But he did not want to take the initiative, to be a supplicant. He calculated that if Lobanov informed the Center that he was receptive, the assignment would come to him.

But before Sakharov could even bid him good morning, Lobanov asked, "Have you heard the news from Cairo?"

"No, I have been swimming," replied Sakharov.

"They have wiped us out!" exclaimed Lobanov. "Sadat arrested all our people—Sabry, Gomaa, Fawzi— everybody!"

"Was there a man named Sharaf?" asked Sakharov.

"The intelligence chief? Yes, him too," responded Lobanov.

President Anwar Sadat had not "wiped out" all KGB agents in the Egyptian government. But he had crushed an imminent coup and created absolute pandemonium at the Kremlin.

In another Middle East miscalculation, the Russians had totally misjudged Sadat. When he succeeded Nasser in September 1970, they looked upon him as a colorless mediocrity, an inoffensive bureaucrat who, after a decent interval, could be displaced by their own men. However, he soon demonstrated both a shrewd competence and an alarming inclination to govern Egypt in terms of its own interests rather than those of the Soviet Union. Though Sadat was neither pro-Western nor anti-Soviet, he was sufficiently independent that, by the spring of 1971, the Russians concluded they should dispose of him.

A ranking Egyptian delegation departed from Moscow on April 15 after observing the 24th Party Congress. One member, Sami Sharaf, stayed behind, it was announced, for a "medical checkup." Actually, Sharaf remained to consult with the KGB about a coup—a coup by which the Soviet Union intended to install its own New Class of Egyptian rulers and transform the country openly into a "Soviet Egyptian Republic." Somehow, Sadat learned of the plot and crushed it, arresting Sharaf and ninety other conspirators.

In the Kremlin the arrests raised a specter of disaster. The whole Soviet position in the Middle East, as well as its multibillion-dollar investment, now seemed jeopardized. Fearing mob assault on their embassy in Cairo, the Russians hurriedly erected a wall around it and stationed soldiers with machine guns on the roof. Soviet President Nikolai V. Podgorny, who had worked well with the Egyptians before, flew to Cairo to assess and try to repair the damage. Through a combination of threats and promises, he extracted from Sadat a treaty pledging continued Egyptian cooperation.* The treaty notwithstanding, the Egyptians sentenced Sharaf to death for treason, though Sadat commuted the sentence to life imprisonment.

Because Lobanov was so preoccupied with the Egyptian situation that May morning, Sakharov decided to await a more propitious time to broach the subject of joining the KGB. But the KGB Resident left on vacation in early June before Sakharov found occasion to speak to him.

Each day, driving to and from the embassy, Sakharov rounded a certain traffic circle and scrutinized a Volkswagen sedan that often parked there. Sometimes books, toys, and other items were visible in the rear window of the car. The afternoon of July 10, 1971, Sakharov as usual slowed to inspect the Volkswagen. In the rear window he saw something that made his hands tremble and his heart pound—a bouquet of flowers. It was an emergency signal from the American

---

*In an effort to liberate the arrested Soviet agents and sympathizers, Podgorny told President Sadat, "Everyone in the Soviet Union greatly admires Ali Sabry."

Sadat replied: "All Egyptians greatly admire Nikita Khrushchev."

Central Intelligence Agency. Vladimir Nikolaevich Sakharov was a CIA agent and had long been one. Now, by placing the flowers in the car, the CIA was telling him that he was in danger and must flee.

To Sakharov, espionage represented the only effective, practical form of rebellion. It caused him neither feelings of guilt nor disloyalty. For like others of his generation and class, he never had acquired a sense of personal identity with the Soviet Union or an allegiance to it. He thought of the Soviet Union simply as the place where by reason of birth the calculated, pitiless pursuit of his own self-interest was to occur.

Both in orgies with his New Class peers and in the despair of the collective farm, Sakharov experienced a degradation that ultimately caused him to reject the values he had been taught to prize. His rejection of these New Class values turned to hatred of the system that spawned them. But he knew that to strike at the prevailing order successfully, he would have to strike at it secretly. Thus, even while a student, Sakharov resolved to seek, inside and outside the Soviet Union, an opportunity to establish relations with a Western intelligence service.

When he approached the Americans, Sakharov stated that he wanted neither payment nor asylum. He asked only opportunity to help subvert the system by undermining the KGB. For that opportunity he daily risked his life but gave it a sustaining purpose.

The second time he met the Americans, they began drilling him in emergency escape procedures. He could hear the words of the American officer: "If it happens, stay calm; above all else, stay calm. Right up to the moment you meet us, there can be no deviation from your normal behavior. Remember, if it happens, they may already be watching you." As Sakharov's circumstances changed, the CIA changed the escape plan. The one now in effect required him to meet the Americans at a designated site at 11:20 P.M. Sakharov looked at his Seiko watch, a present from his father on his twelfth birthday. It was 2:11 P.M.

Sakharov feared not only the imminent danger but the unknown future. He had vowed to himself and to the Americans that he would live the rest of his life in the KGB, secretly resisting. He had no idea of the kind of life he would begin at 11:20 P.M., assuming he survived until then. He only knew that the end of his marriage would be merciful for both Natalia and him. But then there was Yekaterina.

His efforts at lunch and a nap were in vain. About 4 P.M. he took a .32-caliber Beretta from beneath his mattress, slipped it in his pocket, and called to Yekaterina. They drove aimlessly until sundown, when he stopped by the sea. He watched her, beautiful and laughing, run up and down the beach, shrieking whenever a small wave washed over her feet. Suddenly she ran straight to him and jumped into his arms. "Papa, why are you crying?" she asked.

"I am not crying, Katushka," he said. "I just have sand in my eyes."

Sakharov wanted to be kind to Natalia, to communicate to her in some way that he respected her. For all the hell of their marriage, she was still an intelligent woman with whom he had shared parenthood and six years of his life. He decided that he could be kindest by leaving her with no remnants of affection for him, by making her believe that his disappearance was a blessing. So, after they put Yekaterina to bed, he provoked an argument. All their grievances against each other poured out in vindictive words until she screamed, "Get out! Get out!" He kissed his sleeping daughter and drove off to the embassy, where the guard let him in as usual.

There, Sakharov removed documents from his safe, then went to the Referentura on the second floor. "Vasili, something urgent has come up," he told the guard. "Could you let me in for a few minutes?"

"Why not, Volodiya?" answered the guard.

At 11:05 P.M. Sakharov said good-night to the guard and walked away toward the desert, leaving the keys in his car. The only personal belongings he carried with him were an automatic pistol and his baptismal cross. About noon the next day, Russians began grimly patrolling the airport and highway border crossings out of Kuwait. By then, Sakharov was thousands of miles away.

The story of Sakharov is unavoidably incomplete because he has refused to disclose when, where, or how he became an agent of the CIA or to reveal precisely what he did in its behalf. The CIA similarly has declined to answer questions about the relationship.

One of the more intriguing unanswered questions is why the CIA chose to withdraw an agent of such value and potential. Apparently it believed he was in danger. But why? Sakharov fled Kuwait shortly after the Egyptian government arrested Sharaf and ninety other Soviet sympathizers. Although he obviously could not have caused the arrests, maybe there was some relation between them and his flight; maybe not.

However, Sakharov by the intelligence he provided doubtless did damage Soviet Middle Eastern strategy, and therein lies the significance of his story. Soviet policies based heavily upon clandestine action are in effect hostage to the conspirators assigned to execute them. At times they can be ruined by the lone individual who elects to betray them. And during the past two decades, disgusted KGB defectors repeatedly have undermined Soviet policies by exposing their clandestine foundations.

Yet despite the reverses and risks incurred, Soviet leaders from Lenin onward have evinced no inclination to diminish their reliance upon clandestine actions. One reason they have not may be found in their philosophy. Former U.S. Ambassador George F. Kennan writes of earlier Soviet leaders: "These, it must be remembered, were all men who had renounced, as a matter of ideological conviction, the view that there were any absolute standards of personal morality to which one owed obedience. Usefulness to the cause of social transformation, as defined by themselves, was the supreme determinant of right and wrong in all human conduct, including their own. With relation to people outside the Party itself, this was indeed the only criterion. Here, dishonesty, trickery, persecution, murder, torture were all in order, if considered to be useful and important at the moment, to the cause." Such men naturally considered it better to steal than to buy from another country; better to seek control of a man than to seek his cooperation; better to compromise an ambassador than to compromise with his government.

Perhaps it would be unfair to impute this exact same mental set to the contemporary Soviet leadership. Nevertheless, the present leaders remain steeped in clandestine ways and addicted to dependency upon the KGB. And as the ensuing chapter demonstrates, the dynamics of Soviet society are such that it will not be easy for them or future Soviet leaders to free themselves of this dependency, whatever they might themselves desire.

III

SWORD AND SHIELD

Copies of an urgent cable from the KGB Resident in New York, Boris Ivanov, were rushed to Politburo members early on the morning of October 30, 1963. Ivanov reported that during the night the FBI had captured three KGB officers in the company of an American engineer, John W. Butenko. Two officers who enjoyed diplomatic immunity because of assignments to the United Nations were released. But the third, Igor Aleksandrovich Ivanov, whose cover as an Amtorg trading corporation chauffeur provided no immunity, had been jailed along with Butenko. The cable emphasized that the FBI had confiscated enough evidence in the form of stolen secret documents and electronic and photographic equipment, to imprison Igor for a long time.

At mid-morning General Oleg Mikhailovich Gribanov, head of the Second Chief Directorate of the KGB, summoned Yuri Ivanovich Nosenko, deputy director of the department responsible for operations against American tourists in the Soviet Union. He explained the crisis and announced that the KGB had resolved to capture an American hostage to force an exchange for Ivanov. "What tourists have you got?" he asked.

"It's the end of the season," Nosenko replied with a shrug.

"There must be somebody," Gribanov insisted.

"Well, there is Professor Barghoorn."

"Who is he?" Gribanov asked eagerly.

Typically, the KGB knew all about the American visitor, and Nosenko recounted his past in detail. A political scientist at Yale University, Frederick C. Barghoorn had served at the U.S. embassy in Moscow during World War II and subsequently with the State Department in Germany. The KGB believed that while in Germany he had talked with Soviet defectors and that some of his postwar visits to the Soviet Union were financed by American foundations.

Gribanov beamed. "It's clear. He's a spy."

Nosenko replied that his department had scrutinized Barghoorn's every action during each of his visits and satisfied itself that he was not a spy. He pointed out that just a few days before, in Tbilisi (Tiflis), the KGB had drugged Barghoorn's coffee and made him so violently ill that he required hospitalization. Its purpose in incapacitating him was to search his clothes and notes, yet nothing incriminating was found. "He is interested in our country; that's his field. He has written three books about the Soviet Union," Nosenko said. "But he is no spy."

"Then make him a spy!" Gribanov commanded.

That afternoon the KGB Disinformation Department gave Nosenko false documents ostensibly containing data about Soviet air defenses, and he drafted an operational plan. Because Khrushchev was away from Moscow, KGB Chairman Vladimir Yefimovich Semichastny on the morning of October 31 telephoned Leonid Brezhnev, who agreed with the "principle of reciprocity" and casually approved the KGB plan on behalf of the Politburo. "We have the go," Gribanov told Nosenko shortly afterward.

The evening of October 31 was Barghoorn's last in Moscow, and he stopped at the apartment of American chargé d'affaires Walter Stoessel for a farewell drink. Stoessel sent the professor back to the Metropole Hotel in Ambassador Foy D. Kohler's official car. As Barghoorn stepped toward the hotel entrance, a young Russian hurried over and tried to hand him some documents. As soon as Barghoorn touched them, KGB agents seized him from behind and carted him off to a militia station. He was then transferred to Lubyanka Prison, where he was locked up alone in a cell with a copy of Theodore Dreiser's *An American Tragedy.*

Ambassador Kohler's Soviet chauffeur, a KGB agent, did not advise the U.S. embassy of what had happened, and the Americans in Moscow assumed that Barghoorn had departed on November 1 as planned. They did not learn of his arrest on espionage charges until the KGB began to transmit the signal: Barghoorn for Ivanov.

President Kennedy asked each division of American intelligence whether Barghoorn was in fact involved in any kind of espionage mission. Assured that Barghoorn was not, Kennedy at a press conference on November 14 denounced the Soviet action and demanded Barghoorn's immediate release. Stunned by the indignant personal intervention of the President, the Kremlin was mortified. Amid alarms and consternation, Khrushchev flew back to Moscow. In his eyes, the crime was not the abduction and framing of an American professor; it was that the American appeared to be a friend of Kennedy's. Which idiot, he demanded to know, authorized this mad venture? Meekly, Semichastny and Gribanov pointed to Brezhnev, who exclaimed: "Oh, no! They didn't tell me he was a friend of Kennedy's. I did not approve such a thing."

On November 16 Soviet Foreign Minister Andrei A. Gromyko, acting upon Khrushchev's orders, informed the United States that despite all Professor Barghoorn had done, he was being released.

That the leaders of a great nation should take time from affairs of state to concern themselves with squalid details of kidnapping and blackmail may seem incongruous. Nonetheless, the intimate, personal involvement of Soviet rulers in the operations of the KGB is commonplace. Moreover, it is the natural outgrowth of a spirit that has suffused the Soviet leadership from Lenin to Brezhnev—the spirit of the Cheka.*

Since the days of the Cheka, the secret political

---

*"Cheka" is formed from the organization's Russian title, which translates as the All-Russian Extraordinary Commission for Combating Counter-Revolution, Speculation, and Sabotage. In Russian, the word *"cheka,"* fittingly enough, means "linchpin."

police has been reorganized and retitled many times, becoming successively the GPU, the OGPU, the GUGB/NKVD, the NKGB, the MGB, and the KGB.* But their mentality, ideals, and aims have always been the same. So has their relationship to Soviet rulers, the Party, and the people. The origins and evolution of this relationship beginning with the Cheka demonstrate why it will be exceedingly difficult for any Soviet leaders to lessen their dependency upon the KGB.

Established as an investigative agency on December 20, 1917, the Cheka swiftly transformed itself into a vengeful political police force committed to extermination of ideological opponents. Ferocious statements by its founding director, Feliks Dzerzhinsky, in 1918 proclaimed its temper: "We stand for organized terror. . . . The Cheka is not a court. . . . The Cheka is obliged to defend the Revolution and conquer the enemy even if its sword does by chance sometimes fall upon the heads of the innocent."

During the Bolshevik Revolution and its aftermath, Chekists shot, drowned, bayoneted, and beat to death an estimated 200,000 people in "official" executions, those more or less authorized. Probably another 300,000 or more died in the executions following suppression of many local uprisings or as a result of conditions in Chekist concentration camps. All these barbarities were perpetrated in accord with sweeping Party mandates that sanctioned terror, indeed demanded it. No one incited the Cheka more enthusiastically than Lenin. When idealistic communists protested Cheka sadism, Lenin in June 1918 retorted: "This is unheard of! The energy and mass nature of terror must be encouraged." He ridiculed the communists who objected to Cheka terror as "narrow-minded intelligentsia" who "sob and fuss" over little mistakes. And he sent telegrams to Cheka officials in Penza commanding them to employ "merciless mass terror."

In theory, the Cheka and its terror no longer were necessary once the communists overcame the last

---

*Appendix A traces the organizational history of the secret political police from the Cheka to the KGB.

armed resistance to the Revolution. A fundamental tenet of Marxism, espoused by Lenin, asserted that workers and peasants, upon being liberated by revolution, would rally to form a "dictatorship of the proletariat." Inspired by this precept, workers in industrial Europe would rise up in contagion to create world revolution, and the resultant society would be governed not by coercion but by "direct rule of the masses."

But at the end of the civil war, reality differed from Marxist theory. Violent opposition to the communists erupted among workers and peasants in the form of strikes, demonstrations, and riots. The most shocking trouble occurred in March 1921 at the Kronstadt naval base near Petrograd. Red sailors, who ever since 1917 had been in the vanguard of the Revolution, issued a manifesto accusing the communists of having "brought the workers, instead of freedom, an ever-present fear of being dragged into the torture chambers of the Cheka, which exceeds by many times in its horrors the gendarmerie administration of the Czarist regime." Now the communists were forced to loose the Cheka on the very people in whose name the Revolution had been undertaken. Lenin despaired. "We have failed to convince the broad masses." The consequences were profound.

Lenin perceived that as a minority representing virtually no one but themselves, the communists could survive and rule only through force. He reiterated that their dictatorship must be based "directly on force." Proposing a new criminal code in 1922, he wrote Justice Commissar Dmitri Ivanovich Kursky: "The courts must not ban terror . . . but must formulate the motives underlying it, legalize it as a principle, plainly without make-believe or embellishment. It is necessary to formulate it as widely as possible."

While terrorizing the general population, Lenin also turned on the socialist factions that had fought alongside the communists, arrested their leaders, and, in 1922, staged the first of the Moscow show trials. Then he proceeded to eradicate democracy within the Communist Party itself.

As Lenin destroyed the right of members to debate,

disagree, and advocate their own ideas, the Party became an exclusive order through which the privileged could gain preferred status and perquisites in exchange for unquestioning obedience. Members formed what Milovan Djilas terms the New Class and acquired an overriding selfish interest in sustaining the Party that favored them with income, status, housing, food, merchandise, and leisure denied the general population. But the whole power of the Party resided with whichever oligarchs succeeded in capturing control of the leadership. As Robert Conquest states in his epic *The Great Terror:* "The answer to the question 'Who will rule Russia?' became simply, 'Who will win a faction fight confined to a narrow section of the leadership?' "

By 1924, when Lenin lay disabled and dying from strokes, he had already cast the mold of future Soviet society. He had bequeathed the Russian people dictatorship by an oligarchy, supported by a privileged New Class, wholly dependent upon a political secret police force. He had securely established the principle, practice, and mechanism of political police force and terror as the foundation of the dictatorship. Concentration camps, arrests on the basis of class, sentences and executions without trial, the extorted confession for purposes of a show trial, the hidden informant, the concept of "merciless mass terror" were introduced not by Stalin but by Lenin. The terror decried decades later as Stalinism was pure Leninism, practiced on a grandiose and insane scale.

Stalin merely took the Soviet people further down the path Lenin clearly charted, with ghastly consequences that now have been well documented, notably by Conquest. The terror under him consumed at least twenty million lives and spared no sector of society from the "sword and shield" of the Party. Generals and privates, laborers and scientists, students and professors, artists and bureaucrats, wives and children, members of the political police themselves, all were among the massacred. But Stalin was only following "the scientific concept of dictatorship," relying on the force supplied by the secret police.

After the death of Stalin in March 1953, a band led

by Khrushchev ultimately won "a faction fight confined to a narrow section of the leadership," thereby gaining control of the Party and the Soviet Union. After liquidating Beria and at least twenty-four of his henchmen, Khrushchev and his confederates relaxed the terror by closing many concentration camps, freeing many prisoners, and introducing other benign changes. They also reorganized the entire political and civilian police structure, creating the KGB on March 13, 1954, and enveloping it in a complex web of controls to ensure that it could not threaten the oligarchy.

All the changes were made for practical reasons quite unrelated to considerations of humanity or idealistic Marxism. The first Stalin pogrom against the peasants made a kind of macabre sense in that, despite disastrous economic consequences, it shackled the last large segment of the population capable of opposing the dictatorship. But the subsequent massacres were insanely counterproductive. The oligarchy under Khrushchev realized that to rule the country they did not have to bleed it perpetually. Having participated in the purges themselves, the new leaders had seen that, once Stalinist terror began, literally no one was safe from it. They wanted it stopped in the interests of their self-preservation, and they reached a tacit agreement that in the future power struggles the victors would not kill the vanquished.*

Khrushchev climaxed the liberalization with his fa-

---

*No one could better appreciate the consequences of the terror than Khrushchev, who had been a zealous agent of the purges and a shameless sycophant to Stalin. While presiding over the purges in the Ukraine, Khrushchev referred to himself variously as: "Friend and comrade in arms of Stalin. . . . Closest pupil and comrade in arms of Stalin . . . Stalinist leader of the Ukrainian Bolsheviks . . . closest companion in arms of the Great Stalin." In January 1937 at a Red Square rally celebrating the execution of purge victims, Khrushchev bellowed: "The sentence passed on these Trotskyite murderers, diversionists, and agents of fascism is a warning to all enemies of the people, to all those who might conceive the idea of lifting their hands against our Stalin." The secret police chief of the Ukraine, A. I. Uspensky, told his men on June 24, 1938: "Nikita Sergeevich Khrushchev asked me to transmit to you his regards and to prepare yourselves in a Bolshevik manner for the collection of a rich Stalinist harvest [of bodies]." Khrushchev in 1944 induced thirteen Ukrainian poets to write a collective poem,

mous secret speech to the 20th Party Congress on February 25, 1956. The speech confirmed in horrific detail the tortures, enslavement, and slaughter of innocent people that had taken place under Stalin—atrocities the Soviet Union and its sympathizers had belligerently denied for decades.*

Many construed the Khrushchev confession as heralding an end to abject tyranny and the beginning of enlightened change in the Soviet Union. Nowhere was the hope greater than among the Soviet people, who

---

To the Great Stalin from the Ukrainian People, which was delivered with 9,316,972 [*sic*] signatures affixed. A typical stanza:

> Today and forever O Stalin be praised,
>   For the light that the plants and the fields do emit.
> Thou art the heart of the people, the truth and the faith,
>   We're thankful to Thee for the sun Thou hast lit!

*Bertram D. Wolfe eloquently sums up the import of the speech thus:

"The speech itself is perhaps the most important document ever to have come from the communist movement. . . . It is the most revealing indictment of communism ever to have been made by a communist, the most damning indictment of the Soviet system ever to have been made by a Soviet leader.

"There is about it a nightmare quality, felt alike by those who believe in communism and those who do not. To see one of the chief creators of the atmosphere of terror and of the monstrous cult of the living God calmly reporting to a Congress of those who were all terrorized agents of the terror and votaries of the cult; to hear the confidences as to what went on behind the scenes, torture, false confessions, judicial murder, perfidious destruction of the bodies and souls and very names of devoted comrades and intimates; to see that the Reporter expects absolution and forgiveness and even continuance in absolute power because at long last he has revealed *some* of the guilty secrets in which he shared; to note the broad self-satisfied smile which deprives the fearful avowals of any of the value of repentance; to catch in all the flood of words only a *sua culpa* and not one syllable of *mea culpa* or a *nostra culpa;* to sense how much greater crimes have been committed against a helpless people by this little band whose deeds against each other are in part being recited; to think that men who are capable of doing such things to each other and tolerating, sanctioning and applauding such actions, have managed to vest themselves of absolute power over belief and action, over manners and morals, over life and death and the good name of the dead, over industry and agriculture and politics and communication and expression and culture; and then to hear that the system which spawned these monstrous things is still the best in the world, and that the surviving members of this band are still in their collective wisdom infallible and in their collective power unlimited—who can read this recital without a sense of horror and revulsion?"

heard of the speech by word of mouth. But on June 30, 1956, the Party formally warned both the Soviet people and the world that there would be no fundamental change in the Soviet system: "It would be a serious mistake to deduce from the past existence of the cult of personality some kind of changes in the social order in the U.S.S.R. or to look for the source of this cult in the nature of the Soviet social order." On July 6 *Pravda* put it more bluntly: "As for our country, the Communist Party has been and will be the only master of the minds, thoughts, the spokesman, leader, and organizer of the people."

The basic structure and the dynamics of Soviet society had not changed in the least. The Soviet Union still was ruled by a tiny oligarchy, supported by the New Class of the Party bureaucracy, whose power rested directly on the force supplied by the secret political police, now the KGB. And Khrushchev, while he secretly decried the past genocide of the political police, publicly praised the KGB, using a historically hated term: "Our Chekists in their overwhelming majority are honest workers . . . we have confidence in these cadres." Speaking of capitalist spies and wreckers, he added: "We must strengthen in every way revolutionary vigilance and the organs of State Security." In tribute to the KGB, Khrushchev ordered a statue of Dzerzhinsky erected outside Lubyanka Prison. More significantly, in 1961 he increased both its budget and manpower to permit intensification of foreign operations.

The structure of the Soviet system has in no way changed since October 1964, when Khrushchev was ousted. The new Party boss, Leonid Brezhnev, has evinced even more sensitivity to the oligarchy's dependency upon the KGB, and more of a disposition to employ it prominently. Soon after gaining power, Khrushchev's successors loosed a veritable flood of panegyrics glorifying the "organs of State Security." The Library of Congress has compiled a bibliography of more than 2,400 laudatory books and articles published in the Soviet Union between 1964 and 1972.

As Richard Pipes has observed: "The Soviet leadership of today finds itself in a situation in all essential respects identical to the one Lenin had left on his death, that is, devoid of a popular mandate or any other kind of legitimacy to justify its monopoly of political power except the alleged exigencies of class war." Having never ruled with the consent of the governed, the Soviet leadership of today perceives no feasible way to rule except through the compulsion of the KGB. That is why they are willing to give it any power the Soviet Union has except that which might endanger their own.

IV

BEHIND THE GUARDED GATES

The KGB by necessity is a creature of disguises, deceptions, secrecy, and darkness. It naturally abhors and shrinks from illumination. Over the years, many of its individual operations have been exposed. But the KGB has largely succeeded in concealing the internal structure and procedures that give it a distinct organizational anatomy and personality.

The following delineation of the KGB organization is based upon heretofore unpublished data provided by former KGB personnel and Western security services. Because of their assistance, it now is possible to look into the many hidden compartments of KGB headquarters and to observe the routine of the officers who staff them. Such a survey shows, as nothing else can, all the KGB does. It reveals, too, weaknesses and strengths peculiar to the KGB.

KGB headquarters are located in a complex of unmarked buildings two long blocks from the Kremlin. The main building, 2 Dzerzhinsky Square, is a gray stone structure which before the Revolution belonged to the All-Russian Insurance Company. Political prisoners and captured German soldiers constructed a nine-story addition after World War II. The old section of the building encloses a courtyard, on one side of which is Lubyanka Prison. Here hundreds of men famous in Soviet history, including at least three chiefs of the state security apparatus, have been marched or dragged to execution chambers. To men and women

working with urban guerrillas in Latin America, training Palestinian terrorists in Syria, posing as Americans
in New York tenements, suppressing religious expression in the Ukraine, stamping out dissidence in Siberia
—to some 90,000* staff officers around the world, the
Dzerzhinsky Square complex is known as the Center.

Many "workers of the organs of State Security" begin
arriving at the six pedestrian gates of headquarters
shortly after 8 A.M., even though the KGB workday
does not start until nine. They come early because the
restaurants in the basement and on the eighth floor of
the main building offer cheap, good breakfasts of fresh
milk, eggs, bacon, sausage, and fruit unavailable elsewhere. An officer planning a party or picnic may stop
by the KGB Club, across the square in Building 12,
where he can obtain caviar, sturgeon, smoked salmon,
or other delicacies at nominal cost. He can also find
apples and oranges for his children and buy a bottle
of Scotch whisky for the equivalent of about a dollar.

The standard offices in the headquarters buildings
originally were spacious, but as the KGB expanded,
they contracted, having been partitioned to create more
offices. The walls and corridors are painted a uniform
light green, and except in the offices of the generals, the
parquet floors are uncarpeted. Illumination is provided
by ceiling fixtures with big white globes encasing the
bulbs and topped by a shade. The typical office may
contain a wooden desk forty years old and brand-new
chairs; usually it has a combination safe that each night
is sealed with wax when locked. Most windows opening
on the courtyard are shielded with steel bars or heavy
screens. Personnel in offices with unscreened windows
are warned about letting loose papers blow into the
courtyard. Directors of all principal KGB components
retain offices in the Dzerzhinsky Square complex, but
many operational offices are scattered about Moscow in

---

*The figure represents an estimate by two Western intelligence ser-
vices. In addition to the estimated 90,000 staff officers, the KGB
probably employs about 400,000 personnel as clerical workers,
building guards, border guards, and special troops. The number
of informants and spies it commands doubtless runs into the hundreds of thousands. However, the exact personnel strength of the
KGB cannot be ascertained from verifiable data now available.

disguised buildings and apartments. In the summer of 1972, the offices of most units concerned with foreign operations were transferred to a new building on the circumferential highway outside Moscow.

Yuri Vladimirovich Andropov, who as of 1973 directed the KGB, is a tall, scholarly-looking man with cultured and reserved manners. Born in Russia on June 15, 1914, he worked as a telegraph operator and as an apprentice movie projectionist before enrolling in the Technical School of Water Transportation in Rybinsk. He began his Party career as a Komsomol organizer soon after his graduation in 1936. In World War II he fought with partisan bands behind German lines. As Soviet ambassador in Budapest during the 1956 Hungarian revolt, he demonstrated a first-rate capacity for intrigue by helping lure Hungarian leaders to their deaths.*

Andropov lives in Kutuzovsky Prospekt in the same building as Leonid Brezhnev. Standing in the entry foyer of his apartment, one sees a short hall to the left, leading to the bathroom, and a wide center corridor. Down this corridor on the right is a large dining room and on the left a kitchen, unusually spacious by Soviet

---

*On November 1, 1956, Andropov deceived the newly independent Hungarian government, headed by Imre Nagy, with assurances that the Russians were willing to negotiate withdrawal of their troops. The same night, at the Soviet embassy, he began to conspire with János Kádár to install a puppet regime propped up by Red Army tanks. Next Andropov lured Hungarian Defense Minister Pál Maleter to a banquet on the night of November 3, with a promise of further negotiations. During the dinner, KGB Chairman Ivan Serov and his men stormed into the hall and seized the entire Hungarian delegation. Maleter, hero of the uprising, later was shot. Andropov undoubtedly also contributed to the final Soviet triumph in Budapest. Kádár, now taking orders from the Russians, provided written guarantees that Nagy and other Hungarians who had taken refuge in the Yugoslav embassy could proceed safely to their homes without fear of reprisals. On the evening of November 22, as the Hungarians left the embassy, Soviet officers forced their way into the bus that was to take them home and delivered them to the Soviet military. Nagy was deported to Romania and subsequently executed.

After his return from Hungary in 1957, Andropov became chief of the Central Committee department which is in charge of relations with Communist Parties. He remained in this position until his appointment as KGB chairman in 1967.

standards. Farther down the hall, on the right and left, are two bedrooms. At the end is a commodious living room, furnished with a piano, a stereo, a television set, and a large table in the middle. A cupboard serves as a bar, and there are shelves filled with books, some in English, which Andropov speaks well. As befits any proper member of the New Class elite, Andropov has filled his home with the ultimate Soviet status symbol, foreign furnishings. Many were given to him in 1957 by the Hungarian government, grateful for his assistance in saving it from the Hungarian people.

Accompanied by a bodyguard, Andropov normally arrives at 2 Dzerzhinsky Square in a limousine driven by a KGB chauffeur. His third-floor office, which straddles the old and new sections of the building, is a big, ornate room with rich oriental carpets, embroidered sofas, mahogany-paneled walls, a high ceiling, and tall windows overlooking the square on Marx Prospekt. Adjoining it is a secluded bedroom with a shower. A portrait of Cheka chief Dzerzhinsky hangs on one wall of the office, but there is none of any of his successors. The portrait of Stalin, who for a quarter of a century smiled down on chiefs of the secret political police, of course is gone.

A battery of telephones lines the chairman's immense desk. One, the Kremlevka, provides a direct line to the Kremlin; another, the Vertushka, links Andropov with a circuit reserved for Politburo and ranking Central Committee members. Others connect through high-frequency circuits with the principal KGB offices throughout the Soviet Union and Eastern Europe. Andropov also has a direct line to the Ministry of Defense and the GRU. The sixth phone enables him to summon privately his six deputies—Semen Kuzmich Tsvigun, Vladimir Petrovich Pirozhkov, Lev Ivanovich Pankratov, Ardalion Nikolaevich Malygin, Georgi Karpovich Tsinev, and Viktor Mikhailovich Chebrikov—whose offices are also on the third floor.

Andropov, his deputies, and KGB personnel of all echelons are tightly bound by a web of interlocking controls, which the Party oligarchy enforces for its own protection. Although the KGB theoretically is subordinate to the Soviet Council of Ministers, in practice it answers to the Politburo. Andropov, himself more of a Party bureaucrat than a professional intelligence officer, reports directly to the First Secretary of the Party, Brezhnev. The Politburo approves, and in many cases initiates, major KGB operations. It oversees the KGB's daily functioning through the Administrative Organs Department of the Central Committee. The KGB may not hire anyone as a staff officer without permission of this department. All assignments of KGB personnel abroad, and all but the most inconsequential assignments within the Soviet Union, must be sanctioned by the department. So must all promotions. Thus, from recruitment to retirement, a KGB officer undergoes special political scrutiny at each milestone of his career. Additionally, virtually every officer must become a Party member, submit personally to Party discipline, attend interminable indoctrination sessions, and fulfill his communist duty to inform on colleagues. The watchdogs of the Soviet people are themselves forever watched.

The political controls are so strong and pervasive that the KGB probably never will break its leash and turn against its Party masters. The controls also ensure that KGB operations faithfully reflect the calculated desires of the ruling oligarchy. Thus, no matter how brutal or dangerous, significant KGB actions may not be regarded as unauthorized aberrations.

However, political interference contributes heavily to some of the more conspicuous KGB weaknesses. The Party tries to run the KGB through centralized bureaucratic planning, just as it does other Soviet institutions. Every spring, the KGB leadership, known as the Collegium, must prepare and present to the Politburo an overall operational plan for the forthcoming work year that begins July 1. This plan is based in part on proposals from foreign Residents and chiefs of domestic divisions, who are required to stipulate their objectives for the coming year and to specify in detail exactly what the officers in their commands should do to help fulfill them. Once the master plan is approved in Moscow, it becomes binding and in effect saddles individual officers in the field with production quotas or norms.

The quota system subjects officers to enormous and often counterproductive pressures. To safeguard their careers, they must recruit their given quota of agents and handle a prescribed number of cases. Anxious to please the Center, they often exaggerate the value of contacts they have made or their progress in cases. Trapped by their own exaggerations, they are compelled by the Center to proceed with recruitments that may not be feasible or may turn out to be relatively worthless. Such pressures often make for squandering of resources, errors of judgment, disruption of operations, and embarrassment to the Soviet Union.

Political interference reinforces the bureaucratic propensities inherent in the Soviet system; it also discourages innovation and perpetuates outmoded procedures within the KGB. Simply by recognizing one minor procedure the KGB has followed for years throughout the world, Western security services have detected many of its operations. At the Center, officers assigned to oversee given operations must take all incoming documents pertaining to it and sew them—literally, with a needle and thread—into their case file. While a few KGB veterans defend this practice as a ritual symbolizing authority and responsibility, most view it as an archaic and ludicrous exercise.

The Soviet obsession with secrecy creates further inefficiencies. The KGB keeps such sketchy records at its foreign Residencies that a sudden illness, accident, or expulsion can temporarily paralyze an operation because the lost officer is the only one thoroughly familiar with all its details. When an officer defects or an operation goes awry, the Center has difficulty reconstructing what actually happened and assessing the damage. Aware of this difficulty, KGB Residents sometimes minimize and even falsify damage reports filed in the aftermath of defections. Because information is often pigeonholed, rather than disseminated to those who need to know about it, the KGB sometimes mounts operations to obtain information already in its files.

The passion for secrecy has resulted in rigid and extreme compartmentalization. Officers are locked into niches in a vertical chain of command, dependent upon what their superiors choose to tell them and say about them. To remain abreast of headquarters developments affecting his career, to gain a favored assignment or to extricate himself from difficulty, an officer needs the influence and private channel of communication that friends can provide. The need gives rise to influence peddling and "old boy" networks, through which rumor and authentic intelligence are exchanged in flagrant violation of the security the compartmentalization is designed to maintain.

The KGB overcomes such encumbrances largely because the Party endows it with vast resources and authorizes it to persevere, regardless of the casualties suffered. The tremendous size and scope of the KGB's resources and responsibilities are reflected in its internal organization. The KGB is broadly organized into four Chief Directorates, seven independent Directorates, and six independent Departments, most of which have numerous subdivisions, variously called Directorates, Departments, Services, and Directions. The First Chief Directorate conducts foreign operations. The Second Chief Directorate supervises operations against the Soviet populace and foreigners inside the Soviet Union. The Chief Border Guards Directorate, which is not numbered, patrols the frontiers and, currently, fights the Chinese. The new Fifth Chief Directorate—there are no Third or Fourth Chief Directorates—has special responsibilities for operations against the Soviet population. The seven independent Directorates are Armed Forces, Technical Operations, Administration, Personnel, Surveillance, Communications/Cryptography, and Guards. The six independent Departments are concerned with Special Investigations, Finance, Operational Analysis, State Communications, Physical Security of the KGB, and the Operational Registry and Archives. The First, Second, and Fifth Chief Directorates, together with the Armed Forces Directorate, constitute the most significant part of the KGB, and their components accordingly merit most attention.

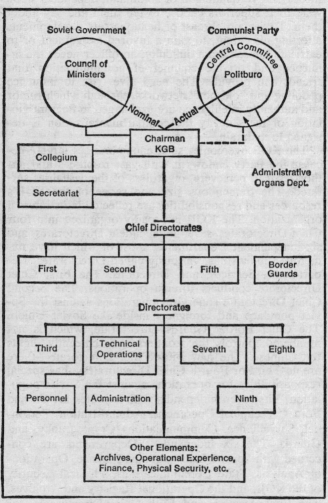

Simplified Diagram of KGB Organization

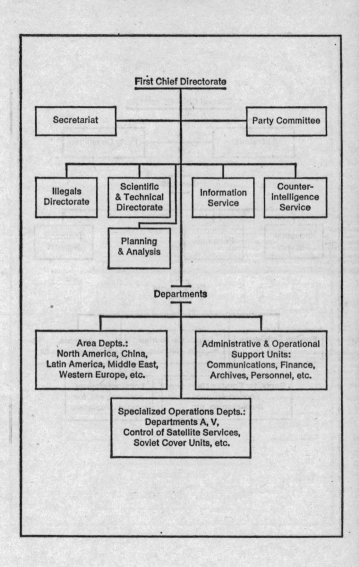

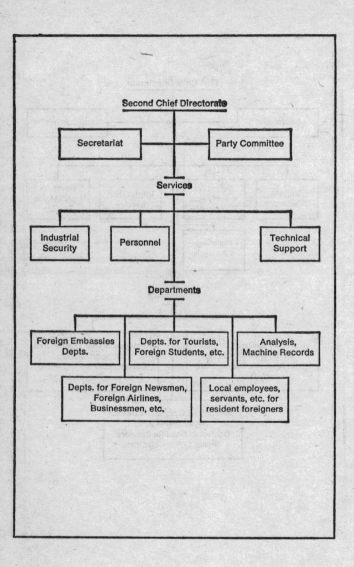

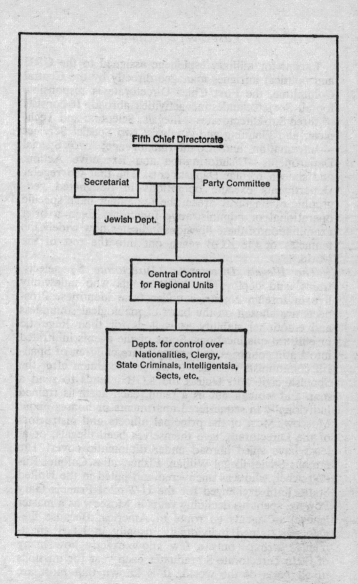

First Chief Directorate

Except for military espionage assigned to the GRU and political intrigues managed directly by the Central Committee, the First Chief Directorate is responsible for all Soviet clandestine activities abroad. It consists of three Sub-directorates—Illegals, Scientific and Technical, and Planning and Analysis; two Special Services —Information and Counterintelligence; two Special Departments—Disinformation and Executive Action; and sixteen regular Departments. The first ten regular Departments execute operations in designated geographic or linguistic areas; the remainder have specific operational or administrative functions. Even a brief examination of these divisions indicates how widely the tentacles of the KGB reach out into the rest of the world.

The Illegals Directorate (Directorate S) selects, trains, and deploys the KGB agents who unlawfully live in foreign countries under false identities. Prospects are chosen on the basis of ideological soundness and emotional stability as well as for their linguistic or cultural qualifications. Some of the agents infiltrated into Latin countries, for example, are children of Spanish communists who fled to the Soviet Union after the Spanish civil war. Unless the KGB intends to send a man and woman out as a team, each agent is trained individually in sequestered apartments or houses about Moscow. Most of the principal officers and instructors of the Directorate have themselves been illegals, or at least have spied abroad under diplomatic cover. The famous Soviet illegal William Fisher, alias Colonel Rudolf Abel, who was uncovered and jailed in the United States until exchanged for the U-2 pilot Francis Gary Powers, spent his declining years in Moscow as a master teacher of agents en route to America. Because illegals are trained individually, usually in KGB apartments, perhaps only a few know exactly how many of them Directorate S graduates each year for missions in all parts of the world. It is known that most are still being consigned to Western Europe, North America, and China. There are indications, from repeated Central Committee demands for improvement of operations against China, that the KGB is having difficulty sustaining illegals there. The Chinese, like the Russians, do not temporize in dealing with suspected spies.

The Scientific and Technical Directorate (Directorate T) was created out of the former Department 10 in 1963 to intensify the theft of Western data about nuclear, missile, and space research, the strategic sciences, cybernetics, and industrial processes. The Directorate engages in operations itself and coordinates the scientific, industrial, and technical espionage of all other KGB divisions. It has a large voice within the State Scientific and Technical Committee (GNTK), which allocates Soviet scientific resources. It also determines which Soviet scientists may attend international conferences, and places some of its officers among each scientific group leaving the country. Having increased steadily in size since its inception, by 1972 Directorate T had a headquarters staff of several hundred officers plus specialists in each major Soviet embassy abroad. Additionally, it has at its disposal numerous consultants from all fields of Soviet science. It is subdivided into four Departments.

In recent years the Soviet leaders have come to realize that their economy is often too backward to transform raw data into production. Thus, more and more, they are trying to induce Western companies to build plants in the Soviet Union and to bring with them managerial as well as technological know-how. Nevertheless, the KGB passion for stealing scientific, technical, and industrial secrets remains unabated.

The Planning and Analysis Directorate (Directorate I) was established in 1969, ostensibly to review past operations and glean from them techniques and principles the KGB could use in the future. To date, though, it has done little more than provide a prestigious sinecure for aging officers and misfits with patrons in the Party.

The Information Service (Special Service I) is of concern to Western intelligence authorities, not because

of what it does but because of what it fails to do.
The Service assembles and distributes all the routine
intelligence gathered by branches of the First Chief Directorate except that processed by the Scientific and
Technical Directorate. It also publishes a weekly intelligence bulletin for Party rulers, briefs officers leaving the country, and, when instructed by the Central
Committee, undertakes special studies of given subjects.

The KGB strives to verify the authenticity of stolen
documents and the accuracy of agent reports. However, neither the Information Service nor any other
KGB division maintains an independent body of professional analysts who attempt to distill the underlying
meaning and import from intelligence. The most important reports go directly through Chairman Andropov
to the Politburo and other members of the oligarchy,
who make their own evaluations. Even the weekly
bulletin consists of raw reports, which the recipients
interpret for themselves. Thus, outside the realm of
science and technology, interpretation of the most significant intelligence is left to Soviet leaders themselves
—men who have matured in the narrow, intellectually
cramped confines of the Party, whose views have been
partially shaped by their own propaganda and who,
with few exceptions, have little personal understanding
of foreign countries.

The absence of a professional panel, empowered,
equipped, and willing to make objective, candid assessments of information and its implications, has cost the
Russians much. From Tokyo, on May 17, 1941, Richard Sorge warned that the Germans were massing between 170 and 190 divisions to attack the Soviet Union.
And Winston Churchill conveyed an even more precise
warning of the imminent German invasion. But Stalin,
acting as his own intelligence evaluator and toadying
to the Nazis until the very end, dismissed the warnings
as a provocation. He consequently left the Red Army
so pitifully unprepared* that when the Wehrmacht on-

---

*The army was also unprepared because so many of its officers
had been slaughtered in the Stalin purges of 1936–38.

slaught began, a Soviet commander at the front radioed his headquarters: "We are being fired upon. What shall we do?" Soviet agents who penetrated the German General Staff in 1941 relayed Nazi military plans to Moscow, sometimes even before they reached German generals in the field. Yet for nearly a year, Stalin and the sycophants around him ignored this utterly accurate and priceless intelligence.

The Counterintelligence Service (Special Service II), despite the defensive connotations of its title, is basically an offensive operating division. It seeks to penetrate foreign security and intelligence services, not so much to prevent them from spying on the Soviet Union as to prevent them from interfering with the KGB. The mission of Special Service II is summed up in an order issued by the Center to KGB Residencies in Western Europe. As intercepted and translated by a Western service, the directive states: "In accordance with the decision of the Collegium, it is imperative that you take immediate steps to utilize all available possibilities for acquiring or injecting our agents in the intelligence and counterintelligence services of the U.S.A., U.K., German Federal Republic, and France. You and the Residency must clearly understand that without the presence of agents in the specified organization . . . we will not be able to conduct operations successfully under difficult circumstances; and we are not in a position to guarantee the security of the work of Soviet intelligence services abroad and the safety of Soviet nationals [illegals] in the countries of your assignments."

Special Service II additionally controls the lives of all Soviet civilians stationed abroad. The security officer from the Service is generally the most feared man in any Soviet embassy. He continuously watches everyone, from the ambassador on down, for "unhealthy signs." Soviet nationals working outside the embassy as correspondents, trade representatives, Aeroflot clerks, or in any other capacity are also subject to his discipline. Each knows that an adverse report from the security officer can bring recall and the destruction of a career.

The Disinformation Department (Department A)

plots clandestine acts and campaigns calculated to influence the decisions of foreign governments as well as schemes intended to demoralize foreign societies and defame individuals or groups hostile to the Soviet Union. It is called upon in attempts to cover up embarrassing messes left by KGB failures around the world, and it assists in the duping, as opposed to the recruitment, of foreigners visiting the Soviet Union. Although the Department executes some operations through its own illegals or officers, most are accomplished through other KGB divisions or agencies of the Soviet government. Since the late 1950s, the Disinformation Department has emerged as one of the most important in the entire KGB. Its activities are analyzed separately in Chapter VIII.

The Executive Action Department (Department V— as in Victor) is the one the KGB most wishes to hide from the world. For this ultrasecret department is responsible for the Soviet Union's political murders, kidnappings, and sabotage—actions which, in KGB parlance, are called "wet affairs" *(mokrie dela)* because they often entail the spilling of blood. Formerly known as the Thirteenth Department of Line F, Department V was expanded and retitled in 1969. Since then it has stressed the development of an ability to sabotage foreign public utilities, transportation and communications facilities, and other nerve centers in peacetime. Its purpose is to give Soviet rulers the option of immobilizing Western countries through internal chaos during future international crises.

The Department stations officers in major Soviet embassies, from which they build and direct agent networks. It also places its own illegals abroad, and trains KGB personnel for individual assassination or sabotage missions. On occasion, in Germany, Ireland, and Mexico it has made use of professional gangsters and perhaps has done so elsewhere. Contemporary operations of Department V, as well as the bloody history of its antecedents, are chronicled in Chapter XIII.

Important as the foregoing divisions are, the greatest striking power of the First Chief Directorate is concentrated in its ten geographic Departments. Most KGB personnel encountered outside the Soviet Union belong to one of these Departments, and they undertake a majority of the KGB enterprises abroad. Their respective targets are:

1st Department — United States and Canada

2nd Department — Latin America

3rd Department — United Kingdom, Australia, New Zealand, and Scandinavia

4th Department — Federal Republic of Germany, Austria

5th Department — France, Italy, Spain, the Netherlands, Belgium, Luxembourg, and Ireland

6th Department — China, North Vietnam, North Korea

7th Department — Japan, India, Indonesia, the Philippines, and the rest of Asia

8th Department — the Arab nations, Yugoslavia, Turkey, Greece, Iran, Afghanistan, and Albania

9th Department — the English-speaking nations of Africa

10th Department — the French-speaking nations of Africa

The duties of the 1st Department are typical of those of all the geographic Departments. From the Center, the Department supervises, maintains, and largely staffs the KGB "legal" Residencies at the Soviet embassy in Washington, the United Nations mission in New York, the embassy in Ottawa, and the consulate in San Francisco. With the exception of agents sent on special missions by the Executive Action and Disinformation Departments, it supports all KGB illegals hidden in North America. It oversees efforts to suborn U.S. government employees, businessmen, students, professors, scientists, journalists, and tourists wherever the KGB can approach them inside or outside the United States. And it manages operations initiated against the United States through international communist-front organizations. The Department bears overall responsibility for penetrating the U.S. government with spies, for developing agents of influence in the Congress, the press, business, labor, and the universities, and for undermining U.S. interests throughout the world. Each of the other geographic Departments has comparable responsibility for operations against the nations within its target area.

The 11th Department of the First Chief Directorate, formerly known as the Advisers Department, conducts the daily KGB relations with the clandestine services of Cuba and the East European satellites. It has some 110 officers posted at service headquarters in Havana, East Berlin, Warsaw, Prague, Budapest, Bucharest, and Sofia. The Russians, whom the Czechs and Poles refer to as "the uncles," inform the Center of all significant actions of the satellite organizations and forward copies of all reports of interest. Simultaneously, they secretly direct agents recruited by the KGB in the satellite services. Sometimes they also recruit civilians in the satellite nations for KGB assignments in the West.

The 12th Department often is referred to as the Cover Organs Department because it places KGB personnel in "cover" jobs with other Soviet government agencies. The Department makes the arrangements for KGB officers to live or travel abroad as diplomats, journalists, trade representatives, clergymen, tourists, or delegates to international conferences. It also arranges for special services the KGB at times requires from the military or other government ministries.

The 13th Department arranges communications with Residencies, officers, and agents abroad, enciphers outgoing messages, and deciphers those arriving from foreign countries. The codes and signals it devises for agents are sometimes rather romantic. Frank Clifton Bossard, an employee of the British Ministry of Defence recruited by the KGB in 1961, had to listen to Radio Moscow on designated nights. His instructions were conveyed in a code based on five melodies: "Song of the Volga Boatmen," "Swan Lake," "Moscow Nights," "Saber Dance," and "Kalinka." James Allen Mintkenbaugh, an American who worked for the KGB more than a decade, was told that should an emergency require him to flee the country, an anonymous caller would telephone the message "When the deep purple falls over sleepy garden walls. . . ."

The 14th Department supplies forged passports, false documents, invisible writing materials, incapacitating chemicals, and other technical devices required in Foreign Directorate operations. Specialists from the Department serve in Soviet embassies to eavesdrop on local communications and provide technical assistance to the Residency.

The 15th Department maintains the operational files and archives of the First Chief Directorate. Since only minimal files are retained in the field, these constitute the only complete record of current foreign operations.

The 16th Department performs routine personnel functions and recruits prospective staff officers for the First Chief Directorate. Many officer candidates are taken from the Institutes of International Affairs and Eastern Languages in Moscow. In former years, relatively few students rejected an opportunity to join the KGB because it offered pay and privileges few other Soviet employers could match. Reportedly, however, increasing numbers of educated youth now disdain the KGB, and it no longer can count on their automatic acceptance of recruitment offers.

Second Chief Directorate

The Second Chief Directorate is generally responsible for controlling the Soviet people and foreigners inside the Soviet Union. Although some of its functions have been shifted to the new Fifth Chief Directorate, it still bears much of the burden of internal repression. The Directorate is composed of twelve numbered Departments, the Political Security Service, the Industrial Security Directorate, and a Technical Support Group.

Of the twelve numbered Departments, six are charged with the twofold task of subverting foreign diplomats and denying them any unapproved contact with Soviet citizens. Their assignments by country are:

1st Department	—	United States and Latin America
2nd Department	—	nations of the British Commonwealth
3rd Department	—	Federal Republic of Germany, Austria, Scandinavia
4th Department	—	all other Western European nations
5th Department	—	non-European nations the KGB considers developed
6th Department	—	non-European nations considered undeveloped

A glance at the resources of the 1st Department suggests just how determined the KGB is in its pursuit of foreign diplomats. The Department is manned by a chief, two deputies, about fifty staff officers, and recruiters, agent handlers, a corps of active reservists, and three hundred professional surveillants on permanent loan from the Surveillance Directorate. Its headquarters are hidden half a mile from the United States embassy in a five-story building that has the facade of a warehouse. But it also owns apartments where it seeks to entrap Americans or to persuade them they are meeting ordinary Russians in their own homes.

The Department has five Sections. The 1st Section attempts the actual recruitment of U.S. embassy personnel. The 2nd Section strives to neutralize any intelligence operations emanating from the embassy. The 3rd Section identifies, investigates, interrogates, and maintains a permanent dossier on each Soviet citizen detected in any contact with an American in the Soviet Union. The 4th Section tries to prearrange and stage-manage contacts Americans may have with Russians while traveling outside Moscow. The 5th Section works among diplomats from Latin-American nations, with a view to enlisting them in operations against the United States or as agents of influence in their own countries.

The 7th Department, the largest of the numbered Departments, preys upon tourists. It employs about a hundred staff officers in Moscow, an equivalent number in the provinces, and some sixteen hundred agents and part-time informants, many of whom are prominent in the arts and sciences. Among its most effective agents are non-Soviet citizens employed by foreign airlines and businesses with offices in Moscow. Of the Department's six Sections, the 1st Section concentrates upon American, British, and Canadian tourists, and the 2nd Section deals with other nationalities. The 3rd Section oversees hotels where foreigners are booked, and the restaurants to which they are usually guided. The 4th Section controls Intourist, through which unofficial visitors must make their travel arrangements, and Sputnik, a travel agency that offers foreign youth economy trips into the Soviet Union. The 5th Section arranges contacts between tourists and the people and investigates any contacts not preplanned. Members of the 6th Section man observation posts at motels, campsites, gasoline stations, and garages along highways traveled by tourists and watch foreigners crossing the Soviet Union by plane or train. This Section also administers a nationwide communication system that enables the 7th Department to transmit both photographs and information about tourists rapidly.

The 8th Department operates computers for the Second Chief Directorate. With increasing KGB reliance upon computers, the Department continues to grow in size and importance.

The 9th Department concentrates upon surveillance and recruitment of foreign students. To this end, it enlists informants among the faculties and student bodies of all Soviet universities to which foreigners are admitted. On occasion, Soviet students have bravely confided to Americans that they were informants and explicitly warned them about KGB traps.

The 10th Department watches and tries to influence or recruit foreign journalists. It ensures favored treatment of correspondents who please Soviet authorities and harasses those who do not. Within the past two years, it has subjected some writers to conspicuous surveillance and provocations in an effort to isolate them from Soviet intellectuals. The Department also staffs the Directorate for Servicing the Diplomatic Corps

(UPDK) in the Foreign Ministry. If a diplomat wishes to make an appointment with a Soviet official or schedule a trip or merely have some balky plumbing repaired, he usually has to call the UPDK—in other words, the KGB.

The 11th Department approves and regulates the travel abroad of all Soviet citizens, except senior Party members and persons in sensitive positions. It scrutinizes the background and circumstances of each prospective voyager, looking for indications or proof of ideological devotion or, on the other hand, of an intention to defect. Ordinarily, either a staff officer or a part-time agent of the Department accompanies each departing group. His reports on the behavior of the travelers become a permanent part of the dossiers kept on every Soviet citizen who ever has been abroad.

The 12th Department investigates major cases of corruption, graft, and waste in government enterprises.

The Political Security Service, which KGB officers refer to simply as the Service (*Sluzhba*), is one of the most important divisions in the entire KGB. For through it, the KGB administers most of the daily controls of Soviet life and most of the informant networks honeycombing the country. The Service formerly consisted of twelve major units called Directions (*Napravleniye*). But in 1969 the functions of the 5th, 6th, 7th, 8th, and 9th Directions were transferred to the Fifth Chief Directorate.

The 1st, 2nd, 3rd, and 4th Directions, which remain in the Second Chief Directorate, supervise general investigations and work with local KGB offices in the four geographic sectors into which Moscow secretly has partitioned the Soviet Union for administrative convenience. A majority of the informant nets are run by the local KGB offices which the four Directions oversee.

The 10th Direction endeavors to catch "economic criminals," including people guilty of currency speculation, black-market dealings, and proscribed private enterprise.

The 11th Direction publishes secret manuals and journals for the Service, reporting problems of discontent and dissidence among other topics.

The 12th Direction is something of a curiosity. It was created in 1963 to subvert Chinese diplomats and penetrate the Chinese embassy in Moscow. Operations against all other foreign embassies are mounted by numbered Departments of the Second Chief Directorate. But the Russians turned the Chinese over to the Service, ordinarily responsible only for internal political matters, because they especially feared the effects of Chinese propaganda and subversion against the Soviet people.

The Technical Support Group of the Second Chief Directorate is actually a professional burglary unit. It has twenty or more specialists in surreptitious entry, who also are trained as safecrackers, locksmiths, photographers, or "flap-and-seal artists" (experts in opening and resealing documents). They assist the numbered Departments in penetrations of foreign embassies and help other KGB divisions rifle Soviet homes and offices.

The Industrial Security Directorate keeps watch over critical production and research centers through its own network of informants. It also exploits Soviet commercial relations with other countries for clandestine ends. The Directorate has six Departments. The first four share stewardship over heavy industry, arms factories, nuclear research, and production centers. Officers of the 5th Department, who permeate the Ministry of Foreign Trade, supervise Soviet commercial exhibitions abroad, monitor foreign exhibitions in the Soviet Union, spot potential recruits among visiting foreign businessmen, and run all Soviet trade associations, such as the Chamber of Commerce. The 6th Department tries to recruit foreign seamen allowed ashore at Soviet ports.

The Fifth Chief Directorate

Alarmed by outbreaks of open dissidence, the Politburo in 1969 created the Fifth Chief Directorate to obliterate political dissent and reinforce controls over the general population. The perversion of psychiatry for political purposes and most of the other intensified repressions reported since 1969 are traceable to this new Directorate. To the embarrassment of the KGB, it failed to track down all the sponsors of the underground *Chronicle of Current Events,* whose accurate reporting infuriated the Kremlin. But late in 1972 the Directorate circulated names of selected Soviet intellectuals and warned that if another issue of the *Chronicle* appeared, all would be arrested even though they were innocent. Out of compassion for the intellectuals rather than fear for themselves, sponsors of the *Chronicle* finally suspended publication.

Most operational divisions of the Fifth Chief Directorate were previously part of the Second Chief Directorate. They include former 9th Department elements responsible for Soviet students; former 10th Department units specializing in operations against the Soviet intelligentsia; and the special Jewish Department. The Fifth Chief Directorate additionally absorbed the 5th, 6th, 7th, 8th, and 9th Directions of the Political Security Service.

The 5th Direction clandestinely controls religion in the Soviet Union. It tries to identify all religious believers and to ensure that the Russian Orthodox Church and all other churches serve as instruments of Soviet policy. The Direction places KGB officers within the church hierarchy and recruits bona fide clergymen as agents. Much of its work is accomplished through the Council for the Affairs of Religious Sects. The Council, which is officially responsible for religion, is heavily staffed with retired or disabled KGB officers.

The 6th Direction has the formidable and critical task of suppressing nationalism among the hundred-odd ethnic minorities that compose about half the Soviet population. Some of the most violent KGB repressions of recent years have been those undertaken by the 6th Direction against minority groups, particularly the Tatars and Ukrainians.

The 7th Direction watches Soviet citizens who have relatives, however distant, living abroad, as well as foreigners who come to the Soviet Union to visit relatives.

The 8th Direction works to negate any influence

Russian émigré groups may exert by slipping literature and agents into the Soviet Union.

The 9th Direction might well be described as the thought-control unit of the KGB. It suppresses unauthorized literature, persecutes heretical writers, and hunts down authors of anonymous books, leaflets, letters, posters, and slogans. It also searches for hidden printing presses, tries to trace typewriters used in "self-publishing," and investigates any misuse of photocopying machines. The Party considers these machines so dangerous that they are kept under lock and key, sometimes even in armored rooms. No one is allowed to use a photocopying machine except in the presence of officially designated witnesses.

The special *Jewish Department* was established in 1971 to intimidate Soviet Jewry, halt public protests, and discourage emigration attempts. Partially because the department is comparatively new, verifiable intelligence about its organization and operations is incomplete. However, the Department at its birth was commanded to recruit more Jewish informants and to ferret out individual dissenters. Department representatives have been stationed in areas containing sizable Jewish communities. Ever since, nonconforming or suspect Jews increasingly have been fired from their jobs, suddenly called into military service, or arrested on bogus criminal charges. While the Soviet Union claims to have relaxed the prohibitive emigration tax, citizens applying for permission to emigrate to Israel still are subject to KGB harassment or arrest.

Chief Border Guards Directorate (Unnumbered)

The Border Guards Directorate constitutes an elite army and navy of about 300,000 personnel belonging to the KGB. It is equipped with the latest weaponry, including artillery and armor, and on occasion its ships range far beyond Soviet coastal waters.

Created by Lenin in 1918, the Directorate has sought ever since to keep the Soviet population caged inside Soviet borders. It guards and patrols the frontiers with the aid of dogs, watchtowers, electronic sensors, and desolate strips of no-man's-land. In 1972 a reporter from the Soviet youth magazine *Yunost* described an exercise in which border guards were being trained to catch citizens trying to slip out of the country. "An imitation frontier line had been marked out across the stadium ground," he wrote. "The 'villain,' dressed in special padded clothing, moved towards it. The onlookers' stands fell silent. A short order rang out, and the dogs sprang forward at the 'enemy.' He tried to get away, but the dogs pulled him down. General applause."

Officers from the Border Guards Directorate served as advisers in Hanoi during the Vietnam war. The Directorate's troops, distinguishable by green piping on their uniforms, have borne the brunt against the Chinese along the Sino-Soviet frontier.

Armed Forces Directorate (*Third Directorate*)

The organization and functions of this important Directorate were analyzed in Chapter I, pages 19–21.

Technical Operations Directorate (*Unnumbered*)

This Directorate develops and produces most of the technical devices used in KGB operations, with the exception of communications equipment. Its scientists and laboratories doubtless lead the world in the invention of incapacitating chemicals, poisons without known antidotes, and instruments that kill while making the cause of death seem natural. The exotic form of mustard gas that so tortured the German technician Horst Schwirkmann was a product of the Technical Operations Directorate.

Officers of the Directorate sometimes travel abroad to provide Residencies with technical assistance. They also covertly inspect the Soviet mails and supply the false documentation needed for clandestine activities inside the Soviet Union.

Administration Directorate (Unnumbered)

This Directorate performs the routine housekeeping chores of the KGB, acquiring and managing property needed for offices or operations inside the country, arranging legal travel, managing the stores, resorts, and apartment complexes set aside for KGB personnel. It has no say over expenditures for operations.

Personnel Directorate (Unnumbered)

A nerve center of the KGB, the Personnel Directorate is strictly controlled by the Administrative Organs Department of the Party's Central Committee. The Directorate tries to anticipate and fulfill all manpower needs, through recruitment of new officers and transfers among divisions. It must approve all hirings wherever they are initiated, all foreign assignments, and all promotions. It also administers and plans the curricula of KGB schools, but not the individual specialized courses given by the Illegals Directorate and the Executive Action Department.

In recruiting young people as future staff officers, the Directorate stresses ideological credentials and, consciously or not, family background. KGB recruits today are predominantly children of the New Class, not the sons and daughters of workers or rural families. Most recruits are nominated by KGB officers from among their friends. A relative of a KGB officer is virtually assured of acceptance unless he has some glaring disability. Unsolicited applications are rarely accepted. Soviet civilians from the lower classes who serve the KGB as informants are sometimes allowed to become officers.

Surveillance Directorate (Seventh Directorate)

As part of their basic training, all KGB officers and agents are taught about surveillance—how to conduct it, recognize it, avoid it. But the Surveillance Directorate, in addition to supervisors, case officers, analysts, and technicians, employs some 3,500 men and women who spend their professional lives doing nothing but following people.

The Directorate is divided, rather illogically, into twelve Departments. The 1st Department follows citizens of the United States and Latin America. The 2nd Department, which formerly hounded people from the British Commonwealth, now trails selected foreign journalists, students, and businessmen. The 3rd and 4th Departments share surveillance of non-Americans. The 5th Department supervises the militia guards posted at each foreign embassy to prevent unauthorized visits by Russians. The 6th Department investigates Soviet citizens being considered for KGB employment. The 7th Department develops and maintains surveillance equipment, from cars and infrared cameras to television cameras and two-way mirrors. The 9th Department patrols the streets that members of the Party oligarchy use in traveling to and from their offices.

The 10th Department, the largest, covers Moscow locales that both foreigners and prominent Soviet citizens are likely to visit. It employs nearly four hundred staff officers and a large corps of part-time spies, mostly retired KGB personnel, to watch parks, museums, theaters, stores, barbershops, stadiums, and air and rail terminals. It also operates the special taxi fleet and Intourist motor pool that enable the KGB to pick up anybody calling a cab or hiring a car. In addition, the 10th Department stations teams in hotels to gather blackmail data by means of photographic and electronic equipment. The 11th Department designs and procures disguises, wigs, mustaches, clothes, and other paraphernalia employed in surveillance. The 12th Department consists of a dozen expert and highly mobile surveillance teams utilized in especially sensitive operations, such as the entrapment of a foreign dignitary or the surveillance of a ranking member of the oligarchy.

The Communications Directorate (Eighth Directorate)

With the aid of space satellites, electronically outfitted "trawlers," or the forests of antennas that spring up on the roofs of Soviet embassies around the world, this Directorate tries to monitor and decipher foreign communications. Its specialists exploited the equipment and documents from the *Pueblo*, seized by the North Koreans in 1968. In addition to intercepting foreign communications, the Directorate prepares the ciphers used by all KGB divisions, transmits communications to foreign KGB posts, and develops Soviet communication equipment.

Guards Directorate (Ninth Directorate)

The personnel of this Directorate are the most thoroughly and intensively screened of all. They are the only men in the Soviet Union allowed to carry loaded weapons near Party rulers, and the leadership literally entrusts its lives to them. Its officers serve as bodyguards for principal Party leaders and their families, both in Moscow and the provinces, and guard the Kremlin and major government offices throughout the country. A testimonial to the effectiveness of the Guards Directorate is the fact that since Lenin was shot and wounded in 1918, no Party leader has been wounded or assassinated—except, like Sergei Kirov in 1934, on orders of the reigning oligarchy itself.*

In addition to its Chief Directorates and Directorates, the KGB has six independent Departments.

Special Investigations Department

This Department makes sensitive investigations in cases involving suspected treason or espionage, pene-

---

*On January 22, 1969, a would-be assassin did attempt to shoot Brezhnev near the Kremlin. He fired at the wrong person, and Brezhnev was unhurt.

trations of the KGB or GRU by foreign intelligence services, and criminality or gross dereliction by important Party members or government officials. It also investigates the circumstances, fixes the responsibility, and assesses the damages of each defection.

Department for Collation of Operational Experience

Analysts from this Department study intelligence operations of the Soviet Union and foreign nations for useful lessons. Findings are reported in a top-secret journal of extremely limited circulation.

Department of State Communications

KGB signal troops from this Department maintain the telephone and radio systems used by all Soviet government agencies.

Department of Physical Security

The guards who patrol KGB offices day and night belong to this Department. The guards examine every employee, regardless of rank, every time he enters or leaves a headquarters building, requiring him to display an identification card no matter how well they know him. At the end of the workday, they inspect each office to ensure that windows are secured, all papers locked up, and all safes sealed. The KGB has two security classifications, secret and top secret. Actually, all papers and documents are treated as at least secret, whether or not they are so stamped.

Finance Department

The Finance Department manages the payroll, disburses and accounts for operational funds, and arranges transfers into foreign currencies. Though willing to expend large sums on demonstrably productive operations, the KGB does not squander money. It often entices a recruit by initially paying him far more than his services are worth. Once the recruitment is solidified, payments are usually made on a piecemeal basis, according to the worth of what is produced, and few KGB agents have grown rich. Case officers must provide a brief, strict accounting of their expenditures. However, they have largely abandoned the practice of requiring receipts from agents. The KGB prefers to do business in U.S. dollars, and officers of the Foreign Directorate are taught the convenience of American Express Travelers Cheques.

The size of the KGB budget is not known. Thousands of KGB personnel are paid by the factory, institution, or government agency to which they are assigned. The KGB receives free logistical support and numerous services from the Soviet military and other branches of government. It well may be that no one in the Soviet Union knows exactly how much the KGB costs the nation.

Registry and Archives Department

Current operational files and KGB records are ordinarily kept by the division concerned with them. The Registry and Archives Department maintains a master index that summarizes the contents of each file and gives its physical location. The archives contain records of investigations and operations dating back to the days of the Cheka.

KGB files include dossiers on all agents and informants, known dissidents and suspects, prisoners, former prisoners, Soviet citizens who have traveled abroad or have relatives abroad, and foreigners in the Soviet Union, as well as prison records and trial records. The files also list petty criminals whom the KGB has elected not to prosecute because it may someday want to blackmail them into becoming informants. Since the reorganizations of 1954, biographical records detailing the residence, work history, and other pertinent data about each Soviet citizen have been kept by the militia. These, of course, are at the constant disposal of the KGB. Both the KGB and the militia are currently trying to modernize their record keeping through the computerization of dossiers.

Since its inception in 1954, the KGB has undergone many organizational changes. More can be expected. But the missions and methods reflected by the present organization of the KGB will not change—unless the whole Soviet Union changes radically.

V

HOW TO RUN A TYRANNY

While endeavoring to shatter the status quo in foreign lands, the KGB strives even more fiercely to preserve the status quo in the Soviet Union. To this end, it engages in far more multitudinous and brutal operations against the Soviet people than against any other. Their subjugation remains both its foremost mission and its greatest accomplishment. Indeed, the continuing feat of the KGB in compelling a vast population daily to obey their rulers is nothing short of epic. The scope of this achievement becomes more apparent upon consideration of the character of the people who must be suppressed and the conditions they are forced to endure.

Of the 246.3 million Soviet citizens recorded in the 1970 census, little more than half are Russians. The remainder are made up of some hundred ethnic or national minorities, many of which struggle to perpetuate their own language and culture while acrimoniously resisting assimilation, or "Russification." Because of their higher birthrates, the non-Russians almost certainly will form a majority of the populace by 1980. Their agitation and demonstrations for a measure of cultural autonomy, for rights promised by Soviet law but denied in practice, have provoked hundreds of arrests and some of the harshest KGB repressions of this decade. In 1972 the KGB even required the aid of paratroopers to quell nationalistic demonstrations in Lithuania. While such public protests are routine in the West, they are extraordinary in the Soviet Union,

and their occurrence is symptomatic of profound strains
to which the nationality problem continues to subject
Soviet society. A good measure of the severity of the
problem is the rising volume of official assertions that
the minorities problem has been solved.*

The Soviet Union is disparate in religion as well as
in race. Despite persecution of the sects and massive
atheistic propaganda, many millions of Soviet citizens
remain religious believers. Paul B. Anderson, a leading
authority on religion in the Soviet Union, in 1964 calculated that there were at least 64 million. He estimated that there were 35 million adherents of the
Russian Orthodox Church, fifteen million Muslims, five
million Old Believers, four million Baptists, 3.5 million
Roman Catholics, 900,000 Lutherans, 500,000 Jews
who profess religious faith, 90,000 Calvinists, and
10,000 Mennonites. Aleksandr Yesenin-Volpin, a noted
mathematician and avowed atheist, stated after his arrival in the West in 1972 that the Soviet Union is experiencing a significant religious revival. Moreover, it
appears that religion is particularly resurgent among
young people.

After more than five decades of famines, pogroms,
deprivations, and tyranny, the Soviet people today reap
fewer benefits from their toil than do the people of any
other advanced nation. It can be argued that a society
should not be measured by its material accomplishments. But the Soviet Union chooses to judge itself by
material criteria and to compare itself economically with
the United States. Therefore, it seems both fair and
useful to apply the standards the Soviet Union has set
for itself.

Even if one accepts Soviet statistics unquestioningly
and makes other charitable allowances, the Soviet stan-

---

*The Soviet Union today embodies the last of the great nineteenth-
century colonial empires, which the Czars built by establishing
Russian hegemony over other nationalities in the Ukraine, the
Caucasus, and vast areas of Central Asia. By keeping intact and
even expanding this inherited empire, the communists have per-
petuated the nationality problem. The largest of the minority groups
are the Ukrainians, Uzbeks, Tatars, Kazakhs, Azerbaijanis, Arme-
nians, Georgians, Moldavians, Lithuanians, Jews, Tadzhiks, Volga
Germans, Chuvash, Kirghiz, Turkmenians, and Latvians.

dard of living emerges in any objective comparison as drastically inferior to that of Western Europe, North America, and Japan. It is lower than that of East Germany, Hungary, and Czechoslovakia. Disparities of income between agricultural and industrial workers, between ordinary professionals and the privileged Party elite, are enormous. In any other industrialized country, comparable economic conditions by themselves probably would suffice to cause political convulsions if not open rebellion.

The Soviet Union occupies nearly one sixth of the earth's land surface, has far more arable agricultural acreage than the United States and more natural resources. Yet, even though fully a third of the entire Soviet labor force is engaged in agriculture, food shortages recur chronically and massive importations of grain are required. The average diet, while adequate in calories, is drably deficient in meat, fruit, and vegetables. Under the Soviet system, the average agricultural worker annually produces enough food for only seven people. In the United States, where less than 4 percent of the work force is involved in agriculture, the average farmer grows enough food for forty-eight people. Although the Soviet farm system has demonstrated itself to be a grotesque failure, Soviet leaders cannot abandon it without permitting far-reaching social and political changes they are unwilling to risk.

The Soviet people are undoubtedly more poorly housed than the citizens of any other industrial state. At least 40 percent of the population still lives in rural areas, and the greater part of rural housing is without electricity, plumbing, or heat, except that provided by stoves burning wood or dried dung. Much of the privately owned urban housing, which constitutes about 30 percent of city dwellings, is made up of log cabins or shacks. Even in the best urban housing, the "socialized" apartments built by the state, a substantial proportion of families still must share kitchens and baths. The Soviet Union has consistently failed to fulfill production quotas for the consumer economy. Even if the government should fulfill its published housing goals for 1975, 18 percent of all "socialized" urban dwellings still would be without running water, 21 percent without sewers, and 38 percent without baths.

Although the Soviet standard of living has risen steadily since World War II, the rate of improvement in recent years has not been as rapid as in France, Italy, Sweden, West Germany, and the United States. Swiss economist Jovan Pavlevski calculates that not until 1963 did the real wages of the Soviet industrial worker *attain the level of 1913*. Pavlevski further finds that in 1969 the real income of Soviet agricultural workers—one third of the labor force—*was only 1.2 percent higher than in 1913*. The take-home pay of the average industrial worker is about a fifth that of his American counterpart, and his effective purchasing power is far less. The variety, not to mention the quality, of goods available is much poorer than that available in Japan or Western countries, and many products commonplace in the West simply are not available.

The economic lot of a Soviet physicist, Alexey Levin, who fled in 1968, was fairly typical. With nine years of higher education, he earned 150 rubles a month. After deductions for income tax, the childlessness tax, and union dues, his net pay was 125 rubles. His wife, an engineer, earned 140 rubles monthly. They lived in a one-room apartment of eighteen square meters, or less than two hundred square feet, sharing a kitchen and bath with five other people. Their monthly rent was ten rubles. Food and the very limited entertainment they granted themselves cost 160 to 180 rubles a month. A suit cost Levin the equivalent of a month's pay. Though he could wear the same suit day in and day out, his wife needed several dresses, and clothes for her were an expensive problem. The Levins had no savings and no prospect of accumulating any.

There is little to justify expectations that the economic plight of the typical Soviet citizen will improve significantly in the near future. Soviet sources express concern that in certain areas critical to economic growth, notably computer technology, automation, and petrochemicals, the Soviet Union is lagging further and further behind the West. Obsolescent machinery is not being replaced in many segments of industry at a pace sufficient to guarantee future economic health. Premier Aleksei N. Kosygin stated that in 1972 the Soviet Union experienced its lowest rate of economic growth in a decade. All the while, according to the nuclear physicist Andrei Sakharov, it spends 40 percent of its national income on armaments—a vastly higher portion than any Western nation spends.*

Manifestly, to compel 246 million people to suffer such an existence, while depriving them of liberty and hope of attaining it, is a momentous task. The KGB continues to accomplish it in large part because the Party has placed at its disposal multiple layers of controls that envelop the individual throughout his life. The daily administration of many of the controls is left to the militia or to special regulatory bureaus; but each constitutes a lever the KGB can pull to bend or break the individual in the interest of the Party. In the workings of these controls one can see the routine of repression and the sophisticated mechanisms of modern tyranny. One can see in them, too, how a tiny oligarchy manages to cow a huge population without having to indulge in the wasteful mass murder of former times.

The Soviet citizen almost immediately upon birth falls under the regulation of the state and the eye of the KGB. Stationed in nearly every apartment building of the Soviet Union is a uniquely communist character known as the *upravdom*—a contraction of *"upravlyayushchy domom,"* which means "director of the house." The *upravdom* acts as the warden of all occupants of the building; he is a combination spy, concierge, janitor, rent collector, and apartment manager. Routinely he reports to the militia, whose services

---

*Two Soviet economists, through an elaborate analysis of unclassified statistics, have concluded that the Soviet Union in 1969 spent between 40 and 50 percent of its gross national product on armaments. The U.S. military budget in 1969 consumed 9 percent of the GNP—in a year the United States still was heavily involved in Vietnam.

The same Soviet economists, incidentally, assert that Western economists have been overestimating the value of the Soviet GNP by as much as 100 percent.

and records are totally at the command of the KGB. However, he also reports directly to the KGB if it develops a special interest in any of his wards. Both the militia and the KGB expect the *upravdom* to detect and report any untoward happening or sustained deviation from normal behavior in the building. If a citizen comes home at 2 A.M. after a party, for example, that may be deemed all right. But if he comes home at 2 A.M. three or four times a month, the *upravdom* will inform the authorities, who forthwith ascertain just why the citizen has started staying out so late.

The *upravdom* maintains for the benefit of the militia and KGB a registration book listing all occupants of his building and any visitor remaining more than seventy-two hours. When a mother brings home a baby, he duly notes the arrival of the infant, who subsequently is carded and pigeonholed in state files. The residential registration books thus enable the KGB to keep track of where everyone in the Soviet Union, including newborn babies, lives.

This scrutiny of the citizen that begins at birth continues until death. For the KGB follows people literally to the grave. Agents sometimes infiltrate funeral mourners to make sure that restrictions upon religious rites are not violated, to identify participants in Christian ceremonies, and to note ideological heresy to which grief may give voice. Tax collectors also have been known to observe funerals in an effort to catch priests receiving gifts from a bereaved family.

At any moment between birth and death, even in childhood, the Soviet citizen is vulnerable to the KGB. A Soviet law pertaining to marriage and family requires parents to raise children in accord with the "Moral Code of a Builder of Communism." The state may deprive parents of their children if the Party or KGB judges that they are flagging in adherence to this code. It appears that the law has been invoked primarily against religious believers, particularly Baptists, but it can be used against any parent the KGB wishes to intimidate. Indeed, its whole purpose is to equip the KGB with another vise with which to squeeze parents into line. However, as the ordeal of one Soviet family illustrates, the children also suffer.

In the village of Dubrovy, Byelorussia, in April 1966, plainclothesmen dragged two sisters, Galya and Shura Sloboda, aged eleven and nine, from their classroom. Ivan, their father, who was working near the schoolhouse, heard his daughters' screams and ran to help them. The plainclothesmen shoved him away, and when he held onto their car as it started off, they beat his hands until he fell to the ground. The screams of the two girls so unnerved the driver that he gunned the engine to muffle them. When the car stopped, one of the girls jumped out and ran toward home, but the plainsclothesmen caught her. The driver recalled that by the time they arrived at the district capital of Vitebsk, the girls were so exhausted they could only whimper. The Slobodas had become Baptist believers, and for that reason alone the KGB took away the two eldest of their five children.

Galya and Shura escaped from the state orphanage in January 1968 and made their way home. Their parents successfully hid them from a search party, but authorities later abducted them from school and transported them back to the state institution.

On December 11, 1968, their mother was sentenced to four years in a concentration camp because of her religious activities. According to recent accounts, the authorities have also taken away the three youngest Sloboda children. Apparently recognizing their earlier mistake in permitting Galya and Shura to stay together, they dispersed the five children in separate orphanages. To tidy up the case, the KGB confiscated Ivan Sloboda's radio through which he had heard religious broadcasts from the West.

An authoritative Soviet source confirms that today the abduction of children is not a rarity. The July 1971 issue of *Science and Religion* (*Nauka i Religia*), which speaks for the Party in matters of religion, states that a large majority of children in Soviet orphanages are confined not because they have no parents but "for various reasons." Thus, Soviet fathers and mothers who

love their children had best be careful about displaying
any behavior that the KGB might construe as violating
the "Moral Code of a Builder of Communism."

At the age of sixteen the Soviet citizen may receive
an internal passport, a document that constitutes one
of the handiest overt controls the communists have
devised. The police increasingly accompany its issuance
with a ceremony that they try to invest with the
solemnity of religious confirmation. The teen-ager is
encouraged to show up in his best clothes, with his
parents, at the local militia station, where the police
take on the role of priests of the state, explaining the
mysteries, beauties, and duties of communism.

Acquisition of an internal passport is indeed a milestone. Without one, the Soviet citizen cannot travel,
much less move permanently to another locality. He
must present the passport to obtain any sort of public
accommodation; and if he visits anywhere for more
than seventy-two hours, he must register it with the
local militia. If he is caught traveling or attempting to
buy a rail, bus, or air ticket without a passport, he is
liable to arrest.

The KGB may cause to be inserted in the passport
restrictions that bar the holder from entering specified
areas or that require him to reside only in a stated zone.
By restricting or withdrawing the passport, the KGB
can put the citizen wherever it wants him. Moreover,
a citizen cannot change his residence permanently unless the local militia places a "deregistration" stamp in
his passport. Merely by signaling the militia not to
"deregister" an applicant, the KGB also can keep him
where it wants him.

While an internal passport is an absolute requisite
to moving, it alone does not assure a citizen the
right to move into a major city. To establish legal
residence in any of the principal cities, the citizen must
prove that he has a job there. To obtain a job, he
must prove that he has an apartment. *But to obtain an
apartment, he must prove that he has a job.* Thus,
unless he is transferred upon orders of the state, the
citizen may not go to the big city without the influence
of someone important—in the Party, bureaucracy, or

KGB—who can arrange for him to receive a job and apartment simultaneously.*

The laws governing internal passports significantly omit any mention of their issuance to rural residents, who, by Soviet classification, compose at least 40 percent of the population. *The reason is that collective farmers, with few exceptions, are denied passports.* Thus, the Party forces many millions to remain in regions most would abandon if they could, and keeps manageable the problems of urbanization that beset most advanced nations. It is possible to escape to the cities through marriage, military service, Party work, personal influence, or joining the KGB. For its own convenience, the state does sometimes grant passports to rural residents if it wants to transfer people to a new industrial area or has some other need. An inhabitant of a collective farm in good standing may obtain a note authorizing a one-day visit to a nearby village or a longer journey to the funeral of a close relative. But for the most part, because they are denied internal passports, the collective farmers are just as effectively chained to the soil as were the serfs of the last century.

The internal passport facilitates regulation of the individual in other ways. Its fourteen pages comprise a detailed personal dossier that enables a KGB officer, a militiaman, or any other authority quickly to ascertain volumes about the bearer. Entry No. 3 discloses the passport holder's ethnic origin—Russian, Ukrainian, Armenian, etc.—according to the region of his birth. However, if the citizen happens to be Jewish, he is listed only as *Yevrey*—Jew—no matter where he comes from. Other entries reveal the social class of the citizen; his complete employment history; his marital history, as well as births and deaths of close relatives; his draft status; and the location of his birth certificate. A section containing the equivalent of internal visas shows every place the citizen has ever lived and every place he has ever visited for more than three days.

The Soviet male at the age of seventeen normally

---

*Usually, but not always, a provincial marrying someone in the city is allowed to join the new spouse if he or she already has an apartment.

becomes liable to the military draft, which authorities on occasion use punitively to control those who incur their disfavor. At current conscription rates, chances are that about 40 percent of all physically qualified young men eventually will serve three to five years in some branch of the military, the KGB Border Guards, or the internal troops of the MVD (Ministry of Internal Affairs). However, every male is subject to mobilization at any time up to the age of fifty-five. In May 1972 scores of Russians identified by the KGB as dissidents suddenly were mobilized to prevent them from demonstrating or circulating petitions during the visit of President Nixon. Some Jews of comparatively advanced age have been called to the army after applying for permission to emigrate to Israel.

When the Soviet citizen takes his first civilian job, the enterprise or office employing him establishes in his name a workbook that provides the Party and the KGB with yet another means of manipulating his life. The workbook records every significant detail of employment—salary, types of duties performed, promotions, transfers, demotions, commendations, and reprimands or other disciplinary actions. Each entry is dated and affixed with an "order number" of the employer. The KGB through its representative, who is ensconced in the personnel office, can seriously limit the future employment possibilities of the individual by inserting in the workbook adverse comments about his political reliability or professional competence. By law, the employee cannot change jobs without submitting to a prospective employer his workbook, which is retained in the personnel office wherever he works. Today Soviet factories and offices ordinarily do not prevent people from leaving by refusing to release their workbooks, as they did in the Stalin era. But the implied threat of a ruinous entry can dissuade a worker from quitting against the wishes of the employer. The workbook follows the employee from his first job through his last and forms another window through which the KGB can look into the life of the individual.

The KGB sometimes uses the Soviet parasite law in tandem with the workbook to deal with nonconformists or otherwise troublesome individuals. According to the law, anyone who is able to work and who is voluntarily unemployed more than thirty days is a "parasite" and, as such, subject to exile or internment in a labor camp. The KGB can arrange the dismissal of a victim with workbook notations that make it difficult for him to find a job, and after thirty days exile him as a parasite.

A young Russian told the British journalist John Morgan: "Suppose that they are angry with you and sack you from your job, and you cannot find other work in your line, say, in the arts. You don't want just to rot, but for a month you find yourself without any kind of work, even though you may have something to live on. They can then declare you a 'do-nothing' and bar you from living in Moscow . . . Migration into Moscow is strictly forbidden, and there is around the city an invisible wall, an invisible curtain, and people from other cities are not allowed to live here. The right to live here is withdrawn from you. You get sent to another town although you have not committed any crime. There is a special law about this."

The parasite law, incidentally, also serves rather effectively to inhibit development of nomadic or hippie subcultures comparable to those which emerged among Western youth in the 1960s.

Perhaps the most basic right any society may grant a citizen is the right to quit, to leave. However, Soviet rulers look upon the individual citizen as state property, a chattel whose loss is not to be permitted.

Normally, no Soviet citizen is allowed to leave the country except as a reward for services to the state or as a result of a judgment that his presence abroad is necessary to state purposes.* The citizen desiring to

---

*A combination of internal and external pressures persuaded the Soviet leadership in 1969 that it would be expedient to allow some Jews to emigrate. Still, the regime insisted upon charging a ransom for the privilege of leaving. The price, exacted in the form of "Education Tax," ranged from $13,200 for a citizen with a normal university degree to $26,400 for one with a doctoral degree. After the U.S. Senate threatened to block trade with the Soviet Union unless the tax was rescinded, Soviet authorities in the spring of 1973 claimed it no longer would be imposed. Nevertheless, the KGB continued to harass and intimidate Jews asking to leave.

travel abroad submits an application to OVIR, the Office of Visas and Registration. This bureaucracy processes the mountainous paperwork that follows during the ensuing six to nine months before the application is approved or rejected. But all along, it is the KGB that makes the crucial evaluations and the final verdict.

The applicant must present documents from his employer, the militia, the local military kommissariat, the courts, the local Party secretary, the health clinic in his district, and even from his spouse. They must prove that he never has been in trouble at work, with the police, the courts, the Party; that he never has been under psychiatric care; that his or her spouse understands and approves of the proposed trip. (Single people with no close relatives to leave behind as hostages rarely survive the processing.) If, after all this, the authorities are disposed to let the applicant out, the chances are at least one in five that he will receive a personal and secret visit from the KGB. The story of this processing and what happens when the KGB officers arrive has been told again and again by former Soviet citizens, and its basics seldom vary.

The Soviet author Anatoli Kuznetsov, who escaped to Great Britain in 1969, recounts a visit by two KGB officers who came to him before he was leaving for France in 1951:

"You realize of course why we've come. One of our comrades will be traveling as usual with your delegation. But it will be difficult for him to cope on his own. So you will help him. You just keep an eye out to see that nobody slips away and stays abroad; to see who talks to whom and to see how people behave."

"No, I don't want to."

"You must."

"Let somebody else do it."

"Others will be doing it."

"I don't want to."

"Well, then, we shall have to reconsider. In that case, what's the point of your going?"

For the overwhelming majority of Soviet citizens, the right to emigrate remains nonexistent.

Kuznetsov ultimately acquiesced, paying the moral price the KGB can exact from any citizen it agrees to let out. However, he proved to be such a poor informant that the KGB rejected his subsequent applications for foreign travel. He got out eighteen years later after fabricating a conspiracy and thereby persuading the KGB that he was a good Soviet citizen.

The KGB further regulates the individual through dominance of institutions that affect his life. Although the tactical methods of KGB personnel necessarily vary with the character of differing institutions, the underlying pattern by which dominance is achieved is the same. It emerges clearly in the KGB regulation of the organized church.

The mere existence of the church in a communist society is of course an anomaly, and the Russians strive mightily to confuse foreigners about the actual status of religion in the Soviet Union. The communists never have recanted in their avowed determination to eradicate religion eventually. Nor have they withdrawn their endorsement of Lenin's declaration: "Precisely because any religious notion, any notion of a Lord God, even any trifling with a Lord God is an unspeakable abomination, which is taken up by the democratic bourgeoisie with particular tolerance (often even with goodwill)—it is for that very reason the most dangerous abomination, the most loathsome pestilence." In recent years the Party has intensified antireligious campaigns, some of which are conducted through the Zaniye (Knowledge) Society, which boasts nearly two million members.*

---

*In an article commemorating the society's twentieth anniversary, *Science and Religion* in June 1968 said: "From the first day of its existence, the society has pursued a policy of far-reaching, many-layered atheist propaganda. Thousands of active atheist propagandists are working in its ranks. . . . During every year the institutions of the society organize hundreds of thousands of atheist lectures and discussions in cities and villages; they edit popular-scientific pamphlets; atheist lecturers are active with contributions in newspapers and reviews. Intensification of the quality of atheist propaganda and its degree of understandability and efficacy is remarkable, showing constant development in its forms and methods. In connection with atheist work, not only are lectures and talks organized but also evenings for discussion meetings, meetings for questions, the

Probably only World War II saved organized religion from annihilation. Their ideological contempt buttressed by a conviction that the church was counter-revolutionary, the communists beginning in the late 1920s attempted to dismantle it. Religious leaders were imprisoned, churches closed, church property confiscated, religious monuments and relics destroyed. William C. Fletcher, an eminent Western scholar of religion in the Soviet Union, writes that "by 1939 the Russian Orthodox Church was on the brink of complete dissolution, and as an institution in society it had virtually disappeared." However, in the extremity of war Stalin recognized that the church could help rally the people to defense of Mother Russia. On September 4, 1943, he received the three ranking Russian Orthodox leaders in a private audience and consummated with them a deal that has governed church-state relations ever since. "Essentially," states Fletcher, "the State granted certain minimal concessions to the Church, marginally sufficient to ensure its continued survival in the country, in return for the Church's unwavering support in political activities."

To control the churches and guarantee that they kept their bargain, the Party established the Council for the Affairs of the Russian Orthodox Church and the Council for the Affairs of Religious Sects, responsible for all other denominations. In 1966 the two councils were merged into a single Council for Religious affairs. The first chairman of the Council for Affairs of the Russian Orthodox Church was an NKVD general, G. G. Karpov. Ever since, the regulatory councils have been dominated by the KGB. Whenever it wants the council to order the church to do something, it can count upon an obliging response.

No one may become a clergyman in the Soviet Union without obtaining a permit from the local representative of the council. It is valid only for service in a designated parish and must be renewed periodically.

reading of articles and reviews, scientific-atheist exhibitions, the showing of films, radio programs, television sessions, conferences, seminars, etc."

The church hierarchy may not promote or reassign a priest or pastor unless the council issues a permit sanctioning his new position. The council has promulgated a variety of restrictions prohibiting clergymen from offering prayers, sacraments, and baptismal or other rites in homes and hospitals. At its own discretion, the council may withdraw or decline to renew the permit of a clergyman who transgresses the rules or who for any other reason becomes unacceptable to the state. Thus, the KGB, through the council, has the power to determine who may serve in the church and to veto all assignments of church personnel.

Technically and overtly, the council may not compel the church hierarchy to promote or place a clergyman in a given position. Therefore, the KGB recruits members of the hierarchy to serve both as informants and the internal equivalent of the agents of influence implanted in foreign institutions. Through them, it usually can station cooperative priests and pastors wherever they best can uphold the interests of the Party.

There is no evidence that clergymen are exempt in the least from the rules, procedures, and customs governing foreign travel by other Soviet citizens. On the contrary, the experiences of a Soviet priest who gained asylum in Switzerland in 1968 suggest that clergymen allowed abroad must be acceptable to the KGB and, if asked, agree to do its bidding.

The supervision of Soviet science is even more stringent than the regulation of religion. The Party both needs and fears scientists. It must allow them to engage in objective scientific inquiry if the nation is to progress; yet it dares not allow them to apply the methods of scientific inquiry to political, economic, or social subjects. It must accord them access to Western research data while inoculating them against the effects of Western ideas. It must grant them sufficient liberties and incentives to do creative work, but not so much freedom and status that they are emboldened to speak out publicly, as the eminent physicist Sakharov has done. To enforce workable resolutions of the dilemma, the Party typically relies greatly upon the KGB.

The State Scientific and Technical Committee

(GNTK), which is heavily staffed with KGB officers, regulates and coordinates basic scientific research in consonance with policy directives from the Central Committee. Assisted by the KGB, the GNTK dictates scientific priorities and the allocation of scientific resources. It also decides which needs should be fulfilled through original research and which best can be met through scientific and technical espionage in North America and Europe.

The KGB on its own watches all scientific institutions, from the Academy of Sciences on down, to make sure they are headed by ideologically acceptable men and are complying with Party directives. The scientist who deviates from Party ideology and policy ordinarily finds that his career possibilities are, at the very least, drastically curtailed. Ironically, the greater a Soviet scientist is, the smaller the chances are that the KGB will let him exchange ideas with foreigners inside or outside the Soviet Union.

Universal censorship provides another control affecting all Soviet institutions and citizens. Glavlit, the Chief Administration for Safeguarding State Secrets in Print, employs throughout the land a veritable army of some 70,000 full-time censors. *Literaturnaya Gazeta* for June 7, 1972, reported that Glavlit staged a festive meeting in the October Hall of Moscow (scene of the Stalin show trials) to celebrate the fiftieth anniversary of censorship. And *Sovietskaya Rossiya,* the day before, announced that the representatives of the Union of Writers attended the meeting with "great enthusiasm" to praise their censors.

The power of Glavlit over what may be legally printed or broadcast in the Soviet Union is all-encompassing. Virtually everything printed, even a bus ticket, must bear a censor's code mark, usually consisting of a letter and five numerals, certifying that publication is officially authorized. In the offices of every Soviet newspaper and publisher is a door with a sign warning "Entry Forbidden" behind which sits the censor. The censorship agency can confiscate or require deletions in material already in circulation, and it determines which foreign literature is acceptable for Soviet readers.

Glavlit, of course, is primarily preoccupied not with military secrets but with ideological and political content. It consults regularly with the KGB, whose chief literary specialist has been identified as General Mikhail Petrovich Svetlichny. However, it refers major problems of policy or interpretation to the Central Committee for final decision. Once a decision is handed down, no matter how capricious or silly, a Soviet editor violates it at personal peril. Leonid Finkelstein, formerly an editor of a leading Soviet scientific magazine, was once ordered to delete a figure denoting the diameter of the earth. "Has this now become secret too?" he asked.

"Yes, there is a directive not to publish the exact size of the planet," the censor replied.

Because the Party so minutely controls the printed word, Soviet citizens have learned to study whatever is published for covert meanings and omens or portents of change. "Our people are such," remarked Khrushchev, "that it is enough to wink and they understand." When an authorized literary work openly and radically breaks with the prevailing orthodoxy, it has an enormous impact, as did Solzhenitsyn's *One Day in the Life of Ivan Denisovich*. There were comparatively few Soviet families without at least one close relative who had been sentenced to a concentration camp, and many felt shame at kinship with an "enemy of the people." Recalling her past to this writer, a young Russian woman whose father died in a camp averted her eyes and, as if confessing some dark personal impurity, said, "You must realize that I am the daughter of an enemy of the people."

Solzhenitsyn's poignant novel, published with the authorization of Khrushchev in November 1962, was the first sanctioned literary revelation of life in the concentration camps. The populace interpreted its publication as a formal exculpation of guilt, as a signal that anyone could now speak of past terrors. Artists and writers interpreted its publication as heralding a new intellectual freedom, and manuscripts detailing the horrors of Stalinism and the injustices of communist society flooded into the publishing houses. To the Soviet leadership, the reaction was frightening confirmation that ideas can be more lethal than guns. Ever since, the power and authority of the KGB to silence dissident writers have been progressively increased.

In 1966 Andrei Sinyavsky and Yuli Daniel were sentenced to concentration camps for writing without a permit and publishing abroad. The poet Vladimir Batshev was found guilty of "engaging in so-called literary activities without being a member of the Writers' Union." To facilitate KGB repression of intellectuals, the Presidium of the Supreme Court on December 16, 1966, promulgated Article 190-1 of the Soviet legal code making it a crime to disseminate "falsehoods derogatory to the Soviet state and social system." In practice, this has proved to mean whatever the KGB wants it to mean.

In literature, the other arts, science and religion, in the factories and on the farms, Soviet citizens who yield to all these controls and secretly assist the KGB in enforcing them are rewarded. The rewards are distributed in the form of professional advancement, honors and prizes, or special privileges to travel and associate with foreigners, as well as in the form of cash payments. The KGB also promises collaborators protection from the vicissitudes of Soviet life, and ordinarily it delivers.

The poet Robert Rodzhestvensky, in the late 1950s, ranked along with Yevgenni Yevtushenko in artistic promise. But rather than fulfill the potential some imputed to him, he became a KGB informant, betraying both foreigners and fellow Soviet artists. Now he lives as a wealthy man, and his mediocre works are widely published in the Soviet Union. Ilya Sergeevich Glazunov emerged on the Moscow artistic scene in the mid-1950s as a painter whose work faintly resembled the old Russian ikon school. It was sufficiently different to make Glazunov popular among young intellectuals, who construed innovation as evidence of honesty and courage. Strangely, he obtained an unusually large apartment that became a gathering place for poets, writers, and artists. Stranger still, Glazunov in time was authorized to show his paintings abroad, though not publicly in the Soviet Union, and to mingle at will with foreign diplomats and especially their wives. What is not surprising, however, is that Glazunov earns all these privileges by informing against Soviet intellectuals and the foreigners.

The KGB of course protects and advances the careers of its secret collaborators and public allies in the arts. The novelist Mikhail Sholokhov offers perhaps the most fascinating example of a Soviet artist who has benefited from the patronage of the masters he openly and slavishly serves. In fact, Sholokhov very well may owe his entire reputation to the protection afforded him by the KGB and the Party.

This reputation rests upon one work, *Tikhi Don* (*Quiet Don*), a great novel of the Russian civil war written from the perspective of a White Guards officer. The novel is distinguished by profound and compassionate human understanding, surging action, and vivid scenes. It is all the more remarkable because when it was first published in 1928 Sholokhov was only twenty-three.*

The subsequent works of Sholokhov evince none of the genius or compassion of *Tikhi Don*. Indeed, they are so undistinguished that they might have been written by any of the hacks who grind out servile Soviet propaganda.** In fact, he was awarded the Nobel Prize

---

*The English version of *Tikhi Don* has generally been published under the title *And Quiet Flows the Don*. Sholokhov published a sequel in 1939 that has appeared in English as *The Don Flows Home to the Sea*. In Russian, the two novels are known simply as *Tikhi Don I* and *Tikhi Don II*. It is the first novel that merits and has received the more critical acclaim.

**The most notable of these later works is *The Science of Hate*, published in 1942. Commenting on it, Khrushchev said: "The works of Sholokhov are deeply human, shot through with love for the human toiler. This is revolutionary socialist humanism which derives from the fact that the happiness of a people is attained in battle with its enemies. During the war Sholokhov wrote *The Science of Hate*, which clearly explained this idea of socialist humanism, showing that it is impossible to vanquish an enemy without first learning to hate him with all the powers of your soul."

for this one work. Because of the stark differences between his one great novel and the rest of Sholokhov's output, Soviet intellectuals long have questioned whether he actually wrote *Tikhi Don*. Stalin's daughter, Svetlana Alliluyeva, recalls from her days in Moscow: "It was common knowledge. Everyone has understood that he just stole these papers from a White Russian officer who had died and included them in the book. It was a joke that the only thing he had ever written that was any good was what he had stolen." Natalia Belinkova, widow of the intellectual Arkady Belinkov, corroborates Svetlana. The literary analyst Viktor Vinogradov, whose expert testimony was used to convict Sinyavsky, once told the philosopher Aleksei Yakushev that he was certain Sholokhov did not write *Tikhi Don*. Then in 1968, shortly before his escape to the West, Yakushev heard from the editors of the literary magazine *Novy Mir* an explicit explanation of how Sholokhov might have stolen materials for the novel. The account may be summarized as follows.

The editorial board early in 1968 received a long handwritten letter from a woman in Leningrad. She stated that her brother* had written a story about his experiences as a White Guards officer in the civil war. Arrested by the communists in the early 1920s and facing execution, the brother, fearing that with his death his work would be lost, confided the location of the manuscript to a fellow prisoner, a priest.

At the time of her brother's arrest, the woman fled the Donbas village where they had been living. When she returned later, she learned about the manuscript and the priest from a message written by her brother before his execution. She also learned from neighbors in the village that the OGPU or court interrogator of the priest was none other than Mikhail Sholokhov.

The woman did not find the manuscript to which her brother referred. But she did find an earlier rough draft of it together with copious notes used in its writing, and she kept them all. She said in her letter that

_____
*From the information given Yakushev in Moscow, it is unclear whether the name of the brother was Sentuchov or Kuzmin.

except for minor changes, chiefly in names and dialogue, the draft she retained was essentially the same as the version of *Tikhi Don* published under Sholokhov's name. Having finally overcome her fear of raising the issue publicly and wishing to act before she too died, the woman now solicited the help of *Novy Mir* in arranging an official inquiry to establish the true authorship of the novel.

The chairman of the editorial board, Aleksandr T. Tvardovsky, replied immediately, urging her to institute formal proceedings by presenting the manuscript together with her explanations to the procurator in Leningrad. Not long afterward, Tvardovsky visited the woman there. She acknowledged writing the letter and told him that upon his advice she had delivered the draft and notes to the procurator. But, obviously terrified, she said she was not at liberty to discuss the matter further. Thereupon, Tvardovsky went himself to see the procurator and asked to examine the manuscript. The procurator advised him that the issue was closed and none of his concern. Subsequently, friends told Tvardovsky that a few days before, Sholokhov himself had been at the procurator's office in Leningrad "in a high state of agitation." There the matter ended.

Professor Yakushev, whose integrity and reputation are beyond reproach, was told the foregoing story first by Tvardovsky's assistant, A. M. Maryamov, then by Tvardovsky himself, who showed him a copy of the letter from the woman. Admittedly, the story they shared with Yakushev does not, in the absence of independent investigation, constitute proof of plagiarism. However, it is consistent with the wide belief of Soviet intellectuals about the authorship of *Tikhi Don,* and it would seem to warrant an impartial, scholarly inquiry into the legitimacy of Sholokhov's Nobel Prize and literary reputation.

It should be added that Sholokhov, who is loathed by decent Soviet writers, is not alone. Members of the Soviet Writers' Union are under unremitting KGB pressure, and some collaborate. What other "union" of writers in the world would send representatives to praise their censors? What other "union" of writers would watch imprisonment of their colleagues and persecution of their nation's greatest living author in mute subservience?

The mere fact that most of the Soviet population docilely submits to this multitude of controls attests to their effectiveness and to the skill of the KGB in overseeing them. Some Soviet citizens, of course, do protest openly. Arrested by the KGB, they are consigned to concentration camps or mental institutions. The most recent data indicate that as of 1972 more than two million people were incarcerated, and countless others were living in forced exile. Certainly, many of the inmates would be considered common criminals by the norms of any society, and it is impossible to determine precisely how many are political prisoners. But undoubtedly the percentage of political prisoners is substantial.

Consider some of the crimes and sentences of people arrested by the KGB since 1969:

Y. M. SUSLENSKY, forty-two, teacher of English, seven years' imprisonment for protesting Soviet actions, including the invasion of Czechoslovakia.

M. Y. MAKARENKO, forty-one, manager of an art gallery, eight years' hard labor and confiscation of property for "anti-Soviet agitation."

JUOZAS ZDEBSKIS, age unknown, priest, one year hard labor for preparing children for confirmation.

NATALIA GORBANEVSKAYA, thirty-five, poet, unlimited confinement in mental institution for demonstrating against invasion of Czechoslovakia and reporting trials of dissenters.

G. ALTUNYAN, age unknown, army officer, three years for circulating "falsehoods derogatory to the Soviet state and social system."

OLGA IOFFE, nineteen, student, unlimited confinement in insane asylum for opposing a celebration of Stalin's birthday.

I. YAKHIMOVICH, forty, former collective-farm chairman, "forcible treatment" in a mental institution for anti-Soviet activities such as protesting the invasion of Czechoslovakia.

A. E. LEVITIN, fifty-five, religious writer, three years imprisonment for violating "separation of church and state."

VALENTIN MOROZ, thirty-five, professor of history, six years' imprisonment plus three years in a concentration camp plus five years' exile, for writing that some of the same men who ran the concentration camps under Stalin continued to run them under Brezhnev.

LEV UBOZHKO, age unknown, student three years in concentration camp for possessing writings of Amalrik, Andrei Sakharov, Solzhenitsyn, and the *Chronicle*.

SIMAS KUDIRKA, thirty-eight, sailor, ten years' imprisonment for trying to flee Soviet Union.

NIKOLAI BOGACH, twenty-eight, student, three years' imprisonment for attempting to establish the "organization for the struggle for social justice."

VLADIMIR GERSHUNI, thirty-nine, bricklayer, indefinite confinement in psychiatric institution for dissemination of "falsehoods about the Soviet State and social system."

V. N. NIKITENKOV, forty-three, doctor, "forcible treatment" in psychiatric hospital of special type for visiting United States embassy and asking about possibility of emigration.

V. MARKMAN, thirty-four, three years' hard labor for "slandering the Soviet state" during long-distance calls to friends abroad.

V. NOVODVORSKAYA, nineteen, student, confinement in a special psychiatric institution for "anti-Soviet agitation and propaganda."

V. VELICHKOVSKY, Roman Catholic bishop, three years' imprisonment for "teaching the faithful to hate everything Soviet."

A. STATKYAVICHUS, thirty-five, state official, "forcible treatment" in a psychiatric hospital for "anti-Soviet writings."

D. F. MIKHEYEV, thirty-one, graduate physics student, eight years in concentration camp for trying to leave Soviet Union illegally and seek asylum abroad.

A. KEKILOVA, poet, forcibly taken to a psychiatric

hospital for sending a letter to the 24th Congress protesting local conditions and renouncing her Soviet citizenship; judged sane but ordered to remain in hospital until she signed a statement that she wrote a petition "while in nervous condition."

M. BARTOSHUK, Baptist leader, five years' imprisonment for instructing children in religion.

A. SEITMURATOVA, history teacher, three years' imprisonment for "preparing and circulating slander against the Soviet social and political system."

L. IBRAGIMOV, teacher, two years' imprisonment for "preparing and circulating slander against the Soviet social and political system."

P. BUBNIS, priest, one year in concentration camp for "organized instruction of children" in religion.

ENVER ODABASHEV, sixty, history teacher, two years' imprisonment for "unlawful seizure and use of collective farmland"—he increased the size of his vegetable plot.

V. DREMLYUGA, age unknown, three years in a concentration camp for dissemination of "falsehoods derogatory to Soviet state and social system"—he charged there was no freedom of speech.

These sentences obviously are more lenient and humane than those of the Stalin era, when such offenders simply were shot. However, under Brezhnev the KGB has been allowed to inflict a convenient new form of punishment as cruel as any imposed under Stalin: "forcible treatment" in mental institutions. The practice of locking up ideological deviants in asylums obviates the need for even pretending to observe formal legal procedures. Rules regarding length of detention, evidence, public trials, and similar "legalities" all can be discarded. By labeling a dissenter insane, the KGB creates at least some doubt about the validity of his or her complaints. By subjecting some political dissenters to drug tortures in the asylums and inflicting on them permanent psychological or physiological damage, the KGB doubtless discourages dissent.

If the evidence of KGB terror within these special Soviet mental institutions were confined to the accounts of a few people or reached us through only a few sources, it might be suspect. But the evidence emanates from sources as varied as poets and a general, from obscure teachers and famous scientists, from witnesses young and old, who have been incarcerated at different times and in different institutions. Their individual accounts differ in detail, but there are in their reports a basic sameness and internal consistency that give them an overwhelming credibility.

The distinguished Canadian psychiatrist Norman B. Hirt has spent a year interviewing former inmates of the KGB hospitals as well as former Soviet psychiatrists now in Israel. He has made public many of his findings, which he plans to publish in book form. In Great Britain, forty-four psychiatrists studied diagnoses made by KGB-controlled psychiatrists of six political dissidents. They judged that the Soviet diagnoses were made "purely in consequence of actions in which they [the prisoners] were exercising fundamental freedoms." In Moscow in October 1971, forty-eight leading Soviet intellectuals on the basis of their own findings petitioned the Ministry of Health to stop the KGB perversion of psychiatry. Dr. Aldwyn Stokes, president of the Canadian Psychiatric Association, states: "We recognize that the evidence of misuse of psychiatric hospitals in the Soviet Union is as hard as it can be. And while we don't have the whole story, there seems not the slightest doubt that these abuses have been going on."

The famed Soviet biochemist Zhores A. Medvedev, together with his brother, Roy A., has written a book, *A Question of Madness,* now available in the West, about his "treatment" for "paranoid delusions of reforming society." General Petr Grigorevich Grigorenko, whom a panel of bona fide Soviet psychiatrists certified as quite sane before the KGB delivered him to its own doctors, kept a diary of his agonies in the first year of his incarceration, and it has been published in the West. The civil libertarian Vladimir Bukovsky smuggled documents and letters to the International Committee for the Defense of Human Rights in Paris.

An Associated Press dispatch from Moscow dated

January 20, 1972, stated that "hundreds of mentally healthy workers, students, artists, and intellectuals" have been herded into KGB mental institutions "for disagreement with official doctrine." It is doubtful that anyone in the West knows the exact number of "patients" interned by the KGB. But in addition to the Serbsky Institute, described in Chapter I, Western sources have located special KGB hospitals in Leningrad, Kazan, Chernyakhovsk, Minsk, Dnepropetrovsk, Orel, Poltava, and Kiev. Moreover, fifteen psychiatric hospitals ostensibly not under KGB control maintain a special section for "political" patients, as do many prison hospitals. Regarding the fate of inmates in these institutions, Solzhenitsyn says: "The commitment of free-thinking people to psychiatric hospitals is spiritual murder, it is another version of the gas chamber, but even more cruel: The sufferings of those being killed are more painful and more prolonged."

The KGB procedures have become efficiently standardized. The arrest party, composed of two to four officers plus one or two "doctors," who may or may not be physicians, usually arrives at night when the victim is likely to be in his apartment. If he resists, the KGB officers twist his arms behind his back and drag him away—to the Serbsky Institute should the arrest occur in the Moscow area. There Colonel-Doctor Daniel L. Lunts pronounces the diagnosis, which usually turns out to be some form of "schizophrenia." On one occasion, the colonel-doctor discovered a strain of schizophrenia "which has no clear symptoms." On another, he is said to have told prisoners: "When I say a man is schizophrenic, he is schizophrenic; just as if I say an ashtray is schizophrenic, it is schizophrenic."

On December 5, 1969, before an opera performance at the Kremlin Convention Palace, a nineteen-year-old girl, Valeria Novodvorskaya, passed out leaflets bearing a poem she had written:

> *Thank you, Party,*
> *For our bitterness and despair,*
> *For our foul silence,*
> *Thank you, Party.*

Thank you, Party,
For the weight of doomed truth,
And for the shots of coming battles,
Thank you, Party.

The psychiatrists at the Serbsky Institute concluded that Valeria suffered from "schizophrenia with a paranoid development of character." Her sole symptoms were "strong emotions" exhibited when answering their questions. Her sentence: "forcible treatment."

The medical findings, sometimes accompanied by the findings of an "ideological diagnostic team," are presented to a court. The accused, being manifestly insane, is not permitted to attend his trial; often he is not even told that it is occurring. His relatives may succeed in finding a lawyer to represent him, and the lawyer may even try his best to defend him. But the lawyer is restricted to questioning the KGB representatives and is not allowed to present any contravening psychiatric testimony. The standard sentence is "forcible treatment."

The prisoner is clearly informed why he has been interned and precisely what he must do to secure his release. Viktor Fainberg, declared insane after protesting the invasion of Czechoslovakia, was informed, "Your ailment is your dissident way of thinking." To overcome the "ailment," the prisoner has only to repent his convictions and affirm that his sentence was proper, that is, admit that he was insane at the time he committed the ideological transgression that aroused the KGB.

The initial treatment may consist of no more than shutting the dissenter up in a cell with unfortunates who are authentically and dangerously insane. Usually denied all contact with his relatives, during this phase he is left to meditate his plight and agonize over whether his loved ones, from whom he daily hopes to hear, have rejected him. However, some inmates allege that they have been beaten and subjected to other physical degradation. Some witnesses who spoke to Dr. Hirt stated that Colonel-Doctor Lunts has required women "patients" to stand naked before him while he stuck pins in their breasts to measure "hypersensitivity" and through it "pathological characteristics."

Periodically the prisoner is offered renewed opportunity to renounce his beliefs and confirm his insanity. If he remains recalcitrant, drug therapy begins. While use of a variety of drugs has been reported, the most frequently mentioned are aminazin, sulfazin, and reserpine. Aminazin can produce extreme depression and shock reaction. Prolonged or excessive injections can cause exhaustive collapse, severe skin reactions, destruction of the memory system, a spasmodic lack of control of muscular movements, and, in some cases, malignant tumors.

After the bricklayer patient Vladimir Gershuni criticized the regime, Lunts's staff and an "ideological diagnostic team" found that he suffered from "chronic schizophrenia." Gershuni describes the effects of aminazin thus: "You no sooner lie down than you want to rise again. You no sooner take a step than you are yearning to sit down again. And if you sit down, you want to begin walking again, and there is nowhere to walk." Sulfazin shoots the temperature up to 104 degrees and makes the least bodily movement extremely painful for about seventy-two hours after an injection. Autopsies performed on victims of reserpine injections have shown extensive brain damage.

Just as the Stalin purges killed idealistic communists who had given their whole lives to the Party, the KGB mental hospitals destroy some men who haved served the Party selflessly and earned its highest honors. One such man is Ivan Yakhimovich. An idealist, he felt it his socialist duty to forsake a comfortable job teaching philosophy and to go to a collective farm. Appointed chairman of a kolkhoz in Latvia, he insisted on a salary equal to the lowest paid his workers—thirty rubles a month. He became a charismatic leader for whom the workers exerted unusual effort, and the kolkhoz so prospered that Khrushchev publicly singled him out as the prototype of the "new Soviet man." His altruism and dedication inspired a laudatory article in the October 30, 1964, issue of *Komsomolskaya Pravda,* which also portrayed him as the model of all a communist should be.

Precisely because he was an idealistic communist, he was shocked by a 1968 trial of young intellectuals arrested because of their beliefs. He wrote to Politburo member Mikhail Suslov denouncing those who think ideas can "be murdered with bullets, prisons, or exile." That August he condemned the invasion of Czechoslovakia. He lost his job, then his residency permit, which made it impossible to find another job, and on March 24, 1969, the KGB arrested him. The charge was defamation of the "Soviet state and social system." A host of friends rallied to testify to his patriotism, his character, his sense of honor and justice. But the KGB found one witness against him, a peasant who remembered that Yakhimovich had attended kolkhoz meetings in dirty clothes and displayed excessive energy. So psychiatric commissions were convened, and it was obvious to them that Yakhimovich was "schizophrenic." The court committed him to a psychiatric hospital in Riga.

Thus far, the international reputations of Solzhenitsyn and Andrei Sakharov have kept them out of the lunatic asylum. But untold numbers of lesser Soviet citizens enjoy no such immunity. Through letters smuggled out by relatives or patients who have "repented," they try to make themselves known and their pleas heard. Hear the plea of V. I. Chernyshov:

"Having been buried, it is hard to prove that you're alive—except perhaps if a miracle should happen and someone dug up your grave before you died for good. It is hard to prove one's soundness of mind from within the walls of a psychiatric hospital.

"I finished the mechanics-mathematics course at LSU [Leningrad State University], then worked as an instructor of math with the title of assistant in the Leningrad branch of the Moscow Institute. I got carried away with collecting books and records, wrote poems for myself, short stories and philosophical essays. I typed up all my writings and bound them in three notebooks: poems and aphorisms, short stories and abstract dissertations, philosophical essays and statements of my ideas, of an anti-communist nature. During my five years of writing philosophical studies, I gave them to only two people. In March 1970 I was arrested for 'anti-Soviet propaganda.' One of the readers of my writings repented at once and was given his freedom. The other, a graduate of the Art Academy, V. Popov, whose guilt was in having drawn a bookplate in my notebook, was arrested.

"In prison I was examined for 30 minutes, and a diagnosis was reached: chronic schizophrenia of a paranoid type. I didn't see a lawyer, was not present at the trial and wasn't even told of the diagnosis or about the trial for a month and a half. My wife told me about it during a visit after the trial. The same diagnosis was reached for Popov. . . .

"In America Angela Davis was arrested. The whole world up to now knows about her fate, she has lawyers, people protest in her favor. But I, I have no rights, not once did I meet a lawyer, I wasn't present at the trial, I have no right to complain, I have no right to go on a hunger strike. I myself have seen how in psychiatric hospitals they tie protesting political prisoners, who refuse to take food or 'medicine,' give them a shot after which they cannot move, and forcibly feed and 'treat' them. A man called V. Borisov has protested for the past two years—they treat him with aminazin, which results in a loss of individuality, his intellect gets blunt, his emotions are destroyed, and his memory disappears. This is the death of creativity: those are given aminazin cannot even read afterward.

"Even though I am afraid of death, let them rather shoot me. How vile, how repulsive is the thought that they will defile, crush my soul! I appeal to believers. N. I. Broslavsky, a Christian, has languished here for over 25 years. And Timonin, whose guilt consists solely of having poured ink in a voting urn. They jeer at Timonin's religious feelings, they demand that he repudiate his faith, otherwise they won't let him out. Christians! Your brothers in Christ are suffering. Stand up for their souls! Christians! . . .

"I am afraid of death, but I'll accept it. I'm terribly afraid of torture. But there is a worse torture, and it awaits me—the introduction of chemicals into my mind. The vivisectors of the twentieth century will not hesitate to seize my soul; maybe I will remain alive, but after this I won't be able to write even one poem. I won't be able to think. I have already been informed of the decision for my 'treatment.' Farewell."

The treatment of Popov, to whom Chernyshov referred, continued. He had been an architect. The doctor advised his wife to draw up official documents about her husband's "disability," explaining that after conclusion of his "treatment," Popov will have to be vocationally reclassified because he never will have the capacity to work as an architect again.

And V. I. Chernyshov will not be able to write even one poem.

VI

SURVEILLANCE AND SEDUCTION

Upon entering the State Historical Archives in Leningrad, Richard Marshall saw that the other American exchange scholars who customarily studied there were unaccountably absent.* A seemingly embarrassed female archivist almost apologetically announced that a "gentleman" wished to see him. Thinking that the "gentleman" perhaps was a director of the archives, Marshall followed the woman to a basement room where a Russian wearing a baggy brown suit was seated behind a table.

The Russian chatted informally for a few minutes without introducing himself. Then he abruptly began accusing Marshall of being a "CIA plant" bent upon "disaffecting" Soviet students. Patronizingly addressing the young American by his first name, he charged that Marshall's fastidious behavior in the Soviet Union was proof of his ulterior motives. Marshall angrily rejected the charges as preposterous. But the Russian persisted and let it be known that Soviet authorities were interested in "certain information" he could provide.

Recognizing the beginning of a KGB recruitment attempt, Marshall started to leave. When he discovered the door was locked, he demanded to be released.

---

*For valid professional reasons, the American scholar has asked that his true identity not be stated, and thus the name Richard Marshall is a pseudonym. The account is based upon interviews with the scholar concerned, other scholars, and official sources. The incidents recounted occurred within the past few years.

"You are in no position to demand anything!" the Russian replied ominously, waving a thick dossier. Trying to break the American psychologically, the Russian read from reports about his finances, the financial condition of his parents, even about his life in the small town where he grew up. The KGB investigation had uncovered not a single blemish or defect which would make the American subject to blackmail. But it had shown that Marshall was a gifted scholar with a promising future in academe or public affairs, precisely the kind of young man the KGB prizes as an agent. So the KGB decided to try to cow him with fabricated charges of moral turpitude.

"We will destroy your reputation in the United States," the Russian threatened. "We have the means of following you wherever you go."

"Evidence is cheaply manufactured in your country," Richard retorted.

Perceiving that Marshall was unintimidated, the KGB officer now made the cruelest threat. Marshall and his wife had covered the walls of their dormitory room with photographs of the baby daughter they left in the United States. From the pictures and doubtless from monitored conversations, the KGB realized that Marshall was a proud and loving father.

"You have a two-year-old daughter back home," said the Russian. "Don't you ever want to see her again?"

The mention of his daughter and the implicit threat of imprisonment did alarm Marshall. Determined to escape and obtain help, he said: "Look, I need some time to think. Let me out and I'll be back at three o'clock with my answer."

At the dormitory, other American students explained that they had been summoned to an "emergency meeting," only to be told upon arrival that a mistake had been made. While his wife packed, Marshall contacted a visiting U.S. cultural attaché who arranged for them to fly to Moscow, where he could gain some protection from the American embassy. Before they arrived, a Soviet official called at the embassy and ordered Marshall out of the Soviet Union.

Jan Fredrik Borge, a Norwegian employed by a Soviet-controlled export firm in Scandinavia, frequently traveled to Moscow. Having heard stories of KGB entrapments, he behaved cautiously, brushing aside Russian girls who sought him out as well as strangers proposing illegal currency transactions. In April 1972 when Borge arrived with a group of Norwegian businessmen, Intourist lodged him alone at the Hotel Ukraina and placed his countrymen in another hotel. On April 30, as he stepped from his room, two KGB officers waiting in the corridor hustled him into a nearby room. Professing an interest in his future, they promised him rapid promotions, cash bonuses, and other perquisites, including compliant women. All he had to do in return was spy against British and American citizens in Norway. Stalling, Borge requested time to consider the proposition, which he reported two days later to security police in Oslo.

In June his firm sent him back to Moscow, where the two KGB officers now demanded his answer. Pointing out that espionage is a crime in Norway and that only a few months before a Soviet engineer had been expelled from Oslo for spying, Borge refused. Thereupon the KGB officers produced a letter from a Soviet citizen charging him with illicit currency transactions and angrily threatened to ruin his career unless he cooperated. Unintimidated, Borge returned to Norway and, wanting nothing more to do with Russians, quit the Soviet-controlled company. The KGB retaliated on August 10, 1972, with an article in *Komsomolskaya Pravda*. Portraying Borge as the personification of imperialistic corruption, it accused him, among other things, of attempted espionage, provocative behavior, anti-Soviet activity, and currency swindling.

A thirty-one-year-old American engineer engaged in top-secret research for an Air Force contractor vacationed in the Soviet Union during the summer of 1966. Both in Leningrad and Moscow he met attractive women, and his pleasant experiences with them belied cold-war bugaboos about the perils Westerners might encounter in the Soviet Union. At a restaurant in Kharkov, a waiter ushered him to a table occupied by a pretty blonde, and the next night they dined together at a café in a park. Afterward, she led him down a dark, narrow path to a bench near an amphitheater. She accepted his embraces and warmly returned them until suddenly she started screaming in Russian.

Flashbulbs popped like strings of firecrackers, and at least ten men sprang from surrounding bushes. The bewildered American was arrested for attempted rape.

"If you confess your obvious guilt, your sentence will be from three to eight years," said a KGB officer calling himself Major Sobolov. "However, if you insist upon denying the obvious, you will be imprisoned from six to sixteen years."

"Let me talk to someone from the U.S. embassy," the engineer said.

"You will be allowed to contact the embassy after you are tried and sentenced," the KGB officer replied. "Of course, if you are willing to cooperate with the Soviet government . . ."

Held incommunicado and facing indeterminate imprisonment in an alien land, the American felt he had no recourse but to "cooperate." KGB officers interrogated him for three days in Kharkov, then flew him to Moscow. There the KGB kept him locked in a hotel suite for six days while specialists extracted technical details of his secret work. They also extorted from him a pledge to become a spy and to rendezvous with a KGB officer in Mexico City the following December. His conscience impelled the American to inform his employer of what he had done. He lost his security clearance and job.

Lorraine DeVries was a kindly woman in her late forties who had given up all hope of marriage.* But while working as a secretary at the Netherlands embassy in Moscow, she met a dashing Russian some ten

---

*The facts of this case were obtained from official sources on the condition that the true name of the woman and dates that would serve to identify her be omitted. Thus, Lorraine DeVries is a pseudonym.

years her junior who shared her interest in ikons. He was Boris Sergeevich Kudinkin, a theological-seminary graduate employed in the foreign section of the Russian Orthodox Church. Advancing from strolls in the park to evenings at the theater and candlelight dinners, Kudinkin courted the older woman. He told her that he was trapped in a miserable marriage to a lamentably dull woman who, unlike herself, could not offer him the intellectual stimulation requisite to true sexual fulfillment. Eventually he became a frequent overnight guest in Miss DeVries's apartment.

Some months later, she and two friends journeyed to Leningrad for a brief holiday. Though she had booked a reservation at the Astoria Hotel, Intourist "mistakenly" gave her a commodious room on the second floor of the Yevropaiski Hotel. By felicitous concidence, Kudinkin happened to be in Leningrad and to have a room on the same floor. He invited her to his room for a lunch of wine and cheese, and soon became amorous. Fearing hidden cameras and microphones, Miss DeVries demurred, but a joint search of the room assured her they were safe from eavesdropping devices. Kudinkin drew the curtains as a further precaution.

A week later, he telephoned the Netherlands embassy in apparent panic and asked her to meet him immediately in a park. That very morning, he said, the KGB had taken him from the Moscow Patriarchate to Lubyanka Prison and harshly interrogated him about their relationship. An officer showed him photographs of them walking together and hinted that the KGB possessed far more incriminating evidence. Claiming that he was already suspect because of his "well-known pro-Western views," the despondent Kudinkin saw his career in ruins. How could this wretched scandal be suppressed? Almost simultaneously he and Miss DeVries thought of the same answer—perhaps Nikolai Alekseevich Butov could help.

Kudinkin had introduced her to Butov months before, representing him vaguely as a "high official" with "important connections." At dinner that night, Butov was not reassuring: "They deal only with the most serious cases at Lubyanka. What were the pair of you up to in Leningrad? Well, never mind, I'll do what I can."

The following evening Butov invited Miss DeVries to dinner alone at an apartment that he said belonged to an absent uncle and confided that he had managed to obtain Kudinkin's "file." It contained some film which he preferred not to look at but which she might want to study for herself. On the film she saw all the scenes of her intimacies in Leningrad. "There is also a tape," Butov remarked. "Would you like to listen to it?" Miss DeVries began to cry.

However, the helpful Butov offered a solution. He simply would keep the whole file in his personal safe, and no one would be the wiser. Of course, he would require a signed statement from her thanking him and pledging cooperation with him in the future. Having signed the statement he dictated, Miss DeVries asked forlornly, "Are you a member of the KGB?"

Butov answered coolly, "Yes, I am."

Netherlands security officers had thoroughly briefed Miss DeVries about KGB tactics before her Moscow tour. But she could not bring herself to disclose anything that might harm her lover Kudinkin, in whom she still believed. Overcome by guilt and anxiety, she suffered a nervous breakdown, and the government transferred her out of Moscow.

About a year later, Miss DeVries was parking her car after driving home from the Netherlands embassy in a Middle Eastern capital. Out of the shadows a man called to her in Russian, "One never forgets those who are in one's heart." It was Butov, who had come to activate her as a spy and introduce her new KGB boss, Viktor Prokovevich Verkovinin. But Verkovinin's demands for secrets from the embassy were so crude and voracious that she soon declared she would see him no more. The KGB countered by threatening to circulate the compromising photographs. She chose to confess to her own people rather than submit further to the KGB.

Security officers at The Hague listened to her story sympathetically. Their most distasteful duty was to inform her that Kudinkin, the one man she thought had loved her, was an agent of the KGB.

Implausible as these tragicomedies seem, they are nevertheless fairly representative of operations the KGB routinely mounts against selected foreigners in the Soviet Union. Embarrassment often inhibits the victims from protesting publicly, but many do report privately to their own governments. The files of Western security services proliferate with personal accounts of such KGB provocations and entrapments. In 1969 the British government published an explicit warning of the hazards awaiting visitors to communist countries, particularly businessmen. The FBI states: "The Soviets never hesitate to employ blackmail, especially against Americans visiting Russia. Sex offers a particularly fertile field—especially perverted sexuality. Suddenly the American is confronted with unpleasant and embarrassing photographs, either legitimate or forged." Professor Robert F. Byrnes of Indiana University, who long helped direct academic exchanges with the Soviet Union, complained in 1970 that KGB depredations against American scholars constitute a serious impediment to normal cultural relations.

Yet they continue year in and year out, because the KGB ranks the control and exploitation of foreigners within the Soviet Union second in importance only to the suppression of the Soviet people themselves. To subvert foreigners, the KGB has constructed, in its Second Chief Directorate, ponderous bureaucratic machinery manned by at least 25,000 staff officers, agents, and civilian informants drawn from all strata of society. This machinery grinds on inexorably and often mindlessly, largely through inertia. Several officers and agents, such as Major Yuri Nosenko, who helped run it, have escaped to the West, and from their firsthand reports its inner workings can be diagrammed rather precisely.

The gears automatically begin to turn in Moscow whenever someone applies for a visa to enter the Soviet Union. The visa application, possibly accompanied by a report from the KGB Residency in the country where it was submitted, is ordinarily referred to an evaluating officer in the 7th (Tourist) Department of the Second Chief Directorate. He requests from the computerized records of the 8th Department, the central KGB archives, and the operational archives of the Foreign Directorate all information that the KGB possesses about the applicant. This may include intelligence gathered over the years by KGB agents as well as data from open sources. The evaluating officer then notifies other KGB departments likely to have a special interest in the foreigner because of his occupation or background. Department V, for example, is interested in employees of public utilities and transit systems because of their access to sabotage targets. The Scientific and Technical Directorate is briefed about proposed visits by scientists, and the Industrial Security Directorate about those by businessmen. The Disinformation Department may be informed about journalists and authors.

After consultations among various Departments and evaluation of what is known about the foreigner, the KGB decides whether to grant the visa. If it is issued, the KGB tentatively decides whether it will try to neutralize, influence, recruit, or merely watch him. This decision is based upon estimates of whether the visitor is a spy, his potential value as a controlled Soviet agent or unwitting purveyor of disinformation, and his vulnerability to recruitment. Other factors, such as age, health, and current needs of the KGB, also may be considered. If the visitor is deemed likely to return to the Soviet Union, the KGB may content itself with gathering intelligence or compromising evidence about him for future use. The official British warning to businessmen states: "Alternatively, the 'evidence' may be stored away for use at a later date, perhaps when the circumstances have changed; for example, after the visitor has married. . . . There are many cases on record where people have been compromised and left to think that their troubles were over, only to find themselves some years later subject to a threatening approach." Even the season of the year can be a factor. During the cold months when foreigners are in relatively short supply, the KGB may hungrily pounce on people of doubtful utility or none at all, simply to fulfill recruitment quotas.

No matter what the initial KGB evaluation is, before a foreigner ever steps on Soviet soil at least one officer is placed in unseen charge of him. If the KGB has no special interest in him, the responsible officer may simultaneously oversee ten to twenty other ordinary visitors, receiving and analyzing daily surveillance reports on the activities of each foreigner for whom he is responsible. Surveillance of any visitor is facilitated by imposition of a rather rigid itinerary approved in advance by the KGB. Escorts from Intourist or other Soviet organizations, all of whom must account daily to the KGB, are prohibited from allowing significant deviations from the itinerary. The difficulties foreigners experience in trying to change travel plans once they are inside the Soviet Union are mostly due to the inconvenience such changes cause the KGB. The hotels, restaurants, stores, and tourist sites frequented by foreigners are peopled with informants. Any scheduled associations with Soviet citizens are arranged by the KGB. Should the foreigner chance to have unplanned contact with a Soviet citizen, that citizen is investigated, interrogated, and in some cases enlisted as an informant.

Certainly the machinery of the Second Chief Directorate does not always function properly or efficiently. The KGB occasionally does lose track of some of the Western tourists, and it cannot always trail each member of the foreign colony living in Moscow. The hunger of many Soviet citizens, particularly youths, for communication and human kinship with foreigners is such that some do approach Westerners without ulterior motives. However, the chances of maintaining normal contact with an ordinary Soviet citizen, free from KGB control, drop precipitously with each renewal of the contact. Generally, a visitor unknowingly passes through the Soviet Union wrapped in an invisible KGB cocoon that effectively shields him from what the KGB does not want him to see or hear.

If the KGB, for any reason, has other than a routine interest in the foreigner, the surveillance is much more elaborate. The visitor is secretly photographed at his point of entry, and his picture precedes him by KGB wirephoto wherever he goes. His hotel room contains not only the standard microphones and television cameras but also infrared cameras that can record his actions in the dark. Some rooms and even railway sleeping cars contain ducts for the introduction of vapors that have been used to incapacitate diplomatic couriers so that their pouches could be searched.

KGB laboratories have developed a special chemical powder to spot letters mailed by foreigners. A hotel chambermaid slips into the foreigner's room and dusts the pockets of his clothes with the powder, which is too fine to be seen or felt. Having put his hands into his pockets, the visitor leaves microscopic traces of the chemical on whatever he touches. Should he mail a letter, devices at the central post office detect the powder on the envelope. Nosenko notes that the KGB can also code the powder by color to identify the sender of the letter. The powder is effective for only about two weeks, so a timetable is inserted in the foreigner's file at the center to show when his pockets must be dusted again. The chambermaid may also paint his shoes with a colorless liquid that enables KGB agents with trained dogs to track him while remaining out of sight.

The visitor in whom there is a priority interest is steered to restaurants where microphones are installed in each table, enabling the KGB to tune in wherever he sits. The Soviet citizens he meets as if by chance are experienced officers or agents assigned to assess his attitudes, character, and weaknesses. The KGB is likely to test him further by exposing him to desirable women, homosexuals, black marketeers, and other provocateurs pretending to be intellectual dissidents or Western sympathizers. His reactions often suggest to the KGB which pressures or appeals are apt to be most effective.

Some operations against visitors are so petty and crude that they require no elaborate preparation. During the 1972 hockey matches between Canada and the Soviet Union, for example, the KGB harassed the Canadian team members by disrupting their pregame naps with anonymous phone calls and absconding with most of the three hundred pounds of steaks they brought along.

A visitor whose person and effects the KGB wishes to search may suddenly find himself violently ill, suffering such acute symptoms of food poisoning that he loses consciousness or requires hospitalization. An Intourist guide in the fall of 1967 insisted that two touring British and American attachés sample the product of a winery near the city of Kishinev. Back in their hotel room, the attachés collapsed with agonizing nausea. Some six hours later, they awoke to find their room a shambles. They were naked and had nightmarish recollections of being roughly searched while in their drugged stupor. Peter Frank, a General Electric scientist being transferred from Tokyo to Zurich, made a tourist stop in Bukhara while flying across the Soviet Union in May 1969. An Intourist guide at the airport pressed him to try some spicy Uzbek food, but he declined, mentioning that he recently had an upset stomach. Unable to drug Frank, his Soviet escorts seized upon this trivial malady as a pretext for shanghaiing him to a hospital and forcibly detaining him as a cholera suspect while the KGB searched his clothes and belongings.

However, serious KGB operations usually are more Byzantine. If the KGB's purpose is to influence the views of a visitor, Soviet citizens authorized to talk with him are briefed about questions he is likely to ask and the answers he should receive. To persuade the foreigner that he is free to see whatever he wishes, he may be allowed time to explore on his own within certain confines. In such instances, the KGB arranges for agents to meet him as if by chance and, through seemingly natural conversation, to inculcate him with whatever impressions it desires.

In recruitment operations, the KGB often tries to ensnare the foreigner in shameful, illegal, or otherwise unbearable circumstances, then convince him that he can extricate himself only by collaborating. Thus, a heterosexual liaison is interrupted by a irate "husband" belligerently demanding justice; a homosexual liaison often brings stern militiamen righteously outraged by the disgusting transgression against Soviet law and morality. To Westerners accustomed to the protections of judicial processes and a free press, these episodes may seem like amusing burlesques. But to the Westerner locked in a Soviet militia station at 2 A.M. surrounded by threatening strangers, denied counsel, and confronted by humiliation or imprisonment, they appear markedly different.

Most recruitment operations against transient visitors or tourists lack subtlety because they are executed hastily. But those directed against diplomats, journalists, and businessmen living in the Soviet Union are put into effect slowly, often with great subtlety, over many months or even years. Each conforms to an operational plan that is reviewed periodically throughout the year. The plan begins with a biography of the foreigner, encompassing his family background, marital status, education, and occupational history. Next comes a minute analysis of his behavioral and personality traits, financial condition, drinking habits, sexual proclivities, political ideology, and attitude toward the Soviet Union. This is followed by a statement showing clearly whether the purpose of the operation is to neutralize the foreigner, shape his opinions, or recruit him as an agent. The operational plan concludes with a detailed chronology of all actions contemplated in the next twelve months, listing technical resources and agents to be employed and specifying what each is expected to accomplish. Depending on the importance of the foreigner, half a dozen separate KGB teams may approach him simultaneously along different routes. One of them endeavors to gain his good will by bestowing professional and personal favors; another tries to reach him through his wife; another may attempt to induce him to spend profligately so that he will come to need money and be susceptible to bribery. Meanwhile, others set the assorted sexual traps.

The KGB undertook one of its most massive entrapment operations since World War II in hope of insinuating a Soviet agent of influence into the highest governmental councils of France. It hoped to install at

the side of General Charles de Gaulle a man who could
warp French policies to the detriment of the whole
Western world. Well over a hundred KGB officers and
agents, including prominent Soviet intellectuals and
fashionable prostitutes, participated in the plot, which
entailed a siege of the entire French embassy and
caused the death of an honorable Frenchman. The
operation was dangerously far advanced when a principal KGB participant fled the country to expose it.
From his testimony, since corroborated and amplified
by other defectors as well as independent investigations
in the West, the anatomy of this grand scheme to
capture and corrupt an ambassador can now be reconstructed.

On an unusually warm day in June 1956, Yuri
Vasilevich Krotkov was summoned to a comfortable
room of the Moskva Hotel to meet his KGB chief,
Colonel Leonid Petrovich Kunavin. A big man with
chestnut hair, hard hazel eyes, and a truculent face,
Kunavin was renowned for zeal and ruthlessness. Once
at a Moscow soccer match, Krotkov saw him beat two
fans senseless after they cursed the KGB team. He had
a voracious capacity for work, and his consuming passion was the intrigue of the KGB.

Over the years, Krotkov had participated in so many
KGB operations that he felt himself incapable of surprise. But Kunavin did surprise him by announcing
that the KGB had resolved to suborn the ambassador
of France. "The order comes from the very top," the
colonel said, obviously elated by the challenge ahead.
"Nikita Sergeevich himself wants him caught."

Krotkov asked who the ambassador was. "His name
is Maurice Dejean," answered Kunavin. "We know
everything about him there is to know."

The KGB did know a lot. Ever since the early years
of World War II when Dejean served as a senior
member of General de Gaulle's Free French government in London, it had been compiling a dossier on
him. The file slowly expanded as Soviet agents filed
reports from New York, Paris, London, and Tokyo,
where Dejean served as a diplomat. After the ambas-

sador and his wife, Marie-Claire, arrived in Moscow in December 1955, the KGB subjected them to unceasing surveillance. Microphones secreted in their apartment and at the embassy recorded their most unguarded words. The Russian chauffeur referred to the ambassador by the Soviet Foreign Ministry was a trained KGB informant, as was Madame Dejean's personal maid. At diplomatic receptions KGB officers introduced as Soviet "officials" watched and evaluated the French couple. From all this scrutiny, the KGB perceived in Dejean not the least disposition to be disloyal to France. But it noted that at the age of fifty-six he retained a vigorous interest in women, an interest agents had discerned at his previous posts. To the KGB, this made him a natural candidate for entrapment.

In such operations, Yuri Krotkov was a KGB star. Since World War II he had tried to lure scores of officials and journalists into traps—including diplomats from America, Australia, England, Canada, France, India, Mexico, Pakistan, and Yugoslavia.

Krotkov was actually a dramatist and film writer, not a regular KGB staff officer. But from childhood his life had been intertwined with the KGB. He grew up in Tbilisi, Georgia, where his father was an artist and his mother an actress. In 1936 his father painted a portrait of Lavrenti Beria, who then headed the Communist Party in Georgia. Beria so treasured the work that after Stalin elevated him to command of the state security apparatus, copies were hung throughout the Soviet Union. Until the artist's death, Beria remained his protector.

Arriving in Moscow to study literature, Krotkov naturally looked up old KGB* friends of the family and thought nothing of asking them for help. Evacuated with his classmates when the Germans threatened to overrun the city in 1941, he returned eighteen months later to find that a family had appropriated

---

*For convenience and simplification, the term "KGB" is used throughout, even though the organization may have been the NKVD or OGPU or MGB at the time.

his room. He appealed to the KGB, which summarily evicted the family. It also helped him obtain a job at Tass and later with Radio Moscow.

When Krotkov began to meet foreigners, the KGB approached him, and in 1946, at the age of twenty-eight, he willingly enlisted in the legion of "co-opted" agents. He was still free to pursue his literary career. Indeed, the KGB wanted him to do well, for the further he advanced, the more useful he could be. But from then on he could never be wholly free of the KGB.

As a writer, intellectual, and friend of the Boris Pasternak family, Krotkov was welcomed by foreigners in Moscow. This tall, slender man, with a handsome shock of dark brown hair and an intense, expressive face, could talk suavely in English or Russian about the arts, history, and prominent Soviet personalities. Soon he learned to exploit the hunger of visitors for communication with the Soviet people.

All the while, Krotkov was instructed to look for attractive girls whom the KGB could use to tempt foreigners into trouble. He picked them primarily from among actresses he met while writing film scenarios. The KGB offered them various inducements—the promise of better roles, money, clothes, a measure of liberty and gaiety absent from normal Soviet life. The recruited girls were known within the KGB as "swallows." During an operation, they often were allowed temporary use of a "swallow's nest" consisting of two adjoining single-room apartments. In one, the girl entertained the foreigner she was assigned to compromise. From the other, KGB technicians recorded on film and tape whatever boudoir events occurred.

Two days after announcing the operation, Kunavin summoned Krotkov for a more detailed briefing. "The ambassador is the ultimate target," Kunavin explained, "but we are also interested in the assistant air attaché at the embassy, a Colonel Louis Guibaud. Your job is Madame Dejean. You must gain control of her; make her ours. You must get her in bed.

"Forget about the ambassador for now. While you're

working on Madame Dejean, others will be dealing with him. When the time comes, it all will fit together. You'll see; we have something special in mind. There is one thing in our favor. Dejean really is trying to do his job. He wants to get out among the people—and his wife is trying to help him. He really wants to be friends." Kunavin started to laugh. "Well, we'll show him how friendly our girls can be."

Kunavin detailed the backgrounds of the ambassador and Madame Dejean, several times quoting from conversations recorded by Soviet microphones. "She is no fool," Kunavin warned. "She watches over the ambassador constantly and tries to protect him. That's another reason why we must get a hold on her."

A few days later, Kunavin introduced Krotkov to the co-opted KGB agent picked to seduce Ginette Guibaud, wife of the assistant air attaché. He was Misha Orlov, an actor and singer idolized by Moscow teen-agers. A gypsylike giant of a man, Orlov frequently was used to seduce foreign women. Only recently the KGB had given him an apartment as a reward for his accomplishments with Americans. Also present at the third meeting was Boris Cherkashin, a young KGB lieutenant then posing as a diplomat named Karelin.

A couple of months before this, Cherkashin and Orlov, masquerading as vacationing bachelors, had been ordered to trail a group of French wives to a Black Sea resort. There, Cherkashin "accidentally" met Madame Dejean, and back in Moscow he continued to see her at official functions. Now the KGB felt that he was sufficiently acquainted to invite her on an outing with "friends" so that Krotkov could meet her. After consulting her husband, Madame Dejean accepted the invitation, adding that she also would bring Madame Guibaud and the daughter of another attaché.

Kunavin and Krotkov planned the outing meticulously, commandeering a high-powered police cutter at a militia headquarters on the Khimki Reservoir and a fat militiaman as a pilot. The cutter was painted and refurbished to make it appear less like a police boat.

Wines, cheeses, fruits, and pastries were ordered from KGB stores, and choice shashlik was made ready for broiling.

Krotkov first saw Madame Dejean when she arrived at the river pier with Madame Guibaud. Her hair was lustrous in the sunlight, and her delicate face reminded him of fine china. She seemed to smile with both her lips and eyes. Still very slender in her early forties, she looked in every way like the aristocrat the KGB had portrayed her to be.

"What a beautiful boat!" she exclaimed. "Is it yours?"

Krotkov smiled and answered as if sharing a confidence. "A friend of mine is an official in the Sports Administration. I lent him my car for his vacation, so he owed me a favor and—this is it. May I have the pleasure of showing you aboard?"

As the cutter gathered speed out into the reservoir, following the precise course charted by the KGB, Orlov courted Madame Guibaud and Krotkov chatted with Madame Dejean.

"Tell me your impressions of the Soviet Union," he said.

"We are delighted," she responded. "All the officials we have met have been so kind to us. I had a long talk with Shepilov* the other night, and I thought he was fascinating."

"Still, you must find Moscow rather drab after Paris," Krotkov said.

"I love Paris, of course," she replied. "But Moscow is also a great city. There is grandeur here too."

Frowning, Krotkov lowered his voice and affected great sincerity. "Would you have me believe that you like everything you have seen?"

Madame Dejean thought about her answer for a moment. "I am a guest. We did not come here to criticize. We came to help our countries to be friends."

"And I hope you succeed," Krotkov replied. "But we should be honest, and I might as well tell you that

---

*Dmitri Trofimovich Shepilov was Minister of Foreign Affairs from June 1956 through May 1957.

there is much in Soviet reality that I detest. As a writer, I would be interested to know if we see the same reality."

"If you insist," Madame Dejean replied gently. "One difference between France and the Soviet Union: a conversation over a glass of wine can bring a Frenchman to the verge of revolution, while your people seem willing to tolerate anything. I think it very sad when people lose their capacity to be outraged."

"I can see that you and I are going to be good friends," Krotkov said.

The cutter glided to a small pier at a deserted pastoral island near the Pestovskove Reservoir. The agents and their French guests did some exploring, swam, and then enjoyed the KGB cuisine. Madame Dejean insisted that the militiaman-pilot join them and broiled a shashlik for him herself.

Their spirits buoyed by wine and cognac, the party laughed and sang on the return trip. Orlov, rather drunk, danced on the bow and created much mirth by nearly falling overboard. At the pier Madame Dejean said: "You are three fine Russian musketeers, and we are indebted to you for an enchanting outing. I want to return your kindness. Will you come to our Bastille Day reception?"

The KGB considered the invitation a triumph. Cherkashin, whom French security had spotted as a KGB officer while he was in Paris, made excuses, but Krotkov and Orlov promised to come. At the Bastille reception, Madame Dejean immediately introduced them to her husband, who welcomed them in passable Russian. Though the ambassador was neither tall nor distinctively handsome, his alert blue eyes, healthy complexion, and slightly graying hair gave him the appearance of a man of substance, an impression heightened by his poise. Later in the evening, Krotkov watched as Dejean and Khrushchev, the guest of honor, drank champagne and traded jokes, occasionally poking each other in the ribs amid the laughter.

While the guests maneuvered around an elegant buffet, Ginette Guibaud steered Krotkov and Orlov to her husband, who spoke to the two Russians in stiffly correct English and regarded them coldly, even contemptuously. Uncomfortable in his presence, Krotkov concluded that Guibaud would not be easy prey for the KGB. Still, the evening ended successfully for Krotkov when Madame Dejean and Madame Guibaud agreed to another picnic the next week.

As the relationship between Krotkov and Madame Dejean progressed, the KGB made elaborate arrangements to open a second front in the fall against the ambassador. This was an essential part of the original plan, and it required an entry into French embassy society of the man responsible for the whole operation —Lieutenant General Oleg Mikhailovich Gribanov, boss of the Second Chief Directorate.

Stocky and baldish, in baggy pants and rimless glasses, Gribanov looked like a run-of-the-mill Soviet bureaucrat. Actually, he was a daring thinker and one of the seven or eight most important men in the KGB. For his work in effecting mass arrests during the Hungarian revolt in 1956, Gribanov (and Kunavin) had been decorated for "distinguished service to socialism." His brilliant, calculating mind and overpowering personality had earned him the sobriquet "Little Napoleon."

To dupe the Dejeans into an association, Gribanov assumed the identity of Oleg Mikhailovich Gorbunov, "an important official of the Council of Ministers." He also equipped himself with a "wife," KGB Major Vera Ivanovina Andreyeva. Next he devised a complicated scheme to meet the Dejeans through his "wife" Vera so that the relationship would seem to develop naturally. Chosen to make the introduction were two prominent co-opted KGB agents—Sergei Mikhalkov, writer and coauthor of the Soviet national anthem,* and his wife, Natalia Konchalovskaya, a popular author of children's stories. At a diplomatic reception they presented Vera as "Madame Gorbunova, a translator in the Ministry of Culture and the wife of an important official of the Council of Ministers."

---

*In March 1970 KGB agent Mikhalkov became chairman of the Writers' Union of the Russian Republic.

Plump, matronly Vera spoke French well, having served with the KGB in France, and her flattering reminiscences of France pleased the Dejeans. Vera also talked a great deal about her "husband," depicting him as an overworked confidant of the Soviet leadership—just the kind of man an ambassador would like to know. Thus the Dejeans were delighted to accept a dinner invitation from the Gorbunovs.

To entertain the ambassador, the KGB requisitioned and furnished a spacious apartment as the Moscow home of the Gorbunovs. More important, Ivan Aleksandrovich Serov, then KGB chairman, lent Gribanov-Gorbunov his dacha in Kurkino-Mashkino some fourteen miles outside the city. A great old Russian country house built of logs with ornate porticoes and window frames and expansive rooms, the dacha became the scene of pleasant parties at which the Gorbunovs admitted the Dejeans into a congenial circle of writers, artists, actors and actresses, and "officials." Virtually all were KGB agents or "swallows." Occasionally Gribanov confided accurate information calculated to be useful to the ambassador, while Vera began to condition Madame Dejean to separations from her husband by taking her on out-of-town trips "to see the country."

At the same time, Krotkov continued to cultivate Madame Dejean with his own squad of disguised agents. She came to refer to him as "my best Russian friend," but the physical intimacy the KGB desired never developed between them. And during a luncheon at the Guibauds' apartment, Orlov drank so much that he fell into a drunken, snoring slumber. KGB microphones recorded the episode. Gribanov angrily banished Orlov from the operation permanently.

Thus, by early 1958—some eighteen months after the siege began—none of the original KGB plans for seducing the French had succeeded. But the friendship between Krotkov and Madame Dejean was a significant asset. Gribanov now decided to capitalize on it by employing Krotkov to arrange the entrapment of Dejean.

The woman Gribanov selected for the mission was

Lydia Khovanskaya, a buxom, sensual, doe-eyed di-
vorcée in her early thirties. She had acquired Western
manners and an excellent command of French in Paris,
where her former husband served as a diplomat. To
insinuate her into Dejean's company, Gribanov played
upon the French desire for better cultural relations.
He "requested" that the Ministry of Culture stage a
special film exhibition of the ballet "Giselle" and invite the ambassador, ostensibly to meet prominent
Soviet motion-picture personalities. Krotkov was designated master of ceremonies, and he compiled the list
of Soviet guests. On it appeared "Lydia Khovanskaya
—translator." For added decoration the KGB rounded
up a dozen Bolshoi ballerinas, including the renowned
Maya Plisetskaya.

At the exhibition, held in an old mansion on
Gnezdnikovski Lane, the freshly coiffured and per-
fumed Lydia sat beside Dejean. Several times during
the film she pressed lightly against him or brushed her
hair against his face while leaning over to whisper
comments about the ballet. Afterward, though, she artfully deferred to Krotkov and devoted herself to translations for Madame Dejean.

Three days later, Krotkov telephoned Madame
Dejean and duped her into helping arrange another
meeting between her husband and Lydia. "I'm giving
a dinner party Friday," he began. "My friends were
greatly impressed by the ambassador, and it would be
quite an honor for me if I could persuade you both
to come." Then he added: "By the way, Marie-Claire,
I have started work on a joint Soviet-French production of the film *Dubrovski*. It would not hurt me to
be seen with the ambassador."

"Oh, I'm certain he will accept with pleasure, Yuri,"
she replied.

The KGB reserved the main dining room of the
Praga Restaurant and allocated nine hundred rubles
for the dinner. Though the purpose of the evening was
to provide Lydia with a further opportunity to entice
the ambassador, Kunavin and Krotkov offered him two
other swallows as alternatives—Nadya Cherednichenko
and Larissa ("Lora") Kronberg-Sobolevskaya, both

stunning blonde actresses in their late twenties. Krotkov knew them well.

Half an hour before the dinner, Kunavin deployed KGB officers throughout the restaurant to monitor the party and prevent it from being disturbed. Lydia, Nadya, and Lora looked radiant. The playwright George Mdivani, another well-known artist co-opted by the KGB, established an air of irreverent frivolity with witty toasts mocking socialism. Dejean, comporting himself as a masterly and affable diplomat, warmed to the occasion and deftly danced with the women. He so enjoyed the evening that he invited everyone to dine at the embassy the next week.

The night of the embassy dinner, the Dejeans were such natural and engaging hosts that they almost made Krotkov, Mdivani, and the three swallows forget their missions. Genuinely pleased to be among Russians they considered friends, the Dejeans escorted the guests through the embassy, magnificently furnished with French antiques. Listening to classical music and sipping champagne after dining on partridge, Dejean charmed and flirted with each of the beautiful women. But Krotkov could not discern which of the three would be most likely to succeed with him.

"Lydia is still our best bet," Kunavin said, upon studying his report of the dinner. "We've got to figure out some way to bring them together by themselves."

Soon thereafter, Vera invited Madame Dejean to join her on a trip. Krotkov then telephoned the ambassador. "There is an artist from Georgia—Lado Gudiashvili, an old friend of my family—who is having an exhibition here," he said. "He spent his student days in Paris, and all his life he has loved France. Now he is quite an old man, and it would mean a great deal to him if you could drop by his show Sunday."

"Certainly," Dejean replied. "I should think it my duty to attend."

The ambassador arrived at the gallery in the embassy's black Chevrolet driven by the KGB chauffeur. Joining Krotkov and Lydia, he automatically accepted her services as an interpreter. Dejean generously complimented the venerable painter, who long had been in official disfavor because his rather romantic work lacked "socialist realism."

As Dejean started to leave, Lydia said, "Mr. Ambassador, would it be too much to ask you to drop me off at my apartment?"

"It would be an honor," he replied.

Alighting from the car, Lydia asked, as if by afterthought, "Would you like to come up for a cup of coffee and see how an ordinary Soviet woman lives?"

When Dejean emerged from the apartment, as the chauffeur carefully noted, nearly two hours had elapsed.

Krotkov called Kunavin in the morning. "The ambassador took Lydia home," he said.

But Kunavin had already heard from Lydia. "Yes, I know. They've done it!" he said triumphantly.

The KGB had no thought of attempting to blackmail Dejean on the basis of his afternoon with Lydia. For the moment, it merely sought to further the liaison and persuade him that he could safely engage in an affair in Moscow just as he might in Paris, London, or Washington.

"Gradually build up the relationship," Kunavin instructed Lydia, "but don't appear too available for a while." Lydia discharged her assignment faultlessly. At embassy functions, to which members of the Krotkov team were increasingly invited, she remained friendly yet respectful toward the ambassador. Flattering Madame Dejean, Lydia became such a good friend that they regularly embraced upon meeting—even as elsewhere she privately received the ambassador with ardor and affection.

In May 1958 the operation against the French suddenly gained new significance in the eyes of the KGB when Soviet agents in Paris reported that within the next few weeks de Gaulle almost certainly would become Premier of France. Presuming that Dejean was still an intimate of de Gaulle's, the KGB reasoned that his eventual ascent to an influential government position now was assured. "This always was important," Kunavin told Krotkov jubilantly. "Now it's ten times as important."

At an embassy party Krotkov attended in June,

Dejean offered resounding toasts to de Gaulle and the new era of grandeur he promised France. Though he never alluded to his personal ties with the general, he doubtless felt that de Gaulle's rise augured a new era for him as well.

Krotkov now expected that the KGB soon would close the trap against Dejean. Thus he was dumfounded when Kunavin announced, "We're going to have to pull Lydia out of the operation."

"*What?!*" exclaimed Krotkov.

"It's not her fault. A mistake has been made," Kunavin said calmly. "In this operation we've got to have a husband. Dejean must believe the girl is married if what we have in mind is going to work. Unfortunately, Lydia's husband was pretty well known in Paris, and there are a couple of people in the French embassy who probably know they're divorced."

"Why in hell didn't someone think about that before?" Krotkov exploded.

"There's no use whining about it now," Kunavin replied. "The point is, we have to start all over."

Kunavin ordered Lydia to tell Dejean that she would be away from Moscow for some time filming a new picture on location. As her replacement, Gribanov selected one of the other actresses previously introduced to the ambassador, Larissa ("Lora") Kronberg-Sobolevskaya. Of all the KGB women Krotkov knew, Lora was the most spectacular. Long-legged and seductive, she was a waif with a beautiful face and a haunting laugh. Not even the KGB could completely harness her wild, adventuresome spirit. She did not have official permission to reside in Moscow, which meant she could not legally obtain a room. So she lived with whoever would take her in, constantly subject to exile, drifting from one affair to another. She occasionally drank too much, sometimes impudently showing up on a set intoxicated and half clad.

According to the KGB legend created for her, she was married to a geologist who had to spend much of the year exploring in Siberia. Now Gribanov instructed her to portray her husband to Dejean as cruel and pathologically jealous.

"For once," Gribanov warned Lora, "you must follow orders strictly. You are not to do a single thing that we have not planned and approved."

Lora smiled and, looking him straight in the eye, replied, "I don't need to be told how to handle a man."

Restraining himself, Gribanov casually delivered the one message the KGB calculated would tame Lora. "If you *do* obey orders and if you succeed, I'll see to it that you get a room, a nice one. And we'll make this your last job."

With Lydia supposedly gone, Lora reappeared at parties staged for the ambassador by Krotkov. In late June after a luncheon at the house of retired KGB Colonel George Bryantsev, Lora whispered to Krotkov: "Hurry! Take me to the apartment. The ambassador asked me to meet him there in an hour!"

On the way, she asked, "Yuri, what should I do with him?"

"That's a ridiculous question," Krotkov replied.

"I'm serious," she said. "Oleg Mikhailovich warned me not to do anything without permission. Nobody told me I could make a date today. The proposition just popped up at lunch, and I took advantage of it."

"Very well," Krotkov agreed, "we'll call from the apartment." From the KGB apartment assigned Lora, Krotkov telephoned Kunavin, then Vera, then Gribanov's office, but no one answered.

"I've called everyone I can," he said. "I don't know what else to do."

Lora began to laugh. "Do I go to bed with him or not? This is the first time in my life the answer to that question depends on somebody besides me."

"Go ahead, Lora," Krotkov ordered.

That afternoon Dejean entered into an affair more passionate than the liaison he had formed with Lydia. Lora, who ardently gave love in hope of finding it, totally won him. And when Madame Dejean flew to Europe for a vacation, Gribanov decided to try through Lora what the KGB had planned for more than two years.

For about ten days, the KGB kept Lora away from

Dejean and deprived him of all amorous companionship. Gribanov brought to Moscow a strapping KGB thug, a Tatar named Misha, and recalled Kunavin from vacation. Special surveillance squads were readied, and KGB technicians installed radio transmitters in the apartment next to the one Lora was to use. Then Krotkov telephoned Dejean.

"Mr. Ambassador," he said, "I promised Marie-Claire that I would keep you amused while she's away. How about a picnic tomorrow? I'll bring along a lady who is a special friend of mine plus Lora and . . ." Krotkov did not need to finish. At the mention of Lora, Dejean accepted.

As the ambassador looked forward to the pleasures of another rendezvous with Lora, Gribanov assembled his team in a suite at the Metropole Hotel. Present were Kunavin, Lora, Vera, and several other KGB officers. After a veritable banquet he delivered a final briefing. "I want you to beat hell out of him," he told Kunavin and Misha. "Really hurt him. Terrify him. But I warn you, if you leave one mark on his face, I'll put you both in jail. And, Lora, the same goes for you if he is not in your apartment by five o'clock. This must go exactly according to schedule."

The next morning Krotkov and his "special friend," Alla Golubova, drove into the countryside followed by Dejean with Lora, with the two cars at all times under KGB surveillance. Eventually Krotkov stopped in a secluded grove on a gentle slope overlooking a brook.

During the picnic, Lora acted her role as seductress so magnificently that Alla whispered to Krotkov, "The ambassador is looking at her like a cat looks at cream!"

Miles away in the apartment adjacent to Lora's, Gribanov, Kunavin, and Misha received continuing reports radioed by KGB agents hidden in the woods. Misha, Lora's "husband," and Kunavin, his "friend," were dressed as geological explorers, complete with cleated shoes and knapsacks.

At midafternoon Krotkov, mindful of the rigid KGB schedule, suggested it was time to go back. About ten miles from the city, Krotkov through his rear-view mirror saw the ambassador's car stopping. He braked, got out of his car, and hurried back to Dejean. "What's wrong?"

"Everything's fine," Dejean said with a broad smile. "Lora's just decided she wants to take a swim in the pond over there."

Krotkov was at once furious and frantic. With a supreme effort of control he turned to Lora. "My dear," he asked, "why would a beautiful girl like you want to swim in a dirty cattle pond?"

Betraying the effects of the wine she had been drinking at the picnic, Lora only laughed at him as she began to take off her clothes.

The news of her caprice, radioed by a surveillance car, enraged Gribanov. He stormed through the apartment shouting, "That whore! I *knew* we shouldn't use her. I tell you, from now on we're going to use only high-class women!"

Lora had no bathing outfit, so she swam in her underwear, and each time she emerged from the water she looked more than naked. "We'd better get the ambassador out of here before he has a heart attack!" Alla whispered.

The excitement Lora generated more than compensated for the time lost by her swim. As soon as they entered the swallow's nest at 2 Ananyevski Lane, Dejean embraced her. "Maurice, there is something I forgot to tell you," Lora said. "I have got a telegram from my husband. He's coming home tomorrow."

Listening to the sounds from Lora's apartment, Gribanov impatiently waited for Lora to give the signal that would serve as the one for Misha and Kunavin. "Why doesn't she say the word?" he muttered again and again. Finally Lora did speak the code word: "Kiev." Instantly Misha, followed by Kunavin, ran to her apartment and unlocked the door.

"It's my husband!" Lora screamed.

"I can't believe it!" Misha shouted. "All day I flew just to be with you a few hours earlier, and what do I find!"

"Misha, oh, please," Lora pleaded. "He is an ambassador."

"I don't give a damn who he is!" roared Misha. "I'm going to teach him a lesson."

Now Misha and Kunavin set upon Dejean, viciously beating him. Kunavin, who destested everything French anyway, went about his mission with relish. Lora, too, was slapped and pummeled.

All the while, Lora put on a superlative performance, crying and screaming, "Stop! You're going to kill him! He's the ambassador of France!"

Finally, as planned, Kunavin grabbed Misha as if to restrain him. "Listen," he said, "if he really is an ambassador, maybe we'd better stop."

"All right, all right," Misha agreed, still feigning fury. "But it's not going to end here. I'm going to the authorities. I'm just a plain Soviet citizen, but we have laws in our country. If you *are* an ambassador, I'm going to see to it that you're expelled. The whole world will know what a filthy swine you are."

Amid continuing threats, Dejean gathered his clothes with as much dignity as the circumstances permitted and left. Nearly collapsing in the back seat of his car, he said to the chauffeur, "The embassy." The chauffeur, watching in the mirror, saw him bury his face in his hands.

In the apartment the scene now resembled that of a locker room of a team that has just won a world's championship. While champagne spilled into glasses and onto the floor, Kunavin and Misha shouted congratulations to each other and to the still naked Lora. Laughing uproariously, they reenacted all that had happened for other KGB agents who crowded in from the street and elsewhere in the building.

Gribanov briefly joined the celebration. "Lora, I too want to congratulate you," he said earnestly. "You were just perfect."

Then in some embarrassment he added, "But, Lora, you ought to be more modest in the presence of men."

Lora laughed at him. "You forget," she said, "I am an actress."

Turning to leave, Gribanov replied: "Yes, but a *Soviet* actress."

Pointing to the many bruises appearing on her body,

Lora glared at Kunavin. "Look what you did to me!"

"I'm sorry," he apologized. "It had to be done. Please, take a few days off and *rest* in bed."

"And my room?" she asked. "Do I get my room?"

"Yes, Lora. You will have your room."

Punctually at eight o'clock that evening, Dejean arrived at the Serov dacha to keep a dinner appointment. Waiting for him was a friendly host—the same man who three hours before had secretly presided over his beating and degradation. Days earlier, Gribanov, playing his role as Gorbunov, had arranged for a party to follow closely upon the beating. The KGB wanted to accord Dejean an opportunity to ask for the help he now desperately required.

Through dinner and afterward over brandy, the ambassador betrayed nothing of what had happened, although he ached from his ordeal. Late in the evening, however, he took Gribanov aside and finally said what the KGB had worked so hard to make him say: "I am in rather bad trouble. I need your help." Thereupon he told of his relationship with Lora and of all that had happened in her apartment just hours before.

"This is extremely serious," commented Gribanov. "The husband has the law on his side. If he goes to court, he could make quite a scandal."

"I would be indebted to you for anything you could do," said Dejean.

"I will do all I can," Gribanov replied. "But, Mr. Ambassador, I must be candid. I'm not sure we'll succeed in hushing this up."

Gribanov toyed with Dejean during the next days. Appeals were being made, he reported, but the husband was obstinate and unreasonable. Everything hung in the balance. Then he eased the ambassador off the hook. "It took a lot of doing, but I believe we have persuaded the man to keep quiet in the interests of Soviet-French relations," he said. "Unless he changes his mind, we're all right."

The KGB decorated Kunavin with another Order of the Red Star and honored Krotkov at an unusual dinner in a private room of the Aragvi Restaurant. Over hors d'oeuvres, cheeses, Tabak chickens, Georgian wine, and five-star brandy, several KGB generals reminisced with Kunavin and Krotkov about the Dejean project. After dinner, a general stood and spoke formally: "The operation was one of the most brilliant ever consummated by the organs of State Security. Without your vital contributions, Yuri Vasilevich, it is doubtful that we would have achieved our goal."

The general paused and took a gold Doxa watch with a gold wristband from his pocket. (It had been confiscated by the KGB from a foreigner.) "On behalf of the Committee for State Security of the Council of Ministers of the Union of Soviet Socialist Republics, it is my pleasure to present you with this gift," he told Krotkov. "Regard it as a symbol of our gratitude for your patriotic activity. We only regret the impossibility of engraving on it the reason for its reward."

By now all the leading participants understood the scope of the KGB plot against the ambassador. The secret Dejean and Gribanov shared formed a special bond between them. The ambassador was profoundly grateful and indebted to the general. The KGB could wait until he attained the high position it believed he would eventually occupy in Paris before seeking any repayment of the hidden debt. Even then, it contemplated no crude confrontation. Gribanov would gently ask a favor in return for the one owed. Once Dejean had acted in the interest of a foreign power, he would be vulnerable to more demands. One favor would lead imperceptibly to another and another until Dejean crossed the threshold of treason from which there could be no return.

For the moment the KGB strategy required only that Gribanov solidify his friendship with Dejean. The friendlier they became, the easier the ultimate approach in Paris would be. To keep the ambassador happy, Gribanov ordered Lydia restored to his company. "Dejean doesn't like to live on Lenten fare," Kunavin commented to Krotkov. In their pose as the Gorbunovs, Gribanov and Vera entertained the Dejeans more lavishly than ever. They took them to a government dacha on the Black Sea, then on a two-week trip through Baltic areas normally proscribed to foreigners.

Gribanov never afterward alluded to the affair with Lora. The ambassador in turn never realized that his good friend Gorbunov, with whom he consulted and confided, actually was the commanding general of the Second Chief Directorate of the KGB. Neither did he ever suspect that Lydia was an agent who reported his every word and action to the KGB. So it was only natural that Dejean should discuss with the Russian friend the attitudes, personalities, and conversations of other Western diplomats he often saw in Moscow. And it was equally natural that he would value information which his trusted friends confided for transmission to Paris.

Because Gribanov could not devote himself entirely to Dejean, he chose a polished and handsome KGB officer, Aleksei Suntsov, to help tend to the ambassador. When Dejean flew to Paris to attend Big Four conferences in 1960, Suntsov went along also, and he turned up at Moscow functions Gribanov could not attend to take care of the ambassador. Once when Suntsov was ill, Gribanov took Nosenko to an Indian embassy reception held in a Moscow hotel. The Indians served no alcoholic beverages, but the waiters, who were KGB agents, stocked a supply of vodka for Gribanov in mineral-water bottles. Spotting Dejean, Gribanov ordered Major Nosenko to take him a bottle. The two smiled and waved at each other across the room before hoisting a toast.

Meanwhile, a host of KGB agents constantly tried to pick and prey on Dejean's subordinates at the embassy. Many entrapments were attempted though in most cases the KGB had no real reason to expect success. Krotkov, for example, was ordered to seduce a French cipher clerk, but she refused even to see him. Still, the KGB kept spying and probing among the embassy staff, searching for any vulnerabilities, and in the summer of 1961 it found one.

Colonel Louis Guibaud and Ginette, targets in the early days of the Dejean operation, left Moscow in 1958. But they had returned for a second tour of duty, and microphones secreted in their apartment soon disclosed that they quarreled frequently and fiercely. To the KGB, this was a signal for action.

Just as it had done with Dejean, the KGB exposed Guibaud to a succession of women until one succeeded in luring him into an affair. It throve until early summer of 1962, when Guibaud was confronted by three men in civilian clothes. Polite but blunt, they spread before him an array of photographs documenting his liaison. Then they gave him a brutal choice: secret collaboration with the KGB or public disgrace.

Ginette soon sensed that her husband was gravely disturbed. A few moments after he left for work on July 30, she became so worried that she ran after him. Before she could stop him, he drove off to his office near the embassy. Ginette hesitated, then hurried out into the street to hunt for a cab.

Some twenty minutes later, Dejean received a call at the embassy. "Mr. Ambassador, there has been an accident," a voice said. "Colonel Guibaud is hurt."

Perceiving that something extraordinary was wrong, Dejean commanded: "Tell me what has happened. I want to know."

"Colonel Guibaud is dead."

Dejean found the colonel sprawled on the floor in a mass of blood by his desk, a revolver at his side. Three Russian Red Cross attendants stood mutely by. Kneeling over the body, sobbing and caressing her husband's face, was Ginette.

For a few hours, news of the death created near panic within the Second Chief Directorate. Its great fear was that Guibaud had left a note exposing the entrapment. Once its agents discovered this was not so, the KGB relaxed, planting reports in the diplomatic colony that Colonel Guibaud had shot himself because of psychotic depression.

Ginette, dressed in black, left Moscow for the last time with the body of her husband, who had died rather than succumb to the KGB. And the KGB resumed normal operations against the embassy.

It had become almost brazenly confident of ultimate success with Dejean. Vera and even Gribanov openly referred to him as "our friend." Vera gleefully talked about the great dividends the KGB would reap from its investment once Dejean was ensconced in Paris. But in fact the whole plot, so artfully conceived and executed over the years, was doomed. For Yuri Vasilevich Krotkov had resolved to disclose it to the West.

To Krotkov, the death of Colonel Guibaud was not suicide but murder. It forced him to a decision he had been struggling with for months: to break away from his life of hack writing, daily deceit, and spiritual squalor. Secretly he began recording and transposing to microfilm the history of his life as an agent of the KGB. At the same time he searched for a way to flee the Soviet Union.

On September 2, 1963, he landed in London with a touring group of Soviet writers and artists. Eleven days later, Krotkov slipped out of the shabby London hotel where the Soviet delegation was staying, hurried through the crowds along Bayswater Road, hurried into Hyde Park, and vanished. That evening, under heavy protective guard, he began talking to British intelligence officers. Krotkov's revelations stunned the British. Soon they called in a senior French counterintelligence officer. After listening less than two hours, the French officer became so alarmed that he flew back to Paris. Determined to report as quickly as possible at the highest level, he managed to obtain a confidential audience with an aide to President de Gaulle. Soon after, appalled but unflinching, de Gaulle issued a personal order: find out the complete truth, whatever it is.

The British shared Krotkov's disclosures with the French and Americans because they raised grave questions affecting all three nations. Was Krotkov telling the truth? If so, had the KGB actually gone much further with Dejean than he knew? Or was Krotkov in fact still a KGB agent sent out to poison relations among the allies and divert suspicions from important Soviet spies by casting doubts upon an innocent man?

In a brief story on February 9, 1964, the Paris newspaper *Le Monde* announced that Ambassador Maurice Dejean was returning from the Soviet Union. It further reported that his farewells were being said "in an atmosphere of cordiality in part due to the personal relations Monsieur Dejean was able to establish with Soviet leaders during his eight years in Moscow." Because he had been in Moscow so long, his withdrawal seemed entirely normal.

Upon Dejean's return, French counterintelligence officers subjected him to a withering secret interrogation that lasted for days. They scrutinized all his dispatches from Moscow. They questioned his associates, Madame Guibaud, and a large number of others named in Krotkov's accounts.

Upon analyzing all the data, French intelligence concluded that the Krotkov story was true in all essential respects. However, it could find no proof that Dejean ever had committed any act of disloyalty to France. The KGB had vastly overestimated Dejean's influence with de Gaulle. By waiting for Dejean to obtain a lofty position that de Gaulle never intended to bestow, the KGB had lost its chance to exploit the hold it had on the ambassador.

Informed that Krotkov's account was true, the British, in whose custody he remained, now had to decide what to do. Krotkov passionately declared that he had forsaken his culture and country to cleanse himself by exposing all he had done.

But Western intelligence experts were tormented by the potential effects of the story even though it was true. In frustration and despair they had watched the KGB steadily advancing toward the fundamental Soviet goal of splitting France from the Western Alliance. In Paris, KGB agents constantly sought to rekindle in de Gaulle old grievances he harbored as a result of his often difficult wartime relations with the Anglo-Americans. During the very days when Krotkov was revealing his story, the KGB was seeking to convince de Gaulle that the Americans and British were still conspiring against him. The British feared that if they permitted release of the story, de Gaulle would think they were plotting against him again, this time by linking him, through a friend, to scandal. So they extracted a pledge of silence from Krotkov.

In Paris, de Gaulle studied the final French intelligence report, then summoned his old friend to his of-

fice. Raising his spectacles and looking down his great
nose, he dismissed him with one sentence: "So, Dejean,
one enjoys the women!" (*Eh bien, Dejean, on couche.*)

Lora received her room and later married one of
her lovers.

Kunavin, even before Krotkov's flight, was dismissed
from the KGB for drunkenness and embezzlement.
Eventually, Gribanov took care of him by making him
manager of an Intourist hotel specially outfitted to
"handle" foreigners.

Gribanov, hero of Budapest, master of entrapment,
retreated into the recesses of the KGB, and Gorbunov,
the man he pretended to be, vanished.

Dejean retired to the comfort of his elegantly furnished apartment on a tree-lined boulevard in Paris.
He has refused to comment—for the record—about
what happened to him in Moscow. But he did become
president of the Franco-Soviet Society for Industrial
Cooperation and continued to visit Moscow.

Krotkov published a book about life in the Soviet
Union, omitting any mention of his work with the KGB.
Then in 1969 the Senate Internal Security Subcommittee invited him to testify in Washington about the
entrapment of Dejean and others. Since then, he has
lived in the United States as a writer. During my long
interviews with him, he often seemed preoccupied with
contemplation of death and with a quest for a god.
He remarked, "I know there will be a day of reckon-
ing, and I expect no mercy."

However, friends report that in the intervening years
he has fashioned a meaningful new life for himself.
France and all other Western democracies are in his
debt.

VII

DANGEROUS LITTLE BROTHERS

The stately Knights of the Cross Monastery on the Vltava (Moldau) River is a historic Prague landmark. Though construction began in the sixth century, the present structure, with its huge cupola and somber, finely sculpted facade, is largely an early eighteenth-century restoration. Inside the monastery, vaulted corridors lead along a rectangular courtyard to rooms of stone where countless monks have meditated and prayed. The most impressive and serene chamber is the domed chapel. One of its walls is lined with ancient paintings of saints. Sometimes when sunlight filtering through the tall stained-glass windows strikes them at a certain angle, the saints seem to smile. Beneath their gaze, worldlier men today regularly gather over Turkish coffee and Pilsner beer to plot the slander and subversion of individuals and whole nations. For the chapel is the principal conference room of the Czechoslovakian intelligence service, the STB,* which has made the monastery its headquarters since 1961.

The STB chieftains are sometimes joined in the chapel by their "uncles"—their term for KGB advisers stationed in the monastery. According to former Czech officers, in the early 1960s the KGB personnel became less obtrusive and more courteous. They now endeavor

---

*The Czech foreign intelligence service actually is the First Section of the Intelligence Directorate of the Ministry of the Interior. But Czech citizens and Western authorities alike commonly refer to it as State Secret Security, Statni Tajna Bezpecnost, or the STB.

to couch their orders in the form of requests or suggestions; some even exchange with the Czechs the standard salutation with which the day begins and ends: "Honor the work, Comrade!" Yet Soviet control over the STB is as real, total, and effective as ever. The Czechs undertake no significant operation without prior approval of the senior KGB adviser, and STB department heads often submit plans to him before showing them to their own boss, Radko Kaska. KGB officers continuously observe operations in progress, at times modifying or redirecting them. They automatically see and, if they desire, receive copies of the reports that pour into the monastery from agents around the world. The prudent STB officer never contradicts Soviet policy or betrays any anti-Soviet attitude because he knows that some of his colleagues are loyal not to Czechoslovakia but to the Soviet Union. They have been recruited as clandestine KGB agents, usually while undergoing training in Moscow. The more sophisticated Czech officers also know that major policy directives and operational orders issued by their own government have been dictated by the Central Committee of the Communist Party in Moscow.

Most enterprises born in the monastery are conceived in the ultimate interests of the Soviet Union, although the Czechoslovak people must bear their costs. The Czechs pay for an extensive worldwide diplomatic establishment and aid programs that are sustained not on the basis of Czech needs but of Soviet desires. They also pay to sustain STB agents in African, Asian, and Latin-American nations with which Czechoslovakia has no natural ties or concerns. While accomplishing little for Czechoslovakia, the contributions of these agents to the KGB over the years have been remarkable.

There is strong circumstantial evidence that the KGB in May 1962 called upon the most valuable of all Czech agents to help kill a man. The Czechs had recruited an official highly placed in the Austrian security service. They considered him so important that few STB officers knew of his existence, and those who did never mentioned his name. When it was necessary to refer to him, he was called Agent Seven. His reports and records were locked in a secret room of the monastery which only one officer, Osvald Hotovy, was allowed to enter.

On May 9, 1962, a twenty-four-year-old lieutenant of the Hungarian secret police, Béla Lapusnyik, fled to Austria. He carried with him precise knowledge of communist operations against both Westerners and Hungaria refugees. The Hungarians had no means of liquidating Lapusnyik, and they of course were ignorant of Agent Seven. But the KGB knew about him.

The Austrians placed Lapusnyik, for his own protection, in a maximum-security cell of police headquarters at Rossauer Lände in Vienna. His food was specially prepared in the prison kitchen, and selected guards attended him twenty-four hours a day. His assassination seemed impossible. It could be accomplished only by someone trusted to enter the prison or to escort him to interrogations at police headquarters—someone such as Agent Seven.

Despite all precautions, Lapusnyik repeatedly expressed fears that he would be killed, and pleaded to be transferred to the United States. At his insistence, arrangements were finally made on June 5 to fly him to Washington, where he could be safely and expertly interrogated. But on June 2, Lapusnyik clutched his throat and called for help. Burning with fever and convulsed with stomach cramps, he gasped, "I've been poisoned!"

Austrian physicians suspected that he had been infected with some deadly but unknown form of bacteria. They fought by the hour to save him, applying every conceivable antidote, but to no avail. At 5:45 A.M. on June 4, the day before he was to fly to the safety of America, Béla Lapusnyik died. Austrian authorities stated that death was caused by paralysis of the brain possibly induced by bacteria. They said they could find no trace of poison. In all probability they could not because the KGB laboratory in Moscow and Agent Seven in Vienna had done their jobs well.

Three years later László Szabó, a defector from the Hungarian intelligence service, revealed that the Czechs had poisoned Lapusnyik. Through subsequent defectors from the STB and other sources, Western security services identified Agent Seven and established that he was one of the few people with access to the prison when Lapusnyik was poisoned. However, their sources were not the sort who could appear in court, so the Austrians were unable to prosecute. Instead, they quietly neutralized Agent Seven by shunting him to an innocuous job.

Czech exploits in the realms of espionage, subversion, and disinformation have significantly augmented the work of the KGB. The STB in the 1950s recruited West German Bundestag member Alfred Frenzel, who served on the Bundestag defense committee. He looted the Federal Republic of military secrets that the STB handed directly to the KGB. According to Ladislav Bittman, a former deputy director of Czech disinformation operations, the Czechs also paid a Bundestag member to help establish a new party, the German Peace Union, as a Soviet force in German politics. In 1970 the British arrested a member of Parliament, William Owen, on charges of espionage. He confessed that he had accepted from Czech intelligence officers payments totaling some $6,000 over a period of nine years. A frail, white-haired, sixty-nine-year-old man suffering from a heart condition and failing eyesight, Owen denied in court that he ever had transmitted anything important to the Czechs, and the jury acquitted him. However, his own attorney characterized his conduct as "shocking, disgusting and dishonorable."

During the 1964 American Presidential campaign, the STB printed tens of thousands of pamphlets containing fictitious quotations and statements depicting Barry Goldwater as a vile racist. The pamphlets were smuggled to Washington in diplomatic pouches, then mailed to citizens throughout the United States. The Czechs also distributed the pamphlets in Africa and Asia, representing them as authentic American political campaign tracts. STB forgeries, ostensibly "exposing" foreign intrigues of the U.S. State Department, the CIA, and even the FBI, have provoked outbursts of anti-American hysteria in Latin America, Africa, and

Asia. Bittman has disclosed that in 1964 the STB leaked three forgeries to President Julius K. Nyerere of Tanzania, outlining an American plot against his government. "And that," Bittman testified, "was the start of a big anti-American campaign, not only in Tanzania, but I would say all over the African continent. President Nyerere hesitated to believe in these forgeries, he asked the American authorities for proof, and shortly after that, the American authorities presented the facts proving that all these documents were forgeries. President Nyerere accepted that, but the campaign continued because the press did not want to believe that they were forgeries."

These few examples of STB accomplishments merely suggest how much the clandestine service of one small country can do for the KGB. To the Czech contributions must be added those from the clandestine services of East Germany, Poland, Hungary, Bulgaria, Romania, and most recently, Cuba. At negligible expense to the Soviet Union, they greatly enlarge the operational capabilities of the KGB and sometimes enable it to achieve objectives that it could not easily attain on its own.

Because of failure to appreciate that all satellite services are an integral part of the same KGB team, foreigners usually are far less wary of satellite representatives than of Soviet representatives. With satellite personnel serving as auxiliaries in many foreign capitals, the KGB can overwhelm local security services with sheer manpower. Constantin Melnik, who formerly supervised French security, stated that of some one thousand Soviet-bloc representatives in France in 1971, six hundred were "professional espionage officers." Melnik pointed out that ten counter-intelligence agents are required to maintain even a routine watch on one trained spy. Thus, six thousand security men would be required to watch the six hundred communist-bloc officers reported in France. In smaller countries the Soviet bloc can put into the streets more intelligence officers than the local government can deploy security agents against them.

The satellite services work well against their own countrymen who have emigrated to the West and take

advantage of historic cultural bonds such as exist between Romania and France. The French unraveled a
Romanian espionage network in 1969 that reached into
the atomic-energy program, the Quai d'Orsay, the foreign intelligence service, and NATO. Belgian police in
1968 detected another dangerous Romanian agent,
Nahit Imre, a Turk who was NATO's financial con-
troller. Arrested on a Brussels street corner, Imre had
microfilm of 1,440 secret NATO documents in his
briefcase.

Many KGB agents originally were developed by one
of the satellite services. The KGB commandeered Henry
Houghton, a British subject recruited by the Poles, and
made him a leading member of the network that stole
extremely valuable technical secrets from the British
naval research center at Portland. The KGB similarly
took over an East German agent, Heinz Sütterlin, and
dispatched him to Bonn with instructions to woo and
marry one of three secretaries employed by the West
German Foreign Ministry.

Taking along a bouquet of roses, Sütterlin called at
the apartment of Leonore Heinz, a pleasant but plain
thirty-one-year-old. Sütterlin, who had a rugged face
with a scar that enchanted women, captivated her, and
they were married in December 1960. Soon, out of love
for Sütterlin and fear of losing him, Leonore began
slipping Foreign Office documents into her purse at
lunchtime for her husband to photograph. After Willy
Brandt became Foreign Minister in 1966, the KGB
was unsuccessful in its efforts to make her his secretary.
Nevertheless, Leonore managed to gain access to hundreds of documents revealing West German apprehensions, weaknesses, and secret policies, all of which the
Soviet Union was able to exploit in formulating its own
policy.

Sütterlin and Leonore were directed by a KGB illegal,
Lieutenant Colonel Eugen Runge, who defected to the
CIA in 1968. The KGB told him in Moscow that over
the years Leonore had supplied 2,900 documents, 969
of which were classified top secret or secret. "We copied
the personal files of the diplomats and functionaries of
the Foreign Service—an ideal starting point for sub-

sequent blackmail," said Runge. "We found out ahead of time whenever an investigation was ordered in the Foreign Office against one of our contact people. We received documents before they moved across Leonore's desk and on to the code room, and we read the reports of diplomatic couriers from abroad, mostly even before German Foreign Minister [Gerhard] Schröder got them."

Arrested after Runge's defection, Leonore tried to protect her beloved husband and steadfastly denied all charges. Then the police confronted her with a confession in which Sütterlin stated that he married her not for love but on orders from the KGB. Thereupon, Leonore hanged herself in her cell.

Since the mid-1960s the KGB has allowed the satellite services to exchange some information and to consult directly with one another on particular issues of mutual concern. However, the Center in Moscow determines how important intelligence shall be distributed and coordinates all Soviet-bloc operations. The French uncovered a case that illustrates how well the Center discharges this responsibility.

Air France in 1959 assigned Jean-Marie Augros, a trim thirty-seven-year-old bachelor with a dark mustache, to Prague as its Central European representative. Staying at the Palace Hotel, Augros became friends with the bartender, Bohumil Pavliček, who was an STB agent. He introduced the Frenchman to a female agent, who subsequently reported that Augros had homosexual proclivities. The bartender then introduced Augros to a homosexual agent, and a series of orgies involving several people, young and old, ensued. Eventually a Czech dressed as a policeman visited Augros with the inevitable photographs. "I have come about a matter that is rather serious for you," he said, making himself at home. "These pictures are the work of a team of blackmailers. You may rest assured that they now are behind bars.

"But we still have a serious problem. Your position does not give you diplomatic immunity. What you have done, and these pictures leave no doubt about it, is a criminal offense here as well as in your own country.

I believe the penalty in France is five to ten years. Then there is the scandal. It would disgrace the French embassy and certainly cost your job." Thus in December 1960 did the STB recruit Augros. He supplied a wealth of information about the French embassy, Air France passengers, and many other foreigners he met in the course of his work and active social life.

In June 1962, Augros was transferred to Bucharest. After he got settled in his new post, the "policeman" from Prague unexpectedly called at his apartment accompanied by another man. "This is my friend Stefanescu," he said. "He has your file, and from now on you will work for him." So the Air France representative reported to the Romanians until January 1965, when he was promoted and sent to Phnom Penh, Cambodia. There he married a French embassy secretary he had known in Bucharest. Shortly after his marriage, he and his bride attended a reception at the Yugoslav embassy in Phnom Penh. A Soviet press attaché approached Augros, looked him in the eye, and casually murmured, "Prague 1960." This time Augros worked directly for the KGB, which assigned him to spy primarily on Americans. Pleased with his reports, the Russians so increased their contacts with him that French security officers became suspicious. They arranged for Augros to be recalled temporarily to Paris in February 1966, and after three days of interrogation he confessed everything. A court sentenced him to seven years' imprisonment.

During the pretrial investigation, a keen French officer noted that an international bartending contest was in progress at the Georges V Hotel in Paris. The security officer examined the list of contestants and, sure enough, spotted the name of Bohumil Pavliček, the Prague bartender who led Augros into the entrapment. With Gallic aplomb, security agents marched into the hotel and ceremoniously arrested the Czech. The State Security Court of France on September 30, 1966, sentenced Pavliček to three years.

However valuable the East European satellite services are to the Soviet Union, the service with the greatest potential for furthering Soviet ambitions may be the

Dirección General de Inteligencia, or DGI, of Cuba. Aside from their proximity to the United States, the Cubans possess a glamour which gives them an entrée to Latin America and the Third World that no other Soviet-bloc nation enjoys. For years, the DGI eluded KGB domination. The story of how the KGB finally captured the DGI is part of a larger story of how the KGB tried to destroy Fidel Castro and convert Cuba into a Soviet colony as servile as any in Eastern Europe. The Cuban and Soviet regimes have wanted to conceal the essence of this history, each for different reasons. It merits recounting in some detail.

Soviet rulers historically have distrusted and feared whatever they do not control absolutely, and in 1961 they became apprehensive about their ability to control Castro. As seen from the Kremlin, he was erratic, volatile, undisciplined, and often nonsensical. His wholesale executions, mass arrests, and unproductive terrorist forays against Latin neighbors, together with the sight of hundreds of thousands of Cubans attempting to flee his rule, raised the very Stalinist specter Khrushchev was trying to dispel. Moreover, while making a shambles of the Cuban economy, Castro neglected to heed orders from Moscow. Thus, the Kremlin concluded that he must be deposed and replaced by old-time communists obedient to the Soviet Union.

The first effort to topple him began in the fall of 1961 with the return from the Soviet Union of one such Cuban communist, Blas Roca. Under the broad direction of Ambassador Sergei M. Kudryavtsev, pro-Soviet communists moved swiftly. They occupied critical political positions, ousted Castro as head of the important agrarian reform movement, and, in early 1962, dared to ridicule him publicly.

However, the Soviet Union was frustrated by its own handiwork. The KGB had created an internal security system for Castro modeled after that by which the Soviet Union is ruled—a network of informants stretching into every city block, factory, farm, and office. Neighborhood committees of vigilantes, Comités de Defensa de la Revolución, provided further watch over each area of the island. This informant system, a gift of the KGB, became extremely efficient and accurately advised Fidel and his brother Raúl of the Soviet-sponsored machinations against them.

On March 27, 1962, Fidel appeared on nationwide television to denounce the conspirators. During a three-hour harangue, he accused them of "organizing a yoke, a straitjacket . . . an army of domesticated and coached revolutionaries." He and Raúl then quickly dismantled the monolithic political party by which the Soviet sympathizers expected to rule. They also instituted widespread purges, exiling some old-time communists such as Aníbal Escalante. Then they told Kudryavtsev to leave.

The stunned Russians were powerless. Their clandestine installation of nuclear missiles in Cuba was well advanced, and they needed Castro's cooperation. So they attempted conciliation, naming as ambassador a skilled KGB officer, Aleksandr I. Shitov, alias Aleksandr Alekseev, who was a personal friend of Castro's. They tried to influence the infant Cuban intelligence service by offering fraternal help. The KGB, utilizing both its own officers and a few from the Czech STB, taught the DGI the basic tradecraft of espionage and subversion. In 1963 it started training DGI officers in Moscow, recruiting those it could as Soviet agents. A few KGB officers who were *"niños"*—sons of Spanish parents who took refuge in the Soviet Union during and after the Spanish civil war in the late 1930s—posed as Cubans and actually joined the DGI. Yet the Soviet Union remained unable to exert full control over either the DGI or Castro.

Khrushchev's successors eventually made their own assessment of the Cuban situation. Their findings were even more discouraging than those which had spawned the first anti-Castro plot. The Cuban economy still was a mess, and the Soviet Union was spending an estimated million dollars a day to sustain it. The guerrilla antics of Che Guevara, while making him a romantic hero, were arousing hostility to communism in Latin America and impairing subversive operations of the KGB. And the Kremlin feared that some wild, unpredictable action by Castro might drag the Soviet Union into a disadvantageous confrontation with the United States. Again the Kremlin decided that Castro must be removed. This time the operation was much more determined and massive.

The most authoritative source of information about the second Soviet plot against Fidel is Raúl Castro. On January 24, 1968, before a secret session of the Central Committee of the Cuban Communist Party, Raúl reconstructed the operation in colorful detail. Each Central Committee member present was issued a numbered booklet bearing his name, which had to be returned at the end of the meeting. It contained an index referring to films, documents, reproduced statements, photographs, and tape recordings assembled to substantiate charges against the Soviet Union and the KGB.

Raúl stated that the Castro regime uncovered "the first seeds of conspiratorial activities" in mid-1966. These seeds matured until the "conspiracy" ultimately included anti-Castro Cubans working in the Ministry of Industries, the official newspaper *Granma,* the Radio Broadcasting Institute, the University of Havana, the Academy of Sciences, the fruit, fishing, and cigar industries, offices of the Party Central Committee, the Ministry of the Interior, and even Raúl's own Ministry of the Revolutionary Armed Forces.

The proclaimed objective of the secret movement, according to Raúl, was to oust Fidel and install an unreservedly pro-Soviet regime. He quoted one of the arrested plotters as having said of the aims: "We would draw much closer to all [Soviet] policies. . . . The group would work in the interest of defending the Soviet Union's stand on current events such as, for example, the recent conflict in the Middle East, as well as clarifying that country's stand in its policy of peaceful coexistence. It would instill in the masses the necessary confidence in the Soviet Union's solidarity with our Revolution and with all revolutionary movements. It would assure the masses that the Soviet Union would never leave us to face the imperialists alone."

The chief Cuban engineers of the plot identified by Raúl were the same cadre of old-time communists who had challenged Fidel before, including Aníbal Escalante, who had been allowed back in the country. But Raúl spoke with more venom about the Soviet representatives who consorted with the anti-Castro faction, and he named numerous KGB officers. Among them were Rudolf P. Shlyapnikov, second secretary of the Soviet embassy; Mikhail Roy of Novosti; another "journalist," Vadim Lestov; and several KGB advisers to the DGI, to whom Raúl referred only by their Spanish code names.

Reporting that two Cuban communists had rendezvoused with KGB officer Roy "on a street corner in Vedado [the western coastal section of Havana] and went for a long ride in the automobile owned by the Soviet 'journalist,'" Raúl declared: "If you want to ask a person some ordinary questions, you invite him to your house or you go to his house, to his office, or here or there; but when you're involved in conspiratorial activities . . . utilizing the classic method to gather information, you make a date on a street corner, you are picked up, you go for a long, slow ride." Manuel Pineiro Losada, then chief of the DGI, caught Escalante in a meeting near the Soviet embassy with the senior KGB adviser to the DGI. Raúl told of another meeting between anti-Castro communists and a KGB officer aboard a Soviet trawler. He quoted one of them as having said to the KGB officer: "The problem is that Fidel wants Cuba to be the hub of the whole world and he himself to become more important than Marx." Another conspirator said: "Nobody can understand Fidel; he is crazy."

Perhaps Raúl inundated the Party leaders with so much detail because of the harshness of the retribution Castro intended to inflict. Escalante, a stalwart of the Cuban Communist Party since 1932, was sentenced to fifteen years' imprisonment, and thirty-four other prominent communists received terms ranging from two to twelve years. These sentences were accompanied by renewed purges of Cubans suspected of disloyalty to Fidel. Again, Castro and his effective internal spy system had frustrated the Soviet Union. Soviet-Cuban relations sank to their lowest ebb since Castro's rise to power.

In the spring of 1968, the Soviet Union suddenly curtailed the flow of Soviet oil to Cuba. Economic paralysis crept over the island as sugar mills, factories, and vehicles stopped running for lack of fuel. Frantically Raúl diverted a third of the military petroleum reserves to the civilian economy. But the Russians halted other supplies and thereby closed more Cuban factories, forcing the workers to be sent into the fields. Having waited long enough for Fidel and Raúl to see complete economic collapse in the offing, the Kremlin proposed a deal.

It offered to reopen the supply lines, improve the quality of the raw materials it was shipping, increase exports of agricultural machinery, purchase more Cuban products, and equip Cuba with a nuclear power plant. In return, the Russians demanded that Castro permanently cease any and all criticism of the Soviet Union, that he permit at least five thousand Soviet specialists to come and supervise all facets of the economy, and that he make the DGI completely subservient to the KGB. Their most fundamental demand was implicit: henceforth Castro must do as told.

In August 1968, while foreign communist leaders the world over, from China to Chile, denounced the invasion of Czechoslovakia, Fidel Castro, the great foe of imperialism, defended it. The Soviet Union was justified, he said, in preventing the breakdown of a socialist country "one way or another." And he has remained a docile follower of the Soviet line ever since. In a 1970 interview published by *Izvestia,* Raúl Castro said: "We have learned a lot in the past. We have matured. Therefore, we believe that the possibilities for friendship and cooperation between Cuba and the Soviet Union are now more positive." And since the 1968 Cuban capitulation, Castro's brother has served as the strongest link between Moscow and Havana.

Slowly but firmly, the Soviet Union took possession of its new property, the DGI, installing the same controls by which it dominates all other satellite services.

To make their subservience more palatable to DGI officers, the Central Committee in Moscow transmits basic orders governing policy, reorganization, and new operations through Raúl Castro. However, to ensure that these orders are in fact executed, the KGB has intensified its recruitment of DGI personnel as Soviet agents and ensconced General Viktor Simenov in an office next to that of the DGI chief. Simenov must approve the annual operational plans of all DGI divisions. He and his KGB subordinates monitor all operations and communications involving any DGI agent of sensitivity or importance. The KGB, though Raúl, disposed of Manuel Pineiro Losada ("Redbeard"), the anti-Soviet DGI director, and established the pro-Soviet José Méndez Cominches as the de facto chief. Pineiro, as First Vice Minister of the Ministry of Interior, theoretically has authority over the DGI, but in practice he is permitted only to supervise Cuban support of "wars of liberation," and Méndez does his best to keep him ignorant of DGI operations.

Raúl returned from Moscow in the spring of 1970 with a host of orders that resulted in fundamental reorganization of the DGI plus other significant changes. At Soviet insistence, the Cuban army was reduced in manpower, and the money saved was diverted to clandestine operations. The DGI began building toward a goal of two thousand staff officers, in addition to the four hundred fomenting terrorism and guerrilla warfare under Pineiro. Overriding angry objections of the Ministry of External Affairs, the DGI usurped an additional 130 to 140 diplomatic posts in Cuban embassies around the world. For the first time outside Africa, the Cubans appointed intelligence officers as ambassadors. In 1971, eight of the ten Cubans at the embassy in London were DGI officers. That year, DGI officer Ricardo Cabisas Ruiz was named ambassador to Japan. Such diplomats regularly tote pistols, and Cuban embassies have assumed the character of armories, with stacks of machine guns, hand grenades, and Soviet explosives imported by diplomatic pouch.

The Central Committee has compelled the DGI to embark upon a series of high-risk or politically dangerous operations, from which only the Soviet Union can benefit. Although Castro had flirted with the Front de Libération Québecois and other separatists in Canada, he was reluctant to embrace them lest he jeopardize diplomatic relations. But at Soviet command, the DGI in 1969 inaugurated clandestine relations with the FLQ and expanded them after Raúl visited Moscow in 1970. The DGI officer responsible for overseeing training and support of FLQ personnel is Joaquín García Alonso, whose code name is Camilo. FLQ leaders now fly under false documentation to Havana, where meetings can be conducted in secrecy and security.

The DGI operational plan for 1972, drafted under KGB supervision, stipulated that the Cubans would train Irish Republican Army personnel in the tactics of terrorism and guerrilla warfare. Liaison with the IRA is effected by DGI officers in London through British communists. Cuba, of course, has never had any interest in Irish affairs. Its willingness to risk British wrath through clandestine intervention in Ireland is but another manifestation of its subservience to the Soviet Union.

The DGI also is preparing for more sophisticated operations against the United States. Heretofore, it has attempted espionage and subversion mostly through Cuban representatives at the United Nations. In 1962 the FBI arrested three Cuban "diplomats" stationed at the U.N. and seized a cache of explosives with which they planned to blow up department stores and sections of the New York subway system. The U.S. expelled two more Cubans from the U.N., one in 1968 and another in 1969, for directing and financing violence by black extremists. And in August 1969 it ousted the third secretary of the Cuban mission to the U.N., Lázaro Eddy Espinosa Bonet. He had tried to obtain photographs, floor plans, and details of security precautions at President Nixon's home in Key Biscayne as well as information about the President's travel arrangements to the Florida retreat.

The DGI in late 1970 established an Illegals Center to train staff officers for sabotage and espionage missions in the United States. The projected infiltration of professional illegals represents a new and ominous departure in DGI tactics. It could give Castro a much more serious ability to incite violence and commit sabotage in North America.

In terms of efficiency and technique, the DGI remains inferior to the more experienced satellite services. The quality of its officers varies, many having been chosen in the early 1960s on the basis of political rather than personal qualifications. Most are under thirty-five, and quite a few lack education as well as experience. But under KGB tutelage and control, these deficiencies are rapidly being corrected. And the Cubans have one great advantage none of the other Soviet-bloc services can match. Whereas Soviet representatives are nowhere regarded as romantic and heroic, Cubans are still heroes to numerous young people throughout the world. Youthful demonstrators in the United States parade with placards of Che, not Brezhnev, and girls swoon over Fidel, not Kosygin. The story of one lovely South African girl demonstrates how valuable the appeal of the Cubans can be in the world of subversion and espionage.

She was twenty-six, tall, blonde, beautiful, and so proportioned that to look at her was to be excited. When she chose, she could make her blue eyes and shy smile combine to convey an unspoken invitation no man could mistake. She could evaluate a man quickly and intuitively, then fashion an individualized approach that suggested she was powerless to resist him. Demurely, she left each of her paramours with the impression that he was the most wonderful of all; discreetly, she assured each of her own discretion.

For all her liaisons, her words and manners were ladylike, and she created about herself an aura of innocent vulnerability. No one felt threatened by her, and everyone wished to help her. Women liked her almost as much as men did, and those who thought they knew her the best liked her the most. Next to "beautiful," the words most frequently used to characterize her were "sweet" and "considerate." She was a superb and punctilious worker endowed with enormous reserves of energy. Though she might have been up until four, she invariably arrived at the office before nine o'clock, fresh and flawlessly groomed. She shunned expensive clothes and cosmetics, needing neither. Everything about her seemed natural and healthy.

By the summer of 1970 she had become a rising and dazzling star in the social firmament of official Washington. Government limousines sometimes called for her in the evening; Senators, Representatives, ambassadors, and government officials greeted her at diplomatic parties and at State Department receptions. Still, she was dissatisfied. Her ultimate goal was to gain entry into the inner society of the White House, that "special circle," as she called it. She was prepared to do anything, to make any sacrifice, to achieve the goal. For she was a spy who had consecrated her whole life to succeeding in her mission.

Jennifer Miles had grown up in the diamond-mining center of Kimberley, South Africa, the third child of a happy middle-class family. Influences at home and the vestiges of South Africa's pioneer culture imbued her with the work ethic, frugality, self-reliance, daring, and a spirit of adventure. After graduating from secondary school, she worked as a clerk, and at night often performed as a chorus girl in local theatrical revues. In July 1964, at twenty, she set off with her savings and two girl friends to explore as much of the world as she could. They traveled by ship from Capetown to England, then toured Europe. In January 1965 Jennifer and another girl went on to Canada, where she found a job as a secretary with a Toronto stock-brokerage firm. Efficient and popular, she attended night school and qualified as a stockbroker. Soon the director of the brokerage firm selected her as his private secretary. For a while she lived with a young South African immigrant. She insisted on paying her share of the housekeeping expenses and never accepted a cent from him or any other man.

In April 1967, Jennifer contracted a severe case of hepatitis requiring prolonged convalescence during which she had little to do but read. Articles in the

Canadian press about Cuba and Che Guevara's exploits in Bolivia fascinated her and inspired her to serious study. Through books, bought and borrowed, she
saw Cuba as a romantic, sunny island being transformed into a utopia by dashing, brave men of vision.
In the fantasies, she imagined herself at Che's side in
the jungles, comforting and caring for him, sharing his
dangers and ideals. With the capture, execution, and
martyrdom of Che in October, her fascination turned
to obsession. Her destiny now was clear. She had to
become a revolutionary and give herself wholly to
building the new world for which Che died and Fidel
lived. For spiritual fulfillment and to take the orders
of a revolutionary, she had to go to Cuba.

To convince the Cubans of her sincerity, she volunteered to work for the Fair Play for Cuba Committee
in Canada. Her enthusiastic efforts in their behalf were
such that she had no difficulty obtaining an entry visa
in December. At the time, however, the only route to
Cuba was through Mexico. The Mexicans, disturbed by
Cuban terrorism, refused to issue her a reentry visa,
which she needed to return from Cuba. As happened
often, Jennifer found a man to help her. An Italian
she met at her Mexico City hotel recommended that
she pretend to be an anthropologist studying an Indian
tribe that practices voodoo. He taught her enough
terminology to pose as an anthropologist, and the guise
succeeded. Jennifer had no place to stay in Havana,
but an American she had charmed on the plane took
her to the Veradero Hotel. After he spoke to the manager, a room was suddenly available.

On January 1, 1968, she stood with the Cuban multitude, enthralled and transported, listening to Castro
deliver his address on the ninth anniversary of the Revolution. Although most of the speech was incompre-
hensible to her, a fact she attributed to her own political
immaturity, she thought Fidel was manly and marvelous. Afterward, she was told that cameras televising
the occasion often focused on her, and she felt honored.
Her predisposition and commitment to Cuba were so
strong they allowed her to invert the import of what

she observed. Public transport, elevators, and hotel ventilation that did not function, lines in front of sparsely stocked stores, the peeling paint and physical deterioration of buildings, all were evidence not of inherent deficiencies in the economic system but of popular concern with higher values. The maze of police and bureaucratic regulations restricting daily life was evidence not of totalitarianism but of the people's willingness to subordinate individual interests to the welfare of society. The government herded townspeople into the fields on weekends in a desperate and inefficient effort to avert agricultural disaster. To Jennifer this meant not that agricultural policies had failed but that people were joyously dedicated to the Revolution.

Proving her own fidelity, Jennifer went into the fields to harvest crops, laboring twelve hours a day and sleeping in dormitory barns. The hard work and Spartan conditions gave her a gratifying sense of identity with the cause. Indeed, she so identified herself with it that one morning she cried upon seeing tobacco plants that had been flattened by a thunderstorm during the night.

Touring the island with a government escort, she proclaimed to one and all her love of Cuba and her determination to become an authentic revolutionary in its service. Doubtless the DGI was watching her closely and skeptically, for she was simply too good to be true. Had she been a lesser girl, the Cubans probably would have expelled her summarily because in her eagerness she resembled a foreign agent sent in to be recruited. But her potential was so obvious and great that the DGI elected to play along with her on the chance that she might be genuine.

When Jennifer returned from a visit to the Isle of Pines in late January 1968, her guide, whom she knew as Bernardo, informed her that she was being moved to the Hotel Riviera as a guest of the government. The Riviera is the Havana hotel whose rooms are best equipped with microphones, one-way mirrors, and television cameras for surveillance of guests. Soon Bernardo introduced her to a DGI officer who used the name George Sánchez. Assigned to be her guide and nightly escort, after a few hours' acquaintance he also became her lover.

While taking Jennifer to nightclubs and otherwise entertaining her, Sánchez analyzed and tested her. He ridiculed her revolutionary ambitions, and when she asked him to arrange a guerrilla mission for her in Latin America so she could emulate Che, he laughed uproariously. "You would do better to stay here and teach school," he said. "Find yourself a good man and produce beautiful blond children for us." But ultimately it was Sánchez who succumbed and Jennifer who prevailed. Leading her to her room one evening in mid-February, he confided: "I am convinced you are genuine. I have written a report today saying that you really do support Fidel."

Two or three days later, a man who obdurately refused to identify himself telephoned her at the hotel. He spoke English in short, abrupt sentences punctuated by frustrating pauses. "If you wish to help, listen," he began. "You want to go to Latin America. That is ridiculous. And you cannot be of particular service in Canada. The best thing is to go to the United States, to Washington. Think about it." With that he hung up, leaving Jennifer exasperated and hurt. She had anticipated some kind of recruitment ceremony, perhaps in the hidden garden of a mysterious villa surrounded by dark, mustachioed men unable to conceal their admiration of her. And she felt cheated and resentful at being deprived of formal baptism into the faith. Soon, though, she rationalized that there must be an occult purpose in the Cuban methods that she, in her naïveté, could not comprehend.

The Ghost, as Jennifer dubbed the anonymous caller, telephoned the next day. "Have you been thinking?" he asked.

"Yes, I am willing to go, but you must explain what I shall do," she replied.

"Your first duty will be to meet people. Meet as many important men in the U.S. government as you can," the DGI officer said. "Instructions will be given to you from time to time, as you need them. Prepare now to return to Toronto. Cover all traces of your interest in Cuba. Say nothing about it. Have nothing to do with the [Fair Play for Cuba] Committee. Your passport shows you have been here. Destroy it and say you lost it so you can get a new one. Wait about six months, then apply for jobs in Washington. Try your embassy and international organizations that employ foreigners. Do not discuss our conversations with anyone. I will call again." Before Jennifer could ask questions, he again hung up.

The anonymous DGI officer telephoned once or twice a day during the next two weeks, emphasizing the necessity of living a sedately normal life in Canada and advising her about how best to meet people in Washington. "Join the English-Speaking Union. Go to National Day parties at embassies. It is not necessary to show an invitation." His final calls concerned the location and use of drops in Canada. The DGI instructed her to leave a report in an alley wall two blocks from McGill University, Montreal, in October. In December she was to put a second message in a hole in a wall surrounding a suburban Montreal residence.

"By what name do you wish to be called?" the Ghost asked the day before she flew from Havana to Mexico City in early March.

"Call me Mary," Jennifer said.

"And our representative. Have you a name for him?"

"Let's call him José," said Jennifer.

"Good," said the DGI officer. "Whenever you hear from José, obey him." The Cubans never offered money for salary or expenses, and Jennifer never asked for any.

The first Saturday in October 1968, Jennifer slipped a note into the alley wall near McGill University reporting no progress in finding a job in Washington. But her message in December announced that she was leaving late that month to take a temporary position at the South African embassy there. Against a chilling wind, she walked along the suburban street to the site of the drop, stopped, and uttered one word, "Damn!"

The hole in the wall had been sealed. So she returned to the drop in the alley near the university and left her message there.

At the South African embassy in Washington, Jennifer, through charm and diligence, immediately endeared herself. Staff members vied for her services as a baby sitter because she was so dependable and their children adored her. An opening for a clerk-typist developed in April 1969, and the embassy gladly appointed her to a permanent position. Now Jennifer began to operate.

She rented an attractive efficiency apartment with a picture window looking out on the woods behind upper Wisconsin Avenue, furnished it colorfully, and stocked a large supply of duty-free liquor from the embassy. Joining the English-Speaking Union, she met young diplomats who invited her to embassy parties where she began to meet Americans. She regarded most of her dates as rungs in the ladder the DGI had assigned her to climb, although she did respond emotionally to a few. Generally, she was not attracted to what she termed "straight Americans"—clean-cut men in conservative suits, with neatly trimmed hair. She preferred swarthy males with long hair and perhaps a mustache —men who fitted her image of Cubans. A Latin diplomat pursued her with suggestions of marriage, and an American became possessively jealous of her, but she disposed of both gracefully.

The DGI called for the first time in late April, having obtained her home number simply by telephoning the South African embassy. In thickly accented English, "José" described the drop in New York where she was to deposit messages. It was another hole in another wall, this one next to an apartment building on Eighty-second Street in Jackson Heights, Queens. Jennifer delivered her initial progress report without incident in May. In late June she received telephone instructions from José to submit another report the first Saturday evening in July. Jennifer wrapped her message in plastic, which she bound with black cloth and tied with a black ribbon to form a cylindrical package the size of a screwdriver handle. She flew to New York the afternoon of July 5 and in the twilight of early evening inserted the little package in a crevice at the base of the apartment-building wall.

Shortly after Jennifer hurried away, the superintendent of the apartment building decided to finish trimming flowers planted on top of the wall. He dropped his shears and, stooping to retrieve them, saw the little black package, as only someone bending close to the ground could have done. Curious, he picked it up, took it to his workshop, and found the letter. Everything about it seemed strange.

Addressed to "My dear friends" and signed "Mary," the letter recounted visits to various embassies, mentioned names of journalists, diplomats, and businessmen in Washington, then said:

"Also through the English-Speaking Union I was invited to the Sulgrave Club, to a cocktail party to welcome the new British Ambassador. I met the Ambassador but no one else of any significance.

"I also went to a party at the New Zealand embassy and met Ambassador Vaughn from Barbados. . . .

"At the moment there does not seem to be anyone of much use to me. I keep going out—I accept every invitation that I think could lead to me meeting someone of some importance. But Washington is snobbish and I just don't seem to be able to get into that 'special circle' of people. . . .

"There is one thing I can do through my work which may be of some use to you. I can give you the names of American Diplomatic Couriers. These will only be the ones applying to us for visas, but thought you may be interested. . . .

"I can also give you names of any official or diplomatic passport holders that pass through my hands. I have records for the past two-three years. . . .

"I am still going to join the Watergate Club. I am saving my money for the Annual Dues—it costs $300 to join. I just hope it pays off and I meet some Senators!"

The superintendent hesitated; reluctant to make himself appear foolish, he nevertheless was troubled by the letter. All the talk about meeting important people might be innocuous, but the statement about supplying names of diplomatic couriers connoted something sinister. After about an hour he overcame his reservations and called the FBI.

The effort to ascertain the identity of agent Mary began that Sunday morning, July 6, 1969, in the Washington field office of the FBI. From the letter, the FBI easily concluded that she was probably a relatively young unmarried woman, a member of the English-Speaking Union, and an employee of a British Commonwealth or former Commonwealth country. A State Department list showed that South Africa was one of the nations requiring visas from American diplomatic couriers. On Monday morning investigators learned that among members of the English-Speaking Union attending the reception at the Sulgrave Club for the British ambassador the preceding May was a Miss Jennifer M̶i̶l̶e̶s̶, ̶a̶n̶ employee of the South African embassy. Inquiries confirmed that a man mentioned in the ̶l̶e̶t̶t̶e̶r̶ dated Jennifer Miles. By midafternoon Monday ̶t̶h̶e̶ FBI was virtually certain that Jennifer was M̶a̶r̶y̶ ̶b̶u̶t̶ it had no proof. Nor did it know with w̶h̶o̶m̶ ̶s̶h̶e̶ was communicating clandestinely.

S̶u̶r̶v̶eillance of Jennifer began that Monday night. W̶h̶a̶t̶ the FBI observed during the summer caused increas̶ing concern. She was seeing, and frequently entertaining in her apartment, half a dozen government officials with access to secrets any enemy would like to have. The FBI had no reason to suspect them of leaking information, much less of disloyalty. But, discerning a progression in the importance of the men Jennifer captivated, it was extremely apprehensive about where her associations might eventually lead. Clearly, if she was a controlled enemy agent, she represented trouble and, potentially, serious danger.

Whatever doubts the FBI still had ended in late September when agents followed her to a clandestine meeting in New York. Excited by the prospect of her first personal rendezvous, Jennifer flew from Washington immediately after work on September 26. She registered at a New York hotel, took a taxi to Queens, and at 8 P.M. stood near the intersection of Fifty-sixth Street and Woodside Avenue wondering what José would look like. She hoped that each approaching man would be the one to speak the recognition signal, "Good evening, Mary." But after fifteen minutes, the maximum time she was supposed to wait, José had not come. Out of eagerness to meet him, she lingered another twenty minutes before resigning herself to attempting the meeting a week later on the alternative date given her, October 3.

The next Saturday she arrived at the Queens intersection at 7:59 P.M. and heard a voice behind her say, "Good evening, Mary." The man she saw, Rogelio Rodríguez López, counselor of the Cuban mission to the United Nations, did not look like the spymaster she had envisioned. Short and heavy-set, he had changed his appearance for the meeting by putting on black horn-rimmed glasses and slicking back his thick, black hair, which he normally wore in disarray. His life and work in New York kept him under severe strain, and he had about him the air of a perpetually harassed, nervous, and perspiring man for whom each act was a struggle. He had to spend his days at the U.N., his nights dealing with agents, and his weekends searching for new drops and rendezvous points. Legal restrictions limiting his movements to a twenty-five-mile radius of the United Nations compounded his difficulties and afflicted his family with a sense of claustrophobia. Always he and his wife worried about encounters with anti-Castro Cuban émigrés, who would not hesitate to assault him if they caught and recognized him.

"I am José. Permit me to offer you a cocktail," said Rodríguez, leading Jennifer to a neighborhood bar. He asked her about her life in Washington and each of her male acquaintances. Taking notes, he interrupted only to verify the spelling of the names she mentioned. "I feel terribly frustrated," Jennifer concluded. "I have been in the States nine months, and I can't see that I've accomplished a thing."

"You are magnificent, Mary," Rodríguez assured her. "You have built a base, a very strong base. You cannot expect miracles overnight. We have been worried about you, though. Why didn't you report in July as we told you?"

"But José, I did!" Jennifer exclaimed.

"Are you sure, Mary?" asked Rodríguez, studying her closely. Jennifer rapidly and emphatically told how she had drafted, wrapped, and deposited the message at the base of the wall, concluding: "I wouldn't lie to you!"

Rodríguez motioned her to speak more quietly. "I believe you, but we did not find it. Maybe the rain washed it away, maybe an animal took it; I don't know. In any case, what you can do is so important that we have decided to take no risks. It is too dangerous to meet you in the United States. From now on ur contacts will be made outside this country. Start nning a vacation in Spain, so that you can be at Avenida Hotel in Madrid by December 28. José call and give you instructions."

ne meeting and the compliments were gratifying ards for Jennifer. She rationalized that the Cubans wonderfully clever in picking as a spy a man who not look like her concept of a spy, and she reed to Washington with an even more vigorous sense nission. In the fall, she met her first Congressman a entered into affairs with an American diplomatic corier and a State Department officer. Flying to Spain after Christmas on a ticket purchased with her own savings, she proudly felt that she could report concrete progress.

A DGI agent identifying himself as José telephoned her at the hotel at 3 P.M. December 28, and told her to enter a certain café at 5 P.M. However, he spoke English so poorly that Jennifer misunderstood and went to the wrong address. In the early evening the agent called again, repeated the correct address, and rescheduled the meeting for 8:30 P.M. Jennifer sat in the café more than an hour drinking sangria. Several Spaniards tried to entice her into conversation, but none referred to her as Mary or to himself as José.

Minutes after Jennifer returned to the hotel, José telephoned a third time. "There is danger. You must leave at once. Take the first Iberia flight to Paris in the morning."

"What must I do in Paris?" Jennifer asked anxiously.

"Take the first Iberia flight," the Cuban agent again commanded. He hung up without further explanation.

Jennifer dutifully boarded the plane, bewildered at her orders, alarmed by the unspecified "danger" and fearful of what would happen next. She had no idea where to go in Paris or how to communicate again with the Cubans. It was a choppy, crowded flight aggravated by a squalling baby, and she was miserable. As she stood in the aisle of the plane waiting to disembark in Paris, a fellow passenger, a middle-aged Spanish woman, touched her hand. Jennifer looked down, and the woman silently gave her a piece of paper folded into a tight, small square. It directed her to a café opposite the Eiffel Tower at noon on December 30.

As Jennifer stepped into the café the next day, a handsome, well-dressed Latin in his early thirties came forward, embraced her, and said in excellent English: "Good afternoon, Mary. How wonderful to see you." After a waiter seated them, he whispered, "Relax and look happy. People should think you are reunited with an old friend."

"I'm quite confused and frightened," Jennifer said. "What is happening?"

"We believe that you were being watched in Madrid," the Cuban replied. "We cannot be sure. Any man might follow you for innocent reasons." The DGI officer interrupted himself with a laugh. "I mean, for reasons that are not sinister. However, the fact that a man was watching you could be a signal. And the fact that your message disappeared could be a signal."

Comprehending instantly, Jennifer said, "If the Americans know and I go back, they will arrest me."

"For what? What crime have you committed?" responded the Cuban. "No, you are doing too beautifully to stop now. Return and continue just as before. We simply must be careful and have no contact for a year or so. Probably we are alarmed at nothing."

Back in Washington, Jennifer gradually reassured

herself. Nothing in the demeanor of the embassy staff suggested that her position there was any less secure and comfortable than before. Nothing in the behavior of her American acquaintances suggested that anyone regarded her as anything other than a delightful and desirable young woman. In fact, invitations from Americans and various embassies increased, and she reasoned that if the authorities suspected her, they would not allow her to circulate so unimpeded.

In February 1970, a Chilean diplomat introduced Jennifer to an American who beguiled her at once with both his position and appearance. He was Saeed A. Khan, a deputy protocol officer of the State Department. A native of Pakistan, Khan was a tall, suave forty-two-year-old diplomat who retained a formidable mustache from his days as a captain in the Sixth Bengal Lancers. He became a U.S. citizen, married, and had five children before separating from his wife. Khan excited Jennifer as a man. As a State Department officer whose duties placed him in the very highest social milieu of Washington, he excited her even more. The protocol officer was equally attracted to Jennifer for personal and professional reasons. Aside from her sexual allure, she would adorn any of the diplomatic parties he had to attend almost nightly.

Soon Jennifer began accompanying Khan to official functions, sometimes visiting as many as three embassies an evening. She attended a reception for West German Chancellor Willy Brandt at Blair House, the guest residence of the President, on April 10. Less than two weeks later she was back for a party for the Vice Premier of Nationalist China. At an embassy reception in honor of President Urho Kekkonen of Finland, her South African boss was astonished to see her chatting with the visiting chief of state. When he mentioned the party to her in the morning, she replied: "Oh, I had a marvelous time. Afterward, I went to Blair House and had dinner. I eat there all the time."

"My God!" exclaimed the South African diplomat. "I have been here six years, and I've never had dinner there."

As the guest of a ranking State Department officer,

she was presented to Cabinet officers, Senators, and other prominent U.S. government officials. Often when they met her, their judgment and protective mechanisms had been weakened by the fatigue of a long day of tension and by three or four drinks. And here was a fresh, appealing young woman, subtly flattering, subtly inviting. On more than one occasion, the conversation that followed her introduction ended with Jennifer giving her telephone number and receiving the promise of a call.

Jennifer never tried to pry state secrets from any man, and insofar as is known, nobody ever betrayed any to her. In the spring of 1970 her objective was still to establish herself in that "special circle" of Washington officialdom. There would be time enough later to seek, through amours or marriage, the intelligence she might be instructed to gather. She had already begun to amass intimate knowledge of personal attitudes, weaknesses, predilections, and eccentricities that form the essence of recruitment dossiers. The ability to supply such personality data, which the KGB in particular amasses, studies, and exploits, alone made her an agent of extraordinary value.

The FBI continued to watch Jennifer in the hope that she would eventually lead them to important Cuban or even Soviet contacts. By May, though, they found it necessary to send circumspect warnings about her to officials in all branches of government. As she deftly maneuvered among the famous, the FBI had to weigh prospective advantages against the growing risks of allowing Jennifer to continue to operate.

As soon as it had established that Jennifer was a Cuban agent in the fall of 1969, the FBI advised South African intelligence. The South Africans skillfully cooperated in the continuing investigation and surveillance. The morning of October 3, 1970, the FBI delivered a priority message to their embassy in Washington: Jennifer had graduated from a potential menace to a real and present danger. The case had to be terminated.

Next day a South African diplomat asked Jennifer into his office. "Miss Miles, I have a rather important item here that must be delivered personally," he announced, handing her an envelope. He asked her to take it to a specified room at a Washington hotel.

Jennifer knocked on the door of the hotel room, and a perfectly groomed, conservatively dressed man, a "straight American," greeted her. "Please come in, Miss Miles." Another man stood up in the room and both displayed FBI identification cards.

Jennifer charmingly and bravely denied that she was a Cuban agent. "This is very thrilling," she said. "But I'm rather afraid you have confused me with someone else."

"Do you recognize this?" asked an agent, showing her the letter she delivered to the New York drop in July 1969. Before she answered, he produced photographs of her with Rodríguez at the Queens intersection and in the nearby bar. "Is it necessary to show you more?"

Near tears, Jennifer said, "I will do nothing to hurt Cuba."

On the chance that her reactions to the confrontation might reveal something more about her contact, the FBI let her leave. But the evening of October 5 Jennifer unexpectedly appeared at the Washington field office of the FBI and volunteered to confess the details of her relations with the Cubans and all her other adventures. In part because of her cooperation, she was allowed to return to South Africa rather than be prosecuted. Khan, who had violated neither security nor the law, quietly left the State Department, his employment contract having expired. The United States expelled Rodríguez and his DGI boss at the United Nations, Orlando Prendes Gutiérrez. A State Department spokesman issued a cryptic statement accusing them of receiving information from "a quite attractive and personable" employee of a foreign embassy in Washington.

In South Africa, Jennifer publicly denied ever having been a Cuban spy. She did write, or allow to be written in her name, a magazine article romanticizing Cuba and her visit there. The article, like Jennifer herself, was sweet and considerate.

VIII

DISINFORMATION: POISONING PUBLIC OPINION

In practicing what it calls disinformation, the Soviet Union has for years sponsored grand deceptions calculated to mislead, confound, or inflame foreign opinion. Some of these subterfuges have had considerable impact on world affairs. Some also have had unforeseeable consequences severely detrimental to Soviet interests. Ultimately, they have made the Soviet Union the victim of its own deceit.

After World War II, when the Russians were threatening Greece, Iran, and Berlin, they leaked data grossly exaggerating the strength of the Red Army. They intended to intimidate the West. Instead, they provided an added stimulus to Western rearmament and the formation of NATO.

With KGB approval and support, the Czech STB in the autumn of 1964 initiated a vast deception campaign to arouse Indonesian passions against the United States. Through an Indonesian ambassador they had compromised with female agents, the Czechs purveyed to President Sukarno a series of forged documents and fictitious reports conjuring up CIA plots against him. One forgery suggested that the CIA planned to assassinate Sukarno; another "revealed" a joint American-British plan to invade Indonesia from Malaysia. The unstable Sukarno responded with anti-American diatribes, which some Indonesian journalists in the pay

of the KGB and STB amplified and Radio Moscow
played back to the Indonesian people. Incited mobs
besieged American offices in Djakarta, anti-American
hysteria raged throughout the country, and U.S. influence was eradicated. The former STB deception specialist Ladislav Bittman has written a history and analysis of the operation in which he participated. He
states, "We ourselves were surprised by the monstrous
proportions to which the provocation grew."

This brilliant tactical success, however, ended in a
debacle. Bittman notes: "Czechoslovak and Soviet disinformation departments, intoxicated by potential gains
in the battle against the main enemy, deliberately shut
their eyes to the danger that the consequences could
also be the heightening of internal tension and intensification of Chinese influence in the country." Encouraged by the increasingly influential Chinese and misled
by the climate the Czechs and Russians had created,
Indonesian communists concluded that the time was
propitious for a coup. The night of September 30,
1965, they murdered six Indonesian generals and attempted to seize the government. The Indonesian military reacted by slaughtering tens of thousands of communists and annihilating the Party, then one of the
largest in the world.* Indonesia, which seemed destined
to slip irretrievably into the communist orbit, emerged
as an independent nation with a strong government
determined to retain its independence.

Despite such fiascos, Soviet rulers have shown no
disposition to abandon organized deception as an instrument of national policy. The practice is another
legacy of Lenin imbedded in Soviet custom. Just as
Lenin admired terror, he extolled the "poisoned weapons" of deceit, duplicity, and slander. He wrote: "The
communists must be prepared to make every sacrifice
and, if necessary, even resort to all sorts of cunning,
schemes and stratagems to employ illegal methods, to
evade and conceal the truth. . . . The practical part of
communist policy is to incite one [enemy] against an-

---

*Several sources have estimated the number killed at 500,000, but
Western intelligence sources have concluded that 50,000 is probably a much more accurate figure.

other. . . . We communists must use one country against another. . . . My words were calculated to evoke hatred, aversion, and contempt . . . not to convince but to break up the ranks of the opponent, not to correct an opponent's mistake but to destroy him, to wipe his organization off the face of the earth. This formulation is indeed of such a nature as to evoke the worst thoughts, the worst suspicions about the opponent."

Out of these "Principles of Leninism" the contemporary Soviet concept of *dezinformatsiya,* or disinformation, has evolved. The Russians define disinformation as "the dissemination of false and provocative information." As practiced by the KGB, disinformation is far more complex than the definition implies. It entails the distribution of forged or fabricated documents, letters, manuscripts, and photographs; the propagation of misleading or malicious rumors and erroneous intelligence by agents; the duping of visitors to the Soviet Union; and physical acts committed for psychological effect. These techniques are used variously to influence policies of foreign governments, disrupt relations among other nations, undermine the confidence of foreign populations in their leaders and institutions, discredit individuals and groups opposed to Soviet policies, deceive foreigners about Soviet intentions and conditions within the Soviet Union, and, at times, simply to obscure depredations and blunders of the KGB itself.

Disinformation operations differ from conventional propaganda in that their true origins are concealed, and they usually involve some form of clandestine action. For this reason, Soviet rulers always have charged their clandestine apparatus with primary responsibility for disinformation.

The Cheka and each of its organizational descendants had a "Disinformation Desk" until reorganization of the KGB in 1959 produced a full-fledged Disinformation Department known as Department D of the First Chief Directorate. The first director was General Ivan Ivanovich Agayants, a tall, aloof Armenian with grizzled hair and a thin gray mustache. Ascetic and solemn, Agayants combined personal puritanism with a penchant for professional ruthlessness. He gathered a

staff of some fifty officers at the Center and stationed
another fifteen to twenty at the KGB's Karlshorst Residency in East Berlin. Additionally, he received authorization to engage scientists, technical specialists, and
military officers as consultants whenever needed. After
the death of Agayants and another reorganization in
1968, the Disinformation Department became Department A, acquiring more stature in the Foreign Directorate bureaucracy and, reportedly, more personnel.

Occasionally Disinformation Department officers
travel abroad to participate in operations. Agayants
slipped into Sweden in 1963 and Pakistan in 1965. He
also went to Indonesia in 1965 and periodically visited
Eastern Europe to inspect satellite disinformation departments. His deputy, Sergei Aleksandrovich Kondrashev, traveled to Bonn in 1966 hunting material for
slandering West German political leaders. Another Disinformation Department officer, Yuri Ivanovich Lyudin, using the alias Yuri Ivanovich Modin, spent ten
months in New Delhi preparing the forgeries that the
KGB released to influence the 1967 Indian elections. A
few disinformation officers, such as Vladimir Aleksandrovich Chuchukin, a first secretary of the Soviet U.N.
mission in New York, are permanently stationed
abroad. However, for most field work abroad, Department A relies upon officers and agents of the First
Chief Directorate's geographic divisions. It also may
avail itself of saboteurs from Department V or bona
fide Soviet diplomats who at times are employed to
plant rumors, wittingly or unwittingly.

Department A executes disinformation operations
against foreigners in the Soviet Union both through its
own officers and various divisions of the Second Chief
Directorate. A Westerner who requests to meet a specialist in his particular field very well may be introduced instead to a disinformation specialist. The KGB
today, for example, arranges for selected Westerners to
meet the distinguished "Professor Nikitin of the Institute of History." Professor Nikitin actually is Anatoli
Gorsky, an old-time KGB officer who also has used the
name Anatoli Gromov. Working out of the Soviet embassy in London from 1936 to 1944, Gorsky helped

direct Soviet agents Harold A. R. ("Kim") Philby, Donald Maclean, and Guy Burgess. He followed Maclean to Washington in 1944 to run high-level espionage and agent-of-influence operations against the United States. Now unable to go abroad safely, Gorsky devotes himself to deceiving foreigners in Moscow.

Visiting politicians, scholars, journalists, clergymen, and other professionals whose opinions are influential are the most common targets of concerned disinformation efforts. Typically, the KGB strives to control what the foreigner sees while persuading him that he is freely seeing what he wishes. It tries to shape his conclusions while making him think that he is reaching them on his own. The KGB often succeeds because of its ability to control the Soviet environment. The record reveals many illustrious victims of its manipulations.

Sir John Maynard, a British agricultural expert, went on an OGPU-guided tour of the Ukraine at the height of the 1932–33 famine that, according to Robert Conquest's calculations, took five to six million lives. Back in London, Maynard assured the world there was no famine; isolated food scarcities perhaps, but certainly no widespread hunger. Similarly, George Bernard Shaw returned from an OGPU tour to aver that there was no evidence of starvation. After all, he noted, the hotels where he dined abounded with food.

The most barbarous of the Stalinist concentration camps were those run by an NKVD front called Dalstroy in the Kolyma gold-mining region of northeastern Siberia. Temperatures much of the year ranged between twenty and forty degrees below zero, and surgeons regularly sheared off the frozen hands, feet, and limbs of inadequately clad inmates. Most of the political prisoners—scientists, artists, intellectuals, teachers, and Party officials—were unaccustomed to the arduous physical labor demanded of them twelve hours a day. When they failed to meet their daily work quota, their already meager rations were reduced as punishment. Given less nourishment, they grew weaker and less able to work or to defend themselves against the common criminals who preyed upon them. Prisoners were routinely clubbed, beaten, or, in many thousands of cases, shot. The annual mortality rate in the mines was 30 percent, and Conquest concludes that between 1937 and 1941 alone, at least a million Dalstroy prisoners perished.

The prisoners in the Dalstroy camps at Magadan were honored in 1944 by the extraordinary visit of two eminent Americans, Henry A. Wallace, Vice President of the United States, and Professor Owen Lattimore, representing the Office of War Information. Dalstroy, as a good host, made special preparations to receive them. In a single night NKVD personnel dismantled the camp watchtowers around Magadan. From private stocks, they hastily gathered Russian goods to fill the shelves of stores serving NKVD and civilian supervisors in the town. The emaciated women prisoners who toiled as swineherds at the nearby farm were replaced by the most presentable NKVD women available. Strong, healthy, happy-looking young men showed up in the mines to relieve the gaunt prisoners. During the three days the Americans visited the camps, all prisoners were kept out of sight under guard and, for the first and last time, shown motion pictures so they would create no disturbance.

Both Lattimore and Wallace subsequently published reports of their tour of the Magadan area. Lattimore, writing in the December 1944 issue of *National Geographic* ("New Road to Asia," pp. 641–76), stated: "There has probably never been a more orderly phase of pioneering than the opening up of Russia's Far North under the Soviet.

"Magadan is also part of the domain of a remarkable concern, the Dalstroi (Far Northern Construction Company) [sic] *which can be roughly compared to a combination Hudson's Bay Company and TVA* [italics supplied]. It constructs and operates ports, roads and railroads, and operates gold mines and municipalities, including, at Magadan, a first-class orchestra and a good light-opera company.

". . . As one American remarked, high-grade entertainment just naturally seems to go with gold, and so does high-powered executive ability."

Referring to NKVD Lieutenant General Ivan Fedorovich Nikishov, who was in charge of the slave-labor complex, Lattimore wrote: "Mr. Nikishov, the head of Dalstroi, had just been decorated with the Order of Hero of the Soviet Union for his extraordinary achievements. Both he and his wife have a trained and sensitive interest in art and music and also a deep sense of civic responsibility. . . . It was interesting to find, instead of the sin, gin and brawling of an old-time gold rush, extensive greenhouses growing tomatoes, cucumbers and even melons, to make sure that the hardy miners got enough vitamins!"

Wallace in his book *Soviet Asia Mission* wrote: "The Kolyma goldminers are big, husky young men who came out to the Far East from European Russia. . . . The miners asked me to take back a message of solidarity to the people of the United States. *Their trade union leader,* N. I. Adagin, sent his best regards to Sidney Hillman and Philip Murray [italics supplied]. . . . It can therefore be said that in the north of Siberia today the Russians have a development of urban life comparable in general to that of our Northwestern states and Alaska. . . . Compared to mine laborers in old Russia, the men in overalls on the Kolyma had many more rubles to spend. . . . The spirit and meaning of life in Siberia today is certainly not to be compared to that of the old exile days. . . ."

Yuri Nosenko states that while he was helping direct operations against Americans in Moscow, the Central Committee expressly ordered the KGB to intensify efforts to influence the opinions of visiting foreigners. Today performance of this mission is greatly facilitated by the basic controls that allow the KGB invisibly to restrict the lodging, travel, and contacts of visitors. Simply by ensuring that the foreigner talks to the right officials, by determining what he may and may not see, the KGB can shape his impressions without mounting a complicated operation. Respectable foreigners who come away from the controlled Soviet society with erroneous impressions, whether fostered directly by the KGB or not, sometimes affect attitudes in their own countries. Occasionally it is possible to trace the effects of misinformation purveyed in good faith by honorable but misled men.

The single problem of Soviet life that should most defy disguise or concealment is the acute shortage and gross inadequacy of housing. Theoretically, each Soviet citizen is allotted at least nine square meters (about a hundred square feet) of living space, but in 1965 the average available in urban areas was 6.42 meters, slightly less than in 1923. At some unspecified future date, the Soviet Union hopes to provide one room for each person. But in 1965 the ratio was about one room for 2.3 urban residents. Soviet data show that even if all current construction goals are achieved, in 1975 a substantial portion of all state-owned urban housing still will be without baths or running water. The condition of privately owned dwellings, which make up about 30 percent of urban housing, is far worse.

Despite comparatively great investment in housing construction during recent years, production goals have been met only twice in Soviet history. In the nonurban areas where approximately 45 percent of the population resides, the general condition of housing can only be described as primitive. Professor Karl-Eugen Wädekin of the University of Giessen in Germany states: "The technical amenities of modern civilization are scarce: many villages are still without electricity; and running water, sewage systems and piped gas are rarely to be found." The lack of privacy, the sharing of bedrooms by children and parents, and the sharing of kitchens and baths with other families, represent a daily oppression felt by a majority of Soviet citizens.

There is no secret about this general condition because it cannot be kept secret. As Professor Donald D. Barry of Lehigh University notes, "The rundown condition of even newer residential buildings has been a constant subject of complaint in the [Soviet] press." Premier Kosygin in 1966 termed housing "one of the greatest social problems" and stated that even with construction of new homes (apartments) for 65 million people, "the housing problem still will not be wholly solved." First Secretary Brezhnev told the 23rd

Party Congress the same year, "We are building a great deal, but the housing problem still remains extremely acute."

Nevertheless Howard J. Samuels, when Under Secretary of Commerce, declared at the outset of a speech on May 7, 1968: "The Soviet Union has far surpassed the United States in solving the low-cost housing needs of its people and may well be on its way to becoming the first large nation in the world to eliminate the blight of slums." One had to wonder. What did Samuels know about Soviet housing that Kosygin, Brezhnev, and the Soviet press did not?

An inquiry to the Department of Commerce was referred to a former Samuels aide, Thomas Langman, who wrote the speech. He stated that the references to Soviet housing were based largely upon data provided by A. Allan Bates, director of the Office of Standards Policy of the Commerce Department. Langman was impressed by the findings of Bates. "Sure, the quality of the Russian housing may be poorer than ours, but at least they have solved the problem of taking care of the people living there," he told an interviewer. "The bathrooms are not as fancy maybe, but, you know, I mean that they are using industrialized technology while we don't. . . . We need to do what the Russians are doing." Langman characterized Bates as "a great exponent of the Russian housing experience." Indeed he is.

The Joint Economic Committee of the United States Congress published in April 1969 a compendium report containing a treatise by Bates on Soviet housing. It began: "The Soviet Union is the first and thus far the only nation which *has solved* the problem of providing acceptable low-cost housing for its masses of citizens [italics supplied].

"Within a few years—perhaps a decade—it will probably be generally acknowledged internationally that the best housed inhabitants of any large country in the world are those of the U.S.S.R. The political impact of this situation will be profound. The United States will suffer devastating comparisons."

Praising the Soviet Union for "carrying out unexampled pioneering in the fields of human mass motivation and organization," Bates noted that Soviet designers, unlike Americans, waste no space on "lavish facilities for home sports, entertaining or private prestige." As he explained, "The Soviet urban ideal is to exalt communal life to a new level of human experience." Bates concluded that "all urbanized nations," presumably including the United States, ultimately will be driven to emulate "Soviet housing policies and operations."

But nowhere in his treatise did Bates cite a single independent source or adduce any objective data, Soviet or otherwise, to support his striking findings. Interviewers asked on what grounds he had reached his unique conclusions. He replied that he had been traveling to the Soviet Union since 1959. "My statements about Soviet housing are based on personal observation," he said. "I have gone all over the world; seen more than any other American what is going on in the Soviet Union. No, I can't refer you to any government reports or data; my statements are based on personal observations. My testimony before the Joint Economic Committee? Well, again, that was based on my personal observations." Bates declined to offer substantiation of any of his extravagant assertions. "I have been in over 100 cities and communities in the Soviet Union, and I know what is going on. My contacts? Well, I don't have time to tell you the dozens and dozens of high authorities I have talked to. Anyway, you must realize that I gather my information by going to factories, talking to workmen. More than any other American, I have done this." Bates acknowledges, though, that he can neither speak nor read Russian.

Thus, the statements by Bates about Soviet housing accomplishments rest on his personal impressions, gained while traveling under the escort of Soviet officials and interpreters. Nevertheless, they have prompted an American Under Secretary of Commerce to make the ludicrous claim that "The Soviet Union has far surpassed the United States in solving the low-cost housing needs of its people and may well be on its way to becoming the first large nation in the world to eliminate the blight of slums." In a long letter published by the Washington *Post* on July 8, 1969, Professor Almont Lindsey of Mary Washington College quoted this claim as evidence of significant Soviet economic achievement. The treatise by Bates, published without critical comment by the prestigious Joint Economic Committee, now is a permanent part of the literature on Soviet housing. As such, it well may influence scholars for years to come.

Outside the Soviet Union, the KGB has initiated important disinformation operations through physical actions calculated to arouse popular fears or prejudices. French authorities have reconstructed the chronology of one such operation that culminated in murder.

Under KGB guidance, the Czech STB in 1956 started mailing virulent neo-Nazi tracts to French, British, and American officials in Europe. They bore the imprimatur of a nonexistent organization called the Fighting Group for an Independent Germany (*Kampfverband für Unabhängiges Deutschland*). Continuing propaganda from this phantom organization created the impression that a gang of fanatical resurgent Nazis was active in West Germany.

In the spring of 1957, four Czech intelligence officers—Miloslav Kouba, Robert Ther, Milan Kopecky, and Stanislav Tomes—journeyed to Paris. Kouba, an explosives expert, built a powerful bomb that could be fitted into a cigar box. The Czechs then went to the post office at 25 Boulevard Diderot in Paris and mailed what appeared to be a box of fine cigars. It was addressed to André-Marie Trémeaud, the prefect of Bas-Rhin Department, and timed to arrive at his home in Strasbourg the morning of May 17. The evening of the seventeenth, the prefect was to be host at a dinner for a French parliamentary delegation that had been meeting at Strasbourg. The Russians and Czechs expected that he would offer his guests after-dinner cigars. He might have if his wife had not first lifted the lid of the box that arrived in the morning mail.

The KGB had hoped to blow up the parliamentarians and blame the nonexistent neo-Nazis. Instead, it succeeded only in killing a housewife. Still, KGB rumors and speculation in the European press implicated

the "Nazis." And Radio Moscow specifically accused the
Fighting Group for an Independent Germany of the
murder. The killing inspired by the KGB was cited as
proof that West Germans at heart were unregenerate
Nazis who deserved the trust of no one.

Not long after the murder of Madame Trémeaud the
KGB perceived another means of defaming West Germany. A West German high-school teacher in 1958
made vile anti-Jewish remarks, juvenile delinquents de-
filed gravestones in a Jewish cemetery, and a few Jewish families received anonymous hate letters. The incidents angered the German press and stimulated a
spate of stories in the foreign press speculating about
a possible rebirth of Nazism. They also bred an idea
in the mind of General Agayants.

On Christmas Eve 1959, a twenty-five-year-old German, aided by an accomplice, smeared swastikas and a
slogan, "Germans Demand That Jews Get Out," on the
Synagogue in Cologne. A Jewish memorial a mile away
also was defaced. In the next few nights, swastikas and
anti-Semitic slogans were painted on synagogues, tombstones, and Jewish-owned stores in more than twenty
West German towns and cities. Jews received threatening anonymous telephone calls and letters. During the
New Year's weekend, swastikas and slogans were
daubed on synagogues and Jewish buildings in London,
Oslo, Vienna, Paris, Parma, Glasgow, Copenhagen,
Stockholm, Milan, Antwerp, and New York. On January 3, further outbreaks of anti-Semitism were reported
in Melbourne, Manchester, Athens, and Perth, Australia.
On January 6, more desecrations occurred in Bogotá,
Buenos Aires, Milan, Oslo, Vienna, and the summer
home of King Frederik IX of Denmark. A Jewish member of the British Parliament was provided a bodyguard after his life was threatened by an anonymous
caller purporting to be a representative of the "British
Nazi Party." Meanwhile, the epidemic of desecrations
intensified and spread throughout West Germany.

The worldwide reaction was instant and almost uniformly disparaging of West Germany. The American
poet Carl Sandburg advocated death for anyone caught
painting swastikas. In London, Lord Robert Boothby,

saying he had been told of a "rising tide of Nazism," announced that he was going to Germany to investigate the situation. West German diplomats were ostracized. British businessmen canceled contracts for purchases of West German products, fired German employees, and removed German goods from their shelves. British newspapers voiced doubts about whether West Germany could be trusted as a partner in NATO. The attitude of leading newspapers in Europe and America was typified by a headline in the New York *Herald Tribune:* "Bonn Unable to Eliminate Nazi Poison." The loudest shrieks came from Moscow. "These disgusting fascist provocations and manifestations of the swastika are directed toward the fanning of the cold war and toward the poisoning of peoples against peoples," intoned *Pravda.* West German leaders were reduced to offering abject apologies and statements of self-abasement. Bishop Otto Dibelius termed the outbreaks proof that the German nation had not overcome its past. West Germany found few defenders. One foreign leader who came publicly to its defense was Israeli Prime Minister David Ben-Gurion. "The young generation in Germany is not Hitlerist but the opposite," he declared.

Between Christmas Eve 1959 and mid-February 1960, West German authorities recorded 833 separate anti-Jewish acts. Then the epidemic ceased almost as suddenly and mysteriously as it had begun. Police arrested and interrogated 234 people. Analyzing their motives, the government concluded that 24 percent acted out of "subconscious Nazi motives"; 8 percent were inspired by extreme rightist or leftist beliefs; 48 percent were drunks or thugs; 15 percent were children; and 5 percent were mentally deranged.

Responsibility for a majority of the acts remained unfixed. All along, West German spokesmen expressed a vague suspicion of organized, clandestine communist involvement. The young German and his accomplice who were convicted of desecrating the Cologne synagogue on Christmas Eve belonged to a small rightwing political party and at their trial unrepentantly mouthed Nazilike statements. But police established that both frequently had visited East Germany, and one had a Communist Party badge hidden behind his coat lapel. In a separate case, Bernhard Schlottmann, the twenty-two-year-old treasurer of a neo-Nazi organization in West Berlin, confessed after his arrest that he was an East German agent under orders to infiltrate and foment anti-Semitism among extremist factions. The simultaneous appearance of swastikas in many cities on different continents as well as the sudden abatement of the campaign suggest an organized operation. But in the absence of proof, insinuations of communist complicity sounded unpersuasive at the time.

Western security services did not begin to learn what actually happened until later in the 1960s, when defectors revealed that the whole swastika operation had been conceived by General Agayants himself. In the shocked reaction to the early isolated incidents of anti-Semitism in 1959, Agayants discerned the world's sensitivity to anything smacking of resurgent Nazism. He reasoned that if a few acts caused concern, a massive and continuing rash of them would generate great fear and distrust of the West Germans. To test the feasibility and practicality of desecrating Jewish shrines, he sent a team of KGB agents to a village about fifty miles from Moscow. One night they smeared swastikas, kicked over tombstones, and painted anti-Jewish slogans, then escaped undetected. KGB agents stationed in the village to gauge the public reaction reported that most people were disturbed or frightened by the swastikas. But appearance of the Nazi insignia also awakened latent anti-Semitism among a few Russians and inspired them to commit a variety of anti-Jewish acts on their own. Some weeks after this trial run in the Soviet village, the KGB began the operation, relying upon East Germans in West Germany and its own agents in other parts of the world. A later defector, Rupert Sigl, who worked for the KGB in East Berlin from 1957 to 1969, corroborated the reports received from other KGB officers. He stated that at the height of the swastika campaign, he was ordered to translate hate letters from Russian into German for mailing to Jewish families in West Germany.

The most common form of KGB disinformation is based upon forged documents and fraudulent literature. The KGB and satellite services throughout the world regularly collect signatures of prominent foreigners, letterheads, and governmental forms for use in forgeries. The STB perceived some years ago that many Westerners receiving a Christmas card feel socially obligated to send one in return. So Czech embassies adopted the custom of mailing handsome Christmas greetings to government officials and prominent people. The signatures harvested in response are filed away at the monastery in Prague, but are also shared with the KGB. Occasionally the KGB distributes forged documents through communist agents. More often, the bogus documents are mailed to newspapers, magazines, and government offices with a covering letter bearing an illegible signature or none at all.

The Bombay daily newspaper *Free Press Journal* in February 1968 published a letter purportedly written to the editor by Gordon Goldstein of the U.S. Office of Naval Research. It ostentatiously assured Asians that the United States meant no harm by stockpiling bacteriological warfare weapons in Vietnam and Thailand (something, in fact, which the United States had not done). The *Times* of London on March 7 reported the letter, and the same day broadcasts beamed to Asia from Moscow cited it as evidence that the United States had caused an epidemic of contagious diseases in Vietnam. The Indian weekly *Blitz* on March 9 published a story headlined "U.S. Admits Biological and Nuclear Warfare." The signature and letterhead of the forged letter were obtained from an invitation issued by Goldstein a year earlier to an international scientific symposium of which he was joint chairman.

In Turkey, Senator Haydar Tunckanat on July 7, 1966, produced "documents" showing that the United States was plotting to purge certain Turkish military officers and to undermine Turkish liberals in the interests of the ruling Justice Party. One "document" appeared to be a letter from a spy in the Justice Party to someone identified only as "E.M." The second purported to be a letter from "E.M." to the U.S. Defense

attaché in Ankara, Colonel Donald D. Dickson. Together, the contents of the two "documents" amply
sustained his charges of arrogant and outrageous U.S.
meddling in Turkish internal affairs, and they produced
an anti-American sensation.

Turkish newspapers quickly pointed out that Edwin
Martin, U.S. embassy counselor-minister in Ankara
from 1964, and Navy Captain E. M. Morgan, a former
U.S. representative to CENTO, the Central Treaty
Organization, both had the initials "E.M." The press
just as quickly concluded that Colonel Dickson was
really a master CIA operative engaged in manipulating Turkish affairs. Responsible Turkish politicians accepted the "documents" as authentic, and even some
of those normally friendly toward the United States expressed anger. Many Turkish military officers were even
more bitter.

Because the KGB has never quite mastered the art
of precisely duplicating American bureaucratese, U.S.
representatives were able to show Turkish officials numerous errors in form and style that proved the "documents" to be forgeries. But this did not erase the impression of "American imperialism" the forgeries had
left with many Turkish citizens, especially army officers.

Department A employed Tunckanat to utter another forgery in late 1969 when a book, *The Inside Story
of the Bilateral Agreements,* was published under his
name. A rather plodding anti-American diatribe, the
book contained an alleged photocopy of a directive from
"James E. Lazenby, Colonel, GS," ordering intelligence
action against officers of the Turkish General Staff. This
directive was dated 22 November 1965, though the
form on which it was written had not been used by the
U.S. military since 1962, and it incorrectly identified
Lazenby, an Air Force colonel, as an Army officer.
Nevertheless, the forgery produced another spasm of
anti-Americanism in Turkey.

Opportunities for disinformation operations sometimes present themselves unexpectedly. The Cypriot
Communist Party in early 1970 informed the Soviet
embassy in Nicosia that Greek military officers were

planning a coup against the government of Cyprus. The KGB investigated the report and advised the Center that it was erroneous, but at Department A the erroneous intelligence spawned an idea. Late one night in March, the Soviet ambassador in Ankara, Vasili Fedorovich Grubyakov, a veteran KGB officer, requested an urgent audience at the Turkish Foreign Office. He stated that the Soviet Union had reliable intelligence indicating that the ruling junta in Greece, acting in concert with American and NATO forces, contemplated an imminent coup against Cyprus. The objective, he said, was to absorb Cyprus into Greece and NATO.

The alarmed Turkish government announced the next morning that a coup was impending. The KGB disseminated official-looking press releases to Turkish newspapers about the alleged Greek-American-NATO coup. Further amplification was offered in rumors spread by Bulgarian diplomats. The consequent uproar gradually subsided, inasmuch as neither the coup nor any provable evidence of it ever materialized. The Soviet Union, however, claimed that it had saved Cyprus, and Turkish interests there, by aborting the coup through its timely exposure.

The most celebrated KGB agent of disinformation, Vitali Yevgennevich Lui, is an unctuous operative better known as Victor Louis. Born in 1928, Louis stands just under six feet tall, has a pale, pink face that smiles often, blue eyes, and wavy brown hair. He possesses a quick mind, and some people profess to find him charming. Twice Louis has been received at the White House: by Vice President Hubert H. Humphrey on October 17, 1966, and by Presidential Adviser Henry A. Kissinger on November 13, 1971. His writings, or those of the Disinformation Department promulgated under his name, have appeared in numerous Western newspapers, including the New York *Times* and the Washington *Post*. The London *Evening News* provides him with a European outlet and press credentials that contribute to his journalistic cover. Louis travels the world in a style allowed no ordinary Soviet citizen, flashing his Diners Club card and relishing the role of a mysterious celebrity. But there is nothing mysterious about his work. His job demonstrably is to sow confusion, plant lies, peddle fraudulent or stolen manuscripts, and smear the reputations of dissenting Soviet intellectuals such as Solzhenitsyn.

While in his late teens, Louis worked as a messenger and petty political police informer at the New Zealand embassy in Moscow and later at the Brazilian embassy. Reportedly, he studied languages at Moscow University before disappearing into a concentration camp. Louis has claimed that he was arrested because of his association with foreigners and charged with black marketeering. Peter Worthington, a leading Canadian journalist specializing in Soviet affairs, reports that in fact he was arrested as a common black marketeer. In camp Louis bought preferred treatment by betraying his fellow prisoners. The late author Arkadi Belinkov knew him in the summer of 1954 at the Ninth Spassky Department Camp in Kazakhstan. Belinkov stated that Louis arrived in style, wearing a pith helmet and an outfit resembling a British tropical dress uniform, which inspired rumors that the Soviet Union was at war with Great Britain. Louis promptly sought out interned intellectuals who, after they confided in him, found themselves undergoing rigorous new interrogations. The prisoners soon recognized him for what he was and beat him up, whereupon the authorities considerately transferred him to another camp.

Louis reappeared on the Moscow scene as a black marketeer in 1956. Carrying his wares in a suitcase, he circulated among the diplomatic community as a dealer and fixer eager to ingratiate himself. Quite openly, he sold ikons and exchanged currency, acts for which other Soviet citizens have been shot. He also arranged supposedly furtive meetings between Westerners and avant-garde painters whose works were banned from public exhibition. Some artists he enticed to such meetings afterward were arrested on charges of illicit dealings with foreigners, according to the New York *Times*.

These and numerous other proscribed activities, which could have continued only with official sanction, clearly suggested that Louis was a KGB agent, and some Western publications have branded him as that or insinuated as much. However, authoritative evidence from a witness who could testify out of personal knowledge about the relationship of Louis and the KGB was lacking. Major Yuri Nosenko, in breaking the silence he maintained ever since his flight to the West in 1964, now has provided some. He explains that in the late 1950s Louis was employed by the local Moscow district of the KGB, rather than the Second Chief Directorate, which ordinarily conducts the major operations against foreigners. The Second Chief Directorate at the time declined to entrust Louis with significant assignments because his personal demeanor, as well as his record as a Judas in the camps, aroused the contempt of some officers. More significantly, General Oleg Gribanov distrusted him.

In 1960 Louis began overtures to a certain American whom Nosenko's agents already were trying to recruit. "Gribanov ordered the Moscow district to get him away from our operation and keep him away," says Nosenko. "But you must understand that the local KGB got only the crumbs of operations, and to them Victor was a big thing. He could work against foreigners very well, and they thought that through him they could get into important operations. They kept telling us, 'This Victor, he is a very good agent; our best agent.' They kept pushing him and promoting him."

Nosenko notes that since his own departure and the retirement of Gribanov, Louis seems to have overcome the reservations, if not the aversion, of the Center. He has acquired expensive foreign cars, a luxurious Moscow apartment, and a country mansion complete with swimming pool. Though he claims they are fruits of his entrepreneurship, they are actually KGB-supplied props necessary to the particular act he puts on for foreigners. At his homes he treats Westerners to fine whisky and caviar and even more delicious intrigue, scheduling interviews with intellectuals and sometimes demonstrating his good will by cautioning his guests to be discreet. To make him more attractive to foreigners, the KGB allows him on occasion to feed them useful intelligence. He has warned Western embassies of impending mob demonstrations against them; he was the first to tell the world of the fall of Khrushchev; and he supplies rumors and stories that are, if not entirely true, at least interesting.

Louis served as a principal agent in the vicious KGB campaign to defame Stalin's daughter, Svetlana Alliluyeva. Shortly after her flight to the United States in 1967, he falsely reported that Svetlana had denounced her good friend, the liberal writer Andrei Sinyavsky. Next Louis interviewed Svetlana's two children in the Moscow apartment they had shared with their mother and induced the son, under emotional pressure, to denounce his mother. Louis then traveled to Europe to peddle an early draft of Svetlana's first book, *Twenty Letters to a Friend,* and some intimate family photographs. (The KGB had confiscated both the manuscript and the snapshots from Svetlana's desk after her flight.) The KGB expected that by offering another version of Svetlana's book for sale, it could create legal problems that would delay publication of any version until after the fiftieth anniversary of the Bolshevik Revolution. But the scheme misfired. To avoid legal problems, the American publisher rushed the book into print in September 1967, and its appearance did embarrass the Soviet Union on the anniversary of the Revolution.

While in Europe, Louis also offered for sale an article about Svetlana, allegedly based on an interview with her aunt, Anna Redens. A German magazine bought the interview, unaware that Anna Redens had died years before.

Louis returned to Europe in the spring of 1968, this time peddling a stolen copy of Solzhenitsyn's then unpublished *Cancer Ward.* Had Louis's machinations not been exposed by the émigré publishing house of Grani, the KGB could have arrested Solzhenitsyn on grounds of unauthorized publication abroad and justified its suppression of his book in the Soviet Union on the pretext that the work was being exploited as anticommunist propaganda abroad. In another disinformation effort against Solzhenitsyn, Louis on March 16, 1969, published in the Washington *Post* an article purportedly based on an "interview" with the author. The statements Louis attributes to him smack of sheer fabrication. Solzhenitsyn has demonstrated personal courage, integrity, and selflessness, yet the quotations Louis ascribes to him are those of a whining, self-pitying, selfish seeker of martyrdom. The Louis article suggests that Solzhenitsyn viewed Russia's wartime occupation by the Nazis favorably and that the horrors of the concentration camps were the fault of Beria rather than Stalin.

In September 1969, after Aleksei Kosygin returned from unsatisfactory conferences in Peking, the KGB, through Louis, initiated a disinformation operation that produced worldwide headlines. In a dispatch to the London *Evening News,* Louis indicated that the Soviet Union was considering a preemptive nuclear strike against China. Simultaneously, KGB officers stationed at Soviet embassies in Europe and America began hinting to influential Americans that the Russians were seriously considering such a surprise attack. This dangerous disinformation campaign represents still another example of one that succeeded tactically but redounded ultimately to the detriment of the Soviet Union. Without officially threatening the Chinese and exposing themselves to a charge of warmongering, the Russians pressured them into reentering negotiations in the Sino-Soviet border dispute. Soon thereafter, though, the alarmed Chinese entered into secret talks that resulted in the visit to Peking of President Nixon and a measure of rapproachement with the United States. Undoubtedly many factors influenced the Chinese decision to talk to the U.S. It seems likely that the fear of a preemptive Soviet strike, spread by the KGB, was one of them.

The KGB continuously searches for means to neutralize or destroy intelligent and effective foreign opponents of Soviet policies through disinformation operations. Commander Anthony Courtney, a tough, keen former heavyweight boxing champion of the Royal Navy, was one of the members of the British Parliament who most vexed the KGB in the early 1960s. Fluent in Russian, Courtney understood both the Soviet Union and the KGB and feared neither. Repeatedly he cited in the House of Commons the absurdity of permitting the Soviet, Hungarian, Czech, and Bulgarian embassies in London to have more than twenty "chauffeurs" enjoying full diplomatic immunity, while British diplomats in Soviet-bloc countries were driven about by secret police informants. Courtney on July 6, 1965, led a group of Conservatives in demanding investigation of communist perversion of diplomatic privileges for purposes of espionage and subversion.

Less than a month later, a fellow MP telephoned Courtney and asked that he come at once to the House. "Something extremely important has happened," he said. When they met, the colleague handed Courtney a broadsheet containing photographs, accompanied by vulgar captions, showing him and a woman in various bedroom postures. Courtney recognized the woman as Zinaida Grigorievna Volkova, who had been his Intourist guide while he visited Moscow in 1961, after the death of his wife. One night she had come to his hotel room, and they spent a few hours together. It was a brief, casual contact between two unmarried adults, and he had almost forgotten about it.

Copies of the broadsheet were mailed to members of Parliament representing all political parties, as well as to magazines, Courtney's business associates, and his second wife. With the John Profumo sex scandal still fresh in their memories, some of Courtney's fellow Conservatives were reluctant to rally to his aid. After the magazine *Private Eye* printed the material, Courtney's business suffered. Despite his forthright explanations, Courtney was not quite able to dispel the cloud of scandal in which the KGB had enveloped him. In the 1966 elections he lost his seat by 378 votes.

But like other disinformation operations, the slander of Commander Courtney ultimately boomeranged against the Soviet Union. For although the KGB pushed Courtney out of Parliament, it did not silence him. He continued to speak out forcefully and persuasively, citing his own experience as evidence of the necessity of combating the KGB. Some British observers believe that his vocal stand over the years contributed to the

British decision to act so resolutely against the KGB in September 1971.

Whenever the KGB is caught red-handed in an outrageous action that threatens the Soviet Union with serious embarrassment, it hurriedly commences disinformation operations to divert world attention from the event. Frequently the KGB simply accuses others of doing precisely what it has been shown to have done. Thus, after Great Britain expelled 105 KGB and GRU officers in October 1971, the KGB agent "Kim" Philby, in statements distributed by Tass, accused the British of the most perfidious sort of spying. However, Philby falsely identified as British spies three prominent Lebanese, who promptly sued Tass and won substantial judgments. Tass, which had always solemnly proclaimed itself a private journalistic agency independent of the Soviet government, then sought to have the judgments set aside on grounds that it is an official agency of the Soviet government, immune to local libel laws. This belated admission has caused some foreign journalists to challenge the right of Tass correspondents, many of whom are KGB officers anyway, to belong to press associations and clubs whose membership is restricted to authentic journalists.

Nevertheless, the KGB has successfully employed disinformation techniques to transform egregious Soviet affronts into non-events. It at times has made the world ignore Soviet acts which, had they been committed by any other nation, would have provoked a worldwide uproar. Consider how KGB disinformation specialists coped with the story of a two-million-dollar bribe and its bloody aftermath.

Sitting in his Beirut apartment, Hassan Badawi put the question coolly and bluntly: "How would you like to make a lot of money?"

Lieutenant Mahmoud Mattar, a darkly handsome Lebanese fighter pilot, shrugged. "Who wouldn't? The problem always is, how." He knew his questioner well enough to be wary. A charming renegade and adventurer, Badawi once had been his flight instructor in the Lebanese air force. But after a succession of escapades, including smuggling, narcotics peddling, and various

moral offenses, Badawi had been cashiered. Mysterious-
ly, though, he had prospered. He wangled a job as a
Middle East Airlines pilot, ensconced himself in a
Beirut apartment overlooking the Mediterranean, and
often had large sums of cash, especially after flights to
India.

"I have friends who need something you can deliver," Badawi replied.

The proposition transmitted to Mattar that sultry
night in late August 1969 was the first gambit in a
Soviet plot to steal one of the world's finest military
aircraft, a French-built Mirage III-E interceptor.

A number of nations depend upon the Mirage. Some
250 Mirages guard the skies of Western Europe, and
in recurrent Israeli-Arab combat the plane repeatedly
has proved itself equal—in some respects superior—to
the most advanced Soviet MIGs. When outfitted with
special electronic equipment, the Mirage can penetrate
Soviet air defenses and deliver nuclear weapons. Soviet
spies in France did succeed in 1966 in pilfering some
plans of the plane; but to devise effective aerial tactics
against it, the Russians needed an actual aircraft to
fly under controlled conditions in mock combat.

Assessing the worldwide possibilities of theft, the
KGB and GRU seized upon Lebanon as the nation
least able to resist. A civilized, lovely country, its population numbered only 2.5 million and its army only
about fifteen thousand. The KGB, which is responsible
for evaluating and neutralizing foreign security services, concluded that Lebanese counterintelligence was
impotent to thwart a determined Soviet operation.
Equally biased, the GRU reasoned that no Arab
would refuse the kind of bribe it was prepared to offer
for the plane.

Eight days after they first talked, Badawi telephoned
Mattar. "My friends have been asking. Have you decided?"

"Yes," Mattar replied. "I agree to the terms you
stated."

Two nights later Badawi introduced Mattar to
Vladimir Vasilyev, a mousy-looking GRU officer mas-

querading as a Soviet trade representative in Beirut. The Russian courteously but formally questioned Mattar about his personal background, military record, and flying experience. Apparently satisfied, he said: "Our plan is simple. You will take off on a routine training flight, go out over the sea, and radio that you are experiencing mechanical difficulty. A minute or so later you will signal Mayday [the international distress signal]. Then you will drop below radar coverage and change course for Baku [in the Soviet Union]. It will be thought that you crashed at sea."

"How and where will you pay the three million dollars?"

"Three million!" Vasilyev cried. "No, no, one million."

To entice Mattar, Badawi had exaggerated the actual Soviet offer and so a prolonged haggling ensued. Finally Mattar dropped his price to two million, but insisted on an advance cash payment of $600,000. Vasilyev hesitated. "I must consult others," he said.

On September 9 Vasilyev and his GRU boss, Aleksandr Komiakov, first secretary of the Soviet embassy in Beirut, flew by Aeroflot to Moscow. Komiakov, a somewhat corpulent man of forty-five with a handsome, ruddy face and gray hair, was a veteran of clandestine operations in the Middle East. He had spied off and on for nine years in Turkey, where, among other actions, he helped engineer a prison break to free Soviet agents. Blunt, hard-driving, and daring to the point of foolhardiness, he was known among Lebanese as "the Russian bull in the china shop."

On the basis of known Soviet procedures, it is reasonable to surmise that in Moscow the GRU, after consultations with Komiakov and Vasilyev, submitted a detailed operational plan for Politburo approval. Given the nature and risks of the operations, the Politburo probably requested a KGB assessment. In any case, the two GRU officers left Moscow with orders emanating from the highest levels of the Soviet government to proceed immediately. They also carried with them a series of specific instructions, written both in

Russian and French, to ensure that neither they nor Mattar would misunderstand precisely what was to be done.

Returning to Beirut in mid-September, Vasilyev summoned Mattar to his seventh-floor apartment three blocks from the Soviet embassy. There Komiakov announced: "We are prepared to meet your request for two million. However, our advance will be $200,000. Ten percent seems more businesslike."

Mattar grimaced but nodded a reluctant acceptance.

"When can you make the trip?" Komiakov asked.

"I am scheduled for a training flight October 3," Mattar replied.

"Good," said Komiakov. "We will make all necessary preparations to receive you then." The Russian explained a plan to take Mattar's wife and children to Moscow via Berlin and Helsinki. "All of you can live the rest of your lives in luxury in the Soviet Union," he assured.

"My wife and I have discussed it. We would prefer to live in Switzerland," Mattar said.

Komiakov appeared not the least abashed by the implied rejection of Soviet life. "That's your affair," he said. "You go anywhere you want. You do the job for us, and we'll take care of you for life. You deceive us, we'll also take care of you—for life."

"I'll do my job," Mattar replied coldly. "But I must have the $200,000 before I take off."

"Yes, yes, you will have it," Komiakov said impatiently.

"I don't want cash," Mattar announced. "I want it in the form of a cashier's check, payable to my father."

"A check!" Komiakov exclaimed. "Not cash?"

"I'm no good at spotting counterfeit dollars," Mattar responded. Komiakov grinned, perhaps out of professional admiration. He gave the pilot two thousand Lebanese pounds (then about $610) to help his family make ready for the journey to Europe, and they agreed to a final review of the flight plan on the evening of September 30.

It is not known when the Soviet ambassador to Lebanon, Sarvar Azimov, was first informed of the operation, but by September 30 he was extremely apprehensive about it. In the early evening that day, the second secretary of the Soviet embassy telephoned a political officer of the American embassy at his home to cancel a protocol visit that Azimov was to receive from the U.S. ambassador on October 1. He explained only that the cancellation was necessitated by *force majeure* (an extraordinary happening). As such appointments are quite formal and not lightly disregarded, the American was surprised by the breach of diplomatic etiquette. "Well, when will Ambassador Azimov be prepared to receive our ambassador?" he asked.

The Russian momentarily excused himself from the phone. "Any time after October 3," he said upon returning.

A little later the same evening, Lieutenant Mattar, obviously tense, entered Vasilyev's apartment for his final briefing before the flight. To reassure him, Komiakov presented a $200,000 cashier's check drawn on the Moscow Narodny Bank, Ltd. Dated September 29, 1969, it was, as Mattar had demanded, payable to his father. Komiakov also gave the lieutenant $2,500 for his wife. "You see," he said, "we keep our word."

Vasilyev, who evinced some aeronautical background, slowly read from the French draft of the flight plan that listed the precise bearings and altitudes at which Mattar was to fly for prescribed periods: "Upon attaining an altitude of 3,000 feet, radio the Beirut tower that you are experiencing generator trouble and your controls are malfunctioning. Then declare an emergency. Thereafter, acknowledge no radio transmissions. . . . Four minutes after you cross the Soviet frontier, three interceptors will meet you and guide you to Baku in Azerbaijan. . . . Should rendezvous fail, contact the base there on a frequency of 322 kilocycles. . . ."

The three were still discussing the flight when they heard an insistent knocking on the door. Vasilyev opened it slightly. In the hallway stood a dozen uniformed Lebanese with drawn revolvers.

"Soldiers!" Vasilyev shouted in Russian. He tried to slam the door, but a Lebanese wedged it open with his foot. Pushing against the door, the Russian grabbed a dumbbell and began swinging wildly at the soldier's foot. While Komiakov stared, momentarily transfixed with horror and rage, Mattar dashed across the room and tackled Vasilyev. As the Lebanese stormed into the apartment, Komiakov pulled out a Polish revolver and opened fire. His first three shots ripped into the stomach and legs of Lebanese Captain Abbas Hamdan. Vasilyev, meanwhile, picked himself up and shot a Lebanese sergeant in the chest.

The Lebanese blazed back, and the apartment became a bedlam of ricocheting bullets and cursing men fighting for their lives. A single slug collapsed Vasilyev, and the Lebanese pounced on him. Komiakov, though hit four times, retreated into an adjoining room, reloaded, and kept firing until a fifth bullet shattered his arm. Bleeding profusely, he staggered across the room and pushed open a window, attempting to jump to his death. He realized now that Mattar was a Lebanese agent who had engineered a Soviet disaster from the plot. But as Komiakov struggled to leap from the window, two soldiers grabbed him while another scooped up the $200,000 check and the flight plan.

Other Russians living in the apartment building ran to the nearby Soviet embassy with the news of the gun battle. The KGB instantly took charge, radioing a fragmentary report to Moscow and dispatching a female Soviet doctor to the military hospital where Komiakov and Vasilyev were being treated.

The senior Lebanese physician attending Komiakov was glad to see her. "This man urgently requires a blood transfusion, at least five pints," he reported. "But he has absolutely no will to live. He won't let us give him any blood. So I'm going to give him an anesthetic, then administer the transfusion."

"I cannot permit that," the Russian doctor said.

The Lebanese physician looked at her incredulously. "Madame, do you realize that this man will die?"

"I cannot permit any anesthetic," said the Soviet doctor, fearful of what Komiakov might reveal when not fully conscious.

The Lebanese pleaded: "As one physician to another, I appeal to you. If you will not allow anesthetics, then persuade this patient to accept a transfusion." The Soviet doctor talked in Russian with Komiakov, who then forlornly agreed.

At 1 A.M. the Lebanese government issued a bulletin announcing the arrest of Komiakov, Vasilyev, and Badawi. A fuller official statement soon disclosed the magnitude of the Soviet debacle. After his first meeting with Badawi, Lieutenant Mattar had reported immediately to his commanding officers, who consulted Lebanese counterintelligence, known as the Second Bureau of the army. Correctly judging the Soviets' view of them, the Lebanese security officer instructed Mattar to accept the proposal and play the role of a greedy, haggling Arab concerned only with money. They outfitted him with a tiny high-frequency radio transmitter which, concealed in his clothes, broadcast into tape recorders all his subsequent conversations with the Russians. To make him more convincing to the Russians, they told him to say he preferred to live in Switzerland; and to obtain documentary evidence, they ordered him to demand a check. The countermeasures the Lebanese authorities conceived were highly professional, and Lieutenant Mattar executed them flawlessly and bravely.

In contrast, the Russians, blinded by their own bigotry toward Arabs, committed one ruinous blunder after another. In Badawi they had relied upon a notorious knave. They accepted Mattar for the cynical mercenary he pretended to be without making any searching, objective assessment of his character. Scornful of the Second Bureau, they flouted fundamental principles of conspiracy. They conducted clandestine meetings in one of their own apartments, failed to make the elementary electronic check that would have detected Mattar's transmitter, and neglected to guard against surveillance. And they let the Lebanese talk them into paying with an incriminating official check issued by a Soviet government bank. Finally, they started a gunfight they had no chance of winning.

The Soviet Union resolved to brazen and lie its way out of the mess, and the KGB hastily began a massive

disinformation campaign. By midmorning of October 1,
KGB agents were closeted with influential Soviet sympathizers in Lebanon, Egypt, Syria, and Iraq, telling
them what to say: the whole Mirage affair was an
American provocation from beginning to end, contrived to sabotage Soviet-Lebanese relations. Novosti
flooded Arab newspapers with stories stressing all that
the Russians had done for the Arabs. In Beirut,
Vladislav Petrovich Zhukov, a KGB officer assigned to
work with Palestinian guerrillas, went quickly to the
Lebanese Foreign Office. Hissing his words because of
a dental problem, Zhukov threatened the expulsion of
all Lebanese diplomats from Moscow if the Lebanese
government continued to publicize the incident.

At 11 A.M. Ambassador Azimov confronted the
President of Lebanon, Charles Helou, with formal Soviet demands. Lebanon must free the two Russians, repudiate all charges against them, pledge to punish key
Lebanese intelligence officers, and publicly apologize
to the Soviet Union. Additionally, it must officially
disseminate the Soviet government statement depicting
the affair as an "American provocation."

Lebanon rejected all of these Soviet demands. But
the pressures generated by the KGB began to have
their effects. "A provocation and fabrication!" shrieked
Radio Damascus in Syria. "All indications point to a
foreign intelligence conspiracy," declared the semiofficial Egyptian newspaper *Al Ahram*. "A cheap American conspiracy to undermine our relations with the
Soviet Union," charged Kamal Jumblatt, a leading leftist
member of the Lebanese Parliament. Other leftists denounced the Second Bureau for daring to embarrass
Lebanon's good friend, the Soviet Union.

More important than the public bombast were the
private visitations by representatives of other Arab
states, especially Egypt and Syria, all of whom conveyed the same message: hush up the Mirage affair
immediately and get our Russian friends off the hook.

The pressure intensified all day on October 2, and
that afternoon little Lebanon, which survives by the
sufferance of its bigger Arab neighbors, capitulated.
The government issued a censorship ban prohibiting

press mention of the case and forbidding foreign correspondents from filing any more dispatches about it. Further references would be "extremely harmful to Lebanon's higher interests," said the censorship decree.

The story of the Soviet plot to steal the Mirage flashed only fleetingly before world attention, then vanished entirely. Confronted by the censorship order, foreign journalists wondered whether the government did not, in fact, have something to hide, and few publications troubled to pursue the story further. The KGB had succeeded in making the happening a non-event.

On October 4 a special Aeroflot plane landed at Beirut airport and parked on a remote corner of the field, as if trying to hide. Vasilyev and Komiakov were helped aboard, the latter on a stretcher. Mattar, the officer who valued honor more than two million dollars, was quietly promoted to captain. KGB-inspired threats against his life reached such ominous proportions that the Lebanese military temporarily sent him into protective hiding. Today he is esteemed by his fellow officers as an authentic hero. But always Captain Mattar must carry with him the thought: Will tomorrow bring a KGB agent to fulfill Komiakov's vow to "take care of you—for life"?

IX

THE ART AND SCIENCE OF ESPIONAGE

"Espionage is needed by those who prepare for attack, for aggression. The Soviet Union is deeply dedicated to the cause of peace and does not intend to attack anyone. Therefore, it has no intention of engaging in espionage."

So wrote Nikita Khrushchev to the chairman of the Japanese Communist Party, Saneo Nozaka, in June 1962.* By Soviet definition, the truth is whatever enhances Soviet interests of the moment, and thus perhaps it would be unfair to accuse Khrushchev of lying. Still, he must have had difficulty restraining himself from laughter at his own words. For his statement was comically at variance with reality as he knew it, and as the world increasingly has come to know it.

Major nations, of course, have spied on each other throughout history, although not always for aggressive or malign purposes. (Intelligence acquired through espionage, after all, may be used to defend against surprise attacks and other aggressions as well as to commit them.) However, probably no nation ever has practiced espionage as massively and aggressively as has the Soviet Union. For decades, the Soviet Union has systematically employed spies to steal the scientific, in-

---

*Radio Moscow quoted the Khrushchev assurance in an English-language broadcast of June 28, 1962.

dustrial, and military inventions of other nations. It relies upon spies to find foreigners who can be recruited as agents of influence and to provide the intelligence necessary to sustain subversion in both emerging and advanced nations. It counts heavily upon spies to discern weaknesses in political resolve and military preparedness that Soviet policy can exploit. And while espionage is but one activity of the KGB, it remains the one activity that consumes most of the time of KGB officers abroad and the one most frequently exposed to public view.

Even in 1962, when Khrushchev offered assurances that the Soviet Union did not intend to spy on anyone, the evidence of worldwide Soviet espionage abounded in public records. It had been provided as early as the 1930s by prominent Soviet defectors such as General Alexander Orlov, author of a basic Soviet espionage manual, and by Walter Krivitsky, who tried in vain to warn of high-level penetrations in Western societies. In September 1945 cipher clerk Igor Gouzenko fled the Soviet embassy in Ottawa with the first revelations that the Soviet Union had stolen the secrets of the atomic bomb while engaging in massive scientific and industrial espionage against its wartime allies. Subsequently, royal commissions in Canada and Australia, and official investigations in Great Britain and the United States, demonstrated that Soviet spies had throughly infiltrated Western governments, scientific institutions, and intellectual circles.

Among Soviet agents identified in the United States were Elizabeth T. Bentley, Edward Joseph Fitzgerald, William Ludwig Ullmann, William Walter Remington, Franklin Victor Reno, Judith Coplon, Harry Gold, David Greenglass, Julius and Ethel Rosenberg, Morton Sobell, William Perl, Alfred Dean Slack, Jack Soble, Ilya Wolston, Alfred and Martha Stern.* Important

---

*No claim is made that this list is complete. It consists of Soviet agents who were convicted of espionage or falsifying information or perjury and/or contempt charges following espionage indictments or who fled to the Soviet bloc to avoid prosecution. The conviction of Judith Coplon was set aside on a legal technicality. However, in ruling that she was entitled to a new trial, Judge Learned Hand stated her guilt was plain. Ultimately, the government

agents exposed in Great Britain included the nuclear physicists Klaus Fuchs and Alan Nunn May; the diplomats Guy Burgess and Donald Maclean; and Harold A. R. Philby, a senior British intelligence officer. In 1960 the Senate Internal Security Subcommittee listed thirty-seven proven cases of Soviet espionage against the United States uncovered in the 1950s. And beginning in 1961, Khrushchev, far from curtailing Soviet espionage, intensified it. Each succeeding year has yielded new examples of Soviet attempts to steal the scientific, industrial, military, and political secrets of other nations.

In September 1962, less than three months after Khrushchev declared the Soviet Union had no intention of engaging in espionage, the FBI arrested a Soviet spy, U.S. Navy Yeoman Nelson C. Drummond. Recruited while stationed in London, Drummond supplied the Russians with Navy secrets for nearly five years. The United States had to spend $200 million revising plans, procedures, and manuals he compromised. The damage was judged so serious that Drummond was sentenced to life imprisonment.

In 1963, Sweden found that many of its most vital defenses had been laid bare to the Russians by another Soviet spy, Stig Eric Wennerström. A Swedish air force colonel, Wennerström additionally gave the Russians data about American weaponry while serving as an attaché in Washington. Wennerström also received a life sentence, in 1964.

In 1964, Great Britain caught Soviet trade representative Vladimir I. Solomatin trying to obtain specifications and samples of electronic equipment banned for export to the Soviet bloc. Solomatin was expelled.

In 1965, Canada ousted two Soviet "diplomats," Anatoli Y. Bychkov and Vladimir N. Poluchkin, after

---

dropped the charges because it could not disclose information obtained by wiretap. It might also be noted that Whittaker Chambers, a former *Time* magazine editor who confessed that he had been a Soviet agent, repeatedly charged that Alger Hiss was one of his fellow conspirators. Hiss, who served as an adviser to President Roosevelt at Yalta and later became director of the Office of Special Political Affairs in the State Department, always denied Chambers' allegations. However, Hiss was convicted of perjury on the basis of some of his denials and sentenced to five years' imprisonment.

they attempted to bribe Canadian civil servants into working for the KGB. The Russians were particularly interested in industrial and technical intelligence and details about pipelines marked for possible sabotage.

In 1966, the FBI arrested retired U.S. Army Lieutenant Colonel William Henry Whalen, whose last assignment had been with the Joint Chiefs of Staff. Whalen confessed that he had been a Soviet spy, and was sentenced to fifteen years.

In 1967, Italian authorities unearthed a huge espionage network that reached into at least eight countries. They began by capturing Giorgio Rinaldi, an antiques dealer and amateur parachutist, who was a principal member of the network. His admissions quickly resulted in the apprehension of twenty-nine other Soviet agents in Italy, Austria, Japan, Cyprus, Greece, Spain, Morocco, and Tunisia. Italy, Cyprus, and Greece immediately expelled five more. Other Soviet "diplomats," who apparently were implicated, disappeared overnight from Japan, Austria, and Morocco.

In 1968, West Germany found that one of its most trusted scientists, Josef Eitzenberger, had been a KGB agent for a decade. Eitzenberger had been entrusted to design a supposedly unbreakable code used by NATO and sensitive navigational systems for German aircraft.

In 1969, Japanese police arrested an Indonesian exchange student, Maba Odantara, for stealing Japanese industrial secrets. The Indonesian previously had studied at a Soviet university, and probably it was there that he was recruited by the KGB.

In 1970, Argentine police seized two Soviet trade officials, Yuri Ivanovich Ryabov and Yuri Leonidovich Mamontov, as they picked up microfilm of documents from a drop in a residential neighborhood of Buenos Aires.

In 1971, an engineer in the French atomic-energy program, Dmitri Volokov, admitted that he had been a Soviet agent for a decade. Over the years, Volokov passed the Russians numerous documents and technical data about French nuclear research. Premier Pierre

Messmer has stated that his espionage seriously damaged the effectiveness of France's nuclear deterrent force.

In 1972, two Russians in Copenhagen, Mikhail Kirillovich Makarov and Anatoli Aleksandrovich Lobanov, were exposed trying to bribe a Danish politician and blackmail foreign diplomats in Denmark.

In 1973, Norway expelled the Soviet "diplomat" Valeri Nikolaevich Yerofeyev after he attempted to recruit Norwegian citizens as spies.

These cases, of course, represent merely a smattering of those that have become known publicly in the past decade. And the cases which come to public attention, in turn, are but a small fraction of those that occur. For a variety of reasons, many manifestations of Soviet espionage are not revealed to the public. A confidential U.S. government study, for example, shows that between 1960 and 1970, Soviet agents made subversive overtures to American diplomats and citizens in seventy-eight countries. In India alone, they approached seventy diplomats and twenty-five employees of the U.S. embassy. These recruitment attempts were symptomatic of an unrelenting, determined KGB effort to suborn Americans throughout the world. Yet because none of the attempts tallied in the study succeeded, hardly any have ever been publicly divulged. Because of diplomatic considerations, real or fancied, governments sometimes do not announce arrests of Soviet spies or expulsions of KGB officers. Security services, upon discovering a KGB espionage network, often try to penetrate it rather than openly destroy it through arrests or expulsions. Nevertheless, from the public record available, the unpublicized case files of security services, and the testimony of former spies themselves, the aims and methods of Soviet espionage can be defined rather precisely.

From the late 1940s to the early 1960s, the major targets of Soviet espionage were, in order of their priority, the United States, NATO, West Germany, the British Commonwealth, France, and Japan. Authentic information from inside the KGB about the relative priority of other nations is lacking. But the pattern of

KGB activity discerned abroad suggests that by 1960 it also had developed a serious espionage interest in Canada, Mexico, Brazil, India, Indonesia, Iran, Iraq, Turkey, Greece, and Yugoslavia. During the 1960s, China ascended rapidly in importance, and today it ranks just behind the United States as a target.

China, incidentally, has proved to be an exceedingly difficult target. Totalitarian controls severely limit the utility of illegal agents and the access of Soviet personnel in Peking to the Chinese population. Consequently, the KGB has been forced to initiate many of its operations against China through other countries. It even stations China specialists in the United States in hope of ferreting out intelligence about the Soviet Union's erstwhile ally from American sources. As of 1973, the senior China expert in Washington was Viktor N. Krasheninnikov, a first secretary of the Soviet embassy. Another was Vladimir S. Kolesnikov, who left his post as a second secretary of the embassy in 1972 but returned to Washington in the spring of 1973. Boris Zanegin, who represents himself as a professor, has traveled to the United States several times in quest of intelligence about China. He spent nine months in America in 1972, questioning scholars and government officials. Igor A. Rogachev, who was a first secretary of the embassy in Washington from 1966 to 1968, is another KGB authority on China.

The KGB also has tried to make use of Hong Kong as a base for espionage against China. British authorities in August 1972 broke up one Soviet network, expelling two Russians and arresting two businessmen of Chinese origin. Press reports at the time noted that during the preceding eighteen months, more than eighty Soviet ships had put into Hong Kong and that many of their crew members obviously knew nothing about the sea.

Sometimes the KGB is comparatively guileless in gathering intelligence. KGB officers in Washington, for example, regularly roam the corridors of the Capitol and other government offices, picking up unclassified publications and interviewing Senators, Congressmen, and public officials. Prior to Brezhnev's visit to the

United States in June 1973, KGB officers approached informed Americans in different sections of the country. They questioned them, for up to two hours, about the impact of the Watergate scandal on American politics and about its possible effect upon impending U.S.-Soviet negotiations. Though Soviet personnel conceal their identity as KGB representatives during such quests for intelligence, they violate no law.

However, KGB intelligence collection in the main does entail illegal methods. For the KGB continues to rely in the extreme upon the individual clandestine agent, the human spy, rather than upon technical means and deductive analysis. Of course the Soviet Union vies with the United States in the development of reconnaissance satellites and an array of sophisticated equipment to monitor electronic emissions and foreign communications. Doubtless the Russians regard such devices as valuable adjuncts to conventional espionage, else they would not invest so much in them. However, in the KGB view, technical means of collection have some crippling limitations. For all the wonders of satellite photography, the camera that can read the intentions of foreign leaders or copy documents locked in safes has yet to be perfected. Satellites and sensors which are useful in assessing the military and productive capacity of industrial nations are of little use against Third World countries where the KGB is not interested in scientific, industrial, or military intelligence. They cannot provide the intimate personality data necessary to recruit agents of influence or the political secrets needed to support subversion.

The KGB also remains wary of intelligence derived from analysis or scholarship based upon overt sources. General Orlov explains the KGB attitude thus:

"The Russians take the view that important secrets of foreign states can and should be procured directly from the classified files in the government departments of those states and from foreign civil servants who agree to turn over state secrets to the Soviet Union. When the Russians suspect that another country is trying to form a coalition against the Soviet Union, they do not seek information about it in newspaper editorials, panel discussions or in historical precedents that show how the countries concerned had acted in similar situations in the past, although all these sources may be enlightening to a certain extent. The Russian intelligence service goes out to steal the secret diplomatic correspondence between the conspiring states or to recruit a secret informant on the staff of the negotiators if they do not have one there already. When the Russians want to know the number of bombers in the air force of a potential adversary, they arrive at a figure—not by library research on the productive capacity of certain plants or by collecting educated guesses or rumors on the subject, but by interviewing their secret informers in the foreign air force or war ministry and by stealing the coveted information from governmental files."

Orlov notes that the Russians consider only information so obtained as real *intelligence* and regard all other information as mere *research data*. "According to the views of Russian officers, it takes a *man* to do the creative and highly dangerous work of underground intelligence on foreign soil; as to the digging up of research data in the safety of the home office or library, this can be left to women or young lieutenants who have just begun their intelligence careers."

In view of this great stress upon the individual spy, the highest art of Soviet espionage is his recruitment. Without the recruitment, an operation is impossible; with it, everything begins. If there is a single subject that reveals the most about the general clandestine techniques of the KGB, it is recruitment practices. For the methods of recruiting an agent for espionage are basically the same as those employed to enlist agents for other clandestine purposes.

By remarkable legerdemain, a Western security service has obtained from Higher Intelligence School 101 outside Moscow a top-secret KGB textbook entitled *The Practice of Recruiting Americans in the USA and Third Countries*. The KGB considered the textbook so sensitive that it printed only a hundred copies. Obviously, the text was intended to be seen by only a small group of select officers. Hence the document affords outsiders an extraordinary opportunity to see the world of espionage against the United States just as the KGB looks at it. The text also makes clear that the KGB is determined to penetrate all important institutions of American government and society—from the White House on down. The more significant targets, in the order the textbook lists them, include:

"The President's Cabinet and the National Security Council;

"The State Department, including its representatives in New York, the U.S. Delegation to the UN, the Passport Office of the State Department, etc.;

"The U.S. Department of Defense (Pentagon), the military intelligence organs of this department and the Permanent Military Group of the NATO Staff in the U.S.;

"The Central Intelligence Agency and the Federal Bureau of Investigation;

"The National Association of Manufacturers and the most important monopolies and banking houses, which have a direct influence on the U.S. government;

"The most important scientific centers and laboratories. . . . [In the copy of the text available to the author, a page on which the target list is continued is illegible. The list resumes on the next page as follows.]

"The governing organs of the leading political parties in the U.S. and other influential public and political organizations—trade unions, youth [organizations], journalistic [organizations], etc.;

"The diplomatic and commercial representations of foreign countries in the U.S., and also the Secretariat of the UN and foreign representations in the UN."

To illustrate recruitment methods, the textbook recites a number of case histories of actual KGB operations in the United States. The Soviet authors—Y. M. Bruslov, N. S. Skvortsov, L. A. Byzov, V. M. Ivanov, and N. G. Dyukov—endeavored to disguise the cases by using pseudonyms for Americans and omitting the true names of KGB officers invoved. Nevertheless, their examples were sufficiently factual and explicit to enable the FBI to identify some of the Soviet agents to whom they referred. Thus, there is no doubt about the authenticity of the textbook.*

It shows that the KGB divides the recruitment process into three phases: (1) the spotting and assessment of the American; (2) development of personal relations with him; (3) consummation of a clandestine relationship. In trying to spot prospective spies, the KGB concentrates upon:

"Employees of government institutions who are cleared for secret political, economic, military, scientific and technical, and intelligence and counter-intelligence information;

"Employees of nongovernmental institutions and organizations who, because of their activities or interests, have access to the state secrets . . . correspondents, employees of technical bureaus and firms, representatives of emigrant groups and foreign intelligence agents;

"Employees of private firms who have access to secret scientific and technical and economic information;

"Persons who have good prospects of joining government organizations. . . ."

The KGB always searches for Americans ideologically sympathetic to the Soviet Union. However, the text frankly warns that "It would be a mistake to assume that there are many such people in U.S. government institutions." Therefore, KGB officers are instructed to look for Americans who can be recruited on the basis of personal grievances against the government, financial need or greed, past wrongdoing, or personality defects. In approaching businessmen, officers are advised to play upon "the desire to trade with the Soviet Union or with other countries of the socialist system." They

---

*Those interested in analyzing the KGB text for themselves will find a verbatim translation of most of it in Appendix C.

also are told to exploit "the desire of scientists to establish scientific contacts with representatives of the U.S.S.R."

The hunt for vulnerable Americans in the right places is endless. The text states: "Our Residencies systematically collect information on Americans who have intelligence potential in order to make their acquaintance later on. They use agents and confidential contacts for this. In those cases where the Residency uses such information, it attempts to camouflage the source.

"Soviet Intelligence Residencies in the U.S. receive considerable assistance from the Center, which reports the results of spotting activity by our Residencies in third countries.

"Use is also made of information received from 'unwitting' individuals. . . ."

Having fixed its interest on a particular American, the KGB contrives means to meet him and begin the development phase of the recruitment. Development may be assigned to a KGB officer protected by diplomatic immunity, to an American agent of the KGB, or to a team of officers and agents. The first meeting may occur "accidentally" at a restaurant, store, office, or other locale the KGB has ascertained the American regularly frequents. Sometimes the KGB officer will find a pretext to call upon the American at work or at his home, and occasionally he will present a forged letter of introduction from a presumably mutual acquaintance. Initially, the recruiter strives to build personal ties on the basis of a common interest or purpose. The KGB textbook stresses: "Our intelligence officer must establish confidential relations with the American in such a way that the latter does not surmise his connection with Soviet intelligence and his true intentions."

Usually during the development phase, the KGB representative tries to condition the American to transmit information, preferably printed materials. He asks a scholar for copies of his writings, a businessman for trade journals, a scientist for technical dissertations. The material requested at first almost invariably is the type that could be procured from a library or other open sources. But its transmission creates a precedent for delivery of information by the American to the Russian. The KGB representative ordinarily offers presents, an honorarium, or a "research fee" in an effort to accustom the American to accepting rewards for services requested. If the development succeeds, the American gradually is induced to provide secret data. At some point, he finds that he has broken the law and is locked into an illegal clandestine relationship. The recruitment is considered accomplished when he consciously submits to KGB discipline and begins purveying information with the knowledge that it is destined for the Soviet Union.

The KGB textbook emphasizes that even when an American voluntarily collaborates on ideological grounds, his motivation must be reinforced by cash payments. "Disregard for the material incentives of an agent," it says, "sometimes causes recruitment development to miscarry and may even result in the loss of an American already recruited." However, the text notes that payments should be made tactfully. It cites the development in New York of "a valuable agent who was obtaining for us samples of equipment and top-secret material concerning research in the field of atomic energy."

The agent was of Russian parentage and sympathetic to the Soviet Union. "At a regular meeting with the agent, the intelligence officer told the agent that the directors of the entire intelligence service had expressed gratitude for the material which had been received earlier and had awarded them a bonus—$100 to the intelligence officer and $500 to the agent. The agent was flattered by this. However, when the intelligence officer offered him the package with the money, the agent announced that he was working with us for patriotic reasons and would not take money.

" 'Are you trying to say that I'm not a patriot?' asked the intelligence officer. 'I need the money, and it will be very difficult for me if I also refuse it. But still, I will have to do this if you refuse.'

" 'And do you need the money very much?' asked the agent.

" 'Very much,' answered the intelligence officer.

" 'Well, all right,' agreed the agent.

"Therefore, as a result of using a correct approach to the agent, it became possible to further consolidate the relationship through the use of material incentive. After this, the agent frequently accepted money from us without any argument."

As a model example of how a recruitment should be planned and accomplished, the textbook reconstructs the penetration of an important scientific laboratory. An officer of the New York Residency accompanied a visiting Soviet scholar to the laboratory, posing as his interpreter. Among the laboratory personnel, he spotted an assistant who, in the words of the textbook, "was a poorly dressed young American and looked like a typical Jew." The Residency subsequently ascertained that he was the son of a poor immigrant family from Poland. He was writing his doctoral dissertation and studying Russian, which of course made him interested in the Soviet Union. To supplement his small stipend, he worked at the laboratory and also for a consulting firm. Still, he was hard pressed for money.

The KGB officer who had posed as an interpreter waited outside the laboratory at a time when the director normally was away. When the young American returned from lunch, the officer asked him how he might see the director. Having thus begun a conversation, he mentioned that he was doing research at a nearby library.

A week later, the officer telephoned the American, stated that he had completed one of his research projects, and proposed that they lunch together in celebration. Thereafter, the officer assessed and cultivated the American during a series of picnics and other outings. Then at a time when the KGB calculated that the American's monthly bills would be falling due, the officer approached him for advice.

According to the KGB legend prepared for the occasion, a friend of the officer had sent him several hundred dollars to purchase from some consulting firm unclassified information about a certain kind of radio tubes—tubes that happened to be the American's specialty. Could the American recommend a consulting firm? The KGB text reports:

"The meeting went as follows: Having just received his bills, Kolumb [the KGB pseudonym for the American] was in a bad mood, and when the intelligence officer told of the information he wanted, Kolumb suddenly became quiet.

"We can assume that Kolumb was having the following thoughts, as anticipated in the plan: 'If I recommend my firm, I will be undoubtedly assigned the job, and I would then get 10 to 15 percent of the money my friends pays the firm. It would be better if the firm had no part in this deal.' " So the American volunteered to write the technical report himself.

Eventually the KGB officer persuaded the American to join him in a "partnership" to sell technical data. "After this, it became easy to place all sorts of new requirements on Kolumb and to demand—literally demand—secret information from him. . . . Since he 'obtained' the money, the intelligence officer at all times remained the principal member of the firm and assigned tasks to Kolumb. Formation of the 'firm' gave the relationship between our intelligence officer and the agent a spirit of 'partnership' and doubtlessly made it easier to consolidate Kolumb's ties with Soviet Foreign Intelligence."

The textbook warns that American security agencies are aware of KGB techniques and utilize sophisticated techniques of their own to counter them. It cites as a problem "the comparatively rapid reaction of U.S. counterintelligence organs to individual changes in the methods and approaches used by Soviet intelligence officers."

To dodge the hazards presented by the FBI and other security agencies, the KGB increasingly tries to recruit Americans outside the United States. The text refers to a KGB directive expressly ordering intensification of efforts to subvert Americans abroad. It suggests that students at foreign universities are among the best prospects.

"As a rule, American students studying in Latin America are short of funds. Most come from the middle

classes of the U.S. Frequently, grants received for service in the Army . . . or limited assistance by relatives
comprise their sole means of livelihood. Persons in this
category are more liberal in their outlook. They are
sympathetic to the local nationalist feelings and sometimes do not approve of the influence of monopolies
in the economy and foreign policy of the U.S. or of
the U.S. colonial policy with regard to the Latin-American countries. The financial situation of the American
students, their convictions, and the general operational
climate facilitate our work. The fact that some of the
students are preparing to enter government service
(and in some cases they can be directed toward this
type of work) indicates that students can form a basis
for organizing future agent networks to penetrate U.S.
government organizations."

However, the textbook as a whole tacitly recognizes
that the number of Americans the KGB can expect to
attract ideologically now is comparatively small. This
was not always true. Most of the important Soviet
agents uncovered in American and Europe prior to
the 1960s were ideologically motivated men and wom-
en. They had seen in communism the means of coping
with the great economic and social problems that beset
the West during the depression of the 1930s. But today
communism, at least as represented by the Soviet Union,
exerts little ideological appeal. To be sure, there remains in the United States as in other Western nations
an apparently irreducible core of communists and
Soviet sympathizers willing to stomach, rationalize, and
apologize for any Soviet aggression or failing. They are
useful to the KGB in propaganda and disruption operations, and some still may be hidden in sensitive positions. But generally they have little espionage potential
because they are known to counterintelligence services
and barred from positions of trust.

A U.S. Army analysis of the motivations of American military personnel known to have committed
treason during the 1960s concluded that none acted
out of an affinity for communism or the Soviet Union.
Each sought in espionage an escape from the consequences of his own misconduct, which in turn resulted

from problems of marriage, sex, alcohol, or sheer greed. This is why the KGB now lays such strong stress on recruitment of Americans on the basis of their personal weaknesses.

Such people, of course, tend to be rather sorry samples of humanity. But the KGB has made an art of fashioning the most miserable human material into lethal weapons of espionage. The next chapter narrates a story that illustrates perfectly the KGB practice of this art. It is the story of an epic case of KGB espionage against the United States, the true details of which heretofore have been kept secret.

X

TREASURES FROM THE VAULT

It was a squat, square concrete building isolated behind barbed wire on a remote corner of Orly Airport outside Paris. No other installation in all of Europe was more vital to the United States, and armed guards protected it day and night.

Military couriers from Washington came to the little building two or three times a week with leather satchels handcuffed to their wrists. Inside, top-secret documents from their satchels were inventoried, then shut up in a massive steel vault behind steel bars. Here the documents stayed until other armed men arrived to deliver them to their ultimate destinations in France, Germany, and Great Britain.

This was the Armed Forces Courier Center. The secrets flowing through it could reveal the fundamental defense plans of the West, the most important strengths and weaknesses of the United States, the cipher systems in which ultrasensitive messages were transmitted. They were secrets worth almost any price to the Soviet Union.

The KGB long had watched the courier center. But it always had been like an alluring and beguiling mirage beyond reach. The KGB knew, as did the United States, that the center and its vault were impenetrable. Still, the KGB searched for the one chance to a million that would enable it to enter and mine the treasures of the vault.

The morning of October 2, 1964, Sergeant Robert Lee Johnson pleaded in vain with the receptionist at

Walter Reed Army Hospital in Washington. "Lady, I tell you, something ought to be done today," he said for the third time.

"I'm sorry, Sergeant," the receptionist replied with finality. "Tuesday is the earliest a psychiatrist can see Mrs. Johnson. Since there's no emergency, why can't she wait a few more days?"

Unable to confess the nature and depth of his desperation, Johnson had no answer. Crossing the hospital parking lot, he shuddered at the sight of his Austrian wife waiting in the car. At forty-one, Hedwig Pipek Johnson retained few vestiges of the beauty that had first attracted him sixteen years before when she was a lithe girl in Vienna. Her face was sallow and puffy, her blue eyes faded and watery, her once seductive figure lost in fat. And she regarded him with the malign, leering grin that portended another mad outburst. As they started down Nebraska Avenue toward their home in Alexandria, Virginia, it began.

"You filthy man, I hate you," she said in a husky, vicious voice. "You're a pervert, a gambler, a drunk, a rapist. You're a filthy Russian general."

"For Christ's sake, Hedy," Johnson interrupted, so shaken that he nearly rammed the car ahead, which had stopped for a traffic light.

Hedy's grin returned, and she leaned across the front seat, thrusting her face truculently close to his. "You know why I hate you most?" she whispered. "Because you're a spy."

Johnson froze until the cars behind began honking. As they drove away, he tried to speak deliberately. "If you ever say that again, I'll beat the hell out of you." But Hedy was beyond fear.

"Spy, spy, spy," she sang defiantly. "You're a spy. And you know what? If you don't do what I say, I'm going to tell the FBI."

"Go ahead! Go ahead, you goddam lunatic!" Johnson shouted. "You're so crazy nobody'll believe anything you say. They'll put *you* away, not me."

Hedy giggled and sang, "Then take me to the FBI, spy."

Johnson could bear her no longer. Five times in

three years she had been released after psychiatric treatment, only to lapse into ever worsening seizures of paranoia that left him in perpetual dread. He had lured her to the hospital, under the pretense of having a prescription filled, hoping to persuade Army doctors to commit her on the spot to an institution. It was like most of his plans—vague, unrealistic, unsuccessful. Now that it had failed, Johnson knew only that he must escape her, whatever the cost. Back home, he began drinking heavily and thinking of suicide.

At 2:45 P.M. Johnson left home, ostensibly to report for duty at the Pentagon, where he was a courier of secret documents. He never arrived. Six days later a back-page story in the Washington *Post* reported his disappearance. "It's quite a mystery," a Pentagon spokesman told the newspaper.

It was a far greater mystery than anyone at the Pentagon imagined. Nobody there could know that the missing sergeant was one of the most destructive spies the KGB ever implanted in the United States Armed Forces. Neither could anyone realize that if he escaped, the defenses of all of Western Europe would remain in unknown peril.

Johnson, his prostitute wife, and another derelict sergeant formed perhaps the most bizarre and improbable trio in modern espionage. Like his two partners, he was distinguished by disabling personal defects. He had no qualifications of intellect, character, or spirit. He was not impelled by any of the classic motivations of espionage—greed, idealism, fear, or adventure. Indeed, he first delivered himself to the KGB out of the pettiest of grievances.

Working as a military clerk in Berlin in the fall of 1952, Johnson considered himself maltreated and unappreciated by the Army. A rival sergeant received a promotion he coveted, and his commanding officer refused to act against another sergeant whom he accused of being a loan shark. The Army had been the only life he had known since dropping out of a New Jersey high school early in World War II. Just as a child seeks to punish his parents by running away from home, Johnson decided to punish the Army by running away to the Russians. He imagined himself as a celebrated defector whose nightly propaganda broadcasts over Radio Moscow would engulf the Pentagon in despair.

Uncertain about how to communicate with the Russians himself, Johnson turned to Hedy. She had lived with him first when he was stationed in Vienna in 1948, then joined him in Berlin on the chance that she could make him her husband. Johnson knew that above all else she craved the security of marriage, and so on Christmas Day 1952 he proposed a bargain. "If you'll go over and fix me up with the Russians," he told her, "I'll marry you."

But Hedy, who had witnessed the behavior of the first Soviet troops in Vienna, was terrified of Russians, and for weeks she walked the winter streets unable to gather enough courage to approach them. It was easy enough in those days, before the Wall, to cross into East Berlin. Once she followed a Soviet officer for blocks along Stalin Allee, yet she could not bring herself to speak to him. She invented excuses to justify her failures and sometimes feigned illness to avoid going out. Belatedly, Johnson saw through her pretenses and threatened to abandon her. Fearful of losing him, she presented herself at the Soviet compound in the Karlshorst district of the city.

"We have no need of vagabonds or parasites in the Soviet Union," a seemingly uninterested Russian civilian responded after listening to her story. "But if you like, you may bring this sergeant over to talk to us."

February 22, 1953, George Washington's Birthday, was a holiday for American forces in Berlin. About 10 A.M. Johnson and Hedy stepped from the elevated train at the Karlshorst station. They were met by two KGB officers, a stocky baldish man and a big buxom woman, who identified themselves as Mr. and Mrs. White. They drove, by a purposely circuitous route, to a massively built gray stone house, whose windows were covered on the outside by heavy wooden shutters and on the inside by thick curtains. The electricity was off, and what light there was emanated from candles. A middle-aged Russian introduced as Mr. Brown sat at an oval table in the center of the room. Without bothering to rise or shake hands, he filled five glasses with cognac and mumbled a toast "to peace."

"Your friend tells us you want to live in the Soviet Union," White said to Johnson. "Do you believe in socialism?"

"Well, to be honest, I don't know much about it one way or another," Johnson replied. "But I'm sure not against it, if that's what you mean."

"Are you a religious believer?" White asked.

"No, I never did believe in God or that church stuff," Johnson answered.

"And why do you want to be a Soviet citizen?" White inquired.

"I'm fed up with the Army," Johnson explained.

"I suppose many soldiers in many armies often have been, as you put it, fed up," White commented. "I can recall times when I myself was unhappy in our army. But that was not reason enough to desert my country. Why don't you just leave the Army?"

"No, no, I want to get even," Johnson replied quickly. "Listen, I can do you fellows a lot of good."

"How?" inquired White.

"I can make propaganda," Johnson said. "I can give press conferences, go on the radio, stuff like that."

Concealing their amusement, the Soviet officers deftly questioned him about his past life, military experiences, and current associates. All the while, Johnson accepted glass after glass of cognac, and by early afternoon he was in an incoherent stupor. As the Russians helped him out through the snow into a Soviet car, he gloomily concluded that he had accomplished nothing, and his grandiose plans for a career in Moscow collapsed in his blurry thoughts. The Russians had made no commitment beyond an invitation to talk again two weeks hence.

They were friendlier when he returned to East Berlin with Hedy in early March. "We have analyzed your situation carefully," began the officer who called himself White. "You of course could have asylum in the Soviet Union or the German Democratic Republic. But why? You want to avenge the injustices you have suffered. You can best do that by staying in the Army.

We belive that if you stay, you can become a strong fighter for peace."

"How do you do that?" asked Johnson.

"From time to time you can supply information," White explained. "It is important to peace that we be informed about the militarists who threaten peace."

"You mean, be a spy!" Johnson exclaimed.

"A fighter for peace," White corrected him.

"I never thought about spying," Johnson said. "I don't know anything about it."

"One must always learn," the Russian responded.

"Well, if you're going to teach me, help me along," Johnson said hesitantly, "I guess I could give it a try."

Any clandestine organization that has to justify undertakings to its controllers in terms of probable and definable results would have shunned Johnson. The Soviet interrogations revealed him to be an utterly amoral man, bereft of any beliefs whatsoever. Beyond drinking, gambling, and liaisons with prostitutes, he had no perceptible interests. Anyone willing to desert his country for reasons as trivial as those he cited could scarcely be regarded as reliable. Except for a certain vulgar and selfish cunning, Johnson would have been downright comical. By any objective assessment, the prospects of his ever accomplishing anything important in espionage were exceedingly slight.

Yet the KGB decision to recruit him was virtually automatic. Whatever face the Soviet Union chooses to present to the world at any given time, the KGB remains organized and deployed for clandestine warfare lasting beyond the foreseeable future Thus, it constantly cultivates agents who, though of no discernible present use, might become of value—five, ten, even twenty years hence. There was at least a chance that in time Johnson would drift into a position from which he could be exploited. It was a remote chance, but one the KGB had no difficulty in electing to take.

Prodded by Hedy, Johnson kept his promise, and they were married on April 23, 1953, in a civil ceremony lasting about three minutes. He arranged for a leave, telling the Army he planned to vacation in Bavaria. Instead, he and Hedy crossed into East Berlin, took a train to the town of Brandenburg, and spent their honeymoon as guests of the KGB. They lived in a house with a steeply arched red-tile roof and a small winter garden off the living room. Russians came daily to instruct them in the rudiments of espionage. Hedy was trained as a courier, given false identification papers and shoes with hollow heels in which film could be concealed. Toward the end of their stay, an elderly German psychiatrist talked to them for several hours and gave Johnson a verbal intelligence test.

How much the findings of the psychiatrist may have influenced the KGB can only be surmised. But soon after Johnson and Hedy returned to Berlin, a new and enduring pattern of treatment emerged. It first was evidenced by Paula, a twenty-seven-year-old KGB officer, who replaced the first three Russians.

Paula was Vladimir Vasilevich Krivoshey, newly arrived in Germany on his first foreign mission. He had a handsome face with narrow, deeply set dark eyes, a straight nose, and a mass of curly black hair that made him look even younger than he was. Casual and confident, he had mastered the English language and Americana so well that he often passed as an American.

He treated Hedy with the consideration one might bestow on a retarded child. Contrary to KGB custom, he made no attempt to keep her ignorant of Johnson's relations with the Russians. He welcomed her to clandestine meetings, and whenever time permitted flattered her with gentlemanly attentions.

Toward Johnson, the KGB attitude was more that of a patient animal trainer toward a dog. Paula established himself as the master upon whom Johnson's new secret life depended. He rewarded each act of obedience, but never lavishly, and he reprimanded the slightest deviation from instructions, but never too harshly. Beginning with Paula, the Russians avoided any mention of politics or effort to motivate Johnson ideologically. Instead, they sought to engender in him the idea that through them he could become an important and valued person.

Initially, Johnson reacted by doing his best to

please the KGB. Guided by Paula, he obtained a transfer to a clerical job in the G-2 (intelligence) section of the Berlin Command. There he began indiscriminately photographing masses of unclassified papers, which he slipped out overnight. Soon he churned up such a blizzard of worthless material that the KGB had to order him to desist. "We admire your energy, but we want only secret documents," Paula told him.

Trying harder, while his office was empty during lunch hour Johnson photographed a wall map showing the disposition of Soviet forces in East Germany. "What did you think of the map?" he asked proudly at the next monthly meeting with Paula in East Berlin.

"Really, we do not need an American map to tell us where our own troops are," Paula replied.

After the East German uprisings in June 1953, Paula pressured Johnson to produce proof that the United States had incited the revolt. But the Americans were as astonished by it as the Russians, and despite renewed KGB demands, Johnson could not find the nonexistent proof. His frustration was such that he now considered severing ties with the Russians. He probably would have done so except for the arrival of a man who was destined to appear unexpectedly as an influence in his life again and again.

"How are you, Bob?" a voice quietly called to Johnson in the corridor outside his office. It was his best friend, Sergeant James Allen Mintkenbaugh, whom he had last seen three years before at Fort Hood, Texas. Mintkenbaugh, thirty-five, was tall and rather strong, with a vacuous face and equally empty brown eyes that shifted away from a direct gaze. Johnson had heard other soldiers refer to him as "unreal," "a zombie," "a weirdo." In many respects the two were dissimilar. Johnson was gluttonous and recklessly impulsive; Mintkenbaugh was fastidious and extremely cautious, even timid. Johnson drank heavily and slept with any woman he could. Mintkenbaugh disliked drunkenness, and though he sometimes bragged about his exploits with women, Johnson had never known him to be in the company of one. Yet, in Texas, each had become the best friend the other had, perhaps because they were both in a way outcasts, devoid of purpose or values.

Johnson saw in Mintkenbaugh a means of enhancing his stature with the KGB. He reasoned that with his friend serving as a lookout while he rummaged through offices during off-duty hours, he could increase his productivity as a spy. Then one day he would present to the Russians the gift of a new recruit for whom they would be grateful. Johnson broached the subject deviously over wine and wurst in a beer garden. "This is a great town," he said. "I'm making good money on the side."

Recalling Johnson's triumphs gambling with teen-age draftees in Texas, Mintkenbaugh remarked, "You mean gypping the kids at cards?"

"No, no. Spying," Johnson responded. "That's the big game here. Me, I'm selling the Russians phony skinny. I only give them a little real stuff now and then to make it look good. I'd be willing to cut you in if you'd give me some help."

Mintkenbaugh wavered but eventually agreed, probably out of curiosity and a desire to be accommodating. Before long, he sensed that Johnson actually was hunting valuable intelligence for the Russians. To his surprise, he found that he didn't care. In fact, the realization that he was helping betray the United States gave him a strange gratification.

Meanwhile the two sergeants joined in a scheme to make money by producing pornographic movies for sale to fellow soldiers. One night they hired a prostitute to come to Johnson's apartment and star in their show. Hedy's raucous shrieking and the drunken commotion in the apartment so antagonized some of the neighbors that they called the police, who in turn notified the Army. The next day counterintelligence agents interrogated Johnson and Mintkenbaugh and searched the apartment. They found nothing incriminating because Johnson had loaded his movie camera improperly and the film was blank. Both men were dismissed after a lecture about the necessity of respecting German civilians.

Johnson was alarmed, convinced that the Army was actually searching for evidence of his espionage. That night he parked his Volkswagen on a side street and sought to infect Mintkenbaugh with his own panic. "Some way, they've found out about us," he declared. "That's why they came around today. We've got to get out of here, go over to the Russians."

Sitting phlegmatically in the darkness, Mintkenbaugh said nothing, and Johnson interpreted his silence as disagreement.

"Christ! You want to go to jail?" he shouted. "Now listen, Mink, I lied to you a little. I've given the Russians some real good stuff. They'll take care of us."

Slowly Mintkenbaugh replied, "Bob, there's something I've got to tell you. You're not going to like it. But I better tell you before we go any further."

With those words, Johnson was sure he was doomed. He remembered a cryptic statement Mintkenbaugh had made back at Fort Hood, and suddenly everything was catastrophically clear. Mintkenbaugh had mentioned that he once attended Army counterintelligence school at Fort Holabird, Maryland, but had dropped out for reasons he didn't explain. It was a lie, Johnson now thought. Mintkenbaugh must have been a counterintelligence agent all along, sent to watch and trap him. Expecting to feel handcuffs slapped on his wrists momentarily, Johnson tremulously asked, "What do you have to tell me?"

Mintkenbaugh answered sorrowfully, "Bob, I'm queer."

"Oh, thank God!" Johnson blurted.

Waiting on Friedrichstrasse in East Berlin, Paula was outraged to see Johnson approaching in the company of a stranger. He took the two Americans to a café, pointed angrily at Mintkenbaugh, and demanded, "Who is this man? What is he doing here?"

Johnson defensively explained his friendship with Mintkenbaugh, their collaboration, and the circumstances that made them fear arrest. "That's perfectly idiotic," Paula declared. "If they actually suspected you, they would have confronted you with accusations or left you entirely alone. Pull yourself together and forget these insane notions of running away. The question of your future was settled months ago."

Turning to Mintkenbaugh, he commanded, "Tell me about yourself. What do you do in the Army? Do you have a family? Why did you get involved in this?"

After listening for a while, Paula relaxed. Now he was quite interested in the new American, and his brusqueness gave way to friendly politeness. Schooled to analyze character and behavior, Paula detected that Mintkenbaugh was a homosexual; and homosexuality, especially when not readily apparent, is an affliction the KGB delights in discovering.

Contrary to popular supposition, the KGB is not primarily interested in homosexuals because of their presumed susceptibility to blackmail. In its judgment, homosexuality often is accompanied by personality disorders that make the victim potentially unstable and vulnerable to adroit manipulation. It hunts the particular homosexual who, while more or less a functioning member of his society, is nevertheless subconsciously at war with it and himself. Compulsively driven into tortured relations that never gratify, he cannot escape awareness that he is different. Being different, he easily rationalizes that he is not morally bound by the mores, values, and allegiances that unite others in community or society. Moreover, he nurtures a dormant impulse to strike back at the society which he feels has conspired to make him a secret leper. To such a man, treason offers the weapon of retaliation. And Mintkenbaugh was such a man.

Paula asked him to return to East Berlin alone, and during the next few weeks ushered him into meetings with other Russians at KGB houses in Karlshorst. They subtly communicated an awareness of his homosexuality without referring to it specifically. Since Mintkenbaugh had already indirectly collaborated with the KGB through Johnson, the Russians did not trouble with any formalities of recruitment. Their conversations assumed that he was under their command. Mintkenbaugh passively acquiesced in this assumption without really understanding why. It would be more than a decade before he could articulate the reason for his disloyalty.

Paula instructed Mintkenbaugh to spot homosexuals in the American community, and mentioned that the KGB might establish him as an antiques dealer in Berlin after his discharge from the Army. Then one evening, about six months after their first meeting, Paula abruptly ordered him to terminate his association with Johnson and to cease all activity entailing risk. The KGB had conceived of much more sophisticated uses for Mintkenbaugh back in the United States. Again it was thinking far ahead.

Johnson continued to supply occasional intelligence, including a few copies of the confidential weekly summaries prepared for the Berlin Command. Paula patiently sought to guide and encourage him. But in time the original allure of espionage for the Russians faded, and Johnson's interest waned. When he was transferred to an Army finance office near Rochefort, France, in April 1955, he skipped his last scheduled meeting with Paula and left Berlin without provision for further contact. The KGB, having ascertained that his new post was of no interest, was content to let him go for the time being.

Still embittered with the Army, Johnson accepted a discharge in July 1956. He was thirty-six, uneducated and unprepared for any particular civilian work. But he had a plan. He imagined that by gambling he could multiply his savings of some $3,000 into a respectable fortune. Then he would enroll in a correspondence course in creative writing and become a famous author. So he took Hedy to Las Vegas. They slept in their car and spent their waking hours in the casinos. Withing two months their money was gone, and Johnson urged Hedy to go back to prostitution to provide them with a livelihood.

Hedy was quite successful. She was still attractive, and her foreign accent augmented her appeal. It pleased her to be needed, to be asked to help. And her sex drive was such that prostitution was exciting rather than degrading. On some days she earned as much as

$200, and once a customer paid her $500 to stay a week with him in a mountain cabin. With her earnings Johnson bought a mobile home, and they moved into a trailer camp. During the day he worked on his correspondence course; at night he drank and gambled with Hedy's money. But late in 1956 Hedy became ill and could not work. Again they were destitute.

On a Saturday morning in January 1957, Johnson groggily answered a knock at the trailer door. "Well, I'll be damned!" he shouted. "Hedy, get up. Fix some coffee. Look who's here." Standing outside, smiling and as impassive as ever, was Mintkenbaugh. He told them that he had left the Army in the spring of 1956, and since then had been working in a northern California ice-cream parlor. After a while, he also mentioned that he was just back from Berlin.

His fixed smile unchanging, Mintkenbaugh handed Johnson an envelope containing twenty-five musty twenty-dollar bills. "It's a present from Paula," he said. "They want you to go back into the service. You'll work with me, and they'll pay you $300 a month."

Johnson regarded both the money and the invitation as providential. Without deliberating further or consulting Hedy, he agreed.

The immediate KGB objective in reactivating Johnson was to gather intelligence about American missiles, which were just beginning to be deployed in numbers. The Russians recognized that he probably could not gain a technical assignment, but they thought that from some peripheral billet he might photograph equipment and documents. Besides, he was a potential asset acquired at next to no cost, and they had little to lose by attempting to exploit him now.

Turned down by the Air Force, which the KGB wanted him to join, Johnson was able to rejoin the Army and retain his former grade. As KGB luck would have it, the Army stationed him as a guard at a new Nike-Hercules missile site on the Palos Verdes Peninsula in California. In meetings with Mintkenbaugh between the springs of 1957 and 1958, Johnson transmitted photographs and diagrams of the missile, together with overheard comments about its characteristics. He also succeeded in siphoning off a sample of the rocket fuel, which the Russians had ordered. The KGB rewarded him with bonuses of $900 and $1,200. Though small in comparison to the value of the information received, the payments represented the maximum the KGB judged he could absorb without becoming conspicuous.

The Army transferred Johnson to Fort Bliss outside El Paso, Texas, where he continued to pass missile data and other secret information to Mintkenbaugh. After each rendezvous with Johnson at the El Paso airport, Mintkenbaugh flew to Washington to report to Petr Nikolaevich Yeliseev, a thirty-five-year-old protocol officer at the Soviet embassy. Yeliseev tended to perspire profusely in the humid Washington summers, and a habit of repeatedly removing his glasses to rub his nose gave him the look of a man forever harried. He preferred to arrange meetings near burlesque theaters so that before or after he could watch a strip show on KGB time. Driving along the Potomac between the Jefferson and Lincoln Memorials in July 1959, Yeliseev, whom Mintkenbaugh knew as Charles, told him to prepare for a journey that would keep him out of the country for four months.

"Where am I going?" Mintkenbaugh asked.

"I can only give you the following instructions," Charles replied. "A letter will come from Germany. It will say somewhere the word 'match.' Fourteen days from the date of that letter, at 1935 hours, you must stand on the street corner in East Berlin where you formerly met our representative."

In early September of 1959, Mintkenbaugh received a letter that appeared to have been written by German friends. The last sentence read, "We still have foreign friends, but none can match you." Thus signaled, Mintkenbaugh took an SAS flight from Los Angeles over the North Pole to Copenhagen, then flew to West Berlin. Waiting on Friedrichstrasse in East Berlin, he saw a squat, snaggle-toothed man walking toward him with his shoulders hunched forward in a manner that suggested the gait of a gorilla. "Excuse me, but did we not meet in Las Vegas?" the stranger said to Mintkenbaugh in a raspy voice with an almost comically thick Russian accent.

"No, it might have been Los Angeles," Mintken-baugh replied.

"Yes, I remember," said the Russian. "I bring greetings from Paula."

"Where is Paula?" Mintkenbaugh asked.

"Far away," answered the Russian. The secret credentials properly exchanged, he extended a pudgy hand and hurt Mintkenbaugh with the strength of his grip. "Relax," he commanded. "I am Nick, your traveling companion."

Western security services knew Nick as Nikolai Semenovich Skvortsov, a diligent but conspicuous spy. Expelled from Canada for espionage in 1949, he soon showed up as a United Nations employee in New York. Before long, he was caught again and booted out of the United States. *"Nekulturny"* ("uncultured"), younger officers said of him because of his peasant origins and bulldozer style. No one ever derided Nick to his face, though, for he was a powerful man who inspired physical fear, and besides he was rumored to have influential patrons within the KGB.*

"I want somebody to tell me why I am here and where I am going," Mintkenbaugh said.

"Save your questions," Nick responded, leading him to a car parked two blocks away. They drove through East Berlin to another of the fine old German houses confiscated by the KGB in the Karlshorst district. "We are going to Moscow to prepare your future," Nick announced after dismissing the German maid who received them. "People want to see you. It is easier to work with a man whose face you have seen."

It was still dark when they climbed into a Soviet Illyushin-28 transport at Schoenefeld airport. A Soviet general and a pretty girl, perhaps his daughter, were the only other passengers. They nodded a greeting but kept to themselves throughout the uneventful, uncomfortable flight.

---

*This Nikolai Semenovich Skvortsov may very well be the N. S. Skvortsov who is identified as one of the authors of the KGB espionage manual (pages 262 and 466).

The first sensation of Mintkenbaugh on Soviet soil was that of pitiless cold. Wearing the light suit and raincoat in which he had left southern California, he quivered uncontrollably as they waited for a car at the airfield outside Moscow. "For God's sake, get us out of here, Nick," he pleaded. "I'm freezing."

In Moscow the KGB settled Mintkenbaugh in a pleasant third-floor apartment attended by an elderly housekeeper, and in the morning Nick brought him heavy Russian clothes—a woolen suit, long overcoat, round fur hat. Initially his routine and training differed little from that of numberless other agents spirited to Moscow from throughout the world. Instructors came daily to indoctrinate him in the use of drops, microdots, invisible writing, photography, recognition signals, surveillance, and the Morse code. They told him that in an emergency he was to flee to Mexico City and stand in front of a specified barbershop with a copy of *Time* in his hand until a man also carrying a copy of *Time* approached him. If the KGB wanted him to flee, an anonymous caller would telephone and say, "When the deep purple falls over sleepy garden walls." He also had to master a code devised for him and based on the sentence "Capitalism is a constant menace to peace."

All the while the KGB exerted a special effort to keep Mintkenbaugh happy and develop rapport with him. Nick and another officer known as Harry escorted him on walks in the vicinity of a compound occupied by foreigners. One evening Paula, his mentor in Berlin, along with his pretty young wife, took him to a restaurant. They drove in a decrepit, rattling car which Mintkenbaugh considered an unsafe jalopy, and on the way the police gave Paula a ticket because the car was dirty. Paula was so proud of owning an automobile and so fearful that it might be stolen that he disconnected the ignition wires before entering the restaurant.

Mintkenbaugh also received attention from a senior KGB officer, introduced as Alex, whose visits were frequently an occasion for festive steak dinners with champagne. Alex was Aleksandr M. Fomin, soon to become KGB Resident in Washington and later a central figure in the Cuban missile crisis. With nuclear war threatening, the Soviet Union characteristically chose to negotiate with the United States clandestinely through the KGB. Twice Fomin arranged furtive meetings with the news commentator John Scali, later U.S. Ambassador to the United Nations, who the Russians knew had access to the White House, and asked him to transmit messages from the Kremlin. The assignment of an officer of Fomin's caliber to coach, counsel, and entertain Mintkenbaugh suggested that the KGB expected much from him.

Midway through his third week in Moscow, Mintkenbaugh realized the importance of what was expected when Alex, Harry, and Nick asked him if he would be willing to marry and live with a female illegal, whom the KGB wished to station in the United States. Such professional marriages provide the female partner with the cover of a housewife and, by relieving her of the necessity of earning an income, make her almost entirely free for clandestine work. But there also are disadvantages. The normal tensions and conflicts that sometimes develop between a man and a woman have disrupted marital teams of illegals. There is also the danger that the man and woman will actually fall in love and become more concerned with the pursuit of their life together than with their secret duties. The KGB evidently reasoned that both risks could be averted by a marriage involving a homosexual husband.

For reasons he could not explain to himself, Mintkenbaugh consented to the proposal. Next evening the three officers took him to a theater, where he sensed that a woman was watching him. She had red hair, blue eyes, a pert face, and a willowy, attractive figure, and he guessed she was in her early thirties. Two evenings later, Alex, Harry, and Nick brought her to the apartment and introduced her as Irene.

"You must excuse my English," she said, offering her hand. "I am afraid I have not spoken it for some time." Actually she spoke very well, with an American accent.

"What do you do in Moscow? I mean, what is your work?" Mintkenbaugh asked.

"I serve socialism, just like you," she replied.

For a week or so, KGB officers chaperoned Mintkenbaugh and Irene at restaurants, the theater, and the ballet, then allowed them to visit alone at each other's apartments. Irene revealed that as a teen-ager during World War II she had served as a radio operator with Soviet partisans and had worked in clandestine operations ever since. She indicated that she had been married before for the period of another assignment as an illegal abroad. Apparently well informed about the United States, she said she understood religion and would have no difficulty attending church.

As Irene started to leave his apartment the night of their third or fourth meeting alone, Mintkenbaugh, on impulse, asked her to go to bed with him. He had compelled himself to try to make love to women before and his efforts had always ended in humiliation. He did not know why he now suddenly invited Irene. Hesitating momentarily, she said, "I would like to, but we'd better not. The maid would report us and I don't know what is authorized at this stage." She kissed him lightly on the cheek as if to say "later."

As a further test of compatibility, the KGB sent them on a holiday to Leningrad. At the hotel Irene insisted on separate rooms. "I have been told about you," she said. "But it doesn't matter. We will be friends and get along." The KGB thought so, too. Back in Moscow, Alex advised Mintkenbaugh that the marriage had been approved and that sometime after his return to the United States he would receive instructions to meet and wed Irene in New Jersey. "We want you to live in Washington. You must become a businessman. We do not care whether you make money; it is only important that you have reason to be in Washington, to meet interesting people. In time, you will be informed of specific tasks."

The KGB did have one immediate task for Mintkenbaugh. Although simple, it was to be the most important he ever performed. The Russians knew that Johnson had been transferred from Texas to an Army base in Orléans, France, in late 1959 and they wanted to reactivate him. So Mintkenbaugh flew via Berlin to

Paris, then traveled by train to Orléans, where he
found Johnson and Hedy were living in a seedy hotel
near the railroad station. He stayed with them three or
four days, departing for the United States only after instructing Johnson how to meet the KGB in Paris.

On New Year's Day of 1960, Mintkenbaugh rendezvoused with Charles at the Washington Monument.
The Russian stressed that he must find a job or business that would make him master of his own time,
enabling him to travel at will and meet people. He also
gave him some specific assignments: pinpoint the location of a reserve "Pentagon" the KGB believed was
buried under the Pennsylvania hills around Gettys-
burg; chart the route of an oil pipeline being constructed from Texas to Pennsylvania; and locate a new
radio transmitter that the KGB erroneously thought
was being erected for clandestine purposes near War-
renton, Virginia. "Of course, these are long-range assignments," Charles said. "We don't expect you to fulfill them immediately. In all things, you must creep,
not run."

As they parted, Mintkenbaugh asked, "Will you find
out when Irene is coming?"

"Yes, I'll inquire," Charles promised.

Mintkenbaugh asked about Irene often. She was one
of the few women with whom he had enjoyed a personal relationship, and she had been kind. He rented a
commodious duplex apartment on a quiet residential
street in Arlington, thinking it would be the home they
would share. He crammed the apartment with furnishings, piling three expensive Persian rugs on top of each
other in the living room in his eagerness to make it
pleasing. But at the end of a Sunday morning meeting in Washington, Charles mentioned, as an afterthought: "This woman you have been asking about.
She is very sick with tuberculosis. She will not be joining you." Mintkenbaugh shook his head with the bit-
terness and despair of a man defrauded of a last slim
hope.

Meanwhile, in France, Johnson drove to Paris following Mintkenbaugh's instructions. He and Hedy
stood before a theater on the Rue d'Athènes studying

the advertisements. A handsome young man who in his black beret looked very French paused beside them and also looked at the advertisements. "Excuse me, are you British?" he asked with a slight Russian accent.

"No, I am American," Johnson replied.

"I wonder if you have change for ten francs," the Russian went on.

Johnson presented a German five-mark coin Mintkenbaugh had given him. The Russian in turn handed him a two-mark coin, smiled, shook hands, and said, "My name is Viktor. Why don't we have a drink?"

Viktor was Vitali Sergeevich Orzhurmov, then a twenty-nine-year-old attaché of the Soviet embassy in Paris. Like Paula, he belonged to the new breed of poised and polished officers the KGB began grooming for foreign operations in the 1950s. He moved easily among Westerners, who were charmed by the novelty of meeting a civilized Soviet representative, particularly one who hinted that he favored democratic reform of the Soviet system. His behavior toward Johnson and Hedy reflected a careful study of the KGB files and its judgment of them. From the moment they sat down in a little corner café, he devoted himself to Hedy, trying to make her comfortable and secure in the relationship he was inaugurating. And he suggested to Johnson that he was now a very important man upon whom Moscow counted heavily.

After chatting with Hedy for a while, Viktor gave Johnson $500 tightly wadded in a cigarette package. "It's a Christmas present," he said. "You know, we are very glad to have you with us here. You bring a good record. It shows that we can rely on you to use your own initiative in discovering information of interest."

Thereafter Johnson, sometimes accompanied by Hedy, met Viktor on the first Saturday evening of every month in cafés near the Porte d'Orléans in Paris. His first assignment in France, with an ordnance battalion, gave him no access to data of importance, and by the summer of 1960 Viktor started urging him to request duty at Supreme Allied Headquarters in Paris. Hedy suffered her first breakdown in the fall and entered an Army hospital near Paris. With the permission of a sympathetic commanding officer, Johnson asked for a compassionate transfer to the Paris area on grounds that his wife needed to live closer to the hospital.

After an unsuccessful interview at SHAPE in March 1961, he fell into conversation with a sergeant serving as a receptionist who told him, "If you want to get to Paris, you might try the Armed Forces Courier Center out at Orly Field," the sergant advised him.

"What's that?" Johnson asked.

"It's a sort of post office for top-secret materials," the sergeant explained. "They guard the hell out of it, so lots of times there's openings for guards."

The description was accurate so far as it went. The courier center was the European citadel of many of the most important military and diplomatic secrets the United States possessed. All vital documents, cipher systems, and cryptographic equipment sent from Washington to NATO, American commands in Europe, and the Sixth Fleet in the Mediterranean were first delivered to the center. There they were sorted and rerouted to their final destination. All materials bearing top-secret or higher classification originating from commands in Europe were also housed in the center, pending transshipment to Washington.

The Army had devised a labyrinth of security barriers to make the little concrete building housing the center physically inviolate. The only outside door opened into a front office where clerks processed the documents. Behind it was a huge steel vault. To enter the vault, it was necessary to pass through two steel doors. The first was secured by a metal bar with combination locks at either end. The second, the door to the vault itself, had a complicated key lock. Thus, no one could open the vault without the combination to two locks and a key to the third. No one, from general to private, ever was allowed in the vault alone. Regulations required the constant presence of at least one officer whenever it was opened. Additionally, an armed guard was posted in the office twenty-four hours a day, 365 days a year. Seemingly, it was impenetrable.

Johnson's request for transfer was routinely approved. When Johnson reported his assignment to the courier center as guard, Viktor slapped him on the back and exclaimed, "Fantastic!" With the assignment, the miserable, ridiculous sergeant, who eight years before had drifted into the hands of the KGB like so much human flotsam, suddenly was transformed into an agent of incredible potential. Much still stood between the KGB and the treasures of the vault. But with an agent unexpectedly stationed a few feet away, the KGB was now closer than it had ever conceived possible. Now all of its ingenuity, imagination, and technical resources were concentrated into a plan to span those last few feet.

Viktor increased the frequency of meetings with Johnson and questioned him interminably about the routine of the center, the rotation of guards, and the methods of selecting personnel admitted to the vault itself. Relaying instructions from the KGB Center in Moscow, he eventually said, "As a first step, you must become one of the clerks who work inside."

"To do that I need a top-secret clearance," Johnson replied. "That means an investigation."

"That is a chance we must take," Viktor responded.

Johnson worried most about what the increasingly unpredictable Hedy might do or say. During her recurrent fits of irrationality, neighbors had heard her babble about espionage and accuse her husband of being a spy. So had the medical personnel who treated her. All dismissed her rantings as delusions. But Johnson could not be sure that if some conscientious investigator heard of the accusations, he might not talk to Hedy, then look further.

However, circumstances were to spare Johnson the thorough background investigation that is supposed to precede the granting of a top-secret clearance. The agreement by which France permitted American troops on its soil prohibited Army investigators from interrogating French citizens, and no interviews of Johnson's French neighbors were attempted. A cursory check, consisting of a review of his past service and a routine written inquiry to his commanding officer, cast no disqualifying doubts upon him. It did not even note Hedy's mental illness, because Johnson, on the pretext of verifying some dates, had checked out his personnel folder and removed all references to her condition. So, late in 1961, he received the clearance and was admitted to the vault as a clerk.

The documents Johnson now sorted ordinarily arrived in large manila envelopes, often bearing red or blue wax seals. Some had laconic labels denoting special security classifications. Most of the security terms were meaningless to Johnson. But the KGB knew that in American parlance the designations referred to ultrasensitive crypographic material, sensitive data about NATO strengths and strategies, and nuclear strike plans.

The KGB was concerned that the courier center might be equipped with a hidden alarm system set to sound a warning if any effort was made to open the vault during nonworking hours. Viktor showed Johnson illustrations, probably extracted from trade magazines, of various systems used in American banks, and ordered him to look for wiring or tiny boxes that would betray the presence of an alarm.

"You must examine the whole building centimeter by centimeter," he said. "You say it is painted?"

"Yes, white," Johnson replied.

"Then eventually it will have to be repainted?" remarked Viktor.

"I guess so," said Johnson.

"Who will paint it?" Viktor asked.

"Some of us poor bastards, I suppose," Johnson replied.

"If there is the opportunity, you must be the one to paint it," Viktor instructed him.

When the Army did decide to brighten the center with a new coat of paint, Johnson volunteered to do the job and was able to examine the building "centimeter by centimeter." He reported that in his opinion it contained no alarm system. He was correct.

The most formidable and seemingly insuperable obstacles, of course, were the three locks. Viktor gave Johnson modeling clay in a French cigarette box and directed him to carry it at all times on the chance that he might be able to steal the vault key for a few minutes. Johnson protested that there was no such chance because the key was always kept in the custody of an officer. "We must not overlook any possibility," Viktor replied.

On a Monday morning in 1962, a young lieutenant with whom Johnson was working complained of nausea. Suddenly ordering Johnson from the vault, he dashed outside to vomit. He slammed the vault door shut and locked it, but in his haste neglected to remove the key. Johnson grabbed it and quickly made an impression in the clay.

Two meetings later, Viktor told him that the impression was too indistinct. Johnson had bungled an opportunity that might not repeat itself, but there was no reproof in either Viktor's words or tone, for Johnson was now too valuable to antagonize. "Mistakes occur," Viktor said. "Let us hope there will be another opportunity and more time."

There was. More in idle conversation than from curiosity, Johnson pointed to a small metal cabinet in the vault and asked the supervising officer, "What do we keep in there?"

"Nothing now," replied the officer, swinging open the unlocked cabinet. "See, it's empty."

Johnson saw that the cabinet was empty except for a key in the corner—a spare key to the vault. Late in the afternoon he slipped it in his pocket and kept it overnight, carefully making three separate impressions in the clay. The next morning while an officer absorbed himself with a new batch of documents, he returned it unnoticed. Some three weeks later Viktor handed him a shiny key made in Moscow. He smiled and commented, "You have a saying, one down and two to go."

Johnson, in compliance with KGB orders, often tried to memorize the combinations by watching officers open the locks. Once an officer abruptly turned on him and snapped, "Stand back, Johnson. Don't hover over my shoulder when I'm doing this." The incident frightened Viktor more than Johnson. "From

now on, stay away when it is being opened; don't
show any interest at all," he ordered.

In June 1962 the Army, in accordance with routine
security procedure, changed the combination to one of
the locks. A captain who had been on leave telephoned
another officer to ask for the new combination. The
officer refused to release it over the phone, but after
some argument consented to list numbers which, when
appropriately added to the old combination, would
yield the new. The captain recorded the numbers and
performed the necessary addition on a slip of paper,
which he carelessly discarded in his wastebasket.

"You are to be congratulated," said Viktor after
Johnson gave him the paper retrieved from the wastebasket. "Of course, we must make certain this is the
combination. I believe it is time you volunteered for
weekend work."

In addition to their regular duties, the clerical personnel took turns standing watch at the center when it
was closed at night and on weekends. These were the
only times the installation was protected by one man
only. During weekday nights, couriers sometimes arrived at odd hours, causing the sentry to summon officers to reopen the center. Therefore the KGB concluded that if the vault was ever to be penetrated, the
attempt would have to be made on weekends, when
couriers almost never came and the area was deserted.

With the pleasures of Paris only a few miles away,
the lonely, boring weekend duty was universally un-
popular. Most disliked of all was the shift lasting from
6 P.M. Saturday to 6 A.M. Sunday. In an effort to make
it more palatable, the Army offered two weekdays off
to anyone who volunteered for it. Still, there were few
volunteers, and Johnson had no difficulty obtaining a
permanent assignment to the Saturday-night watch. He
explained that he needed a weekday free to take his
wife to the doctor. The first night he stood guard, he
waited until nearly 2 A.M. before testing the combination. "Two down," he thought, as the lock clicked
open.

"Our scientists think they may have a way to figure
out the combination of the other lock," Viktor con-

fided in August. "But first we need many good close-up pictures of it from all angles. Use the Minox and take exposures this weekend. I will receive the film from you on the way to work Monday at 0700." Holding up a map, Viktor pointed out a meeting site beside a bridge along a country lane not far from Orly Airport.

Driving through heavy rain, Johnson detoured off the main road to the airport and halted his old Citroën by the bridge. He saw Viktor running out of the woods followed by a small, dark, slender man who looked out of place in an elegant blue suit. They both jumped into the car, and Viktor said, "Let me present my replacement, Feliks."

"Where are you going?" Johnson asked.

"I will still be here, still working with you. We will see each other again," Viktor replied. "However, we feel that two men now are required for your good care, and our mutual success."

Viktor basically told the truth. As the possibilities of success increased, the operation had assumed transcendent importance to the KGB. Preparations for its decisive moments had grown so complex that many officers, both in Moscow and Paris, were now devoting themselves to it. The KGB needed at least two officers in Paris able to deal personally and easily with Johnson, in case one should become incapacitated. In addition it wanted an extra officer available to watch future meetings with Johnson, to guard against enemy surveillance.

Feliks—Feliks Aleksandrovich Ivanov, who sometimes posed as a diplomat, sometimes as a United Nations official—knew Johnson well as a result of Viktor's briefings and his own study of the files. By nature Feliks was much more restless, authoritarian, and intense than Viktor, yet he too treated Johnson considerately. He behaved like a patient tutor determined to extract the most from a dull and unstable pupil.

He met Johnson in early October at the café L'Etoile d'Or on the corner of the Boulevard Brune and the Rue des Plantes, to transmit critical instructions. "You must listen very carefully. If at any time you do not understand me, please say so," Feliks began. "A special device soon will come from Moscow. It looks like this." He unfolded a piece of onionskin paper bearing draftsman's designs and Russian lettering. One illustration showed a flat, circular metal plate about four inches in diameter and a thick metal cone perhaps nine inches long. Another depicted the plate being held behind the combination lock. A third showed the cone being fitted over the lock against the plate.

"You might call this a little X-ray machine," Feliks explained. "Once you place it over the lock, it will automatically X-ray the mechanism of the lock. Our scientists believe that from the X-rays they can calculate the combination.

"As you can see, what you must do is simple. But there is danger. When fitted together, the apparatus becomes extremely radioactive. As soon as you place it over the lock, you must go to the farthest part of the room and wait thirty minutes. Is that all clear?"

"You mean, all I got to do is stick it over the lock?" Johnson asked.

"And then stay away for thirty minutes, then take it off and bring it to me," Feliks replied.

Along the same country lane where Johnson first met Feliks, the KGB delivered the device in two packages on a Friday night. Johnson stopped his Citroën just long enough for Viktor to pass one part through the window. About a mile down the lane, Feliks stepped from the woods and sat in the front seat with the second. Then he drilled Johnson once more in the procedures he was to follow.

In the courier center, at 3 o'clock Sunday morning, Johnson planted the plate and cone over the lock. They fitted perfectly, and instantly began to emit a barely audible humming sound, which Feliks had neglected to mention. Johnson crouched in the darkness against a corner wall, continuously checking his watch, as the device did its work. After exactly thirty minutes the hum ceased, and he replaced the cone and the plate in their respective boxes. Three weeks later, on November 30, Feliks handed him a slip of paper inscribed with a series of numbers. "That is it!" he said triumphantly.

"How do you know it's right?" Johnson asked.

"We know. There is no doubt," Feliks replied with a smile. "We have scheduled your first entry for December 15. There is much to do between now and then. We shall begin with a tour."

That night Feliks drove Johnson in his gray Mercedes to Orly Field and turned onto a service road leading to the administration building, stopping on a bend near an overpass. "At fifteen minutes past midnight, I will be standing here by my car," he said. "I will wave as you approach in your car. It will seem that I am seeking assistance. You will stop and give me the documents. We estimate that you will be away from your post less than five minutes."

From the airport they traveled about five miles into the countryside, where Feliks parked his car on a dirt road by a forsaken little cemetery and said, "At 0315 hours I will return the documents to you here." The wind moaning through the tombstones and the forbidding cemetery itself made Johnson uneasy.

"Why'd you pick such a creepy damned place?" he asked.

"What would you prefer? The Arc de Triomphe?" Feliks rejoined. "No one is likely to disturb us here. It is the best nearby site we could locate."

Feliks got out of the car and took two identical blue Air France flight bags from the trunk. Giving one to Johnson, he said, "You are to place the documents in this bag. When you hand it to me at the airport, I will give you this one in return. Look inside."

Inside the second bag were a bottle of cognac, four sandwiches, an apple, and four white tablets wrapped in a napkin.

Feliks explained that the cognac contained a drug that would quickly induce pleasant sleep. "Should anyone come to your post between our first and second appointments, give him a drink," he instructed. "Then you can safely leave to recover the documents from us. If it is necessary for you to drink also, take two of the tablets at once and the other two five minutes later. They will prevent the drug from affecting you."

The methodical rehearsals continued almost daily

now, and they reflected the scope of the KGB's preparations. Feliks led Johnson two hundred yards into a field off Highway D33 exactly 13.6 miles outside Paris. At the base of a tree he picked up a large rock, and as Johnson watched wonderingly, unscrewed it so that it formed two hollow parts. "In an emergency, you will find a Canadian passport here with your photograph, personal credentials, money, instructions, a 1921 American silver dollar," Feliks said. "Make your way to Brussels. With a copy of the London *Times* in your left hand, come daily at 11 A.M. to the 100 block of Chaussée de Forêt. Our representative will approach you with a 1921 American silver dollar and ask if you dropped it. You will then display your silver dollar and abide by his orders."

"How do you expect me to remember all that?" Johnson grumbled.

"We will practice until you can," Feliks calmly replied. "Now, let us begin the lesson again. . . ."

Feliks stressed that the KGB escape plan would automatically go into effect unless Johnson, immediately after leaving the courier center on Sunday, signaled that all was well. To give the signal, he had to drop a Lucky Strike pack, with an "X" penciled inside it, by a telephone booth on his way home.

The final rehearsal was Friday night, December 14. Once more Feliks drove Johnson to the bend on the Orly Field road, then to the cemetery. "I will be waiting for you. Many people will be waiting," he said in parting. "Good luck."

At the courier center, Johnson turned on a transistor radio and set his watch by the 11 P.M. time signal sounded by the U.S. Armed Forces Radio network. In Paris, twenty-four miles away, Feliks did the same. Meanwhile, at the Soviet embassy in Paris, a team of KGB technicians, flown in from Moscow via Algeria, gathered in a small room on the third floor. They knew that they would have scarcely more than an hour to break the seal of the envelopes, photograph the contents, and reseal the envelopes in a manner that could not be detected.

Johnson took less than two minutes to open the three

locks to the vault. Inside, he stuffed envelopes—some eleven by thirteen inches, others eight by eleven—into the blue flight bag. Locking the vault and then the outer door of the center, he ran to his Citroën and drove off to meet Feliks. All went precisely as rehearsed. At 3:15 A.M. Johnson recovered the envelopes by the cemetery and replaced them in the vault. By the time he reached home Sunday morning, a mass of American cryptographic and military secrets—some so sensitive they were classified higher than top secret —were already en route to Moscow.

The next Saturday night, December 22, Johnson again looted the vault without the least difficulty. This time he selected new envelopes that had arrived during the preceding two or three days. About a third contained cryptographic materials.

The day after Christmas, Feliks greeted Johnson jubilantly: "On behalf of the Council of Ministers of the U.S.S.R., I have been directed to congratulate you on the great contribution you have made to peace. I am told that some of the material we sent was so interesting that it was read by Comrade Khrushchev himself. In appreciation, you have been awarded the rank of major in the Red Army. I also have been authorized to give you a bonus of $2,000. Take a holiday and go to Monte Carlo and live it up."

The supposed rank of major of course represented a fictitious award bestowed to stimulate Johnson's ego and motivate him further. But there is independent testimony to the effect that an excited Khrushchev did study the materials Johnson purveyed. Yuri Nosenko, who in 1963 was still stationed at the Center, states that the arrival of the first documents from the vault created such a sensation that rumors of a momentous new penetration in France spread through the upper echelons of the KGB. According to what he was told, the documents were adjudged so important that immediately after translation, copies were rushed to Khrushchev and certain Politburo members. Nosenko also heard that some of the stolen data disclosed numbers and locations of American nuclear warheads stored in Europe.

Clearly, the documents from the vault were extraordinary, not only because of their content but also because of their indisputable authenticity. Anyone studying them might as well have been admitted to the highest councils of the United States and been allowed to take notes. Some of the ultrasecret papers outlined major modifications or additions to the basic American strategic plan for the defense of Western Europe. No one document, by itself, provided an overall blueprint of the plan, but collectively they laid it bare to the KGB. The Soviet Union could now identify with certainty strengths to be countered and vulnerabilities that could be exploited. Great and decisive battles have been won with less intelligence than these first two penetrations yielded. And this was only the beginning.

Indeed, the initial yield was so spectacular that the Soviet Union adopted further precautions to safeguard the operation. Nosenko says that all subsequent entries into the vault required direct approval from the Politburo, and that with the approach of each, an air of tension and excitement pervaded the KGB command. This corresponds with instructions Johnson received in January 1963 from Feliks, who advised that henceforth the vault would be looted only at intervals of from four to six weeks, and that each entry would be scheduled a minimum of fourteen days in advance. "We must bring people in specially from Moscow," Feliks said. "The arrangements are very complicated."

A team of technicians was required to process the documents Johnson removed, but the KGB dared not station them permanently in Paris. It knew that French security would eventually recognize them as the specialists they were, and realize that their presence signified a leakage of considerable importance. The KGB also knew the technicians probably would be detected if they shuttled in and out of Paris too often. Therefore it chose to reduce the frequency of their journeys and to have them come to Paris individually and by various routes—via Germany, Algeria, Belgium, or Denmark.

Additionally, the KGB recognized that although Johnson had twice taken documents from the vault with ease, each penetration still entailed high risks. If anyone chanced to find him missing during the two crucial ten- to fifteen-minute absences from the center, there was no way he could explain himself. The Russians did not bother to equip him with a cover story because they knew that any excuse would be futile. Moreover, although Johnson, by virtue of his position, had become a priceless agent, the KGB had no admiration for him as a person. It knew that he was irresponsible and that if he were ever subjected to serious interrogation, he would soon collapse and confess.

The night was cold and mist-laden when Johnson met Feliks at 3:15 A.M. in late February to retrieve documents he had passed three hours before. As usual, they quickly shook hands and silently exchanged the blue flight bags. Johnson hurriedly started to drive away, but the engine of his old Citroën refused to turn over. "Let me try," Feliks insisted. Neither of them could make the weary car respond. Then they heard another automobile braking to a stop behind them. Both Feliks and Johnson jumped out and froze before the silhouette of a man approaching with a revolver. It was Viktor, who had been guarding the rendezvous from a distance. For about twenty minutes—each second increasing the probability of disaster—they struggled in vain to start the Citroën. Finally, after Viktor in his car had pushed it nearly half a mile, the engine coughed and began to run. The next week, on orders from the KGB, Johnson bought a used Mercedes with money from Moscow.

One Sunday in March, after one of Johnson's forays into the vault, he stepped out of his apartment in early afternoon to buy bread. To his astonishment, he saw both Feliks and Viktor parked near the entrance to the building. When they spotted him, they drove off without a nod of recognition or greeting. Johnson was puzzled. His entry into the vault the night before had been accomplished smoothly. Then he realized that he had forgotten to leave the cigarette package by the telephone booth to signal that he was safe.

"You cannot imagine what trouble your negligence caused," Feliks said angrily at the Wednesday critique that regularly followed each theft of documents. "To prepare for your escape, we had to alarm people all the way from Paris to Moscow. I will have to waste two days now writing reports to explain."

"Christ, I'm sorry," Johnson replied. "I just forgot."

"Never let it happen again," Feliks warned. "This is the kind of carelessness that will put you in prison."

On April 20, 1963, Johnson prepared to enter the vault for the seventh time. By now he had supplied the KGB with some ninety large envelopes filled with documents and cipher systems. Tonight he was intent on grabbing two particular envelopes that had arrived from Washington the day before. At 12:15 A.M. on April 21, Johnson handed the bagful of secrets to Feliks without incident. But at 3:15 A.M. he failed to appear by the cemetery as scheduled.

Feliks began a torturous wait. Possibly someone had come to the center, and Johnson had not yet succeeded in drugging him with the doctored cognac. Perhaps he had sustained an accident en route, or maybe he had been caught and had already told about the Russian standing on the cemetery road. Maybe at this very moment platoons of armed Americans were on their way.

About 5 A.M. Feliks realized he could wait no longer. Soon dawn would break over Orly Field, and with daylight there would be no chance of replacing the documents. Johnson would be arrested, the great operation destroyed. Feliks took the only gamble he could. He drove to Orly Field, and stopped his car no more than ten yards from the courier center. Leaving the engine running, he dropped the flight bag containing the documents into the front seat of Johnson's car. He left with little hope that his daring could overcome the catastrophe he was certain had befallen both Johnson and the KGB.

However, Johnson was not the victim of any misfortune. He simply had fallen asleep at about 2 A.M. Around 5:30 he awoke in clear daylight. Frantically, he ran to the car. There was the bag. He had just shut the vault and still had his hand on one of the locks to the outer door when someone said, "Making sure no one sneaked in on you during the night, eh?"

"You scared hell out of me!" Johnson exclaimed. "I didn't expect you until six."

"I couldn't sleep, so I thought I might as well let you off early," said the young corporal who had arrived to relieve him for breakfast.

Johnson could not force himself to admit to the KGB that he had been so stupid that he had endangered himself and the entire operation by merely falling asleep. So he concocted the story that an officer had come at 3 A.M. to pick up documents for a special delivery and had decided to take a nap before departing.

"The son of a bitch stayed until after five," he told Feliks. "There was nothing I could do."

"You couldn't persuade him to take a drink?" Feliks calmly asked.

"Hell, no. I tried, but he claimed he was on duty and couldn't drink."

"I see," Feliks remarked. "It must have been a difficult time."

"You can say that again," Johnson replied, thinking that his lies had been accepted.

They had not been. The KGB was aware that withdrawals from the center were never made on Sunday, and that no officer in any case could remove documents without submitting to inventory control by a second officer. Therefore, it well knew that Johnson was lying. But it could not imagine why. Least of all could it imagine the truth.

Thus in doubt, the KGB decided in May to retire temporarily from the game while it still was an immense winner. The KGB had gained minute knowledge of the NATO defense system, and beyond that had information about what the United States intended to do in a variety of world contingencies. It had discovered hidden discords among NATO partners that the Soviet Union could exacerbate. And it had learned which Soviet weaknesses the West had secretly pinpointed. Some of the damage the loss of these secrets inflicted upon the United States was irreparable. Nothing, for example, could nullify the insights into American cipher methods gained by Soviet cryptologists. However, much of the value of what the KGB had

stolen depended upon keeping the United States ignorant of the thefts. Should the Americans find out, they
could begin repairing the damage, though at great cost,
by revising plans and redistributing forces. Thus, until
it knew the real reason for Johnson's lie, the KGB
wanted to take no more risks.

Feliks explained the suspension to Johnson on the
basis that with the coming of summer, the nights would
be too short. "We don't want to take any unnecessary
risks; you are much too valuable," he said. "We can
resume in the fall when the nights are again long and
dark."

During the summer, the KGB found no evidence
that Johnson had compromised himself, and it prepared to resume operations in the fall. It was reassured
when Johnson received a promotion in September.
But to its dismay, with the promotion came a transfer
to the Seine Area Command in Sainte-Honorine. The
vault had been rifled for the last time.

In May 1964, the Army sent Johnson to the Penta-
gon to be near Hedy, who had been flown to Walter
Reed Hospital for psychiatric treatment. Just before
leaving France, he dined with Feliks and Viktor in
Paris. "Do you know what your duties will be at the
Pentagon?" Feliks asked.

"Well, in this outfit you never know for sure until
you get there," Johnson replied. "But I hear I might be
working for the courier service."

"Just what does that mean?" inquired Feliks.

"More of the same old shit, I guess," mumbled Johnson. "Shuffling secret papers, hauling 'em around."

Both Feliks and Viktor beamed over such unbelievable luck. "Well, that could be a very interesting assignment for us," Viktor commented.

"Yes, you must do all you can to gain that assignment," Feliks chimed in. "Perhaps your wife could
help. Perhaps she could entertain officers who have influence." Somewhat embarrassed by his own suggestion, he added, "Of course, by 'entertain' I mean she
could have parties at your home."

"Yeah, you bastard, I know what you mean," Johnson responded.

A KGB GALLERY OF AGENTS, ASSASSINS, SEDUCTRESSES AND VICTIMS.

The main building of KGB headquarters on Dzerzhinsky Square in Moscow. The old portion of the structure, on the left, housed offices of the All-Russian Insurance Company before the Revolution. It was occupied by the Cheka in 1918. The notorious Lubyanka Prison is inside this part of the building. The addition, on the right, was built by political prisoners and captured German soldiers after World War II.

The new headquarters that most elements of the KGB First Chief Directorate, responsible for foreign operations, moved into in the summer of 1972. The building is hidden off the circum-ferential highway outside Moscow, much as the U.S. Central Intelligence Agency headquarters is sequestered in the Virginia countryside near the highway encircling Washington. Soviet designers also seem to have been very much influenced by CIA architecture.

Yuri Andropov,
chairman of the KGB

General Anatoli
Ivanovich Lazarev,
chief of the KGB
Illegals Department
and a former operative
in France

vasili Romanovich
Sitnikov, deputy
director of the KGB
Disinformation
Department

Nikolai A. Korznikov,
deputy director of the
KGB Illegals Department

Soviet Ambassador to Morocco Sergei Petrovich
Kiktev and his wife. A veteran of subversive
operations in the Arab world, Kiktev hastily fled
Afghanistan in September, 1972, after a prominent
anticommunist editor was murdered by assassins
traveling in a Soviet jeep and firing Soviet
weapons.

Former United Nations Secretary General U Thant
and his personal assistant, KGB officer Viktor
Lessiovsky. Engaging and gregarious, Lessiovsky
used the U.N. sanctuary for a variety of KGB
activities until his departure from New York
in 1973.

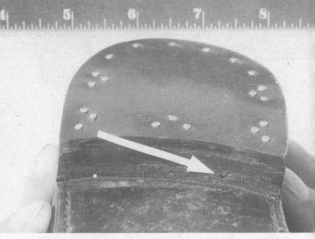

Shoe worn by a U.S. diplomat stationed at the American embassy in Bucharest. The arrow points to a tiny hole housing a pin that a maid could depress to turn the hidden transmitter on or off.

Removal of the lower part of the heel reveals the transmitter implanted when the diplomat sent his shoes for repair.

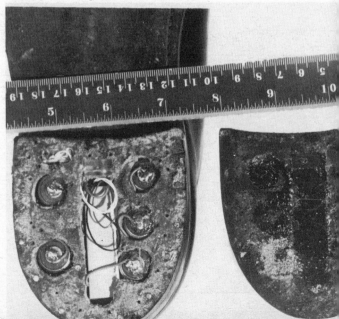

KGB General Yevgenni Petrovich Pitovranov, senior vice president of the Soviet Chamber of Commerce, who concentrates on subversion of Western businessmen seeking to trade with the Soviet bloc. He is considered one of the three or four most gifted officers in the KGB.

Vladimir Pavlovich Pavlichenko, a United Nations employee who has specialized in disinformation and recruitment operations in the American academic community. Although the New York _Times_ exposed him as a KGB officer in October, 1971, the U.N. promptly renewed his employment contract.

Mikhail Stepanovich Tsymbal (alias Rogov), deputy director of KGB foreign operations. As KGB Resident in Paris from 1953 to 1959, he developed agents of influence and helped spread disinformation extremely damaging to the Western alliance.

Vladimir Aleksandrovich Chuchukin, a KGB officer assigned to work against Western journalists under the cover of a United Nations appointment

(UPPER LEFT) Assassination weapons produced by
the KGB laboratory in Moscow for use by Captain
Nikolai Khokhlov.

(LOWER LEFT) Dismantled, the cigarette case
yields an electric pistol designed to fire
poisoned bullets noiselessly.

(ABOVE) The battery-powered pistol given to
Khokhlov fired both poisoned and dumdum bullets.

FILATOV SHADRIN'S WIFE SHADRIN WITH BRIEFCASE
BEFORE EXCHANGE IN PARK

SHADRIN'S WIFE FILATOV & WIFE SOLIS SHADRIN

(UPPER LEFT) A surveillance camera photographs a Soviet team en route to a clandestine meeting at a park in Quito, Ecuador, in January, 1971. At far right of photo, KGB Resident Anatoli Mikhailovich Shadrin strides ahead carrying a black briefcase. Shadrin is followed by his wife and GRU Resident Robespier Nikolaevich Filatov.

(LOWER LEFT) The Russians tarry in a small park, as if enjoying a casual outing. Awaiting them there is Jose Raphael Solis Castro, an Ecuadorian Communist leader, who stands (partly obscured) close to Shadrin at far right of photo

(BELOW) The Russians and Solis leave the park. Solis now has the KGB briefcase. Shadrin and Filatov were expelled in July, 1971, for trying to incite labor strife and otherwise interfering in Ecuadorian internal affairs.

FILATOV   SHADRIN'S   FILATOV'S   SOLIS   SHADRIN
           WIFE   WIFE

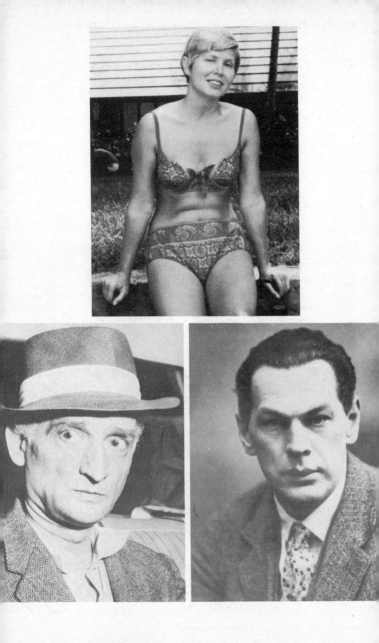

(FACING TOP) Raya Kiselnikova, a one-time secretary and intimate of senior KGB officers at the Soviet embassy in Mexico City.

(FACING LEFT) William Fisher (alias Colonel Rudolf Abel), the KGB illegal arrested by the FBI for espionage in 1957 and exchanged for U-2 pilot Francis Gary Powers in 1962.

(FACING RIGHT) Richard Sorge, one of the most valuable Soviet agents of all time. A native of Russia who became a German citizen, he worked as a correspondent in Tokyo and made himself the confidant of two German ambassadors. He provided the Soviets with advance warning of the 1941 German invasion and later intelligence that permitted the Red Army to rush troops from Siberia to defend Moscow. The Japanese executed Sorge in 1944.

(BELOW) Yuri Nikolaevich Loginov, who spent eight years preparing to be a spy in the United States. South African authorities arrested him in 1967 in Johannesburg, where he was familiarizing himself with scenes that were to be part of his fictitious past when he came to America. He was freed in return for the release of ten West German citizens held in East Germany.

Anatoli Borisovich Gorsky (alias Gromov) as he appeared in the mid-1940's when he was the case officer of Soviet spies Harold A. R. Philby, Guy Burgess and Donald Maclean

Gorsky (alias Professor Nikitin) as he looks today, in Moscow, where he conducts KGB disinformation operations against foreign diplomats and visitors

Robert Lee Johnson, the sergeant who became one of the most devastating KGB agents ever uncovered in the United States armed forces

James Allen Mintkenbaugh, a KGB agent and confederate of Johnson

The Soviet embassy in Mexico City which is staffed largely by KGB and GRU officers.

(BELOW LEFT) Oleg Nechiporenko and his wife, Lydia, who used her husband's authority to intimidate and degrade other Soviet wives at the embassy in Mexico City.

(BELOW RIGHT) Raya Kiselnikova at a press conference in Mexico City. After her defection in February, 1970, she provided details about the KGB's exploitation of Mexico City as a base for espionage and subversion in the Western Hemisphere.

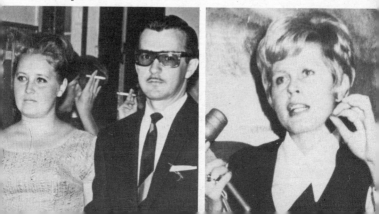

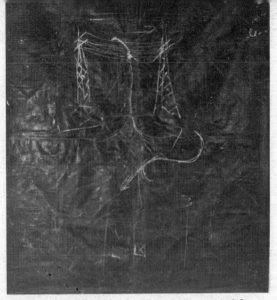

(ABOVE) Early in 1971 a Mexican constable discovered some young men in a shack gathered around a crude blackboard. He arrested them when they belligerently refused to answer his questions about their drawing. Subsequent interrogation yielded clues to an incipient KGB guerrilla operation in Mexico. The blackboard and drawing (left) show electrical transmission towers the guerrillas were training to sabotage.

(BELOW LEFT) Fabricio Gómez Souza, a Mexican schoolteacher recruited by the KGB while studying at Patrice Lumumba University

(BELOW RIGHT) Angel Bravo Cisneros, a deputy guerrilla leader whose confessions helped the Mexican government destroy the KGB operation.

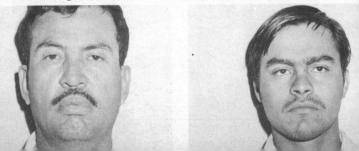

(UPPER LEFT) Kaarlo Tuomi in 1951

(UPPER RIGHT) Aleksei Ivanovich Galkin, one of
Kaarlo Tuomi's mentors in Moscow

Tuomi (left) at the riverbank reunion with
Galkin, as photographed by the FBI with a
telescopic lens.

Ukrainian exile leader
Stefan Bandera in life

Lev Rebet, murdered by
KGB assassin Bogdan
Stashinsky

Bandera in his
funeral bier,
after assassination
by Stashinsky

"In any case, rent a nice house," Feliks said. "Modest but nice. Concentrate the first months on learning all about your work and the procedures in your office. Do nothing, absolutely nothing, that might arouse suspicion." They parted with an understanding that Johnson would meet a KGB representative at La Guardia Airport in New York on December 1, 1964.

Johnson did rent a pleasant brick house on a tree-lined street in Alexandria, Virginia, and after her release from the hospital, Hedy joined him, seemingly much better. Coming home from the Pentagon one afternoon in July, he stopped on Columbia Pike in Arlington to buy a pizza for dinner. While he stood in line, a man called to him from the doorway. "How are you, Bob?" They were the same words with which Mintkenbaugh had greeted him in Berlin, in Las Vegas, in Orléans.

Reunited over beer and pizza that evening, Johnson and Mintkenbaugh recounted their espionage experiences since they had last seen each other five years before. Mintkenbaugh had performed a variety of useful if unspectacular chores for the KGB. He lived six week in Canada collecting birth certificates and other documents for use by KGB illegals infiltrating into the United States. Eventually he became a real-estate salesman in Arlington, a job that enabled him to supply the Russians with information about government employees looking for housing. He also had much free time. During the Cuban missile crisis of October 1962, the KGB dispatched him on an emergency trip to report about a massive military mobilization in southern Florida.

"Well, I'm gonna see them again in December," Johnson confided. But he soon forgot about the Russians, his duties at the Pentagon, and everything else. In September, Hedy's spasms of insanity and jealousy had returned with such a violence that fear of them obsessed him. Once, in a restaurant, she fancied that a woman at a nearby table was courting Johnson's attention. Suddenly she jumped up, threw over the table, and began pulling the woman's hair with one hand while slapping her with the other. In a supermarket she

imagined that Johnson was flirting with a shopping
housewife. Stealthily, she slipped up behind him and
kicked him so hard that he stumbled forward, knocked
over a display of canned goods, and sprawled in the
aisle on his face. Shrieking vile language, she created
terrifying scenes. All the while, day and night, she demanded impossible sexual feats of Johnson. In self-
defense, he urged her to return to prostitution. Such
proposals only worsened her condition and intensified
the ferocity of her onslaughts against him. So on the
afternoon of October 2, 1964, after failing to have
Hedy committed at the hospital, Johnson chose to flee.

At the Old Dominion Bank in Arlington, he withdrew $2,200 in savings, then drove aimlessly about un-
til he saw a highway sign pointing to Richmond, Virginia. There he abandoned his car, bought a bottle of
whisky, and embarked on a drunken bus journey to
Las Vegas via Cincinnati, St. Louis, and Denver. In
Las Vegas he rented a dingy little room for $24 a
month and began to gamble.

Thirty days after Johnson vanished, the Army classified him as a deserter and asked law-enforcement
agencies, including the FBI, to track him down. Two
FBI agents called on Hedy in quest of routine information. Though obviously disturbed, she answered
their questions more or less rationally. She acknowledged that she and her husband had been quarreling a
lot, but professed concern about his disappearance and
welfare. It looked like the most mundane of cases—an
Army sergeant off on a binge, in quest of respite from
the nagging of a mentally ill wife. In view of the available evidence, no one could have reproached the two
FBI men if they had simply filed their report and considered their duty done. They chose, however, to explore the case a little further. Within a few days they
discovered that while being treated at Walter Reed,
Hedy had called her husband a spy.

"Mrs. Johnson, we wonder if there isn't something
troubling you, something you would like to talk about,"
one of the agents said during a second visit.

"Oh, there is," Hedy replied. "But if I tell, they'll
kill me."

"Who will kill you?" the agent asked.

"The Russians," she answered. "And they'll kill my papa too."

"Why don't you tell us about it and let us try to help you?" the agent said.

The three of them sat in silence for perhaps two full minutes while Hedy kept her head bowed and her hands over her face. "My husband, he's a bad man," she finally said. "And Hedy is a very bad girl."

"What do you mean, Mrs. Johnson?" the agent asked.

"He's a spy," she said. "And so am I. And I know someone else who is too."

The appalling narrative Hedy then offered was sometimes incoherent, often rambling, and inherently incredible. She confused dates and places, and on occasion her memory failed entirely. Yet, deranged as she was, Hedy offered too many specific details to be ignored. Those fragments of her story which could be subjected to verification through quick consultation with military authorities proved to be true.

Doubt diminished and alarm multiplied the next morning when the FBI agents went to Mintkenbaugh's Arlington apartment. He too had disappeared. The FBI found him three days later hiding at an old address in northern California. Pale and trembling, he denied any involvement in espionage. But on being confronted with specific allegations, he began to sob and confess. His confession continued for days, interrupted by his tearful attempts to explain himself.

"I couldn't understand for a long time why I was doing it," Mintkenbaugh told the FBI. "Now I know that revenge got into me. You see, God makes mistakes, and I'm one of them. I wish I had died as a baby."

The accounts of Hedy and Mintkenbaugh conclusively demonstrated that Johnson was a spy, and Hedy made some indecipherable references to secret documents. But neither she nor Mintkenbaugh knew about the looting of the vault. To the Defense Department and FBI, the critical question remained: What had Johnson given the Russians? Only he and the KGB

had the answer. Now FBI teletypes advised field offices throughout the country that apprehension of
Johnson was of urgent national importance.

While FBI agents and police watched for him at
airports, rail and bus terminals, bars, and hotels, Johnson on the morning of November 25, 1964, awoke
despondent and groggy from alcohol. The day before,
he had pawned his last two salable possessions, a
trench coat and a German army knife. He reached in
his pocket and counted all the money he had left—
four pennies. Unshaven and bedraggled, he walked into a police station in Reno, identified himself as a
deserter, and surrendered. The police locked him in a
cell with an old one-legged vagabond.

The military police escorted Johnson to Washington
and eventually he confessed. He evinced not the least
remorse or even any awareness that he had done anything very wrong. It was not until an interrogator mentioned the possibility of execution that Johnson seemed
to worry. "Listen, you guys are going about this the
wrong way," he said. "I can do you fellows a lot of
good."

"What do you mean?" asked an FBI agent.

"I can be a counterspy," Johnson answered seriously.

Two FBI agents and two Army officers present
stared at him in disbelief, perhaps the same kind of
disbelief with which KGB officers had regarded him
twelve years before in Karlshorst when he proposed
that he be made a commentator on Radio Moscow.
During hundreds of subsequent interrogations, Johnson seemed to enjoy reliving his life as a KGB agent,
and he supplied the FBI with mountainous details
about it.

On July 30, 1965, in the Federal District Court at
Alexandria, Johnson and Mintkenbaugh were each
sentenced to twenty-five years' imprisonment. They
pleaded guilty to conspiracy charges, and no evidence
was presented in court. From the brief proceedings,
the public derived no intimation of the enormity of
the losses the United States had sustained. In Moscow,
meanwhile, Paula, Viktor, Feliks, and at least four
other KGB officers who participated in the Johnson-

Mintkenbaugh operation were awarded the Order of Lenin, the highest decoration of the Soviet Union.

Because Johnson could not identify all the documents he delivered to the KGB, the United States had to assume that the Russians had copied every one that passed through the courier center between December 15, 1962, and April 21, 1963. The Army needed months just to trace them all. Many more weeks were required to assess the full consequences of their theft. On grounds of national security, the Department of Defense declines to comment about the possibility that the documents enabled the KGB to break American cipher systems. It also refuses to discuss the countermeasures that had to be adopted.

"It is accurate to characterize our losses as enormous. Some are irreparable and incalculable," a Department of Defense spokesman has stated. "It is also impossible to reckon precisely in dollars the cost of repairing that damage which would be repaired. There is, however, a more fundamental consideration. Had we not discovered the losses, and had there been war, the damage might very well have been fatal."

The story and consequences of Johnson's espionage did not end with his imprisonment. The West German magazines *Stern* and *Der Spiegel* in September 1969 published articles purportedly based on authentic copies of top-secret U.S. contingency plans. The contents of the alleged plans as reported by the magazines were enough to horrify friends and foes of America alike. For they suggested that should Soviet forces overrun Western Europe, the United States intended to devastate the continent by waging bacteriological and nuclear warfare against the civilian population.

Circulation of the alleged documents bore some basic and familiar characteristics of a KGB disinformation operation. They earlier had been mailed to other European journals and first appeared in a publication in Italy, *Paese Sera,* to which no one paid any attention. Subsequently the "documents" were mailed from Rome to the two German magazines by an unknown source whose signature was illegible. The "documents" were not originals but copies, and therefore not subject to technical tests that could prove them to be either authentic or bogus. *Der Spiegel* asserted that they were circulated as part of a KGB disinformation operation. Nevertheless, the reported American plans engendered alarm in Western Europe and doubtless sowed much distrust of the United States.

In its issue dated February 1, 1970, *Stern* published an even more incendiary article ostensibly based on another top-secret American document, *Handbook of Nuclear Yield Requirements,* which it said came from a "Big Unknown." Excerpts from this alleged document showed that the United States, in event of war, intended to blow up more than a thousand civilian targets in Egypt, Syria, Iraq, and even Iran, as well as in Western and Eastern Europe. Another understandable anti-American furore ensued.

Time and study have usually permitted American authorities to expose Soviet forgeries as such, by citing errors in style or terminology. But the "documents" the KGB disseminated in 1969 and 1970 were almost perfect in form—because the Russians were able to pattern them after similar, authentic documents Johnson had mined from the vault.* With an original of the *Handbook of Nuclear Requirements,* which did enumerate Soviet-bloc targets, the KGB easily added targets in Western European and neutral nations.

The story of Robert Lee Johnson finally ended May 18, 1972. Johnson and Hedy had a son, Robert, whom I had not intended to mention. Events now require otherwise.

The illness of Hedy and the character of Johnson made their home a hell, and Robert was eventually placed in a foster home. He joined the Army at nineteen and fought in Vietnam, and there he began to brood about his traitor father.

---

*The KGB did make one error in its version of the *Handbook.* According to *Stern,* the document contained a special caveat: "The information contained in this document must not fall into the hands of foreign citizens or their representatives." Any one familiar with U.S. security classifications will recognize the fraudulence of this phraseology. Documents whose circulation is supposed to be restricted solely to U.S. personnel simply are labeled "NOFORN"—meaning "No Foreigners."

Johnson must have been pleased when notified that Robert, back from Vietnam, wished to visit him on Thursday afternoon, May 18. Robert had come to see him at the Federal penitentiary in Lewisburg, Pennsylvania, only once before, and had written rarely. Smiling, Johnson walked into the prison reception room and reached to shake hands with his son. Without a word, Robert lunged at him and plunged a knife deep into his chest. Johnson died within the hour. He was fifty-two.

Robert has consistently refused to explain. To the FBI he will only say, "It was a personal matter."

XI

THE PLOT TO DESTROY MEXICO

Just before midnight on March 12, 1971, five of the most important men in the government of Mexico met at the National Palace. A senior intelligence officer distributed a formal report and a stack of photographs. Silently the officials studied the documents, at first with dismay, then with the anger of men betrayed.

The import of what the Mexican leaders read was staggering. The detailed intelligence summary revealed a KGB plot conceived in Moscow to plunge Mexico into a civil war and destroy its government by armed force. In the words of a Mexican servant of the KGB, it would make of Mexico "another Vietnam."

In an epic counterintelligence coup, the Mexican security service had uncovered not only the Soviet plan but the identities of the principal KGB officers and Mexican agents involved. Security men had seized caches of arms and explosives, located clandestine training centers and hideouts, and captured guerrilla chieftains. It was a near thing. For the evidence showed that soon the first fires were to be set, the first bombs detonated, the first policemen killed.

"We will, of course, act—and act decisively," declared the President of Mexico, Luis Echeverría Alvarez.

The adviser who had drafted the intelligence report spoke up quickly. "Strike at the embassy, Mr. President. All begins with the embassy. And with Nechiporenko. He is Número Uno."

It was true. During the 1960s the KGB had completely taken over the Soviet embassy in Mexico City and developed it into one of the world's great sanctuaries of subversion. And of all the Russians, the most skilled and dangerous was Oleg Maksimovich Nechiporenko, justifiably considered by the KGB to be one of its top agents.

Slender and darkly handsome, he cultivated a debonair mustache, and with his wavy black hair and olive complexion looked utterly Latin. Indeed, Mexican authorities theorized that he was either the child of Spanish communists who had fled to Russia after the Spanish civil war or perhaps the son of a Russian father and a Spanish mother. He kept himself in superb condition by jogging daily and playing tennis the year around. Strangers often guessed him to be ten years younger than his actual age—forty. His Spanish was flawless; he spoke the idioms of laborers, diplomats, and students with equal fluency. Westerners found him charming, quick-witted, and inordinately aggressive. Alone among the Russians, he understood that the best way for any foreigner to approach any Mexican is with respect.

Nechiporenko had trained himself to adapt, chameleonlike, to disparate environments. He could and sometimes did don the clothes of a *campesino,* go out into the countryside, and win automatic acceptance as a farmer or laborer. Similarly, at the universities, where he spent many of his working hours, students thought of him as one of themselves. With the same ease, he could affect the manners of a bright young Mexican business or professional man. He once assumed just such a pose and strode into the United States embassy. For more than an hour he wandered about, gleaning what information he could, until a security officer recognized him as a KGB officer.

Nechiporenko simply was the best KGB field operative in Latin America. He knew it; so did everybody else in the embassy. Few KGB officers, though, felt comfortable around him. He disdained intellectual inferiors and scarcely condescended to speak to the Russians he considered stupid or unimportant. Sometimes he insulted colleagues by ignoring a dull comment and walking away without a word. But the primary reason no one relaxed around Nechiporenko was that he also was the SK officer—the officer charged with preserving the security of the *Sovyetskaya koloniya,* or Soviet colony, in Mexico.

In that capacity, he constantly scrutinized everyone for the least portent of disaffection or psychological breakdown. KGB officers, conditioned from their earliest training to watch each other, realized that in his eyes deviation from prescribed behavior had to be cause for official suspicion. So they feared Nechiporenko, and he had almost no real friends. He was not the kind who needed them.

Nechiporenko had arrived in Mexico City with his wife and two small children in 1961. Although he had been thoroughly briefed in Moscow, the life and routine of the embassy still demanded some unexpected adjustments. The embassy itself surprised and amused him. Everything about it reeked of conspiracy.

A somber gray Victorian villa with ornate cupolas and shuttered windows, it stood partially hidden behind trees at Calzada de Tacubaya 204. A tall iron fence encircled the grounds, which armed sentries patrolled. At night an armed guard paced the roof. A concealed camera photographed everyone admitted through the gate. At embassy receptions, guards ensured that no guests ventured beyond the reception rooms on the first floor. Foreigners never were allowed in the small, sterile offices and apartments on the second floor.

But the most inaccessible area of the embassy was a large section of the third floor known among KGB officers as the "dungeon." This was the Referentura, the heart and brain of any Soviet embassy. Here all operations of the KGB were planned and administered. Here the secrets of Soviet subversion in the Western Hemisphere were stored.

Testimony of Russians who have fled from Soviet embassies in various countries indicates that Referenturas the world over are much the same. They normally are divided into soundproofed rooms designed for conferences, study, and the drafting of messages. The most restricted area houses the files as well as cipher and radio equipment for communications with Moscow. No documents may ever be removed from a Referentura; no briefcases, cameras, or recording equipment ever brought in. A Referentura staff includes a chief, his deputy, and cipher personnel who live under virtual house arrest. Rarely does the KGB permit them to leave the embassy grounds, and then only in a group accompanied by armed security personnel.

To enter the Referentura in Mexico City, an officer walked down a narrow corridor and pressed a buzzer that opened the door of an antechamber and signaled his approach to the watch. At the end of the chamber was a steel door with a peephole through which he was inspected.

All outside windows of the Referentura had been blocked out with cement to block long-range electronic or photographic surveillance. KGB officers complained that with sunlight and fresh air thus shut out, the atmosphere inside was perpetually dark, dank, and musty. They grumbled also because, as a result of this dungeonlike atmosphere, smoking was forbidden.

The Referentura never closed. And during the ensuing years, Nechiporenko was to come to it at all hours of the day and night. It was the one place in Mexico where he could feel completely secure and speak of his work freely.

In Moscow the KGB had advised Nechiporenko that his wife would be expected to "help out" at the embassy. He did not understand that this meant a fulltime job. Because the KGB refused to permit employment of even one Mexican, most Soviet wives had to labor as secretaries, file clerks, telephone operators, typists, or petty administrators.

When a reception was held at the embassy, a list of duties for the wives was posted. Some were to attend as guests, some as maids, and others as kitchen helpers. Nechiporenko had to inform his wife that at her first party in Mexico she would be a maid. After the guests left, he and all the other Russian men waited around while their wives did the dishes.

Nechiporenko soon accepted, as necessary to securi-

ty, the rules that bound all Russians in Mexico City.
He perceived that the embassy, regarded by the KGB
as one of its four or five most important installations
outside the Soviet Union, offered boundless professional opportunities. Energetically he set out to make the
most of them.

His work began in the Referentura with study and
briefings about some of the KGB operations against
Mexico. They revealed that the KGB was less interested
in collecting intelligence about the country than in developing agents who could influence Mexican policies
and create disorder. In 1959 it almost had succeeded
in bringing significant segments of the Mexican economy to a standstill. That year the KGB bribed the labor leader Demetrio Vallejo to paralyze the national
railway system with wildcat strikes. Caught consorting
with KGB officers Nikolai M. Remizov and Nikolai V.
Aksenov, Vallejo admitted taking a million pesos
($80,000) from them to organize the strikes.

Nechiporenko saw that now the KGB was attempting to plant female agents in key secretarial positions
within the most important government ministries. It
also was seeking to position in the Foreign Ministry
an agent who could affect assignments of Mexican diplomats throughout the world. In an even more sinister
operation, the KGB was trying to establish its own
private detective force, composed of a corrupt ex-
police official and cashiered cops. Through them it
planned to gather data for blackmailing Mexicans, to
harass anti-Castro Cuban exiles, and to execute "wet
affairs."

Nechiporenko was to be involved in all these operations. But his primary assignment was to infiltrate the
universities and recruit students for future subversion.
Prospects usually were spotted through the Communist Party or the Institute of Mexican-Russian Cultural
Exchange. The latter was directed by the Soviet cultural attaché, a KGB officer; it was financed by the
KGB; its daily affairs were administered by Mexican
communists handpicked by the KGB. Openly, the Institute disseminated Soviet propaganda and sponsored
meetings of communist sympathizers. Covertly, it

served other functions. With offices strategically located throughout the country, it offered KGB officers a ready pretext to travel to any section of Mexico. Youths attracted by its films, book exhibits, and free lessons in Russian unknowingly were evaluated by the KGB. Those who appeared particularly promising eventually were approached and offered scholarships to Patrice Lumumba Friendship University in Moscow, where the KGB could develop their potential for subversion.

Hearing about the scholarships, an embittered Mexican named Fabricio Gómez Souza addressed an inquiry to the Soviet embassy. Invited to the Institute's office in Mexico City for an interview, he arrived on a summer afternoon in 1963 and was courteously greeted in Spanish by Nechiporenko.

"There is nothing I care to say to you," Gómez announced. "I came to see the Russians." Nechiporenko coolly surveyed the Mexican, spoke a few sentences in Russian, then said in Spanish: "I am Russian. Now please sit down and let me see if I can help you."

Gómez was a squat, muscular thirty-one-year-old schoolteacher with black eyes and a scowling, swarthy face. Since finishing college ten years before, he had taught school in the small town of Nanchital. Long interested in communism, he had read extensively about Marxist and other revolutionary theory. Early in 1963 he married. While still honeymooning, his bride fell ill and died of an ailment that doctors could not diagnose. In his grief and rage, Gómez blamed Mexico, its culture and institutions, for failing to provide the kind of medical care that might have saved her life. Now he believed that Mexican society must be destroyed so that it might be rebuilt, and he had concluded that the most practical way to destroy it was to work with the Russians.

As the two men talked late into the evening, Nechiporenko knew that here was a man for the KGB. Gómez was no posturing student caught up in a fad. Rather, he emerged in Nechiporenko's judgment as a tough, realistic convert whose malicious motivation of the moment could be harnessed, a man who could be trained to endure, obey, and do whatever was necessary for the KGB.

So strong was Nechiporenko's recommendation that the KGB acted swiftly to spirit Gómez out of the country. Processing by the KGB for Patrice Lumumba ordinarily required months. But within three weeks Nechiporenko handed Gómez cash for a flight to Moscow. From the moment he landed, the KGB treated him as a very special student, as indeed he was: Fabricio Gómez Souza was destined to lead the guerrilla force that the Soviet Union years later was to unleash upon Mexico.

During the next two years, Nechiporenko sent at least a dozen others off to Moscow and at the same time recruited agents for the KGB directly from Mexican universities. Yet the Center kept demanding more. From his own briefings in Moscow, Nechiporenko could understand why.

The pressure reflected the KGB's judgment that Mexico was the most important target in Latin America, not only because of its proximity to the United States but also because of the great potential of its abundant natural resources and varied climate. A succession of national administrations had been making dramatic social and economic progress. Allocating more money to education than to any other purpose, the government reduced adult illiteracy from 63 percent in 1940 to 17 percent in 1970. Between 1960 and 1970, annual per capita income increased from $330 to $660.

Poverty, exacerbated by rapid population growth, endured. But the average Mexican, who enjoyed incomparably more freedom than a Soviet citizen, could see proof of continuing betterment and thereby derive hope for the future. Thus, if Soviet subversion was to succeed in Mexico, this government had to be undermined.

Accordingly, in the mid-1960s the KGB slipped more and more officers into Mexico City in the guise of diplomats. In the fall of 1966 it assigned one of its best staff specialists in Latin-American affairs as Resident. He was Boris Pavlovich Kolomyakov, an officer who, like Nechiporenko, had never suffered serious failure.

At forty-seven, Kolomyakov was nearly bald but trim and vigorous. Comfortable with authority and responsibility, he was proud of his assignment and of his reputation. He was known in Moscow as the complete professional, a perfectionist ruthlessly intolerant of mistakes by others or himself. The first to arrive at the embassy and the last to leave, he worked and studied constantly, daily reading as many as twenty Mexican, U.S., and Canadian newspapers. No matter what the pressures of work, he reserved at least half an hour a day to improve his English, and his wife privately complained to others that he spent too much of their money on books and periodicals.

In purely personal matters, Kolomyakov was kind. An inflexible caste system prevailed throughout the Soviet colony, rank being the sole determinant of perquisites and social standing. The few nonintelligence personnel were the outcasts, openly referred to as "lesser mortals." Kolomyakov flouted these distinctions. An illness in any Soviet family brought a visit from him, flowers, and assurances of all help needed. He lent money readily and could be a compassionate counselor when marital difficulties arose.

If Kolomyakov was kind to his subordinates personally, he was mercilessly demanding of them professionally. He required that all match his own energy and insisted upon measurable "production," which he could chart and report to Moscow. Laxity or errors evoked withering reprimands that could turn even veteran KGB officers pale. Once he summoned a highly regarded subordinate and upbraided him for nearly an hour. When the officer emerged from his office, a secretary saw him weeping. Three days later, he abruptly departed for the Soviet Union. His banishment was never explained officially; the rumor that swept through the embassy was simply, "He failed."

By 1968 the number of Russians over whom Kolomyakov presided at the embassy had grown to a preposterous fifty-seven, all but eight of whom were professional intelligence officers or co-opted agents. The

Soviet embassy staff was more than three times as large as those of the embassies of Great Britain, West Germany, France, or Japan. And while these nations have extensive trade and other ties with Mexico requiring diplomatic representation, the Soviet Union had virtually none.

Among Mexico's world trading partners, the Soviet Union in 1968 ranked almost last. That year it purchased only $368 worth of Mexican goods. There were only 216 legal travelers between the two countries. Few Soviet ships called at Mexican ports. Cultural relations between the two nations were virtually nonexistent, and Mexico found that it needed only five diplomats in Moscow.

Indeed, the Russians barely bothered to pretend that they were engaged in diplomacy. Weeks often passed without any Soviet "diplomat" making an official visit to a Mexican government office. The Russians opened their consular and cultural offices only four hours a week. Thus, armored with the protection of diplomatic status, they were almost entirely free to attend to their real business, which was subversion.

More than half the KGB personnel were engaged primarily in operations against the United States, but a sizable contingent, led by Nechiporenko, worked exclusively against Mexico. By 1968 they had developed in the universities a corps of agents who gave the KGB a new capability for violence. As the 1968 Olympic Games approached, the KGB perceived a way to use these youthful agents with devastating effect.

The trouble began with a commonplace incident on July 23 when dozens of students from two preparatory schools got into a brawl. Police intervened to break it up and bloodied some heads. On July 26 the Young Communist Party staged a long-planned rally to celebrate the Cuban revolution and demand the release of Demetrio Vallejo, the labor leader bribed by the KGB to instigate railroad strikes. When the young communists attempted to march on the National Palace, the police moved to halt them, the communists attacked with clubs and rocks, and another brawl ensued.

Demonstrations called to protest "police brutality"

culminated in destructive rioting the next three nights as mobs shattered windows, set buses afire, and hurled Molotov cocktails in downtown Mexico City. A quickly formed National Strike Council appealed to all Mexican students to boycott classes. Students seized the National University and the Polytechnic Institute, whose combined enrollment exceeded 120,000. In August these schools became sanctuaries from which a band of zealots sallied forth to demonstrate and riot. As the violence intensified, foreign journalists speculated that the Olympics, scheduled to begin on October 12, El Día de la Raza or Columbus Day, might have to be canceled.

After the initial outbreaks in July, only a minute fraction of the thousands of rioters were communists; fewer still had ever heard of the KGB. Usually, however, the actual violence was initiated by so-called Brigadas de Choque, or shock brigades. These were disciplined groups of fifteen to thirty men, often including paid thugs. Many were organized, financed, and led by members of the Young Communist Party or youths directed by the KGB through the Institute for Mexican-Russian Cultural Exchange. Communists constituted only a small minority on the two-hundred-member National Strike Council. Yet eight of the most vigorous, effective, and intransigent leaders in the disturbances were agents of the KGB—four of them recruited by Nechiporenko.

During the turmoil, the KGB maintained contact with its young agents through the Communist Party. Moreover, the second week in September, KGB agent Boris N. Voskoboynikov, who masqueraded as Soviet cultural attaché, rendezvoused with students outside Preparatory School No. 1. And KGB officer Valentin Loginov, the same week, met two separate groups of students near a downtown theater.

As the disturbances continued, the army on September 18 took over the National University, across the street from the Olympic Stadium. The next week Mexico suffered its worst violence since the revolutionary battles of the 1920s. Students and adult anarchists managed to acquire large quantities of arms, and fierce gunfights broke out nightly between them and troops. Around schools, students battled police with pistols, knives, clubs, and gasoline bombs.

Disaster appeared imminent when the government learned that riot leaders were secretly planning a climactic assault on the Polytechnic Institute, now occupied by the army. Their purpose was to create casualties and chaos that would doom the Olympics once and for all. Preparing for the attack, they stored, in apartments of the sprawling Tlatelolco housing project, explosives and hundreds of weapons, including .22-caliber machine guns and high-powered rifles with telescopic sights.

The afternoon of October 2, some six thousand youths gathered for a rally in the Plaza of Three Cultures, adjacent to the apartment project. The government authorized a rally but stationed troops in the vicinity to prevent any march. The gathering was peaceful enough until the eighth speaker took the podium. He was Sócrates Amado Campos Lemus, a radical fugitive whom authorities had hunted for weeks. As plainclothesmen moved to arrest him, an army helicopter dropped a flare, signaling the troops to advance into the plaza.

Using a bullhorn, General José Hernández Toledo declared the rally over and urged the students to disband. Suddenly, volleys of sniper fire rang out from apartment balconies, and Hernández was critically wounded by three bullets, two in the back, one in a leg.

A terrible battle lasted about ten minutes, with troops shooting up into the balconies at the snipers and the revolutionaries spraying bullets down into the plaza. Twenty-six civilians and two soldiers, almost all in the plaza, died. But as some eighty hard-core members of the National Strike Council attempted to flee through the rear of the project, police captured them. Without their leadership, the uprising ended and the Olympics proceeded.

The KGB had come close but had failed. With most of its young Mexican agents arrested, the KGB had lost its capacity to foment violence. But within a month a new onslaught was planned, to be led by Fabricio Gómez Souza, whose potential Nechiporenko had so quickly perceived five years before. Now the KGB turned to him and to Patrice Lumumba Friendship University.

Nikita Khrushchev had announced in 1960 that Patrice Lumumba University was being established to train "intelligentsia cadres" for the nations of Africa, Asia, and Latin America. Within the Soviet Union, Russian authorities stated the university's mission more plainly: "To educate students from underdeveloped countries so they can return to their homelands to become the nucleus for pro-Soviet activities."

The first vice rector of Patrice Lumumba was Pavl Erzin, a major general of the KGB. Other KGB officers and agents serve on the faculty, which must obey the dictates of the KGB. Students are selected primarily on the basis of their potential usefulness to the KGB. (If the Russians really want to educate a foreigner to work, for instance, on a Russian foreign-aid project back home, the student does not attend Patrice Lumumba; he goes to a first-rate Soviet university or technical school.)

Upon arrival at Patrice Lumumba in the fall of 1963, Gómez joined thirty other Mexicans, many of whom had come to Moscow without the knowledge of their government. After studying Russian for a year, he was put into a special class of students who had demonstrated the greatest revolutionary zeal. Even in this elite, he distinguished himself during the next four years of indoctrination by his cold fanaticism and obedience to the Russians. In October 1968, when the KGB gave Gómez his initial assignment, it probably had as much confidence in him as it ever places in any foreigner.

He began the assignment as leading actor in an elaborate fiction staged by the KGB. One morning Mexican students in Moscow were called together, ostensibly to hear a fresh report about the recent violence in their country. An unfamiliar Russian, who purportedly had talked with travelers just back from Mexico City, appeared before them. He gravely stated that the Mexican army had killed hundreds of students, arrested thousands more, and was now hunting down all remaining "progressives" in a murderous purge of the universities. "They are slaughtering students in the streets as if they were insects," he concluded. "And today there is no Pancho Villa, no Emiliano Zapata to defend them."

Gómez stood up as if rising spontaneously to the challenge. "I request permission of the university to conduct a meeting of only Mexicans," he said formally. "I mean no disrespect, but we would prefer that no one else be present. We Mexicans must redeem our own honor."

Passionately Gómez harangued his fellow countrymen on the necessity of avenging the dead students and sweeping Mexico with Marxist revolution. "I say it is time to stop musing about theory!" he cried. "It is time to act. All of us must prepare ourselves as guerrilla warriors."

That evening Gómez invited to his dormitory ten or so selected Mexicans, including two entrusted with supporting roles in the KGB theater. Inspired by more oratory, bravado, and vodka, the group proclaimed the birth of the Movimiento de Acción Revolucionaria (MAR). At the suggestion of Gómez, the students also agreed to solicit guerrilla training from Cuba and North Vietnam.

With addresses supplied by an obliging Russian "professor," the Mexicans first visited the Cuban embassy in Moscow. Two Cubans received them hospitably, offering coffee and cigars, while listening attentively to their proposals. "Of course we are sympathetic to your objectives," said one Cuban. "However, our diplomatic relations with Mexico form an extremely valuable channel into the nonsocialist camp. At this time it would not be in the greater interests of revolution for us to provoke a break in relations."

The North Vietnamese were more brusque. "We are already fighting a guerrilla war," said a wizened, bespectacled functionary. "Our lives are at stake, and we have absolutely no resources to spare."

Back at the university, Gómez dutifully affected dejection as he recounted the Mexicans' experiences to the Russian "professor." "An idea occurs to me," remarked the Russian. "Have you thought of the North Koreans? Perhaps they would be helpful."

At the North Korean embassy, Gómez spoke the same preliminary lines the KGB had cued him to use at the other embassies. The North Koreans dispensed with pretenses. "Yes, yes, we have agreed; it is arranged," an officer said to Gómez. "Are you the one appointed to fly to Pyongyang?"

The KGB had dictated, directed, and managed each act of this scenario—beginning with the "report" to assembled Mexican students and ending with the visit to the North Korean embassy—all in order to conceal its sponsorship of the guerrillas. It sought to create the illusion that Mexican students had spontaneously decided to form a guerrilla force, and on their own initiative had found a patron in North Korea, which had no diplomatic ties with Mexico. This is what most Mexicans subsequently drawn into the movement would be led to believe. Through this deception the Russians expected to escape retaliation and avoid the loss of their vital embassy in Mexico.

Early in November, Gómez flew via Aeroflot to the North Korean capital of Pyongyang, where he conferred with intelligence and military officers. Again the Koreans were well prepared. They advised Gómez that no more than fifty dedicated revolutionaries were required. Each would be developed into a leader and teacher of future recruits. Once the force of fifty was deployed, it would multiply like a cancer through the cities and mountainous countryside of Mexico. To permit time for careful selection of trainees and to avoid attention a large exodus might attract, the Koreans recommended that the fifty Mexicans be brought to Pyongyang in three successive contingents.

Back in Moscow, Gómez picked up $25,000 from the North Korean embassy and divided it among four other students chosen by the KGB to return with him to Mexico as recruiters. Traveling singly by separate routes, they landed in Mexico City in late December 1968 and early January 1969.

At the same time, the Russians dispatched to Mexico City a senior KGB officer who, in the temporary absence of the ambassador, became chargé d'affaires. He was Dmitri Alekseevich Diakanov, whom the other Russians promptly dubbed "the Clown." In private they laughed at his appearance and manners. His pate was totally bald except for tufts protruding angularly from either side of his head. If he let the hair grow, he looked as if he had horns; if he cut it, he looked as if he had just been scalped. His hair, combined with huge, sunken eyes and a guttural voice, made him seem like a caricature of a bomb-throwing Bolshevik of the early 1900s. When attempting to make a speech, he was virtually powerless to control his hands. He alternately stuck his thumbs in his pockets and leaned backward or clutched his hands behind his back and leaned forward. In either posture, he created the impression of a man about to topple.

Moreover, Diakanov was a stern puritan appalled by the adultery and lewd references to sex commonplace in the isolated Soviet colony. At a weekly Communist Party meeting, he stood up to call for reform. "I am shocked," he began, "to hear within an embassy of the Soviet Union dirty talk about sex. Such talk is contrary to communist morality. Yet it is heard all the time, even, I am ashamed to say, among the female comrades." Waves of giggles from the women interrupted, embarrassed, and mystified Diakanov.

All the women knew that the worst offender against his concept of communist morality was Lydia Nechiporenko, Oleg's wife. When Nechiporenko had first met her, Lydia was a nineteen-year-old salesclerk with a lithe figure and the face of a Madonna. Her physical appeal initially obscured in his eyes her lack of education and her coarseness. While KGB training and travel transformed him into a sophisticated, cosmopolitan man, Lydia utterly failed to grow intellectually, and deteriorated physically into dumpiness. Her obscene jokes, which once had seemed amusing to Nechiporenko, now shamed him. After a couple of drinks at parties, she would make vulgar advances to other KGB officers who dared not offend either her or her husband.

Lydia cunningly used her husband's power, appointing herself watch-bitch over the Russian wives. Their private lives became her official domain. She pried incessantly and maliciously tried to set woman against woman by asking questions of one that might incriminate or debase another. She delighted in degrading a woman by making false accusations, then forcing her to disprove them. Nechiporenko came to loathe her, and so did everybody else.

Ignorant of this background, Diakanov stumbled on with his speech. "I want you to know something else. I am shocked by the statements some of you make about the Mexicans. They are naïve and can be manipulated, but it must not be said that they are dirty, that they are lazy, that they have no culture."

Giggles and smirks again greeted Diakanov, for again Lydia was the prime culprit. Then suddenly, the laughter stopped as if turned off by a switch. Kolomyakov was on his feet, clearly enraged. "Why do you insult Comrade Diakanov?" he shouted. "He is absolutely correct. Comrade Diakanov speaks for the Party. He also speaks for the organs of state security. Do you understand?" Everybody understood.

However foolish Diakanov may have appeared to the Russian women, he was not the clown they thought him. In the back alleys of the world, he had proved himself the equal of the most violent men. The government of Argentina threw him out of Buenos Aires in 1959 after he created chaos by instigating labor riots. In 1963 he turned up in Brazil as a member of a Soviet "Peace Prize Commission." His labors there culminated in a rebellion by noncommissioned officers of the Brazilian army, and he was kicked out of the country. A specialist in strikes, riots, and violence, Diakanov was admirably equipped to deal with guerrillas. And that was his mission in Mexico.

Through Diakanov, the KGB was kept informed of the recruitment progress being made by Gómez and his Mexican subordinates. Kolomyakov in turn suggested prospective recruits spotted by Nechiporenko or the KGB apparatus in Mexico.

One name that long had been in the Referentura

file of prospects was that of Angel Bravo Cisneros, a mustachioed student radical who looked a little like a pudgy Hitler. On a cool evening in April 1969, Gómez traveled to the lovely colonial city of Morelia to seek him out. At a café frequented by students near the University of Michoacán, the two talked fervently for an hour or so about Vietnam, Cuba, and revolution in general.

Bravo seldom used one word when he could find three. His conversation was larded with revolutionary slogans and hoary Marxist clichés, which he declaimed as if he had originated them. Unable to achieve distinction in scholarship, he had turned to anarchy. In this he had attained some success, joining a variety of extremist groups and helping foment a series of student riots.

"You have demonstrated energy," Gómez said, "but that is no substitute for knowledge and skill. We must leave the country and be trained by experts."

"Such training would be an honor of which I would always strive to be worthy," Bravo responded.

"Good," Gómez replied. "I want you to establish residence in Mexico City. In the months ahead, I will send to you comrades who are to undergo training. You will serve as liaison between them and me, and also ensure that they obtain all necessary travel documents. At the proper time, you will lead them on the journey out of the country."

"Perhaps you have observed that I am possessed of great intellectual curiosity," Bravo said grandly. "I would be pleased to know the land to which I will journey."

"Gómez glowered at him. "You are to take orders, not ask questions. I will tell you only this: our duty is to make of Mexico another Vietnam."

Through the summer, a succession of young people checked in with Bravo in Mexico City. Fourteen men and two women were gathered in the city when Gómez visited Bravo in mid-August. "Your journey is about to begin," said Gómez, unwrapping a package containing nearly $9,000.

"Divide the comrades into groups of two or three

and give each person $500. Instruct each group to make its own arrangements to fly to Paris. But make certain that each group leaves on a different day and uses a different airline. Tell everyone to assemble at 10 A.M. on September 7 at the Eiffel Tower."

"Are we to be trained in France?" Bravo asked with excitement.

"Pay attention," Gómez ordered. "You are to tell the comrades no more than I have told you. However, after you gather in Paris, you are to guide them to West Berlin, where you will stay at the Hotel Colombia. Each day you must cross into East Berlin and, beginning at 1 P.M., stand on the corner by the Moscow Restaurant. Sooner or later you will see a man you know. From him you will receive further orders."

All seventeen Mexicans appeared as planned at the Eiffel Tower on September 7. Though some grumbled about being kept in ignorance of their ultimate destination, they willingly flew on to Berlin. After failing on three successive days to meet anyone he recognized in East Berlin, Bravo began to worry. The Mexicans didn't have enough money left to pay their hotel bills, and soon there would be none for meals. On the fourth day, however, as Bravo stood by the Restaurant Moscow, he felt a tap on his shoulder, and there was Gómez.

After listening to Bravo's account of the trip and the group's financial plight, Gómez said, "I will see what can be done. Walk around for a while and meet me here in a couple of hours." Gómez returned in mid-afternoon with about $1,000. "Tomorrow bring me passport photographs of each of the comrades, including yourself," he instructed Bravo. "We should be able to depart in three or four days. Until then, you and I will meet here daily." On their seventh day in Germany, Gómez told Bravo: "We go tomorrow. Bring everyone to the main railway station of East Berlin at noon."

In the dark, cavernous old railroad terminal, four somber North Koreans awaited the Mexicans. They handed each a Korean passport bearing his photograph and a Korean name. In return, they required each to surrender his Mexican passport and all other papers reflecting his true identity. At 5 P.M. Gómez led the Mexicans aboard the night train to Moscow. Only after it started to move did he reveal that their final destination was Pyongyang.

To the customs and immigration officials who boarded the train at the Polish and Soviet borders, it was obvious that the Mexicans were not the Koreans their passports represented them to be. When a Soviet inspector approached, the youngest of the future guerrillas, Felipe Penaloza, nervously pulled from his pocket both his Korean passport and his Mexican draft card, which he had neglected to give the Koreans in Berlin. *"Nyet, nyet!"* exclaimed the Russian, grabbing the Mexican document. But seeing the boy's fright, the inspector smiled, patted his shoulder, and walked away with the draft card. The KGB had prepared the way thoroughly.

More North Koreans greeted the Mexicans in Moscow and drove them in embassy cars to a hotel where they were confined for five days pending the flight to Pyongyang. The KGB had, of course, supervised all travel arrangements. But the trip was so contrived that at no time in Moscow or during the entire passage across the Soviet Union did any Mexican except Gómez converse with a Russian. To all but Gómez, it seemed that the Koreans were in charge.

Whatever the Mexicans may have expected in North Korea, doubtless none anticipated the grueling regimen that awaited them. The guerrilla training camp, set in a valley between two mountain ranges some thirty-five miles northwest of the capital, was bleak and forbidding. It consisted of wooden barracks, a mess hall, frame buildings housing classrooms and administrative offices, and ranges for practice in small arms, demolition, and hand-to-hand combat. The training day, beginning with an hour of exercise, lasted from 6 A.M. to 11 P.M. The trainees were told that they must henceforth forsake both sex and alcohol, which were labeled useless and disruptive distractions from fighting. Except for an occasional visit to a circus or outing in the countryside, no recreation was provided. There were excursions to factories and villages—but only to teach the Mexicans how to destroy them.

They received zealous instruction in all the tools of terror, including arson, explosives, karate, assassination, extortion, ambush, disguises, clandestine travel, recruitment, communications, and weaponry. In learning about weapons, the students practiced almost exclusively with American-made equipment. A humorless little Korean known as Comrade Lee explained why.

"In the initial phase of guerrilla warfare, you must make the enemy supply you with arms and money," he began. "To obtain guns, kill the policemen and soldiers who have them. To obtain money, rob banks and stores. While sustaining you, these assassinations and expropriations contribute to the terrorization of the enemy. For a time they can also mislead him into thinking he is confronted merely by common criminals.

"The Mexican army and police buy mostly American arms. They are what you will be using, at least in the first years."

The most realistic and brutal of the training exercises pitted the young guerrillas against regular elements of the North Korean army. The Mexicans were required to infiltrate military bases, sabotage guarded vehicles, set ambushes, fight the soldiers with their bare hands, and flee pursuing patrols. The women trainees received no special consideration, except that in the field their packs were not as heavy as the men's. Fatigue, injury, or illness excused no one from the nightly seminars at which the day's lessons were rigorously reviewed.

In its harshness, the training had a purpose beyond making the Mexicans physically strong and technically proficient. The communists strove to develop each into a disciplined fanatic consumed by the objective of destroying the Mexican government. A senior instructor called Comrade Sung repeatedly stressed the concept of selflessness and sacrifice.

"Some comrades will die lonely deaths of wounds which cannot be attended," he warned. "Some will be imprisoned with no hope of liberation until victory. Many of you will have to discharge your revolutionary duties in the night, then work all day at ordinary jobs in which you have no interest. No matter what the hour, when the order comes to move, to bomb, to kill, you must obey instantly."

As in Moscow, Gómez was a prize pupil. But he did not really need all the tactical training, for his was a higher mission of organization, planning, and leadership. So after less than three months, Gómez slipped out of the North Korean camp. Picking up another $10,000 in Moscow, he flew in early January 1970 to Berlin, then on to Mexico. There he began assembling the final contingent of would-be guerrillas.

Locked in the Mexico City Referentura reading the reports that charted the progress of Gómez and the Movimiento de Acción Revolucionaria, Nechiporenko could be proud of himself. Gómez had justified every expectation and thereby had enhanced Nechiporenko's already glittering reputation at the Center. Then something every Soviet embassy dreads happened, something that suddenly clouded Nechiporenko's prospects.

On the morning of February 7, 1970, Kolomyakov received a telephone call from the Soviet commercial office located in a small villa adjacent to the embassy. "Raya has vanished," an attaché said.

Kolomyakov called Nechiporenko to the Referentura and informed him that Raya Kiselnikova apparently had fled. To Nechiporenko, the news had special and terrible meaning.

The widow of a Soviet physicist who had died of radiation, Raya was thirty, blonde, blue-eyed, pretty, and sensuous. Officially she was a secretary in the commercial section of the embassy; actually she was much more. As a student of literature, she had known many intellectuals who enriched her intellect and inspired her imagination. Later, study in East Berlin, with opportunities to venture into West Berlin, had given her furtive, delicious tastes of Western life. Ever since, she had continued to quest intellectually, to explore, to educate herself. Soviet men were almost compulsively attracted to her, not only because of her seductive appearance but because she could talk to them about the world as few of their wives could.

Moreover, she had about her a girlish openness that tempted men to trust and confide.

Even KGB officers felt at ease with Raya. They sometimes commanded her presence in the evening, ostensibly as a cover for some secret assignment. Usually this was merely a pretext to enjoy her company, but on occasion she did serve as a genuine decoy and thereby witnessed clandestine meetings between the KGB and its Mexican agents. A few officers flaunted their secret exploits in an attempt to impress her with their importance. Even Kolomyakov, who harbored no amorous designs on Raya, liked and relied upon her.

But the man who most trusted and confided in her was Nechiporenko himself. She was all he yearned for in a wife, all that Lydia was not. If he had one genuine friend in Mexico, it was Raya. Now he had to ask himself tormenting questions. Exactly what had he told her in the many unguarded moments they had shared? How much did she know? Many another KGB officer had to search his memory with the same questions.

As the security officer responsible for recovering any defector, Nechiporenko immediately organized a hunt for Raya. All other business of the KGB halted while every available Russian joined the search. The corrupt ex-police official who commanded a squad of cashiered cops for the KGB was summoned. The KGB did not have to tell him what to do if his detectives found Raya. He knew that he was to retrieve or kill.

All efforts were in vain. On February 10 the Mexican government announced that Raya Kiselnikova had requested and received political asylum. The Soviet embassy demanded an interview with her, and Kolomyakov sent Nechiporenko. Before leaving Moscow, Raya had pledged not to associate on her own with Mexicans or discuss with them problems of Soviet life. Yet, beguiled by her, KGB officers winked at the regulations and allowed her some freedom. She went to the Anthropological Museum, danced at discotheques, and, above all, talked to Mexicans. Having tasted the gaiety, liberty, and promise of Mexican life, Raya had come to look upon the Soviet embassy as an Orwellian anthill. And ultimately she saw it, permeated as it was by pettiness, mistrust, fear, regimentation and conspiracy, as a microcosm of Soviet society.

Nechiporenko was magnificent in his tender appeals. Never referring to communism or the Soviet state, he spoke of her love of Russian culture and their bond with each other. Constantly he stressed, as the KGB always does in such a situation, that if she returned now, she would be guilty of no more than a foolish peccadillo which would be promptly and permanently forgiven.

She began to cry. "Oleg, I am sorry, I am sorry," she said. "You must know I can never go back." As Mexican security officers stepped forward to end the interview, Nechiporenko kissed her and left, also in tears.

KGB interrogations of embassy personnel permitted no illusions about the value of the intelligence Raya might disclose to the Mexican government. She knew that Nechiporenko had recruited some of the students who emerged as prominent leaders in the 1968 riots. She had accompanied Valentin Loginov to his clandestine meeting with students at the height of the riots. She had heard KGB officers brag about bribing certain magazine and newspaper editors to publish pro-Soviet stories. She could recite in clear, meaningful detail what went on inside the embassy.

But one question concerned Kolomyakov and Nechiporenko more than any other. Could Raya conceivably know anything about Gómez and the guerrillas? Strenuous reconstructions of associations, conversations, and all data to which Raya might have had access yielded no evidence that she did. Neither could clandestine KGB sources discover any indication that the Mexican government had become aware of the incipient guerrilla movement. Thus, the KGB elected to let the operation continue. As the months passed without disaster, it seemed that Raya's defection would be nothing more than a minor blemish on Nechiporenko's brilliant record.

The guerrilla training in North Korea for the final twenty-three recruits and the seventeen members of the second contingent ended in August 1970. They split into three groups for the journey home via Moscow. By late September, all were back, mentally and physically ready for their secret labors.

The morning after the last group landed in Mexico City, Gómez convened his chief deputies, including Bravo, in an apartment at Calle Medellín 27. "Our immediate objective is to increase our numbers as rapidly as possible without making any sacrifice in quality of personnel," he announced. "Our cadre will be organized into three sections. The first will recruit new comrades; the second will train the recruits; the third will execute the expropriations. Once our numbers are sufficient, we will divide into an urban guerrilla force and a rural guerrilla force. Comrades, we are ready to begin."

The Movimiento de Acción Revolucionaria indeed progressed with astonishing swiftness. In less than two months it doubled in size by adding some fifty recruits spotted and screened by the first ten guerrillas who had returned from North Korea in 1969. Clandestine schools were established in Zamora, San Miguel de Allende, Querétaro, Puebla, Chapala, and Mexico City. A special school for the training of future instructors was founded in Salamanca. Apartments or houses where guerrillas could hide and mount operations were acquired in Mexico City, Acapulco, and Jalapa.

Some of the guerrillas took jobs, both to earn money for the movement and to cloak themselves in an aura of respectability. One of the most ruthless, Alejandro López Murillo, opened a beauty salon in Mexico City. The idea was good. The police were unlikely to look for terrorists among hairdressers or women in a beauty parlor. Neither were they likely to search parlors for weapons and explosives.

The first robbery was plotted in late November, with all the military precision learned in North Korea. López, who had worked at the Banco de Comercio in Morelia for a while, suggested the target. He recalled that about three times a month the bank sent a courier by bus to deposit U.S. dollars in a central bank in Mexico City. With the approval of Gómez, the plotters decided to waylay the courier.

Four guerrillas visited Morelia to familiarize themselves with the appearance of the courier, a thin, elderly man. One, Comrade Hilda, remained in Morelia to watch the terminal of the Three Star Bus Company. The night of December 18 she telephoned Mexico City to report that the courier had departed on a bus due in the capital at 6 A.M.

About 4 A.M. in Mexico City, three guerrillas hailed a taxi. They knocked the driver unconscious with a pistol and, binding and gagging him, threw him on the rear floor. Shortly before six o'clock, they drove to the bus station where Bravo and two more members of the squad were waiting.

When the courier stepped from the bus, the six guerrillas saw that he was escorted by a young man they believed was a police detective. They quickly wrestled both men to the ground, then grabbed the courier's satchel, ran to the stolen taxi, and escaped. Hurriedly, Bravo ripped open the satchel, passed out handfuls of dollars, and stuffed some into his own pockets. Abandoning the cab, the guerrillas fled. In the safety of an apartment, Bravo counted out the money he had kept—almost $30,000. Not until he read the afternoon papers did he learn that the total loot was $84,000.

With money allocated by Gómez, Bravo bought a Volkswagen and a Datsun van. Gómez also sent a courier to the Texas border to purchase wigs for disguises and walkie-talkies. The remainder of the $84,000 was allotted for weapons and operating expenses.

While his men plotted additional robberies and trained more and more recruits, Gómez scheduled the first guerrilla attack for July 1971. He planned to detonate bombs simultaneously at fifteen airports, hotels, restaurants, and public buildings throughout Mexico.

The explosions would proclaim the existence of the Movimiento de Acción Revolucionaria and a siege of the Mexican government. Each subsequent bombing, robbery, and assassination would be committed to achieve maximum shock and publicity at minimum risk. Continuing and intensifying terror, first in one part of the country, then another, would create a growing illusion of the guerrillas' invincibility and the government's impotence to protect its citizens. Such an aura could be expected to attract to the movement extremist groups and opportunists who thought to secure their future by joining the winning side. Additionally, through atrocities against police and public officials, the guerrillas hoped to provoke the government into retaliatory measures that would alienate many citizens and drive them into MAR ranks.

The movement would also gather strength in the Mexican mountains, in whose virtually uncharted areas bandits and fugitives had long found refuge. At the outset, only small raiding parties would venture out of the mountains to sabotage railways, bridges, power lines, and factories. In time, organized battalions would descend to ambush army units and sack whole towns.

These terrorist tactics would be accompanied by unremitting psychological warfare. In Moscow, Gómez had learned to understand that most events are not as important as how they are perceived. The strategy taught him required creation of a propaganda section to "educate" the masses, and particularly journalists. All propaganda would sound one underlying theme: the inevitability of guerrilla triumph over the "injustices" of Mexican society and government. Each attempt of the government to defend against the guerrillas would be seized upon as proof of its repressive, totalitarian character. Selected sympathetic foreign correspondents would be invited to melodramatic interviews portraying the romance of revolution, the idealism of young men impelled by conscience to take up arms. All the while the KGB through its worldwide resources would surreptitiously foster the impression that the masses were rising up against another degenerate Latin-American oligarchy.

But no one, in Mexico or Moscow, could have foreseen the chance encounter that occurred in February 1971. An elderly constable was walking homeward outside a small mountain village some thirty miles from Jalapa. It was a long walk, and often he stopped to rest at an abandoned shack about halfway to his house. On this afternoon, as he approached, he heard voices from the shack. Looking inside, he saw four young men, one of whom was drawing a diagram on a blackboard. More out of curiosity than suspicion, the constable said, "Good afternoon, friends. What are you drawing?"

"None of your damned business, old man," one of the young men answered comtemptuously. "Get out of here."

"Just a moment," said the constable. "I am a police officer. I have asked a proper question."

"Get away or we'll beat hell out of you!" shouted the youth.

As two of the young men advanced on him, the constable drew his revolver. "I warn you, I'm a good shot," he said. "Take the blackboard and march."

The constable delivered the four to the police. To them the diagram was a mystery, and had the youths offered the slightest explanation, they doubtless would have been released. But their insolent refusal to say anything motivated the police to telephone Mexico City.

The next morning a man who was introduced only as "the Colonel" arrived. He saw at once that the blackboard diagram was of electrical transmission towers—towers being marked for destruction. A gifted interrogator, the Colonel soon extracted all that the four youths knew—which was not very much. They said that a Comrade Antonio had persuaded them to become "guerrilla warriors" so they could "fight for Mexico." He told them that he would return in a month or so to inform them of plans for their training. Meanwhile, they were to practice shooting and making bombs. One youth did remember that Comrade Antonio had mentioned a Movimiento de Acción Revolucionaria. Another thought they would be trained somewhere in Jalapa. The search for an MAR hideout in Jalapa began.

About a month later, in Mexico City, Gómez ordered Bravo to inspect the clandestine MAR center in Jalapa. Bravo took a bus to Jalapa and knocked on the door of the guerrilla house at Guadalupe Victoria 121. He did not recognize whoever it was that politely opened the door, but this was not surprising because by now the movement had many new members. As soon as he stepped inside, he heard a shout: *"Manos arriba, traidor!"* ("Hands up, traitor!") Looking into the muzzle of a submachine gun and the fierce eyes of the man who held it, Bravo sensed that he stood very near death.

Shortly after midnight, he was ushered into a room at the police station and left alone with the Colonel. For four or five minutes the Colonel stared at him silently, responding to nothing he said. Then the Colonel began a methodical interrogation, and soon Bravo had told everything. The KGB had never dealt with Bravo and Gómez had withheld much from him. But as leader of a contingent to Korea and an accomplice in the robbery, he knew a great deal, including the importance of Gómez and the location of several guerrilla centers.

Four days later, Gómez, having heard nothing from Bravo, traveled to Jalapa himself in search of him. The guerrilla house appeared dark and empty as he unlocked the front door. But suddenly a beam from a flashlight struck his face; then the lights flashed on. "Ah, Señor Gómez," said a man pointing a cocked .38-caliber revolver. "It is you for whom we have waited most."

Led away to jail, Gómez screamed curses and vows to kill all who might have betrayed him. It was useless. Within the week, the Mexican security service devastated the Movimiento de Acción Revolucionaria, raiding its centers, capturing its nineteen most important leaders, and laying traps that would ensnare many more.

When the intelligence advisers presented their report the night of March 12, they were able to accompany it with voluminous and concrete evidence. It was the kind of proof any responsible chief of state covets on the eve of a momentous decision. Photographs showed the American M-1 rifles and .45-caliber pistols, hand grenades, cartridges, short-wave radios, even some of the money remaining from the $84,000 robbery. Signed confessions and captured diaries recorded the training of the guerrillas and their plans for terror. Dossiers on Kolomyakov, Nechiporenko, and Diakanov detailed their involvement and that of the KGB.

It was clear that Mexico had barely escaped grievous damage. The Russians might never have realized their ultimate goal of creating "another Vietnam." But they were only months away from achieving their minimum objective of serious social disruption. Had the guerrillas multiplied and mounted sustained attacks, Mexico would have had to waste its resources on new arms and armies. These could have been raised only at the expense of education, industrial development, transportation, rural electrification, and social reforms.

On March 15 the government announced the capture of the guerrillas and indicated that arrests were continuing. The announcement shocked Mexico, but doubtless the consternation was greatest in the Referentura at the Soviet embassy. The ripening fruits of years of planning, hundreds of clandestine meetings, and painstaking recruitment suddenly were destroyed. And momentarily, Moscow would be demanding explanations.

There was, however, one consolation for the KGB in the official announcement. It offered no intimation that the Mexican government had the least suspicion of the true sponsorship of the Movimiento de Acción Revolucionaria. Apparently Gómez had not talked; seemingly, Nechiporenko, Kolomyakov, and Diakanov were safe.

Then, on March 17, Mexico ordered its ambassador to leave Moscow quietly. The following morning Diakanov, the Soviet chargé d'affaires, received a curt message. His presence at the Foreign Ministry was required immediately. Foreign Minister Emilio Rabasa greeted him with none of the customary niceties.

"The continued presence of you, Dmitri A. Diakanov, Boris P. Kolomyakov, Oleg M. Nechiporenko, Boris A. Voskoboynikov, and Aleksandr V. Bolshakov [the latter a KGB official involved in recruiting students] is intolerable to my government," the Foreign Minister announced. "You are hereby ordered to depart the territory of Mexico immediately."

"What is the reason for this?" asked Diakanov.

"Señor Diakanov, you, I, and the State Security Committee of the Soviet Union all know the reason why," replied Rabasa. "There will be no further discussion. This interview is at an end."

The expulsion of five diplomats, including the chargé d'affaires, was an extraordinary diplomatic slap in the face for the Soviet Union. Mexico was aware that whenever a nation dares to expel KGB officers, the Soviet Union retaliates with a belligerent denunciation and the arbitrary ouster of an equal number of diplomats from Moscow. However, since the recall of its ambassador, Mexico now had only four diplomats left in the Soviet Union. If the Russians retaliated in kind, they would in effect sever diplomatic relations. Thereupon, the Mexicans could order all Russians out of Mexico and close the great Soviet sanctuary of subversion once and for all. So the Soviet Union swallowed its humiliation without protest.

Other Latin-American nations rallied to the support of Mexico. Colombia and Honduras sent their ambassadors to the Foreign Ministry to declare their endorsement of the Mexican action. Leading newspapers throughout the hemisphere denounced the Russians and praised the Mexicans. Costa Rica consulted the Mexican government, then announced suspension of negotiations which had been expected to result momentarily in diplomatic relations with the Soviet Union.

On March 21 the expelled Russians waited at the airport for a plane home. Their enforced departure was probably regretted most by Nechiporenko, whose life had been so imtimately intertwined with a country he would never be allowed to see again. But he was a good actor to the end, smiling and bantering with reporters. Kolomyakov, the KGB boss who never forgave a mistake, also was in character. Just as their flight was announced, he jumped out of line and took a swing at a photographer. His last blow in Mexico missed.

What happened in Mexico is merely part of a worldwide pattern of continuing KGB subversion. Tactics vary from nation to nation, according to risks involved, political conditions, culture, geography, and the resources the KGB can concentrate in a given area. But the strategy is uniform: strikes, riots, demonstrations, disinformation, sabotage, and terrorism. The KGB aim is to spread Soviet power by creating costly, debilitating crises, or strife that make the target nation more vulnerable to Soviet pressures. In some instances, the Soviet Union pursues the same aim by relatively peaceful or parliamentary means, but clandestine KGB operations continue simultaneously. Despite all the precautions the KGB takes to conceal Soviet sponsorship of subversion, evidence of its efforts to disrupt other societies has emerged repeatedly.

Before dawn on February 24, 1966, anticommunist insurgents in Ghana attacked Flagstaff House, the residence and headquarters of President Kwame Nkrumah, who at the time was en route to Peking. Subduing the Presidential Guard after a battle lasting nearly ten hours, the insurgents stormed into Flagstaff House and discovered eleven KGB officers. The attackers marched the Russians into the garden, lined them up against a wall, and shot them all on the spot. These summary executions have never been revealed publicly. The Soviet Union, not wanting the world to know that KGB officers were actually sitting in the Ghanian President's office running the country, chose not to mention the deaths. The National Liberation Council that deposed Nkrumah saw no reason to announce them either.

But the new Ghanian government assigned teams to study and analyze the copious secret files of the Nkrumah regime. Subsequently, it publicized its findings in the form of a White Paper. Ghana also sent official apologies to other African states and gave detailed briefings to numerous foreign governments. The evidence distributed shows that the KGB had converted Ghana into one vast base of subversion, which the Soviet Union fully intended to use to capture the continent of Africa. As the White Paper states at the outset: ". . . the discoveries made by the government of Ghana revealed that the danger to Africa was one hundred times more serious than anyone outside a small circle had realized."

The Soviet operation began in 1962. Nkrumah, fearing for his life after an assassination attempt and frustrated in his own imperialist adventures in Africa, turned to the communists for help. The KGB offered to organize a special force of bodyguards and at the same time to equip him for the subversion of neighboring countries. Once he accepted, KGB personnel flooded into Ghana literally by the hundreds. They were joined by Chinese, East Germans, Czechs, Poles, North Koreans, and Cubans. The majority were either intelligence officers or instructors in various phases of terrorism and guerrilla warfare.

The KGB officer directing the operation in Accra, the capital, was Robert Issakovich Akhmerov, whose mother had been the secretary of Lavrenti Beria and whose father was a KGB colonel. His deputy was Nikolai Ivanovich Gladky, who had served as Khrushchev's personal bodyguard. Gladky was present in 1960 when Khrushchev pounded his shoe on his desk at the United Nations. While in New York he got into a fist fight on the street with one of Fidel Castro's bodyguards and broke his jaw. The KGB supervisors were assisted by two East German intelligence officers, Jürgen Rogalla and Rolf Stollmeyer. Rogalla, who used the alias Jürgen Krüger, was notorious in Europe for his beatings of prisoners suspected of anticommunism.*

The KGB swiftly established a secret political police apparatus in Ghana called the National Security Service, modeled exactly after the one in the Soviet Union. About thirty Ghanians were flown to Moscow for training in maintenance of informant networks, provocation, surveillance, and all the other techniques the KGB uses to control the Soviet people. Many more were trained locally. The White Paper states that as a result: "Nkrumah's security officers, both men and women, were placed everywhere—in factories, offices, drinking bars, political rallies and even in churches,

---

*The East Germans so esteemed him that after he was arrested in Ghana they held 350 Ghanian students and eight diplomats as hostages for his release.

not forgetting the taxi drivers, bus drivers, shop assistants, peddlers and seemingly unemployed persons who were all acting as informants." To further ensure Nkrumah's power, the KGB kept its word and organized a special force of three hundred bodyguards who were instructed by officers from the Ninth or Guards Directorate in Moscow. As a counter against the army, it began building an elite Presidential Regiment answerable only to Nkrumah.

Meanwhile, the KGB created, much in its own image, a huge clandestine organization for espionage, subversion, and guerrilla warfare throughout Africa. Known publicly as the Bureau for Technical Assistance and secretly as the Special African Service, it was divided into geographic departments, as is the Foreign Directorate of the KGB. Its files revealed plans for infiltration of terrorists or agents into Cameroon, Ivory Coast, Upper Volta, Niger, Togo, Congo Léopoldville (now Zaïre), Chad, Nigeria, Sierra Leone, Sudan, Liberia, Gambia, Swaziland, Tanzania, Malawi, Zambia, Mali, Guinea, Burundi, Rwanda, Congo Brazzaville, Rhodesia, Angola, Mozambique, and Portuguese Guinea. Secret jungle camps were set up to train terrorists, and the Special African Service also prepared for political assassinations. An early target appears to have been President Sylvanus Olympio of neighboring Togo, but he was murdered by dissidents in his own country before the KGB/Nkrumah operatives could act.

A prisoner of his own delusions of grandeur, the vain Nkrumah was easily manipulated by the KGB officers surrounding him. But the whole clandestine structure was so constructed that the KGB could control it with or without his assent. With Soviet arms piling up in the country, the training of terrorists proceeded efficiently, and by the end of 1965 some 350 men, half of whom were from other African nations, had been graduated from the jungle camps. And some agents had infiltrated most of the target countries when anticommunist elements of the army took over in February 1966.

In retrospect, it appears that the ensuing Soviet debacle resulted from three mistakes by the KGB: it failed to penetrate the army sufficiently; it failed to develop the Presidential Regiment rapidly enough to neutralize the army; and it underestimated the nationalist loyalties of its Ghanian informants, who did not report preparations for the coup. Regardless, as the White Paper declares: "The liberation of Ghana was a bitter blow to all these communists. Like animals running in front of a forest fire, they fled the country. Planes and ships took away 1100 Russians, 430 Chinese and scores of people from the countries already named."

The Ghana operation followed an old communist blueprint whereby the KGB wrests control of a regime by making it first beholden to and then totally dependent upon the Soviet Union. Traditionally, the Soviet Union has distrusted and even been hostile to international movements it felt were permanently beyond its control. But in recent years the KGB has supported underground organizations over which it cannot expect to exert absolute control but which have the capacity to inflict considerable damage on other nations. The adoption and workings of this comparatively new tactic can be seen in the evolution of Soviet relations with the Irish Republican Army.

As early as the mid-1920s, the IRA dispatched representatives to Moscow in quest of Soviet aid. The OGPU defector Walter Krivitsky recalled that their braggadocio and grandiose military titles produced much mirth among the Russians. Considering the IRA a joke and at the time reluctant to antagonize Great Britain any more than necessary, the Politburo turned them down. The Russians did recruit Irish agents for espionage against Great Britain in the 1930s, and Dublin became a favored site for rendezvous with spies. The KGB passively watched Ireland after World War II through Czech and East German business firms clandestinely founded to gather intelligence and import strategic embargoed goods to the Soviet bloc. Still, the Russians remained aloof from the IRA.

With the outbreak of more violence and communal rioting in 1969, the KGB displayed its first serious interest in the IRA. It endeavored to establish clandestine ties through the Irish and British Communist Parties. By early 1970 the IRA had openly split into two hostile factions: the Marxist "Official" IRA, which has between 800 and 1,000 active members, and the less doctrinaire but more violent "Provisional" IRA, with between 900 and 1,000 active members. The Official faction, though not repudiating violence, advocates more peaceful "national liberation front" tactics to unite all of Ireland under a "socialist" regime allied with the Soviet Union. The Provisionals favor urban terrorism and sabotage aimed at collapsing the governments in both Dublin and Ulster. To the extent that the Provisionals have a coherent political philosophy, it resembles fascism more than anything else.

There is virtually no chance that either objective ever can be achieved. But between the onset of violence in 1969 and May 1973, the IRA succeeded in killing 521 civilians, 37 police, and 194 British soldiers, most of whom have been blown up by bombs or shot from ambush by snipers. The strife has exacerbated ancient religious enmities between the Catholic minority and Protestant majority in Northern Ireland and made redress of legitimate Catholic grievances much more difficult.

To sustain the terror and goad on the IRA, the KGB sends representatives rather openly into Ireland. KGB officer Yuri Ustimenko, the Tass correspondent in Dublin, deals regularly with Irish Communist Party Secretary-General Michael O'Riordan, who is closely associated with leaders of the pro-Marxist faction of the IRA. Posing as an Intourist representative, KGB officer N. V. Glavatsky has visited Irish trade unionists associated with the IRA. *Pravda* correspondent Yuri Yasnev utilizes his journalistic cover to meet with IRA personnel and even has succeeded in talking to some who are interned. Official Soviet delegations, including Central Committee representatives, confer with IRA leaders, both in Great Britain and Ireland.

Meanwhile, the KGB has worked secretly through Czech, Cuban, and Arab terrorist intermediaries to arm and train both wings of the IRA. In October 1971

Dutch authorities intercepted Czech arms at Schipol Airport. They had been bought by David O'Connell of the Provisional IRA from Ominipol, a subsidiary of Czech intelligence which in turn is controlled by the KGB. Since November 1972 the Provisionals have used Soviet RPG-7 rocket launchers in attacks on police and British troops. The Irish navy on March 29, 1973, boarded a ship off the south coast and captured five tons of arms and ammunition, including 250 Kalashnilov automatic rifles. The Soviet arms had been forwarded through Al Fatah in the Middle East.

One can almost pick any area of the world at random and find evidence of some form of subversion being instigated by the KGB. Colombian police, alerted by Mexican authorities in April 1968, relieved two communist couriers of $100,000 they had received from KGB officer Nikolai Sergeevich Leonov in Mexico City. The couriers, Feliciano Pachón Chocanta and Librada Morena Leal, eventually admitted that the $100,000 was destined for the most murderous band of terrorists in Colombia, the Fuerzas Armadas Revolucionarias.

The Congo (now the Republic of Zaïre) threw out the entire Soviet embassy staff of one hundred after the KGB openly supported an armed rebellion against the government in 1963. Subsequently, the Soviet Union signed a protocol specifically limiting it to seven diplomats in the Congo. By spring of 1970 the number had swelled to forty-two. Then the Congolese unraveled a KGB network that reached into student organizations, the army, the Ministry of Information, the Ministry of Foreign Affairs, and the National Documentation Center. The Congo immediately expelled four KGB officers and ordered the embassy staff reduced to seven.

After an abortive pro-Soviet coup in July 1971, the Sudan banished the Soviet and Bulgarian ambassadors, ousted hundreds of Soviet "technicians," and executed many local communists. President Gaafar Mohamed El Nimeri declared that the plot had failed because "Moscow was as stupid as the conspirators." The same month Ecuador expelled two KGB officers and a GRU officer paying a workers' group to instigate a nationwide strike.

Student terrorism in Turkey has produced kidnappings and murders that have taken the lives of the Israeli consul general and three British radar technicians. It has also retarded development of Turkish democracy, forcing imposition of a curfew in Ankara and martial law in eleven provinces. The terror is partly the handiwork of mindless, nihilistic youths whose only motivation is anarchy. But police have ascertained that some of the terrorists have undergone training in Syria arranged by a Soviet "diplomat" in Damascus, Vadim A. Shatrov, and a Soviet "chauffeur," Nikolai Chernenkov.

Actually, there should be nothing surprising about all this. The Soviet Union never has disguised its ultimate objective of establishing Soviet hegemony over the world. Neither does it disguise its continuing commitment to the violent methods of subversion and revolution in pursuit of this objective. In 1905 Lenin commanded: "Give every company short and simple bomb formulae. Some will immediately kill a spy or blow up a police station; others will organize an attack on a bank, in order to confiscate funds for the uprising."

In 1971 Boris Ponomarev, who speaks most authoritatively for the Soviet leadership on foreign affairs, published in *Kommunist* a remarkable article whose import is equally clear. Surveying the world, Ponomarev was fairly bedazzled by the opportunities for revolution he saw on all continents. Exhorting communists everywhere to exploit these revolutionary opportunities, Ponomarev declared: "The communists always remain the party of socialist revolution, a party which never tolerates the capitalist order and is always ready to head the struggle for the total political power of the working class and for the establishment of the dictatorship of the proletariat in one or another form."

XII

THE SPY WHO CHANGED HIS MIND

At the Yaroslavsky railroad station in Moscow, a handsome Nordic-looking traveler stepped off the Trans-Siberian express and stood apart from the other disembarking passengers. He was known by many names, but in reality he was Kaarlo Rudolph Tuomi, combat veteran of the Red Army, instructor in English, and secret informant to the KGB. Why he had been summoned to Moscow or who would meet him, he did not know. But following a prearranged set of signals, he cradled an umbrella under his left arm and waited.

"Good morning," said a stranger. "Tell me, how is your Uncle Efim?"

"I'm sorry to say he just passed away," Tuomi answered.

"That's too bad. Come with me, please."

In silence the two men rode in a little Moskvich sedan to a military hotel where Tuomi was taken to a third-floor suite. "These will be your quarters," his escort advised him. "You'll be having visitors after a while, so don't go out."

The luxury of the suite awed Tuomi. The bedroom alone was bigger than the one-room apartment in Kirov far to the northeast, where he lived with his wife and three small children. The adjoining living room, decorated with freshly cut spring flowers, was larger still. On the center table stood a bowl of oranges, apples, bananas, and grapes along with bottles of cognac,

Scotch, and vodka. The bathroom even had a tile tub and bidet.

An hour or so after he had entered the suite, Tuomi heard the living-room door being unlocked. As an army major general and a colonel entered, he stood at attention.

"Please, sit down and relax," the trim little colonel said. "There is no need for formality among us. Do you find your quarters satisfactory?"

"I cannot believe I am here," Tuomi replied.

"Well, you have a big decision to make, and we want you to be comfortable while making it," the colonel commented cryptically. "Besides, this is an indication of what you may expect someday if your choice is correct."

The general, a broad-shouldered officer with a jagged scar on his forehead and a thick shock of unkempt black hair, wore a pair of dark sunglasses and chain-smoked. "We might as well come right to the point," he said brusquely. "We are considering sending you on an important and dangerous assignment to the United States. You would have to enter the country and work there illegally. Should you be caught, the best you could expect would be a long prison sentence. If you succeed, however, the rewards would be great."

The sudden prospect of becoming a spy in America overwhelmed Tuomi. "I have never imagined such an assignment," he said. "I'm not sure I am qualified . . ."

"Your record, your whole life, have been thoroughly analyzed," the general interrupted. "We are confident you have the capacity to do what is needed. The question is your will. You have a free choice, and nobody can make it for you."

The general paused, and Tuomi realized both officers were watching him intently, seeking to measure his reactions. Uncertain about what to say, he kept silent.

"Actually, the mission is not as difficult as it must seem to you," the general resumed. "But there are some unpleasant considerations we want you to face. We cannot control what happens to you once you are beyond our borders. You would have to live and work like any other American but still accomplish your real task. Never for a moment could you relax. You would also be separated from your family for a long time."

"How long?" Tuomi asked.

"Your training here in Moscow probably would last three years," the general replied. "Having invested so much in you, we would want to keep you over there a minimum of three years, maybe more. The better you do, the longer you will stay."

"What will happen to my family?" Tuomi asked.

"Don't worry about that," the general replied. "We can assure you that they will want for nothing."

"Could they possibly have a new apartment?"

"It might take some time, but we can guarantee it," the general pledged. "There will be even bigger compensations. Your salary will be tripled, and you can give it all to your family because we will supply you with all the dollars you need. Every year you spend abroad will count as two years toward your retirement. When you come back, you will not have to worry about anything for the rest of your days. But there is something far more important. You will enjoy the pride of having truly served your socialist fatherland. You will know that you have done something significant with your life."

Both officers rose abruptly. "Do not answer now," said the general. "We want you to think hard first. We will be back tomorrow."

Despite weariness from the train trip, Tuomi could not sleep that night. Sometimes pacing across the suite, sometimes sitting by the window looking out over the lights of Moscow, he thought back on all that had led him to this moment. Events and remarks that he had not understood at the time now acquired meaning. They made him wonder if the KGB had not been planning for years to confront him with the decision he had to make within the next few hours.

Kaarlo Tuomi had been born in the United States, but from his childhood on, he was indoctrinated in communism by his earnest, evangelistic Finnish stepfather. In 1933, when he was sixteen, the family moved from Michigan to Russia, and they became Soviet citizens. Four years later, during the Stalinist purges, the secret political police came in the night and took his stepfather, who never returned.

To support his mother and sister, Tuomi worked as a lumberjack until drafted into the army in 1939. Although trained for combat intelligence duty, he was shifted to the infantry when the Nazis attacked. After years of combat, he was mustered out in May 1946, one of two survivors of his original infantry battalion. In the wartime chaos his sister had disappeared, and his mother died of "heart failure," then a Soviet euphemism for starvation. His possessions consisted of a dirty uniform, a patched overcoat, a pair of German boots, a duffel bag stuffed with towels and underwear, and discharge pay equivalent to twenty dollars. He also had in his tunic pocket a faded letter, the last from his mother. It ended, "I would give all for just the tail of a fish, I am so hungry."

Yet Tuomi felt no self-pity. His whole life had conditioned him to privation and adversity. And his plight differed little from millions of others' in the Soviet Union.

In hopes of becoming a professor of English, Tuomi enrolled at the Teachers Institute at Kirov, an ancient city on the forested plains 475 miles northeast of Moscow. For a nominal rental, he shared a fifteen-by-seventeen-foot room with a widow and her two daughters. It had a fireplace but no kitchen or bath. Nearby, a communal garbage pit bred foul odors and rats the size of small cats. On Sunday afternoons he took the elder daughter, Nina, for walks and to the movies at the Palace Theater on the main square. Once they visited one of the two remaining churches in Kirov, a city formerly famous for its ecclesiastical architecture. Hesitantly Nina confessed that she had been unable to forsake an inherited faith in God.

She and Tuomi never really fell in love. But mutual respect and affection developed, and they were married in the fall. The wedding took place during a lunch period, and they spent their wedding night with her mother and sister sleeping a few feet away. To augment the meager salary Nina earned as a clothing-store clerk, Tuomi chopped wood and hauled bread after school for State Teahouse No. 3. He received the equivalent of fifty dollars a month and his meals, enabling him to give most of his rations to the women. Still, food shortages occurred frequently, and one of them led Tuomi to commit the first of two errors that were to change his life forever.

In late December 1947, Tuomi was pulling a sled loaded with bread through the snow toward the teahouse. Noticing that the bread box seemed heavier than usual, he opened it. Vapors from fresh-baked French rolls steamed out into the cold air as he counted the trays, then counted them again. There was no doubt. The bakery had included an extra tray of a hundred succulent rolls. If he kept them and was discovered, he could receive a ten-year sentence for stealing state property. But who would find out?

Bending nearly double, he towed the sled past the local KGB* office, known because of its forbidding character and color as the Gray Building. For a moment he trembled, then hurried home. "My God!" exclaimed Nina as he rushed into the room with the rolls. "Where did you get them?"

"Never mind," Tuomi commanded. "Buy some vodka and butter while I finish my delivery. We're having a party tonight!"

When he returned from the teahouse, the room was transformed by candlelight and the scent of the rolls heating in the fireplace. Nina proudly displayed half a kilo of black-market butter and a liter of 100-proof vodka she had chilled in a pan of snow. Sitting at the hearth, the family ate hot buttered rolls and drank cold vodka late into the night. Nina's mother, now dying of cancer, led them in singing carols remembered from her childhood. It was the best Christmas Tuomi ever had in the Soviet Union.

Tuomi made his second mistake the following win-

*The state security apparatus, which in 1947 was known as the MGB, had a number of different titles during the years Tuomi was in the Soviet Union. All are explained in Appendix A, which provides an organizational history of the apparatus. For simplicity of reference, the term "KGB" is used throughout this narrative.

ter. When a firewood shortage threatened to close the teahouse, the manager conspired with a night watchman to loot a state depot of enough wood for the season. He persuaded Tuomi to borrow a truck from a friend at the state garage to transport the wood and as compensation gave him half a truckload for himself.

Tuomi forgot about both incidents until the night of December 8, 1949. He was finishing work at the teahouse when a man entered, flashed a KGB card, and commanded, "Follow me."

At the local KGB headquarters, Tuomi was led down a dark stairway and into a basement room dimly illuminated by a single bulb hanging from a ceiling cord. Seated at a wooden table was KGB Major Serafim Alekseevich,* a stocky man with a disproportionately large head and cold blue eyes. Flanking him, barely visible, were two somber figures in civilian dress.

"Sit down, thief, and explain why you have turned into an enemy of the people!" the major shouted.

"I don't understand," Tuomi said.

"You have failed miserably in your duty to socialism," Serafim declared. "You are guilty of sabotage, and you shall be punished."

The KGB had arrested the night watchman for another offense and wrung from him the story of the stolen wood. As the officer detailed evidence of the crime, a sickening fear flooded through Tuomi. "We took the wood only to keep the shop open," he said. "Don't I deserve some leniency? I fought in many battles. I was decorated for bravery. I never have done anything else wrong."

Drumming his fingers on the table, Serafim slowly replied, "And what about the rolls? Tell us how you stole a hundred rolls and gorged yourself like a swine while your comrades went hungry. You see! You not only steal, you lie!"

Benumbed, Tuomi felt drained of hope. "All I can say is that I am sorry," he apologized in despair.

The major grunted contemptuously. After a minute

---

*As often happened, Tuomi knew only the first and patronymic names of this KGB officer.

or so of silence, one of the men spoke from the shadows. "Your family will suffer terribly while you are in prison," he said. "That would be a shame. Possibly there is a way out for you."

"What do you mean?" Tuomi asked.

"It is enough to say that we have a lot of work to do, and you can help us," the man replied.

Serafim shoved paper and pen across the desk. "Write," he ordered. Tuomi dutifully wrote out an oath pledging eternal secrecy and faithful execution of all secret-police orders. Next, the major handed him a slip of paper bearing a street address. "Meet me there at 9 P.M. a week from tonight," he instructed him.

It was a classic KGB recruitment. As Tuomi was to learn years later, the KGB had planted the rolls and tempted him to steal them. Then it had waited patiently to discover still another act for which he could be blackmailed. Now it owned him.

On a cold moonlit night one week later, Tuomi knocked at a two-story frame house on a side street near downtown Kirov. Outside, the house looked like any other on the block. Inside, it was partitioned into a series of offices on the first floor and two self-contained apartments on the second. This was the first of many "safe houses" Tuomi was to visit—sanctuaries where the KGB meets and instructs its informants.

"Pour yourself a drink, and we will get started," Serafim said, motioning to a decanter of Georgian brandy. Then he began to outline Tuomi's duties:

"First you will report attitudes at the Teachers Institute toward Party policies, conditions of life, and especially the West. We want to know everything your teachers and fellow students say, the bad and the good. Tell us exactly what you hear, not what you think we want to hear.

"In the eyes of your comrades, you should appear as an intellectual, curious about the world. Whenever you hear an anti-Soviet statement, hint that you might agree. Venture cautious criticisms occasionally. You may even make a mildly favorable comment or two about the West. As your reputation spreads, you will attract those who think privately what you suggest

openly. This takes time. Never go too far, or you'll
frighten the fish away. But once you learn the sport,
you will be surprised at how many you bring into the
net. Pay special attention to your English professor,
Petr Filimonov. We know he listens to foreign broadcasts. You must win his confidence so that he will invite you to listen with him."

Tuomi could get nowhere with Filimonov, a thin,
bald man who wore a long waxed mustache curled up
at the ends. Reserved by nature, he betrayed no visible
reaction to any of the heretical remarks Tuomi made
in his presence.

After Tuomi was graduated, the KGB arranged to
have the Ministry of Education appoint him a junior
English instructor at the Institute. Filimonov, as head
of the English Department, was his immediate supervisor, and now Tuomi was in a position to cultivate a
personal relationship. One night in November 1950, he
went back to the Institute to look for a missing foun-
tain pen and found himself in the midst of a drunken
party. It had developed spontaneously after two students smuggled several liters of grain alcohol out of the
local machine-gun factory. Standing alone in a corner
was Filimonov, smiling serenely, a teacup of alcohol in
one hand, a cup of water in the other.

"Good evening, sir," Tuomi greeted him in English.

"My dear fellow, how good to see you," the professor responded in what he imagined was an Oxford
accent. As they drank together, Filimonov grew progressively euphoric, effusively complimenting his subordinate's scholarship and command of English.

"Someday I hope to find a radio powerful enough to
pick up foreign broadcasts," Tuomi confided. "I want
to hear the language as it is actually spoken. More than
that, I think every Soviet scholar ought to learn for
himself about the outside world, don't you?"

"I have a very good radio, a German Grundig liberated in Prussia," Filimonov whispered. "It receives
broadcasts from everywhere. Sometimes when conditions are right, I can even hear an American station in
Del Rio, Texas. Perhaps you would like to stop by,
and we can practice English together."

During the following months Tuomi and Filimonov listened to the radio once or twice a week, and the professor did begin to make dangerous statements. Tuomi faithfully reported his remarks, and in May Serafim patted him on the back and announced, "Your assignment with Filimonov is finished."

"But why?" asked Tuomi.

"Never mind," Serafim Alekseevich told him. "You have done a good job at the Institute. We already have another position in mind for you."

The next morning at school, Filimonov did not speak to Tuomi. For a moment he simply stared at him, his whole face contorted with pure hatred. Tuomi was never sure, but he suspected that the KGB had used his report to intimidate the professor, forcing him to become an informant like himself.

No rewards had been promised, but Tuomi began to discover that the KGB did bestow secret benefits. He was given another job, as a teacher at the Kirov adult education center. Party membership was essential for long-term advancement within the teaching profession or the KGB itself. When Tuomi's application was stymied because he could not account for his missing sister, the KGB searched the Soviet Union until it found her—working as a hod carrier in Archangel. With the birth of his first two children in 1948 and 1951, Tuomi's regular salary became increasingly inadequate. The major supplemented it with gifts of several hundred rubles before holidays and vacations.

With coaching and experience, Tuomi grew adept at conspiracy. He had many attributes of a good spy: courage, intelligence, curiosity, a keen memory, and an ability to make people like him. He laughed easily, his blue eyes radiated good humor, his broad, pleasant face invited trust. As often happens to people who remain in espionage, he came to like intrigue for intrigue's sake. The guilt he initially felt at betraying his colleagues gradually subsided as he succeeded in thinking of himself as a patriot.

There was one man he could not bring himself to betray—Nikolai Vasilevich, a scholar of Russian literature beloved for his wit, honesty, and generosity of spirit. Tall, frail and gentle, he had a great teacher's ability to inspire, and his classes were always crowded. Because he repeatedly refused to join the Party, the KGB kept him under periodic surveillance, and in December 1955 Tuomi was assigned the watch.

At a New Year's party soon thereafter, Tuomi heard a student ask Nikolai why he declined Party membership. "Communism is a cage," he answered. "I was not born to be in a cage. I was born an eagle."

Tuomi omitted any mention of the statement at his next KGB meeting. Four days later Serafim telephoned him at school, something he never had done before. "Make any excuse you want, but meet me in fifteen minutes," he ordered. When Tuomi entered the safe house, the major's face told him he was in trouble. " 'Communism is a cage. I was not born to be in a cage,' " the KGB officer repeated. "Have you ever heard those words?"

"Yes, Nikolai Vasilevich spoke them," answered Tuomi, chilled by the realization that there had been another spy at the party.

"Why then did you not report them?"

"I thought them unimportant."

"Don't make it worse than it already is," Serafim said. "You are just lucky that I, instead of somebody else, found out about this. I am going to let it pass only because we have worked together so long and because I have an idea of what is in store for you if you don't ruin it."

As Tuomi was dismissed, the major added a final warning. "I hope this experience teaches you something," he said. *"Never* try to deceive us."

In the fall of 1956, Alevtina Stepanovna, a widow of twenty-nine, enrolled in Tuomi's class. Although she was not beautiful, her blonde hair, soft hazel eyes, and seductive figure made her decidedly attractive. She taught French in high school and was determined to master English. "I wonder if you could give me extra lessons," she asked Tuomi one day after class. Her smiling entreaty seemed so earnest that he agreed to meet her for a couple of hours every Sunday.

Alevtina was an excellent pupil. During the tutoring

sessions she concentrated completely on English, but afterward she would insist that Tuomi stay for tea and cake. The two-room apartment in which she lived with her mother and small son was warm and bright. Talking with her as the sun slanted through the windows, Tuomi was glad he had agreed to the lessons.

In time, Alevtina induced him to talk about himself. Unexpectedly she would throw a personal question at him, always smiling, sometimes lowering her voice as if to invite an exchange of confidences. "Is it true you were born in the United States?" she once inquired.

"Yes."

"Wouldn't you like to live there if you could?" she asked softly.

The intuitive antenna a wise Soviet citizen develops warned Tuomi to be careful. "I suppose everyone longs to visit his birthplace again," he replied. "But live there, no. The future belongs to the Soviet Union, not to America."

Bedecked in a new blue dress, Alevtina looked especially alluring when he came to give a lesson one Sunday in January 1957. From the window she called, "Come look at the sun on the snow." As he joined her, she stood so close that their bodies touched. "We are alone today," she whispered.

For an instant Tuomi wavered between temptation and the dictates of all his KGB experience. Then, stepping away, he said, "I'm sorry, we cannot have your lesson today. My children are sick, and I have to help Nina take care of them." A few days later Alevtina curtly told him that she was giving up the class.

Walking home a few weeks later, Tuomi saw a figure scurrying along the street ahead of him, looking neither left nor right. It was Alevtina, and as she turned down a side street, he followed her. But as she entered a house, he stopped abruptly. It was one of the KGB safe houses at which he had met with Serafim.

Two months later Tuomi received the summons to Moscow. Now, in the spacious suite, he understood why the KGB had tested him through Alevtina. It had sought to fathom his inner feelings about the United States. But more important, by his reactions to her sexual blandishments, it had tried to gauge his devotion to his family. Only if he truly cared for them could they serve as effective hostages.

As dawn broke over the city, Tuomi tried to weigh the costs and rewards of accepting the mission to America, the consequences of rejecting it. He thought of his children—Viktor at nine, Irina at six, Nadezhda at four—and the years with them that would be irretrievably lost. But he thought too of the benefits his new income and status would afford his family. They would have a better apartment, a refrigerator, television, all the food and clothes they needed. The KGB would ensure the children a good education.

What if he refused the assignment? He could be branded "unreliable." Just as the KGB had arranged his employment, it could arrange his dismissal. Without explanation, it could bring destitution upon him and his family, and there would be no appeal.

What if he undertook the espionage mission and failed? Fear of imprisonment, even death, tormented him. Yet patriotism and devotion to communism made him want to do what his country asked.

The faces of the KGB general and colonel were expressionless when they entered the apartment. After they were seated, the general leaned forward. "Have you given the matter the most careful consideration?"

"I want to do my duty," Tuomi answered.

"You can be proud of yourself," the general said as both officers smiled and perceptibly relaxed. "This still must be approved at the highest level, but I think it will go through. You will hear from us within a few weeks."

Back in Kirov, Tuomi told Nina and his fellow teachers that he had taken tests for admission to an interpreters' school and was awaiting the results. They came on April 26, 1957, in a telegram from Moscow: "You have been accepted for the course."

The colonel was waiting when Tuomi arrived in Moscow on May Day. They drove to one of the city's finest apartment buildings, on Kutuzovsky Prospekt, and took the elevator to the fifth floor. There the colonel opened what appeared to be a broom closet. It was actually the entrance to a hidden stairway leading to an apartment on the sixth floor.

"Come in," said the colonel. "Let me show you your new home."

The apartment consisted of a large, elegantly furnished living-dining room carpeted with Oriental rugs, a master bedroom, a smaller bedroom, an American-type kitchen, and a modern bathroom. A narrow spiral staircase wound upward to a huge sunlit recreation room on the roof. Among the furnishings were two red leather sofas, a mahogany writing desk, a movie projector and screen, a television set, record player, radio, a Ping-Pong table, and a safe. One wall was lined with bookshelves filled with American magazines and copies of the New York *Times*. There also were many works by Western authors popular in the Soviet Union— Dickens, Mark Twain, Jack London, Dreiser, Steinbeck, and Hemingway. Far to the north, Tuomi could see the blue Moscow River and to the east the spires of the Kremlin churches, which in sunlight looked like golden turnips. This room was the spy school.

"Everyone is on vacation, so you will have to take care of yourself for a while," the colonel told him. "Go see the city, sleep all you can, and relax until you hear from us. The neighbors know they are not to ask questions. If you meet them on the elevator, you may say hello but no more. Let me wish you all success in your new life."

The interlude of privacy and freedom ended on the sixth day. Just before 8 A.M. he was awakened by the ringing of the telephone. "Don't go out this morning," a voice told him. "Somebody is coming by."

Tuomi was in the recreation room an hour later when he heard someone call from the living room below, "Hello! Anybody home?" Hurrying down the spiral staircase, he saw a short, rather ugly man with slightly jowly cheeks, a wide nose, steel-rimmed glasses, and a mass of thick black hair combed straight back. "I am Aleksei Ivanovich, your chief instructor and adviser," he said, extending his hand. "Excuse me for letting myself in."

The visitor was Aleksei Ivanovich Galkin. As a young communist, this son of peasant parents had worked on the Moscow subway while obtaining an education. By obedience, industry, and scholarship, he rose swiftly in Soviet intelligence. From 1951 to 1956 he served as an agent in the United States while masquerading as a United Nations employee. He devoted himself primarily to acquiring firsthand knowledge that would equip him to train spies for espionage in America. Every few months he changed residences so as to familiarize himself with different sections of New York City and its suburbs. He continually sought invitations into homes so he could see for himself how Americans live and thus how Soviet agents should behave among them.

"Let me brief you generally about what is ahead; then I will try to answer questions," Galkin began in heavily accented but understandable English. "Your training will last three years. Your main subject will be the theory and practice of intelligence, which I will teach. You will also study the philosophy of Marx, Engels, and Lenin as applied to intelligence, as well as technical subjects such as cryptography, photography, and secret writing. Along the way we will give you a real understanding of the United States: its history, geography, politics, military establishment, and contemporary life. Naturally, we will work intensively on your English. I know you speak it well, but language is ever-changing. You have years of colloquialisms to learn, and we want to shave away your accent as much as possible. Incidentally, I hope you like movies," he said, pointing to the projector. "We will show you American films constantly. We have quite a library of them."

Galkin paused, then picked up the pad on which Tuomi was jotting notes. "Please, from now on, nothing in writing," he said. "You must memorize everything."

"I'm sorry," Tuomi apologized.

"No, no," Galkin continued, patting Tuomi on the shoulder. "You must not confuse a correction with a reprimand. Someday your life will depend upon what you learn here, so all your instructors will be pointing out mistakes that could be fatal. We simply want to help you; I especially, because as your counselor I shall be graded according to how well you do. You must not hesitate to raise any question or problem with me, no matter how personal or trivial. How about some tea?"

While he was boiling water in a silver samovar, Galkin remarked, "You know, the Americans actually put ice in their tea."

"It can taste pretty good on a hot day," Tuomi said.

"That's right. I almost forgot about your boyhood in the States," Galkin replied. "That's an advantage you have over most of the illegals we send there. Still, you have a terrific amount to learn."

Sipping tea, Galkin continued, "The second phase of your studies will be entirely practical. We will concentrate on building an identity for you which will stand up in America. A whole life must be invented for you, and you must know it as if you had actually lived it."

"Can you tell me what I am expected to do in America?" inquired Tuomi.

"Not specifically. But your first task will be to establish yourself as an American and get a job. Then you will want to spot Americans who might work for us. If all goes well, some American agents we already have might be turned over for you to handle. In any case, I'm pretty certain you will work out of New York City."

"Will I be able to see my family while I'm here?" Tuomi asked.

"Certainly," Galkin assured him. "From time to time you may make brief visits to Kirov, and we'll bring them here for a holiday or two. Incidentally, here's an address where they can write you. If you have any family problems, let me know.

"One last thing. In educating the masses, sometimes simplifications, even exaggerations, are necessary. But for you, accurate knowledge is vital. So don't be shocked if what we tell you differs from what the public is told. Now let's meet Yelena, the best cook in Moscow."

A portly, gray-haired woman in her fifties welcomed Tuomi. For years she had been an assistant chef at the Kremlin. Now she acted as a kind of housemother to spies in training. She served a delicious lunch of pea soup, spiced beef and rice baked in light dough, red cabbage, tomato salad, and melon, accompanied by red wine. "I'll do better once I learn what you like," she promised. "I will take good care of you."

Unaccustomed to so much food and wine at midday, Tuomi dozed on the sofa. He was awakened by a sultry-voiced greeting: "How are you, comrade?" Staring at him was a striking brunette in her late twenties. She wore a dress bought in New York. It outlined the curves of her slender body in a way that distinguished her from any woman in the provinces of the Soviet Union.

This was Fainna Solasko, daughter of a Russian woman who for years had served in the United States as a courtesan to KGB officers and visiting Soviet officials. Fainna had grown up in New York, where her mother was on the payroll of Amtorg, the Soviet trading company. After studying at Columbia and New York University, she entered into an unhappy marriage with an American employee of Tass. In 1955 she slipped away to Moscow, ideally suited by background, intellect, and disposition to teach spies about the United States.

Her announced duty was to perfect Tuomi's English and to indoctrinate him thoroughly in contemporary American life. She also had the more important, covert assignment of continuously assessing his psychological state, character, and native ability.

"Why are your fingernails so filthy?" she asked.

Tuomi looked at his hands. It occurred to him that his fingernails had always been dirty from the menial jobs he had to perform in order to scrape up extras for his family. Before he could say anything, Fainna mocked him again.

"Which collective farm do you come from?"

"I am a teacher," Tuomi replied.

"Your shoes make that difficult to believe," Fainna retorted. "Have you ever shined them?"

"It was not the custom in Kirov," he answered.

"You will have to learn to shine your shoes by yourself," said Fainna. "But *I* will teach you to tie your tie so people will not think you moonlight as a hangman. Come into the bedroom."

Positioning Tuomi before a full-length mirror, Fainna stood behind him, put her arms around his neck, and tugged at the knot in his tie. The feel of her lithe body, the touch of her hair on his neck, the faint fragrance of powder and perfume, produced the natural male effect for which she was watching in the mirror. Stepping away, she sought further to shame him. "Haven't you ever been near a woman before?" she snapped, feigning indignation. "My God, you're hopeless!"

Humiliated and enraged, Tuomi was tempted to hit her. But over the years the KGB had put him through too much for him not to sense that Fainna was provoking him purposely.

"My background has been such that I have not had an opportunity to acquire all the manners I should," he said as casually as he could. "But given the opportunity, I am sure I can learn them."

For a moment Fainna silently searched him with her dark, taunting eyes. "You handled that very well," she said finally. "I can see that you are going to be a good student and that we will get along fine. Just to show you there is no ill will, I'm going to give you a present." She handed him an American shoeshine kit.

After the first few days of classes, Tuomi felt as if an entire university had been created solely to educate him. The instructors who visited the apartment daily from nine to five were all experienced, professional intelligence officers. At one time or another, most had been spies in the United States. The quality of their English varied, but the mastery of their particular subjects was uniformly excellent.

The instructor in the philosophy of intelligence was a handsome blond man with a resonant voice. He looked and talked remarkably like the evangelist Billy

Graham. And when he lectured about the importance of intelligence to the Soviet Union, he spoke with the sincerity and fervor of an evangelist.

"Materially the United States remains far more advanced than we, with its standard of living. As the strongest military and economic power in the world, it is thus the foremost enemy of socialism," he declared.

"It always will be until capitalism is liquidated and the American people are brought into the socialist camp. The laws of history decree that this is inevitable. But Lenin believed that they best can be accelerated through intelligence, and history has proved them right.

"One of our agents actually saved Moscow from the Nazis. We would not have had the atomic bomb until much later had it not been for our spies in Canada and America. Today the Western countries are advancing very rapidly technically. By learning their military, technical, and political secrets, we who are momentarily weaker will become the stronger."

The instructor paused for emphasis. "You must absolutely understand the morality of socialist intelligence," he said. "You must think of humanity—past, present, and future—as one great body that requires surgery. You cannot perform surgery without severing membranes, destroying tissue, spilling blood. Similarly, in intelligence we sometimes destroy individuals who are expendable tissues on the body of humanity. Occasionally we must perform unpleasant acts, even kidnapping and liquidation. But none of this is immoral. All acts that further history and socialism are moral acts."

There were aspects of America the teacher frankly admired. "Over there, if you want to go somewhere, you just get in a car, bus, train, or plane and go, and nobody asks any questions," he informed Tuomi with wonder in his voice. "The highway system is unbelievable, and they're about to spend billions more to improve it."

"Capitalism has nothing to do with this, does it?" Tuomi asked jokingly.

"In a way it does," the teacher replied seriously.

"Just as feudalism had a place in history, so did capitalism. But its time is past. The American economy owes its strength to three primary factors that have nothing to do with capitalism. First, the United States has immense natural resources. Second, its territory has escaped the devastation of war for nearly a century. Third, America was settled by the bravest and most industrious people of Europe. Americans today are descendants of good stock, and they remain industrious and tough. It would be folly to pretend otherwise."

Of all the instructors, Tuomi liked and respected Galkin the most. But Fainna Solasko ranked close behind. She made each session an entertaining though serious game. At the outset she would describe a typical scene in American life, then assign Tuomi one role and herself another to act out in English. Thus, Tuomi went to a patio party at a suburban home, and she was the hostess. He checked into a hotel, and she was the registration clerk. He applied for a job, and she was the personnel director. He went to a restaurant, and she was his date. Always she emphasized the use of idiom, jokes, and profanity in his speech.

Most of the instructors referred, one way or another, to the perils of promiscuity and alcohol. But Fainna was chosen to deliver the formal lecture about sex. "It is not expected that you will go for years without sexual experiences," she said matter-of-factly. "But as they can be extremely dangerous, it is necessary to define what you may and may not do. You must have nothing to do with prostitutes because they can give you diseases. Don't attempt to seduce young girls or married women. We are investing too much in you to risk senseless trouble with parents or a jealous husband. A mature, independent woman is the safest partner, but do not get emotionally entangled with *any* woman."

Fainna was the first to exploit the library of American films for classroom purposes. Literally every type of Hollywood production was available—silent films of the 1920s, the latest Technicolor releases, mysteries, melodramas, comedies, musicals, Westerns, crime, war, and horror movies; the good, bad, and indifferent. To test Tuomi's comprehension she required him to watch a film, then recount the plot in English and explain its meaning.

Other instructors selected films for more specialized purposes. Galkin stressed those which portrayed the techniques of American law-enforcement agencies. He repeatedly showed a picture in which Yul Brynner headed a ring of narcotics smugglers. Each time, he stopped the film to rerun a scene in which U.S. customs officers ripped open and relentlessly searched the luggage of a suspected heroin courier. "This is what you could be up against," he said. "It is a very realistic scene."

Galkin also painstakingly instructed Tuomi about how to meet Americans and discern those who might be lured into espionage. He stressed the importance of a wide circle of acquaintances. "Go to church," he told Tuomi. "It's a good place to make friends, and the mere fact that you're there suggests that you're harmless. Join clubs such as the Lions or Rotary. Remember, even if a person you meet isn't interesting, he might lead you to someone who is."

The best prospects were people who had hidden problems—money, sex, gambling, drinking—any weakness that might make them susceptible to enticement or manipulation.

"In America a man may have a $20,000 house, a car, good furniture and clothes, and still not be satisfied," Galkin explained. "He knows others who are living even better. He wants a $40,000 house. So he moves, and his mortgage payments go way up. He has to join a club, buy a second car, new furniture. He falls deeper and deeper in debt trying to maintain his status.

"This is where you step in and give him a helping hand with a loan. Let him know you're in no hurry to get the money back and hint there's more available if needed. You advance him more and more until he is hopelessly in your debt. Then suddenly you demand repayment, which he cannot possibly make. Now he is desperate, and he will be tempted by your subtle offer: for one sweetly disguised little act of treason, you will wipe out all his debts. You will persuade him that the information or document or favor you ask isn't very important and that you will ask no more. Everything will be forgotten. Of course," Galkin concluded with a smile, "once he commits this single act, he is ours for life."

Though Galkin usually guarded against any display of emotion, one day in September 1957 he burst into the apartment flushed with excitement. "Guess who I just came up on the elevator with!" he yelled. "Eleanor Roosevelt! I stood right next to her!"

"What's she doing here?" Tuomi asked incredulously.

"That's what's so funny," Galkin answered. "They're taking her through the fanciest apartments in Moscow so she can see how the typical Soviet worker lives. I thought about bringing her up here to meet you, a fellow American."

They laughed, speculating about what Mrs. Roosevelt was being told one floor beneath a Soviet espionage school. "Maybe she would like to sit in on some of your classes," said Galkin. "She could see for herself how much we really want to understand her country."

The training gradually became more technical. Tuomi was introduced to all the professional terminology of Soviet intelligence. He learned that the "Center" meant Moscow headquarters, to "swim" meant to travel, "illness" meant arrest, a "wet affair" meant assassination. A "legend" was a cover story, a "shoe" a false passport, a "cobbler" a technician who forges passports, a "music box" a radio transmitter, a "neighbor" another arm of Soviet intelligence.

He mastered microphotography, reducing a page of writing to the size of a period on a postcard or letter. He learned how to use and develop invisible writing, how to encipher and decipher messages with code books disguised as pocket calendars the size of a pack of matches. He was taught how to detect and evade surveillance by jumping on a bus, entering a crowded store with multiple exits, or switching taxis. And he went out on the streets to practice communicating with

the Center through "drops"—hiding places where one
agent deposits messages, money, or documents to be
picked up by another.

One day while taking pictures of the Defense Ministry, Tuomi was grabbed by two KGB plainclothesmen
who had been summoned by a suspicious citizen. His
photography instructor ran up and whispered, "I am
responsible for this man. Let him go." A profane argument ensued, but the instructor's superior credentials
prevailed. As he hurried his charge away, the instructor was furious. "I've told you a thousand times, when
you take pictures in public, you've got to do it quickly." It was one of the few lapses in Tuomi's performance.

In February 1958, an officer who periodically
brought supplies and equipment drove Tuomi to an unmarked compound in the inner ring of Moscow just a
few blocks from the American embassy. Entering
through a wooden gate, they crossed a courtyard and
stopped at a long flat building. Inside, Tuomi found
himself in a men's clothing store, one that seemed very
strange. Suddenly Tuomi realized why: everything he
saw was American! He was standing in a small but
complete storehouse for spies on their way to the
United States.

"We want this man dressed up," the supply officer
said to the tailor in charge, who recorded Tuomi's mea-
surements, then proceeded through the room gathering
up clothing. The officer carefully checked off each article on a printed form as the tailor handed over shirts,
ties, one black and one brown pair of shoes, a hat,
nylon socks, T-shirts, boxer shorts, a cashmere sweat-
er, handkerchiefs, a silver tie clasp, cuff links, and a
self-winding watch.

"Your suits and coat will have to be altered before
they're ready," he explained. "But we want you to wear
all this just enough so nothing will look new when
you leave. Incidentally, that's a very fine watch. Don't
be tempted to hock it on the black market. One fool
tried that. I won't tell you where he is now. But it isn't
the United States."

Two weeks later, Tuomi, Galkin, and Fainna were

finishing one of Yelena's superb lunches when the supply officer walked in with a brown cowhide suitcase. He opened it and presented Tuomi with a dark-blue sharkskin suit, a gray tweed suit, and a tan topcoat with a zip-out lining. Everyone demanded that Tuomi try on his clothes immediately. In the bedroom he dressed himself in the tweed suit, a white shirt, a black knit tie, and black shoes and socks. Then he folded a handkerchief in his jacket pocket the way he had seen it done in the most recent American movies. When he reappeared, the others all joined in laughing and clapping. "You look just like an American!" Fainna exclaimed. "You will pass anywhere."

In mid-March of 1958, Galkin arrived unexpectedly at the apartment looking tired and preoccupied. "I have been at the Center, and I must tell you that you will be leaving much sooner than I had hoped," he said. "Relations with the United States are very turbulent. We must plant you soon so that if two or three years from now there is a break in relations, you will be ready. Should there be war, people like you will be all we have to rely on."

"How soon?" Tuomi interrupted.

"I don't know exactly," Galkin replied. "In any case, you're going to have to pass some very stiff examinations. That's not my idea; the Center insists. Afterward, maybe you can have a little time with your family. Then we will have to work at building up your legend, and you will take a European trip. You must have some practice posing as an American outside the Soviet Union."

The examinations took five days and covered every aspect of his training. Strangers who were never identified joined the regular teachers in interrogating Tuomi. Some of their questions went so far beyond the bounds of anything he had been taught that he feared they were determined to flunk him.

Tuomi did not learn how he had done for three days. Then Galkin brought a message from the Center. "You are officially advised that the results of your examinations are as follows. Theory and Practice of Intelligence: Excellent, with the qualification that improvement is needed in surveillance detection. Philosophy of Intelligence: Excellent. Photography: Satisfactory. Cryptography: Excellent. American Studies and English: Excellent. I congratulate you. Chief."

Beaming, Galkin added, "I have more good news. Your family is getting the apartment, a brand-new one."

"That's wonderful!" Tuomi exclaimed. "Can you tell me about it?"

"I'll let your wife do that," Galkin said. "She and the children arrive in Moscow the day after tomorrow. We have a house for you outside the city; a whole house, mind you! After a week here, all of you go to the Black Sea for a month."

Galkin had been almost mirthful in his role of benefactor. Now, as he started to say farewell, he became serious to the point of melancholy. "This will be your last chance really to be with your family for perhaps many years," he said. "Make the most of it. When you come back, I will still look in on you now and then. But others will take over. They will work out your mission with you in detail. From here on, everything is for keeps."

Returning from his vacation tanned and refreshed, Tuomi met a number of new instructors. All were army officers, a status they revealed by their authoritarian manners as much as by the uniforms they occasionally wore. About a week after he was back, an officer ceremoniously informed him that he had been awarded the rank of lieutenant in Soviet military intelligence.

Having served the KGB for more than a decade, Tuomi naturally had assumed that he was being sent to the United States as a KGB agent. Now he realized that the KGB had turned him over to the GRU and that he had been in its hands ever since coming to Moscow. But the distinction between the KGB and GRU meant little to him. He thought of himself as working simply for Soviet intelligence or, more particularly, the Center. His training was precisely the same as that given a KGB illegal and the clandestine procedures he was to follow in America were exactly the same as those used by the KGB. The only real difference the transfer to the GRU made was in the emphasis of his future assignment.

Tuomi learned in the next weeks that New York would be his first target area in America. After securely settling himself, he was to watch the movement of missiles, munitions, and troops through New York Harbor and to search for prospective recruits. He was told that if all went well, he might eventually be shifted to Washington to handle Soviet agents already recruited.

The officers who came to the apartment each day now began to prepare the legend, or fictitious past, that was to mask all Tuomi had done for the last twenty-five years. They questioned him minutely and intimately, hunting authentic details of his life which would be blended with fiction to create a plausible past. For example, the fact that Tuomi actually knew something about lumbering and carpentry caused these activities to be included in his fictitious biography.

According to the legend ultimately approved by the Center, Tuomi was born in Michigan and grew up in small towns there. After his sister died in 1932, his stepfather abandoned the family, never to be seen again. The next year he and his mother moved to Minnesota, to help with his grandmother's farm. Vacationing in the Upper Peninsula of Michigan five years later, he married a childhood sweetheart, Helen Matson. The farm began to fail in 1941 and Tuomi went job hunting in New York, living in a Bronx apartment building on Decatur Avenue. A draft board exempted him because his wife, mother, and ailing grandmother in Minnesota were dependents.

Unable to find work he liked in New York, Tuomi got a job in a lumber camp on the Fraser River near Vancouver, Canada. He later was transferred to a lumberyard in Vancouver, remaining there until 1949, when he moved to Milwaukee. There he was employed at a machine shop and later in the shipping department of the General Electric plant. Next he opened a small cabinetmaking shop of his own. In 1956 his unfaithful wife deserted him.

Because of emotional problems caused by the break-up of his marriage, his cabinetry shop foundered, and he closed it in 1957. He then moved to New York, intending to study bookkeeping and start anew. His most recent employment had been at a Bronx lumber company. At the moment he was looking for an apartment because he had been forced to move from a building condemned to permit construction of a new approach to the George Washington Bridge. To help his legend blend with reality, he was to use the name he had been given at birth, Kaarlo R. Tuomi.

As Tuomi learned the factual foundations of the biography, he realized that Soviet agents in the United States over the years must have spent thousands of hours gathering seemingly innocuous details. There was a real Helen Matson who left an upper Michigan town in 1938 to be married and was never heard from again. The grandmother was dead, and her farm long since had been merged with others. The Bronx apartment building where he allegedly lived had been demolished. Ownership of the Vancouver lumberyard had changed, and the present proprietors would not know who had worked there years before. The owner of the Milwaukee machine shop had died, and the personnel turnover in the GE shipping department was such that it was assumed anyone *could* have worked there without being remembered. Moreover, the skeleton of the story was fleshed out with names and characterizations of numerous people whom Tuomi would have known in the locales where he supposedly lived and worked.

Through the next weeks, Tuomi rehearsed his legend endlessly while his teachers played the roles of American police and employers, probing and challenging in an attempt to trap him in a fatal inconsistency. The Russians had managed to take motion pictures inside three of the establishments where Tuomi was supposed to have been employed. Studying the films, he watched his "colleagues" working while the instructors briefed him about their names, personalities, and habits.

In midsummer, Tuomi embarked on a two-month training trip into Western Europe. Posing as an Ameri-

can tourist, he took off from Vnukovo Airport outside
Moscow on a plane bound for Copenhagen. This trip
to the West, a crucial part of the training of most Soviet
illegals, was designed to familiarize him further with
the customs he would encounter during his actual mission, including travel arrangements, casual conversation with strangers, and currency requirements. The
journey was also expected to ease the effect of cultural
shock that agents often experience when first exposed
to Western society.

At Copenhagen, Tuomi boarded a flight to Paris.
Upon arrival, he began the furtive ritual often employed by a Soviet agent after his illegal arrival in a
foreign country. He checked into a hotel under the
name he had used to enter France, spent the night, and
tore up his passport and flushed it down the toilet.
Then he registered at another hotel under a name appearing on a second passport. If the French authorities
had suspicions, they would be looking for a man who
had vanished.

During the next forty-eight hours Tuomi walked the
streets and rode buses and cabs to make sure he was
not being followed. Satisfied, he mailed a picture postcard, signaling he was safe, to a mail drop in Vienna.

Now Tuomi had two weeks to enjoy Paris as would
any energetic American. Camera in hand, he visited
the Eiffel Tower, Notre-Dame, the Arc de Triomphe,
Sacre-Coeur, and other tourist attractions. He dined
at restaurants and nightclubs, strolled along the Seine,
and window-shopped. He bought a wristwatch for Nina, a camera for Viktor, ice skates and winter skating
costumes for the girls. The beauty of the city, the ele-
gance of the women, the streams of honking traffic, the
dazzling shops, the melody of speech—all made Paris
seem dreamlike and unreal. Nothing in his experience
had prepared him for such a world. Sipping wine at
a sidewalk café, Tuomi felt ashamed that he found
Western "decadence" so enjoyable.

After a week at the Brussels World's Fair, he went
to Scandinavia. He could not entirely rid himself of the
fear of detection that is the permanent companion of
any spy, but he relaxed more and more as he saw that

everywhere Europeans thought he was American. Dining alone at a Finnish resort, he glanced up to find a fierce Finn, weighing at least 250 pounds, glowering at him.

"My name is Olavi, and I want to talk to you," the Finn said belligerently. "Come over to my table."

Prepared for trouble, Tuomi obeyed. Olavi declared that he was violently anticommunist, having fought the Russians as a guerrilla. Now he had a conviction, approaching an obsession, that the Russians were infiltrating Finland with Americans who actually were Soviet spies. "I see that you are an American," he said ominously. "What I want to know is—are you a Russian spy? Let's have the truth!"

The Finn's suspicions, at once preposterous and accurate, caused Tuomi to break into laughter. This persuaded Olavi that he was in the company of an authentic American. Tuomi had no choice but to spend a long, drunken evening listening to curses about everything Russian.

A few days later, Tuomi flew back to Moscow. Galkin, whom he had not seen for several months, welcomed him at the apartment.

"The pressure is on to get you over to the United States, and we're going to have to exploit every minute," he said. "I'm afraid that the rush means you can have only a few days with your family. Actually, it may be better that way. Any longer would probably just be torture for you all."

"I would like to buy some things for my wife," Tuomi said.

"Fine," said Galkin. "That reminds me—your salary is being tripled." That made it $550 a month, a princely sum by prevailing Soviet standards.

"If you need anything major, all you have to do is tell me, and we'll arrange to have it shipped."

"I would like my wife to have either a refrigerator or a washing machine," Tuomi said.

"She will receive both within the month," Galkin promised.

When Tuomi got off the train in Kirov, Irina jumped into his arms and hugged his neck as if she never would let go. "My papa, my papa," she kept repeating. Nina had to pull her away so he could embrace the rest of the family.

They shared the new apartment with two other families, though each family had a large room of its own. At the end of the hallway running the length of the apartment were a bathroom and a kitchen with a sink and wood-burning stove. By comparison with their old home, the new one was magnificent.

The presents from Paris excited the children. They listened raptly as Tuomi told them of his travels, and in turn Viktor and Irina proudly recounted their progress in school.

Although it was snowing in the afternoon, Tuomi asked his son to walk with him. They passed the square where he had discovered the extra tray of rolls, the KGB headquarters where it had all begun, and Tuomi had difficulty summoning up the words to speak to his son.

"Viktor, tomorrow I will go away on an assignment for our government," he began. "I will be gone a very long time. You are only ten, but while I am away, you must be the man who looks after Mama and your sisters. If something should keep me from coming back, you must look after them all their lives."

In the morning the family went out together to watch Nadezhda and Irina skate in their bright Parisian outfits. Tuomi found his hand trembling almost uncontrollably as he tried to take a last picture. In the taxi to the station, Nina and the girls began to cry. As the train slowly gathered speed out of Kirov, Tuomi stood on the rear platform watching his family huddled together waving to him. When he could no longer see them, he wept.

On Tuomi's last night in Moscow, Fainna came to say good-by. She seemed warm and feminine as never before. It was as if she were lowering the wall of reserve which had always separated them even after they became friends. "This is perhaps the last time I will ever see you," she said. "I wish you all success in your assignment."

Spontaneously Tuomi reached out to embrace her.

"No!" she said, pushing him away. "That wouldn't be right. Whatever you or I might want, in our work we can trust only the brain, never the heart. Good-by, comrade."

At the airport the next evening, Tuomi waited alone for the plane. He carried with him a forged passport and 150 American twenty-dollar bills. Secreted in his luggage were other forged passports and documents, including letters of reference from the Milwaukee machine shop, General Electric, and the New York lumber company. Sewn into his shaving kit were materials for invisible writing and a cipher pad. Having produced a visa and passport that identified him as an American tourist, Tuomi walked directly to the plane. As it gained altitude, he looked down on the lights of Moscow and wondered if he ever would see them again.

On December 17, 1958, after a week in Paris and another in Brussels, Tuomi landed in Montreal, posing as a Finnish American. Once past customs, he destroyed his first passport and became Robert B. White, a businessman from Chicago. When he had convinced himself he was not being watched, he made an advance Pullman reservation for December 30 to Chicago from Montreal, then took a transcontinental train to Vancouver. It was Christmas Eve when he arrived there. As he stood outside the lumberyard where he had supposedly worked in his fictitious past, a group of caroling teen-agers came by. "Merry Christmas!" they shouted.

"And a happy New Year to you!" he answered.

After two days in Vancouver, Tuomi returned to Montreal. On December 30 he waited until the night train to Chicago started to move out of the station, then jumped aboard. He closed the curtain to his berth and once more rehearsed his story. Myriad warnings and instructions drilled into him in Moscow tumbled through his thoughts. As the train lurched to a halt amid snowdrifts in Port Huron, Michigan, he took off his glasses and wiped perspiration from the palms of his hands. Soon he heard customs officers awakening and questioning passengers. Then came the knock.

"May I see your identification, please?" asked a U.S. inspector. He glanced at it casually and handed it back.

"Did you make any purchases in Canada or order any goods for delivery in the United States?" he asked.

"Only a shirt," Tuomi replied.

"Well, have a good trip home," said the customs official. "Sorry to wake you at this hour."

A young man clutching a pint of bourbon came weaving down the aisle and to Tuomi's consternation threw his arm around his shoulder. "How about a drink, buddy?" he asked.

"Thanks," replied Tuomi disengaging himself, "but I'd better get some sleep."

Soon Tuomi felt the train start to move, and he knew he was inside the United States. He could not believe it had been so easy.

From Chicago he went to New York, and on January 3, 1959, the long journey from Moscow ended. Exhausted, Tuomi hailed a cab and registered at the George Washington Hotel as Kaarlo R. Tuomi, his permanent name in the United States. Tipping the bellhop, as Fainna had taught him, he fell into bed and for the first time in twenty-six days slept soundly.

Next day he looked over the Bronx lumber company and the site of the razed apartment building that were part of his legend. Because the Center preferred that his messages be typewritten, he also bought a portable typewriter and began practicing on it in his room.

To establish communications with Moscow, he had to find the four drops selected for him in New York. The first was located in Queens beneath a railroad bridge; the second, also in Queens, was by a lamppost at the northeast corner of St. Michael's Cemetery; the third was in the Bronx under a subway bridge; the fourth was in Yonkers under a bush near McLean and Van Cortlandt Avenues.

By sending a crank postcard to the Soviet U.N. delegation, Tuomi advised the Center that he would leave a message at the Bronx drop on January 10. In it he reported his travels and stated that unless instructed otherwise, he would leave January 26 on a two-month trip to inspect locales of his legend in Minnesota and Wisconsin.

Just after 9 P.M. on January 17 he strolled under the Bronx bridge. There he spotted a magnetic metal container stuck to a girder and pocketed it with one easy motion. Opening it in his hotel room, he found an enciphered note: "Congratulations on your successful arrival. Trip approved. Family is well and sends warm regards. All the best. Chief."

The journey through the Midwest was pleasant. Riding buses, occasionally hitchhiking between small towns, Tuomi felt a growing sense of well-being. Everything was just as described in Moscow. No one seemed even interested in him, much less suspicious of him. He had always reasoned that he might succeed; now he began to believe he would.

Completing his "education" in Minnesota, in early March he took a room at a boardinghouse in Milwaukee where eight different locations were important to his legend. The morning of March 9 the cook served a good breakfast. Tuomi snapped her picture and, intending to give it to her as a present, started out for a camera shop to have the film developed. He had walked about ten yards when he heard a voice say:

"Mr. Tuomi, we would like to talk with you."

He spun around. Staring at him were two men who looked young, athletic, and well dressed—just the way FBI men had always appeared in the American movies Tuomi had seen. Then, in terror, he slowly recognized one of the men. He was the friendly "drunk" who had offered Tuomi a drink on the train. Tuomi felt near collapse. He realized he had been followed all the way from the border.

He thought his training in Moscow had steeled him for every emergency, but nothing could really have prepared him for this moment. It seemed inconceivable that all the years of labor and planning could evaporate so suddenly on this street in Milwaukee. Yet somehow the FBI had found him. Desperately he tried to order his thoughts. But the sole advice he could remember from his schooling was: Your legend is your only defense. No matter what happens, stick with your legend.

"Who are you?" he asked.

"Mr. Tuomi, I think you understand who we are."

"There must be some mistake," Tuomi said.

"Yes," the man replied. "The question is, what do we do about it? Do we take you directly to jail, or do you want to talk and see what might be worked out?"

"Gentlemen, there must be some mistake," he said. "I'll be glad to straighten it out if I can."

"All right, then, get into the car," one of the men ordered, motioning to a black Dodge sedan occupied by two other men.

They were well into the countryside before the man in the right front seat spoke. "We might as well get acquainted. I'm Don, and this is Gene," he said, pointing to the driver. "Steve is on your left, Jack on your right." Don was tall, slender, and handsome. It was his voice that Tuomi had heard first on the street, and he was clearly in command. Gene was freckle-faced and boyish. Steve had wavy blond hair, a ruddy complexion, and the quiet, quizzical look of a professor, which in fact he once had been. But Jack looked like a professional wrestler who had progressed to better things. His black eyes fixed on Tuomi with a stare of unconcealed contempt.

After a drive of about an hour, the car turned off a back road down a dark, narrow lane that ended at a hunting lodge set deep in the woods. There a young man admitted Tuomi and the group. As the door shut behind them, Don ordered, "Take off your clothes."

"But why?" Tuomi protested.

"It's our duty to make sure you're not carrying anything to harm yourself with," Jack answered.

Tuomi stripped and stood in the middle of the main room of the lodge. It had a high vaulted ceiling, random-width floorboards, and a huge stone fireplace where four or five big logs were beginning to blaze. Overhead, an open balcony lined with bunks evidently served as a dormitory. To the right were two bedrooms, a bathroom, and a kitchen. Faintly, from a room behind the fireplace wall, Tuomi could hear bits of unintelligible conversation being conducted by radio.

Tuomi held his hands against his ribs to keep them from trembling as Steve, wearing rubber gloves, methodically examined him. The other three agents went through his clothes, briefcase, and wallet. "You're shaking," Don observed when the physical search ended. "Would you like something to eat or drink?"

After a lunch of soup and sandwiches, the interrogation began. Tuomi sat on a sofa facing the fire. So intent was he on maintaining his legend that he seldom was conscious of which interrogator asked which question.

"What are you doing in Milwaukee?"

"Looking for a job."

"Who do you know in Milwaukee?"

"No one, really. I used to work in a machine shop here, then at the General Electric plant, in the shipping department. After that I had a cabinetmaking shop. But my wife walked out on me in 1956, so I went to New York to start over. All my friends here seem to have drifted away."

"Why did you come here, then?"

"I was tired of New York. I grew up around the Lakes, and I wanted to get back."

"Where did you live in New York?"

"In an apartment house at 4738 Decatur Avenue in the Bronx—until last December. I had to move because the building was being torn down. I stayed at the George Washington Hotel until I came here."

"Where did you work?"

"At a lumber company in the Bronx."

"You don't have a driver's license with you. Do you own a car?"

"No."

"How did you get to work in New York?"

"By bus."

"Which bus? Describe its route."

Both in Moscow and during his first weeks in New York, Tuomi had studied the neighborhoods in which the apartment building and the lumber company were located. But no one had foreseen that he would have to know which bus traveled between them, much less its route. "Actually, I don't remember the exact number of the bus," he said.

"You've been riding a bus week in, week out," Jack shouted, "but you can't tell us which one?" Tuomi remained silent.

"Let's put New York aside for a while," Don said. "Tell us about your early life."

Tuomi began to recite the legend, and the agents listened attentively. It all sounded so believable that, for the first time since confronting the FBI, Tuomi thought he might have a chance. But late in the afternoon, a fifth agent emerged from the room behind the fireplace and whispered to Don.

"Kaarlo, our colleagues have been doing some checking," Don said. "We've talked to GE in Milwaukee, the Bronx lumber company, and the last two managers of the apartment building where you claim you lived. There is no record of you anywhere. How do you explain that?"

Tuomi shrugged. "You must have talked to the wrong people."

"I think it is more logical to assume that you're lying," said Don. "Take a look at this picture. Do you recognize that man?"

"Yes," said Tuomi, stunned. "It's my stepfather."

"And these people?" Don asked, handing him another photograph.

"My mother, stepfather, my sister, and me when I was a boy."

"Do you remember when that picture was taken?" Don asked.

"No. I've never seen it before," Tuomi replied.

"Think hard," Don said. "Wasn't it in 1933—just before all four of you went to the Soviet Union?" Tuomi put the photograph down and saw that the agents were smiling at him.

"Let's take a break," Don said.

Standing around the fire, the agents were polite, even friendly. They talked about the weather, speculated

about the severity of an approaching snowstorm. Then
Steve casually said, "By the way, Kaarlo, when you
were staying at the George Washington in New York,
what were you typing in your room all the time?"

He had merely been practicing with a newly purchased portable typewriter. But to Tuomi the question
was devastating. It told him how closely the FBI had
watched him since he had entered the country. And
this evidence, together with the photographs, obtained
perhaps from distant relatives or friends of his parents,
was proof that the FBI knew what he actually was.
His legend was now a shambles. Still, he vowed not to
give up.

At the start of the next interrogation, Tuomi announced, "I've decided to tell you the truth."

The agents stared at him, waiting.

"You were partly right yesterday," Tuomi said. "My
stepfather did take us out of the country back in
1933—but we went to Finland, not to the Soviet
Union. I always planned to get back to America. Last
fall I got a job as a deckhand on a Finnish freighter.
When it docked in Quebec, I jumped ship and came to
the United States. I know this is illegal. But I did it
because I wanted to live in my own country."

A hail of questions instantly beat down on him:
What was the name of the ship? Who was the captain?
The first mate? What was the cargo? From which port
did it sail? What was the date it arrived in Canada?
Where did Tuomi get all his false papers?

Later, Don came out of the room behind the fireplace to confront him again. "I have more bad news
for you, Kaarlo," he said. "Naval authorities tell us
there is no Finnish ship such as you describe. We also
have discovered something else."

He put on the table a bottle of laxative tablets given
to Tuomi in Moscow. "We found this in your briefcase," he said. "What's in it?"

"Medicine," Tuomi answered.

The tablets bore a common American brand name.
Don placed an identical bottle on the table. He took
one tablet from each bottle, placed them side by side,
and sliced each in half with a pocketknife. "Look at

this, Kaarlo," he said. "This tablet is white all the way through. But the one from your bottle is pink on the inside. How do you explain that?"

"I don't know," Tuomi replied.

"Well, our laboratory has a pretty good idea," Don said. "It tells us that your pills contain a special chemical compound not manufactured in the United States. It also advises us that the only conceivable use for this compound would be in developing some sort of invisible writing. What do you say about that?"

"I have nothing to say."

"It's time we talked frankly," Don continued. "All the evidence shows that you are a Soviet agent, sent here on an espionage mission. We happen to know that this is the case. You are in this country illegally. All we have to do is deport you—turn you back to the Russians. They'll take care of you for us." He paused.

"Reason it out for yourself. If you explain what happened over here, nobody will buy it. The people who planned your mission simply will not believe that *they* made the mistakes. At best, they will think you are lying to cover up some stupid blunder, and you will be stigmatized as a failure. More likely, you will be suspected of something far worse. Nothing you do or say will quite convince your superiors that you didn't make a deal with us and that we didn't send you back as an American agent. In either case, your future back home won't be very promising, will it?

"Now, on the other hand, should you choose to cooperate with us . . ."

The words were hardly spoken before Tuomi exploded. "Why should I cooperate with representatives of a system that is collapsing?" he shouted. "Your side is losing! We are winning!"

It was the first crack in Tuomi's facade, and the agents took advantage of it.

"You've been traveling around the country quite a bit the last couple of months," Jack retorted. "Does the system look as if it's collapsing?"

"It won't happen overnight," answered Tuomi. "But historically the collapse of capitalism is inevitable."

Thereupon, Tuomi and the FBI agents plunged into

ardent ideological argument. Tuomi earnestly repeated all the Marxist, socialist, anti-American doctrine absorbed during twenty-five years in the Soviet Union. The agents granted certain points and ridiculed others. "Kaarlo, we have real problems in this country," Don said. "But at least we can try to solve them with the ballot box." The debate raged through the evening meal and late into the night.

"This is getting us nowhere," Don said finally. "Let me finish what I started to say. If you work with us, we can make it appear that you have accomplished all your assignments. Someday you will be recalled, and you can go home with no one the wiser. You will enjoy all the rewards given a successful illegal. You can lead a normal life in your own country.

"I know that at the moment things look very black to you," Don went on. "And I realize that the decision you have to make is hard. But you're going to have to make it soon. Every day you stay out of circulation increases the danger to you. The Center often makes secret checks on its illegals. It could have a man out looking for you today."

Tuomi sank into a profound depression. The prospect of betraying his teachers, his country, and all he believed in made him feel weak and sick. He thought of feigning collaboration with the FBI just long enough to flee to Mexico or perhaps take refuge in the Soviet embassy in Washington. Yet no matter what escape he charted, it always ended in a confrontation with the Soviet interrogators. Ultimately he would have to convince them that he had not sold out, that he had been discovered through no fault of his own. And the more he reflected, the more he doubted that he could make anyone in Moscow believe him.

He feared most of all for his family. On the ugliest of all his KGB assignments in the Soviet Union, he had seen for himself how whole families could be made to suffer. It concerned a young Finnish couple who illegally crossed the Soviet border in 1953. The couple walked into a militia station and requested Soviet citizenship, but the KGB jailed them. Continuous ques-

tioning during the next eleven months indicated only
that the couple believed communist propaganda and
sincerely sought to enjoy the life it promised. Nevertheless, the KGB consigned them to an exile camp for
"suspects" in Kirov Province.

Because Tuomi spoke Finnish, the KGB sent him
into the camp as a "prisoner," with instructions to become friends with the couple. Hardened as he was to
privation, he still was aghast at what he saw in the
camp. Whole families subsisted in five-by-eight-foot
wooden stalls or cells in communal barracks. Each
morning at six, trucks hauled all the men away to peat
bogs where they labored until dark. Small children,
Tuomi observed, regularly died of ordinary maladies
because of inadequate medical care. Worse still, the
camp inmates, who had committed no crime, had no
idea when, if ever, they might be released. After only
three days Tuomi persuaded himself that the forlorn
Finns were concealing nothing, and he signaled the
camp administrator to remove him.

"That place is just hell," he later told Serafim, his
KGB supervisor. "Those people are living like slaves."

"I understand," Serafim said. "But don't get so excited. There's nothing you or I can do about it."

Now, as if in a delirium, Tuomi saw grotesque
images of prisoners. Irrationally, he pictured himself,
Nina, and the children huddled in despair inside a
KGB camp. More than anything else, it was concern
for his family that made him ask Don, "This cooperation—what would it mean?"

"Well, first you would proceed just as if you had
never met us," Don answered. "You'd get a job, build
up your cover, maintain normal communications with
the Center, and carry out every assignment it gave you.
Of course, you would report everything to us."

"What would you do?" Tuomi asked.

"We would give you guidance and some assistance
in getting set up. But it is very important, especially at
first, that you do things for yourself just as you normally would. If we helped you advance too fast, the Center
would wonder why you were doing so much better

than the average illegal and would become suspicious."

"Would I draft the messages to the Center, or would you?" Tuomi inquired.

"By and large, you would," Don replied. "But we would have the final say about what goes out."

Tuomi shook his head. "It won't work. Some way the Center will find out."

"Kaarlo, I assure you that it has worked before, and it will work again," Don said.

Tuomi brooded in silence. "All right," he said. "I will try, if you will agree to something. I'll tell you all about my mission and what happens from here on. But not about my training or my teachers or my colleagues, or any other secrets I learned in the Soviet Union."

"Fair enough," said Don. "Naturally, there are a lot of things we would like to know. But we won't press you. Eventually, I think you'll want to tell us of your own free will. Whenever you're ready, just pass the word to Jack or Steve. They will be taking care of you from now on."

Tuomi traveled to New York alone by bus and moved into the Seville Hotel at Madison Avenue and Twenty-ninth Street. The next afternoon he spent nearly two hours switching from subway to bus to taxi before slipping into the Statler Hilton Hotel to meet Jack and Steve. The three of them carefully composed a letter informing the Center that Tuomi's familiarization tour of the Midwest had been an uneventful success. Jack relayed the proposed text to FBI headquarters, and within the hour Washington telephoned approval. As Tuomi wrote the final draft of the letter in invisible ink, he was aware that both agents were scrutinizing every movement of his hand, and he sensed why.

"I didn't put in any signal, if that's what you're worried about," he said as he finished.

"Kaarlo, that's something we've been waiting for you to bring up," said Steve. "Were you given any signal for use in event of detection?"

"No," Tuomi replied, "and I can't understand why not. It would have been so easy. Just by leaving out a comma, I could have let them know."

Tuomi addressed the envelope to an office in Helsinki and handed it to Jack, who handed it back. "You're going to trust me to mail it?" Tuomi asked.

"From now on we have no choice but to trust each other."

In the following weeks, Tuomi's dejection and fear intensified. He could conceive no real alternative to the deal he had made with the FBI, yet he felt guilt and shame over collaborating with the enemy. He lost weight, and at night he awoke with terrifying nightmares. Every stranger on the street became a possible assassin from Moscow, every ring of the phone or knock on the door a sound of danger. He dreaded the next message from the Center, fearing it might contain some proclamation of his doom.

The message was due April 21. As dawn broke over Queens that morning, Tuomi followed instructions that he had memorized in Moscow. He warily approached an underpass beneath a railroad bridge at Sixty-ninth Street, the site of one of the "drops" where he was to leave or pick up messages. The area was deserted, and his footsteps echoed. Crouching down, he pretended to tie his shoelace. Quickly he plucked a magnetic metal container from a bridge girder and hid it in a rolled copy of the New York *Times*. He reached the Statler Hilton back in Manhattan two hours later. Jack and Steve were waiting with hot coffee.

The container yielded $3,000 in twenties, plus two sheets of secret writing. "Why don't you develop that sheet, and we'll work on this one," Jack said. Tuomi watched as the tray of chemicals he held brought the message slowly to life. It said: "Congratulations on your successful trip. Legalization is proceeding normally. Remain cautious and do not hurry. All the best. Chief."

Steve patted Tuomi on the shoulder. "You see, they have no idea of what has happened. You've been worrying for nothing."

With unusual politeness, Jack passed over the second sheet, still wet with chemicals. It contained three brief letters that the Center had rewritten in invisible ink. As Tuomi read them, he could almost hear the voices of his family. His wife wrote: "My Dearest One . . . My work is hard, but all difficulties disappear when I see our children. . . . We all kiss you." From Viktor: "I am very glad to get your presents. But the best thing I am dreaming of is to see you." From Irina: "Papa, please come back to us. Good-by, Papa."

He reread the words, saying nothing.

"Kaarlo, let's knock off early this afternoon and go out to my place for the evening," Jack said. "I'd like you to meet my family and see what a great cook my wife is."

Jack's home stood on a tree-shaded side street in a Long Island town, about an hour's drive from Manhattan. It was a white two-story frame house of eight rooms built in the early 1930s. Jack had added a second bath and a small den, remodeled the kitchen, built a stone patio, and fenced the back yard.

In the living room, Jack's wife, a handsome redhead of about forty, greeted Tuomi with a warm handshake. "We're delighted you could come. It's always a treat for us to meet Jack's friends."

Tuomi could not discern precisely how much his hostess knew about him, but it soon became obvious that she was aware he was an alien and alone in New York. After they had chatted for a while, she invited him into the kitchen. "If you'll excuse the mess, I'll try to give you some tips that might help when you start housekeeping for yourself." As she finished making dinner, she instructed Tuomi about various frozen foods, explained the merits of various detergents and cleaning powders, and suggested menus for quick meals. Tuomi marveled at the array of products but was even more impressed by the ingenuity with which the kitchen was designed and equipped.

Just before dinner, Jack's two teen-aged sons appeared in the dining room and introduced themselves. When all sat down, Jack offered grace, and Tuomi remembered a Soviet instructor's admonition to bow his head and close his eyes. Dinner—roast veal with gravy, and hot biscuits—was excellent. The conversation was easy and natural. No one seemed inhibited by Tuomi's presence, and the family routinely discussed private questions as if he were one of them. Whose turn was it to use the car on Saturday night? The television set needed repairs for the second time in five weeks. Would it be best to have it fixed again, buy a new one, or use the money to replace the aging hi-fi? Would everyone be willing to get up for six-o'clock Mass on Sunday so Jack could accept a nine-o'clock golf invitation?

Jack's sons helped clear the table, and his wife served coffee and dessert. After the first bite, Tuomi put down his fork and exclaimed, "I've never tasted anything so delicious!"

Jack's wife smiled. "It's blueberry pie. I baked it this afternoon."

Later, the boys excused themselves to attend to homework, and Jack proposed a quick tour of the house. Tuomi was astonished to see an unused bedroom set aside for guests. In the den he saw hanging above Jack's desk a bachelor's degree from one university, a law degree from another, and four framed FBI commendations. On the bookshelves he spotted *Das Kapital* and a dozen or so other volumes pertaining to communism. He grinned and pulled out a 1958 English edition of *Fundamentals of Marxism-Leninism,* published in Moscow. "I didn't know the FBI had any Marxists," he said.

"You can't fight what you don't understand," Jack answered. "But no shoptalk tonight. How about a nightcap before I drive you back? We ought to leave fairly soon because it wouldn't be wise for me to take you all the way to the hotel. I'll drop you off near the subway."

When they left, Tuomi told Jack's wife, "You have a wonderful family and a wonderful home. It meant a great deal to me to be here."

"It was fun having you," she replied. "Oh, just a minutes. I forgot something." Returning from the kitchen, she handed Tuomi a blueberry pie wrapped in foil. "I baked two," she said.

Alone with the roar of the subway, Tuomi felt another wave of guilt as he acknowledged to himself just how much he appreciated the evening. The fact that Jack had a home luxurious by Soviet standards was explainable in terms of Tuomi's training; the freedom from fear, the atmosphere of trust that permeated it, was not. Jack had knowingly exposed his own family to a Soviet agent, and they had accepted him as a friend. To Tuomi, the United States was still an enemy. He knew that he should also regard Jack as an enemy. But he realized now that he did not.

It had been an unusual evening for Jack as well. Normally, an FBI agent would not reveal his true name or anything else to a double agent, much less admit him into his home. But the FBI considered the winning of Tuomi's allegiance so vital that it authorized Jack to employ any prudent means to establish a personal relationship. Jack concluded that the best way to make a friend was to be a real one himself.

Because the FBI insisted that Tuomi do everything possible for himself, he had to find an apartment on his own. He located one on Eightieth Street off Roosevelt Avenue in the Jackson Heights section of Queens. It was on the fifth floor of an old building ideally suited for conspiracy. The building had four entrances, two in front and two in the rear. Most of the occupants were transients or short-term residents who paid little heed to each other. Equally important, the FBI was able to locate and lease an apartment nearby—a secure, convenient hideout where Tuomi could rendezvous with Jack and Steve.

As he had been told to do in Moscow, Tuomi enrolled in a bookkeeping and clerical course at a business school. He studied so diligently that he completed the course three months ahead of schedule—in late September 1959—and with the help of a Manhattan employment agency began job hunting. "I think we may have something for you," a girl at the agency told him in mid-October. "There's a clerical opening at Tiffany's. That's a lovely place to work."

To Tuomi, who had worked as a lumberjack in the backwoods of eastern Karelia before being drafted into the Red Army in 1939, it seemed almost ludicrous to seek employment in the jeweled magnificence of

Tiffany's, a symbolic citadel of capitalism. But Jack said: "Hell, go ahead. What have you got to lose?"

The personnel manager at Tiffany's interviewed Tuomi for some fifty minutes, inquiring about his schooling, interests, and past employment. Tuomi recounted his legend and presented his certificate from the bookkeeping school. "I think you're a good bet," the man concluded. "We'll give you a three-month trial in the auditing department at sixty-five a week. If that works out, you'll have a good future here."

The Center was delighted, three months later, when Tuomi received tenure as a cost-analysis clerk, along with a five-dollar raise. It recognized Tiffany's as a perfect haven in which its man could hide while building his credentials as an American and readying himself for espionage missions. "Continue to solidify your position," the Center instructed. "Begin to widen your circle of acquaintances." The regular flow of money and messages showed that from the perspective of Moscow, the operation appeared to be developing flawlessly.

For Tuomi personally, Tiffany's unveiled a glittering and heretofore unimagined world. The first evening he had to work overtime, he found himself alone amid millions of dollars' worth of jewelry. Back in Kirov, even after years of KGB service, he knew that he was still spied upon, that traps were still set for him. Yet here, after only a few months, Tiffany's trusted him to wander about at will, unwatched and unguarded.

While taking inventory with another clerk late one afternoon, Tuomi picked up a dazzling diamond bracelet that bore no tag. He started to take it to the Registry Department so the price could be ascertained and a tag affixed. Just then the phone rang, and he dropped the bracelet into his jacket pocket as he hurried to answer. "Come on, Kaarlo," his partner pleaded when he hung up. "We'll have to hurry if we're going to finish before closing."

While he was hanging up the jacket at his apartment that night, Tuomi felt the bracelet. Panic nearly overcame him. As he stared at the diamonds, he imagined swarms of detectives heading up the stairway after him and television bulletins announcing his imminent arrest. He saw himself reading a *Daily News* headline: "Soviet Spy Steals Tiffany Bracelet."

The next morning, pale from sleeplessness, Tuomi waited outside Tiffany's until a guard opened the door. "Here's an item without a price tag on it," he said urgently to the manager of the Registry Department. "Please make out a proper one."

Picking up his magnifying glass, the manager calmly analyzed the price code scratched inside the bracelet. "Eighteen thousand dollars," he said. "It's beautiful, isn't it?" Tuomi was too relieved to reply.

Throughout these months, Tuomi still considered himself an unrepentant if captive communist. He continued to provoke debates with Jack and Steve, disparaging the United States and extolling the Soviet Union. With the beginning of the 1960 Presidential campaign, both FBI agents often cited the forthcoming election as an example of the basic freedoms in America.

"It doesn't mean a thing," Tuomi retorted. "Both parties are dedicated to exploiting the masses. It doesn't matter which wins."

But after the nomination of Kennedy, Tuomi changed. He got up early to read campaign news, and in the afternoons he rushed home from work to listen to the early evening telecasts. Kennedy came to personify for him a kind of glamor foreign to Soviet politics. When several public-opinion polls in September indicated that Nixon was leading, Tuomi was beside himself with alarm, as if he himself were on the verge of a personal disaster.

One day he asked Jack, "Don't you think I should register to vote?"

"Well, every good citizen should vote," Jack agreed, "and it's our job to make sure you're a good citizen."

He became so deeply involved that he studied registration procedures and qualified as a New York voter. On Election Day he joined other Americans at the polls, thus becoming probably the only man who ever cast ballots for both Nikita Khrushchev and John Kennedy. At 7 P.M. he settled before his television set to watch the returns. At 3:20 A.M., when Nixon in effect conceded defeat, Tuomi grabbed the phone, called Jack, and fairly shouted, "Did you hear? Kennedy's won!"

"You woke me up to tell me that?" Jack replied. "I thought it didn't make any difference who won."

The two agents urged Tuomi to explore America by himself. Partly at their suggestion, he bought an excellent 1954 sedan. No American teen-ager could have been prouder of his first car. After work, Tuomi often drove about the city just for the sheer pleasure of driving. He ventured out on his own to the Catskills and the Poconos, to Philadelphia, Washington, Chesapeake Bay, and Williamsburg. During his first two-week vacation from Tiffany's, he toured the Michigan and Minnesota woods and lakes where he had spent his boyhood.

One Sunday, Jack casually suggested that Tuomi join him at Mass. Both by his fanatical Finnish stepfather and by communism, Tuomi had been trained to be a militant atheist. Yet his Soviet instructors had emphasized that he should attend church. So he agreed to go along, expecting to be amused by superstitious ceremonies. But the quiet of the church, the solemnity of the service, the hymns and the worshipers' sincerity left him with an unexpected feeling of respect.

Thereafter, he sometimes went to church on his own, usually to small Lutheran or Methodist churches. He neither accepted nor understood all that the ministers preached. But ultimately he asked himself, "If this means so much to so many people, what's so bad about it?" Consciously he changed from an atheist to an agnostic.

In February 1961 the Center sent a new cipher system, and Tuomi flew with Jack to Washington on a Saturday afternoon to study it with FBI cryptologists. Ironically, Tuomi felt more secure in Washington than in New York. For, as a "deep cover" illegal, he was confident that Soviet diplomats in Washington were unaware of his existence. And on Sunday morning at the Mayflower Hotel it was he who asked, "Well, where should we go to church?"

"Let's try St. Matthew's," Jack said. "It ought to be

safe enough for us to go there together." As they neared
the cathedral, just off Connecticut Avenue, Jack tapped
Tuomi on the shoulder. "Look, Kaarlo!" he exclaimed.
"There's a friend of yours." Tuomi turned and saw a
handsome bare-headed young man wearing a dark-blue
overcoat striding up the cathedral steps. It was John F.
Kennedy.

"Is it all right to take a picture?" Tuomi whispered.

"It's a free country," Jack told him.

Seeing that Tuomi and others wanted to photograph
him, the President paused momentarily, grinned, and
waved. "Wasn't that something!" said Tuomi. "Wasn't
that really something!"

A few months later Kennedy and Khrushchev met
in Vienna, and Khrushchev threatened war unless the
United States yielded West Berlin. Sober and grim after
the confrontation, Kennedy flew back to Washington
to mobilize reserves and fortify American defenses.
Khrushchev returned to Moscow to begin the elaborate
clandestine operation that was to bring the world the
closest it has ever been to nuclear holocaust. As he
did so, new instructions went out from Moscow to
Soviet spies throughout the United States.

Tuomi's orders arrived in secret writing. "The situation is becoming more complex," it began. "You must
now be more active in your work. On the basis of your
own observations, report to the Center any preparations
for further mobilization of the country. Organize your
recreation in places where military personnel gather,
near the docks, near the warehouses of Army bases in
Brooklyn in the area of Bay Ridge Station, and near
Docks 11, 12, and 13 in Richmond. Ascertain the
character and destination of arms shipments, troop
movements, and the movement of military vessels. Be
more alert. Wife and family are well. Chief."

"Well, Kaarlo, the Center thinks you're ready to play
in the big leagues," Jack said.

"How can I work at Tiffany's and hang around the
waterfront?" Tuomi asked.

"You can't," said Steve. "Some way, you're going
to have to get a job down there, and that may take
some doing."

On a Sunday afternoon, Jack and Steve signaled Tuomi to meet them in the safe apartment. They arrived with a bulging copy of the *Times,* which they opened to the Help Wanted section. "Here's something that looks like it was written just for you," Jack said with an author's pride. He pointed out an ad for a bookkeeper's position at a steamship firm.

After evaluating dozens of potential employers, the FBI had approached Peter Burbank, president of A. L. Burbank & Co. and Pier 8 Terminals, Inc. FBI agents told him only that in the interests of national security, they needed to place a man on the waterfront. Burbank agreed to employ anyone the FBI sent, provided he could actually do the work required. Cordially going through the motions of an interview, Burbank hired Tuomi at $80 a week.

For Tuomi the abrupt shift from Tiffany's to the waterfront was like jumping from civilization into a jungle. The docks were peopled with brawling, profane characters and ruled like baronial fiefs by union bosses. Moreover, his primary duty consisted of trying to collect loading and unloading fees from truckers, many of whom were notorious for their belligerent refusal to pay. But as an ex-lumberjack and a longtime combat infantryman, Tuomi was ready to be tough.

The fourth day at the pier, a waterfront thug stopped in the office and helped himself to a cup of coffee. As he started to leave, Tuomi, who had put himself in charge of the coffeepot, said, "Wait a minute, mister. Everybody here washes their own cup."

"Do you know who you're talking to?" the man said contemptuously.

"I don't give a damn who you are," Tuomi barked. "My rule is that everybody washes his own cup." The hoodlum lunged. Tuomi sidestepped and picked up a crowbar. This he held at the ready until the cup was washed.

Tuomi's real breakthrough came when he decreed that no truck whose owner owed Pier 8 Terminals any money would be allowed on the dock. In spite of vociferous cursing by truck drivers, Tuomi enforced the rule so adamantly that he promptly was titled "a real

S.O.B." Nevertheless, the number of delinquent accounts plummeted to near zero, and Tuomi's salary was raised to $100 a week. In time, he formed warm friendships among his fellow workers, most of whom he considered decent if somewhat rough.

Secure in his new job, Tuomi moved from Jackson Heights to a larger apartment in East Orange, New Jersey. Demands upon his time rapidly mounted as communications to and from Moscow increased. Munching a sandwich, Tuomi sometimes drove during his lunch hour to meetings with Jack and Steve in parks, church parking lots, and out-of-the-way cafés. While one of the agents maintained a protective watch, Tuomi and the other began encoding or decoding messages. The process continued at the FBI safe apartment during the evening.

The Center imposed new and complicated communications arrangements. Each Saturday morning, Tuomi now had to walk past the intersection of 146th Street and Park Avenue looking for an orange peel. Its presence meant that he had to "unload" a drop at ten o'clock that night. Then, to acknowledge receipts of the package or message, he was required to write an anti-Soviet statement on a postcard and mail it to "Public Relations Officer, Mission of the U.S.S.R. to the United Nations," at the mission's New York address. To advise the Center to pick up something that he was putting in a drop, he had to mail a quotation from the Bible inscribed on a religious postcard.

The character of messages from Moscow also changed markedly. Instructions heretofore had been cautious and general, always admonishing against risks. Now the Center increasingly demanded hard intelligence and specific results and insisted that Tuomi begin to develop new sources.

Using the techniques he had been taught in Moscow, Tuomi set to work, and the FBI was impressed by what he was able to accomplish entirely on his own. He began to frequent a Brooklyn bar across the street from the Bethlehem Steel shipyard. Becoming friendly with shipyard workers and subtly prodding them to talk about their jobs, he learned that two

destroyers, the *Calan* and the *Taylor,* were being outfitted with advanced and secret electronic equipment.
Although he had no scientific background, he compiled a detailed technical report, much of which he
himself did not understand.

The material he gathered was so revealing that Jack
confided, "It's going to have to be doctored quite a bit.
We can't afford to send it the way you wrote it."

Through social gatherings, Tuomi made friends with
several other Americans: a Navy radarman, an Army
sergeant who had just finished military intelligence
school and was soon to leave on a sensitive assignment
in the Middle East, an engineer in charge of sales of
all new products developed by one of the nation's most
important defense contractors, a young man employed
at an ultrasecret installation of the Central Intelligence
Agency near Washington.

Moscow regarded Tuomi's new friendships as a considerable accomplishment. From experience it knew
that as the relations became more intimate, he might
discern a quirk or weakness that would make one or
more of his friends susceptible to subversion. Even if
he didn't, the new friends might lead him to associates
who could be suborned.

However, these were all long-range prospects. To
satisfy the demands of the Center for immediate, concrete intelligence, the FBI decided to recruit a source
for him. It chose an official in charge of loading military
supplies at both the Ports of New York and Philadelphia. Assigned the code name of Frank, he knew only
that he was performing a critical service for the FBI.
Escorted by Jack, Tuomi spent two days with him,
memorizing details of his life and work, which he then
reported to Moscow. Information that the FBI thereafter obtained from Frank and gave to Tuomi for
transmission was authentic. For the FBI had no alternative but to give away some secrets in hope of eventually learning many more.

On September 18, 1962, when Tuomi arrived home
from work, he found in his mail the usual advertisements, sports magazines, and a letter from a friend he
had known at Tiffany's. There was also an unusually

large business envelope, postmarked in New York but bearing no return address. Enclosed were two sets of commercial patterns for a folding snack table and tray. The lower left-hand corner was folded, a sign that the reverse side of each sheet contained secret writing.

Steve whistled in astonishment when the message was deciphered at the FBI apartment. It was an order which, in its Byzantine detail, typified Soviet intelligence. But its content was utterly unexpected.

"We announce the conditions of a meeting. Time: Sunday 23 September 0900 hours. Place: bank of the river Hudson opposite the Greystone railway station in Westchester County. With fishing rods, a rose-colored plastic pail, and a fishing license, drive to the northern part of the town ot Yonkers. Then drive along Warburton Avenue to Greystone station and park your car in the parking lot. Cross the pedestrian bridge to the river and then walk along the bank to the telephone pole with a figure 429. Near this pole you should be fishing. Parole:* 'Excuse me, I think we met at the Yonkers Yacht Club last year.' You must answer, 'No, sir, I left that club in 1960.' Legend of contact: you met our representative while fishing. Report your readiness for the meeting by sending a religious postcard to our United Nations mission. Sign the card R. Sands. If you do not understand the conditions of meeting, sign the card D. C. Kott. Chief."

The decision of the Center to risk a personal meeting with Tuomi in the United States was extraordinary. Repeatedly he had been told in Moscow that face-to-face encounters among agents were the most dangerous of all clandestine activities. He remembered the words of Aleksei Ivanovich Galkin, his chief instructor: "You will never be approached by one of our representatives except in an extreme emergency." Rereading the message, Tuomi wondered if it was not really a summons to abduction or liquidation.

"What do you think?" Tuomi asked.

"Well," Jack answered, "obviously there's a possi-

---

*Soviet term for recognition signals.

bility that they've become suspicious of you. But my best guess is that they think you're now so securely established they can take a chance. In any case, they have something important to say to you. We've got a lot of work to do before Sunday."

It was gray and chilly when the alarm clock roused Tuomi from a half sleep at six o'clock Sunday morning. The tautness in his stomach made him reject all thoughts of breakfast. He put on a checkered sport jacket, dark wool trousers, heavy shoes, and a hunting cap, then left his East Orange apartment. Driving north along the Garden State Parkway, he turned off at Route 46 to buy gas and check for surveillance. He stopped again for coffee at a diner to make sure he was not being followed, then crossed the George Washington Bridge and proceeded north to Yonkers.

Parking his car at the Greystone station, he noticed a man polishing an automobile at the corner of the lot. Tuomi was sure he was a Soviet agent assigned to detect possible surveillance by the FBI. As he crossed the New York Central tracks on the footbridge that led to the river, he saw four men in two small boats rocking gently in the swells offshore. In the distance northward, two men appeared to be fishing from rocks above the river. Tuomi also was sure who they were— FBI agents deployed to protect him.

His knees leaden, each step becoming harder and harder, he forced himself to walk toward the designated telephone pole. Then he saw who was standing there—and gasped. There was no need for recognition signals. Waiting for him was a short, rather ugly man with a wide nose, steel-rimmed glasses, and a mass of thick black hair. It was his old teacher from Moscow, Galkin.

Galkin heartily shook hands, and embraced Tuomi. Yet the warmth of the greeting did not reassure Tuomi. If Galkin was serving as the bait of a trap, this was how he would behave.

"I see you're surprised," Galkin said.

"Yes, I never expected to see you here," Tuomi replied.

"You came here to fish," said Galkin. "Put your line in the water, then sit down and tell me all about yourself."

Tuomi obeyed. His trial was beginning, and Galkin was the judge. For the next forty minutes he talked of his life in the United States, telling the truth about everything except his association with the FBI. Galkin took notes, nodded occasionally, and asked only a few questions until Tuomi began to speak about his prospective sources.

"They are all interesting," Galkin commented. "But at the moment Frank is the most important. How good are your relations with him?"

"Very good," Tuomi answered.

"Do you think he could be recruited?" asked Galkin.

"Possibly," said Tuomi. "He's divorced and needs money."

"We will consider it," Galkin said. "Meanwhile, stay close to him. Everything you can get from him in the next weeks about troop movements and arms shipments is terribly important."

Galkin paused. Then he began to speak again. "Now I want to express myself precisely. If you don't understand anything, say so. First of all, we are going to bring you home next year. Do you think you can arrange a vacation for two or three months so you can get away?"

"But why a 'vacation'?" asked Tuomi. "Won't I be staying in the Soviet Union?"

Galkin laughed. "No, my friend. You will be coming back here for a long time."

The announcement was Tuomi's first proof that in the eyes of the Center he was still in good standing. His tension began to evaporate, and he struggled to conceal his relief.

"You have started well," Galkin resumed. "We are going to turn over three sources, three of our best, for you to handle. They are Americans, and they supply a great many vital documents. We want you to start looking for two very good drops outside New York City, large enough to take big packages of documents.

Once the Center approves, the other arrangements will be worked out gradually."

Galkin took a deep breath. "Now pay the strictest attention to my words," he resumed. "The world situation is extremely dangerous. In the next two or three months it will become more so. It is possible that the United States will mobilize for war. Therefore, the instructions I am giving you are urgent.

"You must check the mothball fleet below Bear Mountain Park every weekend from now until further notice. Count the number of ships each time, and notify us immediately if any have been withdrawn.

"You must also go as a tourist to the New London submarine base as often as is safe. Count the number of submarines present, particularly atomic submarines. Also watch for any unusual activity in the vicinity of the base. The presence of extra guards or large numbers of big trucks would be especially significant. Should you find no submarines, notify us at once. In the area of New York Harbor, watch for signs that the old World War II piers might be put into use again. Each morning, find out if during the night there was any abnormal movement of troops or large trucks around the harbor."

By now, Galkin had succumbed to his unconscious habit of speaking rapidly whenever he got excited about the importance of what he was saying. "Through Frank and other friends, keep checking to see if individual reservists are being secretly called to duty. Listen constantly for any rumors that the population or key offices are about to be evacuated from the cities. During the next weeks, you must report *anything* that seems at all unusual. No matter how trivial it looks to you, it could be vital for us to know. Do you understand these instructions?"

"Yes," Tuomi answered.

"Then repeat them to me," Galkin ordered. Tuomi complied flawlessly.

"Very good," said Galkin. He stood up and began reeling in his line. "Your family is well," he said. "I'm pleased to tell you that when you return you'll find them in a brand-new two-room apartment."

"That's very good to hear," Tuomi replied. "But concerning my family, there's something I want to bring up with you. For nearly a year the Center hasn't forwarded any letter. All I get is the stock phrase 'Wife and family are well.' I hoped you would bring a picture."

"You know a picture would be dangerous," Galkin responded a little peevishly. But quickly putting a hand on Tuomi's shoulder, he added, "Besides, you will be seeing them before too long."

"I still would like some letters," said Tuomi.

"All right, I'll look into it," Galkin promised. "You have done well. Always remember we are counting on you. Good luck."

Tuomi drove away from the Greystone station at 11:46 A.M. To assure himself that the Russians were not following, he weaved around the Yonkers hills for nearly an hour before stopping at a telephone booth next to a luncheonette.

"How did it go?" Jack asked.

"There were no problems," Tuomi answered. "But I have a lot to tell you."

Just after 1 P.M., Tuomi joined Jack and Steve at the FBI apartment in Jackson Heights. "Tell us what happened," Jack said. "We'll save the questions for later."

The agents listened with professional detachment, their faces showing flickers of excitement only twice: when Tuomi mentioned that three spies were to be entrusted to him, and when he recounted the new assignments from Galkin. But as soon as the summary was finished, Jack made a brief, cryptic phone call. "We have something here you should see right away," he said over the phone. "Yes, we'll get it ready tonight."

The agents and Tuomi started drafting a report of all Galkin had said. They worked through the afternoon and into the night, omitting dinner in their rush to ready the report for delivery to Washington. It was well after midnight when Tuomi started home, hungry and exhausted yet elated. He had apparently survived as a double agent without arousing suspicion at the

Center. Before long he could see and hold his children once more.

His thoughts now were all entirely personal. He did not realize that the rendezvous on the Hudson and his new assignments might be related to a historic crisis. Even less could he realize how much he had done to strengthen American capacity to contend with that crisis.

Between April 1959 and September 1962, Tuomi had exchanged dozens of communications with Moscow. Some were transmitted in invisible writing through the mails, but many were sent through the four drops selected for him in New York. By watching the drops, the FBI was able to identify the various Soviet agents who came to deliver or pick up messages. Carefully followed, these agents eventually led the FBI to still other drops and other spies. Gradually, a whole pattern of Soviet espionage operations in the United States was uncovered.

Some of the consequences of what the FBI thus discovered endure to this day. For this reason, no one is likely to divulge the full magnitude of all that was gained. However, it is clear that, by analyzing the orders that Moscow was issuing to its agents in America, the FBI acquired invaluable insights into Kremlin thinking. As early as August 1961, FBI Director J. Edgar Hoover informed the White House that the Russians had started looking for any evidence that the United States was about to mobilize for war. Beginning in 1962, instructions to Soviet spies to search for such indications steadily increased in both frequency and urgency.

By early fall, these orders raised disturbing questions in the minds of intelligence analysts in Washington. For the United States was not doing anything—nor did it contemplate anything—that would justify Soviet belief that mobilization might be imminent. Why then did the Russians have this fear? The ultimate, chilling conclusion of some American specialists was that the Soviet Union must be engaged in an action that, if detected, could be expected to provoke the United States to start preparing for war.

The next critical question was: Where would this action most likely be taking place? From all intelligence data available, one answer emerged: Cuba.

Thus, awareness of what was happening within Soviet espionage networks contributed to the United States decision to resume U-2 reconnaissance flights over Cuba. The first of the renewed flights over Cuba's critical San Cristóbal area, on October 14, 1962, produced proof of what the Russians were doing: implanting nuclear-tipped missiles pointed at the heart of America.

Tuomi, of course, knew nothing of the Cuban missile crisis until President Kennedy announced it in an emergency address. But as he listened to the President, he experienced the emotions of most Americans. He was simultaneousely terrified by the prospect of nuclear war and outraged by the Soviet treachery. With a sense of shock, he realized that he completely supported the United States.

The Sunday after the crisis ended with a Soviet pledge to withdraw the missiles, Tuomi went to a pro football game between the New York Giants and the Washington Redskins. The stadium crowd sang "The Star-Spangled Banner" with rare fervor and pride, and when it ended, a great patriotic cheer rose over the stadium. Tuomi was yelling as loud as anybody else.

That night, as he sat by himself in his apartment, Tuomi gave up the last pretenses about his innermost feelings. He finally acknowledged to himself that he had become wholly American. His belief in communism and his dedication to the Soviet Union had gradually eroded since he boarded the airliner at Vnukovo Airport, outside Moscow, in December 1958. He could not define for himself the stages of his ideological evolution, nor did he entirely understand the process. Initially, when confronted by something in America that was superior to what he had known in the Soviet Union, he had fallen back on doctrinaire communist rationalizations, learned by rote. When he encountered facts that could not be explained away, he simply banned them from his mind. But the everyday realities he experienced in the United States had had a cumulative effect.

Moreover, as he was drawn closer to the FBI agents, he increasingly saw conditions from a unique perspective: that of an observer able to view the Soviet Union through the KGB, and the United States through the FBI. Privately, he began to compare the two societies that had produced the KGB and the FBI.

All his life in the Soviet Union, Tuomi had accepted communist promises of free and decent tomorrows. He had believed that the summary arrests, purges, and massacres engineered by the KGB were unpleasant yet essential means to a noble end. But the undeniable realities of contemporary America finally destroyed his faith in Soviet promises. Here, rights, liberties, and opportunities unimaginable in the Soviet Union already existed in fact. For most Americans, freedom from fear and want was not a theoretical abstraction but a reality. In the open clamor and turbulence of American society, Tuomi did not see the "seeds of self-destruction" that Marxism imputed to it. Rather, he saw the means of salvation through democratic change.

He felt none of the passion of the sudden convert, none of the dogmatism of a believer whose faith results from inheritance. Yet his convictions were all the stronger because they had been forged gradually and painfully by his own reasoning. As he picked up the phone to call Jack, he felt a serene pride.

"You remember a long time ago, when we met at the lodge, I said that there were a lot of things I wouldn't tell you?" Tuomi asked. "Well, I'm ready now to tell you everything."

"Kaarlo, you've been ready for a long time," Jack replied. "But we thought it would be best to wait until you realized that yourself. We'll meet you at the apartment tomorrow night at seven."

In January, Tuomi began to prepare for the "vacation trip" to Moscow, as Galkin had instructed. The Center sent him a forged American passport and birth certificate, along with orders to submit a plan that would enable him to depart in May or June. The package from Moscow also included instructions: "Within next two months ascertain if there is a rocket base 2.2 miles south of Swanton in Franklin County, Vermont.

If a base does exist, report on which side of the Missisquoi River it is located and submit a map showing its precise position. Further determine if there is a rocket site eight miles north of Elizabethtown, New York, in the Adirondack Mountains. Use extreme caution and plan ahead so as to be able to explain your presence in these areas if challenged. Wife and family are well. Chief."

In accordance with his order to acknowledge a message by mailing an anti-Soviet statement to the U.N. delegation, Tuomi wrote on a postcard bearing the picture of the Madonna: "Sirs: Most members of the U.N. pay their assessments without fail. I can't figure out how a big and strong country like yours can claim that it can't pay her debts. Yours truly, M. Aclin."

The FBI interceded with Peter Burbank, head of the steamship firm, and Tuomi advised the Center that he had arranged a leave of absence from June through September. He had explained to his boss, he reported, that he yearned to spend a few months in Finland looking up lost relatives of his parents.

The mission to Vermont and upstate New York in late April was a lark. Both bases were where the Russians believed they were (both have since been closed). It was so easy for Tuomi to pinpoint them on a map that he, Jack, and Steve had time to act out their disguises as fishermen. The first night, they fried fresh-caught trout over a fire by a clear stream in Vermont. The next evening, they gorged themselves on sausage and pancakes at the annual Maple Sugar Festival in Elizabethtown. Tuomi drove home rested and relaxed. But at his apartment he found a stunning message from the Center.

"By your reckless and unauthorized action you have jeopardized your security and that of your mission," it began. "You were instructed only to submit a plan for your vacation, not to proceed with any arrangements. Your trip now must be postponed. Cancel all arrangements. Disassociate yourself from all friends so that it will be unnecessary later to explain your absence to anyone. Communicate at once your understanding and readiness to comply. Chief."

To Tuomi, Moscow's reaction was irrational, indeed incredible. He could scarcely offer a plan to leave the country without first having his employer's permission to take time off. And abrupt severance of carefully cultivated relations with his friends would be far more suspicious than anything he had done. Now the Center was ordering him to throw everything away. That night, he encoded a detailed, reasoned protest, beseeching the Center to reconsider.

The reply from Moscow was terse: "Cut off all ties with all friends immediately and await further instructions. Chief." Tuomi was further alarmed when the Center failed to signal that it had received his report and charts of the missile sites. Slipping back to the drop he had visited two nights before, he found them still there in the magnetic container.

"What's gone wrong?' Tuomi asked Jack and Steve.

"Evidently quite a bit," Jack answered. "There's nothing to do but play along and see what happens."

Tuomi could not know that Soviet intelligence in much of the world was suffering traumatic convulsions produced by the discovery that Colonel Oleg Penkovsky was a Western spy. Through career and marriage, Penkovsky was so positioned in Soviet society that he had access to secrets worth almost any price to the West. His information had assured the United States at the time of the Cuban confrontation that it enjoyed decisive military superiority over the Soviet Union—and that the Russians knew it. Moreover, he had knowledge of some vital Soviet espionage personnel and operations. Now the Russians could not be certain who and what had been compromised. General Ivan Serov, chief of military intelligence, and some of his ranking deputies were fired. Operations were being halted in midpoint. Agents were being transferred or brought home en masse, either for their own protection or because they were suspect. The result was disarray bordering on chaos.

On June 8, the Center did acknowledge receipt of the missile-site data that Tuomi had sent through another drop. But it offered no further guidance or hint of his future. So, after work on Friday, June 28, he drove westward, planning to see friends in Chicago and to go on to the northern lakes for a few days. His first night in Chicago, he received a telephone call.

"Sorry to ruin your trip," Jack said, "but something important has come up. You've got to fly to Washington tomorrow afternoon. Make a reservation right away and call me back. I'll meet you at the airport."

At Washington National Airport, Tuomi was met by Jack and Don, the senior agent who had stopped him on the street in Milwaukee four years before. They drove at once to a motel suite in Arlington, Virginia. Two other senior FBI agents were already there.

"Kaarlo, I imagine that sometimes you've wondered what you would do if you had to decide whether you were going to spend the rest of your life in the Soviet Union or the United States," Don began. "I hate to tell you, but the time has come when you have to make that decision. We have reason to believe that very soon you will be called home. We also believe you will not be sent back here.

"I am authorized to assure you that you are completely free to go. The FBI will do everything possible to make your return seem normal. We will do everything we can to help you. And let me add that they are not calling you home because they suspect you.

"On the other hand, Kaarlo—and again I'm speaking with the authority of our government—you are welcome to stay in the United States. If you decide to remain, we can't promise you paradise. You will have to stand on your own feet, earn your own living. But we will do everything we can to ensure your security and to help you get settled."

"If I stay, would there be any way to get my family out?" Tuomi asked.

Don shook his head. "There is no way."

"If I go back, would I still have to work for American intelligence? Would you try to contact me?"

"Absolutely not. You have our word on that," Don pledged. "As far as we are concerned, you will be as free as anyone in the Soviet Union can be. And no one will ever know what went on over here."

Tuomi had assumed—as Galkin had told him—that

after a temporary recall, he would be returned to the United States. He reasoned that he could survive personal scrutiny in the Soviet Union for two or three months, be with his children once more, and find out why he had received no word from his wife for two years. He also nurtured a hope, however unrealistic, that in Moscow he might chance upon means of eventually bringing his family to the West. But now . . .

He had no illusions about the cruelty of the choice suddenly confronting him. To stay in America meant never to see his wife and children again. To go meant never to see America again, to live the remainder of his life in a society he had spiritually repudiated and come to abhor.

What would happen to his family if he refused to return? Would the KGB imprison them? Or would it recognize the futility of punishing a wife and children who were in no way responsible for his actions, who posed no threat to the state?

What would happen to his family if, some time after his return, the KGB learned that he had betrayed the Soviet Union? Could he withstand the countless debriefings without making the one errant remark that would expose his duplicity? Could he live in the Soviet Union, forever suppressing the convictions that had transformed him into an American? He concluded that he could not.

"Don, maybe Kaarlo would like some time alone," he heard Jack say.

"No," Tuomi replied. "I have to decide now. I decide to stay."

The FBI agents stood up and crowded around to shake his hand.

Tuomi, after that day of decision, disappeared into America. In the years since, he has built a normal life for himself. Though he has never earned a great deal of money, he enjoys a comfortable home and most of the material conveniences that the United States offers. But his contentment results primarily from a sense of physical and spiritual liberty. He owns forty acres of isolated woodland where he likes to hunt and roam at will hour after hour. Having cut countless trees in his youth, he now derives satisfaction from planting and nurturing them.

In his community he is known as a moderate Republican, an occasional churchgoer and the personification of respectability. The same disarming grin and manner that sustained him in Moscow, at Tiffany's, and on the New York waterfront have helped fill his new life with good friends.

In spite of the excellence of Tuomi's abilities as a spy, mysteries remain in this story that he knew and lived. How did the FBI know he was coming? How did it know who he was? Tuomi has never been able to ascertain the answers. Neither, it would appear, has the KGB.

The Russians for years evidently were uncertain about what actually happened to Tuomi. Certainly they must have suspected that he had changed allegiance. But they could not be sure that he had not died an anonymous death, the victim of a street thug or an automobile accident. Between 1964 and 1971 his name never appeared on the list of men and women whom the KGB hunts throughout the world. This list, published in a secret book bound in a blue cover, is distributed to all KGB Residencies abroad and all KGB offices in the Soviet Union. It provides brief biographical detail about the wanted man, a statement of his crime, and the sentence pronounced on him, either at a trial or in absentia. The current list, for example, shows that Yuri Nosenko has been sentenced in absentia to the "highest measure of punishment." So have most of the other KGB officers now in the West.

In 1971, after the *Reader's Digest* had published in slightly different form an excerpt from this book manuscript containing the story of Tuomi, the FBI warned him that the KGB now was hunting him. His name had been added to the official list of those upon whom the KGB seeks, by any means it can, to inflict the "highest measure of punishment."

XIII

THE DARK CORE

Party Secretary Leonid Brezhnev on Monday, September 27, 1971, abruptly terminated a tour of Eastern Europe and hastened back to the Soviet Union. Shortly after landing, he joined KGB Chairman Yuri Andropov and members of the Politburo in the dignitaries' lounge at the Moscow airport. The urgency of the meeting necessitated an embarrassing postponement of a long-planned state reception in honor of Indian Prime Minister Indira Gandhi.

Three days earlier, Great Britain had banished 105 Soviet intelligence officers engaged in an increasingly brazen campaign to subvert public officials and steal technological data. Never before had a nation dealt so bluntly and effectively with the KGB—by wiping out a whole base of subversion through mass expulsions. But the announcement that accompanied the ousters gave the Politburo cause for still greater alarm. It told the Russians that the British had accepted into protective custody Oleg Adolfovich Lyalin, a man from the darkest core of the KGB, the ultrasecret division known as Department V, which is responsible for sabotage and assassinations. Over the weekend, the KGB had to inform the Soviet leadership that the defector was liable to expose Department V officers and operations in other countries. The Politburo feared that other nations, upon learning of professional Soviet saboteurs in their midst, might duplicate the British action.

Shortly after the extraordinary Politburo session at

the airport, Department V officers in the Western Hemisphere, Europe, Asia, and Africa received orders to flee their posts. As specialists in sabotage and murder, they had been among the best disguised and most hunted of all KGB personnel abroad. Now by fleeing, they unmasked themselves.

One of the first to scurry home was Valeri Vladimirovich Kostikov, second secretary of the Soviet embassy in Mexico City. An oldtime saboteur, Kostikov had been arrested by Mexican police in December 1968, after he drunkenly pulled a gun on two Mexican engineers employed in the national petroleum industry. One can only speculate about why this Soviet diplomat was carrying a gun, but his interest in the Mexican petroleum industry, a prime target for sabotage, is understandable.

Simultaneously, Department V officer Vyacheslav Nikolaevich Pavlov disappeared from the Soviet consulate general in Montreal, where he used the title of vice consul. Before becoming a diplomat, Pavlov had entered Canada with several other Department V officers who posed as Soviet officials at Expo 67. It is believed that the KGB used the exposition as a cover for reconnoitering sabotage targets along the St. Lawrence Seaway and in the industrial sections of the northeastern United States.

General Viktor Mikhailovich Vladimirov, who also had been at Expo, hastily fled the Soviet embassy in Helsinki, strengthening Western suspicions that he was a ranking officer of Department V. What this senior expert in sabotage and assassination was doing in Finland is as mysterious as what he was doing in Canada.

Other suspected Department V officers hurriedly withdrawn after Lyalin's defection included Ivan Pavlovich Yevdotev from Bonn, Lev Fedorovich Shengalev from Bogotá, Leonid Leontevich Litvak from Athens, Anatoli Baronin from Lagos, and Boris A. Sazanov from Paris.

Among the few Department V officers to escape immediate recall was its chief representative in the United States, Mikhail Mikhailovich Antipov. The Kremlin allowed him to remain as first secretary of the Soviet mission to the United Nations until February 1972. The Russians probably hoped to hide his Department V affiliation by keeping him apart from the wholesale exodus. However, as early as 1958, Antipov was known to have been involved in assassination and sabotage operations. Working out of the United Nations in New York under the cover of diplomatic immunity, Antipov helped plan and supervise Department V operations against the United States from July 1963 until September 1966. After a tour at the Center in Moscow, he returned to the United Nations in October 1969.

The tracks left by various Department V officers flushed into the open were revealing. They showed that Department V was active on all continents, surveying both physical and human targets for destruction. Partial reconstruction of such operations by foreign governments indicated that the Kremlin contemplated sabotage not only in case of war but in certain peacetime circumstances. Threatening as these preparations were, the mentality they mirrored was even more disturbing. For the existence and worldwide deployment of an outfit such as Department V revealed a continuing Soviet commitment to the principle of clandestine violence.

Consonant with the Leninist precept that whatever serves to advance communism is moral by definition, the Soviet Union murdered and kidnapped foreigners as early as 1926, when Stalin fully consolidated his power. That year, OGPU agents gunned down the Ukrainian leader Simon Petlura in Paris. They abducted the Estonian minister to the Soviet Union, Ado Birk, off a Moscow street in broad daylight, his diplomatic immunity notwithstanding. Birk never was heard of again. On January 26, 1930, the OGPU kidnapped the White Russian leader Aleksandr Kutepov in Paris, and, on May 22, 1932, shot a former communist courier, Hans Wissengir, in Hamburg. Soviet intelligence officers who displeased their superiors were also murdered. Valentin Markin, chief of the OGPU in the United States, was liquidated in New York in 1934, and GRU agent Jean Cremet was killed in Macao two years later.

To perpetrate terror abroad more efficiently and on a larger scale, the NKVD in 1936 organized the Administration of Special Tasks, which Russians in time referred to as the department of "wet affairs" (*mokrie dela*). At first, the new administration concentrated on eliminating dissident foreign communists: Trotskyites and Trotsky himself. Among its 1937 victims were Dmitri Navachine, murdered in Paris; Juliet Stuart Poyntz, who disappeared in New York; Ignace Reiss, murdered near Lausanne; Yevgenni Miller, kidnapped in Paris; Henry Moulin, Kurt Landau, Camillo Berneri, and Andrés Nin, all killed in Spain. The Directorate probably was responsible for the disappearance in Spain that year of José Robles, Marc Rein, Erwin Wolf, and Hans Freund. In 1938, NKVD agents in Belgium abducted and killed George Arutiunov, a former OGPU officer, and blew up the Ukrainian leader Evhen Konovalec in Rotterdam. Almost certainly they murdered Rudolf Klement, an associate of Trotsky's son, Leon Sedov, in Paris. Klement's decapitated corpse was found in the Seine on July 16, 1938.

The Administration of Special Tasks also may have caused the death of Sedov himself, who underwent stomach surgery in February 1938, at a small Parisian clinic staffed by Russian émigrés. The surgery was successful, and he appeared to be recovering rapidly. But on the fifth night after the operation, he was found wandering outside his room, naked and delirious, with large bruises on his abdomen. He died three days later. Without explaining what produced the bruises, an inquest attributed his death to postoperative complications.*

A band of some twenty NKVD agents, armed with machine guns and led by painter David Alfaro Siqueiros, assaulted Leon Trotsky's villa in Mexico on May 24, 1940. Although Trotsky was unharmed by the more than two hundred bullets fired into his bedroom, the raiders took away and later killed one of his bodyguards, an American, Robert Sheldon Harte. (Some students of Trotsky have speculated that Harte

---

*Eighteen years later, though, Mark Zborowski, who was Sedov's closest friend, admitted that he had been an NKVD agent assigned to spy on Trotsky's son. It was Zborowski who took Sedov to the clinic and visited him before his death.

actually was a conspirator in the attack and that the NKVD wanted to silence him.) Late in the afternoon of August 20, 1940, NKVD agent Ramón Mercader, also known as Jacques Mornard, who had worked his way into Trotsky's confidence, followed him into his study. Guards heard screams and sounds of a struggle, and Trotsky staggered out drenched with blood, fatally wounded by a blow on the head from a skiing ice ax (piolet). Imprisoned in comfortable style, Mercader went to Czechoslovakia upon his release in 1960.

After the Nazi invasion in 1941, the Administration of Special Tasks grew into the Fourth, or Partisan, Directorate of the NKVD, which conducted espionage, sabotage, assassination, and guerrilla operations behind German lines. Its director was General Pavl Anatolevich Sudoplatov, a poised, extremely intelligent man of medium stature whose countenance was dominated by great dark eyes. He directed wartime operations so ably that he was given command of Special Bureau (Spetsburo) No. 1, established within the NKGB January 1, 1946, to perpetrate peacetime sabotage and murder.

With dispassionate philosophical detachment, Sudoplatov managed the annihilation of people. Discussing recruitment of agents, he told an officer who later defected: "Go search for people who are hurt by fate or nature—the ugly, those suffering from an inferiority complex, craving power and influence but defeated by unfavorable circumstances. . . . The sense of belonging to an influential, powerful organization will give them a feeling of superiority over the handsome and prosperous people around them. For the first time in their lives they will experience a sense of importance. . . . It is sad indeed, and humanly shallow—but we are obliged to profit from it."

Under Sudoplatov the Special Bureau developed the networks in Germany, Austria, and Switzerland that provided the intelligence, surveillance, and other support necessary for kidnappings and killings. Actual abductions ordinarily were carried out by thugs the Russians termed "combat groups" (*boyevaya gruppa*). Although personally supervised by Soviet officers, the gangs were composed mostly of East Germans and Czechs chosen on the basis of their physical strength and, in some cases, their criminal records. They preyed primarily on effective anticommunists and leaders of émigré organizations. One gang abducted Karl Fischer from Austria in January 1947, and the following September Georgi Tregubov disappeared, after being lured into East Berlin by a female Soviet agent, Yelizaveta Klyuchevskaya. The chief inspector of the Vienna police vanished in 1948, and the chief of police in the East Sector of Berlin disappeared in 1949. A year later, the wife of Georgi Sergeevich Okolovich, a prominent official of the Munich-based Russian émigré group NTS (Narodny-Trudovoy Soyuz—People's Labor League), eluded Soviet agents who tried to kidnap her on a Munich street. In 1951 a defector betrayed a plot to kidnap Okolovich himself. West German police subsequently were led to a cache of drugs and a crowbar that agents intended to use to keep him quiet during the trip eastward.

When Dr. Walter Linse, head of the Association of Free German Jurists, walked out of his apartment in a West Berlin suburb about 7 A.M. on July 8, 1952, a stranger approached and asked for a match. As he reached into his pocket, the stranger struck him and another man grabbed him from behind and forced him toward a car parked nearby. Linse fought fiercely until one of the assailants, having taken deliberate aim, calmly shot him in the leg. The noise attracted neighbors, and a West Berlin truck driver pursued the abductors. But as they neared an entrance to the Soviet sector of Berlin, a barrier suddenly rose to admit the abductors' car and just as quickly closed to bar pursuit. U.S. High Commissioner John J. McCloy protested the kidnapping to his Soviet counterpart, Marshal Vasili Ivanovich Chuikov. "You do not think, I hope, that the Soviet Union would have had any complicity in this plot," Chuikov replied. Years later repatriated German prisoners of war reported having seen Linse in 1955, emaciated and in failing health, at a Soviet concentration camp near Vorkuta north of the Urals. The Soviet

Red Cross in 1960 announced that Dr. Linse had died in prison on December 15, 1953. It is impossible to determine which report was true. But the Red Cross announcement was an admission that Dr. Linse was a Soviet prisoner, a fact the Soviet Union had denied, officially and categorically, for years.

The Special Bureau also maintained the *Kamera*, or Chamber, a laboratory that conducted experiments to invent ever better and more undetectable means of exterminating human beings. The Chamber specialized in poisons for which there is no known antidote and devices that kill while making death appear to be the result of natural causes. Planning an assassination in 1953, Sudoplatov's deputy, Colonel Lev Aleksandrovich Studnikov, remarked: "The fellows from the Twelfth [the Chamber] say that they themselves are afraid to walk in their own laboratory. I can understand it. A fearful business. You just touch something by chance—and there's your funeral."

Even within the Party hierarchy the Special Bureau acquired such an infamous reputation that Khrushchev and his associates, upon ascending to power in June 1953, promptly abolished it and closed the Chamber. Seven MVD officers appeared at the office of General Sudoplatov and, while four guarded the exits, three went inside. "General Sudoplatov, a letter for you," one announced, handing him an envelope. As the general extended his hand to take it, the other two officers grabbed his arms and wrenched them behind his back, then dragged him away to Vladimir Prison.

However, as defecting Soviet officers disclosed, the demise of the Special Bureau was temporary. Once Khrushchev and his allies began to exercise power, they concluded they could not rule without such an organization, and so in September 1953 it was reconstituted as the Ninth Section of the First Chief Directorate. With the formation of the KGB the following year, it became Department 13 of the First Chief Directorate.

In a sense, the operations of Department 13 represented more of an affront to the world than those of its predecessors. Stalin, of course, approved a general policy of murder and kidnapping, yet it is not certain that he personally deliberated about and authorized in advance each and every crime committed in accord with this policy. But under Khrushchev, the collective leadership did personally examine and approve in advance the significant operations of Department 13. Two former Department 13 officers, Nikolai Khokhlov and Bogdan Stashinsky, have attested to this effect, and their testimony is corroborated by another former KGB officer, Petr Deriabin. Moreover, it is consistent with the known determination of the Khrushchev oligarchy to control all important actions of the KGB. Thus, the Soviet murders and kidnappings perpetrated under Khrushchev cannot be considered errant offenses by the KGB or its individual officers. They were carefully considered acts of the Soviet leadership. And during their first full year in power, the successors of Stalin resorted to assassination and abduction operations with undiminished ferocity.

In Frankfurt, early on the evening of February 18, 1954, Captain Nikolai Khokhlov, a veteran Soviet agent, knocked on the apartment door of the Russian émigré he had been sent to kill. Marked for death, in an order signed both by Khrushchev and Premier Georgi M. Malenkov, was Georgi Sergeevich Okolovich, the feared NTS leader whom the Russians had tried unsuccessfully to kidnap three years before. "Georgi Sergeevich?" Khokhlov asked, when Okolovich opened the door.

"Yes, I am he," said Okolovich.

Khokhlov smiled. "May I come in?"

"Actually, I don't know you, and . . . ," Okolovich replied hesitantly.

"But," Khokhlov interrupted, "I know you very well." He added, "If you'll permit me to sit down, I'll explain everything. You are home alone?"

"Yes, alone," Okolovich admitted uneasily. "Come in."

"Georgi Sergeevich, I've come to you from Moscow," Khokhlov announced. "The Central Committee of the Communist Party of the Soviet Union ordered your liquidation. The murder is entrusted to my group."

Silently Okolovich nodded slightly, signifying his comprehension.

"I can't let this murder happen," said Khokhlov.

Although he had engaged in terrorism and sent men to kill during the war, Khokhlov could not commit premeditated murder. The day he received the assassination assignment in Moscow, he agreed with his wife that he would not fulfill it. Not knowing what else to do, he decided to inform Okolovich of the KGB plan to kill him. Khokhlov identified two other Soviet agents, Feliks Kukovich and Franz Weber, who had been trained with him in Moscow and sent out to assist in the mission. Captured by American security agents, they corroborated his account. Khokhlov then directed the Americans to an automobile battery hidden in a forest outside Munich. From it, he removed a gold cigarette case which the laboratory in Moscow had transformed into an electric pistol that noiselessly fired poisoned dumdum bullets.

Other disclosures by Khokhlov disrupted some of the Department 13 activities in Europe, but they did not end the vendetta against prominent anticommunists. KGB "combat teams" abducted Dr. Aleksandr R. Trushnovich and the journalist Karl W. Fricke from Berlin, and NTS member Valeri Tremmel from Austria. KGB agent Mikhail Ismailov, in November 1954, tied up Radio Liberty employee Abdul Fatalibeyl with wire, then beat him to death. In December 1955, a German criminal, Wolfgang Wildprett, confessed that he had been ordered to kill NTS president Vladimir Poremsky in Frankfurt. Josef Winkelmüller confessed that he was under orders to murder a U.S. Army employee in Regensburg. Eventually Khokhlov's own name appeared on the list of men doomed by the Kremlin.

The Soviet Union initially tried to cope with the embarrassment of his defection by asserting that his statements were malicious inventions of the CIA. Khokhlov began speaking publicly, and audiences around the world found him to be both credible and persuasive, so the KGB propagated the fiction that he was actually a relative of Okolovich and that both were Nazi war criminals. Unintimidated, Khokhlov persisted in speaking out, and so the KGB was handed a warrant for his death.

While participating in a convention at Frankfurt on September 15, 1957, Khokhlov became ill and later collapsed. Regaining consciousness, he suffered violent nausea that doctors treated as acute gastritis. But the treatment was unavailing. On Khokhlov's fifth morning in a Frankfurt hospital, a nurse entered his room and stared at him transfixed in horror. "What is it?" Khokhlov demanded. Then he looked in a mirror with a horror of his own.

Hideous brown stripes, dark splotches, and black-and-blue swellings disfigured his face and body. A sticky secretion oozed from his eyelids, and blood seeped through his pores; his skin felt dry, shrunken, and aflame. At the mere touch of his hand, great tufts of his hair fell out. An eminent professor of medicine suspected that he had been poisoned with thallium, a rare toxic metal. However, treatment with thallium antidotes had no effect. Tests on September 22 showed that Khokhlov's white corpuscles were being swiftly and fatally destroyed, his bones decaying, his blood turning to plasma, and his saliva glands atrophying. That night doctors told Okolovich that Khokhlov's condition was hopeless, his death imminent.

But Okolovich refused to abandon the man to whom he owed his own life. Desperately he appealed to the Americans, and with approval from Washington Khokhlov was transferred to a U.S. military hospital in Frankfurt. Protected constantly by armed guards, a team of six American physicians now began a duel with the scientists of the Chamber in Moscow. Around the clock they gave him massive injections of cortisone, vitamins, steroids, ACTH, and experimental medications, while keeping him alive with intravenous feeding and almost continuous blood transfusions. An anesthesiologist stood by, preparing solutions for Khokhlov's mouth, which was devoid of saliva, and otherwise trying to ease his agony. More specialists arrived for consultation and analysis and still newer drugs were rushed to Frankfurt. For a week the supreme resources of American medicine barely kept Khokhlov alive. Then, for reasons the physicians themselves did not understand, their intensive treatments and Khokhlov's will to live slowly began to prevail. Though Khokhlov would remain totally bald and scarred for many months, after about three weeks his ultimate recovery was assured. Still, the doctors could not diagnose precisely what had happened to him.

Subsequently a famous American toxicologist, who studied the medical records in consultation with colleagues, found the answer. Khokhlov was poisoned with thallium that had been subjected to intense atomic radiation, which causes the metal to disintegrate into tiny particles. Introduced into his body through food or drink, the radioactive particles disintegrated completely and permeated his system with deadly radiation.

While Khokhlov was being poisoned, Department 13 stalked another Soviet opponent in Germany, Lev Rebet, a leading Ukrainian émigré and political theoretician. His appointed executioner was Bogdan Stashinsky, a handsome, clean-cut twenty-five-year-old KGB agent who had been recruited at the age of nineteen after being caught riding a train without a ticket. A Ukrainian who learned German during the Nazi occupation, Stashinsky was trained to serve as an illegal in West Germany. Four times during 1957 his supervisor in Karlshorst, whom he knew as Sergei, sent Stashinsky to Munich to study Rebet's daily routine and habits. Upon his return to Karlshorst in September, Sergei greeted him simply: "The time has come. A man from Moscow is here."

The Department 13 officer from Moscow unveiled a metal tube about seven inches long and half an inch in diameter, and explained that it contained a firing device and a glass ampule filled with prussic acid. A spring detonated a small charge which crushed the ampule and caused the poison to spray forth from the tube as a vapor. Once inhaled, it quickly induced death by contracting the blood vessels, as in a cardiac arrest. Soon after death, the blood vessels relaxed so that an unsuspecting pathologist performing an autopsy would conclude that the victim had died of a heart attack. The Department 13 officer assured Stashinsky that he would be safe so long as he took an antidote pill before firing the poison and inhaled another antidote from a special ampule immediately afterward. The weapon, he was told, had been used often and had never failed.

The next day Sergei and the officer from Moscow drove Stashinsky to some woods outside Berlin where a friendly, playful dog was leashed to a tree. The officer handed him a pill and the tube and nodded at the dog. Stashinsky pressed the firing spring and heard a dull pop. The dog fell, convulsed, and died in a few moments.

Stashinsky flew to Munich on October 9 under a false identity, carrying the tube concealed in a sausage can, as well as ten antidote pills and antidote ampules. Each morning he took one of the pills, along with a tranquilizer, then began his watch outside Rebet's office building. About 10 A.M. on October 12, he saw Rebet alight from a streetcar. Stashinsky hurried into the building to await him on the stairway. As Rebet passed, he took the tube from his pocket and discharged the vapor into his victim's face. Rebet staggered and collapsed. An autopsy indicated that death was caused by a heart attack.

In May 1958 the KGB sent Stashinsky to a Rotterdam cemetery to observe the people attending a memorial service for the Ukrainian leader Evhen Konovalec, murdered by the NKVD in 1938. Afterward, Sergei asked him to diagram the location of Konovalec's grave and discussed planting a bomb near it to blow up the Ukrainians at some future service. Almost a year later Stashinsky realized that he really had been sent to the memorial service because of the presence there of one man, Stefan Bandera, who was to be his next victim.

At the Center in April 1959, an officer introduced as Georgi Aksentyevich informed him that the "highest authority" had decided to liquidate Bandera, the famous nationalist who led a guerrilla movement in the Ukraine that was not subdued until 1947. Because a bodyguard often accompanied Bandera, Department

13 had produced a doublebarreled weapon capable of killing two men simultaneously. It also had duplicated a key to Bandera's apartment building in Munich.

A month later, Stashinsky spotted Bandera standing alone in the garage of his apartment house. As the young KGB assassin started toward him, he was paralyzed by his conscience. He simply could not kill another human being who never had harmed him. He fled, throwing the poison-filled tubes into a river. Back in Karlshorst he told the KGB that just as he was about to kill Bandera, a stranger appeared in the yard by the garage. To prove that he had tried to fulfill the assignment, he displayed a piece of the key the KGB had given him. Actually, Stashinsky had broken the key in an earlier attempt to open the door of Bandera's apartment house. He took leave to visit his parents in the Ukraine, hoping that the assassination plan now would be canceled. But in October Sergei informed him that "the highest authorities" in Moscow had sent urgent orders that he must exterminate Bandera at once.

Lurking outside the Munich apartment house on October 15, Stashinsky resolved that if Bandera appeared before 1 P.M., he would kill him; if not, he would flee and endure whatever punishment the KGB chose to inflict. Just before 1 P.M., Bandera drove into the apartment yard alone. As he unlocked his apartment door, Stashinsky fired the poison into his face. Bandera was found dead at 1:05 P.M.

Because Bandera was armed and known to fear for his life, German authorities immediately performed an autopsy. They detected flakes of glass from the crushed ampule on his face and traces of prussic acid in his stomach. That Bandera had been murdered was clear; yet there was no clue as to his killer. Quickly the KGB decided to make the most of an opportunity to smear another anticommunist, Dr. Theodor Oberlander, West German Minister for Refugee Affairs. Adducing no evidence whatsoever, the communist press cried out in unison that Dr. Oberlander was the murderer. A *Red Star* article on October 20 typified the Soviet disinformation campaign: "Bandera knew too much about

Oberlander's activities. As public opinion is becoming increasingly insistent that Oberlander should be brought to judgment, Bandera could have become one of the most important witnesses. This made the Bonn Minister and his patrons apprehensive. They decided to liquidate Bandera and obliterate all traces. Thus has one rogue got his own back on another."

A few weeks after the murder, at an East Berlin theater, Stashinsky happened to see a newsreel film of Bandera's funeral. The sight of Bandera lying in an open coffin, his wife and children weeping nearby, struck him like an electric shock. He left the theater, went directly to Sergei, and told him he was overcome with guilt and grief for Bandera's family. "Some day Bandera's children will be thankful to have returned to the Soviet Union," Sergei said.

Aleksandr Nikolaevich Shelepin, then chairman of the KGB, now a Politburo member and president of the Soviet "trade unions," personally received Stashinsky at KGB headquarters early in December 1959. Ceremoniously, Shelepin read a document stating that the Presidium of the Supreme Soviet (as the Politburo was then called), by decree dated November 6, 1959, had awarded Stashinsky the Order of the Red Banner for executing an "important government commission." He pointed out that the document bore the signatures of Marshal Klimenti Yefremovich Voroshilov, chairman of the Presidium, and Mikhail Porfirevich Georgadse, secretary of the Presidium.

At the investiture of Stashinsky into the ranks of Soviet heroes, some KGB generals indicated that they had grand plans to develop him into a truly professional killer as well as a leader of other assassins and saboteurs. They had arranged for him to undergo eighteen months of officer training in Moscow and to study English, a subject that suggested eventual missions in Great Britain or North America. His future work, Shelepin later advised him, would be "difficult but honorable."

Stashinsky might have caused many other "natural deaths" had it not been for a remarkably intelligent, courageous, and idealistic young woman. In Karlshorst, between missions in the West, Stashinsky fell in love with an appealing East German named Inge Pohl who, as it happened, loathed communism. Ignorant of her political views, the KGB tolerated the relationship because it supported the East German identity Stashinsky assumed while in Berlin. Now, though, the KGB insisted that he abandon Inge, give her some money, and forget her. Shelepin urged that he marry a KGB girl who could assist him on illegal assignments. But in the face of Stashinsky's adamant assurances about Inge's political reliability, he reluctantly acquiesced to their marriage.

Stashinsky, in defiance of orders, confided to Inge that he was a Soviet citizen and a KGB agent. Inge was appalled, but for the sake of their love she agreed to feign sympathy for the Soviet Union and a readiness to collaborate with the KGB. Thus did the lovers form a mild conspiracy against the KGB. Soon after their marriage in April 1960, it turned into outright enmity.

To transform Inge into a "Soviet person" and reeducate Stashinsky in "Soviet reality," the KGB frequently took them on tours of factories, collective farms, museums, schools, and other institutions, while requiring them to read volumes of propaganda. Inge undertook her own "reeducation" program, perceptively pointing out to Stashinsky glaring disparities between Soviet claims and what they saw for themselves. Increasingly, she made him see the Soviet Union through Western eyes, and he began to experience a "spiritual change." Sensing it, Inge remarked, "One day you will wake up and find yourself cured." Once, in response to his halfhearted defense of communism, she said: "I don't understand why you are so silly about this, seeing that you are not a stupid person about other things."

Stashinsky's disaffection was completed after Inge became pregnant that summer. Marriage had enhanced their love, and they were eager for a child. But the KGB considered a baby an encumbrance and pressured Inge to submit to an abortion. She indignantly refused, so the KGB proposed that the parents surrender the baby to the state for upbringing. Now Stashinsky told

Inge about the two murders he had committed. He told her also that he intended to atone for his crimes by communicating with West German or American intelligence once they were sent into the West.

Late in 1960, however, KGB General Vladimir Yakovlevich informed them that because the political situation was "fundamentally altered," they could not safely enter the West for some time. Stashinsky did persuade the KGB to allow Inge to visit her parents in Berlin. They devised a code for use in their letters, and he told her to stay in East Germany until he could find a way to join her. But even after the birth of their son on March 31, 1961, the KGB rejected all his requests to go to Berlin. Then, on August 8, Inge telephoned terrible news. Their son had died of pneumonia.

With KGB officer Yuri Aleksandrov guarding him, Stashinsky flew to East Germany on August 10 aboard a military plane for the funeral. Aleksandrov outraged him en route by theorizing that the Americans or Germans had murdered his child to lay a trap for him in Berlin or that Inge had killed the infant just so he would visit her.

In East Berlin the KGB kept Bogdan and Inge under heavy surveillance. Cars parked conspicuously day and night near the house of Inge's parents, and men trailed them wherever they went on the street. On the afternoon of August 12—one day before the Wall sealed off East Berlin—they concluded that they would be forced back to Moscow immediately after the funeral, and the only chance of escape lay in fleeing before the service. So on that same afternoon, they crawled out of the house and, crouching behind a hedge out of sight of the KGB surveillants, crab-walked to a side street. Along paths and alleys Inge knew from her childhood, they ran until they found a taxi that took them to the elevated train that crossed into West Berlin. At the Tempelhof police sation, Stashinsky identified himself and asked to see the Americans.

He begged his interrogators for neither mercy nor favors; indeed, he sought expiation through confession and punishment. On September 1 the Americans delivered him to West German authorities, who announced his arrest for "treasonable activities," making no mention of the murders.

Not until Stashinsky's public trial opened at Karlsruhe in October 1962 did the world begin to see fully what he, Department 13, the KGB, and the rulers of the Soviet Union had done. Both American and German authorities treated Stashinsky skeptically at first. During much of the trial, the formal and punctilious German judges seemed to put him in the position of a defendant forced to prove his own guilt. But German police in investigating his story unearthed myriad documents and several witnesses to corroborate what he said. Down in the lock housing of Bandera's apartment door, they found part of the key he had broken. Stashinsky vividly recalled a woman he had seen upon leaving the murder scene. And he remembered that when he killed Rebet, a police car was parked nearby. The police located the woman and verified that their car had been there. Hotel and travel records confirmed that Stashinsky had been in West Germany at the times he said and under the aliases he mentioned. Scientists testified that the murder weapons he described would function just as he reported.

Psychiatrists found Stashinsky straightforward and mentally healthy. The presiding judge said of him: ". . . an intelligent and gifted person, gentle and peace-loving by nature. Had it not been for the Soviet system, which, just as did the Nazi system, regards political murder on behalf of the state as a necessity, he would today probably be a schoolteacher somewhere in the Ukraine." And it was Stashinsky himself who made the most profound impression on the judges, the press, and spectators with his consistent, intelligent, and reserved testimony. At the end of the seven-day trial, he said to the court and the world:

"I wanted to unburden my conscience, and I wanted to give worldwide publicity to the way in which 'peaceful coexistence' really works in practice. I did not want to go on being used on murder assignments. I wanted to warn all those who live in danger of being liquidated, as were Rebet and Bandera, to take precautions. I hope that my flight to the West will be seen as lessening my guilt, for I have brought a great deal upon myself through my flight. The fate of my parents and relatives will come to pass, or may already have come to pass, as I have described it. This will always remain a heavy spiritual burden for me. . . . My wife and I will always live in the fear that we shall one day be overtaken by retribution from the East. Quite apart from that, we are entirely without means here in the West. Nevertheless, I have decided in favor of the West because I believe that this step was absolutely necessary for the world at large."

Because of his character and contrition, the court, with the concurrence of the families of the murdered men, sentenced Stashinsky to only eight years' imprisonment as an *accomplice* to murder. In pronouncing sentence, the presiding judge declared:

"On the strength of evidence adduced in this trial, the guilt of those from whom he received his orders is far greater. . . . the Soviet Secret Service no longer commits murder at its own discretion. Murder is now carried out on express government orders. Political murder has, so to speak, now become institutionalized."

Stashinsky's defection, trial, and public testimony had a traumatic effect within both the KGB and the Party hierarchy. At least seventeen officers were fired or demoted, according to former KGB Major Anatoli Golitsin. Despite the resources and resourcefulness of Soviet propagandists, the evidence that the Kremlin had cynically plotted the murders of civilians in peacetime could not be explained away. And the Soviet leadership realized that a repetition of the Stashinsky affair could seriously obstruct their efforts to repair international relations in the aftermath of the Cuban crisis.

The Kremlin could not quite bring itself to entirely forswear murder as a tool of Soviet foreign policy. Department 13 was allowed to retain the capacity to kill and to continue its hunt for selected defectors, both from the Soviet Union and the East European satellites. But in late 1962 or early 1963, the leadership did drastically curtail the practice of assassination and told the KGB that henceforth people would be liquidated in peacetime only in special circumstances. Yuri Nosenko, on the basis of evidence he is not at liberty to divulge, believes that the KGB concluded that future assassinations should be entrusted not to Soviet personnel such as Khokhlov and Stashinsky but to hired foreign criminals and illegal agents of other nationalities, who could not be easily linked to the Soviet Union.

During the mid-1960s, Western security services discerned a shift in emphasis in Department 13 operations from assassination to preparations for sabotage. They also began to perceive the outline of a new Soviet concept of sabotage. The KGB, of course, had always sought to establish dormant networks of agents who could be activated in wartime as a fifth column against critical defense installations and military targets. But the immensely successful 1959 disinformation operation in which Department 13 agents desecrated Jewish shrines in West Germany (see pages 234–36) dramatized how physical acts could achieve great psychological effect. Perhaps under the influence of the formidable General Ivan Agayants, who conceived the swastika operation, the KGB concluded that widespread sabotage could be coordinated to paralyze a nation's will and ability to respond to an international crisis short of war. Specifically, it envisioned plunging foreign capitals into panic and disarray by stopping transit systems, shutting off electrical power, disrupting water supply, and blocking key traffic arteries. In KGB theory, the sabotage could be accompanied by mass demonstrations and propaganda against whatever particular action the foreign government was considering to cope with the crisis.

When Department 13 became Department V as a consequence of the 1968–69 reorganization of the KGB, its headquarters staff consisted of between fifty and sixty officers, all trained in sundry forms of violence and familiar with given geographic areas of the world. Additionally, Department V officers were stationed in most major Soviet embassies abroad. Their duties included the assessment of sabotage targets, the recruitment and management of local agents who could be employed either as saboteurs or assassins, and the support of Department V illegals. In keeping with severe secrecy strictures imposed after the Stashinsky defection, Department V officers, both in Moscow and abroad, tried to conceal their affiliation even from their KGB colleagues. Through secrecy and discretion, Department 13 succeeded in hiding its continued existence in its reconstituted form as Department V. Then, beginning in the summer of 1971, a series of events combined to show that it still was very much alive and hard at work.

Paris-Match for August 14, 1971, published an interview with Jan Sejna, a Czechoslovak general who fled to the United States in 1968. Sejna stated that under Soviet direction, Warsaw Pact nations had implanted in Western Europe and North America dormant networks of saboteurs who were to destroy vital installations at the outset of a war. But he also indicated that the Soviet Union contemplated utilization of the saboteurs in circumstances short of war. For example, Sejna reported that a plan had been discussed in secret Warsaw Pact meetings to sabotage the London subway system in the event of "serious political difficulties." According to the plan, communist agents would also incite mass demonstrations and then accuse the British government of deliberately halting the underground to prevent public protests.

As the Party secretary assigned to oversee the Czechoslovak Defense Ministry, Sejna regularly attended Warsaw Pact command conferences, where he came into possession of the kind of information he divulged. Nothing he said was inconsistent with what Western security services already knew from other sources. But in the absence of independent public corroboration, his statements were difficult to accept. And the spector of serious and deliberate communist preparations to sabotage Western cities in peacetime so contravened the spirit of détente that few Westerners wanted to accept it.

A month after the Sejna interview, however, an intelligent and engaging thirty-four-year-old Russian named Oleg Adolfovich Lyalin requested and received asylum in London. In a formal statement issued September 24, 1971, the British Foreign Office said of him: "This man, an officer of the KGB, brought with him certain information and documents, including plans for infiltration of agents for the purpose of sabotage." The British quietly arrested several persons, including two Cypriots working in London as tailors. The *Daily Mail* on October 2 quoted "a high British source" as predicting that the trial would "shock the country." The newspaper reported: "The most sensational revelation may be that the Russians planned to sabotage vital installations even during peacetime." Two weeks later, the Attorney General of Great Britain, Sir Peter Rawlinson, dispelled all doubt about the significance of Lyalin and what he represented. In a written reply to a question in Parliament, Sir Peter said that Lyalin occupied an "official post of importance" in the KGB division whose mission "included the organization of sabotage within the United Kingdom." The Attorney General continued: "After Mr. Lyalin sought asylum, there were substantial grounds for anxiety over his personal safety, enhanced by the fact that the duties of his department of the KGB also included the elimination of individuals judged to be enemies of the U.S.S.R. These anxieties remain."

The spectacular revelations anticipated by a sector of the British press in consequence of Lyalin's flight have yet to appear publicly. Unexpectedly, the two Cypriots pleaded guilty to espionage, and so the government unveiled little of its evidence. Lyalin declined offers from numerous publications eager for the rights to his story. Perhaps out of deference to Lyalin or for counterintelligence purposes, British authorities have refused to make any further comment.

However, the reverberations of Lyalin's disclosures probably have not ended. Energetic investigations of leads he provided continued throughout 1972 in Europe, North America, and Asia. And in illuminating some of the most secret plans and techniques of the KGB, he has undoubtedly made the entire West better able to defend itself against Soviet saboteurs and assassins.

On April 17, 1972, thousands of miles from London, further evidence emerged to demonstrate that the KGB continues to nurture networks of potential saboteurs and assassins in the West. About 9:30 P.M. in Edmonton, Canada, Anton Sabotka* finished work and started toward his car to drive home. Three tall men came out of the darkness to surround him. They displayed identification cards of Royal Canadian Mounted Policemen. "We would like a word with you," one said. "May we please have the keys to your car?"

The Canadians drove Sabotka to a nearby motel, and there the officer in charge remarked, "I believe you know what we want to talk about."

Sabotka slumped in a chair. "I've always known this day would come," he responded. "I'm ready to tell you everything and take the consequences." The story Sabotka told that night and in succeeding days illustrates the tedious, tortuous lengths to which the KGB is willing to go to ensure that it can wreak havoc abroad on signal from Moscow.

Though Sabotka was born in Canada, his immigrant parents took him back to their native Czechoslovakia in 1946 when he was sixteen. His father, for whom communism was a religion, became Party chairman in a rural Slovak district and with Canadian dollars bought an old German army truck. Father and son worked together in a hauling business that was quite profitable until the government nationalized their truck after the communist coup in 1948. As compensation, the government paid less than a tenth of what the truck cost the father, and it thereby planted in Sabotka the first seeds of antipathy toward communism.

Anton Sabotka went to work for a Czech equivalent of a Soviet machine tractor station, dispatching agricultural equipment. At first he willingly supported the communist collectivization of farms. Repeated subdivisions, the result of generations of inheritances, had partitioned most of the tillable land in his area into tiny odd-shaped plots. To him it made sense to consolidate them into large farms where mechanized methods

---

*The true name of the man here described is omitted in an effort to assist him in the new life upon which he has embarked.

could be employed. Thus in 1951, when State Secret Security (the STB) asked him to provide information about resistance to the collectivization, he agreed. By the time he concluded that the farmers were actually being condemned to modern serfdom, he was inextricably part of the political police informant system that dominates the social landscape of communist countries.

His one source of happiness was his wife, a young woman from a neighboring village whom he married in 1953. Their marriage, like that of his parents, was strong and fulfilling. Otherwise, Sabotka saw his future in Czechoslovakia as bleak and barren. He longed for Canada, a land where the future had seemed to him synonymous with hope and promise.

The STB officer with whom Sabotka dealt in the summer of 1957 casually introduced him to a Russian named Mikhail. Gentlemanly, meticulously dressed in Western clothes, considerate and self-effacing, Mikhail was the antithesis of the Ugly Russian. He also was an officer of Department 13. After a few meetings and seemingly idle conversation over beer, all in flawless Czech, Mikhail asked, "How would you like to go back to Canada or some other Western country?"

"If I were to go back, I would want to go to Canada," Sabotka replied.

"Would you be willing to go without your family?"

"No, never," Sabotka answered.

"Very well," said Mikhail. "You must move to Prague to begin your studies. Find yourself a job and a place to live and tell your wife you are going to night school. Of course you may visit her on weekends."

The KGB officer offered no hint as to when Sabotka might go to Canada or what he was to do there. Sabotka only knew that some sort of clandestine activity would be expected, but that scarcely mattered to him at the time. Suddenly given hope of escaping to Canada, he felt as if he had received a reprieve from life imprisonment.

To the KGB, Sabotka had impressive qualifications for the work the KGB had in mind. His parents were confirmed and loyal communists; his record as a relia-

ble police informant was good; he spoke English as a
Canadian native and understood Canadian customs; his
Canadian citizenship entitled him to a valid passport
and legal residence. Still, he was a foreigner, and the
KGB wanted to be even surer.

During the next year, Sabotka worked as a truck driver during the day. In the evenings, STB agents
instructed him in Morse code and surveillance and
countersurveillance at a downtown office. Mikhail saw
him two or three times a week as part of the KGB's
continuing check on his personal qualifications. They
talked about politics, religion, love, marriage, war, and
many other subjects while attending hockey and soccer matches, dining at small restaurants, or merely
driving about Prague. Mikhail, whose interest in religion Sabotka found curious, once mentioned that the
Russians employed priests as intelligence agents. On
another occasion he asked, "Do you have a Bible?"

"No," Sabotka lied.

"Well, there's nothing wrong with having a Bible,"
the Russian said. "I do."

Only once did Mikhail even suggest that Sabotka
was progressing satisfactorily in the judgment of the
KGB. When he admired a passing car, Mikhail said,
"Don't worry. You will have a car someday. And a
lot more." It was not until late October 1958 that
Sabotka knew he had been accepted. A KGB officer
informed him, "Next week you are to go to Moscow
for real training."

At the Moscow airport, a friendly, rather heavy-set
Russian of about forty greeted Sabotka in English.
"Call me Mike," he said. Mike, who was to supervise Sabotka's training, was Mikhail Mikhailovich Antipov, the same Antipov who was later to conduct Department V operations against the United States from
the United Nations haven. The authoritative knowledge
Antipov displayed about both North America and clandestine techniques convinced Sabotka that the Russian
had already worked in Canada or the United States
as an illegal.

The routine of Sabotka's training in Moscow was

standard. The KGB lodged him in a comfortable apartment about half a mile from the Kremlin. A housekeeper prepared his morning and noon meals and kept the refrigerator liberally stocked with cold meats, vodka, and beer for supper. Different instructors arrived punctually at 9 A.M. six days a week and drilled him until 5 P.M., at which time he was encouraged to take a walk to refresh himself for homework in the evening. The instructors were competent, demanding, and impersonal.

However, the substance of Sabotka's training differed from that given regular espionage agents. A professional radioman and a slender woman in her early twenties did school him in all the methods of clandestine communications—ciphers, codes, invisible writing, microdots, drops, recognition signals, and radio procedures. But he was taught virtually nothing about the general theory and practice of intelligence, the spotting, recruitment, and management of agents. He was provided none of the customary briefings about the purposes of Soviet intelligence or his niche in it. Nor did any of his instructors clearly define what his mission would be. When he asked, he received vague answers to the effect that he would be an "organizer."

He soon realized that the KGB intended him for something more menacing. Aside from communications, the subject most emphasized was the identification and evaluation of sabotage targets. He had to report about factories, refineries, and power plants: their location as fixed by three bearings; dimensions and shape; materials used in construction; nature of the facility; source of power; security measures in effect; capacity or output; sites from which it might safely be observed; its peculiar vulnerabilities to sabotage. He was also taught what to ascertain about pipelines: dimensions; number of tubes; location of pumping stations; sources of their power; maintenance procedures; control points; weak points, such as river or highway crossings.

Remarks by Antipov persuaded him that the KGB already had sequestered caches of explosives in Canada for future use. "If they are meeded, they are there," he told Sabotka. "The instructions for their use will come with the package."

One morning Antipov called at the apartment and announced, "Today we are going to a firing range." The range was ostensibly part of a "sporting club," but when Sabotka saw the target, he understood he was not being trained for sport. It consisted of the silhouette of the upper half of a man's body with target circles centered in the middle of the chest. "Always aim at the middle of the body," Antipov advised. Practicing mostly with American pistols, Sabotka learned to fire both carefully aimed single shots and rapid point-blank fusillades. Target practice normally lasted about an hour, and Sabotka became proficient enough to outshoot Antipov occasionally. At the end of their last visit to the range, Antipov asked, "Could you use this weapon if necessary?"

"It would depend on the reason," Sabotka answered.

"If, say, someone knew too much?"

"Yes, I suppose so," replied Sabotka.

Antipov nodded. "If a need for a weapon develops, one will be provided."

Telling him only that he would be informed in due time of his final departure date, the KGB sent Sabotka back to Prague in late December 1958. He resumed his former routine, working during the day, meeting KGB and STB officers at night, until November 1960, when he was again ordered to Moscow and met by Antipov.

With an air of solemnity and secrecy, a gangling Ukrainian named Nikolai showed him a gray metal box roughly the size of a large attaché case. It housed an exceedingly powerful radio transmitter capable, Nikolai assured him, of reaching Moscow from anywhere in Canada. To send a message, the operator used a dial similar to that of a telephone to record five-digit groups on a magnetic tape. He then pressed a button which caused the entire message to be "squirted" through the atmosphere in a few seconds, an insufficient time for security monitors to pinpoint the origin of the transmission.

The KGB was determined that foreigners should not learn the technical secrets of the transmitter. Nikolai warned that it would blow up instantly if anyone attempted to dismantle it. "If it stops working, don't try to fix it," he said. "Notify us and leave it alone." Nikolai further stressed that the transmitter would be delivered to Sabotka only after he was securely established in Canada and had built a safe hiding place for it in a floor, wall, or dry cellar.

Just before Christmas 1960, Sabotka learned the first sparse specifics of his assignment. Antipov informed him that he was to settle in Edmonton, find a job and house, create a normal life, then simply wait. During this settlement period, he had only to keep the Center advised of his whereabouts and status. The KGB gave him two addresses in Prague for messages in invisible writing and an open code for use in letters to his father, with whom it maintained contact in Czechoslovakia. In time, Antipov said, a man would approach him and ask, "Were you by any chance in Brno?" The question would identify the stranger as a representative of the Center, and Sabotka was to obey whatever orders he conveyed.

Beyond these few explicit instructions, the KGB left Sabotka largely ignorant of what it planned for him. He understood that he would be in Canada for several years and eventually might move to the United States. Vague comments by Antipov suggested that he might be required to perform "special" tasks in a time of "crisis." But he was unsure whether the KGB expected him to commit sabotage himself or merely to spot sabotage targets. References to his being an "organizer" made him think that perhaps he would work with other people. But Antipov firmly warned him never to attempt a recruitment himself or deal clandestinely with anyone except emissaries from the Center, and with them only after they had properly identified themselves.

The KGB had neither desire nor reason to enlighten Sabotka further. He had been trained primarily to serve as the communications link between Moscow and a sabotage network in North America. He knew

how to pick up messages from agent drops and relay
them to the Center by radio or mail; how to receive
enciphered instructions by radio and deposit them in
hiding places for unknown men or women to retrieve.
He could survey and assess the vulnerability of installations to which the KGB directed him. And he was
equipped with sufficient rudimentary knowledge to
commit sabotage or kill on his own, if the KGB
so ordered. Edmonton, standing on the edge of the
vast Canadian Northwest, was surrounded by installations, particularly pipelines, whose demolition could
seriously injure the country. Moreover, after settling
into Canadian society there, he could easily fly to the
more populous regions of eastern Canada or slip into
the United States. Specific assignments could be communicated to Sabotka whenever the KGB was ready to
activate him. Until such time, further details would only
burden Sabotka and increase the damage his disclosures
could cause if he were caught. The KGB had made
only one mistake in its preparations of Sabotka. In
him it had picked a man whose dominant motivation
was to escape the Soviet world.

Sabotka had no trouble obtaining a Canadian passport, to which he was entitled by birth, and he landed
in Montreal with his wife and six-year-old son on May
29, 1961. His son carried through customs a toy truck
in which the KGB had concealed cipher pads, microdots containing instructions, a microdot reader, and a
Minox camera. The family also had a valise in whose
lining the KGB had sewn five thousand dollars in old
Canadian currency. In Edmonton, Sabotka took a job
as a door-to-door salesman and bought an old frame
house that he remodeled himself into a comfortable
home. Overcoming their initial bewilderment at the
pace and comparative complexity of Canadian life, the
family swiftly adjusted and soon began to think of themselves as Canadians.

The letters Sabotka regularly wrote to his father kept
the KGB aware of his situation. The KGB was content
to wait patiently while he developed into a normal
Canadian, a man no one would suspect of being a

Soviet assassin and saboteur. For almost four years it did not send so much as a single message. With each year Sabotka's hope that he had been forgotten increased. Then, on the night of March 28, 1965, his phone rang and he heard a voice ask, "Were you by any chance in Brno?"

The caller was Oleg Nikolaevich Khomenko, a counselor from the Soviet embassy in Ottawa, who had journeyed to Edmonton on the pretext of assisting the touring Moiseyev dance company. He commanded Sabotka to meet him in half an hour near a motel. Hopping into Sabotka's car, Khomenko greeted Sabotka cordially and stressed that he had only a few minutes. He told him to buy a powerful radio receiver and handed him a schedule of broadcasts from Moscow. Then, wishing Sabotka good luck, the Russian slipped out of the car and stepped quickly away into the darkness.

Driving home, Sabotka gripped the steering wheel to stop the trembling of his hands. He was tempted to turn toward the police station and surrender. But he feared what the KGB might do to his family, or to his parents in Czechoslovakia. After lying awake most of the night, he bought the receiver, forlornly hoping that time would somehow bring him deliverance.

The Morse code broadcasts from Moscow, beamed across Siberia, arrived between 7 and 9 A.M. Sabotka had trouble explaining to his family his sudden interest in radio, and even more the need for locking himself in the basement at night to decipher the messages. One or two mistakes in transcribing the Morse code digits could add hours to the time required for deciphering. And the messages themselves were often exasperating. Once Sabotka labored until almost 4 A.M., only to read: "Dear Friend. On occasion of May 1 we cordially congratulate and wish you happiness in life and success in your work. Your Friends."

But in September 1965 the Center transmitted a significant message: "We would like for you to come to Ottawa, rent a car, drive to Brockville [a town sixty-five miles away], and be at the entrance of the Grena-

dier Inn at 1 P.M. October 3. Have magazine *Look*
folded in left coat pocket. You will be asked, 'Have I
by any chance met you in Brno?' Best wishes!"

Reluctant to identify himself by renting a car,
Sabotka, after flying to Ottawa, disregarded instructions
and took a train to Brockville. Meanwhile, a KGB
officer, Viktor Mitrofanovich Myaznikov, who had
been in Canada as a Soviet diplomat since the previous year, hitchhiked from Ottawa to Brockville.
Traffic was light that Sunday morning, and the diplomat had difficulty thumbing rides, so he arrived about
half an hour late.

Myaznikov motioned for Sabotka to follow him
down a dirt road that came to an end beside a clump
of bushes in a field. As they silently walked down the
road, Sabotka was terrified by irrational fantasies. He
imagined that the KGB had divined his inner feelings
and that a bullet awaited him at the end of the walk.
A small dog barked at their heels, and he imagined
that its collar hid a microphone belonging to the KGB
or the Royal Canadian Mounted Police. But Myaznikov was totally relaxed, friendly and reassuring.
"Anton, tell me how you are," Myaznikov began.
"How is your family? Your money?" He nodded ap-
provingly as Sabotka described life in Edmonton.
Admonishing him to listen carefully, he explained the
location of a drop beneath a tree near Belanger, On-
tario, where the KGB intended to bury $4,000 the
following month. "You will need it for future assignments," he said.

Handing Sabotka a slip of paper with the address
of a house in the Toronto suburb of Port Credit,
Myaznikov continued: "There is something else you
can do for us while you are in the vicinity. Find out
who owns the house and if there are any permanent
guests. Do the usual things: introduce yourself as a
salesman and get into the house, file a full report. No
real hurry, but it has to be done." Since its first approach in 1957, the KGB had invested more than
eight years in training and emplacing Sabotka. Now
it was ready to begin collecting dividends from its
investment.

The assignment to investigate the house alarmed Sabotka. Clearly the KGB was looking for someone, and he wondered why. He had been trained to seek out targets for destruction. Was the KGB hunting someone to kill? If so, would he not make himself an accomplice to murder by locating the prospective victim? Might he be ordered to kill the victim himself? Parting from Myaznikov, he derived no solace from the cordiality with which the Russian treated him. He realized that because he retained the confidence of the KGB, this small assignment was only the beginning.

Sabotka had booked a hotel room in Brockville, planning to take a train to Toronto and fly on to Edmonton the next day. As he started toward his room, he saw a man enter the lobby, stride over to the desk, and talk to the clerk. The man might have been just another guest, but in his anxiety Sabotka decided he was being followed. In panic, he locked himself in the bathroom and burned two slips of paper Myaznikov had given him containing the Port Credit address and a new address in Prague for emergency use. The next morning, walking away from the ticket counter at the railway station, he observed another man push his way into the line and question the ticket agent. On the train he thought he saw the same man.

In the basement of his Edmonton home, Sabotka compressed a message into a microdot: "Have reason to believe I am being followed by Canadian security agents. Must cease operations pending further investigation." He stuck the microdot into a blandly worded letter and mailed it to the new Prague address he had tried to memorize before burning the paper Myaznikov gave him. However, the next broadcast from the Center made no acknowledgment, saying only, "Urgently require report your activities in East." Sabotka repeated his fears of surveillance in another letter to Prague, but subsequent broadcasts merely upbraided him for not picking up the $4,000 and failing to supply information about the Port Credit house.

Evidently Sabotka had incorrectly remembered the new Prague address. About four months later the Center informed him that his letters had wound up in the

dead-letter file of the Prague post office, where they
finally were retrieved. The KGB agreed that for the
time being he should do nothing to cause suspicion.
It halted the radio transmissions, communicating instead by means of microdots. Periodically Sabotka received messages such as "Greetings Comrade on the
occasion of your birthday, and best wishes for the new
tasks that lie ahead. Your Friends."

Sabotka resigned himself to arrest, hoping only that
his family would not suffer too much privation while he
was in prison, and that afterward they would all be
allowed to remain in Canada. But nothing happened.
There were no indications that he was under surveillance, no signs of official interest in his activities.
Though he was sure at the time that he had been
followed after meeting Myaznikov, eventually he began
to doubt his suspicions. And so did the KGB. In August
1967 a microdot arrived with orders for another clandestine meeting.

On September 2 Sabotka flew to Montreal, and at
exactly 2 P.M. stood in the foyer of St. Joseph's Cathedral, a copy of *Look* in his pocket, waiting for someone
to ask, "Have I by any chance met you in Brno?"

This time his contact was Anatoli Pavlovich Shalnev,
another of the KGB experts in sabotage and assassination who had been sent to Expo 67. Shalnev arrived
late, identified himself with the proper question, and
led Sabotka to a nearby pew near an altar in the
basilica. Whispering in broken English, he asked why
Sabotka had not carried out the assignments issued by
Myaznikov two years before. Patiently Sabotka explained his fear that the Canadians had been watching
him. "Of course you did the right thing," Shalnev said
in a friendly tone. "But they did not pick you up. If
you actually had been followed, don't you think they
would have picked you up by now?"

When Shalnev began talking about "getting back to
work," Sabotka pleaded that he could not finance operations from his own funds. He added that he could
hardly afford to pay for the trip to Montreal. "Look,
Anton," Shalnev replied, "I'm supposed to be a tourist
at Expo, and I just don't have any money to spare.

But I see your problem, and if you think you can start operating now, I'll get you some." In a Montreal park at noon the next day, Shalnev gave Sabotka $400 and another broadcast schedule. He also told him that renewed transmissions would bring further orders. Sabotka's reprieve from KGB missions had ended.

The critical message came in the spring of 1968. It commanded Sabotka to prepare for a trip to East Berlin later in the year. Brooding alone in his basement, Sabotka knew he stood at a point of no return. The KGB would certainly subject him to interrogations to be sure he was still trustworthy. If satisfied, he would be sent back with serious assignments that Canada could never forgive. If less than satisfied, the KGB would simply keep him from returning. He thought once more of going to the RCMP, and again fear for his relatives inhibited him. It was after dawn when he made a decision. He climbed onto his roof, took down his antennas, and put away his radio. He simply would listen no more to the KGB.

Moscow kept calling for almost six months before acknowledging its awareness of trouble by stopping the broadcasts. The KGB tried to recover Sabotka. It sent his father to Canada in 1969 with a warm invitation to return to Czechoslovakia. "I will never go back," Sabotka told him. "I won't do anything against Canada. I'd go to the police right now if I weren't afraid something would happen to you or the family." The next year his father wrote an emotional letter pleading for him to return. Even though his father was a loyal communist, he remained more loyal to his son and adroitly signaled in his letter that it was written under duress. Members of the Soviet embassy telephoned in 1971 demanding that Sabotka return all his clandestine paraphernalia—the cipher pads, broadcast schedules, microdots, and microdot reader that constituted physical evidence of KGB activities directed against Canada.

Through all this, Sabotka awoke each morning fearing that his day would end with either arrest by the RCMP or a bullet from a KGB agent. The ordeal did not end until after the Royal Canadian Mounted Police surrounded him on the street in April 1972. His initial willingness to cooperate with the Canadians was reinforced by his realization of how much the security officers already knew about him. Their questions convinced him they had become aware of him as early as 1965, if not earlier, and had elected to watch rather than arrest him, in hope of learning more about the KGB. He was stunned when they showed him photographs of KGB officers with whom he had dealt in Moscow as well as Canada. Because of his cooperation, the Canadian government chose not to prosecute him. Neither did it announce his apprehension or what he had disclosed. However, a Canadian journalist, Tom Hazlitt of the Toronto *Star,* learned something of him, doggedly tracked him down, and on September 11, 1972, published an account of his experiences. Sabotka, now under protection of the Royal Canadian Mounted Police, subsequently talked to me freely and at length in December 1972.

Although the KGB failed with Sabotka, he was only one of many. Department V officers, whether working out of a world's fair, the halls of the United Nations, or a Soviet embassy, are charged with the management of whole networks of agents. Undoubtedly, numbers of these agents remain invisibly sewn into the fabric of Western society. Despite the substantial reverses Department V had sustained, its grisly business goes on. There is some circumstantial evidence that this business still includes murder.

On the evening of September 7, 1972, six men appeared at the home of Monahajudin Gahiz in Kabul, Afghanistan. Gahiz was the publisher and editor of a newspaper, a fervent Muslim, and one of the foremost anticommunist journalists of the Moslem world. He had exposed subversive KGB activities in the Middle East and repeatedly called Arab attention to antireligious books and propaganda disseminated by the Soviet Union. Several times, anonymous callers had warned Gahiz he would be killed if he did not keep quiet about the Russians. Now two of the six men who entered his home gave him a last chance to cease his anticommunist editorial campaign. When Gahiz defiantly refused, they opened fire, fatally wounding him and also killing a nephew and wounding a guest.

The assassination was deliberately crude. Its intent was not only to eliminate an effective Soviet adversary but also to terrorize potential adversaries into silence. The assassins also purposely left behind discernible Soviet traces. Witnesses testified that the men arrived in a Soviet jeep. Ballistics tests established that the bullets that killed Gahiz and his nephew came from automatic Soviet weapons.

After the assassination, Soviet Ambassador Sergei Petrovich Kiktev suddenly and unceremoniously left the country. Kiktev has been identified as a KGB officer by the *Christian Science Monitor* and the Paris weekly *Valeurs Actuelles*. He directed espionage agents in Turkey in 1947 and 1949, in Egypt from 1950 to 1954, and in Lebanon from 1955 to 1961. In all three countries he also dealt with assorted terrorists. According to *Valeurs Actuelles*, the KGB stationed him in Afghanistan primarily to establish Soviet control over the Peoples Liberation Front for the Arabian Gulf.

The influential Muslim World League convened in Mecca in November to decry the assassination and denounce Soviet complicity in it. The Afghanistan press declared that Kiktev was responsible for the murder and Lebanese newspapers stated that it resulted from "foreign involvement." Kiktev rode out the storm in the tranquillity of the Center. Then, on December 12, 1972, a new Soviet ambassador presented his credentials in Morocco. He was Sergei Petrovich Kiktev.

XIV

A CHOICE FOR THE WORLD

Having always relied upon a clandestine apparatus such as the KGB as their principal instrument of power, Soviet rulers are ill prepared to do otherwise now. While endeavoring to project themselves as reasonable, prudent men, they still display no disposition to diminish the role of the KGB in Soviet domestic or foreign affairs. Indeed, by all objective criteria available, KGB operations against both the Soviet people and foreign nations rather than subsiding have intensified since the beginning of this decade.

Shortly after Leonid Brezhnev visited the United States in June 1973, the Party ideologue Mikhail S. Suslov emphasized that détente in no way heralds abatement of the "ideological struggle" against the Western democracies. On the contrary, he stressed, the Soviet Union remains committed to "uncompromising, implacable struggle against bourgeois ideology." Events quickly gave his words meaning.

On July 21, 1973, the FBI arrested a first secretary of the Soviet embassy, Viktor A. Chernyshev, for espionage after catching him in a rendezvous with Air Force Sergeant James D. Wood. According to U.S. officials, the sergeant had in his possession documents containing counterintelligence secrets—secrets of American efforts to defend against the KGB. Meanwhile, the KGB and the Party orchestrated a chorus of hate, vilifying two of the Soviet Union's greatest intellectuals, the novelist Aleksandr Solzhenitsyn and the physicist Andrei Sakharov. Then in early September, Solzhenitsyn reported that the KGB had interrogated and intimidated a woman in Leningrad for five days until she disclosed the location of one of his manuscripts. He said that upon being released, the woman went home and hanged herself. Disclosing that his own life had been threatened, the great author added that should he suddenly die or disappear, the world must know that "I have been killed with the approval of the KGB or by it." The somber Moscow scene darkened further in September when Soviet authorities publicly exhibited two other victims of the KGB, Petr I. Yakir and Viktor A. Krasin. Having been in custody of the secret political police for more than a year, both of the broken men behaved like trained mice. Their "crimes" consisted mainly of circulating uncensored writings. But now they dispassionately confessed to "illegal activities" and "clandestine meetings with foreigners." It was an exhibition that Lavrenti Beria, his secret-police predecessors, and Stalin himself would have admired.

Refusing to tolerate ideological disagreement at home or abroad, the Soviet leadership continues to loose the KGB on all people who oppose it. However, in the remainder of this century, Soviet rulers well may find that the KGB is more of a cause than a remedy for problems whose dissipation is critical to their own survival. And the risks of continuing their inordinate dependency upon the KGB may be greater than the risks of devising alternative means of dealing with their own people and the world at large.

In an era when technology and communications increasingly blur international boundaries, neither an Iron Curtain nor the KGB can completely seal off the Soviet people from the ideas and impulses of liberty alive in the rest of the world. Ideological ferment in the Soviet Union has not coalesced into unified, organized opposition. Neither is it widely discernible among the Soviet masses, who have never experienced freedom. To the leadership, the current acts of political defiance represent disturbing but manageable pressures—certainly not auguries of imminent upheaval that could overturn the regime. Yet despite vigorous new repres-

sions, the KGB appears unable to smother all the cries
for a measure of reform and liberty. The multiplying
protests by scientists, artists, intellectuals, ethnic minorities, and religious believers raise at least some doubt
that the whole Soviet population can forever be
squeezed into a KGB straitjacket. Unless the leadership
accommodates change and reform, popular pressures
eventually may gather such force that they can be
contained only by return to the mass terror and murder
of Stalin's days. But reimposition of the terror would
endanger all members of the oligarchy, and there is
no assurance that the Soviet people would meekly allow
themselves to be dragged into another Stalinist inferno.

The risks of continued reliance upon the KGB in
foreign affairs are more immediate and evident. Fearful
of the Chinese, economically enslaved to armament
production, perennially on the brink of agricultural disaster, and lagging further and further in technology
requisite to future economic health, the Soviet Union
urgently requires Western assistance. It needs Western
technology, managerial expertise, agricultural produce,
and trade credits; it needs help in developing and
marketing its mineral resources; it needs agreements
that will ease the onerous arms burden; and it needs
to ensure that the United States is not driven into an
anti-Soviet alliance with China.

Recognizing that these needs cannot be permanently
fulfilled without better relations with the West, Soviet
leaders seek some forms of détente. But at the same
time, the leadership expands clandestine KGB aggressions that make a mockery of normal, stable, mu-
tually beneficial international relations. The contradic-
tion between the public politics of détente and the secret
machinations of the KGB can be seen in the realm of
trade. While the Soviet Union solicits broader commercial ties with the West, the KGB prepares to pervert
these ties for its own familiar purposes by installing
General Yevgenni Petrovich Pitovranov and other officers as overseers of the Soviet Chamber of Commerce.

While the Soviet leadership tries to negotiate a relaxation of tensions with the West, the KGB plans to
sabotage Western cities; encourages civil strife in

America; plots to incite civil war in Mexico and Ireland; nurtures the Palestinian guerrillas in their worldwide terrorism; strives to corrupt and subvert Western officials and politicians; and, through a variety of deceits, vilifies the same nations whose economic and political favors the leadership courts. And Soviet embassies the world over remain filled with nests of KGB officers who, under the demands of the Soviet quota system, perpetuate the chicanery that is their calling.

Manifestly, there can be no real détente until this massive KGB aggression stops. Its continuation will not only preclude the enduring commercial, political, and security agreements the Soviet Union needs; it will also jeopardize the limited understandings already achieved. Thus, Soviet rulers must choose between the substantial, tangible benefits of normal relations and the tenuous, uncertain gains that might be realized through the clandestine activities of the KGB.

The world does not have to stand by passively, powerless to influence the Soviet choice. Much can be done to defeat the KGB, to make its activities costly and counterproductive and thereby to persuade Soviet rulers that their interests will be best served by curbing the KGB. The countermeasures most likely to be effective are democratic, honorable, relatively inexpensive, and well within the means of all nations interested in preserving their independence.

First, deferential silence about KGB oppressions and depredations must be shattered. Soviet propagandists and apologists have succeeded remarkably in establishing the proposition that to condemn even the most egregious Soviet affront or injustice is somehow to "fan the flames of the cold war." The reverse is true. Silent acquiescence positively encourages the kind of KGB actions that are the essence of the cold war by suggesting to Soviet rulers that these actions have no deleterious consequences. Intelligent, reasoned protest demonstrates that KGB methods do have injurious consequences.

The Party oligarchy and the KGB are sensitive and in some cases responsive to foreign opinion when it becomes forceful enough to threaten Soviet interests.

Their sensitivity is well illustrated by the abject fear shown by the KGB leadership after Lee Harvey Oswald was arrested as the assassin of President Kennedy. The reaction has been disclosed by Yuri Nosenko, who, as deputy director of the American section of the Seventh Department, became involved with Oswald when he requested Soviet citizenship in 1959. Nosenko states that two panels of psychiatrists independently examined Oswald at KGB behest, and each concluded that though not insane, he was quite abnormal and unstable. Accordingly, the KGB ordered that Oswald be routinely watched, but not recruited or in any way utilized. Oswald returned to the United States in June 1962, then in September 1963 applied at the Soviet embassy in Mexico City for a visa to go back to Moscow. On instructions from the KGB, the embassy blocked his return by insisting that he first obtain an entry visa to Cuba, through which he proposed to travel. The Cubans, in turn, declined to issue a visa until he presented one from the Russians. Shunted back and forth between the two embassies, Oswald finally departed Mexico City in disgust and on November 22 shot the President.

With news of his arrest, the KGB was terrified that, in ignorance or disregard of the headquarters order not to deal with him, an officer in the field might have utilized Oswald for some purpose. According to Nosenko, the anxiety was so intense that the KGB dispatched a bomber to Minsk, where Oswald had lived, to fly his file to Moscow overnight. Nosenko recalls that at the Center officers crowded around the bulky dossier, dreading as they turned each page that the next might reveal some relationship between Oswald and the KGB. All knew that should such a relationship be found to have existed, American public opinion would blame the KGB for the assassination, and the consequences could be horrendous.

Concern over foreign opinion has produced some major restrictions of KGB operations. The revulsion caused by confessions of the KGB assassin Bogdan Stashinsky in 1962 influenced the Politburo to curtail the political murders which the Soviet Union had been committing since the 1920s. In the autumn of 1971 the KGB hastily withdrew all officers assigned to sabotage missions in European capitals because it feared the public reaction should their presence be disclosed by Oleg Lyalin, who had defected in London.

Awareness that the arrests of Aleksandr Solzhenitsyn and Andrei Sakharov would bring down obloquy on the Soviet Union among Western intellectuals is probably all that has kept them out of prison thus far. But whenever the Kremlin concludes that Western opinion is indifferent to the plight of the Soviet people, it loses another inhibition against their repression. In November 1972 Sakharov stated: "Since Nixon's visit, things have gotten worse. The authorities seem more impudent because they feel that with détente they can now ignore Western public opinion, which isn't going to be concerned with the plight of internal freedoms in Russia."

Protests by private individuals against KGB assaults upon liberty within and without the Soviet Union should be accompanied by specific official actions. Politicians and Foreign Offices in particular must disabuse themselves of the illusion that "good relations" with the Soviet Union are contingent upon permitting the KGB to station armies of professional spies, subversives, and saboteurs in their midst. They should also liberate themselves from the corollary illusion that the cause of "good relations" can be served by polite tolerance or appeasement of the KGB. The massive presence of KGB officers in Soviet embassies constitutes an insuperable obstacle to normal relations. Their removal and the disruption of their operations represent a fundamental prerequisite to healthy relations.

Any arrested KGB officers who are unprotected by diplomatic immunity should be swiftly prosecuted and, if convicted, imprisoned. The diplomatic release of proven KGB agents is interpreted by the Soviet leadership not as a gesture of good will but as a sign of impotence, if not simplemindedness, indicating that a nation will tolerate further subversive attacks. Neither should imprisoned KGB personnel be exchanged for Westerners arrested in the Soviet Union. Although effected for humanitarian reasons, such exchanges only encourage Soviet authorities to seize more innocent Westerners such as Professor Barghoorn or Newcomb Mott, who died of a slashed throat while in Soviet custody.

Nations should refuse to accept Soviet "diplomats" other countries have expelled for illegal activities, or who are known to be KGB officers. Eduard V. Ustenko, ousted from London in September 1971, arrived in February 1972 as first secretary of the Soviet embassy in Ceylon (Sri Lanka). Viktor T. Veklenko, also deported from London in September 1971, appeared in May 1972 as third secretary of the embassy in Thailand.

Most important of all, governments should summarily expel the legions of KGB officers entrenched in foreign capitals throughout the world. Continuing defections and patient counterintelligence work have revealed the identities of most KGB personnel legally stationed abroad. Many soon betray themselves through brazen actions or inaction. It is comparatively easy to deduce the true business of a commercial representative where there is virtually no trade, of an Aeroflot man where there are almost no flights, of a correspondent who seldom files a dispatch, and of diplomats who rarely engage in any form of diplomacy.

Wholesale expulsion of KGB officers will doubtless provoke indignant posturing from the Soviet Union, including charges that the banishments represent efforts "to revive the cold war" and an impediment to "good relations." But in fact, elimination of KGB nests around the world will have a salutary effect upon international relations.

Soviet rulers cannot expect other nations to adopt an attitude toward espionage, subversion, and sabotage different from the attitude they themselves take. Mass expulsions of KGB officers from Mexico, Great Britain, Belgium, and Bolivia in recent years did not impair the relations of those nations with the Soviet Union. Veiled Soviet threats to curtail trade with Great Britain never were fulfilled because it is the Soviet Union that needs trade the more. Aside from the face-saving ouster of a relatively few British diplomats from Moscow, the Russians attempted no retaliation: there was no way it could retaliate so long as it wished to maintain diplomatic relations. Moreover, governments that have resolutely rebuffed the KGB have commanded the support of their people. A public-opinion poll in Britain showed that an astonishing 80 percent of the population endorsed the banishment of the 105 Russians. Since the inception of public-opinion polling in Great Britain, seldom has a government policy or action won popular sanction by such a margin.

By purging Soviet embassies of professional subversives, foreign governments will at once blunt much of the KGB onslaught against them. By permanently denying the KGB the sanctuary of Soviet embassies, they will enormously increase the cost of renewing and sustaining the onslaught. Such action will, to a degree, free the authentic Soviet diplomats who remain and afford them more opportunity to practice legitimate diplomacy. And it will communicate, in language especially comprehensible to Soviet rulers, the message that the price of the benefits of membership in civilized international society is civilized behavior.

Given the will, free nations can successfully defend themselves against the KGB. Each time they do, they not only save themselves; they reinforce the arguments and influence of those in the Soviet Union who would have the cold war truly come to an end. But so long as other nations keep silent about the KGB, so long as they tacitly tolerate its assaults by failing to crush them, arguments against the KGB within the Party hierarchy will go unheeded, as will the pleas from the concentration camps and the mental institutions. Soviet rulers will feel no compulsion nor perceive much reason to reduce either the power or the role of the KGB. The KGB will remain the Sword and Shield of the Party, and the sword will remain poised against all peoples.

APPENDIX A

HISTORY OF THE STATE SECURITY APPARATUS

The organizational history of the state security apparatus offers another perspective of how deeply, widely, and firmly the roots of the KGB are imbedded in Soviet life. It shows also how little the basic structure of Soviet society has changed in more than half a century. The terrors the apparatus visited upon the Soviet people under Lenin and Stalin have been thoroughly chronicled and documented by others, so there is no need to dwell on them here.* But it is germane to note that during the terrors of the past the secret political police acquired the institutional credo and spirit that endure in the KGB of today.

THE CHEKA

The state security apparatus was born on December 20, 1917, when the Council of People's Commissars informally established the Cheka.** The first chief was Feliks Edmundo-

---

*Conquest's *The Great Terror* is, of course, the definitive work on the purges and pogroms under Stalin. Other excellent works dealing with the history of state security, particularly insofar as its internal operations are concerned, include: Hingley's *The Russian Secret Police*, E. J. Scott's "The Cheka," and *The Soviet Police System*, edited by Conquest. Useful accounts based in part upon personal experiences include: Nicolaevsky's *Power and the Soviet Elite*, Ginzburg's *Into the Whirlwind*, Gorbatov's *Ten Years Off My Life*.
**The name derived from letters extracted from the organization's full Russian title: *Vse-Rossiyskaya Chrezvychaynaya Komissiya Po Borbe S Kontrrevolitisiey I Sabotazhem*, the All-Russian Extraordinary Commission for Combating Counterrevolution and Sabotage. As local and functional Chekas were organized, the name Ve Cheka sometimes was used to distinguish the All-Russian or central Cheka from the local subsidiaries.

vich Dzerzhinsky, an austere and merciless man who came from an aristocratic Polish family. He soon moved his offices from Petrograd to the confiscated building of the All-Russian Insurance Company in Moscow, where the political police ever since have maintained their headquarters.

Formation of the Cheka was not accompanied by any announcement of its powers or purposes. Soviet explanations given much later suggest that the founders originally intended the Cheka to be essentially an investigative body. But beginning in February 1918, it rapidly and openly emerged as an avowedly terrorist organization committed to the extermination of all Communist opponents. After promulgation of the order "On Red Terror" in September 1918, the Cheka received authority to execute or sentence suspects at will, without reference to any independent tribunal. Many of its victims were liquidated not because of anything they had said or done, but merely because of their social origin or what they were thought capable of doing. The frequent stealth, caprice, and brutality of its actions compounded their psychological effect upon the populace.

However, the Cheka was much more than a vigilante organization created to cope with the transitory exigencies of revolution and civil war. As it grew into a legion of at least 31,000 men, it assumed the characteristics of an institution and started discharging functions that have become permanent features of Soviet society. Its divisions included a Secret Political Department for surveillance of the general population and a Special Department for control of the military. So-called functional Chekas were formed to oversee transport and communications. Newspapers were required to submit three copies of each edition for Cheka scrutiny. Chekists served on the local commissions established to control and combat religion, and the Cheka founded the system of concentration and labor camps. A foreign department attempted to gather intelligence abroad, and to discredit and demoralize anticommunist émigrés. In November 1918, a Chekist leader named Moroz boasted, "There is no sphere of our life where the Cheka does not have its eagle eye."

THE GPU AND OGPU

The communists easily dismissed and even made capital of foreign protests against the atrocities of the Cheka. But they could not so easily ignore the widespread hostility the Cheka had generated among the Soviet people. With the end of the civil war and consolidation of communist power, it became expedient to make some cosmetic changes in the state security apparatus. Accordingly, by a decree issued February 6, 1922, the Cheka was abolished and replaced by the GPU, the State Political Directorate.

The GPU was made a subordinate division of the NKVD, the People's Commissariat of Internal Affairs, which also controlled the militia or conventional police. It lost the power to sentence suspects, but retained all of its investigative powers as well as administrative authority to exile people for up to three years. When the Soviet republics were federated in 1923 to form the U.S.S.R., the GPU became the OGPU or Unified State Political Directorate and was detached from the NKVD.

These changes, by themselves, meant very little. The GPU/OGPU absorbed most of the Cheka personnel and Dzerzhinsky remained director of the apparatus until his death in 1926, when he was succeeded by Vyacheslav Rudolfovich Menzhinsky. During the 1920s, the OGPU formalized the repressive functions of the Cheka and systematically expanded the informant networks into all realms of society. It also helped stage-manage the early show trials and furthered the practice of forced labor.

By a decree of December 27, 1929, Stalin set the OGPU on the peasantry, which he considered the one group left with potential for organized opposition to the dictatorship. During the dispossession and collectivization of some ten million peasants that followed, at least 3.5 million people perished. The OGPU consequently acquired a reputation for terror matching that of the Cheka, and this proved something of an embarrassment at a time when the Soviet Union was seeking admission to the League of Nations and other forms of international recognition. Again, for the sake of appearances, a change was dictated.

THE GUGB/NKVD

After the death of Menzhinsky in 1934, Stalin on July 10 reconstituted the OGPU as the GUGB, the Chief Directorate for State Security, and again made it part of the NKVD. To head the NKVD, he chose Genrikh Grigorevich Yagoda, who as Menzhinsky's deputy had won favor by zealously directing the slaughter of the peasants, terrorizing the intelligentsia, and suppressing political minorities.

In addition to the GUGB, the NKVD controlled the conventional police (militia), the border guards, internal troops, the concentration and labor camps, a goodly segment of the transportation system, and a host of economic enterprises. During the great purges and enslavements that began in 1934, the public failed to distinguish these various elements from their parent organization. Although the secret political police, strictly speaking, were embodied in the GUGB, they were generally referred to as the NKVD.

Stalin in 1936 removed Yagoda, ostensibly because he was prosecuting the purges with insufficient vigor. Yagoda was shot after a show trial at which he was accused of being a murderer and a foreign spy. His successor, Nikolai Ivanovich Yezhov, was a remarkable man, even by standards of the period. Just over five feet tall, he was called the "bloody dwarf" and his character eminently suited him for the tasks of the times. However, Stalin fired him in December 1938 and thereby removed one of the witnesses who knew most about the worst of the purges. Although Yezhov's fate was not announced, he eventually was shot in the Lubyanka cellar where Yagoda perished. Lavrenti Pavlovich Beria, an ambitious disciple of Stalin, replaced Yezhov as chief of the NKVD.

THE NKGB

As a result of ever-expanding forced-labor programs, the NKVD by 1941 was managing a large part of Soviet industry and virtually all of Siberia. These responsibilities were so onerous and unrelated to the basic work of the secret political police that it was decided to detach the GUGB from the parent NKVD. The political police again became an independent organization and were retitled the NKGB or People's Commissariat for State Security. Beria remained chief of the NKVD, but contrived to retain effective control of the new NKGB by persuading Stalin to appoint one of his personal protégés, Vsevolod Nikolaevich Merkulov, as its director.

THE MGB AND KI

In 1946, the NKGB and NKVD were given the status of ministries. The NKGB became the MGB, Ministry for State Security, and the NKVD became the MVD, Ministry for Internal Affairs. Beria was elevated to the Politburo and succeeded as head of the MVD by Lieutenant General Sergei Nikiforovich Kruglov.

Soviet postwar strategy envisioned intensification of clandestine activities abroad, particularly against the United States. Foreign Minister Vyacheslav M. Molotov argued that the strategy best could be implemented by concentrating all such activities under control of a single organization. Merkulov, backed by his patron Beria, vigorously disagreed, fearing that the MGB would lose its foreign responsibilities. Condemning Merkulov for failure to grasp the subversive opportunities created by postwar chaos, Stalin replaced him with Lieutenant General Viktor Semonovich Abakumov, who had headed SMERSH.* Then in 1947 he established a new, independent KI or Committee of Information. Its formation portended the beginning of the cold war.

The KI absorbed all the foreign sections of the MGB, some units of the Ministry of Foreign Affairs, and, much to the outrage of the army, also took over the GRU or the military intelligence service. The KI, which answered directly to Stalin, was headed successively by Molotov, Valerian Aleksandrovich Zorin, and Andrei Yanuarevich Vishinsky. The proliferation of Soviet espionage and subversion in the late 1940s created a need for more personnel in foreign posts. The KI drew them mostly from the internal divisions of the MGB. As they showed up in Western capitals with their baggy suits and belligerent manners, these veterans of the prewar purges reinforced the gangsterlike reputation Soviet intelligence had acquired in the 1930s.

Beria regarded both Abakumov and the KI as threats to his own influence, and his enmity contributed to the demise of each. With his support, the army recovered the GRU in 1948 and thereby weakened the KI. In 1951, Beria, abetted by Georgi Malenkov, destroyed Abakumov by convincing Stalin that he had suppressed evidence of a plot. Stalin arrested Abakumov and abolished the KI. In the autumn of 1951, Semen Denisovich Ignatiev became director of the MGB, which now regained its former responsibilities for clandestine operations abroad.

THE KGB

Upon Stalin's death in March 1953, there began, in Conquest's words, "a faction fight confined to a narrow section of the leadership," to determine who would rule the Party and through it the Soviet Union. Beria maneuvered to depose both Ignatiev and Kruglov, and merged the MGB into the MVD, of which he assumed personal charge. He thereby gathered under his direct control the political police, their foreign operations, the militia, some 300,000 special troops, the concentration camps and their inmates, and a substantial segment of Soviet industry, including the nuclear and missile weapons program.

Other Politburo members, particularly Khrushchev, Malenkov, and Molotov, knew well what awaited them unless they

---

*SMERSH was a special wartime counterintelligence and terrorist organization. The name is an acronym formed from the Russian words *smert shpionam,* meaning "death to spies."

quickly countered Beria. On June 26, they engineered his arrest. *Pravda* on Christmas Eve 1953 announced that Beria had been shot for having been, among other things, a foreign spy.

The new leaders reorganized the whole state security and police power, as Beria had attempted to do. The reorganization culminated on March 13, 1954, in formation of the KGB. It was assigned the traditional political police functions; responsibility for all clandestine operations abroad, except those allowed the GRU; and the duty of guarding the borders. The MVD was left with the conventional police, firefighting personnel, and some responsibility for guarding the transportation system and industrial sites. But most of its industrial functions were dispersed among other ministries. The infamous Special Commission, which, in concert with the political police, had tried and sentenced political prisoners since the 1930s, was abolished, and responsibility for trials was transferred to the Ministry of Justice.

Today, the KGB has the same relationship to the Politburo under Brezhnev that the Cheka had with the Council of People's Commissars under Lenin. Antecedents for virtually all of the KGB's operational divisions may be seen in the Cheka. And the dedicated KGB officer prizes and boasts of his heritage as a Chekist.

The KGB of course is more pervasively and securely established in Soviet society than was the Cheka. The Soviet leadership in 1973 indicated just how great its status is by honoring KGB Chairman Andropov with full membership to the Politburo. Upon entering this, the highest of communist councils, Andropov attained power and influence no representative of the state security apparatus has enjoyed since the days of Stalin and Beria.

APPENDIX B

THE GRU: SOVIET MILITARY INTELLIGENCE

The Glavnoye Razvedyvatelnoye Upravleniye, or Chief Intelligence Directorate, is a division of the Soviet General Staff. The GRU engages primarily in the collection of strategic, tactical, and technical military intelligence, although it is also involved in industrial espionage and guerrilla warfare. Administratively it is independent of the KGB. It has its own schools, its own spaces in Soviet embassies, runs its own operations, and reports to Moscow through its own channels. Virtually all Soviet military attachés belong to the GRU, as do a large number of the Soviet citizens staffing Aeroflot offices abroad. Unquestionably, the GRU forms a significant component of the Soviet clandestine apparatus, and its operations represent a threat to all independent nations. However, in the judgment of this writer, the GRU has fallen so completely under the domination of the KGB that attempts to consider it as a separate entity are really an academic exercise. Certainly many GRU officers would disagree, and my opinion is not shared by some Western security experts. By briefly reviewing the history of the GRU, readers may judge for themselves.

The GRU originated in the spring of 1920. The Polish army, in April of that year, invaded the Soviet Union and drove far into the Ukraine before being repulsed. Deluded by outdated and erroneous intelligence suggesting that the Polish population was ready for revolution, Lenin ordered the Red Army to attack Poland in retaliation. Far from revolting, the Poles held firm and mutilated the Soviet invaders.

As a consequence of the debacle, Dzerzhinsky assigned a competent deputy, Yan Karlovich Berzin, to direct the Cheka

Registry Department, which was then responsible for gathering military intelligence. Shortly afterward, an independent Directorate of Intelligence was organized under Berzin's direction to take over the functions of the Cheka Registry Department. In time it became the Chief Directorate of Intelligence, or GRU, subordinate to the General Staff.

Stalin encouraged rivalry between the GRU and the political police, and the GRU encroached into many areas of clandestine activity beyond military intelligence. During the 1920s and early 1930s many nations withheld diplomatic recognition from the Soviet Union and thereby denied it embassies in which to station spies. The GRU thus had to conduct much of its work through illegals. It became well practiced in clandestine techniques and, until the 1936–38 purges, probably was even more skillful than the political police in external operations.

However, hundreds of its ablest officers, including Director Berzin, perished in the mad purges, and the GRU never really recovered from this loss of talent. Demoralized and depleted, it performed miserably after the Soviet Union attacked Finland in 1939, and its failures contributed to the defeats the Finns inflicted on the Red Army. The GRU functioned well and sometimes brilliantly during World War II, principally because its agents in Germany, Japan, Great Britain, and North America had survived the purges by virtue of being outside the Soviet Union. The feats of GRU agent Richard Sorge in Japan remain among the most important in the published annals of espionage. The intelligence provided by GRU agents within the German military was also important, even though it was not always exploited.

Natural deaths, coupled with arrests and defections, eventually disintegrated these wartime networks. The GRU, with its best surviving officers themselves growing old, then suffered further in morale and efficiency when it was submerged into the KI between 1947 and 1948. Afterward, because of the increasing emphasis upon subversion, disinformation, agents of influence, and other forms of clandestine political warfare, foreign operations were expanded more through the KGB than through military intelligence.

But the real eclipse of the GRU's independence began in 1958, when the KGB discovered that GRU Lieutenant Colonel Yuri Popov was a CIA spy. Khrushchev ordered KGB Chairman Ivan Serov to take personal charge of the GRU and clean it up. Serov, a veteran of the Stalin purges and a professional intelligence officer, did his best. Unfortunately, in 1962 the KGB discovered that another GRU colonel, Oleg Penkovsky, was also a spy, directed jointly by the British MI-6 and the

CIA. Not only was Penkovsky a Western spy; he was an intimate friend of Serov's own daughter and a crony of ranking GRU leaders.

Now the GRU really experienced the wrath of the Politburo. The disgraced Serov was deposed and replaced by First Deputy KGB Chairman Lieutenant General Petr Ivanovich Ivashutin, who had been responsible for controlling the entire Soviet armed forces. A fat man with a bloated, florid face, Ivashutin was already widely despised by the Soviet military because of his personal conceit, overbearing manner, and brutal disregard of subordinates. He demonstrated something of his mentality by opining in an *Izvestia* article that the Soviet people love and trust the KGB. Ivashutin brought with him five senior KGB officers and placed them at the head of the GRU hierarchy.

Thus, today the leadership of Soviet military intelligence consists of professional KGB staff officers rather than military men. The GRU may not employ anyone, either as an officer or agent, without prior clearance from the KGB. In addition, the KGB uses coercion and bribery to recruit informants among GRU officers, just as it does in every other element of Soviet society. Moreover, the KGB can veto any proposed assignments of GRU personnel abroad.

The GRU still contributes vigorously and effectively to the overall Soviet espionage effort. Western security services generally rate the typical GRU officer as at least the professional equal of his KGB counterpart. In the sphere of espionage, the methods of the GRU are the same as those of the KGB. And the GRU in the past decade has achieved some significant penetrations. Colonel Stig Eric Wennerström, arrested in Sweden in 1963, and Lieutenant Colonel William Henry Whalen, arrested in the United States in 1966, were GRU agents. So were the twenty-nine spies arrested in seven countries in 1967 after the capture of the Italian Giorgio Rinaldi.

In the field, the GRU and KGB often work together harmoniously, especially if good personal relations exist between the local GRU and KGB Residents. However, if there is a policy clash, the KGB invariably prevails. The KGB in Moscow remains aware of and reaps the benefits of all GRU operations. It can intercede with the GRU leadership—composed of former KGB officers—to modify or redirect GRU operations in its own interests. And through its authority over personnel and informants, it exercises an invisible but real control over the GRU at all levels.

Thus it seems to this writer that for practical purposes, the GRU must be regarded as a subsidiary of the KGB—a dangerous subsidiary, but a subsidiary.

APPENDIX C

"THE PRACTICE OF RECRUITING AMERICANS IN THE USA AND THIRD COUNTRIES"

A Western security service has obtained a copy of a top secret KGB training manual entitled *The Practice of Recruiting Americans in the USA and Third Countries.* The format states that the manual was "published in accordance with the plan for editorial publishing work of [KGB Higher] School 101, approved by the leadership of the First Chief Directorate of the KGB under the Council of Ministers, USSR." The authors are identified as Y. M. Bruslov, N. S. Skvortsov, L. A. Byzov, V. M. Ivanov, and N. G. Dyukov.

The manual specifies the more important KGB targets in the United States; outlines, step by step, the methods the KGB customarily employs in recruiting Americans; and mentions some of the problems the KGB encounters in attempting to suborn Americans. To illustrate recruitment methods, the authors reconstructed a number of actual KGB operations in the United States. However, they endeavored to disguise these somewhat by using pseudonyms for the Americans involved, omitting the names of KGB personnel, and changing the names of locales and institutions.

The strictures and themes set forth in the manual all are consistent with what is known from other sources about KGB attitudes and practices. But any doubt about its authenticity was removed after the FBI received a copy. For the FBI eventually was able to identify some of the people referred to in the case examples, despite the efforts of the authors to disguise them.

Those who obtained the manual translated it into English

for intelligence rather than literary purposes. As a consequence, the style and expressions are purely Soviet and they reflect the degeneration that has occurred in the Russian language during the past fifty years. Some sections of the manual, composed of standard communist polemics of the sort one may read in the Soviet press, have been deleted as irrelevant. Some other sections have been summarized or omitted because they seemed tediously repetitious or trivial. Unfortunately, an important page of the translated copy of the text procured by the author is illegible; its absence is noted. The relatively few explanatory, transitional, or summary comments deemed necessary appear in italics. Otherwise, what follows is extracted and translated verbatim from *The Practice of Recruiting Americans in the USA and Third Countries.*

The introduction of the textbook begins with the necessary and standard obeisances to the Party couched in vintage communist jargon. Its essence is that the overriding mission of "Soviet intelligence" is to procure information that other nations do not wish the Soviet Union to have. Arriving at the point, it states:

Soviet intelligence can accomplish this task successfully with the aid of a competent agent network capable of obtaining the secret information in which we are interested. The acquisition of such an agent network in the countries of the principal adversary, particularly in the U.S., is the most important operational task of Soviet intelligence.

The recruitment of such an agent network among Americans has a number of peculiar characteristics and difficulties, dependent in large part on whether recruitment is carried out in the U.S. or in third countries.

The purpose of this text is to point out the particular characteristics of recruiting Americans and to disseminate certain beneficial experiences of Soviet Foreign Intelligence Legal Residencies in the recruitment of Americans in the U.S. and in third countries under present conditions, as well as to show how Soviet Foreign Intelligence is solving the task of acquiring an agent network among the Americans.

The text examines such problems as the basis for recruitment [*verbovochnaya baza*], methods of spotting, and methods of assessing Americans, with the aim of subsequently determining the most effective means of inducing them to collaborate with Soviet Foreign Intelligence, and the accomplishment of recruitment itself.

The material is presented in approximately the same sequence as that used in development for recruitment.

The authors hope that this text will be of definite assistance to intelligence officers, particularly to the inexperienced, in organizing and carrying out intelligence operations against the U.S.

1. THE BASIS FOR RECRUITMENT IN THE U.S.

At the present time KGB Residencies in the U.S. are faced with an extremely important task: the development of agent networks capable of obtaining secret information on the military and political plans of the U.S. government; on new discoveries and inventions in science and technology; on the work of American intelligence and counterintelligence organs; and on the activities of international organizations—the U.N. and others—which are located in the United States.

The basic targets of our agent penetration (operations) are as follows:

—The President's Cabinet and the National Security Council;

—The State Department, including its representatives in New York, the U.S. delegation to the U.N., the Passport Office of the State Department, etc.;

—The U.S. Department of Defense (Pentagon), the military intelligence organs of this department, and the Permanent Military Group of the NATO Staff in the U.S.;

—The Central Intelligence Agency and the Federal Bureau of Investigation;

—The National Association of Manufacturers, and the most important monopolies and banking houses, which have a direct influence on the U.S. government;

—The most important scientific centers and laboratories; . . .

(Here a page of the copy available to the author is illegible.)

—The governing organs of the leading political parties in the U.S. and other influential public and political organizations —trade unions, youth [organizations], journalistic [organizations], etc.;

—The diplomatic and commercial representations of foreign countries in the U.S., and also the Secretariat of the U.N. and foreign representations in the U.N.

In carrying out these tasks, our Residencies must, first of all, thoroughly study the basis for recruitment.

Purposefulness in the recruitment operations of our Residencies is achieved through the identification of Americans who have intelligence potential and sufficiently strong motives that could lead them to collaborate with Soviet Foreign Intelligence. The following categories of individuals are of operational interest to Soviet Foreign Intelligence Residencies in this connection:

—Employees of government institutions who are cleared for secret political, economic, military, scientific and technical, and intelligence and counterintelligence information;

—Employees of nongovernmental institutions and organizations who, because of their activities or interests, have access to the state secrets of the country against which intelligence operations are being carried out—correspondents, employees of technical bureaus and firms, representatives of emigrant groups and foreign intelligence agents;

—Employees of private firms who have access to secret scientific and technical and economic information;

—Persons who have good prospects of joining government organizations. This relates primarily to students in educational institutions which supply the personnel for organizations having an interest in intelligence. In addition, our Residencies are also interested in other persons who hold certain jobs and have personal qualities which make their recruitment possible.

Correct determination of the basis for recruitment, that is, of the motives which lead us to conclude that a person of interest can be induced to collaborate, is of great importance to successfully organizing his development for recruitment. Thus, for example, the following factors can serve as a basis for recruiting employees of government institutions:

—Sympathies toward the U.S.S.R., as a consistent striver for peace;

—Dissatisfaction with the rigid policy of the U.S. government toward civil servants—infringement on the rights of the individual;

—Surveillance of government employees; study of their way of life, contacts, etc.;

—Dissatisfaction with the domination by large monopolies which use the U.S. government apparatus for purposes of repression (such dissatisfaction with the uncontrolled activities of the large monopolies is most frequently found in government functionaries, persons from laboring families, and in employees lacking sufficient financial security);

—Availability of confirmed information on the financial difficulties of a government employee or of serious compromising information which could cost him his job.

The following are exploited when establishing relationships with scientists and important specialists:

—The desire of specialists to sell us the technical secrets of their firms;

—The desire of scientists to establish scientific contacts with representatives of the U.S.S.R. (particularly noticeable in persons who have left Russia).

When determining the basis for establishing intelligence relationships with representatives of business circles, account is taken of the fact that businessmen can assist the intelligence service on the basis of such motives as:

—Monetary reward for the passing of technical information and new models;

—The desire to trade with the Soviet Union or with other countries of the socialist system. Particular interest in such trade can be evoked by the possibility of concluding deals which make it possible for the businessman to pay his taxes, which come to large amounts.

The identification of persons in the government apparatus who sympathize with us ideologically is of great importance for our recruitment operations in the U.S.

Here the text digresses into a polemic asserting that the collapse of "monopolistic capitalism" is imminent and that "Marxist-Leninist ideas" are gaining acceptance in the West. Returning to the subject, the text summarizes the recruitment of an American scientist, identified as "Put," whom the Russians had spotted as a prospective ideological sympathizer. This and many other cases to follow are cited as case-study material.

The Soviet intelligence officer established an acquaintance with Put on the recommendation of another of our intelligence officers who had known Put during the Second World War.

This intelligence officer went to Put's home with a letter from his friend and within two or three months became a friend of Put and his family—of his wife, children, and brother. During the first meetings, our intelligence officer succeeded in dissuading Put from phoning him at work or at his apartment and from telling his friends about their acquaintance. These precautions and the clandestine behavior on the part of the intelligence officer prior to his meetings with

Put made it possible to conceal our contact with Put from the FBI.

In the course of their meetings, our intelligence officer convinced Put of the correctness of our activities, and he came to sympathize with the Soviet Union. We learned that Put was planning to present some of his most recent work at one of the international congresses. With this aim, he asked a friend—a well-known progressive who had visited our embassy in Washington—to give this work to the scientific attaché at our embassy. Having learned of this, the intelligence officer chided Put in a friendly way for not asking the intelligence officer's help and for turning to his American acquaintance, which was not entirely safe despite the progressive views of the latter. Put took this conversation seriously. This helped our intelligence officer to convince Put of the need for a subsequent clandestine meeting with him in the city.

Through further work, the intelligence officer developed Put to the point where he began to photograph information and pass it to him on film during brush contacts and through various dead-drops.

As is evident for this example, the development of Put for recruitment was relatively uncomplicated and did not require a great deal of effort on the part of the intelligence officer. This is explained by Put's ideological affinity with us, by his readiness to help us if possible.

When selecting candidates for recruitment, however, it is wrong to consider persons such as Put to be the basic source. It would be a mistake to assume that there are many such people in U.S. government institutions. According to available information, the U.S. counterintelligence organs spend as much as $5,000 to investigate the political views of every candidate for a job in any government institution. The FBI checks on the loyalty of employees throughout the time they serve the government. Politically unsound persons are fired from their jobs or deprived of access to secret work if the smallest signs of insufficient political trustworthiness are found. This is testified to by the fact, which has become known to the Soviet intelligence service, that one American, who because of his convictions was attracted to the Quakers,* was transferred from the intelligence service of the State Department to ordinary line administration within the department. Under such conditions, government employees hide their dissatisfaction with the policies of the government for fear of losing their

---

*(Footnote from the KGB text.) The Quakers are one of the Christian Protestant sects in the U.S. and are currently manifesting pacifist tendencies.

jobs. The aid of an experienced agent network, or of confidential contacts [*doveritel "naya svyaz"*] used as spotters, is needed to identify them.

In recruiting operations in the U.S., much attention is paid both to recruitment on a material basis and to recruitment on the basis of compromising materials.

Correct use of the factor of material interest first of all requires an understanding of the psychological makeup of the American, who soberly regards money as the sole means of ensuring personal freedom and independence, of making it possible for him to satisfy his material and spiritual needs. In the average American, this attitude toward money engenders an indifference to the means by which it is obtained, although sometimes involving risk.

At the same time it should be kept in mind that the relatively high standard of living in the U.S. is maintained by plundering the peoples of other countries. Therefore, it would be wrong to assume that an employee of a U.S. government institution can be encouraged to collaborate with Soviet intelligence for a pittance. In order to understand this question clearly, it is useful to be familiar with the amounts earned by Americans working in government institutions. . . .

These data indicate that during the process of development, and particularly at recruitment, determination of the monetary income of an American is an extremely important matter. On one hand, the money which is offered should not give the person being developed unfounded illusions that he is to receive large amounts of money for his work with us; on the other, the person under development must be firmly convinced of the readiness of our intelligence service to compensate him for services that involve the risk of losing his job in a governmental organization and of being taken to court. Obviously, a government employee who is being developed with the aim of recruitment on a material basis will not agree to collaborate with Soviet intelligence for $50 or $100 a month.

When selecting candidates for recruitment on the basis of compromising materials, great importance is attached to information which, if revealed, could actually do serious harm to the person who is concealing it from those surrounding him. To solve this problem, it is sometimes necessary to have specific knowledge of American legislation and regulations which determine the official policy regarding particular government organizations, private firms, and various institutes engaged in work subsidized by the U.S. government. It should be kept in mind that the most important information that could compromise an American consists of data on the commission of serious crimes at work, usually related to illegal appropriation of large sums of money, and also information to the effect that he is a homosexual.

The text at this point quotes extensively from U.S. statutes prohibiting government employees from accepting bribes and indulging in conflicts of interest. It also notes that the government considers communist affiliations and homosexuality sufficient grounds for dismissing employees from sensitive positions.

These orders of U.S. authorities testify how serious must be the information compromising an American. Information on the commission of such moral crimes as promiscuous relationships with women usually cannot serve as convincing compromising material.

When selecting candidates for development, account should be taken of the fact that, according to existing legislation, a person born in the U.S. automatically becomes a U.S. citizen.* He is not subjected to any discrimination in comparison with native [descended] Americans with regard to admission to educational instutitions and in his progress at work. There are many examples of not only such persons but also immigrants being permitted access to secret material in the U.S. The latter, however, are not always good prospects for our Foreign Intelligence.

As a rule, an immigrant is a man of experience who has seen much of life, but he frequently is somewhat suspect among local police organs. The native American, while not usually having these shortcomings, feels a great love for the U.S. in contrast with first- or, at most, second-generation Americans. Immigrants are of interest due to the fact that, while possessing an equal right to access to secret materials, because of the influence of their parents they do not always consider the U.S. to be their homeland and therefore can more easily be persuaded to work for us.

As experience has shown, it is also useful to look for people of interest to us in the advanced classes of universities, among those who have temporarily left their secret work to complete their education.

---

*(Footnote from KGB text.) Meaning a person who is a child of immigrants.

2. THE ACQUISITION OF USEFUL CONTACTS AND THE SELECTION OF CANDIDATES FOR RECRUITMENT. THE INITIAL STAGE IN DEVELOPMENT FOR RECRUITMENT

The active operations of American counterintelligence force the Soviet intelligence officer to give the most serious consideration to the initial stage of any development for recruitment. Therefore, Soviet Foreign Intelligence Residencies in the U.S. devote great attention to the manners and methods by which intelligence officers acquire useful connections among Americans and establish personal contacts with them. Our intelligence officers seek unusual means for establishing acquaintances, rejecting the use of places controlled by the FBI for this purpose. For example, they rarely use official receptions inasmuch as an acquaintance which is begun there may immediately come to the attention of counterintelligence. For these reasons, under present operational conditions in the U.S., Soviet Intelligence Residencies give particular attention to proper organization of the initial stage of development for recruitment; that is, in establishing a new acquaintance with local citizens, they try to create or find conditions which ensure that the new contact will not attract the attention of American counterintelligence.

For purposes of generalizing some of the valuable operational experience of our Residencies in the U.S., all developments for recruitment carried out by Legal Residencies can be divided into the following groups:

1. Development for recruitment which is begun as a result of a personal acquaintance between our intelligence officer and an American. Development is carried out by the intelligence officer himself in cases when it is not feasible to involve the agent network or when there is no direct need to do so, for example, when development is through the gradual involvement of an American who works with the intelligence officer in the same official organization, etc.

2. Development for recruitment which is carried out through an agent network or by intelligence officers themselves on the basis of data received in advance concerning the American and his intelligence potential. In cases where the intelligence officer participates in the development, these data make it possible, even before personal contact is established with the American, to designate a specific means for drawing him into collaboration with us as an agent. Such data may consist of

compromising materials [or] information concerning the readiness of the American to help us on an ideological and political or material basis.

3. Development for recruitment which is carried out by an agent network that recruits the Americans under a false flag, without the personal participation of intelligence officers. Specially trained recruiters are used to carry out such requirements. . . .

The spotting, assessment, and selection of Americans for recruitment and the accomplishment of recruitment through recruiters remain the principal task of Soviet Foreign Intelligence in the U.S. Under these conditions, as formerly, great importance is attached to the ability of the intelligence officer in our Legal Residency to develop clandestinely and for recruitment the group of Americans to whom he has access.

Depending on the sequence for the assessment of Americans and the establishment of relations with them, all development of Americans for recruitment which is conducted personally by intelligence officers of Legal Residencies can be divided into two categories. The first group includes cases where the intelligence officers first become acquainted with the Americans and then discover their intelligence potential; the second group includes cases where they first receive information about Americans of interest to us, study the basis for establishing confidential or agent relations with them, and only then establish a personal acquaintance with them. The second method is more purposeful and provides better results.

We cannot, however, orient ourselves solely toward the development of Americans whose intelligence potential we know in advance. Our Legal Residencies organize purposeful acquaintances between their intelligence officers and the Americans of known intelligence potential and at the same time conduct operations to establish acquaintances between intelligence officers and Americans in general for the purpose of subsequently discovering persons of interest among them. With this in mind and taking into account the cover possibilities of intelligence officers, our Residencies assign them the task of making acquaintances in circles whose members have direct or indirect access to the targets set for Soviet Foreign Intelligence. This gives the work of the Residencies a purposefulness necessary for agent penetration of the designated intelligence targets.

Let us examine these possibilities.

Usually the cover of a Soviet intelligence officer provides him with the necessary legal basis for being in the country against which our intelligence is operating and makes it possible for him to establish personal acquaintances among Americans.

In the U.S., in addition to ordinary cover, we use various international organizations and our representations in them. The most important of these is the United Nations and its branch institutions. The associations of Soviet representatives with foreigners at various international congresses and conferences, international congresses of scientists and specialists, etc., are also widely used for intelligence purposes. Here it is possible to become acquainted with individuals active in politics and labor unions, with scientific workers, and with persons engaged in cultural affairs and the arts.

The cover used by intelligence officers usually corresponds to the field of their intelligence operations. For example, intelligence officers who are collecting political information work in the press department and in the cultural affairs department of the embassy; intelligence officers collecting scientific and technical information are engaged with questions of technology, under the adviser of the embassy, and also work in Amtorg; intelligence officers who are occupied with questions of foreign counterintelligence and émigré operations work in the consular department, etc.

An intelligence officer's cover position is selected by taking into account his general education, his political and specialized training, work experience, and personal and business qualities. Under these conditions the intelligence officer can become acquainted with foreigners without his behavior being distinguishable from that of Soviet citizens employed by the given organization who are not connected with intelligence.

The wording of the next three paragraphs is abstruse. The meaning: To prevent counterintelligence services from identifying personnel engaged in espionage, the KGB tries to place officers in cover jobs that entail normal contact with foreigners. Additionally, it "enlists the services of" or "co-opts" Russian civilians whose work abroad involves them in legitimate relations with foreigners. The text continues:

The Soviet intelligence officer may become acquainted with an American with good prospects for development who by the nature of his activity has every reason for his overt meetings with Soviet representatives. Such Americans include businessmen and correspondents who are not subject to restrictions concerning friendships with Soviet representatives without notifying their superiors.

In acquiring useful contacts, it is more expedient to establish acquaintances with Americans in places other than those frequented by employees of Soviet organizations. This is explained by the fact that in these [other] places it is more difficult for the FBI to fix their attention on the useful acquaintances with Americans which are established by our intelligence officers and to bring these acquaintances under its own control.

As examples of sites where FBI surveillance best can be avoided, the text mentions business offices, universities, libraries, theaters, concert halls, parks, clubs, restaurants, playgrounds, and similar public places. It stresses that to acquire plausible reasons for meeting Americans, KGB officers should develop hobbies such as golf, fishing, tennis, gardening, and stamp or coin collecting. It also recommends that they acquire specialized knowledge of art, science, or literature to increase the likelihood of having common interests with Americans. Finally, the text warns that Americans met accidentally or through "untested persons" may be FBI counterspies. It continues:

Our Residencies systematically collect information on Americans who have intelligence potential in order to make their acquaintance later on. They use agents and confidential contacts for this. In those cases where the Residency uses such information, it attempts to camouflage the source.

Soviet Intelligence Residencies in the U.S. receive considerable assistance from the Center, which reports the results of spotting activity by our Residencies in third countries.

Use is also made of information received from "unwitting" individuals: personal data which is available from various Soviet missions and agencies; for example, information contained in correspondence between these institutions and foreigners, in visitors' books at exhibitions, in various announcements, etc.

To obtain information on foreigners with intelligence potential, use is also made of legal sources existing in the country against which we are conducting intelligence operations—the press, general information books (for example, *Who's Who*), U.S. diplomatic lists which contain biographical information on State Department employees, reference books on employees of the press, reference books which publish biographies of celebrities, etc.

Having received such information, the Soviet Foreign Intelligence Residency determines the most expedient means of becoming acquainted with the American in whom it is interested, and either an agent or an intelligence officer is selected for these purposes. Depending on the capabilities of the Residency, a plan for making the acquaintance is worked out. Advance planning for establishing acquaintance with specific persons is more effective than the establishment of an acquaintance with Americans who are previously unknown to the Residency. In addition to the above means of establishing a relationship, the intelligence officer can "accidentally" meet the American, can visit him at his home under a convincing pretext, or can prepare a special combination of circumstances for this purpose in order to ensure that contact is established in such a way as to create conditions for further clandestine meetings with him.

For purposes of studying a person under development, experience shows that it is sometimes useful to take advantage of his departure for a third country, where conditions for agent operations are more favorable.

Below are given examples in which intelligence officers have successfully established contact with Americans with intelligence potential. . . .

An intelligence officer of the New York Residency, engaged in the collection of scientific intelligence, during a bus trip struck up a conversation with his neighbor, who worked on problems of radio direction finding. In the given case, the intelligence officer had no reason to suspect that the scientist was a plant, since he previously had not planned to travel by bus, and the idea of using this type of transportation came to him at the very last moment. Having convinced himself that this was not an intentional encounter, the intelligence officer began to talk with the scientist, who expressed an interest in the Soviet Union. The intelligence officer—having studied the attitudes of his conversation partner—touched on questions of interest to himself. The scientist willingly continued this conversation and gave the intelligence officer some useful information. For example, he told about the lines being followed in research at his institution, which is subordinate to the Department of the Navy.

Wishing to consolidate a useful acquaintance, the intelligence officer proposed to the scientist that they meet in Washington, but the scientist did not go along with this proposal. He stated flatly that it wouldn't be healthy for him if his chief, an admiral, learned anything about their conversation. He personally did not share the views of his chief; he was ashamed of the reactionary policy of the American authorities, but he was not able to change anything in this regard and did not wish to subject himself to unpleasantness. He remarked that he would willingly meet with our worker somewhere under noncompromising circumstances and named a number of scientific associations, the meetings of which he attended from time to time.

A useful example can be found in the acquaintanceship of an intelligence officer in our New York Residency with an American of Ukrainian extraction, "Rok," whom we discovered when studying the contacts of one of our agents.*

The forty-year-old Rok was the head of a small engineering and technical planning firm which also filled orders for the International Atomic Energy Agency. The agent characterized Rok as a simple man with little education, who passionately loved his firm but did not possess the necessary business qualities for the firm to be a success. By character, Rok was outgoing and made friends easily. However, because of a serious speech impediment—a bad stutter—he was unable to maintain these friendships. Therefore, he had almost no friends and frequently, in spells of loneliness, drank.

Having analyzed all this information, our Residency assigned the intelligence officer, with the aid of the agent, the task of arranging an "accidental" meeting with Rok in a restaurant. So that Rok would have no suspicions that the agent helped arrange this meeting, the following plan was drawn up.

The agent was to invite Rok to the restaurant twice in a row: the first time, the intelligence officer was to be present in the restaurant during their dinner so as to be able to recognize Rok; the second time, the agent would treat Rok to a good dinner and would leave "on business." After this, the intelligence officer would become acquainted with Rok.

The first meeting took place, but not exactly as planned. The intelligence officer arrived at the bar to carry out the identification. The agent and Rok appeared shortly thereafter. Stuttering, Rok loudly asked the agent to have another drink. The agent quickly adapted himself to the developing situation, refused the drink, and left on his business. Glancing around, Rok sat at the only remaining free place, which was next to the intelligence officer. Having ordered a cocktail, he began to talk to his neighbors. The intelligence officer decided to take advantage of this, to change the plan and become acquainted with him at once. It was easy for him to do this. After talking with Rok for several minutes, the intelligence officer paid for his cocktail and departed.

The next day, our intelligence officer phoned Rok and gave his name, which Rok recalled only after the intelligence officer

---

*As used here, the term "agent" probably denotes an American already recruited by the KGB. However, it could refer to a KGB illegal being employed as a spotter of prospective recruits.

mentioned the restaurant. Rok was pleased to hear from him and suggested that they meet for a drink. At the meeting the intelligence officer did not specifically state his nationality, telling Rok that he worked at the U.N. During this period, his role was mainly that of an "accidental" acquaintance.

During the next two meetings the intelligence officer, using Rok's peculiar characteristics, described above, quickly became close friends with him and began his active development. It was only during the third meeting that Rok learned that his new friend was Russian. He told this to the agent, but the latter replied that Rok's friendship was none of his business and that, in any case, he didn't remember the person Rok had met.

By this time the intelligence officer had firmly consolidated his acquaintance with Rok and had become his friend. The intelligence officer correctly understood that Rok had a yearning for his homeland and for people in general: it was difficult for him, a stutterer, to find someone with whom to talk. Taking advantage of this circumstance, the intelligence officer quickly won his confidence.

In a friendly manner the intelligence officer warned Rok not to call him at work. Rok didn't try to find out specifically why, convinced that his new friend had a good reason. This gave a clandestine character to their relationship, in that the intelligence officer had previously approached Rok only after a careful check. Thus, the possibility of an unwitting breach of security by Rok concerning his acquaintance with the intelligence officer existed only during the period when the intelligence officer was playing the role of a drinking companion previously unknown to Rok. With the aid of the agent network the Residency ascertained that the agent was the only person whom Rok told at that time about his acquaintance with the intelligence officer. Therefore, it was possible to keep the relationship of the Soviet intelligence officer with Rok a secret.

As a friend, the intelligence officer asked Rok to acquire, for a friend in Moscow, a number of materials which were forbidden for sale to Soviet citizens. The intelligence officer paid Rok the cost of the materials he received, photographed them, and then returned them to Rok, who was quite willing to keep them at home. In addition, the intelligence officer paid Rok $300 "commission." Thus, Rok set out on the path of direct intelligence collaboration.

In another case, a person of interest to us was shown to a Soviet intelligence officer in the following manner. The intelligence officer, who had contacts with an agent, went at a set time to a restaurant and sat at a small table. A second intelligence officer arrived later and occupied another small table, from which he could conveniently observe the actions of the first intelligence officer and could see the people entering the restaurant. When the agent appeared with the person of interest to us, the first intelligence officer gave a signal to the second. On the basis of a description, the second intelligence officer recognized the agent and began to observe his companion. Soon the intelligence officer succeeded in "accidentally" making the acquaintance of this American in another restaurant while remaining unknown to the agent who had acted as spotter.

Letters of recommendation are also used to make the acquaintance of Americans.

When approaching a foreigner with a letter of recommendation, a Soviet intelligence officer uses general information concerning the person making the recommendation; he recalls what the person looks like and the circumstances under which he obtained the letter. When handing over the letter, the intelligence officer casually mentions an event known to him from the life of the person making the recommendation and thus confirms his closeness to him. For this purpose, the intelligence officer selects facts which might interest his new acquaintance to whom he is handing the letter. By giving such information, it becomes easier to consolidate the acquaintance of the intelligence officer with the new person. . . .

If they are correctly prepared, these methods of making an acquaintance are used successfully by Soviet intelligence officers. However, a scornful attitude toward preliminary work can place the intelligence officer in a difficult position.

It is necessary to note that the use of letters of recommendation by our intelligence officers is known to U.S. counterintelligence organs. The American press frequently publishes information on this question in order to alert the population to the modus operandi of Soviet intelligence. Still, there is no reason to reject the use of letters of recommendation for intelligence purposes since, as in times past, they are widely used by persons who have no connection with intelligence. It is important that letters of recommendation and recruitment letters [*verbovochnoye pis'mo*] not be used in blackmail operations, as this would make it possible for the person being developed to realize the true intentions of our collaborator.

These are the basic methods of establishing acquaintances between our intelligence officers and Americans.

In their daily work, Soviet Foreign Intelligence Residencies and Soviet intelligence officers, when recruiting Americans, particularly within the U.S., should always bear in mind that American counterintelligence dangles its agents before our Foreign Intelligence Service.

The techniques and approaches used by the counterintelligence services in dangle operations take various forms at the present time. It is sometimes extremely difficult to discover them, and therefore careful analysis must be made of the behavior of persons under development in order to determine their true nature.

Experience has shown that one general feature is characteristic of all dangle operations—the person being dangled either attempts to interest us in his intelligence potential or he takes the initiative and offers to pass us certain secret materials. The display of such initiative is particularly characteristic in cases when our interest in the person being dangled declines or when the plant feels that we are rejecting him outright. A second characteristic feature of the behavior of persons being dangled is their disproportionate interest in money, which at times is manifested in self-seeking (there is every reason to assume that money received from our intelligence service serves as additional compensation for the plant). And finally, when, for one reason or another, we break off contacts with the plant, he takes active steps to restore the severed ties, for example even visiting an operational worker at his home and visiting places to which he normally doesn't go so as to arrange "accidental" meetings.

The Soviet Intelligence Service is aware of the following methods used by the FBI to insert a plant:

—It sends its agent to Soviet installations under the guise of a visitor, figuring that the information which the agent gives about himself or his specific offers to "help" us will arouse our interest and that we will take steps to develop our relationship with him;

—It uses persons in the categories described above as intermediaries to dangle their agents before Soviet intelligence officers as "prospective" contacts;

—It plants its own agents among persons connected with our embassy and other Soviet installations;

—It recruits an agent network among persons with liberal views who have contacts with Soviet institutions.

In some cases, the FBI and other U.S. counterintelligence organs dangle their agents before Soviet intelligence officers through contacts of our workers which they have discovered, using them on an unwitting basis. . . .

3. CARRYING OUT DEVELOPMENT FOR RECRUITMENT

The introduction of this section emphasizes that, except in unusual circumstances, recruitment should ideally be accomplished gradually by subtly changing a "normal" relationship into a conspiratorial one.

Holding a number of meetings of an ideological character makes it possible to develop the American to the point where he himself declares his desire to help the U.S.S.R., to aid in a progressive movement, or personally to help our intelligence service. In this case, the intelligence officer, taking advantage of the initiative displayed by the American, develops their relationship in such a way that it is given an intelligence character:

—Use is made of the times when an American turned to our Intelligence Service with a request for assistance in one or another matter without letting this fact become known to the persons surrounding him or to local authorities.

—The intelligence officer must understand that the establishment of such confidential relations with an American is a step toward intelligence relations. Nevertheless, the intelligence officer must establish confidential relations with the American in such a way that the latter does not surmise his connection with Soviet intelligence and his true intentions. For example, the intelligence officer takes steps to provide other convincing reasons for his interest in the information possessed by the American.

When consolidating relations with the person who is being developed, particular significance is attached to a favorable relationship with his family. As experience shows, during the early stages of development, visits by the intelligence officer to the home of the person being developed, accompanied by his wife, are sometimes expedient. With the aid of his wife, the intelligence officer can clarify some of the data characterizing the American and can decide how to strengthen relations with the person being developed. The expediency of using the wife of the American in his further development depends upon the degree and the direction of her influence on her husband. In no case, however, should the wife of the person being developed know of the intelligence purpose of the development by our worker. If she does, she may have a negative influence on the results of the development.

There is an example of this in the operational experience of our New York Residency. A Soviet intelligence officer established friendly relations with the wife of an American engineer at the beginning of his development. This helped him to become friends with her husband and actively to develop him further. When the American had been recruited and had started to have clandestine meetings with us, his wife turned out to be the main stumbling block. Fearing for the fate of their children, she began to demand that her husband break off relations with our worker.

Our Legal Residencies in the U.S. have had valuable experience in carry-out development for recruitment. For example, the possibility of using a U.S. government employee in the interests of Soviet Intelligence can be seen from an extremely successful development for recruitment which was carried out when our Intelligence Service succeeded in establishing confidential relations with an employee of the State Department (we will call him "Koen") and obtained secret information from him in return for material compensation.

The course of this development was as follows. From a State Department information directory, it was learned that Koen was thirty years old and that he had received a Bachelor of Arts degree in 1953. During the next four years he studied at three universities, including one in Washington. He then enrolled in a six-month preparatory course for employees of the State Department and, having completed it, worked there as an information clerk concerned with countries of the Far East.

Two days after becoming acquainted with him (they met in one of the clubs visited by diplomats), our intelligence officer called Koen at work from a public phone booth and arranged to meet him at the entrance of an international students' club that same evening. At the appointed time, the intelligence officer met Koen but took him to a restaurant rather than the club. Koen told our intelligence officer that he was an American of Anglo-Saxon background and that he came from a rather poor family. At one time he worked for the Veterans Administration. After graduation from the university, he succeeded in finding himself a job as an information clerk in the department for Far Eastern countries. His duties included processing telegrams received from U.S. embassies in the Far East and writing reports based on these telegrams for the directors of the department and for the Deputy Secretary of State. This took a lot of time: Koen frequently had to work until nine or ten o'clock at night. In addition, he was preparing himself for work at a U.S. embassy in the Far East. In this connection, he was taking foreign-language courses at the State Department.

Koen told the intelligence officer that he was a pacifist by conviction, and therefore was interested in the activity of Quaker organizations. Although he was not a member of the organization of Quakers in Washington, he frequently went to its meetings.

The intelligence officer noted a certain acquisitiveness in Koen. As it turned out, Koen lived in a poor section of Washington, where Negro families and low-paid Americans have their homes. Despite the fact that it was winter, Koen came to the meeting without an overcoat and in a rather threadbare suit. He appeared interested in our intelligence officer's remark that weekly English lessons pay $90 to $100 a month. At the end of the meeting, Koen thanked the intelligence officer for the good dinner.

The text proceeds to recount in minute detail how the KGB, exploiting the American's financial condition as well as his pacifist philosophy, slowly induced him to accept money first for innocuous unclassified information, then for significant secret data.

To illustrate that money should ordinarily not be offered crudely, the text next summarizes the recruitment of an American, referred to as Yang, employed by a scientific research firm in the Washington area. A visiting KGB scientist met the American, spoke about the desirability of free exchange of ideas among scientists, and ultimately offered to send a technical film he knew would greatly interest the American's employer.

While the firm was waiting for the film, the intelligence officer, as directed by the Residency, informed Yang that delivery of the desired film was being held up as they wanted to see it at the Soviet embassy in Washington. At the same time, the intelligence officer made the chance remark that a scientist friend badly needed certain nonsecret information from Yang's firm.

As expected, Yang, having already told the firm that he had received the film from us as a result of his good relations with Soviet scientists, began to pass us this information without notifying the head of the firm. Since the intelligence officer did not connect the transfer of the film with the receipt of the information, Yang was very pleased to think of this affair as a personal favor to our scientist. Yang gave us the confidential information of his firm. Incidentally, the second lot of material was received on a semiclandestine basis.

The problem then arose of how to solidify and strengthen this relationship. At this point it was decided that the scientist would offer Yang financial compensation for this information. Yang declined the compensation, declaring that this was a personal favor to the scientist.

Analyzing this refusal, the Residency concluded that possibly the attempt to offer Yang money was a mistake. Yang strove to prove himself an unselfish person in the eyes of the scientist. However, the Residency got the impression that Yang needed money, that his refusal was not genuine and that this was a sort of game with him.

Then it was decided to help him overcome these difficulties. For this purpose, a cover story was worked out according to which our scientist, who by this time was leaving for the U.S.S.R., wanted to give Yang a present for his birthday and for this reason left money with the intelligence officer.

The intelligence officer decided to give Yang the money for the present during a luncheon at a suburban restaurant. Yang so skillfully assumed the pose of mild offense that he even managed to fool our intelligence officer, a young man who had only recently begun practical operations and who, disappointed with such an outcome, took the package of money out of his pocket, looked at it, and was about to put it back. This involuntary action of the intelligence officer was accompanied by an expression of obvious distress. Here Yang ceased to "resist." The intelligence officer felt Yang's hand on his knee, and Yang said in a businesslike tone, "Give me the money under the table."

After this, the development of Yang became easier. Having trained Yang to pass information for compensation on a regular basis, the intelligence officer "excluded" the scientist from the development and proposed that Yang obtain the information supposedly for one of his friends who worked in the Soviet Information Service. This concluded the recruitment. Yang still works effectively but even now always likes the transfer of money to be preceded by a discussion of his unselfish aid to Soviet science.

As an example of another successful recruitment, a Soviet intelligence officer from the very beginning accepted the task of establishing personal contact with the person of interest to him under secure conditions. He thoroughly thought out a plan for making this acquaintance that would guarantee the success of the development.

As an interpreter, an intelligence officer of our New York Residency accompanied a Soviet scholar who visited a number of institutes and firms while in New York. During a visit to a laboratory which was of particular interest to Soviet Scientific and Technical Intelligence, our intelligence officer turned his attention to one of the assistants. He was a poorly dressed young American and looked like a typical Jew. When the Soviet scholar was saying good-by to the leader of the group, who was an old friend, he (with prior agreement with the intelligence officer) said that he would like to send them a number of his scientific works. The intelligence officer interrupted this conversation and offered to help translate these works. "But we have our own translator," said the leader of the group, pointing to the aforementioned assistant. The scientist and the intelligence officer then bade farewell and left.

It was decided to utilize the transfer of this information to solidify the acquaintance with the young Jew, whom we will call "Kolumb." Judging by external appearances, Kolumb was poor, obviously not an Anglo-Saxon, and possibly came from a family of Jewish immigrants from Russia. Since he worked in such an important laboratory, he apparently was an American citizen by birth and not an immigrant. Kolumb was studying Russian and consequently was somewhat interested in our country. This was possibly an avenue to induce him to associate with us on the basis of ideological and political feelings. Since he was young, it would be possible to develop the element of comradeship which is difficult to do with older people.

In order that the acquaintance with Kolumb would not become known to the chief of the laboratory and other workers, the following plan was developed. The Residency sent its intelligence officer to the library of the laboratory and gave him the task of carefully determining the days and times the chief of the laboratory was away at the university giving lectures. On such a day the intelligence officer would come to the laboratory during lunchtime, wait for the workers to appear, and having selected a convenient position to observe the situation would then approach Kolumb and begin a conversation with him.

But the unexpected took place: Kolumb came out of the laboratory with a group of workers, and the intelligence officer was forced to wait for the end of the lunch period. When Kolumb was the first to return from lunch, the intelligence officer approached him and asked, "How does one get to see the chief of the laboratory?" He explained to Kolumb that he wanted to deliver the materials sent to him by the Soviet scientist. The chief of the laboratory naturally was not there. Kolumb recognized the intelligence officer. A conversation then began which the intelligence officer utilized to support an acquaintance with Kolumb outside his institution. The intelligence officer said he was studying certain problems of an international character at the city library located not far from the laboratory. After this, the intelligence officer left without mentioning any future meetings. The following day the intelligence officer brought the material to the chief of the laboratory. After a week he phoned Kolumb to say that he had finished his work at the library on one of the problems and invited him to a simple lunch in order to celebrate its successful conclusion. In this way the development of Kolumb began.

As it turned out, the conclusions of the Residency concerning Kolumb were basically correct. Kolumb was indeed the son of a Jewish immigrant worker from Poland who had come to the U.S. at the beginning of the century. Kolumb had received his education at the cost of severe hardship. This did not help to teach him "patriotism." Besides this, Kolumb was writing his doctor's dissertation. He was receiving a very small stipend, which was not even enough to pay for his education and apartment. Kolumb was married. Having this in mind, the intelligence officer took steps from the beginning of the development to make sure that Kolumb's wife knew as little as possible about the character of his relationship with the intelligence officer. With this in view, the intelligence officer during his discussions with Kolumb characterized their relationship as a friendship between two men who were avoiding the interference of their wives.

It was decided to shorten the period of Kolumb's assessment and to prepare him for collaboration as rapidly as possible. During their long meetings (there were only six meetings—each from ten to twelve hours long, which included picnics, fishing trips, and excursions to the country) all development work was carried out, and after three months the intelligence officer was able to arrange a situation which would lay the foundation for Kolumb's cooperation with the Intelligence Service.

It had been learned that, because of his difficult financial position, Kolumb also worked as a translator-consultant in a firm and was its only specialist in his field. With this in mind, the intelligence officer decided to ask Kolumb to recommend some sort of a consultative firm in that field to him. On the chance that Kolumb would ask who needed this information, the intelligence officer was prepared to answer that a good friend of his, who was working in this field, badly needed some unclassified information on the production of tubes (he named the type of tubes which were Kolumb's specialty). In connection with this, the friend of the intelligence officer had sent him several hundred dollars, figuring that the intelligence officer could place an order for such information with one of the consultative firms. The intelligence officer scheduled this meeting for a time that Kolumb would receive the bills for his apartment and utilities.

The meeting went as follows. Having just received his bills, Kolumb was in a bad mood, and when the intelligence officer told him of the information he wanted, Kolumb became quiet.

We can assume that Kolumb was having the following thoughts, as anticipated in the plan: "If I recommend my firm, I will be undoubtedly assigned the job, and I would then get 10 to 15 percent of the money my friend pays the firm. It would be better if the firm had no part in this deal at all."

The proposal was accepted—Kolumb offered to write the survey. The intelligence officer agreed, saying that he didn't care whom he paid as long as the work was done. After this, it was not difficult over the next four or five months to teach Kolumb to pass to us information clandestinely for money.

The intelligence officer realized that his cover position did not satisfactorily explain to Kolumb his desire to obtain secret information. Therefore, he concocted a material interest in his relations with Kolumb. For this purpose he talked Kolumb into organizing a two-man firm, consisting of Kolumb and our intelligence officer, in which Kolumb would obtain the information and the intelligence officer would sell it. After this, it became easy to press all sorts of new requirements on Kolumb and to demand—literally demand—secret information from him. The formation of the "firm" did not of course make it more difficult for the intelligence officer to maintain control, although in a formal sense he was now dependent upon Kolumb. Since he "obtained" the money, the intelligence officer at all times remained the principal member of the firm and assigned tasks to Kolumb. Formation of the "firm" gave the relationship between our intelligence officer and the agent a spirit of partnership and doubtless made it easier to consolidate Kolumb's ties with Soviet Foreign Intelligence.

A deficiency in this edifice became obvious later when the question of the final recruitment and transfer of Kolumb to another one of our workers came up. It took a long time to talk Kolumb into working with a new intelligence officer.

The necessity of carefully investigating each and every case, no matter how sincere the American, is pointed out in the development of an American journalist who appeared, in the early stages of development, to be a plant.

Our Residency in Washington received a spotting report on a certain "Beys"—an American citizen born in India, who worked in the Washington office of the radio propaganda broadcasting service Voice of America.

A Soviet intelligence officer, after a lengthy search for Beys in the area where he worked, identified him through his automobile license plate and then made his acquaintance in one of the nearby drugstores. During their conversation, the intelligence officer promised to give Beys a book of interest to him at the request of a mutual friend. The intelligence officer arranged to meet him in one of the restaurants in the city. A week later Beys invited the intelligence officer and his wife to his home for dinner along with Beys' wife, who was an American, and his brother. It turned out that Beys' wife worked as a secretary for the military attaché in the embassy of one of the Eastern countries. Beys criticized Western policy in the Asian countries. He asked the intelligence officer to recommend a store where he could buy Marx's *Das Kapital* in the English language. In addition, Beys stated that he was soon going to India on business connected with his work for the Voice of America.

The next meeting took place after Beys had returned from his trip to the East. Besides India, he had visited a number of countries in the Near East. In talking with the intelligence officer, he spoke of the strong anti-American feeling in these countries, resulting primarily from U.S. deliveries of arms to Israel, and of the sincere desire of these countries to cooperate with the Soviet Union.

Beys told the intelligence officer that he had written a number of articles on the situation in the Asian countries but that he didn't intend to give them to the Voice of America. Instead, he planned to publish them under a pen name in a weekly magazine of one of the Eastern countries for which he was a correspondent. Our intelligence officer cautiously asked Beys to tell him about these articles. Beys agreed and expressed a desire to publish one of his articles in some Soviet magazine. The intelligence officer said that this proposal merited attention and that he would try to interest the editor of a Soviet journal in Beys' material. Having thought it over for a moment, Beys promised to give the intelligence officer not only this article but also others which he was writing.

At the end of the meeting, Beys asked where the intelligence officer had called from when setting up their meeting and was relieved to learn that the call hadn't been made from the Soviet embassy. Taking advantage of this, the intelligence officer asked Beys not to phone him at work or at home. Beys proposed that they meet next time somewhere outside the city together with their wives, but the intelligence officer didn't go along with this. Saying that his wife wasn't feeling well, he suggested that they meet a week later in one of the suburban restaurants without their wives.

It is necessary to point out that, in developing relations with Beys, our Residency made an effort to determine the sincerity of his relationship with the intelligence officer on the basis of the information in his articles. It was quite clear to the Residency that in many ways Beys' conduct was similar to that of a plant. Included in this category were his ideological affinity and sympathy for the U.S.S.R., which were incompatible with his position at work; the fact that he had relatives abroad who were members of the Communist Party; his wife's intelligence potential, which might well have been calculated to increase the interest of our Intelligence Service in him; Beys' initiative in writing articles containing information of possible interest to our intelligence; and the fact that he expressed a fear that the FBI would learn of his contact with the intelligence officer.

At the next meeting our intelligence officer carefully determined the intelligence potential of Beys at his place of work. Soon the intelligence officer received the article from him for publication in the Soviet press, along with illustrations for it on film. Beys requested that certain details be altered when publishing the article and photograph—that the figures of two people be deleted from the photograph since the film had been developed by an American company.

In the course of further discussion, Beys again expressed his sympathy toward the Soviet Union as a friend of India, and accepted in principle our intelligence officer's suggestion that he prepare material, not for newspapers but for him personally. For this purpose he was to use nonofficial data received from his wife, friends, and acquaintances. At the same time a regular meeting was arranged with Beys. Beys indicated that he was interested in receiving an honorarium for his article.

At the meeting in late June, Beys received an honorarium of $100 from the intelligence officer for his first article and passed him a second one. He complained that like most Americans, he had no faith in tomorrow and said that his and his wife's combined earnings came to only $600 or $700 a month.

Beys agreed to the intelligence officer's suggestion that they arrive together rather than separately when holding a meeting in a restaurant and that Beys, rather than the intelligence officer, order the meal. He said: "You're right, the waiters might realize that you are a foreigner. If I talk to them and select and order the food, they will think that we are just two American businessmen. And this won't arouse any interest in us. In this country it is customary to enter a bar or restaurant together."

At a regular meeting in the beginning of July he said that he had been called in by an agent of the FBI and had been asked whether he was having contacts with any foreigners. According to Beys, he did not tell the FBI about his acquaintance with the intelligence officer. Subsequently Beys saw that he was under FBI surveillance. Beys said that he didn't know the cause of FBI interest in him—whether this was a routine precautionary investigation or whether the FBI had received information of his contact with the intelligence officer.*

Beys did not bring the promised article to this meeting. He was noticeably upset. It was only after two weeks that Beys calmed down and the intelligence officer could have a long talk with him in order to determine his intelligence potential, with particular emphasis on his contacts and sources from whom he could obtain the information.

The regular and alternate meetings between our intelligence officer and Beys did not take place. It was not until the middle of August that they saw each other again. When the intelligence officer asked Beys whether he had brought the material, he replied: "Besides the risk, I'm spending much of my own time and effort. I am not rich enough to give them away. I realize that if I write such articles for you, sooner or later I will find myself in the electric chair. I'm sure the FBI is watching your every move. Someday they will discover our contacts, and that will be the end of me. I don't want to lay down my life here, in this damned country of gangsters and political criminals. You know that I work in a government institution, and by oath I must inform the security service of all my friends and contacts. If I conceal them, not only can I lose my job but I could also land in jail. Therefore, if you want me to give nonofficial material, I must know specifically the size of my honorarium in order to weigh it against the risks of losing my head and the well-being of my family. Don't think that I am trying to extort money from you. No, I am only concerned with the well-being of my family."

Beys promised to give information orally: "I can tell you everything that I know and everything that you want to know

---

*Often when a KGB officer clandestinely meets an agent, a KGB colleague follows to ensure that the meeting is not under counterintelligence surveillance. Possibly through such procedure the KGB had assured itself that the FBI was not trailing Beys to his rendezvous with the Russian.

about the organization in which I work, but for the time being I am going to refrain from writing it down."

The intelligence officer explained that the amount of the honorarium would depend upon whether Beys could obtain documentary authentic information on the activities of U.S. governmental circles, for which he would receive a lot of money. Apparently this placated Beys, and he gave his word that he would write the article he had promised the intelligence officer and to give it to us at the next meeting.

Ten days later Beys brought a report which he had written on the basis of information from the military attaché of one of the Far Eastern embassies in the U.S.

The intelligence officer gave Beys an advance of $200 and promised more if the information he had given on the plans of the U.S. in the Near and Middle East proved to be accurate. At the same time the intelligence officer instructed Beys to write a detailed report on the activities of the Voice of America and to clear up questions concerning the structure of this organization, its financial setup, and its sources for the information it uses. . . .

Having analyzed the intelligence officer's work with Beys, the Center came to the conclusion that their relationship had now progressed beyond the point of being merely a confidential contact and told the Residency to complete the development and assessment of Beys within two months' time and to present its recommendations concerning his recruitment.

At the end of October Beys supplied information on increased broadcasting activity by the Voice of America directed to Europe, particularly Hungary.

In the beginning of November the intelligence officer could not make his regular meetings with Beys since he was under surveillance. Several days later, having taken appropriate measures, the intelligence officer waited for Beys at the entrance to his home, where he made contact with him and proposed that they meet ten minutes later at another place. At this meeting Beys gave the intelligence officer information on the operating schedule of the Voice of America for the European countries and received $200 from him.

The next meeting took place in two weeks. At this time Beys handed over information on U.S. military installations in the countries of the East, which received a good evaluation from the Center.

The Center decided to train Beys, as an agent, in methods of clandestine communication. At a regular meeting at the end of December, the intelligence officer completed the recruitment and obtained the agreement by Beys to cooperate with Soviet Foreign Intelligence. Beys told the intelligence officer that he had waited a long time for this meeting since he knew that the intelligence officer was interested in secret material information, and he was prepared to sell it to him if necessary measures were taken to ensure his security.

After the recruitment, Beys continued to pass us valuable information for money.

The above example shows that despite a number of circumstances which seriously alarmed our Residency in the course of development, it was possible to determine that the recruitment target was not a plant—his information was reliable, and its receipt did considerable harm to U.S. interests.

The operational experience of Soviet Foreign Intelligence Residencies in the U.S. includes cases in which various approaches to the development target have been successfully combined. This is illustrated by the following example from the experience of our New York Residency.

Glebov, an intelligence officer assigned to this Residency, enrolled in one of the New York universities to study English. On joining the class, he immediately turned his attention to "Poynt," an Italian born in 1925 who worked for the representatives of one of the major Italian airlines in New York, and who had also joined the group in order to improve his English. As it turned out, Poynt planned to remain in the U.S. and become an American citizen. Glebov quickly made friends with Poynt and soon concluded that he could be recruited as he was sympathetic toward the Soviet Union and was in great need of money because of his numerous affairs with women. Because of this combination of the ideological-political and material motivations, Poynt was passing Glebov information, albeit of little value, within about two months after initial contact and was being paid for this in order to consolidate the relationship.

The Residency decided to make a detailed assessment of Poynt's potential. With this aim, it arranged for another of our intelligence officers, Alekseev, to become acquainted with Poynt. Alekseev was an engineer and could develop the intelligence potential of Poynt along the lines of scientific and technical intelligence more successfully than Glebov.

During this period, meetings with Poynt took place openly, as he was not yet trained in clandestinity. For example, prior to meeting with Poynt in a restaurant, our intelligence officers picked him up at home in a taxi. Alekseev noted a somewhat adventuresome spirit in Poynt. From the very start, both Poynt and Alekseev liked one another. After a two-hour discussion, it was clear to Alekseev that Poynt possessed a great deal of intelligence potential.

During the evening of the same day, Glebov obtained Poynt's agreement to work with us; however, Poynt categorically refused to sign a written agreement. Contact with Poynt was transferred to Alekseev.

In passing material to the intelligence officer, Poynt said that he didn't understand the necessity for the "intensified" (as he expressed it) clandestinity of their meetings, since he was engaged in normal business. Having heard him out, Alekseev realized the necessity of instilling appropriate work habits in Poynt, so as to establish agent relations with him in the future. Therefore, he told Poynt that clandestinity was necessary not for Poynt's sake but for the sake of the intelligence officer, who, being a Soviet diplomat, had no legitimate cause for interest in technical matters.

This explanation completely satisfied Poynt, and he didn't question the need for clandestinity again. And when Poynt began to pass us secret materials, he came to recognize the need for clandestinity for himself as well.

After the operation had been going on for five months, it was decided to give Poynt a permanent system of communications. When our intelligence officer began to explain this system to him, Poynt burst into laughter. It turned out that Poynt had run across passwords, recognition signals, alternate meetings, etc., so often in various detective and spy novels that he had come to believe that the authors had thought them all up. He was simply amazed that real intelligence work—and he already understood by this time that he was cooperating with an intelligence service—employs such "antediluvian" methods. The response of the intelligence officer, which lasted about an hour, boiled down to the following: Intelligence itself and all its so-called methods in themselves are not new and have been used for a long time. The specific application of those methods is another matter, which is entirely dependent upon the skill and experience of the intelligence officer. Here, for the first time, Alekseev intentionally called Poynt an intelligence officer.

Posing the problem in this manner, which was necessary in this case, pleased Poynt very much, and he asked the intelligence officer to share his "art" with him. This was utilized when training Poynt to detect external surveillance, to open safes, etc.

After about ten months Poynt was removing secret material from a safe at work. At the same time, the possibility arose of finding him more interesting work in the U.S. after he received his American citizenship.

It became clear that Poynt, because of his amiable personality, was an excellent spotter. He had extensive contacts among people working in industry. Utilizing opportunities arising from his work, he brought us some cards containing their addresses and data about their jobs and announced that he could become acquainted with any one of them. Later on he very carefully studied three of them. These persons were then developed by our Residency.

After about a year, Poynt came to Alekseev with the following request: "A year ago when your friend Glebov proposed that I sign a contract, I refused to do this since, despite my friendship for him, his proposal that I work for you seemed insufficiently serious to me. Now I am convinced of the importance of my cooperation with you. You even called me an intelligence officer once. Therefore, I want to become a staff member of your Intelligence Service. But of course, when I grow old and leave this game, I ask that you guarantee me a pension."

This signing of a contract at the request of Poynt took place at a special organizational meeting. By this time Poynt had become one of the most valuable agents of our Residency.

At one time our Residency in New York got hold of a certain "Del," who was a Spaniard by nationality and the son of a noted Republican who had fled Spain to France after the victory of Franco. Del had dual citizenship—Spanish and French. He was an economic specialist but at the time of contact was out of work. He had an interesting appearance: he had typical sharp Spanish features and enjoyed great success with women. He was married to a Russian whose parents had left Russia during the Revolution. Del's wife had retained her sympathy for her native country.

A member of the Soviet Foreign Intelligence Residency, an employee of the U.N., became acquainted with Del at one of the parties organized by the U.N. for the purpose of introducing its workers to local residents with the aim of popularizing the organization. The acquaintance was made as follows: Del's wife, who worked in a store, took the initiative at the party and approached our intelligence officer, having recognized that he was a Soviet. She later introduced Del to the intelligence officer.

Subsequent meetings with Del took place without his wife, as it was not expedient to include her in the process of developing Del. In order to make the next steps appear natural, our intelligence officer chose a day for the next meeting when

Del's wife would be busy at work. At this meeting the intelligence officer convinced Del that common knowledge of their meetings would principally be injurious to Del, as he did not have American citizenship. They agreed to meet without their wives. Several meetings were held in the city. Up to this time principal attention was given to the establishment of friendly relations with Del, to developing a progressive ideological spirit in him, and to assessing his intelligence potential, which turned out to be rather limited. Being jobless, Del possessed limited contacts which were of no intelligence interest. In order to test Del, the intelligence officer proposed that he buy samples of electrical equipment which Soviet citizens could not obtain. In a confidential manner, it was explained to Del that the purchase of such items by Soviet representatives could attract the attention of the authorities. According to standard business procedure, our intelligence officer offered Del a 10 percent commission, telling him that it would be necessary to pay this amount to any businessman. Del successfully made these purchases.

Subsequently, Del was given a more important assignment, to purchase a sample of a restricted piece of electrical equipment. This was within the realm of possibility for Del, since he had a friend who, according to Del, formerly had been involved in risky operations; for example, he had supplied certain gangsters with weapons at a good price and had even shipped large consignments of weapons to the Cuban army. Del took advantage of his friend and succeeded in talking him into getting the equipment in which we were interested. Del purchased the equipment and safely brought it to our intelligence officer. He also received a commission for this. This completed the initial testing of Del. The intelligence officer began to have clandestine contacts with him. In order to initiate a meeting with the intelligence officer, for example, Del placed a signal in a little-used stairway in the U.N. Building. Soon after this, the recruitment meeting took place, thereby consolidating the relationship which had developed.

In order to increase his intelligence potential, Del got a job as a non-staff correspondent on a local magazine. This helped him to legalize his position and made it possible to intensify his contacts among U.N. employees from various countries and to obtain certain economic and political information from them. Del did well in this work—he was able to establish useful contacts with many acquaintances of his father and to use them for intelligence purposes. However, the information coming from these sources was still of insufficient quality. For example, he was unable to obtain documentary information.

After this, it was decided to use Del as a recruiter. Our Residency had become interested in a female employee who had access to valuable information. The Residency figured that this young American woman might be attracted to Del. Therefore, they recommended that he make the acquaintance of this woman and establish good relations with her. Del successfully coped with this task. Having made the acquaintance of the female employee, he soon began to live with her. After studying his new acquaintance carefully, Del began to exert an influence on her. On Del's recommendation, for example, she changed her job within her organization and immediately obtained direct access to documentary information.

After a certain amount of time, Del began to cultivate his female friend in the interests of our intelligence. Somehow, in conversation with her, he directed her attention to the fact that she spent less on clothes than many of her colleagues. To her reasonable remark that on $70 a week there's not much one can do, Del asked: "And how do the others manage to buy clothes?" Then he explained that her girl friends had supplementary incomes, since they sold the information that comes their way to various correspondents. Del recommended that she do the same thing. After some reflection, Del's female friend agreed with his suggestion. Del convinced her that it would be safer if he were to sell the material. She agreed to this, and he started to pay her money regularly for each document.

In analyzing this recruitment development, it is clear that the intelligence officer took a calculated risk in establishing an agent relationship with a foreigner who did not have American citizenship and who had limited intelligence potential. But as subsequent events proved, this risk was fully justified. The Soviet intelligence officer's correct interpretation of Del's personal qualities showed the expediency of acquiring his cooperation and made it possible for the Residency to acquire a valuable recruit.

Under current conditions, material incentives should be used to consolidate an agent relationship, even in those cases where the basic factor motivating an American to cooperate with our Intelligence Service is ideological. Disregard for the material incentives of an agent sometimes causes recruitment development to miscarry and may even result in the loss of an American already recruited.

Despite the acquisitiveness of an overwhelming majority of Americans, intelligence cooperation based on material incentives should not become a simple "barter" arrangement. Americans understand that unlike commercial activity, agent relationships with Soviet Foreign Intelligence subject them to great risk, and they appraise any relationship which has developed with our workers very carefully. Therefore, considerable tact must be used in giving money, and account must be taken of the degree to which the agent has been prepared for this. . . .

An intelligence officer of our New York Residency had contact with a valuable agent who was obtaining for us samples of equipment and top-secret material concerning research in the field of atomic energy. The intelligence officer took over this agent immediately after his recruitment, on an ideological and political basis, by a worker of the Center. The agent was of Russian extraction and very sympathetic toward the Russian people, a fact which was used in his recruitment.

Even though there was considerable difference in ages (the agent was twenty years older than the intelligence officer), the intelligence officer was able to develop the proper relationship with the agent, who came to consider the intelligence officer to be his only link with the motherland and came to feel toward him as he would toward his own son.

The Residency utilized this attachment, and in order to consolidate the relationship introduced an element of material interest in his relations with our intelligence officer.

At a regular meeting with the agent, the intelligence officer told the agent that the directors of the entire Intelligence Service had expressed gratitude for the material which had been received earlier and had awarded them a bonus—$100 to the intelligence officer and $500 to the agent. The agent was flattered by this. However, when the intelligence officer offered him the package with the money, the agent announced that he was working with us for patriotic reasons and would not take the money.

"Are you trying to say that I'm not a patriot?" asked the intelligence officer. "I need the money, and it will be very difficult for me if I also refuse it. Still, I will have to do this if you refuse."

"And do you need the money very much?" asked the agent.

"Very much," answered the intelligence officer.

"Well, all right," agreed the agent.

Therefore, as a result of using a correct approach to the agent, it became possible to further consolidate the relationship through the use of material incentive. After this, the agent frequently accepted money from us without any argument.

For purposes of development or for consolidating tionship, it is particularly important to note the ex bringing Americans out of the United States to third countries where the operational climate is more suitable. It is especially desirable to use the People's Democracies and in certain cases even the U.S.S.R. When doing this, it is necessary to have a convincing pretext for such a trip.

In conclusion, it is necessary to discuss the more characteristic peculiarities of recruitment in the U.S. At the present time the principal method used to recruit Americans is that of gradual development. This does not mean that a well-prepared recruitment of an American by the direct method cannot be effective. As regards the basis for recruitment, the most effective one at the present time lies in a combination of ideological motivation and material incentives. . . . In carrying out recruitment operations in the U.S., Soviet intelligence officers must take into consideration the following peculiarities of the operational climate:

1. The attempts of U.S. counterintelligence to block the possibilities of Soviet intelligence officers' access to foreigners through the development of an extensive agent network in the area surrounding Soviet installations and targets of interest to Soviet Foreign Intelligence.

2. The availability to American counterintelligence of information on the experience and modus operandi of Soviet Foreign Intelligence in the U.S.

3. Widespread dissemination to the population by the counterintelligence services of information on the methods and approaches used by Soviet intelligence officers in developing that part of the local population which is of recruitment interest to Soviet intelligence.

4. The comparatively rapid reaction of U.S. counterintelligence organs to individual changes in the methods and approaches used by Soviet intelligence officers. In connection with these peculiarities, exceptional importance is attached to clandestinity when a Soviet intelligence officer establishes any initial contact with an American.

To penetrate the more secret targets of the opposition, it is expedient to recruit representatives of the neutral countries in American and international organizations and institutions.

The ability of the recruiter to establish friendly relations with an American under development often has a great influence on the success of a recruitment.

4. THE RECRUITMENT OF AMERICANS IN THIRD COUNTRIES

The directive of the leadership of the Committee for State Security entitled "On Intensifying Intelligence Operations Against the U.S. in Third Countries" sets important tasks for the Residencies of the KGB, U.S.S.R. First of all, the directive calls for increased activity in the recruitment and development of Americans working in U.S. government installations abroad; Americans serving on the staffs of military blocs and international organizations; military personnel; representatives of scientific institutions, firms, and organizations; and American correspondents, students, etc.

Special attention is paid to spotting, developing, and recruiting American intelligence officers engaged in espionage and sabotage activities against the U.S.S.R. and other socialist countries. Great attention is given to the acquisition of agents used to acquire documents in American institutions—primarily those with access to coded and other secret correspondence: code clerks, secretaries and typists, stenographers, cipher-machine operators, and repairmen. At the same time it is urged that more agents be acquired among Americans and local citizens working in various American establishments, principally at U.S. military bases and other strategic targets.

In developing people within this category, it is recommended that skillful use be made of their financial insecurity, their speculative desires, their way of life, their weakness for alcoholic beverages and gambling, etc. Operational workers are required to be bolder in acquiring personal contacts and confidential relationships with Americans who can obtain work in the government organs and scientific organizations of the U.S., as well as in American establishments abroad, or as individual American citizens acting as translators, secretaries, typists, chauffeurs, chefs, domestic help, etc. It was urged that such an agent network be used for thorough study of the staffs and work schedules of American installations in order to procure secret documents and to install listening devices.

The concluding portion of the directive pointed out the duty of the Residency to study carefully the contradictions existing between the U.S. and other capitalist countries, to analyze the information received from the agent network, and to develop and implement active measures to exacerbate these contradictions and to compromise and undermine the prestige of individuals active in U.S. politics and government.

Some 1,500,000 American citizens are now living in countries of the world.

Besides government workers, there are American servicemen, diplomats, businessmen, missionaries, and others living abroad. According to official U.S. data, there were 12,500 American diplomats alone in foreign countries in October 1962. *Newsweek* magazine has pointed out that of 2,668,000 members of the U.S. Armed Forces, there are 400,000 located in Europe alone. Besides those Americans who are abroad for an extended period, there are some 1.5 million American tourists in Europe every year.

Americans are motivated to go abroad by various material benefits: higher salaries, the opportunity to save money because of the lower cost of living abroad, exemption from taxes, the receipt of rent-free quarters and longer vacations, the opportunity to carry out profitable foreign currency operations, etc.

Americans employed by government institutions are of the greatest interest to Soviet Foreign Intelligence.

The operational climate in third countries determines the possibilities for recruiting Americans in them. In this connection, it is possible to delineate the general characteristics of the operations of our Residencies against Americans in the capitalist countries and to divide all countries into two groups: neutral countries and countries belonging to aggressive blocs. Of course, the operations of Soviet Foreign Intelligence Residencies in the second group of countries are of the greatest interest to us, for it is there that the greatest number of Americans with access to valuable secret information is found. In organizing this work, it is naturally necessary to take into account U.S. counterintelligence measures aimed at protecting those secrets. At the present time, targets have already been determined in those countries where Americans are concentrated and which are of interest to our Residencies. In these countries our Residencies are systematically studying the conditions of work against U.S. representatives and are seeking ways to establish contact with employees of these organizations with the aim of recruiting them.

From agent information, meetings with Americans, and personal observation, workers of our Residencies obtain necessary information on the status and behavior of Americans, on their attitudes toward developing acquaintances with Soviets, and also on conditions in the organizations of the principal enemy. All this helps us to operate successfully against the U.S.

In those countries where previously there have been no Soviet Foreign Intelligence Residencies, where the Residencies have not yet shown the necessary interest in operations against U.S. representatives or have not been in a position to overcome existing difficulties, work against these representatives has begun with identification of American citizens located in the country and with development of the more promising targets. For example, the Residency in Sweden developed measures for studying members of the U.S. embassy in Sweden, representatives of American news bureaus and newspapers, students at the international schools of Stockholm University, representatives of tourist, commercial, and transportation firms, and American businessmen traveling to Sweden on business.

Our Residency in India determined that some 150 Americans, including 69 diplomats, work at the U.S. embassy in that country. Many Indian citizens are employed by the embassy. In the chancellery and motor pool alone there are more than 30 of them. . . .

Many Indians work in the embassy as members of the cleaning crew, gardeners, guards, messengers, chauffeurs, servants, etc. Moreover, Indians work in the personnel section of the administrative department of the embassy. In this regard, considerable attention is given to the political views of candidates and to whether they have relatives or even acquaintances in various government and public institutions and organizations. In addition, an investigator (Indian) checks all Indians hired by the U.S. embassy.

Indians fill out a special State Department questionnaire for persons seeking jobs in American establishments abroad. The questionnaire consists of 37 points. A person applying to work for the Americans for the first time must indicate his places of residence during the past ten years, the names of all previous places of employment, and the places of employment of all close relatives and relatives of his wife; he must list all relatives who work in government establishments and all friends in the U.S.; he must give three references who are not related to him and can vouch for his character; he must also indicate whether he has ever been or is now a member of the Communist Party, and if so, he must give the name of the organization and the degree to which he participated in it. The applicant must present recommendations from Americans, highly placed members of the Indian government, or from other individuals who are well known to the American embassy. Indians who are hired by the Americans are fingerprinted.

Indians who work at American installations in Delhi are well paid, particularly at the U.S. embassy. Therefore, they value their positions. However, it is difficult for an Indian to hold his job over a long period of time since the Americans do not want to pay them pensions for longevity. Therefore, there is a frequent turnover among the Indians working in U.S. installations.

In studying Americans, our Residency in Italy identified a number of places visited by Americans working in target installations of interest to our Intelligence Service. It was possible to determine that Americans in Rome systematically frequent the same bars, restaurants, and places of recreation. Americans feel almost at home in these places: they drink a great deal, are very free in their conduct and frequently sing. American women, especially the wives of Americans who are away on temporary assignments, drink and have relations with other men.

Having studied the operation of organizations of the main enemy in Italy, our Residency came to the conclusion that it is difficult for the intelligence officer himself to make friends with and develop Americans who work in these organizations.

This is explained by the fact that American intelligence and counterintelligence organs understand the nature of the problems confronting Soviet Residencies in third countries and of their methods of operation. It is known that in countries which belong to aggressive blocs, U.S. counterintelligence attempts to interfere with the work of our Residencies. It maintains close contact with local counterintelligence organizations and, together with them, attempts to identify Soviet intelligence officers and to learn their methods of operation.

Endeavoring to make the work of Soviet intelligence more difficult, they tell all U.S. citizens going abroad that they will not be punished if they voluntarily report recruitment by foreign intelligence services.

In a number of third countries where there is an efficient counterintelligence effort, the development of Americans directly by our workers as a rule does not pay off. American diplomats who establish personal, unofficial contacts with employees of Soviet establishments in third countries are recalled to the U.S. Only American intelligence and counterintelligence personnel who are trying to assess our citizens willingly establish contacts and friendships with Soviet personnel. In such countries it is advisable to use indigenous agents for development of Americans. Therefore, when assessing Americans working in places that are of interest to us, our Residency in Rome has relied mainly on Italians who have contacts with these Americans or can easily develop such contacts.

In the future, insofar as possible, it is planned to use these Italians as agent recruiters or as intermediaries to establish acquaintance with Americans who are of interest to us. The Residency feels that Americans of interest to the Soviet Intelligence Service are financially well off and are antagonistic toward the Soviet Union. Consequently, these persons can be developed successfully only when the American sees that he can earn good money by collaborating with us.

Having trained a number of Italians with opportunities to develop Americans, our Residency in Rome directed them toward the establishment of friendships and the collection of information concerning those American citizens who work in specific departments of the embassy (political, economic, and the military assistance group), in the Joint Defense Department, and also in the department of cipher communications, the security service, USIS, and NATO forces in Italy.

In designating these measures, our Residency took into account the difficulties connected with using Italians for this purpose: Americans pay them well, and therefore many of them want to hang on to their jobs in American establishments. Afraid of losing their jobs, they dutifully observe instructions concerning their conduct at work, particularly regulations forbidding any kind of nonofficial contacts with Soviet personnel. The Residency also took into account the fact that the official presence of the so-called "security service" of the U.S. embassy, which fulfills the functions of the FBI and works in close contact with local police organs through its Italian employees, has a considerable influence on the conduct of employees at American and NATO installations in Italy. This service investigates the political views of embassy employees. Indigenous employees who are suspected of holding leftist views are immediately fired.

This service has surveillance teams made up of Americans. The security service investigates the local population in the vicinity of NATO staffs and American bases in Italy. When an Italian who lived in Naples and was well known to the Residency changed his home and rented an apartment near the NATO staff headquarters, the local police questioned the janitor about his views and why he had moved and watched him for a time. Despite these difficulties, good results are obtained from the use of local citizens for developing Americans in Italy and other countries.

After targets for development are determined, Soviet Foreign Intelligence Residencies begin to acquire personal contacts. In this regard, it is necessary to organize the operation correctly and to know the methods which make it easier to overcome the difficulties of establishing personal acquaintances with Americans. Our Residencies carefully study the composition of American groups and their peculiarities. As a result of such work by KGB Residencies in Latin America, for example, particular attention has been given to American students studying in those countries. . . .

In Asia and Latin America, for example, the number of visits by Americans to Soviet embassies has increased greatly during recent years: there has been a considerable increase in the number of students coming to the Soviet embassies for information on questions concerning life in the U.S.S.R. It is also noted that representatives of government establishments in these countries, including the U.S. embassy, are more willing to establish personal contacts with Soviet citizens, are less hostile during such encounters, and in some cases one senses that they are sincerely dissatisfied with current U.S. policies.

International events during recent years and the role of the Soviet Union in them have had a considerable influence on most American students studying abroad, especially in Latin-American educational institutions. One important factor is that American students enjoy considerable freedom in obtaining Soviet literature in these countries and run a smaller risk of coming to the attention of U.S. counterintelligence. In Latin-American countries, American students are frequently influenced by the nationalistic sentiments of the local population and in discussions with Americans frequently contrast the peaceful policies and scientific achievements of the U.S.S.R. with the colonial policies and shortcomings of the U.S.

As a rule, American students studying in Latin America are short of funds. Most come from the middle classes of the U.S. Frequently, grants received for service in the Army prior to beginning their studies or limited assistance by relatives comprise their sole means of livelihood. Persons in this category are more liberal in their outlook. They are sympathetic to the local nationalist feelings and sometimes do not approve of the influence of monopolies in the economy and foreign policy of the U.S. or of the U.S. colonial policy with regard to the Latin-American countries. The financial situation of the American students, their convictions, and the general operational climate facilitate our work. The fact that some of the students are preparing to enter government service (and in some cases they can be directed toward this type of work) indicates that students can form a basis for organizing future agent networks to penetrate U.S. government organizations.

Studying the operational climate in Mexico, the Soviet Foreign Intelligence Residency came to the conclusion that employees of the embassy and other U.S. installations on one hand and American students on the other are of the greatest interest to us.

There are important differences in the development of persons falling within each of these two groups. The first group consists of government employees, who are obligated to guard secret information and who know to a certain degree the methods of operation of the Soviet Intelligence Services. They are constantly subjected to political and psychological indoctrination. The second group consists of students. For the most part they are independent, are free in their choice of contacts and topics of conversation, and lack sufficient experience in life. Proper counteraction by our Intelligence Service can prevent the political indoctrination of U.S. propaganda organs from achieving its purpose.

Experience in establishing contacts with and developing individuals in these groups has resulted in the formulation of specific methods and approaches for each.

In establishing contacts with employees of the embassy and other government installations, operations from a legal standpoint are usually carried out within the context of official diplomatic contacts, at official receptions, and at receptions in neutral embassies or private homes. The development of individuals in this category is more effective through agent-recruiters and confidential contacts, since such individuals in Mexico shy away from nonofficial contacts with Soviet citizens.

In order to consolidate a friendship with such Americans, our workers under embassy cover usually present gifts on New Year's Day and other holidays. Frequently the Soviet intelligence officer delivers the gift personally, selecting a time when the American of interest to us is at home in order to ascribe a nonofficial homelike character to the relationship. After this, the American usually presents a gift in return, at the same time visiting our worker at his home.

Tours of Soviet performers are also used for inviting Americans to concerts. Tickets for these concerts can even be given to slight acquaintances, who view such a gesture as natural. During intermission the Soviet intelligence officer can approach the American and ask the usual questions for such an occasion and can consolidate the friendship during the discussion.

Knowledge of the English language and of American history, culture, and way of life is of great importance in the successful development of friendships with Americans. Our worker can ask the American to send to the U.S. for a certain book, can ask him to explain the peculiarities of American football or baseball and the like. In answer to such questions, Americans sometimes invite Soviet intelligence officers to attend scheduled games.

The method of establishing contact through a neutral contact, through members of embassies which have good relations with Americans, is fairly effective. The embassies of India, Burma, and the Arab and Latin-American countries fall within this category. For this purpose, our intelligence officers establish friendly relations with representatives of these countries.

Published in accordance with the plan for editorial and publishing work of School No. 101, approved by the leadership of the First Chief Directorate of the KGB under the Council of Ministers, U.S.S.R.

EDITOR: Colonel A. I. Avdeyev
LITERARY EDITOR: T. V. Mitrofanova
SENIOR PROOFREADER: I. B. Dubenskaya

Copies printed 100   No. ——   Rot. No. ——
Duplicated by rotary press at School No. 101

TOP SECRET

APPENDIX D

SOVIET CITIZENS ENGAGED IN CLANDESTINE OPERATIONS ABROAD

When our researchers began gathering data for this book, they established a master file in which they carded the name of each KGB officer encountered in their research. They additionally noted the names of Soviet citizens who have been detected in clandestine operations but who may represent the GRU or Central Committee rather than the KGB. Many names were obtained from published reports announcing the expulsion of Soviet diplomats for illegal actions. Still more were supplied by former KGB officers such as Yuri Nosenko and Petr Deriabin. Others were recorded during interviews with diverse authorities in numerous nations. By 1973 the file contained names of well over two thousand men and women alleged to belong to the KGB or GRU.

The list that follows includes only those Soviet personnel positively identified by two or more responsible sources as having engaged in clandestine activities against foreign countries. Most are known to be regular staff officers of the KGB, but a few may be co-opted agents. Some are GRU officers, and their status as such is indicated in parenthesis. It is believed that most Soviet ambassadors involved in clandestine work have acted, at least in recent years, under orders of the Central Committee rather than under KGB direction. The names of a number of ambassadors accused, in various published reports, of personal involvement in espionage or subversion have been omitted because of contradictory evidence.

The list states the countries in which each officer is known to have been stationed, the years he served there, and the last year he was spotted abroad. If an officer has been declared *persona non grata* or privately asked to leave a country, the notation EXPELLED appears. An asterisk denotes that the officer used the cover of the United Nations or some other international organization.

In transliterating Russian names for the list and the entire book, we have followed the style used by the U.S. Board on Geographic Names, with some modifications we regard as simplifications. These deviations include the use of "y" for "iy" and "sky" for "skiy" at the end of a name; omission of the short "i," except where it alters the sound of the preceding vowel, as in Sergei; and the apostrophe ordinarily employed to signify a soft sign.

The French transliteration customarily used on Soviet diplomatic passports has been modified thus: "ff" to "v," "ch" to "sh," "j" to "zh," "ou" to "u," "e" to "ye," and "iu" to "yu."

We further have deviated in the transliteration of first names and the transfer of first names into patronymic form. If a first name ends in a vowel, we have used "e" and "vich" but not "y." Thus, Arkadi becomes Arkadevich. In some instances "e" must be used twice because the first name ends in two vowels. For example, Sergei becomes Sergeevich, Aleksei becomes Alekseevich, and Andrei becomes Andreevich. First names ending in consonants are changed by adding "ovich": Borisovich, Pavlovich, Ivanovich. In female names, "ovna" after consonants and "evna" after vowels are used to form the patronyms.

ABALAKIN, Ivan Pavlovich: France 63–69; Switzerland 73

ABDULOV, Safar Nazarovich: Ethiopia 62–64 EXPELLED 64; Sudan 66–69

ABIALIEV, Mikhail S.: Venezuela 52 EXPELLED

ABRAMOV, Vladimir Mikhailovich: (GRU) Sweden 59–62; Ghana 66 EXPELLED; Indonesia 68

ABRAMOV, Vladimir Sergeevich: Norway 64–68

ABRASHKIN, Mikhail Y.: India 55–58; Pakistan 61–64 EXPELLED 64; Zanzibar 68–70

AFANSASIEV, Nikolai: Canada 45

AGADZHANOV, Eduard Bargatovich: Kenya 68

AGAYAN, Guerguen Semonovich: Italy 46–52; Iran 55–56; Italy 59–63

AGRAFENIN, Vladimir Alekseevich: Belgium 59–63; Switzerland 72

AISTOV, Yevgenni Sergeevich: West Germany 69

AKHMEROV, Robert I.: Switzerland 50–54; Ghana 62–66 EXPELLED 66

AKIMOV, Anatoli I.: New York 62–65; Great Britain EXPELLED 71

AKSENOV, Aleksandr Ivanovich: (GRU) Netherlands 69

AKSENOV, Aleksandr Pavlovich: Great Britain EXPELLED 71

AKSENOV, Konstantin: Belgium 52–55; Morocco 64–69

AKSENOV, Nikolai Vasilevich: Mexico 49–53; Mexico 56–59 EXPELLED 59; Cyprus 61–64; India 69–70

AKUTNIKOV, Gennadi Ivanovich: Italy 72

ALADKO, Ivan P.: Italy EXPELLED 54

ALEKSANDROV, Andrei Mikhailovich: (GRU) Sweden 40–47; New York 57*

ALEKSANDROV, Nikolai F.: India 63–66; Great Britain EXPELLED 71

ALEKSANDROV, Vladimir Ivanovich: (GRU) Italy 68–70 EXPELLED 70

ALEKSEEV, Aleksandr Ivanovich (Alias): See SHITOV, A. I.

ALEKSEEV, Dmitri I.: Great Britain 46–51; Great Britain 57–60; West Germany 62–63

ALEKSINSKY, Yuri Nikolaevich: (GRU) Norway 62–64

ALESHKIN, Aleksandr Vasilevich: (GRU) Sweden 45–50

ALFERYEV, Ivan G.: Mexico 60–64; Argentina 68

ALIPOV, Ivan Vasilevich: Great Britain 44–47; New York 50–55*; Iceland 58–61

ALLILUYEV, Nikolai Filipovich: Greece 54–57; Cameroon 63–67

ALYABYEV, Mikhail S.: Venezuela EXPELLED 52

AMOSOV, Igor Aleksandrovich: Washington EXPELLED 54; Cuba 68

ANANYEV, Georgi: Washington 56–60; Turkey 61–63; New York 63–67*

ANDREYEV, Andrei: Ghana 66

ANDREYEV, Igor Ivanovich: New York 58–63*; New York 65–69* EXPELLED 69

ANDREYEV, Mikhail Aleksandrovich: Italy 68–70

ANDREYEV, Vladislav V.: New Zealand 61–62 EXPELLED; Finland 65–70

ANDREYEV, Yevgenni V: Greece EXPELLED 60

ANDRONOV, Vladimir Vladimirovich: Finland 50–51; Italy 58–61; Morocco 64–71; Norway 72

ANDROSSOV, Grigori Vasilevich: Italy 56–60

ANISHCHENKO, Anatoli Dmitrevich: (GRU) Norway 62

ANISIMOV, Viktor: (GRU) Sweden 44–51

ANISIMOV, Yevgenni Ostapovich: (GRU) Canada 56–60; Egypt 62–65; Netherlands 70

ANISOMOV, Yuri Y.: Kenya EXPELLED 65

ANISSENKO, Mikhail: Paris 69–72*

ANISTRATOV, Sergei Ivanovich: Great Britain 56; Netherlands 61–63; West Germany 69–72

ANOSOV, Aleksei: Austria 65–67

ANTIPIN, Venyamin Vasilevich: France 47–51; Luxembourg 62–64; France 66–67; Sweden 70–72

ANTIPOV, Boris Nikitovich: West Germany 69–71

ANTIPOV, Mikhail Mikhailovich: New York 63–66, 69–72*

ANTONOV, Georgi Pavlovich: Italy 66–71

ANTONOV, Sergei N.: Austria 65–67

ANTONOV, Viktor Nikolaevich: Australia 52–54

APANASENKO, Viktor G.: Iran EXPELLED 60

ARTEMYEV, Stefan: (GRU) Sweden 40–42; Norway 45–46

ARTISHEVSKY, Yevgenni Ivanovich: Great Britain EXPELLED 71

ARUTYUNOV, Elmir Arshakovich: Iran EXPELLED 65

ASTAFYEV, Aleksandr Romanovich: Italy 55; Washington 64–68

ASTASKOV, Naum Petrovich: West Germany 58–59; Sweden 60–63; Norway 67–71

AVDEYENKO, Vasili A.: Ethiopia 50–52; Israel 57–63; Yugoslavia 64–67

AVDEYEV, Aleksei Ivanovich: Yugoslavia EXPELLED 57; Italy 67–70

AVETIAN, Norair Akopovich: Lebanon 63–67; France 70–71

AVRAMENKO, Oleg Vasilevich: Greece 58–62; Italy 63–70

AYKAZYAN, Eduard: (GRU) Great Britain EXPELLED 71

AZAROV, Ivan Pavlovich: Washington 51–55; Washington 61–62; Great Britain 67–71 EXPELLED 71

BACHINSKY, Vitali Dmitrevich; Turkey 59–70

BADIM, Mikhail Ilich: Italy 64–67; Austria 66

BAKHOLDIN, Aleksandr P.: Romania 72

BAKHTOV, Konstantin Konstantinovich: France 45–47; Belgium 49; France 50–52; Cuba 60–61; Italy 65–71

BAKURSKY, Aleksis Dmitrevich: (GRU) Sweden 46–47

BAKUSHIN, Nikolai Vasilevich: Thailand 66–70; Italy 72

BALACHOV, Vitali Dmitrevich: Belgium 61–62; Belgium 64–67 EXPELLED 67; North Vietnam 70

BALAKIREV, Nikolai Ivanovich: (GRU) Italy 54–59; France 62–65; Cambodia 67–70

BALAN, Georgi Yevdokimovich: (GRU) Mexico 48–52; Italy 56–60

BARABANOV, Ivan I.: Great Britain EXPELLED 55

BARANCHEYEV, Eduard Grigorevich: (GRU) France 63–66; Belgium 69–72

BELYAYEV, Yevgenni Aleksandrovich: Libya 61–65; Norway 67–71

BERDENNIKOV, Nikolai: Great Britain 62–67

BEREZIN, Aleksei S.: France EXPELLED 47

BEREZIN, Viktor V.: Washington EXPELLED 65

BEREZNOY, Vasili A.: (GRU) Afghanistan 43–45; Washington 48–51; Iran 53–56; Great Britain 57–58; France 64–68; Greece 70–73

BEZUKLADNIKOV, Vladimir Nikolaevich: Rhodesia 72

BIRYUKOV, Aleksei Petrovich: Norway 65–67; West Germany 71

BIRYUKOV, Igor D.: Great Britain 58–61; Great Britain 66–71 EXPELLED 71

BLAGUSHIN, Nikolai: Brazil

BLINOV, Boris Afanasevich: (GRU) Norway 60–64; Italy 69

BOBARYKIN, Nikolai B.: Great Britain EXPELLED 71

BOCHAROV, Ryurik Grigorevich: Denmark 71

BOGACHEV, Aleksandr Mikhailovich: Paris 68*

BOGACHEV, Anatoli Aleksandrovich: West Germany 56–68; Venezuela 61–62; Austria 62–65; Italy 66–69

BOGATY, Nikolai Y.: Yemen EXPELLED 60

BOGDANOV, Radomir Georgevich: Poland 54–56; India 57–59; India 60–67

BOGOMOLOV, Aleksandr: East Germany 54–56; East Germany 57–63; West Germany 66–71

BOGOMOLOV, Yevgenni Vasilevich: Netherlands 65–71

BOGOSLOVSKY, Vadim Aleksandrovich: Cuba 72

BOKAREV, Stepan I.: Ghana EXPELLED 66

BOLDIN, Nikolai Fedorovich: Somalia 62–65; Italy 68–71

BOLDYREV, Boris K.: Iran 72

BOLSHAKOV, Aleksandr V.: Mexico EXPELLED 71

BONDARENKO, Gennadi A.: Pakistan 57–58; Ceylon 58–59; New York 69–73

BONDAREV, Nikolai Vasilevich: Iceland 56–57; Sweden 61–64

BORDACHEV, Yuri Yakovlevich: Italy 57; India 62; Norway 66–69

BORISENKO, Aleksandr Ivanovich: Great Britain 68

BORISOV, Gennadi: Switzerland 49–55; Belgium 59–65

BORISOV, Gennadi Aleksandrovich: (GRU) West Germany 49–50, 53–56, 59–62; Italy 64–69; France 72

BORISOV, Ivan Dmitrevich: New York 49–51;* Sweden 57–60

BORISOV, Kim V.: (GRU) Finland EXPELLED 63

BORISOV, Mikhail Dmitrevich: Hungary 53–55; France 58–62, 67–72; New York 72–73*

BORISOV, Petr P.: China 47; Washington 50

BORISOV, Sergei Aleksandrovich: Greece 50–53; France 56–59; Cyprus 61–65; Italy 67–70

BORISOV, Vasili G.: San Francisco 46–58; Ethiopia 70

BORKUNOV, Aleksandr Pavlovich: Austria 59–63; West Germany 64–69

BORODIN, Viktor Mikhailovich: (GRU) Netherlands 63–65; India 68–70; France 72

BOROVINSKY, Petr Fedorovich: (GRU) Austria 60–64; West Germany 66–70; West Germany EXPELLED 70

BOROVSKY, Vitali N.: Cuba 62

BOYAROV, Vitali K.: Great Britain 63–65 EXPELLED 65

BOYKO, Arkadi Konstantinovich: East Germany 56–57; Netherlands 61–65; Tanzania 66–70

BRAGIN, Lev Alekseevich: New York 56–58*; Great Britain 61–63

BRATUS, Lev Sergeevich: West Germany 69–71

BREYTIGAM, Mikhail Florentevich: Great Britain EX-PELLED 71

BUBCHIKOV. I. A.: Washington EXPELLED 56

BUBNOV, Nikolai Ivanovich: (GRU) Burma 59–62; Norway 64–67

BUBNOV, Vladimir Andreevich: (GRU) Libya 62–65; Iceland 68

BUDAKHIN, Nikolai: West Germany 52

BUDAKOV, Aleksandr Ivanovich: Austria 58–63; Netherlands 65–70; Austria 72

BUDANOV, Viktor Georgevich: Great Britain EXPELLED 71

BUDNIK, Vladimir Sergeevich: France 47–54; Switzerland 56–57; Italy 59–63

BULAY, Boris Alekseevich: West Germany 58–62; East Germany 68

BULGAKOV, Anatoli Yakovlevich: Denmark 70

BULGAKOV, Thomas V.: Nationalist China EXPELLED 49; Thailand EXPELLED 62

BUNIN, Vladislav: Great Britain EXPELLED 71

BURDIN, Vladimir P.: Washington 44–46; Canada 49–55; member Khrushchev entourage 59 visit USA: East Germany 62–66

BURDYUKOV, Lev: New York 52–57;* Canada 59–62

BURINSKY, Mikhail A.: Switzerland 55

BURLAKOV, Viktor G.: Belgium EXPELLED 51

BUROV, Nikolai Ivanovich: New Zealand 49–53; New York* 57–61; Berne* 68

BURTSEV, Ivan V.: Greece 54

BURZOV, Gennadi Fedorovich: Switzerland 49–55; Belgium 59–65; Washington 67; Italy 71

BUTAKOV, Ilya Petrovich: (GRU) Italy 66–67; Italy 67–68

BUTENKO, Vladimir Pavlovich: Washington 63

BUZUNOV, Vladimir Antonovich: France 57–61; Iran 65–67; Denmark 71

BYCHKOV, Anatoli Y.: Canada EXPELLED 65

BYKOV, Nikolai Demidovich: (GRU) Mexico 54–59 EXPELLED 59; Italy 61–65

BYKOV, Yuri Vasilevich: Austria 57–60; Togo 61; New York 67*; Italy 68–72

CHEBRAKIN, Vladimir I.: Congo Kinshasa (Zaïre) 63–67 EXPELLED 67; France 71

CHECHETKINA, Olga I.: Italy EXPELLED 52

CHEGVINTSEV, Georgi Nikiforovich: (GRU) Sweden 55–59; Washington 65–68

CHEKALKIN, Igor Aleksandrovich: Sweden 72

CHEKMASOV, Vadim Grigorevich: Argentina 72

CHEKULAYEV, Yuri: India 65–67

CHEREMUKHIN, Yuri S.: Great Britain EXPELLED 71

CHERETUN, Vladimir I.: (GRU) Belgium 67

CHEREZOV, Boris Ivanovich: Turkey 64–69

CHERNETSOV, Yuri Yevgennevich: Great Britain 67–70 EXPELLED 71

CHERNEVKOV, Nikolai: Syria

CHERNOV, Leonid Ivanovich: Netherlands 55–58 EXPELLED 58

CHERNOV, Sergei Fedorovich: Sweden 62–66; Finland 72

CHERNY, Stefan: (GRU) Sweden 48–51

CHERNYKH, Vyacheslav Dmitrevich: Netherlands 70–73

CHERNYSHEV, Nikolai P.: Greece 53

CHERNYSHOV, Leonid Ivanovich: West Germany 72

CHERVYAKOV, Vladimir Ivanovich: (GRU) Sweden 59–64; Norway 69

CHERVYAKOV, Yevgenni S.: Egypt 52–53; Great Britain 54–56; Norway 59–60

CHESTNOY, Yuri Pavlovich: Argentina 56–60; Cuba 62–64; Geneva 68

CHETVERTUKHIN, Aleksandr Nikolaevich: Great Britain EXPELLED 71

CHISTYAKOV, Oleg V.: West Germany EXPELLED 55

CHIZHOV, Mikhail T.: Great Britain 51–52; Great Britain 56–61; Great Britain 62–66; Ceylon (Sri Lanka) 71

CHOBOTOV, Aleksei Sergeevich: (GRU) Norway 54–59, Norway 66–72

CHUCHUKIN, Vladimir Aleksandrovich: New York*

CHUMAK, Ivan Vasilevich: (GRU) Belgium 49; Sweden 50–54

CHURILIN, Anatoli Khrisanfovich: Austria 48; Finland 55–59; Sweden 64–66; Sweden 72

CHUSOVITIN, Valeri S.: Great Britain EXPELLED 71

CHUVAKHIN, Dmitri Stepanovich: Canada 38–42; Ambassador Canada 53–58; Ambassador Israel 64–67

DANILOCHKIN, Vladilen Ivanovich: India 65–69; Burma 71

DANILOV, Anatoli Aleksandrovich: China 42–49; Great Britain 57–62; Great Britain 63–66; Denmark 69

DANILOV, Vladimir Nikolaevich: Belgium 68–72

DANSHEVSKY, Vasili Ivanovich: Italy 50–53

DARENSKY, Dmitri Afanasevich: (GRU) Sweden 56–58; Afghanistan 61; Netherlands 65–67

DAVIDOV, Aleksandr: Belgium 56–59; Pakistan 60–61; Paris 62–67*

DAVIDOV, Aleksei I.: (GRU) Japan 53

DAVIDOV, Boris: Washington 69

DAVIDOV, Dmitri Dmitrevich: Sweden 55–57; Norway 60–63; Finland 66–70; Austria 72

DAVIDOV, Vladimir Ivanovich: Belgium 67–72

DEDOV, Yuri Sergeevich: Ghana 71

DEGTYAROV, Kusan Illaryonovich: Sweden 45–47

DEMIDOV, Nikolai V.: Argentina EXPELLED 61

DEMIN, Konstantin Alekseevich: New York *63–65; West Germany 67–70

DEMIN, Mikhail Aleksandrovich: (GRU) Israel 64–67; West Germany 69

DENISENKO, Anatoli L.: France EXPELLED 66

DENISKIN, Aleksei N.: (GRU) Great Britain EXPELLED 71

DENISOV, Ivan Aleksandrovich: (GRU) Sweden 48–50

DERYUGIN, Yuri Ivanovich: Sweden 63–66

DIAKANOV, Dmitri Alekseevich: Argentina EXPELLED 59; Brazil 63; Mexico 69–71 EXPELLED 71

DIDENKO, Vasili Semonovich: Canada EXPELLED 68

DIDYATEV, Dmitri: Burma 58–59

DIKUSHIN, Mikhail Aleksandrovich: Indonesia 58–63, 65–68; New York 71–73

DIMETROVSKY, Anatoli: Colombia 70

DMITREVICH, Yuri: West Germany 64

DMITRIEV, Albert V.: West Germany 62–66; Austria 69

DMITRIEV, Lev V.: Iceland EXPELLED 63

DOLGOV, Vladimir A.: Mexico 64–70

DOLYA, Fedor P.: Afghanistan 44–49; Thailand 50–56; India 60–61; Ambassador Nigeria 61–64 (wife also KGB)

DOMOGATSKY, Mikhail Georgevich: Rhodesia EXPELLED 64; Kenya EXPELLED 69

DOROFEEV, Sergei Ivanovich: Italy 57–62

DORONKIN, Kirill Sergeevich: New York EXPELLED 59*

DOZHDALEV, Vasili Alekseevich: South Africa 52–56; Great Britain 59–61

DRACHINSKY, Nikolai I.: Egypt 56

DRANKOV, Vasili Dmitrevich: Netherlands 54–57 EXPELLED 57; East Germany 60–

DROZDOV, Vladislav Alekseevich: Great Britain 68

DUBONOSOV, Andrei Ilich: (GRU) China 36; Great Britain 39–45; Great Britain 59–67; West Germany 72

DUDIN, Anatoli Mikhailovich: France 60–64; Italy 67–70

DUDIN, Yuri Vasilevich: London 63–68; Washington 71–73

DUGANOV, Vladimir M.: Tunisia 61

DUSHKIN, Yuri Aleksandrovich; Great Britain EXPELLED 68

DVIGANTSEV, Lev V.: Egypt 72

DYACHENKO, Oleg: Paris 66*

DYUDIN, Vladimir N.: Great Britain EXPELLED 71

DYUKOV, Nikolai Gavrilovich: Washington 50–55; Mexico 57–60; Cuba 61–63; Peru 71

DZHIRKVELOV, Ilya G.: Turkey EXPELLED; Sudan 71

EFENDIYEV, Fikrat I.: Iran EXPELLED 66

ELLIOTT, Rita (Alias): See YURYN, Esfir

FARAFANOV, Georgi Nikolaevich: Sweden 49–52; Sweden 58–63; Finland 66–71

FARMAKOVSKY, Vadim Vadimovich: (GRU) Sweden 62

FATAYEV, Albert Georgevich: Vienna 67*

FEDASHIN, Georgi: Belgium 59; Congo Kinshasa (Zaïre) 61–63; Belgium 68–72

FEDORENKO, Gennadi Gavrilovich: East Germany 56–58; Austria 60–61 EXPELLED 61

FEDOROV, Aleksandr I.: (GRU) Congo Brazzaville EXPELLED 63

FEDOROV, Ivan F.: Iran EXPELLED 54

FEDOROV, Valeri Alekseevich: (GRU) Great Britain 53–56; Netherlands 58–62; Poland 71–

FEDOROV, Vladilen Nikolaevich: Turkey 55–60; Iraq 65–67; Turkey 69–72

FEDOROV, Vladimir G.: Finland 67

FEDOROVSKY, Vyacheslav Ivanovich: Netherlands 55–61

FEDOSEEV, Mikhail Dmitrevich: India 59–63; Thailand 65–68; Denmark 72–

FEDOSEEV, Pavl Osifovich: (GRU) Denmark 57–61; Cyprus 63–65; Iran 67–69; Belgium 71; India 71–

FEDYANIN, Vladimir Petrovich: Austria 53–55; Sweden 58; Cuba 62–63

FEKLENKO, Vladimir Nikolaevich: Belgium EXPELLED 71

FILATEROV, Vladimir: Belgium 71

FILATOV, Aleksandr S.: Cuba EXPELLED 52

FILATOV, Nikolai A.: France EXPELLED 47

FILATOV, Robespier Nikolaevich: Ecuador EXPELLED 71

FILATOV, Vladimir Gerasimovich: Great Britain 55–58; Disarmament Con. 62; France 62–65; New York 66*; Great Britain 68–71 EXPELLED 71

FILIPOV, Anatoli Vasilevich: (GRU) Great Britain EXPELLED 71

FILIPOV, Ivan Filipovich: (GRU) Ambassador Sierra Leone 72

FILIPOV, Yuri Vladimirovich: New York 46–49*; Washington 59–62; New York 63–70*

FILKOV, Mikhail Kuzmich: (GRU) Sweden 52–56

FILONENKO, Viktor: (GRU) Great Britain EXPELLED 71

FIRSOV, Oleg Aleksandrovich: (GRU) Norway 66–68

FOKIN, Dmitri Fedorovich: Cyprus 71

FOMENKO, Pavl Nikolaevich: (GRU) Sweden 40–41; West Germany 57–61

FOMENKO, Valentin Petrovich: (GRU) Ghana 72

FOMENKO, Viktor, and wife Galina Ivanovna: Paris 62–70*

FOMIN, Aleksandr Mikhailovich: New York 41; Great Britain 47; Washington 60–68

FOMIN, Andrei Andronovich: New York 50–59*; Ambassador Brazil 62–65

FROLOV, Boris Petrovich: Switzerland EXPELLED 60

FROLOV, Konstantin: Argentina 62–67

FROLOV, Mikhail M.: Israel EXPELLED 67

FROLOV, Porfiry Vasilevich: (GRU) Sweden 48–51

FROLOV, Vycheslav Ivanovich: France 67

GALASHIN, Boris A.: Burma 57

GALAYEV, Nikolai Y.: (GRU) Austria EXPELLED 61

GALKIN, Aleksei Ivanovich: New York 63* (as Byelorussian delegate)

GALKIN, Vasili Pavlovich: Belgium 56–61; Italy 63–65; Switzerland 65–70

GAMOV, Prokopi I.: Denmark 60–66; Great Britain EXPELLED 71

GANIN, Vasili Ivanovich: Netherlands 66–70; Laos 70–71; Japan 71–

GAPON, Vsevolod Ivanovich: New York 58*

GAVRICHEV, Sergei Ivanovich: France 50–57; Switzerland 61–65

GAVRILOV, Nikolai Fedorovich: (GRU) Sweden 53–54

GENERALOV, Vsevolod Nikolaevich: (GRU) Washington 62; Great Britain EXPELLED 71

GENIK, Aleksandr A.: France EXPELLED 47

GERGEL, Yevgenni Ivanovich: New Zealand 56–61; Sweden 64–70

GETMAN, Yuri Filipovich: (GRU) West Germany 64–68

GLADKOV, Boris Fedorovich: New York EXPELLED 56*

GLADKY, Nikolai Ivanovich: Ghana 64–66 EXPELLED 66

GLAVATSKY, N. V.: Ireland 72

GLINSKY, Vladimir F.: Washington 60

GLOTOV, Viktor N.: Mexico 44–48; Venezuela 50–52; Mexico 53–57; Mexico 60–62; Uruguay 67–68 EXPELLED 68

GLUKHOV, Vladimir Alekseevich: (GRU) Great Britain 59–62; Netherlands 64–67 EXPELLED 67

GLUKHOVSKY, Vasili Vasilevich: Burma 55–58; Brazil 61–63; Ghana 65–66 EXPELLED 66; Pakistan 66–71

GLUSHCHENKO, Oleg Ivanovich: Belgium EXPELLED 71; Singapore 73

GOLANOV, Vladimir Yevgennevich: Belgium 50–52; Sweden 53–57; Sweden 60–66; Sweden 70–71; Cuba 71–

GOLOSHUBOV, Yuri Ilich: Sweden 61–66; Denmark 68; Finland 70

GOLOSOV, Arkadi Y.: (GRU) Washington 63

GOLOVANOV, Ivan A.: (GRU) Austria EXPELLED 70

GOLOVIN, Leonid Leonidovich: (GRU) Sweden 46–48

GOLOVKIN, Viktor Pavlovich: Netherlands 63–66

GOLUBOV, Sergei Mikhailovich: New York 61*; Washington 63–64; Cairo 67–69; Great Britain EXPELLED 71

GOLUZIN, Valentin Andreevich: Ecuador EXPELLED 71

GOLYAKOV, Anatoli S.: Great Britain EXPELLED 71

GONCHAROV, Gennadi Grigorevich: (GRU) Austria 58–61; Netherlands 63–65

GORBATOV, Yevgenni Nikolaevich: West Germany 70

GORDEYEV, Boris Stepanovich: Great Britain 71

GORDIK, Ivan: Morocco 61

GORLENKO, Yevgenni Yakulevich: Great Britain EXPELLED 71

GOROKHOV, Oleg Anatolevich: Turkey 65–70

GORSHKOV, Georgi Vasilevich: Italy 56–57; Italy 63–64

GORSHKOV, Valeri Petrovich: Colombia 69

GORSKY, Anatoli (alias Professor Nikitin): London 36–44; Washington 44

GORYUNOV, Georgi Vasilevich: Netherlands 56–58

GRACHEV, Aleksandr Fedorovich: Austria 53–56; Switzerland 65–69

GRACHEV, Nikolai Matveevich: (GRU) Sweden 50–53

GRANOV, Yuri Nikolaevich: West Germany 56–57; Austria 58–63; West Germany 64–66

GRAUER, Andrei G.: Sweden EXPELLED 41

GRECHANIN, Vladimir P.: (GRU) Washington EX-PELLED 64

GRECHKO, Ivan Akhminovich: Thailand 50–53; China 59; Ceylon 60–64; Thailand 66

GREMIAKIN, Igor: France 65–72

GRENKOV, Vladimir Fedorovich: Greece 62–66

GRESKO, Aleksandr A.: Great Britain EXPELLED 71

GREYDING, Yuri: Colombia 70

GRIBAN, Dmitri F.: (GRU) Congo Kinshasa (Zaïre) EX-PELLED 60

GRICHAKOV, Aleksei Mikhailovich: Sweden 62–63; Syria 63–67; Belgium 68–71

GRIGORIEV, Sergei Grigorevich: West Germany 58–59; West Germany 61–64

GRIGORIEV, Valentin Gerasimovich: (GRU) France 57–63; Italy 65–70; Denmark 72–

GRIGORIEV, Yuri Alekseevich: Czechoslovakia 68

GRINEV, Mikhail Ivanovich: Italy 64–69

GRISHAKOV, Aleksei Mikhailovich: Sweden 62; Syria 63–66; Belgium 68–72

GRIUCHIN, Arkadi Yakovlevich: France 54–59; Turkey 61

GROZNNY, Andrei V.: Great Britain EXPELLED 58

GRUSHA, Vladimir A.: New York 53–57* EXPELLED 57; Indonesia 59–61; Egypt 67–71

GRUSHKO, Viktor Fedorovich: Norway 54–58; Norway 62–66; Norway 68–72

GUBERMAN, Roman: Sweden 40–44

GUBICHEV, Valentin A.: New York 46–49* EXPELLED 49

GUBKIN, Aleksei P.: (GRU) France EXPELLED 72

GUDKOV, Andrei Fedorovich: Great Britain EXPELLED 54

GUERASSIMOV, Boris: (GRU) France 67–71

GUGIN, Valentin A.: Belgium EXPELLED 71

GULIEV, Leonid Aleksandrovich: (GRU) Brazil 72

GUNDAREV, Ivan Y.: Mexico 55–59; Washington 61–65; Austria 71

GURENKO, Vyacheslav Tikhonovich: (GRU) West Germany 56–60; West Germany 69–71

GUROV, Vasili Nikolaevich: Norway 70

GURYANOV, Aleksandr K.: New York EXPELLED 56*

GURYANOV, Oleg Aleksandrovich: Cuba 65–67; Netherlands 68–72

GUSAROV, Viktor Petrovich: Great Britain 55–61; Netherlands 63–68

GUSEV, Lev: Sweden 71

GUSEV, Petr Mikhailovich: (GRU) Sweden 40–44

GUSEV, Vasili Fedorovich: Cambodia 57–60; Congo Kinshasa (Zaïre) 60–63; West Germany 64–67

GUSHCHIN, Mikhail Ivanovich (Alias): See MUKACHEV, Mikhail F.

GUSHKOV, Ivan: Austria 54

GUSIN, Valentin: Ecuador EXPELLED 71

GUSOVSKY, Aleksandr: Algeria 44; France 44–58

GUZOV, Vladimir Vasilevich: Denmark 62–63; Denmark 67–68; Switzerland 71–

GVOZDEV, Yuri Ivanovich: Mexico 48–53; Washington 56–59; Brazil 65

IAKUKHIN, Dmitri Zakharovich: Romania 53; France 58–64

IBRAGIMOV, Ramiz: India 63–66

IGNATCHENKO, Boris Arkentevich: (GRU) Turkey 46–47; Burma 53–56; Afghanistan 65–69; Denmark 71–

IGNATOV, Vladimir Vasilevich: Laos 67–70

IKONNIKOV, Aleksei: India 57–60; Paris 71*

ILINTSEV, Valentin Ivanovich: Yale Univ 63–64; India 65

ILLARIONOV, Anatoli Nikolaevich: Austria 67–68; Denmark 70; Denmark 71–72

IONCHENKO, Nikolai Vasilevich: Turkey EXPELLED 56

IPPOLITOV, Ivan Ivanovich: Washington 47–51; Great Britain 54–57; Great Britain 69

ISAKOV, Vadim Anatolevich: India 53–58; New York 62–66* EXPELLED 66; Japan 68–71

ISTOMIN, Sergei Mikhailovich: Finland 47–51; Sweden 52–57

IVANOV, Anatoli N.: Great Britain EXPELLED 71

IVANOV, Anatoli Nikolaevich: (GRU) Netherlands 67–69

IVANOV, Anatoli Vasilevich: France 61–66; Belgium 69–71

IVANOV, Boris: New York 63

IVANOV, Feliks: Paris 59–65*; Mali 67–71

IVANOV, Igor Aleksandrovich: New York, convicted of espionage 1964 and sentenced 30 yrs. Presently in U.S.S.R. on $100,000 bail.

IVANOV, Konstantin: (GRU) Sweden 40–42

IVANOV, Mikhail Ivanovich: (GRU) China 72

IVANOV, Nikolai Iosifovich: Uruguay EXPELLED 66; Guinea 69

IVANOV, Oleg Nikolaevich: West Germany 68–71

IVANOV, Valentin Mikhailovich: Norway 48–49; New York 50–52; Washington 57–60 EXPELLED 60; Finland 63–68

IVANOV, Viktor M.: Great Britain 50–55; Iraq 58–62; Brazil 68

IVANOV, Viktor Vasilevich: (GRU) Turkey 52–57; Greece 57–60; Denmark 63–66; Sweden 67–69

IVANOV, Yevgenni M.: (GRU) Great Britain 63

IVANOV, Yuri Alekseevich: Denmark 55–60; Denmark 64–67; West Germany 72

IVASHCHENKO, Vladimir Gavrilovich: Sweden 43–47

IVASHKIN, Vladimir: (GRU) Laos 62–64; France 65–70

IVASHOV, Vasili Yegorovich: Argentina EXPELLED 59

IVLIYEV, Nikolai V.: Great Britain EXPELLED 58

IYYISHEV, Ivan I.: (GRU) Soviet High Commissioner Austria 54

IZVEKOP, Aleksandr Nikolaevich: Washington 60–65; Uganda 70

IZVEKOV, Nikolai Nikolaevich: Washington 45–48; Washington 56–57; East Germany 57–61; Australia 63–67; Netherlands 70–

KABALIN, Vladimir Nikolaevich: (GRU) Sweden 54–57

KABATOV, Yuri B.: New Zealand 64–67; Great Britain EXPELLED 71

KACHALOV, Mikhail: Italy 55–61

KALASHNIKOV, Aleksandr F.: Iran EXPELLED 65

KALENIKOV, Mikhail: Colombia 64

KALIN, Yuri Mikhailovich: Finland 72

KALININ, Mikhail: Burma 53–58

KALININ, Valeri Petrovich: Greece 59–63; Switzerland 68–

KALMYKOV, Grigori D.: Washington EXPELLED 61

KALMYKOV, Valeri Vasilevich: (GRU) Italy 65–68; Greece 70

KALUGIN, Oleg Danilovich: New York 60–64

KALUZHNY, Vladimir Romanovich: Canada 68

KAMAYEV, Yevgenni B.: Ghana EXPELLED 66

KAMCHATOV, Viktor Aleksandrovich: Belgium 55–59; France 62–66

KANAYEV, Georgi Yelisevich: Costa Rica 72

KAPALET, Lev Mikhailovich: Italy 63–68

KAPALKIN, Sergei Vasilevich: (GRU) France 50–53; Italy 60–66; North Vietnam 68–72

KAPITSA, Mikhail Stepanovich: Ambassador Pakistan EXPELLED 60

KAPLIN, Anatoli Stepanovich: Denmark 46–47; Sweden 47–53; Denmark 54–56; Norway 61–65; West Germany 71

KAPTSOV, Nikolai: New York 56–59*; Brazil 61

KARAKOV, Yuri Osipovich: Washington 61

KARELIN, Igor Borisovich: West Germany 70–72

KARELIN, Vladislav B.: Great Britain EXPELLED 71

KARGALTSEV, Ivan S.: Turkey 66

KARMANOV, Vladimir D.: Greece 46–47; Yugoslavia 49–52 EXPELLED 52

KARPEKOV, Nikolai Prokofevich: Great Britain 62

KARPENKO, Gennadi Andreevich: France 62–66; Colombia 68–71

KARPENKOV, Nikolai: New York 44–46; Italy 48–51; Yugoslavia 52–54; Great Britain 59–62

KARPOV, Gennadi: Colombia 72

KARPOV, Konstantin: Turkey 53–57; Turkey 61–66; France 67–72

KARPOVICH, Boris Vladimirovich: New York 54*; New York 57–60*; New York 62*; Washington 63–65 EXPELLED 65

KARPOVICH, Kirill B.: Nigeria 66–70

KARYAGIN, Viktor Vasilevich: West Germany 54–58; Great Britain EXPELLED 71

KARYAKIN, Vladimir M.: (GRU) Belgium EXPELLED 71

KARYUKIN, Aleksandr Sem: Belgium 56–62; France 68–71 EXPELLED 71

KASHLEV, Yuri B.: Austria 58–60*; Great Britain EXPELLED 71

KASHVA, Nikolai S.: France EXPELLED 47

KATACHINSKY, Viktor Semenovich: (GRU) Italy 67–70

KATALOV, Aleksandr Grigorevich: (GRU) Netherlands 54–58

KATASONOV, Sergei V.: (GRU) Great Britain 55

KATAYEV, Valeri V.: Ghana EXPELLED 66

KAUNAFIN, Khabib A.: Congo Brazzaville 62; Congo Kinshasa (Zaïre) 63 EXPELLED 63

KAVERZNEV, Mikhail Kirillovich: East Germany 52

KAZAKEVICH, Vladimir D.: New York 48

KAZAKOV, Viktor Fedorovich: Belgium 59–62; France 64–68

KAZANTSEV, Aleksei Nikolaevich: Ghana EXPELLED 67

KAZIMIROV, Vladimir: Hungary 56; Brazil 64; Ambassador Costa Rica 71

KAZIN, Viktor: Switzerland 57–58; France 68–71

KEDROV, N. (Alias): See PAVLOV, Vitali Grigorevich

KEDROV, Nikolai: Canada 42–46; Australia 52–54; Uruguay 58–61; Austria 66–70

KEDROV, Viktor Nikolaevich: (GRU) Great Britain 64–68; Denmark 71–

KHABALOV, Nikolai Andreanovich: Sweden 62–64

KHACHATUROV, Karen: Uruguay 57–62; Brazil 65

KHALDEYEV, Arkadi Aleksandrovich: New Zealand 60–65; Denmark 66–71

KHARKOVETS, Georgi I.: Australia 51–54 EXPELLED 54; Bern 60–62*; Rhodesia 65–68

KHLOPYANOV, Vasili Ilich: Thailand EXPELLED 71

KHLYSOV, Boris V.: Iraq 53

KHMELEV, Vladimir Aleksandrovich: Japan 57–59; Japan 62–67; Japan 70

KHMYZ, Vasili P.: Great Britain EXPELLED 71

KHOBOTOV, Nikolai I.: Italy EXPELLED 54

KHODNENKO, Paul Vladimirovich: Belgium 48–50; Greece 56–60

KHODZHAYEV, Yuri T.: Great Britain EXPELLED 71

KHOKHLOV, Nikolai Afanasevich: France 54–58; France 61–64; Syria 66; Italy 72–

KHOKHLOV, Nikolai P.: Congo Kinshasa (Zaïre) EXPELLED 65

KHOKHLOV, Valeri Mikhailovich: Italy 67–72

KHOMENKO, Oleg Nikolaevich: Canada 65

KHOMENKO, Viktor V.: Norway EXPELLED 62

KHOMYAKOV, Aleksandr Sergeevich: (GRU) Turkey 50–55; Lebanon EXPELLED 69

KHOTULEV, Bronislav Pavlovich: (GRU) East Germany 56–57; West Germany 59–63; East Germany 65–72

KHRENIN, Pavel Aleksandrovich: (GRU) Great Britain 59–63; New York 69–73

KHRENOV, Vladimir Mikhailovich: Paris 62–64*; New York 71*

KHRISTOFOROV, Yuri I.: Greece 70–73

KHRYACHKOV, Boris Fedorovich: Denmark 53–60; Canada 67; Iceland 69–

KHURBATOV, Georgi Alekseevich: Colombia EXPELLED 72

KHURUMOV, Yuri Petrovich: Italy 72

KIKTEV, Sergei Petrovich: Turkey 47–48; Egypt 50–54; Ambassador Lebanon 55–61; Ambassador Afghanistan 70–72; Ambassador Morocco 72–73

KILDISHEV, Yakov S.: Belgium EXPELLED 60

KIREYEV, Anatoli Tikonovich: New York 53–57*; Washington 59–63; New York 66–67* EXPELLED 67

KIRILYUK, Vadim Aleksandrovich: New York 59–60* EXPELLED 60

KIRPICHENKO, Vadim: Egypt 70

KIRPICHEV, Dmitri Ivanovich: West Germany 61

KIRSANOV, Stepan Mikhailovich: France 61–62; Washington 64–65 EXPELLED 65; Ethiopia 66–69

KIRYANOV, Anatoli: China 61–65; Ethiopia 65–70

KIRYENKOV, Vladimir Mikhailovich: Sweden 59-62

KISAMEDINOV, Maksut Mustarkovich: Ghana EXPELLED 66

KISELEV, Anatoli: (GRU) Sweden 46–51

KISELEV, Ivan Pavlovich: Ghana EXPELLED 66

KISELEV, Lev Sergeevich: Iceland EXPELLED 63

KISELEV, Vladimir Ivanovich: Netherlands 55–59; Brazil 62–64; Peru 69–

KISHILOV, Nikolai Sergeevich: (GRU) Finland 53–58; West Germany 61–66

KISLITSIN, Filip Vasilevich: Great Britain 45–48; Australia 52–54

KITAEV, Yuri Konstantinovich: Netherlands 55–59; Washington 64–69

KLEYMENOV, Mikhail Fedorovich: (GRU) Geneva 67*

KLIMENKO, Anatoli Filipovich: (GRU) Sweden 57–58

KLIMIN, Vadim: Kenya EXPELLED 65

KLIMOV, Dmitri Petrovich: (GRU) Sweden 41–44

KLIMOV, Igor K.: Great Britain EXPELLED 71

KLOKOV, Vladilen Vasilevich: New York EXPELLED 62*

KLYUSOV, Serafim Timofeevich: (GRU) Sweden 53–57; Sweden 63–64

KOBAKHIDZE, Konstantin: France EXPELLED

KOBELEV, Fedor Mikhailovich: West Germany 69

KOBYSH, Vitali Ivanovich: Brazil EXPELLED 66

KOCHEGAROV, Yevgenni Mikhailovich: (GRU) Netherlands 60–62; Geneva 65–69 EXPELLED 69*

KOCHESHKOV, Anatoli N.: Cameroon EXPELLED 67

KOCHETKOV, Aleksandr: (GRU) Italy 60–64

KOCHUBEY, Yuri Nikolaevich: Rome 57*; New York 58–62*; New York 63–68 as Ukrainian*

KODAKOV, Vladimir Aleksandrovich: Sudan 56–59; Ghana 59–62; Kenya 64–66 EXPELLED 66; Libya 68–71

KOKOREV, Genrikh Vasilevich: (GRU) West Germany 59–63; Austria 65–69; West Germany 72

KOLCHIN, Aleksei I.: (GRU) Washington 63

KOLESNICHENKO, Mikhail G.: Rhodesia EXPELLED 64

KOLESNIKOV, Mikhail I.: Colombia EXPELLED 64

KOLESNIKOV, Vladimir S.: Washington 72, 73

KOLESOV, Dmitri Ivanovich: (GRU) Denmark 47–53; Sweden 58–63

KOLK, August Savlovich: Sweden 57–59

KOLODYAZHNY, Boris G.: Great Britain EXPELLED 71

KOLOMYAKOV, Boris Pavlovich: Mexico EXPELLED 71

KOLYCHEV, Yuri Konstantinovich: Great Britain EX-PELLED 71

KOMAROVSKY, Fedor Petrovich: (GRU) Great Britain EX-PELLED 71

KOMIAKOV, Aleksandr: (GRU) Lebanon EXPELLED 69

KOMISAROV, Danil S.: Iran 41–48

KOMUSHKIN, Vladislav: Mexico 68

KONDRASHEV, Sergei Aleksandrovich: Great Britain 53–55; Austria 57–62; West Germany 66–67

KONDRATENKO, Yuri Aleksandrovich: Denmark 61–65; Great Britain 69–71 EXPELLED 71

KONEV, Boris Aleksandrovich: (GRU) West Germany 49–52; Sweden 54–57; Austria 59–61

KONOBEYEV, Valdimir Petrovich: (GRU) Sweden 51–55; Great Britain 60–64; Great Britain 64–72

KONONOV, Lev D.: (GRU) Japan 71

KONOVALEV, Ivan: (GRU) New York EXPELLED 54

KONOVALOV, Aleksei Dmitrevich: Austria 58–60; West Germany 66–68

KONOVALOV, Leonid Nikolaevich: (GRU) Sweden 58–63; Denmark 65–69

KONOVALOV, Mikhail: Belgium 71

KONOVALOV, Vladimir I.: Yugoslavia 64

KONSTANTINOV, Igor Konstantinovich: Great Britain EX-PELLED 71

KOPALIN, Vladimir: Egypt 68–70

KOPEYKIN, Gennadi Nikolaevich: (GRU) Great Britain EX-PELLED 71

KOPTELTSEV, Valentin Alekseevich: West Germany 56–58; East Germany 62–65; West Germany 72

KOPYTIN, Viktor V.: Student California 61–62; New York 64; Washington 65–69 EXPELLED 69

KORETSKY, Vladimir Petrovich: France 57–61; Belgium 65–71

KORINFSKY, Georgi Mikhailovich: Belgium EXPELLED 71

KORMAKOV, Yevstigney Dmitrevich: Norway 63–71; France 71–

KORNEICHUK, Yevgenni Kalinnikovich: Great Britain 57–58; West Germany 58–64; Netherlands 68–70; Italy 72–73

KORNIYENKO, Anatoli Yakovlevich: Washington 57–60; Egypt 63–65; Switzerland 68–73

KORNIYENKO, Yuri Fedorovich: (GRU) Great Britain EX-PELLED 71

KOROBOV, Vladimir I.: Great Britain EXPELLED 71

KOROLEV, Boris: Canada 68

KOROLEV, Viktor I.: Greece 71–73

KOROLEV, Yevgenni Vasilevich: Austria 58–62; West Germany 64

KOROLEV, Yuvenali I.: France 60–65 EXPELLED 65

KOROTKIKH, Nikolai Georgievich: London University 64–65; Denmark 66–70

KOROTKOV, Aleksandr: East Germany 57–61

KOROVIKOV, Valentin Ivanovich: Ghana EXPELLED 67

KOROVYAKOV, Manuil Aleksandrovich: (GRU) Italy 49–51; Netherlands 55–58; France 62–65; North Vietnam 71–73

KORSHUNOV, Mikhail: (GRU) Sweden 46

KORYAKUSKY, Aleksandr P.: (GRU) India 70; Egypt 72

KOSELOV, Dmitri I.: Denmark EXPELLED 53

KOSHELEV, Vladimir: Norway 51

KOSOLAPOV, Anatoli I.: Belgium 64–67; Lebanon 69

KOSOV, Mikhail Borisovich: Hungary 40–41; Sweden 42–45; Denmark 46–50; Norway 63–67; Finland 67–70; Sweden 71–73

KOSOV, Nikolai Antonovich: Washington 48–52; Washington 52–55; Netherlands 57–62

KOSTIKOV, Lev; Paris 67*

KOSTIKOV, Valeri Vladimirovich: Mexico 68 EXPELLED 68

KOSTIN, Valeri Dmitrevich: Netherlands 66–69; Finland 71–

KOSTRYTSIN, Boris Vladimirovich: Latin America 58–61; Brazil 63

KOSTYLEV, Valentin Petrovich: Turkey and Iran 43–51; France 54–58; Belgium 62–65

KOSYUKOV, Yuri Leonidovich: China EXPELLED 66

KOTCHOUBEI, Yuri: New York 61–62*; Paris 71* (as Ukrainian)

KOTIK, Paul: Uruguay 51

KOTOV, Mikhail: Finland 45–48; Finland 55–57; Finland 70–71

KOTOV, Yuri M.: Dahomey 63–65; Mali 65–67; France 68–69

KOTUSOV, Aleksandr I.: Great Britain EXPELLED 71

KOVAL, Nikolai Danilovich: Sweden 56–60; Sweden 63–66

KOVALENKO, Ivan I.: Japan 48; Japan 67

KOVALENKO, Petr Timofeevich: Italy 51–52; Italy 54–59; Italy 62–64; Ivory Coast 67–69; France 72

KOVALEV, Aleksandr Petrovich: New York EXPELLED 54*

KOVALEV, Anatoli Pavlovich: (GRU) Norway 71

KOVALEV, Leonid A.: New York 57–60*; Ceylon (Sri Lanka) 64–68

KOVALEV, Nikolai Grigorevich: Australia 54

KRYLOV, Lev V.: Venezuela EXPELLED 52

KRYLOV, Yuri Pavlovich: Washington EXPELLED 57; China 66

KUCHYUMOV, Aleksandr M.: Greece EXPELLED 67

KUDASHKIN, Fedor D.: New York 58–63*; Cuba 66–69; Somalia 71

KUDRYASHOV, Aleksandr Konstantinovich: West Germany 72

KUDRYASHOV, Vladimir Nikolaevich: (GRU) Netherlands 57–63

KUDRYAVTSEV, Sergei Mikhailovich: Austria 37–38; Germany 40–41; Turkey 41–42; Canada 42–45; West Germany 45–47; Ambassador Austria 52–55; West Germany 55–57; France 59–60; Cuba 60–61; Ambassador Cuba 61–62; West Germany 65–67; Ambassador Cambodia 67–70; Paris 71–72*

KUDRYAVTSEV, Viktor: Egypt 71

KULAKOV, Aleksandr Alekseevich: Great Britain 58–62; Denmark 66–70

KULIKOV, Arkadi: France 50–55

KULIKOV, Ivan Aleksandrovich: Paris 57*; Great Britain 66–71 EXPELLED 71

KUNICHKIN, Dmitri Vasilevich: (GRU) West Germany 57–62

KUPLIAKOV, Yuri V., wife KUPLIAKOVA, Yekaterina A.: Israel 56–58; Uganda 63–66; Mexico 68–71

KUPRIK, Boris Fedorovich: West Germany 65–68

KUPRYANOV, Dmitri Vladimirovich: Belgium 71

KUPRYANOV, Porfiri: Greece 57–61; Cyprus 67–70

KURITSYN, Yuri Vasilevich: Kenya 64–66 EXPELLED 66; Nigeria 70

KURKURIN, Vladimir Ilich: Switzerland 60

KUROCHKIN, Nikolai Ivanovich: Washington EXPELLED 58

KUROCHKIN, Yuri Pavlovich: Italy 55–57

KURSHIN, Arkadi: East Germany 63–64; France 68–71

KURYANOV, Yevgenni Ivanovich: Canada 64–66

KUSHLEVICH, Nikolai F.: Italy 57

KUTUZOV, Yevgenni I.: Great Britain EXPELLED 71

KUZIN, Vladimir: New York 61–63*

KUZIN, Yevgenni F.: Great Britain EXPELLED 71

KUZMIN, Lori T.: Great Britain EXPELLED 71

KUZMINYCH, Nikolai Ivanovich: Sweden 71

KUZNETSOV, Albert Mikhailovich: West Germany 65–66

KUZNETSOV, Anatoli Ivanovich: Iran EXPELLED 56

KUZNETSOV, Anatoli Vasilevich: Great Britain 57–59; New York 62–66; Great Britain EXPELLED 68

LAVRISHCHEV, Aleksandr Andreevich: Bulgaria 47; Ambassador Turkey 48–53

LAVROV, Ivan Mikhailovich: Austria 57–60; West Germany 62–65; Mauritania 65–68; Zaïre 70

LAVROV, Valeri Alekseevich: (GRU) Great Britain EXPELLED 71

LAVRUSHKO, Igor P.: India EXPELLED 68

LAZAREV, Anatoli Ivanovich: France 49–58; France 59–66; Uruguay 67

LAZAREV, Oleg Borisovich: (GRU) Great Britain EXPELLED 71

LEBEDEV, Nikolai Kuzmich: (GRU) Netherlands 46–50; Netherlands 56–59

LEBEDEV, Sergei Mikhailovich: Great Britain 58–64; Norway 67–68; India 70–

LEBEDEV, Yevgenni S.: Japan 51–52; India 62–66

LEBEDINSKI, Roald: China 65–66; France 70

LEMEKHOV, Dmitri Aleksandrovich: (GRU) Sweden 44–48; Denmark 56–58; Netherlands 59–62; Finland 64–65

LEMZENKO, Kir Gavrilovich: (GRU) Italy 62–66 EXPELLED 66

LENEV, Nikolai Ivanovich: (GRU) Belgium 71–73

LENSKY, Yakov K.: West Germany EXPELLED 55

LEONOV, Anatoli Fedorovich: (GRU) Israel 57–60; Norway 61; Iran 62–65; West Germany 66; Norway 67–72

LEONOV, Petr Ivanovich: Netherlands 53–56

LEONOV, Vladimir Alekseevich: (GRU) Great Britain EXPELLED 71

LEONOV, Vladimir F.: Japan 72

LEONTIEV, Konstantin Ivanovich: Belgium EXPELLED 71

LEONTIEV, Leonid A.: Great Britain EXPELLED 71

LEPESHKIN, Leonid Ilich: Sweden 54–57; Norway 60–64; Norway 66–71

LESSIOVSKY, Viktor Mechislavovich: Burma 53–57; Thailand 58; Australia 59; New York 60–73*

LESTOV, Vadim: Cuba EXPELLED 67

LEVCHENKO, Anatoli Mikhailovich: West Germany 71

LEVCHENKO, Nikolai Ivanovich: Sweden 60; Nigeria 66; Japan 70

LEVIN, Yevgenni: East Germany 56–58

LEVINOV, Nikolai Y.: West Germany 56–60

LIPASOV, Viktor Ivanovich: Denmark 72

LISENKO, Igor Aleksandrovich: West Germany 60–63; New York* 69–71

LISOVSKY, Ivan: Hungary 47–50; Sweden 51–56

LITOVKIN, Grigori Yekulevich: Austria 53–54

LITVAK, Leonid Leontevich: Netherlands 63–67; Cyprus 69–71; Greece 71

LITVAK, Lev Fedorovich: Colombia 71

LITVINETS, Sergei Nikolaevich (also known as Sergei Ivanovich and as I. S. Ruban): Norway 63

LITVINOV, Yuri Mikhailovich: Finland 62–64; Norway 70–72

LOBACHEV, Aleksandr Ivanovich: Egypt 72

LOBACHEV, Vladimir C.: Washington 53–56; North Vietnam 60–65; India 65–69

LOBANOV, Anatoli Aleksandrovich: Sweden 56–57; Norway 58–61; Denmark 64–69; Denmark 71–72

LOBANOV, Vitali Ilich: (GRU) Austria 62–64; Italy 66–68

LOBANTSEV, Vladimir: (GRU) France 68

LOGINOV, Anatoli Fedorovich: Canada EXPELLED 61; India 67

LOGINOV, Igor K: (GRU) France 62–65 EXPELLED 65; Switzerland 67–70

LOGINOV, Valentin: Mexico EXPELLED 71

LOGINOV, Vladimir A.: Great Britain 65–68 EXPELLED 68

LOMAKIN, Boris Grigorevich: Egypt 58–59; Italy 69–71

LOMAKIN, Paul Ivanovich: Cyprus 64–67

LOMAKIN, Yakov I.: New York EXPELLED 48

LOPATIN, Aleksandr Georgevich: Sweden 67–72

LOPUKHOV, Georgi: France 63–70

LOSEV, Aleksandr A.: Indonesia 62

LUBIAKO, Igor Mikhailovich: Washington 62–66; France 70

LUI, Vitali Yevgennevich: KGB "newsman" better known as Victor Louis, who frequently travels abroad.

LUKASHIN, Ivan Sergeevich: Sweden 58–63

LUKYANOV, Pavl Pavlovich: New York 50–54*; New York 56–61*; Washington 63–65

LUKYANOV, Sergei Grigorevich: Washington 43–47; Sweden 55–56

LVOV, Valentin: Czechoslovakia 57–59; Paris 63–71*

LYALIN, Mikhail Amosovich: (GRU) Denmark 59–63; Norway 69–72

LYKOV, Stepan Mikhailovich: (GRU) Sweden 53–56

LYSENKO, Igor A.: West Germany 60–63; New York 69–70*

LYSENKO, Nikolai Y.: France 56–62; West Germany 63–65

LYSHCHIN, Mikhail N.: Turkey EXPELLED 57

LYSSYKH, Ivan: Mali EXPELLED 72

LYUBIMOV, Mikhail P.: Finland 58–59; Great Britain 61–65; Denmark 67–70

LYUBIMOV, Viktor Andreevich: (GRU) Washington 53–57; France 61–65; Netherlands 69–72

LYUDIN, Yuri Ivanovich (alias Yuri Ivanovich MODIN): India 67

LYUKSHIN, Ilya P.: Uruguay EXPELLED 66

MACHKOVTSEV, Nikolai: Cyprus 67

MAKARCHENKO, Leonid K.: Italy 52–62; Uruguay 62–66; Chile 69–72

MAKARENKO, Boris V.: Great Britain EXPELLED 71

MAKAREVICH, Igor Vladimirovich: Pakistan 63–66; (GRU) Great Britain EXPELLED 71

MAKAROV, Aleksandr L.: (GRU) Japan 48; Washington 64–67

MAKAROV, Boris Andreevich: Netherlands 64–69

MAKAROV, Leonid Alekseevich: Denmark 67–72

MAKAROV, Mikhail Kirillovich: Great Britain 68–69; Denmark 71–72

MAKAROV, Rudolf Vasilevich: West Germany 68–72

MAKAROV, Vasili Georgevich: Belgium 55–58; Togo 60–63; New York 69–71*

MAKEYEV, Nikolai Gerasimovich: Great Britain 50–56; West Germany 56–57; Finland 60–61

MAKHLUYEV, Vladimir Aleksandrovich: Italy EXPELLED 55

MAKSIMOV, Vladimir Borisovich: Sweden 65–69

MAKSIMOV, Vladimir Mikhailovich: (GRU) Austria 63–67; West Germany 70

MAKSIMOV, Yuri Vladimirovich: Turkey 61–65; Turkey 67–68 EXPELLED 68

MAKURIN, Pavl: France 59–65; Algeria 67–71

MAKUSHKIN, Fedor Semenovich: (GRU) Sweden 43–47

MAKUSKY, Ignet Nikandrovich: (GRU) Finland 45; Austria 55–61; Sweden 63–69

MALAKHOV, Valentin Sergeevich: Netherlands 51–53; Belgium 55–60; Nigeria 63–65; Burma 69–71

MALAKHOV, Vasili Ivanovich: (GRU) Italy 59–63; Somalia 69

MALAKHOV, Vasili P.: Kenya EXPELLED 67

MALIKOV, Aleksei P.: Turkey EXPELLED 57

MALIN, Fyodor Petrovich (Alias): See MELHISHEV, Petr Pavlovich

MALININ, Aleksei Romanovich: Washington EXPELLED 66

MALYSHEV, Aleksei Anatolevich: France 60–66; Italy 71

MALYSHEV, Konstantin Yakovlevich: Iran 57; Netherlands 61; Sweden 62–65; Finland 68

MALYSHEV, Viktor Vasilevich: Belgium 72

MAMEDOV, Riza Mamed Ali Ogli: Turkey 63–67

MAMONTOV, Yuri Leonidovich: Argentina 67–70 EX-PELLED 70

MAMURIN, Leonid Aleksandrovich: Thailand EXPELLED 66

MAMYSHEV, Aleksei F.: Greece 69–73

MANTYUKOV, Boris Fedorovich: Colombia 72

MARAKAZOV, Afansi Iosifovich: Britain 52

MAREYEV, Sergei K.: Switzerland 53–57; Cyprus 63–66; Greece 70

MARKELOV, Valeri Ivanovich: New York 72*

MARKIN, Vasili Petrovich: (GRU) Sweden 52–55

MARKOV, Roman Aleksandrovich: Rhodesia 72

MARLAGIN, Aleksandr N.: Turkey EXPELLED 57

MARTINOV, Maksim Grigorevich: New York EXPELLED 55*

MASHIN, Anatoli Georgevich: Belgium EXPELLED 71

MASHKANTSEV, Gennadi Fedorovich: Washington EX-PELLED 57

MASHNIN, Nikolai V.: New York 65–66; Canada 68–70

MASLENNIKOV, Nikolai: Poland EXPELLED 57

MASLENNIKOV, Petr E.: New York 63*

MASLOVSKI, Georgi Borisovich: Sweden 69–73

MATUKHIN, Georgi Gavrilovich: Uruguay EXPELLED 68

MATUSHIN, Anatoli Nikolaevich: Ghana EXPELLED 66

MATUSHIN, Gennadi F.: India 62–66

MATVEYEV, Viktor: India 52–56; Ethiopia 66–69 EX-PELLED 69

MAYOROV, Ivan Sergeevich: Greece 54–59 EXPELLED 59; Geneva 62*; France 63–64; Morocco 67–72

MAZAYEV, Mikhail Kuzmich: Switzerland 52–55; Japan 57–60; Cyprus 61–67; Norway 70–72

MAZTIKYAN, Ruben G.: Cyprus 69–73

MAZYAKIN, Vladimir Ivanovich: (GRU) Switzerland 54–57; Norway 68–70

MEDNIKOV, Viktor N.: Mexico 68–69 EXPELLED 69

MEDNIS, Vladimir Augustovich: Great Britain 59–63; Sweden 65–69

MEDVEDEV, Yuri Fedorovich: Kenya 64–67; Italy 71–73

MEDVEDOVSKY, Pavl M.: Italy 67

MELEKH, Igor Yakovlevich: New York EXPELLED 61*

MELHISHEV, Petr Pavlovich: (GRU) Consul New York 41–45; Europe 57–62 (handler of Wennerström)

MELNICHENKO, Yevstafi Ivanovich: Turkey 63–66

MELNIK, Vladimir I.: Great Britain EXPELLED 71

MESHEVITINOV, Boris S.: Norway 50–54 EXPELLED 54

MESHKOV, Boris P.: Great Britain EXPELLED 71

MESROPOV, Valeri Moisevich: (GRU) Norway 68–70 EXPELLED 70

METKIN, Mikhail V.: Pakistan EXPELLED 61

METKOV, Vyacheslav: Austria 54

MIAKUSHKO, Vasili: France 55–57; Paris 57–60* EXPELLED 60

MIKHAILOV, Boris A.: Austria 54

MIKHAILOV, Boris Nikolaevich: (GRU) Denmark 58–62; Netherlands 66–71

MIKHAILOV, Georgi: (GRU) Sweden EXPELLED 47

MIKHAILOV, Pavl Petrovich (Alias): See MELHISHEV, Petr Pavlovich

MIKHAILOV, Yevgenni Fedorovich: East Germany 51–56

MIKHAILOVICH, O. M.: Italy 58

MIKHAILOVICH, Yevgenni F.: Canada 67

MIKHEYEV, Vladimir Petrovich; Washington 56

MIKHEYEV, Vladislav Aleksandrovich: West Germany 67–72

MILOVIDOV, Igor V.: Great Britain 58–60

MILOVZOROV, Yuri Dmitrevich: Great Britain 45–49; Netherlands 59–61

MIRONOV, Albert Alekseevich: Denmark 66–67; Denmark 68–

MIRONOV, Andrei Mikhailovich: Turkey 49–55; Lebanon 57; Syria 58–61; Turkey 70–72

MIROSHNICHENKO, Petr Fedorovich: (GRU) Italy 55–61

MIROSHNIKOV, Petr Sergeevich: Sweden 51–56 EXPELLED 56; East Germany 59–64

MISHUKOV, Yuri A.: New York 57–62* EXPELLED 62

MITITEL, Fedor S.: Greece EXPELLED 62

MITKOV, Rotislav L.: Switzerland EXPELLED 59

MITROPOLSKY, Yuri Alekseevich: (GRU) West Germany 55–59; Cuba 62–63; Mexico 64–69; Geneva 71*

MIZIN, Viktor V.: Thailand EXPELLED 71

MOCHALOV, Georgi Aleksandrovich: Denmark 70; Sweden 72–73

MOCHAYEV, Vsevolod Yevgennevich: Finland 53–55

MODIN, Nikolai Konstantinovich: Switzerland 58–60 EXPELLED 60; Dahomey 64–65; Togo 65–68

MODIN, Yuri Ivanovich (Alias): See LYUDIN, Y. I.

MODNOV, Igor Semenovich: West Germany 63–66 EXPELLED 66

MOISEYEV, Boris: Ghana 65

MOKRETSOV, Ilya Alekseevich: Sweden 50–56; Sweden 59–64

MOLCHANOV, Aleksandr Alekseevich: Washington 46–49; Great Britain 53–56; Geneva 69–73*

MOLCHANOV, Valentin M.: Washington EXPELLED 64

MOLEV, Vasili Mikhailovich: Washington EXPELLED 57

MONAKHOV, Konstantin Petrovich: Mexico 43–46; Argentina 48–53; Argentina 58–59; Cuba 60–63; Italy 67–69 EXPELLED 69

MOROZOV, Aleksandr D.: Argentina EXPELLED 56

MOROZOV, Anatoli Grigorevich: (GRU) Finland 61–63; Washington 64–66; Norway 70–72

MOROZOV, Ivan A.: West Germany EXPELLED 65; Indonesia 66

MOROZOV, Ivan Yakovlevich: (GRU) Geneva 72*

MOROZOV, Nikolai Mikhailovich: Sweden 54–58; Norway 63–67

MOROZOV, Oleg Nikolaevich: Italy 68–72

MOROZOV, Yuri V.: Great Britain EXPELLED 71

MOSEVNIN, Yevgenni Ivanovich: East Germany 67–69

MOSKALENKO, Ivan S.: Austria 56–61; France 62–66; Austria 69–72

MOSOLOV, Arnold Ivanovich: Great Britain 59–63; Norway 64–69; Costa Rica 71

MOZHENKO, Yuri: Italy 49–53; Italy 59–63

MUKACHEV, Mikhail Fedorovich (alias Mikhail Ivanovich Gushchin): Venezuela 72

MUKHIN, Mikhail Lukich: Chile EXPELLED 47; Uruguay 66; Costa Rica 70

MUKHITDINOV, Nuridin Akramovich: Syria 67

MURASHEV, Yevgenni: Great Britain 56–60; Canada 63–65

MURATOV, Yevgenni Georgevich: Iran 56–59; Tunisia 61–63; Senegal 67–71

MURAVYEV, Vasili Mikhailovich: Brazil 61–63

MURNIKOV, Mikhail A.: Canada 65–70

MUSATOV, Aleksandr: (GRU) Romania EXPELLED 72

MYAKISHEV, Aleksei Nikolaevich: (GRU) Thailand 57–60; Netherlands 61–64; Singapore 66–71

MYAKOTNIK, Yuri Nikolaevich: Togo 60; Congo Kinshasa (Zaïre) 62–63 EXPELLED 63; Italy 67–70

MYAKOV, Yuri Aleksandrovich: (GRU) West Germany 62

MYATNIKOV, Ivan: Hungary 56; Czechoslovakia 68

MYAZNIKOV, Viktor Mitrofanovich: Canada 64

MYSHKO, Vladimir Ivanovich: Austria 60–63; West Germany 65–69

NALEVAIKO, Boris Yakovlevich: East Germany 46–53; Austria 53–55; East Germany 62–64

NASEDKIN, Dmitri Pavlovich: Mexico 59

NATASHIN, Nikolai Gavrilovich: China EXPELLED 67
NAYDENKOV, Vsevolod Andreevich: Sweden 59–62
NAZAROV, Fedor: Turkey 63
NAZHESTKIN, Oleg Ivanovich: Congo 61; Tunisia 68
NECHIPORENKO, Oleg Maksimovich: Mexico 61–65; Mexico 67–71 EXPELLED 71
NEDORUB, Leonid Vasilevich: (GRU) France 64–66
NEDOSOROV, Valentin Viktorovich: West Germany 71
NEMCHIN, Sergei Sergeevich: Thailand 47–50; Ambassador Syria 55–58; Ambassador Congo Kinshasa (Zaïre) 62–63 EXPELLED 63
NEMTSOV, Vladimir: France 72
NEPOMNYASHCHY, Karl Yefimovich: Austria 54; Novosti International Information 62
NESTEROV, Valerian Sergeevich: London 61–65; Washington 69–73
NESTEROV, Vladimir: (GRU) France 70–72 EXPELLED 72
NETREBSKY, Boris Pavlovich: Netherlands 69–70 EXPELLED 70
NEZNAYEV, Grigori Semenovich: Congo Kinshasa (Zaïre) EXPELLED 63; Denmark 65
NIKANDROV, Yuri Nikolaevich: (GRU) India 54–57; Ethiopia 59–63; Turkey 66–70
NIKIFOROV, Dmitri Semenovich: France 52–56; Ambassador Lebanon 62–66; Ambassador Senegal 68–72
NIKITIN, Aleksandr Aleksandrovich: Mexico 65–70
NIKITIN, Professor (Alias): See GORSKY, Anatoli
NIKITIN, Sergei Sergeevich: Belgium 46–49; Italy 53–55; France 62–66
NIKITIN, Vladimir: France 72
NIKITUCHEV, Nikolai: (GRU) Sweden 39–45
NIKOLAYEV, Aleksei D.: West Germany EXPELLED 63
NIKOLAYEV, Anatoli Nikolaevich: Sudan EXPELLED 71
NIKOLAYEV, Gennadi Akimovich: Washington 61–63; Italy 65–71; France 72
NIKOLAYEV, Paul Ivanovich: Sweden 63–67
NIKOLAYEV, Vasili Fedorovich: Romania 56–60; Czechoslovakia 62–65; Ambassador Iraq 65–69
NIKOLSKY, Nikolai Nikolaevich: Italy 66–68
NIKOLSKY, Vitali Aleksandrovich: (GRU) Sweden EXPELLED 63
NIKOLSKY, Yuri Ivanovich: East Germany 56–57; Austria 58–62; West Germany 65–69; Germany 72
NIKONOROV, Yuri Vladimirovich: Austria 57–60; Netherlands 65–70

NIKULIN, Leonid Nikolaevich: (GRU) Burma 54–56; New York 64–66*

NIKULIN, Viktor Aleksandrovich: Turkey EXPELLED 45; Lebanon 62

NOMOKONOV, Vladimir Petrovich: India EXPELLED 68

NOSKOV, Nikolai Stepanovich: Israel 58–63; France 64–68

NOSKOV, Valentin N.: Iraq EXPELLED 55; Thailand 63

NOVIKOV, Lev Aleksandr: Chile 71

NOVIKOV, Mikhail Maksimovich: Ethiopia EXPELLED 69

NOVIKOV, Nikolai Stepanovich: Washington 50–53; Paris 57–62*

NOVIKOV, Pavel Filipovich: Sweden 49–54; Finland 66–71

NOVIKOV, Vitali: Greece 52–56; Greece 59–65; Congo Kinshasa (Zaïre) 69–70 EXPELLED 70

NOVIKOV, Vladimir: Turkey 71

NOVIKOV, Yuri Vasilevich: Washington 47–53 EXPELLED 53; East Germany 55–65; Great Britain 66

NYUNIN, Viktor I.: Iran EXPELLED 65

OBOLENTSEV, Fedor Romanovich: Sudan 59–62; Libya 64–66 EXPELLED 66

OBUKHOV, Aleksei: Thailand 60–61; Chicago 62–63; Thailand 65–66 EXPELLED 66; Helsinki 66* (Soviet Delegation SALT Conference)

OBYEDKOV, Mai Mikhailovich: (GRU) Italy 57–58; Austria 59–62

OGANESYAN, Khachik G.: Iran 46–51; East Germany 56–58; Iran 60–64

OGNEV, Aleksandr Tikhonovich: Sweden 57–60

OGNIVTZEV, Arkadi Leonidovich: Sweden 43–45; Finland 66–71

OGORODNEV, Igor Alekseevich: (GRU) Great Britain 52–53; Netherlands 54–56

OGORODNIKOV, Anatoli Trifonovich: Belgium EXPELLED 67

OGURTSOV, Anatoli Andreevich: India 56; Washington 61–63; Sweden 66–67

OKULOV, Vasili Nikolaevich: France 54–59; Geneva 72*

OLENEV, Vladimir Ivanovich: New York 61–63* EXPELLED 63

ONUKHOV, Mikhail: Sweden EXPELLED 42

OOS, Vladimir Semenovich: Burma 57

OPEKUNOV, Aleksandr Dmitrevich: Soviet delegate to several international labor union meetings in an effort to organize spy ring Latin America and Africa, *60–70; Colombia EXPELLED 64

OREKHOV, Boris Mikhailovich: Washington EXPELLED 70

ORLENKO, Vladimir Ivanovich: Ghana EXPELLED 66; Senegal 69

ORLOV, Arseni Fedorovich: Brazil 63–67; Peru 69

ORLOV, Konstantin Petrovich: France 48–51; Italy 62–66

ORLOV, Mikhail G.: Iraq 63; Sudan EXPELLED 71

ORLOV, Nikolai Petrovich: (GRU) Sweden 49–51; Poland 56–63; Belgium 63–65

ORLOV, Vladimir Nikolaevich: New York 59–67*; Washington 70–71

OROBINSKY, Anatoli P.: Great Britain EXPELLED 71

ORZHURMOV, Vitali Sergeevich: East Germany 54; France 59–65; Washington 65

OSADCHY, Vilior G.: Israel 55–57; Israel 58–60; Israel 66–68; Afghanistan 68–71

OSHURKOV, Igor Pavlovich: Greece EXPELLED 67

OSIPOV, Igor Aleksandrovich: West Germany 63–66

OSIPOV, Oleg Aleksandrovich: (GRU) Netherlands 64–67

OSKIN, Viktor Nikolaevich: (GRU) Norway 67–71

OSTROVSKY, Yakov Arkadevich: Washington 60; Washington 61–66; Switzerland 67; Italy 71

OVAKIMYAN, Gaik B.: New York EXPELLED 41

OVECHKIN, Vladimir Yevgennevich: Ghana EXPELLED 66

OVSYANNIKOV, Mikhail Dmitrevich: West Germany 61–64

PALYURA, Anton Petrovich: France 56–57; Turkey 61–63; Italy 72

PANIN, Yuri I.: (GRU) Great Britain EXPELLED 71

PANKIN, Mikhail Semenovich: (GRU) Japan 44–49; Geneva* 68–

PANKOV, Ilyador Alekseevich: (GRU) Turkey 53; West Germany 61–65; Washington 66

PANKOVSKY, Viktor M.: Great Britain EXPELLED 71

PANOV, Aleksei: Sweden 40–45

PANOV, Vasili: Burma 57

PANZHEVSKY, Aleksei Afanasevich: Sweden 51–54

PAPOROV, Yuri N.: Mexico 57; Cuba 64

PAPYRIN, Arkadi Sergeevich: Netherlands 70–73

PARAIL, Vladimir Aleksandrovich: Paris 68–72*

PARCHINSKY, Boris A.: New York 65–68; Pakistan 71–72; Greece 72–73

PARFENOV, Yuri Y.: Belgium EXPELLED 71

PASENCHUK, Valentin Mikhailovich: China EXPELLED 67

PASHCHENKO, Grigori S.: Congo Kinshasa (Zaïre) EXPELLED 63

PASHKOV, Y. V.: India EXPELLED 68

PAVLENKO, Yuri Kuzmich: (GRU) Italy 64–67

PAVLICHENKO, Vladimir P.: New York 53–54*; New York 68*

PAVLOV, Aleksandr: (GRU) Sweden 39–44; Denmark 59–64

PAVLOV, Gennadi Mikhailovich: West Germany 57–61; Netherlands 65–68; Austria 71–73

PAVLOV, Georgi N.: India 68

PAVLOV, Gleb: New York 60–63* EXPELLED 63

PAVLOV, Lev Aleksandrovich: (GRU) Great Britain EX-PELLED 71

PAVLOV, Sergei S.: (GRU) France EXPELLED 65

PAVLOV, Stanislav Alekseevich: France 72

PAVLOV, Vitali Grigorevich: Canada 44; United States named him a co-conspirator in Abel case; 67 in West with alias KEDROV, N.

PAVLOV, Vladimir Denisovich: Austria 51–53; West Germany 58–61; East Germany 61–63; East Germany 65–70

PAVLOV, Vyacheslav Nikolaevich: Canada 67–71

PAVLOV, Yuri A.: (GRU) Israel EXPELLED 67

PECHENKO, Vadim Georgevich: (GRU) Iraq 72

PEKIN, Aleksei Fedorovich: (GRU) Japan 72

PERCHIK, Vadim Fedoseevich: Switzerland 67–71

PEREBILLO, Boris Dmitrevich: (GRU) Great Britain EX-PELLED 71

PERFILYEV, Yuri Nikolaevich: Canada 68

PERMINOV, Vilenin Petrovich: (GRU) West Germany EXPELLED 58

PETRIN, Boris M.: Cyprus EXPELLED 67

PETROPAVLUSKY, Vladimir Aleksandrovich: Sweden 45–51

PETROV, Ilya Vyacheslavovich: Italy 57–62; Italy 65–68

PETROV, Ivan Yaklovovich: Geneva 67* EXPELLED 67

PETROV, Nikolai Kirilovich: (GRU) France 68–71

PETROV, Viktor Ivanovich: New York 56* EXPELLED 56

PETROV, Vyacheslav: Greece 57–58; Guinea 62–65; Ivory Coast 67–69; Senegal 71

PETROVICHEV, Leonid Y.: Great Britain 57–61; Washington 62–66; Great Britain 69–71 EXPELLED 71

PETROVICHEVA, Emilya A.: Great Britain EXPELLED 71

PETROVSKY, Illen Nikolaevich: Egypt 54–58; Syria, Lebanon, Iran, Canada 72

PETRUK, Boris Georgevich: Ghana EXPELLED 66

PETRUKHIN, Viktor Georgevich: Cyprus 67

PETRUNIN, Viktor I.: (GRU) New York EXPELLED 56

PETUKHOV, Aleksei Dmitrevich: New York 55–57*; Lebanon 59–63; Turkey 66–69

PIGOROV, Vladimir Yakulevich: (GRU) Egypt 56–59; Belgium 62–63; Belgium 69–73

PIGOROV, Yuri A.: Washington EXPELLED 65

PIOTROVSKY, Vladimir: France 62–64

PISAREV, Lev K.: Netherlands EXPELLED 53; Iran 65

PITOVRANOV, Yevgenni Petrovich: East Germany 53–58; China

PIVNEV, Leonid Yegorovich: Washington EXPELLED 54

PIVOVAROV, Oleg Ivanovich: (GRU) Egypt 54–56; Netherlands 59–63; Great Britain 65–68; Washington 70

PLIGIN, Feliks Aleksandrovich: West Germany 69–71

POCHANKIN, Vitali Aleksandrovich: Mali EXPELLED 72

POCHATAEV, Nikolai Vasilevich: France 61–67; North Vietnam 70

PODKILZIN, Boris: Congo Kinshasa (Zaïre) EXPELLED 70

PODKORYTOV, Yuri P.: Ghana 64–66; Uganda 69

PODOPRIGORA, Gennadi: (GRU) Sweden 46–47

POGIN, Vladimir Dmitrevich: Italy 63–68; Finland 72

POKROVSKY, Georgi P.: Washington 51–53 (Social Sec. to Soviet Amb.); India 59–62; Japan 64–69

POLIKARPOV, Gennadi Ivanovich: France 53–60; Italy 64–68

POLOZHENTSEV, Ivan P.: Finland EXPELLED 63

POLOZOK, Anatoli: Kenya 69

POLUCHKIN, Vladimir Nikolaevich: Canada EXPELLED 65

POLUNIN, Leonty N.: Paris 48–53; New York 59–62, 68–73

POLYAKOV, Boris Alekseevich: (GRU) Norway 68–71

POLYAKOV, Dmitri Fedorovich: New York 59–62*

POLYAKOV, Valentin: Egypt 1970

POLYAKOV, Yuri: Sweden 71

POLYUSHKIN, Yuri Vasilevich: Norway 69–73

PONOMARENKO, Panteleymon K.: Ambassador Netherlands EXPELLED 61

PONOMAREV, Anatoli Vasilevich: Netherlands 57–61; Great Britain 65–67

POPOV, Anatoli A.: (GRU) Washington EXPELLED 56

POPOV, Anatoli Dmitrevich: Netherlands EXPELLED 61

POPOV, Gennadi F.: Great Britain 52–53; Canada 54–56 EXPELLED 56; Sweden 66

POPOV, Nikolai: Turkey 63

POPOV, Nikolai Fedorovich: Washington 67

POPOV, Nikolai Nikolaevich: (GRU) Italy 57–58

POPOV, Nikolai Sergeevich: Ghana EXPELLED 66

POPOV, Yuri Ivanovich: Burma 54–58; Japan 59–65; Japan 69

POROZHNYAKOV, Aleksandr Y.: New York 48–49 (as Ukrainian); Soviet Consul New York 48–49; Pakistan 57; Novosti Photo Chief 67

POSELYANOV, Nikolai Fedorovich: Finland 47–54; Denmark 60–65; Sweden 68–72

POSTNIKOV, Aleksandr Nikolaevich: India EXPELLED 57

POSTNIKOVA, Lyudmila A.: Great Britain EXPELLED 71

POTAPENKO, Leonid Terentevich: (GRU) Afghanistan 59–60; Great Britain 63–65; Italy 70–72

POTAPOV, Yevgenni Georgevich: (GRU) Norway 68–72

POTEMKIN, Gennadi Petrovich: Ghana EXPELLED 71

POTSELUYEV, Yevgenni Aleksandrovich: (GRU) Belgium 68–73

POZHIDAYEV, Dmitri Petrovich: Belgium 48–53; Italy 55–57; Ambassador Switzerland 57–58; Ambassador Morocco 58–62; Ambassador Egypt 65–67

PREDVECHNOV, Aleksandr Yemelyanovich: (GRU) Italy 52–58; Italy 64–67; Cambodia 70

PRESNAKOV, Fedor Fedorovich: Sweden 49–52; Washington 55–58

PRIKHODKO, Ivan Yevseevich: (GRU) New York 52–55*; West Germany 59–62

PRIKHODOV, A. V.: Mexico 59

PRIPOLTSEV, Valentin Aleksandrovich: West Germany EXPELLED 62

PRIVALOV, Anatoli Petrovich: Turkey 55–61; Turkey 66–67

PROKHOROV, Yevgenni M.: New York 62* EXPELLED 62

PRONIN, Vasili I.: Great Britain EXPELLED 71

PROSHIN, Dmitri: Great Britain EXPELLED 71

PROSHIN, Nikolai: Ethiopia 58–62; Libya 64–67

PROSVIRNIN, Vladimir I.: Greece 60–65; 71–73

PROSVIRNIN, Yuri Gennadevich: (GRU) Norway 71

PROZHOGIN, Nikolai Pavlovich: Morocco 60–63; Algeria 63–66; Italy 68

PROZONSKOV, Viktor A.: Burma 57

PRYAKHIN, Vladilen Aleksandrovich: (GRU) West Germany 57–59; Netherlands 63–68

PUCHKOV, Aleksandr: Copenhagen 69* EXPELLED 69

PUPYSHEV, Ivan Vasilevich: Great Britain EXPELLED 54

PUSHKIN, Vladimir A.: Great Britain EXPELLED 71

PUSHKOV, Aleksandr Nikolaevich: Denmark 65–69

PUTILIN, Mikhail Semenovich: (GRU) Great Britain 55–57; France 60–64; Norway 68–70

PUTYATOV, Vladimir Trofimovich: (GRU) Pakistan 58–61; Tanzania 65–68; Turkey 72

RADCHENKO, Vsevolod: Paris 56–59*; Geneva 72*

RADTSIG, Yegenni Sergeevich: Italy 60–66; France 71

RADVONSKA, Tanya Markovina: Canada 59–61

RAGOZKHIN, Ivan Petrovich: (GRU) Great Britain EXPELLED 71

RAINA, Ivan Andreevich: New York (Amtorg) 40s; China 50s (Intelligence Adviser to Mao Tse-tung)

RANOV, Nikolai I.: Cyprus EXPELLED 67

RASKOPOV, Yevgenni Mikhailovich: (GRU) Italy 51–53; Italy 54–56 EXPELLED 56

RASSEIKIN, Aleksandr I.: Somalia 62; Italy 63–68

RATANOV, Anatoli: Cambodia 60–62; Ambassador Cambodia 65–67; Ambassador Guinea 70

RATNIKOV, Valentin Mikhailovich: New York 64*; Turkey 65–67; Italy 69–71

RATUSHNYAK, Vladimir Petrovich: (GRU) Norway 59–64; Denmark 66–70

REDIN, Nikolai G.: Washington EXPELLED 46

REMIZOV, Nikolai Matveevich: Mexico EXPELLED 59

REPIN, Anatoli Fedorovich: Egypt 71

REVIN, Valentin A.: California 59–63; Washington 63–66 EXPELLED 66; Japan 70

RIMYANS, Leonid Vladislavovich: Sweden 57–61

RODIONOV, Aleksandr S.: (GRU) France 71

RODIONOV, Georgi M.: Ambassador Ghana 63–64

ROGACHEV, Igor A.: Washington 66–68

ROGACHEV, Ivan N.: Thailand 53–57; Burma 57–61

ROGOV, Anatoli Vladimirovich: Denmark EXPELLED 57

ROGOV, Leonid A.: Great Britain EXPELLED 71

ROGOV, Mikhail Stepanovich (Alias): See TSYMBAL, M. S.

ROGUCHIN, Fedor Konstantinovich: Italy 66–68

ROMANOV, Anatoli Aleksandrovich: (GRU) Canada 57–60; New York 62–67, 69–73

ROMANOV, Leonid Mikhailovich: Mexico EXPELLED 59; Brazil 62

ROMANOV, Sergei Aleksandrovich: Latin America May 69

ROMASHCHUK, Dmitri Iliodorovich: Denmark 51–56; Norway 63; Greece 67

ROMASHIN, Yuri Anatolevich: New York 63* EXPELLED 63

ROSKOV, Gennadi: Italy EXPELLED 68

ROY, Mikhail: Cuba EXPELLED 67

SAMOKHIN, Yuri Stepanovich: Sweden 46–51; Burma 57–60; Denmark 70

SAMOKHVALOV, Leonid Aleksandrovich: Turkey 57–60; Belgium 63–70; Italy 73

SAMOKICH, Nikita Ivanovich: (GRU) Netherlands 51–56; Austria 58–61; France 63–67

SAMOYLOV, Mikhail K.: Uruguay EXPELLED 61

SAMOYLOV, Vladimir Matveevich: Netherlands 56–59

SANKO, Vasili F.: Australia 54; New York 56–57*; New York 67*

SARMANOV, Sergei S.: Egypt 53–58; Libya 60–61

SAROVNIKOV, Konstantin Grigorevich: Washington 57–61; Greece 63–67; West Germany 70

SARYCHEV, Boris Leonidovich: West Germany 64–66; Kenya 67–71

SAULCHENKO, Fedor A.: Iran 57–61; Iran 65–69

SAVELEV, Mikhail Stepanovich: Great Britain 58–61

SAVICH, Boris Trofimovich: Belgium EXPELLED 70

SAVIN, Nikolai Andreevich: Switzerland EXPELLED 70; Algeria 72

SAVIN, Stanislav A.: Greece EXPELLED 61

SAVIN, Viktor Grigorevich: (GRU) Turkey 67–69; Netherlands 71

SAZANOV, Boris Aleksandrov: Canada 67; France 69–71 EXPELLED 71

SBIRUNOV, Viktor: Egypt 68

SEDOV, Vyacheslav Alekseevich: Japan 64–67

SELEZNEV, Mitrofan Yevlaineevich: Austria 58–62; Washington 70–73

SELUNSKY, Valentin Ivanovich: Sweden 63–66

SELYUTIN, Yuri Dmitrevich: West Germany 61–64; Algeria 70

SELIKH, Aleksandr Sergeevich: Belgium 64–66

SEMENENKO, Stanislav N.: New Zealand 64–67; Great Britain EXPELLED 71

SEMENOV, Aleksandr Aleksandrovich: (GRU) Italy 67–69

SEMENYCHEV, Yuri Konstantinovich: Belgium 58; France 66–72

SEPELEV, Yuri F.: Great Britain EXPELLED 71

SEREBRYAKOV, Fedor Dmitrevich: Japan 49–56; Belgium 58–61; North Vietnam 65–66; Austria 68–71; New York 72–73*

SEREBRYAKOV, Igor Dmitrevich: India 59–61; India 64–69; Pakistan 70

SEREBRYANIKOV, Robert Semenovich: Congo Brazzaville 66; Congo Kinshasa (Zaïre) 67

SEREGIN, Aleksandr Ivanovich: Sweden 63

SEREGIN, Anatoli Semenovich: Denmark 60–65; Denmark 68–72

SEREDA, Aleksei M.: Belgium EXPELLED 71

SERGEYEV, Vladimir Dmitrevich: West Germany 63–66; West Germany 70

SERGEYEV, Vladimir Yefimovich: Mexico EXPELLED 69

SERGEYEV, Yuri Pavlovich: (GRU) Sweden 60–63; Great Britain 65–67

SEVASTYANOV, Gennadi Gavrilovich: Washington 59–63 EXPELLED 63

SHADRIN, Anatoli Mikhailovich: East Germany 59–61; Brazil 62–64; Ecuador 70–71 EXPELLED 71

SHAKHOV, Geli A.: Rhodesia EXPELLED 64; Kenya 66

SHALAYEV, Nikolai Vasilevich: (GRU) Washington 57; West Germany 59–63; West Germany 66–70; Sweden 71; Austria 73

SHALKHAROV, Khairulla Mukhanovich: Thailand EX-PELLED 58; Ceylon (Sri Lanka) EXPELLED 65

SHALNEV, Anatoli Pavlovich: Canada 67

SHAPOVALOV, Rotislav Yefimovich: New York 55–56* EXPELLED 56

SHAPURIN, Yuri Petrovich: Tunisia 65–68

SHARAYEV, Vladimir Ivanovich: Ethiopia 62; Ethiopia 66–69 EXPELLED 69

SHAROVATOV, Vladimir Semyonovich: Netherlands 68–70 EXPELLED 70

SHATROV, Vadim A.: New York 58–60* EXPELLED 60; Syria 68–72

SHCHEDRIN, Vailan Ivanovich: (GRU) Sweden 54–58; West Germany 62–63; Austria 70

SHCHEGOLKOV, Aleksei M.: Iraq 63; Afghanistan 67–70

SHCHEKLIN, Nikolai Arsentevich: Denmark 53–57; Denmark 60–64; Norway 68–69

SHCHERBAKOV, Aleksei Anatolevich: Belgium 67–71 EX-PELLED 71

SHCHERBAKOV, Vladimir Sergeevich: (GRU) Netherlands 70

SHCHERBAKOV, Yuri Ivanovich: West Germany 59–62; West Germany 65–67

SHEBANOV, Yuri Konstantinovich: Sweden 69–71

SHELENKOV, Albert A.: Ghana EXPELLED 66; Washington 67

SHELENKOV, Aleksandr Ivanovich: Yemen 66; Jordan 71

SHENGALEV, Lev Fedorovich: Colombia 71

SHEPELEV, Viktor Petrovich: (GRU) Austria 54–55; Austria 62–67; West Germany 69

SHEPENIN, Mikhail Sergeevich: Geneva 72*

SHERSTNEV, Aleksandr Ivanovich: Italy 59–63

SHERSTNEV, Lev Nikolaevich: Canada 52–53; Norway 59–63; Great Britain EXPELLED 71

SHESHIN, Valentin Valentinovich: (GRU) Sweden 62–66; Japan 69–72

SHESKIN, Vladimir Fedorovich: (GRU) Belgium 54–58; Paris 60–65*; Geneva 69*

SHESTAKOV, Vladimir Vasilevich: Sweden 50–53; East Germany 57–58

SHESTOPALOV, Lev: France EXPELLED 63

SHEVCHENKO, Oleg Andreevich: Mexico 71

SHEVCHENKO, Vladimir Andreevich: (GRU) Italy 66–70

SHIBAYEV, Sergei Vasilevich: Netherlands EXPELLED 61

SHIGAEV, Anatoli Nikolaevich: West Germany 63–64; Belgium 64–67

SHIPOV, Vladilen Nikolaevich: (GRU) Turkey 64–67; Syria 71

SHIROKOV, Oleg Aleksandrovich: Laos and Cambodia 68–70; France 70

SHIROKOV, Yevgenni Aleksandrovich: Great Britain 57–62; Sweden 64–66; India 72

SHISHKIN, Ivan Aleksandrovich: Finland 53–57; East Germany 60–65

SHISHKIN, Yevgenni I.: Austria 51–53; Austria 57–60; Austria 70

SHITOV, Aleksandr I. (alias Aleksandr I. Alekseev): France 46–51; Netherlands 52–54; Argentina 54–58; Cuba 59–62; Ambassador Cuba 62–68; Peru and Chile 70 (as newsman)

SHLYAPNIKOV, Rudolf P.: Cuba EXPELLED 67

SHOLOKHOV, Igor Y.: Bolivia EXPELLED 72

SHPAGIN, Mikhail Mikhailovich: West Germany 63–66 EXPELLED 66

SHPAKEVICH, Vladimir I.: Australia 60–62 EXPELLED 62; Chile 63–65; Uganda 67–69

SHTYKOV, Nikolai Ivanovich: New Zealand EXPELLED 62

SHUBIN, Vitali B.: Mexico 60–64; Chile 65–67; Cuba 69

SHULTSEV, Aleksei Sergeevich: East Germany 57–59; France 66–72

SHUMAKOV, Aleksei Georgevich: Sweden 57–61; Finland 63–68

SHUMAYEV, Mikhail A.: Washington 59–63

SHUMILOV, Yevgenni: Sweden 70

SHUMOVSKY, Stanislav Antonovich: Netherlands 67

SHUMSKY, Vladislav Stanisovich: West Germany EXPELLED 61

SHVEDOV, Aleksei: Ambassador Morocco 63–64

SHVETS, Vladimir Fedorovich: Uruguay EXPELLED 66

SHUVAKIN, Dmitri: Ambassador Israel 68

SIBOROV, Yevgenni Vasilevich: West Germany 58–61; West Germany 66

SIDELNIKOV, Yulian Antonovich: Yugoslavia 53–55; Congo Kinshasa (Zaïre) 61–63; Yugolsavia 65–71

SIDORENKO, Vasili: (GRU) Sweden 41–42

SIDORENKOV, Vladislav: Uruguay 57–58

SIDOROV, Vasili S.: Cyprus 66–67; Greece 68–73

SILIN, Boris A.: Ghana EXPELLED 66

SILKIN, Galina Trofimovna: New Zealand; Geneva*; Belgium; New York*; Congo Kinshasa (Zaïre) 62–63

SILKIN, Vladimir S.: Belgium 59–61; Congo Kinshasa (Zaïre) 62–63; Romania 64–67

SIMANTOVSKY, Oleg Vladimirovich: Congo Kinshasa (Zaïre) 68–70 EXPELLED 70; Dahomey 71

SIMBURTSEVA, Ludmila Serafinovna: Great Britain EXPELLED 71

SIMENOV, Viktor: Cuba 68

SIMINOV, Vladimir A.: India 66–71

SIMSON, Ernst Rudolfovich: Sweden 45–49

SINITSYN, Igor Yelisevich: Sweden 62–69

SINITSYN, Sergei Yakovlevich: Ethiopia 56–61; Rhodesia 64–66

SIOMONCHUK, Leonid Yemilianovich: Austria 47–53; Austria 55; West Germany 58

SITNIKOV, Vasili Romanovich: Austria 50–57; West Germany 58–60

SKOBEYEV, Yevgenni Mikhailovich: Norway 68–72

SKOPTSOV, Yuri V.: Great Britain EXPELLED 71

SKORIDOV, Boris A.: Great Britain 61–65 using alias of ZHILTSOV, Boris A.

SKOTNIKOV, Nikolai: (GRU) Sweden 40–45

SKRIPOV, Ivan Fedorovich: Great Britain 52–59; Australia 59–63 EXPELLED 63

SKVORTSOV, Nikolai Semenovich: New York 50–52*; Austria 53–55; East Germany 56–59

SLAVIN, Grigori Ivanovich: Sweden 43–45: West Germany 56–58; East Germany 58–62

SLEPENKOV, Zakhar: (GRU) Sweden 43–45

SLEPOV, Aleksandr Vladimirovich: Argentina 56–59; West Germany 61–64; Great Britain 71

SLIUCHENKO, Georgi: (GRU) France 70–72 EXPELLED 72

SLYUSARENKO, Petr Konstantinovich: Egypt 66; Ambassador Jordan 67; Ambassador Togo 70

SMIKOV, Oleg A.: Belgium EXPELLED 67

SMIRININ, Nikita: France 47

SMIRNOV, Anatoli Vasilevich: Thailand 63–68; Thailand 71

SMIRNOV, Ivan Georgevich: (GRU) Japan 52–54; Japan 57–60; Japan 66–70

SMIRNOV, Jacob: France 51–52 (alias SKOMOROKHIN); Romania 62

SMIRNOV, Konstantin Nikanovich: Yugoslavia 72

SMIRNOV, Leonid V.: Tunisia 64–66 EXPELLED 66; France 66–71

SMIRNOV, Petr Vasilevich: Netherlands 58–60 (alias PETROV, Serge) EXPELLED 60; Sweden 65

SMIRNOV, Sergei S.: Denmark EXPELLED 57

SMIRNOV, Viktor M.: (GRU) France 64–70

SMIRNOV, Viktor Nikolaevich: Finland 54–58; Sweden 59–62; Australia 70–

SMIRNOV, Viktor Petrovich: Geneva 56–59*; Sweden 61–64; Geneva 66–69*

SMOLIN, Nikolai Vasilevich: Switzerland 49–54; France 56–57; Cambodia 57–60; Tunisia 62–65; Ambassador Togo 66–70

SMOLKOV, Albert Vasilievich: (GRU) Iceland 58–60; Great Britain 63–68; New York 70–73*

SOBOLEV, Igor P.: Austria 57–61; West Germany 64–69

SODAKOV, Vladimir: Turkey 63

SOIDRA, Ivo-Aat A.: Great Britain EXPELLED 71

SOKOL, Nikolai Ilich: (GRU) West Germany 46–49; Sweden 54–56; Norway 64–69

SOKOLOV, Mark Nikolaevich: Sweden 61–65; Sweden 70–

SOKOLOV, Nikolai P.: (GRU) West Germany 66

SOKOLOV, Sergei Nikiforovich: Great Britain EXPELLED 71

SOKOLOV, Viktor Aleksandrovich: (GRU) France 68–72 EXPELLED 72

SOKOLOV, Vladimir Mikhailovich: Denmark 65–68; Great Britain EXPELLED 72

SOKOLOV, Yuri B.: Syria 62–64; Cyprus 69–73

SOKOLSKA, Yekaterina: New York 48* EXPELLED

SOLIAKOV, Leonid Dmitrevich: Kenya 64–66 EXPELLED 66

SOLKOV, Vladimir N.: Mexico 59

SOLNTSEV, Nikolai Ivanovich: West Germany 64–68

SOLOD, Danil Semenovich: Syria 44–48; Ambassador Egypt 53–56; Ambassador Guinea 60–61 EXPELLED 61

SOLODOVNIKOV, Vasili: Nigeria 69

SOLOMATIN, Aleksandr Mikhailovich: West Germany 63–65; East Germany 68–69

SOLOMATIN, Vladimir I.: Great Britain EXPELLED 64; Thailand 66

SOLOMATIN, Yuri Dmitrevich: West Germany 70

SOLONIN, Vyacheslav A.: Finland 63–66; Ethiopia 67–72

SOLOVIEV, Vyacheslav Leonidovich: Denmark 72

SOLOVIEV, Yevgenni: Algeria 72

SOLOVOV, Aleksei Vasilevich: (GRU) Italy 53–58 EX-PELLED 58

SOLOVYEV, Vladimir Ivanovich: New York 61–64; Japan 64–69

SOLYAKOV, Leonid Dmitrevich: Burma; China; Tanzania; Kenya EXPELLED 66

SOROKIN, Aleksandr: New York 60–63*

SOROKIN, Dmitri Ivanovich: Washington 61–64; Great Britain EXPELLED 71

SOROKIN, Stanislas I.: Paris 64–71*

SOROSHKIN, Yevgenni Filipovich: (GRU) West Germany 70

SOTSKOV, Lev Filippovich: Sweden 62–67; Sweden 69–71

SPASSKY, Vladimir: France 67–71

SPICHKIN, Igor: Sweden 42–44

SPOLNIKOV, Viktor: Lebanon 68

STALNOV, Boris C.: Great Britain 66–70 EXPELLED 70

STAROSTIN, Viktor: (GRU) Sweden 40–41 EXPELLED 41; Ceylon 65–68; Finland 70–

STARTSEV, Aleksandr Nikolaevich: Great Britain 50–54; Great Britain 55–58; Norway 60–65

STATSKEVICH, Nikolai Viktorovich: Washington 48–50; Burma 51–53; Yugoslavia 54–58; Sweden 61–64; Sweden 71–73

STEPAKOV, V. I.: Ambassador China 70; Ambassador Yugoslavia 71

STEPANENKO, Nikolai Gavrilovich: France 61–66; Switzerland 69–

STEPANOV, Yuri S.: (GRU) Libya EXPELLED 57

STERLIKOV, Aleksei Petrovich: France 57–58; Switzerland 60–65; Switzerland 69–70 EXPELLED 70

STOROZHKO, Vadim I.: (GRU) United States (Indiana) 59–60; Cuba 64–67; Greece 69

STOVBUN, Ivan Ignatsevich: Israel EXPELLED 67; Congo Kinshasa (Zaïre) EXPELLED 70

STRELBITSKY, Vladimir Vasilevich: (GRU) France 56–61; Belgium 63–66; Switzerland 69–73

STRIGANOV, Aleksei R.: France EXPELLED 60

STRIGANOV, Sergei R.: Washington 45–48; Washington 55–58; Ambassador Uruguay 60–64

STRYKANOV, Nikolai Alekseevich: (GRU) Belgium 70–72

STUDENIKIN, Ivan Yakovlevich: (GRU) Sweden 56–62; Netherlands 65–69

STUDENIKOV, Igor: Chad 67–68; Congo Kinshasa (Zaïre) 68–70 EXPELLED 70; Congo Brazzaville 71–72

STUPAR, Sergei Nikolaevich: Washington 60–64

STYCHKOV, Vladimir M.: Ethiopia EXPELLED 64

SUBOTIN, Aleksandr: Colombia 70

SUDAREV, Igor Nikolaevich: Guiana 59–63; Luxembourg 63–68; Italy 71–73

SUKHACHEV, Georgi Nikanorovich: (GRU) Netherlands 55–58 EXPELLED 58; Egypt 66; Jordan 69–73

SUKHANOV, Iva F.: Greece EXPELLED 61

SUKHAREV, Boris Arsenevich: Cuba; Yugoslavia; France 65–70

SUKHORUCHKIN, Konstantin Nikolaevich: (GRU) Netherlands 55–58 EXPELLED 58

SULDIN, Vasili Andreevich: West Germany 59–61

SULITSKY, Nikolai P.: Canada 46; Romania 49–54; Lebanon 54–60; Ambassador Yemen 60–68

SULTANOV, Yuli A.: Yemen EXPELLED 60

SUMSKOY, Mikhail: New York 53–56*

SURZHANINOV, Vladimir Vasilevich: West Germany 56–58; West Germany 61–65; Czechoslovakia 69

SUSLEV, Vladimir: New York 58*

SUSLIKOV, Yuri V.: Egypt 72

SUVOROV, Georgi Borisovich: Great Britain EXPELLED 64; Japan 69

SUVOROV, Valentin: Belgium 61–64; France 66–69

SVERCHKOV, Vladimir Alekseevich: Cuba 61–63; Ghana 64–66

SVETANKO, Dmitri Andreevich: Great Britain 61–64; Sweden 70–73

SVETAYLO, Nikolai Vasilevich: Italy 56–62; Belgium 67–68

SVIRIDOV, Feliks Aleksandrovich: (GRU) Washington 55–58; Netherlands 66–72

SVIRIN, Mikhail Nikolaevich: Great Britain 44–49; New York 52–57*

SVISTELNIKOV, Paul Mikhailovich: (GRU) Italy 51–54; France 57–64; Belgium 67–71

SYCHEV, Vasili Ivanovich: West Germany 63–65; Iran 70–72

TARABRIN, Yevgenni Anatolevich: Sweden 50–54; Austria 55

TARANKOV, Ivan Y.: India EXPELLED 60

TARASENKO, Sergei Ivanovich: Ghana EXPELLED 66

TARASOV, Vasili Vasilevich: Canada EXPELLED 64

TATISHCHEV, Sergei I.: Washington EXPELLED 63

TCHERNIAK, Leonid Vasilevich: France 68

TEBENKO, Vasili Fedorovich: (GRU) West Germany 62–65

TEPLOV, Mark Ivanovich: Sweden 59–62; Norway 67–72

TEREKHIN, Aleksandr D.: India 65–68

TER-SARKISOV, Yuri M.: Great Britain EXPELLED 71

TIBLYASHIN, Aleksei Viktorovich: France 45–52; Egypt 61–65; Egypt 67

TIKHOMIROV, Aleksandr Vasilevich: New York 70* EXPELLED 70

TIKHONOV, Petr Stepanovich: (GRU) Japan 51–53; Denmark 56–59; Italy 66–69

TIKHVINSKY, Sergei Leonidovich: Japan 56

TIKUNOV, Vadim Stepanovich: Romania 72

TITOV, Anatoli Filipovich: Ethiopia 61

TITOV, Gennadi Fedorovich: Great Britain 61–63; Great Britain 68; Norway 71

TKACHENKO, Vadim Afanaseevich: Great Britain EXPELLED 64; Indonesia 73

TOGULEV, Boris Vasilevich: France 66

TOKAREV, Viktor N.: Great Britain EXPELLED 60

TOOM, Pavel Mikhailovich: Sweden 62–66

TOOMPU, Adolf Yanovich: Sweden 60–63

TOROPOV, Vasili Nikolaevich: Norway 65–70

TOUMASYAN, Suren A.: Soviet Rep. to Ho Chi Minh; Ambassador North Vietnam 61–65; Ambassador Libya 65–70

TRAVIN, Nikolai Aleksandrovich: Italy 64–68

TRAVKIN, Mikhail I.: India 63–68

TRETYAKOV, Konstantin Georgevich; Sweden 55–61; Washington 70–73

TRICHIN, Aleksei Fedorovich: France 56–61

TRISHIN, Boris I.: Belgium EXPELLED 71

TRISHIN, Yuri Fedorovich: Egypt 71

TROFIMOV, Nikolai Ivanovich: Mexico 57

TROFIMOV, Vladimir Ivan V.: Egypt EXPELLED 56

TROFIMOV, Vladimir Vasilevich: Italy 52–57; Somalia 60–64; Italy 70–

TROITSKY, Anatoli Petrovich: Great Britain EXPELLED 71

TRUCHIN, Ivan: (GRU) France 66–70

TRUSHKIN, Yuri Fedorovich: Thailand 55–58 EXPELLED 58; Laos 60–62; Egypt 70

TRUSHKOVSKY, Igor Rotislovich: Pakistan 51–56; Burma 58–60; Burma 63–65

TRUSOV, Aleksandr Vasilevich: Italy 60; Great Britain (Hong Kong) 72

TSAREV, Boris Ivanovich: West Germany 61–63; Austria 67–68

TSAREV, Yuri Ivanovich: Netherlands 71–72

TSELYAYEV, Aleksei Pavlovich: (GRU) Washington 54; Washington 57; Iraq 62–65; Italy 70–72

TSUMAYEV, Stepan: Great Britain (Hong Kong) EXPELLED 72

TSUTSKOV, Nikolai: Sweden 61–65; Great Britain EXPELLED 71

TSVETAYEV, Mikhail Vasilevich: Great Britain 60–61; Syria 62–64; Norway 69–73

TSVETKOV, Yuri Aleksandrovich: Turkey 68–72

TSYGANOV, Vladimir Ilich: (GRU) Austria 61–63; West Germany 65–68; West Germany EXPELLED 68

TSYMBAL, Mikhail Stepanovich (alias M. S. ROGOV): Italy 45–52; France 53–59

TUDIN, Anatoli M.: France 61

TULAYEV, Vladimir: Vienna 63–65*; Australia 70

TUMANOV, Boris G.: Congo Kinshasa (Zaïre) EXPELLED 70

TURALIN, Mikhail Ibytch: France 57–60

TURASOV, Vladimir Ivanovich: Netherlands 66–71; Switzerland 72–

TURAYEV, Nikita Vasilevich: (GRU) Italy 68–71

TURKIN, Nikolai Fedorovich: New York 56* EXPELLED 56

TUROV, Nikolai I.: Ghana 65

TYAZHEV, Nikolai Ivanovich: Switzerland 59–61; Turkey 64–69

TYUKHIN, Leonid Y.: Great Britain 66–67; Great Britain 68–70; Japan 71

TYUPAEV, Anatoli: (GRU) Austria 50–58; East Germany 58–61; West Germany 64–67

UDALOV, Aleksandr Vasilevich: Washington EXPELLED 64

UDALTSOV, Ivan Ivanovich: Czechoslovakia 68

UGOLKOV, Vasili Dmitrevich: (GRU) Turkey 42–46; Turkey 59–63; Turkey 66–70

UMNOV, Valentin Aleksandrovich: (GRU) Austria 60–67; Switzerland 71–

USTENKO, Eduard V.: Australia 64–67; Great Britain EXPELLED 71; Ceylon (Sri Lanka) 72

USTIMENKO, Yuri: Ireland 72

UTEMOV, Adolf: Sweden 48–52

UTKIN, Stanislav Grigorevich: Norway EXPELLED 70

VAKULA, Vladimir: Ohio 60–61; New York 62–65* EXPELLED 65

VALIKOTNY, DeGarcia V.: Turkey EXPELLED 44

VALYALIN, Fedor Fedorovich: Congo Kinshasa (Zaïre) EXPELLED 70

VANAGEL, Viktor I.: Guinea 62; France 69–71 EXPELLED 71

VANOVSKY, Yuri Yakovlevich: Mexico 70

VANYUSHIN, Ivan Petrovich: India 67–70; West Germany 71

VASICHEV, Gennadi Nikitovich: Great Britain EXPELLED 71

VASILYEV, Aleksandr Nikolaevich: (GRU) Sweden 45–48

VASILYEV, Anatoli F.: Canada 62–64; Pakistan 66–70; Greece 70

VASILYEV, Nikolai I.: France EXPELLED 39; Sweden 40–46 EXPELLED 46; Ghana EXPELLED 66

VASILYEV, Sergei V.: Washington 46–50; Washington 52–56; Washington 57–60; India 67–71

VASILYEV, Vladimir: (GRU) Lebanon EXPELLED 69

VASILYEV, Vyacheslav Vladimirovich: Italy 54–58

VAULIN, Gennadi Afanasevich: East Germany 59–64; Thailand 64–69; Burma 71

VAVILOV, Valeri Maksimovich: Norway EXPELLED 63; Pakistan 66

VAYGAUSKAS, Richardas Konstantinovich: New York 60–62*; Canada (Expo) 67; Great Britain 68–71 EXPELLED 71

VDOVIN, Valentin P.: France 59–65; Chad 65–69; Ambassador Laos 72

VEBER, Voldemar Pavlovich: Sweden 65–67; Canada 70–73

VEKLENKO, Viktor T.: Great Britain EXPELLED 71; Thailand 72

VELICHKO, Vladimir G.: West Germany 61–64; Tanzania 66–69; Greece 70–73

VELIKANOV, Avenir Akimovich: Washington EXPELLED 65

VENCHIKOV, Aleksandr Antonovich: Netherlands 60–63; Netherlands 68–73

VESELOV, Yuri A.: (GRU) Congo Brazzaville EXPELLED 63

VESHKIN, Aleksandr Vladimirovich: Sweden 61–65; Norway 68–

VETROV, Yuri Pavlovich: (GRU) Netherlands 58–62; New York 66–68*

VIILOV, Adolf Aleksandrovich: Sweden 52–53

VIKTOROV, Yuri Petrovich: Finland 53; Congo Kinshasa (Zaïre) 62

VILIU, Adolf A.: Sweden EXPELLED 53

VILKOV, Boris Nikolaevich: (GRU) India 51–54; Italy 61–67; France 71

VINOGRADOV, Feliks Vasilevich: (GRU) West Germany 63–67; Austria 69

VINOGRADOV, Konstantin Fedorovich: (GRU) Sweden 42–47; India 62–

VINOGRADOV, Nikolai F.: Syria 48–50; Egypt 57–63

VINOGRADOV, Valter Vladimirovich: Ghana EXPELLED 71

VINOGRADOV, Vladimir M.: Britain 61; Ambassador Japan 62–67; Ambassador Egypt 70

VISHNEVETSKY, Konstantin Mikhailovich: Egypt 63; Philippines 66

VISHNYAKOV, Vladimir Nikolaevich: Belgium 69–72

VISKO, Georgi Stepanovich: India 52–53; Great Britain 54–57; Mexico 62–66

VISKOV, Y. N.: Great Britain EXPELLED 71

VLADIMIROV, Gherman Ivanovich: Hungary 50–52; Austria 55–58; West Germany 61–66; West Germany 70

VLADIMIROV, Viktor Fedorovich: West Germany 63–67

VLADIMIROV, Viktor Mikhailovich: Canada 67; Finland 71

VLASOV, Vasili Pavlovich: France 48–55; Netherlands 55–58; France 58–63 EXPELLED 63

VOLKOV, Gherman A.: Greece 71–73

VOLKOV, Mikhail M.: Iran EXPELLED 59

VOLKOV, Nikolai Fedorovich: New York 57–61*; Paris 66–72*

VOLKOV, Vladimir Ivanovich: France 59–60; France 64–66; Netherlands 70

VOLNOV, Vladimir Grigorevich: Norway 58–61; Norway 63–67

VOLODIN, Viktor Stepanovich: France 68

VOLOKITIN, Sergei Ivanovich: France 51–54; Poland 58–61

VOLOKITIN, Vladimir Ivanovich: (GRU) West Germany 62–66; Austria 71

VOLOSHIN, Paul Trofimovich: Indonesia 54–57; Netherlands 61–63

VOLOSSATOV, Vladimir Alekseevich: Lebanon 56–59; Syria 60–63; Algeria 63–64; France 66–71

VOROBIEV, Lev Ivanovich: Hungary; France 61–63; Mali 71

VOROBIEV, Vasili A.: Greece 56–60; Cyprus 62–67; Greece 69–71

VORONIN, Albert Georgevich: Lebanon 63–65

VORONIN, Aleksei: Iran 45–49; Iran 53–55; Iran 57–60; Turkey 62–64; Ambassador Guinea 64–68

VORONIN, Boris A.: Albania 51–54; Italy 57–61; Congo Kinshasa (Zaïre) 62–63 EXPELLED 63; Mali 65–68; Somalia 70

VORONIN, Yuri N.: Finland 54–58; Finland 60–64; Great Britain 67–71 EXPELLED 71

VORONTSOV, Viktor Nikolaevich: Norway 69–72

VOSKOBOY, Aleksei Savvich: Turkey 55–61; Turkey 62–68

VOSKOBOYNIKOV, Boris Nikolaevich: Chile 65–66; Mexico 67–71 EXPELLED 71

VOSTRIKOV, Aleksei Nikolaevich: Belgium 71

VOTRIN, Sergei Ivanovich: (GRU) Austria 58–62; Switzerland 65–71

VOZNOY, Ivan M.: Burma 57–59; Burma 63–65

VUCHENKO, Valeri Maksimovich: (GRU) Austria 69; West Germany 71

VYBORNOV, Aleksandr Dmitrevich: Sweden 60–66; Norway 68–

VYRODOV, Ivan Yakovlevich: New York 62* EXPELLED 62

YAKOVLEV, Aleksandr Ivanovich: Denmark 53–59; Sweden 62–66

YAKOVLEV, Aleksandr Ivanovich: Kenya 64–66 EXPELLED 66; Indonesia 66–72

YAKOVLEV, Boris Fedorovich: West Germany 66–71

YAKOVLEV, Igor Irinarkhonovich: West Germany 62–66 EXPELLED 66

YAKOVLEV, Mikhail D.: Ambassador Congo Kinshasa (Zaïre) 60; Ambassador Iraq 63; Ambassador Sweden 71

YAKOVLEV, Nikolai Fedorovich: (GRU) Sweden 48–53; Denmark 57–59

YAKOVLEV, Sergei Vasilevich: West Germany 60–62

YAKOVLEV, Viktor N.: Canada 63–69; Cyprus 71

YAKUBOVSKY, Vasili Pavlovich: Mexico 43–45; Argentina 51–54; Brazil 63; Ambassador Guinea 69

YAKUNIN, Viktor V.: India 69

YAKUSHEV, Nikolai Petrovich: Venezuela EXPELLED 52

YAKUSHEVA, Aleksandra Georgevna: Venezuela EXPELLED 52

YANGAYKIN, Sergei Alekseevich: Uruguay EXPELLED 66

YASAKOV, Viacheslav Aleksandrov: New York (Cornell University) 65–66; Great Britain 68–71 EXPELLED 71

YASEV, Valentin Vasilevich: Italy 63–69

YASHCHENKO, Anatoli A.: New York 62–65; Great Britain EXPELLED 71

YASKOV, Nikolai Fedorovich: (GRU) France 51–56

YASNEV, Yuri : Ireland 72

YATISYNA, Lev L.: Congo Kinshasa (Zaïre) EXPELLED 71; Mali EXPELLED 72

YATSENKO, Nikolai Andreevich: Netherlands 57–60

YATSOV, Pavl Antonovich: Mexico 55–57; Washington 57; Mexico 57–60; Mexico 63–67; Italy 71–

YATSYNA, Vladimir: Washington 55; Iran 56–58; New York 60–61*; Paris 61–64*; Mali 71 EXPELLED 71

YEDANOV, Oleg A.: China 64–67 EXPELLED 67; Washington 70–71; San Francisco Consul General 71

YEDEMSKY, Sergei A.: Washington 55–60; Great Britain 66

YEFIMOV, Afansi Ivanovich: Austria 46–54; East Germany 55–59

YEFIMOV, Fedor I.: Congo Kinshasa (Zaïre) EXPELLED 63; Finland 70

YEFIMOV, Gennadi Konstantinovich: Thailand 72

YEFIMOV, Nikolai V.: France 50–57; Morocco 58–63; France 64–69

YEGOROV, Anatoli Grigorevich: (GRU) Denmark 59–63; Netherlands 66–69; Sweden 71–

YEGOROV, Ivan D.: New York 63* EXPELLED 63

YEGOROV, Stanislav Vasilevich: Netherlands 68–70

YEGOROV, Vasili V. (Alias): See LAZAREV, Anatoli I.

YEGOROV, Viktor Mikhailovich: Sweden 48–52 EXPELLED 52

YEGOROV, Yevgenni S.: Japan EXPELLED 52

YEGURNOV, Aleksandr: West Germany 52

YEKIMOV, Konstantin P.: New York 52–56* EXPELLED 56

YEKUCHOV, Ivan Ivanovich: (GRU) Italy 58–62

YELATONTSEV, Anatoli: Brazil 64

YELISEEV, Petr Nikolaevich: Washington 59

YELISEEV, Viktor Alekseevich: Kenya EXPELLED 69

YELISTRATOV, Valentin N.: (GRU) Washington 56–59; Great Britain 64–68; Cyprus 72–73

YEMELIN, Viktor Pavlovich: Brazil 67

YEMELYANOV, Vladimir Vasilevich: Iraq 66; Geneva 69*
YENGIBARYAN, Noraya A.: Greece 71
YENIKEEV, Gennadi: Egypt 70
YENIKYEEV, Oleg Yakovlevich: West Germany 59–61; Switzerland 61–62; Austria 62–65 EXPELLED 65
YERIN, Arkadi Alekseevich: (GRU) Sweden 48–53
YERMAKOV, Aleksandr Ivanovich: (GRU) Italy 70–73
YERMILICHEV, Valeri Dorofevich: (GRU) Norway 70–
YERMOLAYEV, Sergei A.: (GRU) Italy EXPELLED 55
YEROFEYEV, Ivan Alekseevich: East Germany 55–61; Austria 65–70; West Germany 72
YEROFEYEV, Valeri Nikolaevich: Sweden 67; Norway 71–73 EXPELLED 73
YEROFEYEV, Vladimir Ivanovich: Sweden 42–44; France 55–60; Senegal 63–66; France 70–
YEROKHIN, Dmitri: India 62–70
YERSHOV, Yuri Alekseevich: India 65–69
YESENIN, Nikolai Nikolaevich: Finland 62–65; Japan 66–69; Norway 71–
YEVDOKIMOV, Anatoli Ivanovich: Egypt 72
YEVDOKIMOV, Sergei Vasilevich: (GRU) Sweden 54–58; Norway 63–67; Norway 71–
YEVDOTEV, Ivan Pavlovich: West Germany 71
YEVLAMPEV, Igor: (GRU) France 68
YEVSEYEV, Nikolai Konstantinovich: (GRU) Czechoslovakia 46–50; Italy 65–70
YEVSTROTOV, Petr: France 66–71
YEZHOV, Petr Yakovlevich: Washington EXPELLED 60
YORDANSKY, Vladimir Borisovich: Ghana 61–64; France 72
YUDAKOV, Sergei: Congo Kinshasa (Zaïre) 62–63
YUDKIN, Ivan Vasilevich: Italy 58–63; Italy 67–70
YUKALOV, Albert Ivanovich: Colombia 61; Egypt 62–64; Netherlands 64–68; Netherlands 70
YUKALOV, Yuri Alekseevich: Sudan 57–60; Kenya 64–66 EXPELLED 66; Tanganyika 70
YURASOV, Viktor Vladimirovich:, Great Britain EXPELLED 71
YURYN, Esfir (alias Rita Elliott): Australia 55
YUSHENKO, Semen Ivanovich: Sweden 57–60; Austria 63
YUSHIN, Boris G.: (GRU) Washington 65–68; Greece 71–73
ZABIVKIN, Leonid Vladimirovich: (GRU) New York 63–65*; Italy 67–70
ZABOTIN, Nikolai: (GRU) Canada 45
ZADVINSKY, Vasili Vasilevich: Washington EXPELLED 64
ZAGORSKY, Sergei A.: United States 57

ZAKENFELD, Yanis Yanovich: Sweden 64–67

ZAKHARIKHIN, Petr Akimovich: France 51–54; France 58–62; France 66–71

ZAKHAROV, Albert Mikhailovich: Greece EXPELLED 67

ZAKHAROV, Albert Petrovich: Cambodia 60–65; Paris 68*

ZAKHAROV, Veniamin Dmitrevich: Kenya 68 EXPELLED 68; Nigeria 72

ZAKZHEVSKY, Gennadi Aleksandrovich: (GRU) Sweden 52–54

ZALENIN, Andrei N.: Tunisia 62; Algeria 62–65; Morocco 72

ZALOZNY, Boris Vasilevich: Turkey 67–71

ZAMOYSKY, Olly Petrovich: Italy EXPELLED 70

ZAMYATIN, Yuri: Egypt 59–62; Syria 62–64

ZANEGIN, Boris: Washington 72

ZAOSTROVTSEV, Yevgenni A.: Washington 57–58 EXPELLED 59; East Germany 60–64

ZAVARUKHIN, Petr: (GRU) Sweden 44–48

ZAVORIN, Ivan Panfilovich: Argentina EXPELLED 59; Great Britain EXPELLED 71

ZAYTSEV, Ivan Ivanovich: China 47–50; Israel 51–56; West Germany 58–63; West Germany 69–71

ZAYTSEV, Leonid Sergeevich: Great Britain 53–61; Denmark 64–69

ZAYTSEV, Valentin A.: New York 50–53*; New York 60–64*; Belgium 69–71 EXPELLED 71

ZAYTSEV, Yuri Vladimirovich: Washington 55–59; New York 61–62* EXPELLED 62; Belgium 72

ZAZYADKO, Anton Grigorevich: (GRU) Great Britain 55–59; Netherlands 65–69

ZELENEV, Vladimir Aleksandrovich: Great Britain EXPELLED 71

ZELENIN, Andrei N.: Tunisia 62–66

ZELENOV, Sergei Nikolaevich: Austria 51–55

ZENIN, Vasili Sergeevich: (GRU) Netherlands 55–58 EXPELLED 58

ZHEGALOV, Leonid Nikolaevich: Washington EXPELLED 70

ZHELANOV, Vladimir Mikhailovich: (GRU) Switzerland 67–71

ZHEREBTSOV, Aleksandr Vasilevich: (GRU) Italy 62–66

ZHERNOV, Leonid Andrevich: Ceylon 66–67; (GRU) Great Britain EXPELLED 71

ZHIGALIN, Nikolai Matteevich: (GRU) Italy 45–46; Italy 50–53; Italy 58–60; Greece 65–71

ZHIGALOV, Fedor Dmitrevich: Italy 57–62; Somalia 65–69

CHAPTER NOTES

CHAPTER I

Lenin quotation: Lenin, V. 31, p. 326.

Serbsky Institute and interrogation of General Grigorenko: *Der Spiegel* (Hamburg), November 1, 1971; *Chronicle of Current Events* No. 8, as translated by Reddaway; Appeal from Z. M. Grigorenko (the general's wife) to the Chairman of the U.S.S.R. Council of Ministers, A. N. Kosygin, January 13, 1970; Appeal from Z. M. Grigorenko to Freedom Loving Citizens of the World, March 3, 1970; General Grigorenko's diary, as translated by David Floyd, *Sunday Telegraph* (London), April 5, 1970; *Time,* April 6, 1970; *The Guardian* (Manchester), March 30, 1971; *The Economist* (London), July 8, 1972.

Perkins case: Interviews with Thomas D. Fox, Chief, Counter-Intelligence Division, U.S. Defense Intelligence Agency; *New York Times,* October 23, 1971; *Washington Post,* August 4, 1972.

Trial of Father Zdebskis: *Chronicle of Current Events,* Nos. 21, 22, 23.

Davidov case: Interviews with Western security services and with the American scholar involved.

Persecution of Panov: Address by Suzanne Massie, Women's National Democratic Club, Washington, December 11, 1972; *New York Times,* July 2, 1972; *Washington Post,* October 23, 1972; Washington *Evening Star-News,* February 21, 1973.

Seizure of defector at sea: *Dagens Nyheter* (Stockholm), September 29, 1972; *Weekendavisen* (Copenhagen), October 20, 1972.

Background and activities of Pitovranov: Interviews with former KGB officers Yuri Nosenko and Petr Deriabin; John, pp. 247–57; interviews with Western security services.

Incident at U.S. embassy in Bucharest: Interview with G.

Marvin Gentile, Assistant Secretary of State for Security, U.S. Department of State.

Schwirkmann case: Interviews with Western security services, *Die Welt* (Hamburg), September 14 and October 14, 1964; Conquest (*The Soviet Police System*), p. 95; Wise and Ross, pp. 57–60.

KGB role in 1967 Arab-Israeli war: Interviews with Vladimir Nikolaevich Sakharov, former KGB agent, and Daniel Pattir, counselor for press and information, Israeli embassy, Washington; testimony at trial of "plotters" in Cairo, as reported by United Press International, Washington *Post*, February 25, 1968; Washington *Post*, June 2, 1968.

Pavlik Morozov: Conquest, p. 502; *Large Soviet Encyclopedia*, 2nd ed., V. 28, Moscow, 1954, and *Komsomolskaya Pravda*, September 2, 1962, as cited by Conquest.

KGB informant system: Reitz, p. 226; Deriabin, p. 93; Blake, pp. 25, 124; *Wall Street Journal*, October 4, 1972.

KGB role in guarding people and facilities: Reitz, p. 55; *Der Spiegel* (Hamburg), November 22, 1971; Washington *Post*, May 25, 1972.

KGB role in the economy: Hingley, pp. 239–40; Dulles, pp. 90–91; Conquest (*Justice and the Legal System in the U.S.S.R.*), p. 91.

Loginov quotation: Interviews with Western security services.

Amalrik quotation: Amalrik, p. 32.

Executions for economic crimes: Hingley, pp. 239–40; Conquest, letter to *The Listener* (London), January 14, 1971; *Christian Science Monitor*, February 3, 1972.

References to Andropov, Shelepin, Mazurov, and Pelshe: New York *Times*, April 28, 1973; *Prominent Personalities in U.S.S.R.*, pp. 398, 474, 561; Statement by Senator Henry Jackson, *Congressional Record*, Senate, July 9, 1969, p. 57769; Barghoorn, p. 112.

Panyushkin background: Khokhlov, pp. 204–206, 221; Barghoorn, p. 113; *Murder International Inc., Murder and Kidnapping as an Instrument of Soviet Policy*, pp. 14, 76.

References to Bannikov and Chestyakov: Blake, p. 124.

Soviet organizations infiltrated by KGB: *Novosti*, Interdoc, The Hague, 1968; interviews with Father Vladimir Ignaste, former KGB agent; William C. Fletcher, professor and director of the Department of Sino-Soviet Studies, University of Kansas; Penkovsky, p. 72.

KGB activities against foreigners in Soviet Union: Interviews with Yuri Ivanovich Nosenko, former KGB officer, Yuri Krotkov, former KGB agent, and Western security services: *Security Advice about Visits to Communist Countries*, prepared by Her Majesty's Government, London, 1969; Byrnes, pp. 84–104.

KGB manipulation of arts and artists: *Aspects of Intellectual Ferment and Dissent in the Soviet Union*, R SSIS 1968; *Problems of Communism*, September/October, 1968, pp. 55–57; Kuznetsov, New York *Times*, August 10, 1969; Blake, pp. 25, 122, 124, 126, 129.

References to Fadeyev: Struve, p. 215; interviews with Natasha Belinkova.

References to Romanov: *Time*, September 27, 1968; Washington *Post*, September 7, 1972; Western security services.

Sholokhov quotations: *Aspects of Intellectual Ferment and Dissent in the Soviet Union*, R SSIS 1968, p. 44; *Problems of Communism*, September/October, 1968, pp. 55–56.

References to Galanskov: *Problems of Communism*, p. 56; Associated Press Report in Washington *Post*, Baltimore *Sun*, November 13, 1972; *The Times* (London), November 14, 1972.

KGB control of military: Interviews with Western security services; Reitz, pp. 210, 215, 217; Deriabin, p. 93, New York *Times*, November 10, 1967; *Wall Street Journal*, October 4, 1972.

Arrests of army and navy personnel: *Chronicles* Nos. 8, 9, 10, 11, as translated by Reddaway, pp. 161–67, 175–83.

Establishment of special Jewish Department: Interviews with Avraham Shifrin and Western security services.

Sakharov quotation: Andrei Sakharov Memorandum of March 5, 1971, and Postscript of June 1972, as published by New York *Times*, August 18, 1972.

Kuznetsov quotation: New York *Times*, August 10, 1969.

KGB role in execution of Soviet foreign policy: Pipes, pp. 4–5; Kaznacheev, pp. 47, 48, 191–196; Penkovsky, pp. 107–16; interviews with Western security services.

Predominance of KGB personnel in Soviet embassies: Interviews with Dr. Fern C. Stukenbroeker, Federal Bureau of Investigation; Raya Kiselnikova, former secretary in the Soviet embassy, Mexico City; Vladimir Nikolaevich Sakharov and Western security services; Kaznacheev, *Inside a Soviet Embassy*.

References to Pavel Kuznetsov: New York *Times*, June 15–17, 27–28, 1952, July 18, 1952; Washington *Evening Star*, June 14, July 13, 1952; Western security services; Chicago *Tribune*, June 16, 1952; *Il Secolo* (Genoa), September 10, 1966.

References to Belous: New York *Times*, April 4, 5, 7, 8, 1959; *Newsweek*, April 20, 1959.

References to Shitov: Jeremiah O'Leary, Washington *Sunday Star*, March 14, 1971.

References to Kiktev: *Christian Science Monitor*, April 9, 16, 1968; *Valeurs Actuelles* (Paris), January 26, 1970; Kabul *Times*, September 13, 1972; *Al-Hayat* (Beirut), October 29, 1972; *Al-Jamhour* (Beirut), November 2, 1972; *Al-Nadwa* (Jidda), October 15, November 27, December 9, 1972; *Al-Medina* and *Al-Bilad* (Jidda), December 8, 1972; Jakarta *Times*, December 15, 1972.

Comparisons of Soviet representation in foreign capitals and Western representation in Moscow: The figures stated were compiled mainly by the European Editorial Office of the *Reader's Digest* in Paris through inquiries to the governments concerned. The overall total was supplied by a Western security service. Diplomatic representation in most capitals fluctuates from month to month, but the disparities cited are fairly constant.

Expulsions of Soviet representatives accredited to U.N.: Figure provided by U.S. Department of State and the FBI.

Abduction of Soviet seamen: *The Episode of the Russian Seamen*, R SSIS 1956.

References to Pavlichenko: New York *Times*, October 5, 6, 20, 1971; Washington *Post*, October 5, 6, 1971; New York *Daily News*, October 5, 1971.

Arrest of Markelov: Washington *Post*, New York *Times*, February 15, 16, 1972; *Dagens Nyheter* (Stockholm), February 16, 1972; U.S. Department of Justice news release, February 17, 1972.

References to Antipov: Interviews with Anton Sabotka, former KGB agent, and Western security services.

References to Malik: Interviews with former KGB officers, and Western security services.

References to Lessiovsky and U Thant: Interviews with U Thant and Nosenko; Lederer and Burdick, p. 151.

KGB exploitation of U.N. agencies: *Berlingske Tidende* (Copenhagen) and *Politiken* (Copenhagen), April 3, 1969; *Sunday Telegraph* (London), September 12, 1971; Baltimore *Sun*, October 8, 1969; *L'Aurore* (Paris), October 19, 1971; Washington *Daily News*, December 20, 1971.

U.N. statistical data: *Time*, December 4, 1972; U.N. Information Office, Washington.

KGB involvement in businesses abroad: *Wall Street Journal*, September 30, 1971; Washington *Post*, October 19, 1971; Washington *Daily News*, November 5, 1971; Washington *Evening Star*, November 4, 1971; *Dagens Nyheter* (Stockholm), October 21, 1971; *Bon Spécial Tombola* (Brussels), March 22, 1972.

References to Loginov and KGB illegals: Interviews with Western security services and former KGB illegal agents Kaarlo Tuomi and Anton Sabotka.

KGB domination of satellite services: Castro, pp. 104–109; Dulles, pp. 93–94; interviews with Bittman, Castro, Rupert Sigl, a former KGB agent, László Szabó, a former officer of the Hungarian intelligence service; reports by Gerardo Perazo Amerchazurra, a former officer of the Cuban intelligence service.

Paques case: Interviews with Western security services; *New York Times*, September 24, 26, December 4, 1963, July 7, 8, 1964; *L'Express* (Paris), July 2, 1964; *Paris-Match*, October 5, 1963; *Le Figaro* (Paris), October 10, 1963; *Time*, July 17, 1964.

Disinformation operations: Pipes, pp. 10–12; interview with Thomas D. Fox, Chief, Counter-Intelligence Division, U.S. Defense Intelligence Agency; Orlov, p. 22; Dulles, p. 150; *The Guardian* (Manchester), August 12, 1969; *New York Times*, May 15, 1968; Washington *Post*, December 25, 1967.

Support of violence and terrorism: *Soviet Analyst*, Special Report by Crozier (Institute for Study of Conflict); *The Guardian* (Manchester), October 19, 1971; *Christian Science Monitor*, March 27, 1971; *Sunday Telegraph* (London), December 24, 1972; Washington *Evening Star-News*, September 18, 1972; *Les Informations Politiques et Sociales* (Paris), September 23, 1972; reports from Adauto Dos Santos, former agent of Brazilian Communist Party.

References to Neruda: Levine, *The Mind of an Assassin; L'Aurore* (Paris), January 19, 1971; *New York Times*, April 16, 1972; *Time*, November 1, 1971; Paseyro, *Le Mythe Neruda;* Gorkin, *L'Assassinat de Trotsky;* Interview with Paseyro in Paris.

Flink case: *New York Times*, New York *Herald Tribune*, New York *Journal American*, Washington *Post*, September 16, 1962; *This Week Magazine*, December 9, 1962.

Institute for the Study of Conflict Statement: Crozier, *Peacetime Strategy of the Soviet Union.*

Expulsions from Mexico: *The News* (Mexico City), March 22, 1971; Washington *Post*, New York *Times*, Washington *Evening Star*, March 20, 1971.

Expulsions from the Sudan: *New York Times* and Washington *Post*, August 3, 4, 5, 1971; Sudanese embassy, Washington.

Expulsions from Great Britain: Washington *Post*, September 25, 1971; New York *Times*, October 1, 1971.

Expulsions from Belgium: New York *Times*, November 5, 1971.

Subversion in West Germany: Los Angeles *Times*, June 7, 1972.

Expulsions from Bolivia: New York *Times*, March 30, 31, April 6, 8, 1972; *Christian Science Monitor*, April 1, 1972.

Expulsions from Colombia: *El Espectador* (Bogotá), August 4, 1972; *Japan Times*, August 6, 1972.

Brezhnev quotation: Baltimore *Sun* and Washington *Post*, June 28, 1972.

CHAPTER II

The story of Vladimir Nikolaevich Sakharov is narrated primarily on the basis of information which he provided during prolonged interviews with the author. The interviews took place in the United States during February, May, and June of 1972. Sakharov studied the first draft of the chapter and recommended a number of factual corrections. After these were made, he certified in writing that the chapter is accurate to the best of his knowledge and belief insofar as it pertains to him.

Sakharov is the sole firsthand source of information concerning his life in the Soviet Union. All of Sakharov's assignments and some of his more significant experiences outside of the Soviet Union have been corroborated by independent sources. Additionally, research efforts have been made to obtain from overt sources at least circumstantial confirmation of the conditions and events he has described.

Conditions in Yemen: David Ransom, U.S. State Department, affirms that as of 1967 the environmental and political conditions in Yemen were generally as Sakharov states.

Burning of German embassy and assault on U.S. embassy: David Ransom, U.S. State Department.

KGB relationship with Abdullah al Sallal: Western security services have confirmed that al Sallal met clandestinely with Soviet officers in Yemen and (unknown to Sakharov) also in neighboring Aden.

New Class privileges and values: Pertinent published references include Djilas, *The New Class;* "Soviet Parents Push Students," Washington *Post*, June 6, 1971; "Education, Class and Ideology," *Soviet Analyst*, November 30, 1972; Sergei S. Voronitsyn, *Class Distinction in Soviet Higher Education* (Copyright Institute for the Study of the USSR), *East-*

West Contacts, Interdoc, The Hague, V. V. No. 1, January 1971; "The Caste System," *Soviet Analyst,* September 14, 1972; "The Private Lives of Russia's Leaders," *Atlas,* July/August, 1971; "The Soviet Union Nobody Has Written About," a review in the *Mainichi Daily News* (Tokyo), April 30, 1971; "Moscow: The End of a Dreadful Leap Year," Washington *Post,* January 2, 1973.

Purge of military 1936–38: Gorbatov, *Years Off My Life.*

University milieu: Sakharov's description of the environment at the Institute has been corroborated in detail by Vladimir Trofimov, the son of a KGB colonel. Trofimov was a student at the Institute of Eastern Languages at approximately the same time Sakharov was enrolled at the Institute of International Relations. He fled to the United States in 1968 from Afghanistan, where he was on a training assignment comparable to that of Sakharov. Another former Soviet national, Maria Vovchok, has provided details about alcoholism, the informant system, and the importance of the Komsomol among students in "Young Russia's Silent Majority," *Sunday Telegraph* (London), April 18, 1971.

Anti-Soviet attitudes in Estonia: "A Visit to Tallinn, the Capital of Estonia," Washington *Post,* August 1, 1972.

Conditions in rural Soviet Union: Amalrik, *Involuntary Journey into Siberia.*

Attitudes toward marriage: "Marriage for Profit: Matchmaking in Moscow," Washington *Post,* February 7, 1971.

Soviet personnel in Egypt: Names of most of the Soviet personnel Sakharov encountered in Egypt appear in the *List of Diplomatic and Consular Corps,* January 1970, issued by the Egyptian Foreign Office; *Prominent Personalities in the USSR.*

Data regarding Western dependence on Middle East petroleum: Petroleum Industry Research Foundation, New York; Joshua, *Soviet Penetration into the Middle East.*

Soviet aid to Egypt: Joshua, pp. 10–11.

Background of Sharaf: The details of Sharaf's background and activities emanate from various foreign security services as well as from Sakharov. The presence of an extraordinarily important KGB agent of influence in the Egyptian government prior to 1971 has been further confirmed by another KGB defector.

Disinformation operations against Egypt: Interviews with Bittman.

Soviet personnel in Kuwait: Names of most of the Soviet nationals with whom Sakharov dealt in Kuwait appear in the *List of Diplomatic and Consular Corps,* April 1969, issued by the Kuwait Foreign Ministry; *Prominent Personalities in the USSR*.

Terrorism in Turkey: Interviews with Turkish embassy officials, Washington: "The Trade in Troublemaking," *Time*, May 10, 1971.

Exploitation of Palestinian guerrillas: *Soviet Analyst*, June 20, 1972; "L'U.R.S.S. et Les Palestiniens," *Les Informations Politiques et Sociales*, Paris, September 23, 1972.

Trial of 91 Egyptians: New York *Times*, August 25, 1971.

Podgorny-Sadat agreement; *Christian Science Monitor*, August 25, 1971.

Sentencing of Sharaf: *Christian Science Monitor*, December 10, 1971.

Kennan quotation: Introduction by George Kennan to *Power and the Soviet Elite* by Boris I. Nicholaevsky, pp. xiv–xv.

CHAPTER III

Barghoorn case: Nosenko is the sole source of information concerning what transpired within the KGB and Politburo before and after Barghoorn's arrest. The account of the arrest and incarceration is based upon an interview with Professor Barghoorn. President Kennedy's statements were published by the New York *Times*, November 15, 1963, in a transcript of his press conference. Other relevant published reports may be found in Barghoorn's "The Security Police"; New York *Times*, October 31, November 13, 16, 17, 20, 21, 1963; New York *Herald Tribune*, October 30, 31, November 13, 15, 16, 1963.

Establishment of Cheka: Carr, Scott, Hingley, pp. 117–32.

Dzerzhinsky quotation: Scott, p. 8.

Deaths inflicted by Cheka: Conquest, *The Human Cost of Communism*, M SSIS, 1970, p. 11

Lenin quotations: ". . . this is unheard of . . ." Lenin, *Works*, V. 35, p. 275; "narrow minded intelligentsia . . . sob and fuss," V. 28, pp. 331–43, *Pravda* (Moscow), December 18, 1918; "merciless mass terror," V. 35, pp. 287, 288.

Opposition to communists and revolt at Kronstadt: Scott, p. 14; Shub, p. 405.

Lenin quotations: "We have failed . . ." Conquest, p. 3; "resting directly on force," Lenin, *Works*, V. 31, p. 326; letter to Kursky, V. 33, p. 321.

Conquest quotation: Conquest, p. 8.

Deaths inflicted under Stalin: ibid, p. 533.

Execution of Beria cohorts: interview with Deriabin.

Khrushchev as a Stalinist: Pistrak, pp. 123, 145–48, 165.

Khrushchev speech: Speech of Nikita Khrushchev Before a

Closed Session of the XXth Congress of the Communist Party of the Soviet Union on February 25, 1956, SSIS, 1957.

Wolfe quotation: Wolfe, *Khrushchev and Stalin's Ghost*, pp. 67–68.

Party announcement of June 30, 1956: Speech of Nikita Khrushchev . . . SSIS, 1957, p. 21.

Pravda quotation: Cited by Wolfe, *Khrushchev and Stalin's Ghost*, p. 75.

Khrushchev quotation regarding Chekists: ibid., p. 41.

Library of Congress study: *Soviet Intelligence and Security Services, 1964–1970, A Selected Bibliography of Soviet Publications, with Some Additional Titles from Other Sources*, R SSIS, 1972.

Pipes quotation: Pipes, p. 4.

CHAPTER IV

The chapter is based in the main upon heretofore confidential data provided by Western security services and former KGB personnel. All but Nosenko, Deriabin, and Sakharov have requested anonymity. Some published sources can be cited to document portions of the chapter.

Andropov: References to Andropov's background derive from *Prominent Personalities in the USSR; Valeurs Actuelles* (Paris), April 26, 1967; New York *Times*, Toronto *Globe and Mail*, May 20, 1967; *Sunday Star* (Washington, D.C.), May 21, 1967; *Daily Telegraph* (London), April 14, 1971. References to the Hungarian Revolution are based primarily upon the United Nations Report of the Special Committee on the Problem of Hungary, New York, 1957, and *Hungary's Fight for Freedom*, a special issue published by *Life*, 1956. The description of Andropov's apartment was supplied by Vladimir Nikolaevich Sakharov, who several times was a guest of Andropov's son.

References to William Fisher: Los Angeles *Times*, August 22, 1972; New York *Times*, August 27, 1972.

Scientific and Technical Directorate: Some data pertaining to Soviet scientific and technological espionage and provided by Penkovsky, pp. 69, 77, 105, 339.

Sorge report: Deakin and Storry, p. 230.

Stalin's disregard of intelligence: Rauch, p. 307; Conquest, pp. 484–89.

Ciphers, signals, and communications: New York *Times*, April 6, 1965; Washington *Post*, April 6, May 11, 1965; Toronto *Globe and Mail*, May 11, 1965; Wise and Rose, p. 107.

Persecution of Jews: *Observer* (London), December 12, 1971; Washington *Post*, August 12, September 26, 1972, April 20,

1973; *Daily Telegraph* (London), August 14, 1972; *Sunday Telegraph* (London), May 21, 1972; New York *Times*, April 28, 1972; *Soviet Analyst*, September 14, 1972.

Suppression of *Chronicle: Daily Telegraph* (London), February 6, 1973, and Western security services.

Border Guards: Reitz, pp. 30–31; *Economic Performance and the Military Burden in the Soviet Union, A Compendium of Papers*, Subcommittee on Foreign Economic Policy of the Joint Economic Committee (U.S. Congress), 1970.

Yunost quotation: *Daily Telegraph* (London), March 14, 1972.

Attempt to assassinate Brezhnev: Deriabin, *Watchdogs of Terror*, p. 348; Washington *Post*, January 24, 1969.

CHAPTER V

Soviet census: *Union of Soviet Socialist Republics, Background Notes*, Department of State, Washington, April 1972.

Minorities and population growth: *Neue Zuercher Zeitung* (Zurich), April 2, 1972.

Number of religious believers: *Recent Developments in the Soviet Bloc*, Part I, Subcommittee on Europe, House Committee on Foreign Affairs, 1964, pp. 100–101.

Statement of Yesenin-Volpin: *Il Tempo* (Rome), June 13, 1972.

Soviet agriculture: The data cited were obtained primarily from the U.S. Departments of State and Agriculture. Pertinent published references include: *The Nation* (London), June 26, 1972; *U.S. News & World Report*, July 24, 1972; Baltimore *Sun*, October 7, 9, 1972; New York *Times*, September 25, 1972; *Christian Science Monitor*, November 17, 1972; *Current History*, October 1971, pp. 227–42; *Journal de Genève* (Geneva), September 14, 1972.

Soviet housing: Donald D. Barry, "Housing in the USSR: Cities and Towns," and Karl-Eugen Wädekin, "Housing in the USSR: The Countryside," *Problems of Communism*, May/June 1969; *Problemy Ekonomiki*, No. 5, Moscow, May 1972; *The Economist* (London), August 12, 1972; *The Guardian* (Manchester), December 16, 1972.

Economic growth rates: U.S. State Department.

Pavlevski findings: *Economies et Sociétés* (journal of the Institute of Applied Economic Sciences), Geneva, February 1969.

Economic lot of Levin: interview with Alexey Levin.

Soviet economic lag: *U.S. News & World Report*, July 24, 1972; Andrei Sakharov, Memorandum, New York *Times*, July 22, 1968; U.S. State Department.

Kosygin quotation: New York *Times*, December 14, 1972.

Sakharov on arms expenditures: New York *Times*, June 23, 1972.

Findings of Soviet economists concerning arms expenditures: Washington *Post*, April 13, 1973.

Treatment of the Sloboda family: Appeal from Baptist women to Kosygin and U Thant, as cited in *Problems of Communism*, July/August, 1968; Michael Bourdeaux and Albert Boiter, *Baptists in the Soviet Union (1960–1971)*, Radio Liberty Research, Munich, January 31, 1972.

Internal passports: *Giornale d'Italia* (Rome), November 1, 1972; *Bonavia* (Tokyo News Report), January 30, 1971; *Christian Science Monitor*, October 11, 1972; U.S. State Department.

Parasite law: Conquest, *Justice and the Legal System in the USSR*, pp. 122–23; Hingley, p. 232.

Statement made to Morgan: Washington *Post*, January 21, 1968.

Control over emigration and foreign travel: Interview with Avraham Shifrin and Shifrin's testimony published in *U.S.S.R. Labor Camps*, H SSIS, Part I and II, 1973; *Sunday Telegraph* (London), May 21, 1972; New York *Times*, August 20, 1972; Kuznetsov, New York *Times*, August 10, 1969.

Tax on emigrants: New York *Times*, August 20, 1972.

Lenin quotation regarding religion: Lenin, *Works*, V. 35, pp. 89–91.

Religious policies and controls: *Religion and Church in the Communist Orbit*, Interdoc, The Hague, May/June 1969, pp. 16–17; Fletcher, *Religion and Soviet Foreign Policy 1945–1970*, p. 5; Fletcher, *Nikolai*, pp. 23, 51; Bourdeaux, pp. 6–7; interviews with Father Vladimir Ignaste, former KGB agent.

Control of science: Penkovsky, p. 339; Sakharov, New York *Times*, July 22, 1968; *Problems of Communism*, September/October 1968; *Time*, August 2, 1968; Western security services.

Reports by *Literary Gazette* and *Sovietskaya Rossiya*: *Soviet Analyst*, June 22, 1972.

Censorship procedures and Finkelstein quotation: *Sunday Telegraph* (London), September 11, 1966, January 1, 1973; *Studies on the Soviet Union, The Soviet Censorship*, Vol. XI, No. 2, 1971, Institute for the Study of the USSR.

Khrushchev quotation: Moroz, p. 12.

Statement of young Russian woman: Interview with Raya Kiselnikova, a former secretary in Soviet embassy, Mexico City.

Arrests of Siniavsky, Daniel, and Batshev and treatment of writers: Reddaway, p. 11; *Problems of Communism*, September/October 1968, pp. 21, 113; Yosif Brodsky in New York *Times Magazine,* October 1, 1972, pp. 11, 78, 82, 84, 86, 87.

References to Rodzhestvensky and Glazunov: Western security services.

Khrushchev statement about Sholokhov: *Znamya,* Moscow, No. 10, 1959, p. 200.

References to Sholokhov: Interviews with Svetlana Alliluyeva, Natalia Belinkova, Aleksei Yakushev.

Sentences to camps: *Chronicle,* Nos. 16–24; London *Times,* February 17, 1971; Washington *Post,* October 18, 1970, November 13, 1970, August 12, 1972; *Politiken* (Copenhagen), May 19, 1971; New York *Times,* September 28, 1971; Reddaway, *Uncensored Russia.*

Use of psychiatry for political purposes: *The Economist* (London), July 8, 1972; *Time,* February 7, 1972; *Chronicle,* Nos. 22 and 23; Toronto *Telegram,* February 17, 1971; Medvedev, *A Question of Madness; Sunday Telegraph* (London), April 5, 1970; Washington *Post,* January 5, 1970; *Abuse of Psychiatry for Political Repression in the Soviet Union,* H SSIS, 1972; *National Review,* June 9, 1972.

Statements by Lunts: *The Guardian* (Manchester), March 30, 1971.

Arrest and treatment of Valeria Novodvorskaya: *National Review,* June 9, 1972.

Abuse of patients by Lunts: *The Economist* (London), July 8, 1972; *National Review,* June 9, 1972.

Statement of Gershuni: *Guardian of Liberty* (Munich), August/September 1971.

References to Yakhimovich: Reddaway, pp. 146–148; *Chronicle,* No. 20; *Problems of Communism,* July/August 1968; *Christian Science Monitor,* March 17, 1972.

Appeal of Chernyshov: *Chronicle,* No. 18; *National Review,* June 9, 1972.

CHAPTER VI

Case of the American engineer: The account is based on official records made available by U.S. government sources on the condition that their anonymity be preserved and that the engineer involved not be named.

Borge case: *Aftenposten* (Oslo) and *Arbeiderbladet* (Oslo), August 11, 1972.

DeVries case: Written report provided by one Western security service and confirmed by another.

FBI quotation: J. Edgar Hoover, "The U.S. Businessman Faces

the Soviet Spy," *Harvard Business Review*, January/February 1964.

Byrnes statement: Byrnes, "American Scholars in Russia Soon Learn about the KGB."

British warning: *Security Advice about Visits to Communist Countries*, Her Majesty's Government, London, 1969.

General procedures and surveillance techniques used against foreigners: Nosenko and other former KGB personnel are the primary sources of the data presented. Some relevant published sources include: Byrnes; Barghoorn; *Sunday Telegraph* (London), August 8, 1965; *Newsweek*, December 28, 1970; *Dagens Nyheter* (Stockholm), April 3, 1971; *Christian Science Monitor*, June 2, 1971; Washington *Post*, February 7, 1971; Los Angeles *Times*, January 16, 1973.

Harassment of Canadian hockey team: Canadian embassy, Washington, D.C.

Drugging of attachés: U.S. Department of Defense.

Frank case: Washington *Post*, June 29, 1969; General Electric Research and Development Department, Schenectady, New York.

The operation against Ambassador Dejean: This narrative in the main derives from extensive interviews by the author with Yuri Vasilevich Krotkov and with Western security services which became concerned with the case. The dialogue is largely based upon Krotkov's recollection of conversations in which he participated or about which he was told. Relevant, detailed testimony which Krotkov offered to the U.S. Congress may be found in *Testimony of George Karlin, Parts I, II, and III*, H SSIS, November 1969–March 1970.

Nosenko, who while in Moscow learned of the operation and personally knew some of the KGB principals involved, has confirmed the general accuracy of the Krotkov account. He also supplied some additional details.

The author, accompanied by two colleagues, interviewed Ambassador Dejean in Paris on March 18, 1970. Although Dejean was gracious throughout the interview, at its end he unexpectedly insisted that the author might not quote him or otherwise make any use of the statements he made. His wishes have been honored.

CHAPTER VII

Description of STB headquarters: Interviews with Bittman.

Agent Seven: Interviews with Bittman and Western security services.

Assassination of Lapusnyik: Interview with László Szabó; statement of Szabó, CIA Subcommittee, House Committee on Armed Services H 1966; *Die Presse* (Vienna), May 20, 1962; New York *Times*, June 5, 1962; Vienna *Express*, June 6, 1962; *Die Presse* (Vienna), June 7, 1962; New York *Times*, June 10, 1962; Washington *Post*, June 14, 1962; Vienna *Kurier*, June 27, 1962 (English translations of all of the newspaper stories cited along with reproductions of several pertinent Reuters dispatches appear in the subcommittee publication containing Szabó's testimony); Western security services.

Frenzel case: Hagen, p. 108.

Owen case: *The Guardian* (Manchester), April 29, 1970; *Daily Express* (London), April 24, 1970; *The Times* (London), May 6, 7, 1970; Baltimore *Sun*, May 7, 1970.

STB forgeries and slander: *Testimony of Lawrence Britt* (Ladislav Bittman), H SSIS, 1971.

Melnik statements: *L'Express* (Paris), October 4–11, 1971.

Romanian operations: *Life*, December 13, 1968; interviews with Turkish embassy, Washington and Western security services.

Houghton case: Clarke, pp. 55–78; New York *Times*, June 14, 1961; Washington *Post*, November 9, 1969.

Sütterlin case: *Stern* (Hamburg), June 1, 8, 15, 22, 29, July 6, 13, 20, 1969; New York *Times*, November 29, 1969; Washington *Star*, November 19, 1969.

Augros case: "Histoire de L'Espionnage 1945–71," *Historia*, Paris, 1971; interviews with Western security services.

Soviet-Cuban relations and the DGI: This section relies primarily upon accounts by two former DGI officers, Orlando Castro and Gerardo Perazo Amerchazurra, who fled from the Cuban embassy in London in late December 1971. The latter is the source of the new information about the latest Soviet attempt to depose Castro and the secret speech of Raúl. The information of both former DGI officers is substantially confirmed in an excellent and detailed study by Crozier entitled "Soviet Pressures in the Caribbean," *Conflict Studies*, Institute for the Study of Conflict, London, No. 35, May 1973.

Story of Jennifer Miles: The narrative is based primarily upon statements Miss Miles made to various authorities after she was confronted with espionage charges. Some details were obtained through interviews with Saeed Khan and others in Washington acquainted with her.

The existence of a spy called "Mary" and the expulsion of the two DGI officers first was reported by Jeremiah O'Leary in the Washington *Sunday Star*, October 18, 1970. Other published references include: Washington *Evening Star*, October 22, November 2 and 21, 1970; Washington *Post*, October 23, 1970, November 28, 1970; *Rand Daily Mail* (Johannesburg), October 19, 1970; Toronto *Globe and Mail*, October 19, 1970; *Sunday Times* (Johannesburg), November 22 and December 6, 1970; Washington *Daily News*, November 4, 1970; *Scope* (South Africa), November 27, 1970.

CHAPTER VIII

STB-KGB operation in Indonesia: Bittman, pp. 106–122.

Lenin quotations: Lenin, V. 12, pp. 378–89.

Concept of disinformation: "The Soviet and Communist Bloc Defamation Campaign," a study read by Rep. Melvin Price, *Congressional Record*, September 28, 1965, pp. 24477–78; *The Guardian* (Manchester), August 12, 1969; interviews with Western security services; Washington *Post*, December 25, 1967.

Agayants: Bittman, pp. 114, 157; New York *Times*, November 10, 1967, and May 15, 1968; Western security services.

Kondrashev: *Die Welt* (Hamburg) and Washington *Post*, December 10, 1966.

Lyudin: Pretoria *News* (South Africa), September 9, 1967; Western security services.

Gorsky: Western security services.

Maynard: Conquest, pp. 22–23.

Shaw: Henderson, pp. 312–16.

Dalstroy, Lattimore and Wallace: Gorbatov, pp. 122–28; Ginzburg, p. 406; Lipper, *Eleven Years in Soviet Prison Camps;* Conquest, pp. 350–355; Hingley, pp. 148–49; Lattimore, pp. 646, 657; Wallace, pp. 33, 35, 36, 72, 89, 117, 134, 137.

Soviet housing data: Donald D. Barry, "Housing in the USSR: Cities and Towns," and Karl-Eugen Wädekin, "Housing in the USSR: The Countryside," *Problems of Communism*, May/June 1969; *The Economist* (London), August 12, 1972; *The Guardian* (Manchester), December 16, 1972; *Wall Street Journal*, May 19, 1969; *Problemy Ekonomiki*, No. 5, Moscow, May 1972; Kosygin and Brezhnev quotations, as cited by Barry.

Samuels speech: U.S. Department of Commerce press release May 7, 1968.

Langman quotation: Interview with Langman, July 1969.

Bates quotations: *Industrialized Housing*, Subcommittee on Urban Affairs of the Joint Economic Committee, 1969; interviews with Bates July 23 and August 8, 1969, July 5, 1973.

Murder of Madame Trémeaud: Interviews with Western security services; Bittman, pp. 1–3.

Swastika operation: Interviews with Rupert Sigl, former KGB agent, and other former KGB personnel; interviews with Western security services; New York *Herald Tribune*, February 20 and April 13, 1958; New York *Times*, April 13 and August 2, 1958, January 10, April 17, December 26, 28, 31, 1959; New York *Herald Tribune*, January 11, January 28, December 26, 30, 31, 1959; New York *Post*, January 28, 1959; New York *Times*, January 1–3, 5, 7, 10, 15–17, 21, February 7, 18, 1960; New York *Herald Tribune*, January 3–5, 8, 9, 21, 22, February 19, March 18, 1960; Washington *Post*, January 4, 19, April 5, 1960.

Forgeries: *Communist Forgeries (Testimony of Richard Helms, Assistant Director, CIA)*, H SSIS, 1961; *The Statesman* (Calcutta), March 21, 1968; *The Pulse* (Ankara), April 6, 1970; *Bizim Anadolu* (Istanbul), September 12, 1970; interviews with Bittman, Sigl, and Western security services.

Background and activities of Louis: Threatened with a libel action, Canadian journalist Peter Worthington began preparing his defense and on May 7, 1969, interviewed the late Professor Arkady Belinkov of Yale University, who had known Louis in the camps. After Belinkov's death. Worthington generously made his extensive notes of the interview available to the author. Nosenko in interviews with the author provided heretofore unpublished details of Louis' early relationship with the KGB. Otherwise, the recitation of Louis' activities relies on the following sources: New York *Times*, May 24, August 7, 12, 1967, May 5, 1968, September 18, 1969, September 7, 8, 1971, June 2, 1973; New York *Times Magazine*, January 31, 1971, pp. 12–35; Washington *Post*, March 6, 16, 1969, November 30, 1970, November 12, 1971, March 22, 1973; *Problems of Communism*, September/October 1968, p. 50; *Parade* magazine, July 2 and December 31, 1972; *El Tiempo* (Bogotá), March 17, 1970; Washington *Sunday Star*, October 5, 1969; Washington *Daily News*, January 14, 1971; *The Current* (Bombay), June 26, 1971; Worthington, Toronto *Telegram*, March 29, 1969; *Evening News* (London), October 2 and 7, 1971.

Defamation of Courtney: Interview with Commander Courtney, *Sunday Telegraph* (London), October 17, 1965; *Private Eye* (London), November 12, 1965; *Evening Standard* (London), September 28, 1971.

Slander by Tass and Philby: New York *Times* and *Daily Telegraph* (London), October 6, 1971; *Daily Star* (Beirut), July 4, 1972.

Attempt to steal the Mirage: The narrative is based primarily upon data provided by noncommunist security services, including statements made by some of the principals in the case. Information about the size of the Lebanese population and army was provided by the embassy of Lebanon, Washington. The U.S. Department of Defense supplied technical data about the Mirage and lent other assistance. Published references to the Mirage affair include: *Le Jour* (Beirut), October 1–4, 1969; *Arab World* (Beirut), October 2, 6, 1969; *al-Nidda* (Beirut), October 2, 1969; *L'Orient* (Beirut), October 1, 2, 4, 5, 1969; New York *Times,* October 1, 3, 5, 1969; *The Current* (Bombay), October 18, 1969; *March of the Nation* (Bombay), October 25, 1969; Ceylon *Daily News,* November 10, 1969; *Son Havadis* (Istanbul), October 6, 7, 1969; *Milliyet* (Istanbul), October 3, 1969; *Son Saat* (Istanbul), November 1, 1969; *Le Monde* (Paris), October 2, 1969; *Stern* (Hamburg), October 12, 1969; *Der Spiegel* (Hamburg), December 22, 1969.

CHAPTER IX

Khrushchev quotation: *Soviet Intelligence and Security Services, 1964–1970,* S SSIS, 1972, p. 1.

Early Soviet espionage: Orlov, *Handbook of Intelligence and Guerrilla Warfare;* Krivitsky, *I Was Stalin's Agent; The Report of the Royal Commission,* Ottawa, February 5, 1946; Gouzenko, *The Iron Curtain; The Report of the Royal Commission on Espionage,* Sydney, August 22, 1955.

Soviet agents in U.S.: *Exposé of Soviet Espionage (Prepared by the FBI),* R SSIS 1960.

Soviet agents in Great Britain: West, *The New Meaning of Treason;* Wise and Ross, pp. 101–103, 113–115.

Drummond: Washington *Evening Star,* September 29, 1962; New York *Times,* September 30, 1962; Washington *Post,* August 16, 1963; interviews with U.S Department of Defense.

Wennerström: Whiteside, *An Agent in Place;* Washington *Post,* November 30, 1964, and October 7, 1972; *The Wennerstroem Spy Case,* SSIS, 1964.

Solomatin: *The Times* (London), *Daily Express* (London), *Daily Telegraph* (London), March 26, 1964.

Bychkov and Poluchkin: Montreal *Gazette* and Ottawa *Journal,* May 10, 1965.

Whalen: New York *Times,* July 13, 1966; interview with FBI.

Rinaldi: Washington *Sunday Star,* April 9, 1967; Western security services.

Eitzenberger: *Stuttgarter Nachrichten* (Stuttgart), June 23, 1970; Western security services.

Odantara: *Asahi Evening News* (Tokyo), *Japan Times*, May 14, 1969.

Ryabov and Mamontov: *La Prensa* (Buenos Aires), November 6, 1970; Washington *Evening Star*, November 11, 1970.

Volokov: *Le Figaro* (Paris), May 4, 1973; Western security services.

Makarov and Lovanov: *Berlingske Tidende* (Copenhagen), March 28–30, 1972; Western security services.

Yerofeyev: New York *Times*, April 29, 1973.

Subversive overtures to Americans: Western security services.

KGB China experts: *Ibid.*

Espionage in Hong Kong: *South China Morning Post* (Hong Kong), March 16, 1972; Washington *Post*, August 26, 1972.

Orlov quotations: Orlov, *Handbook of Intelligence and Guerrilla Warfare*, pp. 5–7.

CHAPTER X

After Johnson and Mintkenbaugh were arrested, they and, to a lesser extent, Mrs. Johnson repeatedly were questioned over a period of months. During the interrogations, agents of the FBI and military counterintelligence tried to scrutinize literally every detail of their lives in quest of evidence and insights that might contribute to an understanding of the KGB operation. Johnson cooperated fully, seeming almost to enjoy reliving all he had done. Mintkenbaugh and Mrs. Johnson also were quite frank in talking about even their most intimate personal experiences. As a consequence, the interrogation reports of the Johnson-Mintkenbaugh case fill many dozens of volumes in government files. The narrative is based largely on these records. The dialogue has been reconstructed on the basis of what Johnson, Mintkenbaugh, or Mrs. Johnson stated was said on the occasions described.

Thomas D. Fox, who as chief of the counterintelligence division of the Defense Intelligence Agency supervised the military investigation of the case, provided invaluable information, counsel, and criticism. So did another authority on the case, Anthony T. Litrento, who has retired from the FBI after a distinguished career in counterintelligence. General Lyman Lemnitzer, who was Supreme Allied Commander, Europe, at the time Johnson stole documents at Orly Field, supplied details that were most useful in the initial research.

Published references to aspects of the case include: Washington *Post*, April 6, 7, 8, June 8, July 31, 1965, May 20,

1972; Washington *Evening Star,* May 19, 20, 1972; *Der Spiegel* (Hamburg), September 8, 1969; *The Times* (London), September 9, 1969; *Stern* (Hamburg), August 31, September 14, 1969, February 1, 1970; New York *Times,* December 1, 1964, April 6, 7, June 7, July 31, 1965, August 26, 28, 1969; New York *Herald Tribune,* April 6, 7, July 31, 1965; Cincinnati *Enquirer,* April 6, 7, 16, July 31, 1965; Chicago *Tribune,* November 13, 1964, April 5, 7, 1965; Bittman, pp. 220–226.

(Because the full, authentic details of the case never before have been released, none of the published accounts reveal the magnitude, nature, and methods of the espionage Johnson committed. Some of the published references leave the impression that the espionage occurred primarily while Johnson was stationed at the Pentagon in 1964. Although such an inference is understandable, given the previous paucity of official data available to the press, it is totally erroneous. Johnson never communicated with the KGB subsequent to his departure from France in the spring of 1964, and while at the Pentagon he did not have access to any documents of significance.)

CHAPTER XI

The story of the assault upon Mexico is based in large part upon interviews with Raya Kiselnikova, written statements made by some of the guerrillas after their capture, diaries seized from some of the guerrillas, interviews with local Mexican police, and Western security services. Pablo Morales, former editor of the *Reader's Digest* Latin American editions, and his colleague, Miss Susan Sellers, verified aspects of the story through interviews of their own in Mexico. They also compiled from official Mexican and United Nations sources most of the statistical data pertaining to the complement of the Soviet embassy, trade, literacy, and per capita income. Of all documents obtained, the most revealing were the written confessions of Fabricio Gómez Souza and Angel Bravo Cisneros.

Nechiporenko: Raya Kiselnikoya's press conference, reported in the Washington *Star,* March 5, 1970; *El Siglo* (Bogotá), March 11, 1970; Western security services.

Use of Soviet embassy by KGB: *La Nación* (San José), *El Tiempo* (Bogotá), March 22, 1971; *London Observer,* March 28, 1971; *Christian Science Monitor,* April 7, 1971, Western security services.

Description of Referentura: Raya Kiselnikova.

Soviet effort to damage Mexican economy, and bribery of labor leader: Chicago *Daily Tribune,* April 4, 19, 1959; Baltimore *Sun,* April 10, 1959; New York *Herald Tribune,* April 17, 1959; *Newsweek,* April 20, 1959.

KGB recruitment of students for future subversion: Western security services; *El Día* (Mexico City), March 20, 1971; *Christian Science Monitor,* March 31, 1971; *March of the Nation* (Bombay), July 31, 1971.

Gómez and his activities: *Novedades* (Mexico City), *El Universal* (Mexico City), *El Día* (Mexico City), March 16, 1971; *Time,* April 19, 1971; Gómez confession.

Figures on Mexican social and economic progress: Miss Diana Muñoz, Mexican embassy, Washington, D.C.; *El Día* (Mexico City), March 20, 1971.

Kolomyakov: Western security services and Raya Kiselnikova. 1968 student riots:

  Trouble in preparatory schools and later riots: Miami *Herald,* July 28, 1968; New York *Times,* July 30, 31, August 2, 4, September 9, 1968; Morris Rothenberg, former political officer, U.S. Embassy, Mexico, 1968.

  Army takeover of university and ensuing violence: Washington *Post,* September 20, 1968; President Gustavo Díaz Ordaz, Fifth State of the Union Address, September 1, 1969.

  October 2, 1968, battle: New York *Times,* October 1–5, 7, 8, 1968; Washington *Post,* October 5–7, 1968; Rothenberg; Report from U.S. Embassy, Mexico City, to the U.S. State Department, Washington, D.C., October 20, 1968.

  Threat to Olympic Games: *Wall Street Journal,* October 2, 16, 1968; President Díaz, Fifth State of the Union Address, September 1, 1969.

Lumumba University: *Japan Times,* April 2, 1971; New York *Times,* April 18, 1971.

Erzin: Identified as KGB by defector.

Gómez and his group at Lumumba University: *Novedades* (Mexico City), *Excelsior* (Mexico City), *El Universal* (Mexico City), *El Día* (Mexico City), March 16, 1971; *Time,* April 19, 1971.

Training in North Korea: *Ibid., Latin American Report,* V. 3, No. 6, March 1971; *Japan Times,* March 17, 1971; *Korea Times* (Seoul), *Kyonghyang Sinmun* (Seoul), March 20, 1971; *Tachan Ilbo* (Seoul), March 22, 1971.

Background of Diakonov: *O Jornal* (Brasília), September 17, 1963; *La Razón* (Buenos Aires), July 29, 1969; *El Mundo* (Caracas), July 30, 1969; *El Universal Gráfico* (Mexico City), August 9, 1969; *O Estado de São Paulo* (São Paulo), March 21, 1971.

Traveling and training of Mexican guerrillas in North Korea: *The News* (Mexico City), March 22, 1971; Statements by Mexican Prosecutor General Julio Nánchez Vargas, March 15, 1971; Statements of guerrillas after their capture, their diaries, and detailed confession by one guerrilla.

Reason for defection of Raya Kiselnikova, and its effect on the KGB in Mexico: Washington *Daily News,* March 5, 1970; *El Siglo* (Bogotá), March 11, 1970; Washington *Star,* March 16, September 20, 1970.

Robberies by Mexican guerrillas: Statement by Mexican Prosecutor General Julio Nánchez Vargas, March 15, 1971; *The News* (Mexico City), September 11, 12, 15, 17, 18, 19, 1971; the New York *Times,* September 20, 26, 1971; *Christian Science Monitor,* September 29, October 20, 1971.

Expulsion of Russians: Statement by Foreign Minister Emilio Rabasa; Washington *Evening Star,* Washington *Post,* March 19, 1971.

Soviet reaction to expulsion: *El Día* (Mexico City), March 20, 1971; Rowland Evans and Robert Novak, Washington *Post,* March 24, 1971.

Sympathy from Latin America: *El Universal Gráfico* (Mexico City), *El Siglo* (Bogotá), March 19, 1971; *O Estado de São Paulo* (São Paulo), March 21, 1971; *La Nación* (San José), *El Tiempo* (Bogotá), March 22, 1971; *La República* (San José), *La Estrella de Panamá* (Panama City), March 23, 1971; *La Prensa* (Buenos Aires), March 24, 1971; *El Telégrafo* (Guayaquil), March 26, 1971.

Costa Rica's suspension of negotiations with USSR: *La Hora* (San José), March 22, 1971; *U.S. News & World Report,* May 17, 1971.

Subversion in Ghana: Information about the summary executions of the KGB officers was provided by *Reader's Digest* Roving Editor David Reed, who visited Accra shortly after the fall of Nkrumah. His account has been confirmed by Western security services. Other sources include: Ghana White Paper, Accra; Reed, "Ghana: Communism's Big Defeat in Africa," *Reader's Digest,* June 1966; *Ghanian Times* (Accra), March 18, 1966; *The Daily Graphic* (Accra), March 18, 1966, June 7, 1967; *The Times* (London), June 7, 1967; *Evening News* (Accra), June 7, 1967; *Anbaa Al Sudan* (Khartoum), April 8, 1966; *Life,* February 21, 1969.

KGB and IRA: Orlov, *The Secret History of Stalin's Crimes,* p. 227; Crozier, *Peacetime Strategy of the Soviet Union;* interviews with Western security services; casualty figures provided by British Information Service, New York; *Wash-*

ington Report, American Security Council, February 11, 1972; *The Guardian* (Manchester), October 19, 1971, December 8, 1972; *Time,* December 11, 1972; *Christian Science Monitor, Daily Telegraph* (London), December 14, 1972; *Japan Times,* December 11, 1972.

Couriers to Colombia: *El Siglo* (Bogotá), *El Tiempo* (Bogotá), *La República* (Bogotá), July 25, 1969; Western security services.

Subversion in the Congo (Zaïre): Washington *Post,* November 20, 1963; *Le Progrès* (Léopoldville), 1963; *Le Progrès* (Kinshasa), May 16–18, 1970; *La Tribune Diplomatique* (Kinshasa), June 6, 7, 1970; New York *Times,* June 23, September 3, 1972.

Action by Sudanese: Interviews embassy of Sudan, Washington; New York *Times,* July 27, 1971; *The Guardian* (Manchester), July 30, August 28, 1971; Washington *Post,* July 27, September 6, 27, 1971; Baltimore *Sun,* September 24, 1971.

Expulsions from Ecuador: Washington *Post,* July 7, 1971; *Christian Science Monitor,* July 10, 1971; Western security services.

Terrorism in Turkey: Interviews embassy of Turkey, Washington; *Time,* May 10, 31, 1971; New York *Times,* June 6, 1971; *Yeni* (Istanbul), February 24, 1971; *Sunday Telegraph* (London), April 2, 1972; *Daily Telegraph* (London), April 29, 1971; *The Current* (Bombay), June 12, 1971.

Lenin quotation: Wolfe, *Three Who Made a Revolution,* p. 372.

Ponomarev quotation: *Detente and the World Revolutionary Process: An Analysis of Current Soviet Revolutionary Aims,* A SSIS, 1972, p. 5.

CHAPTER XII

The story of Kaarlo Tuomi derives primarily from interviews by the author with Tuomi and FBI agents who worked against, then with him. Additionally, Tuomi made available extensive notes and the rough draft of a manuscript he wrote in 1965 on the chance that he might someday wish to publish his story himself. The author also obtained a variety of photographic evidence, including a surveillance photo of the meeting between Galkin and Tuomi on the Hudson and a picture of the forged passport Tuomi used to enter the United States.

Tuomi is the sole source of information concerning his experiences in the Soviet Union. However, the narrative of events that occurred in the United States is based upon extensive interviews with the FBI agents referred to as Don and Jack as well as with Tuomi. The two agents, both of whom are retired, read early drafts of the chapter and offered valuable criticisms. Further corroboration was obtained from Cartha DeLoach, former Assistant to the Director of the FBI.

CHAPTER XIII

Emergency Politburo meeting: *Financial Times* (London), September 29, 1971.

Expulsions from Great Britain: *The Times* (London), *Daily Express* (London), *Daily Telegraph* (London), *The Guardian* (Manchester), September 25–28, 1971; New York *Times*, September 25–28, 1971; Washington *Post*, September 25–28, 1971.

Arrest of Kostikov: *El Sol* (Mexico City), December 21, 1968; *The News* (Mexico City), December 22, 24, 1968.

Flight of KGB officers: Western security services.

Soviet murders 1926–1938: *Murder International, Inc., Murder and Kidnapping as an Instrument of Soviet Policy*, H SSIS, 1965.

Directorate of Special Tasks: Orlov, *The Secret History of Stalin's Crimes*, p. 223.

Death of Sedov: Poretsky, pp. 264–273; Dewar, p. 50; Levine, pp. 29–31, 38–40, 42.

The stalking of Trotsky: Levine, pp. 69–70, 83–87, 97–98, 124–125, 194.

Admission by Zborowski: *Scope of Soviet Activity in the U.S.* (Testimony of Zborowski), H SSIS, 1956.

Sudoplatov quotation: Khokhlov, pp. 165–66.

Postwar murders: *Murder International, Inc., Murder and Kidnapping as an Instrument of Soviet Policy*, H SSIS, 1965.

Abduction of Linse: *Ibid.*, Deriabin, pp. 22–23, 28–30.

Quotation of Studnikov: Khokhlov, p. 222.

Closing and Reestablishment of Kamera: The references to the Kamera differ somewhat from the scant information previously published. They are based upon comparatively new intelligence which Western security services believe to be valid.

Khokhlov and Okolovich: Khokhlov, pp. 189–190, 245–246; *Activities of Soviet Secret Service* (testimony of N. E. Khokhlov), H SSIS, 1954.

Attempt to kill Khokhlov: Khokhlov, pp. 360–363.

Stashinsky assassinations and defection: *Murder International, Inc., Murder and Kidnapping as an Instrument of Soviet*

Policy, H SSIS 1965; Anders, *Murder to Order;* interviews Western security services.

Organization of Department V: Western security services.

Sejna statements: *Paris-Match,* August 14, 1971; interviews with Sejna.

Statement of British Foreign Office: Washington *Post,* September 25, 1971.

Sir Peter Rawlinson quotation: *Daily Telegraph* (London), October 19, 1971.

The story of Sabotka: Tom Hazlitt, Toronto *Star,* September 11, 1972; interviews with Sabotka, Hazlitt, and Western security services.

Assassination of Gahiz: *Christian Science Monitor,* April 9, 16, 1968; *Valeurs Actuelles* (Paris), January 26, 1970; Kabul *Times,* September 13, 1972; *Al-Hayat* (Beirut), October 29, 1972; *Al-Jamhour* (Beirut), November 2, 1972; *Al-Nadwa* (Jidda), October 15, November 27, December 9, 1972; *Al-Medina* and *Al-Bilad* (Jidda), December 8, 1972; Jakarta *Times,* December 15, 1972.

ACKNOWLEDGMENTS

I am solely responsible for any errors of fact or interpretation that may mar this work. I also am indebted to men an women of many nationalities without whose trust, courage, and intelligence the work never could have been accomplished. Without implying that any benefactor herein named necessarily endorses my findings and conclusions, I wish to thank those whose help I am at liberty to acknowledge publicly:

Father Vladimir Ignaste, Aleksandr Yurevich Kaznacheev, Nikolai Yevgeniyevich Khokhlov, Yuri Vasilevich Krotkov, Yuri Ivanovich Nosenko, Vladimir Nikolaevich Sakharov, Rupert Sigl, and Kaarlo Tuomi, all former officers or agents of the KGB.

Svetlana Alliluyeva, Natalia Belinkova, Raya Kiselnikova, Vladimir Matusevich, Vladimir Trofimov, and Aleksei Yakushev, former Soviet citizens.

Dr. Ladislav Bittman, formerly of the Czechoslovakian intelligence service (Statni Tajna Bezpecnost); László Szabó, formerly of the Hungarian intelligence service (Allami Vedelmi Batoság); Gerardo Perazo Amerchazurra and Orlando Castro Hidalgo, formerly of the Cuban intelligence service (Dirección General de Inteligencia).

William C. Fletcher, professor and director of the Department of Slavic and Soviet Studies, University of Kansas; Brian Crozier, director of the Institute for the Study of Conflict, London; Thomas D. Fox, former chief of the counterintelligence department of the U.S. Defense Intelligence Agency; William King Harvey and Peer de Silva, retired officers of the Central Intelligence Agency; Cartha DeLoach, former Assistant to the Director of the Federal Bureau of Investigation; Anthony P. Litrento and John O'Toole, retired FBI agents.

I owe an especial debt to colleagues at the *Reader's Digest:* Patricia Lawson, Alicia Boyd, and Virginia Lawton of the

Washington office; and John Panitza, John Flint, and Denis Fodor of the European Editorial Office.

Charles M. Stevenson, our former Washington Editor, who was my friend and teacher, allowed and encouraged us to proceed during the early, uncertain stages of the undertaking. DeWitt Wallace, by repeated expressions of personal interest and approbation, sustained us through many frustrations and provided the resources that made the book possible.

Susan Wanner discharged, with determination and diplomacy, the difficult duty of challenging and attempting to verify each statement in the book. In so doing, she purged the first drafts of many mistakes and enhanced the manuscript with factual findings of her own.

Katharine Clark, beyond assembling an immense mass of information and maintaining it in usable form, conducted dozens of interviews, confirmed myriad facts, and by her own ingenuity surmounted numerous research problems.

Fulton Oursler, Jr., and Edward T. Thompson supported the project from its inception, enriched it with gifted editorial thoughts and criticism, offered ideas that improved the final manuscript, and, by courageous professional stands, helped overcome many difficulties and crises.

Kenneth Gilmore conceived the idea of the book; shared with me all major decisions regarding research, form, and content; nurtured the writing and edited each chapter. All the while, he provided the kind of intellectual stimulation and inspiration only a great editor can. The book is as much his as mine.

No one was a closer confidant, critic, counselor, and partner than my wife, Patricia. To her, I give loving thanks.

For permission to reprint copyright material the author and publisher gratefully acknowledge the following:

Will the Soviet Union Survive Until 1984? by Andrei Amalrik, Harper & Row, Publishers.

Transcript of Sakharov's Memo and Postscript, N. Y. *Times,* August 18, 1972: © 1972 by the New York Times Company. Reprinted by permission.

"Russian Writers and the Secret Prize" by Anatoly Kuznetsov, N. Y. *Times,* August 10, 1969: © 1969 by the New York Times Company. Reprinted by permission.

From the "Introduction" by George F. Kennan in *Power and the Soviet Elite,* by Boris I. Nicolaevsky. Excerpted and reprinted by permission of Praeger Publishers, Inc., New York.

"The Cheka" by E. J. Scott, St. Anthony's Papers No. 1, St. Anthony's College, Oxford, published in London by Chatto & Windus 1956.

From *The Grand Tactician: Khrushchev's Rise to Power,* by Lazar Pistrak. © 1961 by Frederick A. Praeger, Inc. Excerpted and reprinted by permission.

From *Khrushchev and Stalin's Ghost* by Bertram D. Wolfe. © 1957 by Bertram D. Wolfe. Excerpted and reprinted by permission of Praeger Publishers, Inc. New York.

Yunost quoted in the *Daily Telegraph,* London, March 14, 1972.

Article by John Morgan in *The Washington Post,* January 21, 1968. © 1968. Reprinted by permission of *The Washington Post.*

Religion and Soviet Foreign Policy 1945–1970 by William C. Fletcher, Oxford University Press, London, 1973.

"Notes from Soviet Asylums," *National Review,* June 9, 1972. Courtesy *National Review,* 150 East 35 Street, New York, N.Y. 10016.

David Markham in the *Daily Telegraph,* London, June 1 and June 7, 1971.

"Histoire de l'Espionnage 1945–1971." *Historia,* Special Issue No. 23: The Secret Services.

Handbook of Intelligence and Guerrilla Warfare by Alexandr Orlov, University of Michigan Press, Ann Arbor, Michigan, 1965.

The Deception Game: Czechoslovak Intelligence in Soviet Political Warfare by Ladislav Bittman. Syracuse, New York: Syracuse University Research Corporation, 1972.

Soviet Asia Mission by Henry A. Wallace, Harcourt Brace Jovanovich, N.Y.

Lenin quotation from *Three Who Made a Revolution: A Biographical History,* copyright © 1948, 1964 by Bertram D. Wolfe. Reprinted with permission of The Dial Press, Inc.

From the book *In the Name of Conscience,* by Nikolai Khokhlov. Copyright © 1959 by Nikolai Khokhlov. Translated by Emily Kingsbery. Reprinted by permission of the publishers, The David McKay Company, Inc.

Sir Peter Rawlinson in the *Daily Telegraph,* London, October 19, 1971.

BIBLIOGRAPHY

ACCOCE, PIERRE, and QUET, PIERRE, *A Man Called Lucy*, trans. by A. M. Sheridan Smith. New York, Coward, 1967.

ALLILUYEVA, SVETLANA, *Twenty Letters to a Friend*, tr. from Russian by Priscilla Johnson. New York, Harper, 1967.

————, *Only One Year*, New York, Harper, 1969.

AMALRIK, ANDREI, *Will the Soviet Union Survive Until 1984?* New York, Harper, 1969.

ANDERS, KARL, *Murder to Order*. New York, Devin, 1967.

BAILEY, GEOFFREY, *The Conspirators*. New York, Harper, 1960.

BARGHOORN, FREDERICK C., "The Security Police," *Interest Groups in Soviet Politics*. Princeton, N.J., Princeton University Press, 1971.

BIALOGUSKI, MICHAEL, *The Case of Colonel Petrov*. New York, McGraw, 1955.

BITTMAN, LADISLAV, *The Deception Game*. Syracuse, N.Y., Syracuse University Research Corp., 1972.

BJÖRKEGREN, HANS, *Aleksandr Solzhenitsyn, A Biography*. New York, Joseph Okpaku Publishing Co., 1972.

BLAKE, PATRICIA, "This Is the Winter of Moscow's Dissent," *New York Times Magazine*, March 24, 1968.

BOURDEAUX, MICHAEL, *Religious Ferment in Russia: Protestant Opposition to Soviet Religious Policy*. New York, St. Martin, 1968.

BRZEZINSKI, ZBIGNIEW, *Ideology and Power in Soviet Politics*. New York, Praeger, 1962.

BULLOCH, JOHN, and MILLER, HENRY, *Spy Ring*. London, Secker, 1961.

BYRNES, ROBERT F., "American Scholars in Russia Soon Learn About the KGB," *New York Times Magazine*, Nov. 16, 1969.

CARR, E. H., "The Origin and Status of the Cheka," *Soviet Studies* (London), Vol. X, No. 1 (July 1958).

CASTRO, ORLANDO HIDALGO, *Spy for Fidel*. Miami, Fla., E. A. Seemann Publishing Co., 1971.

CHAMBERS WHITTAKER, *Witness*. New York, Random, 1952.

CHAPMAN, COLIN, *August 21st: The Rape of Czechoslovakia.* Philadelphia, Lippincott, 1968.

CHESTER, LEWIS, FAY, STEPHEN, and YOUNG, HUGO, *The Zinoviev Letter*. Philadelphia, Lippincott, 1968.

CHORNOVIL, VYACHESLAV, ed., *The Chornovil Papers*. New York, McGraw, 1968.

Chronicle of Current Events, Nos. 16–27, trans. by Amnesty International Publications, London.

CLARKE, COMER, *The War Within*. London, World Distributors, 1961.

CONQUEST, ROBERT, *The Great Terror: Stalin's Purges of the Thirties*. New York, Macmillan, 1968.

CONQUEST, ROBERT, ed., *Justice and the Legal System in the USSR*. London, The Bodley Head, 1968.

———, *The Soviet Police System*. New York, Praeger, 1968.

CROZIER, BRIAN, rapporteur, *European Security and the Soviet Problem*. London, Institute for the Study of Conflict (ISC), July–November 1971.

CROZIER, BRIAN, *Peacetime Strategy of the Soviet Union*. London, ISC, 1973.

Czech Black Book (The), Prepared by the Institute of History, Czechoslovak Academy of Sciences, and published under title *Sedm Prazskych Dnu*, 1968, trans. by Frederick A. Praeger, Inc., ed. Robert Littell. New York, Praeger, 1969.

DALLIN, ALEXANDER, *The Soviet Union at the United Nations*. New York, Praeger, 1962.

DALLIN, DAVID J., *Soviet Espionage*. New Haven, Conn., Yale University Press, 1953.

———, *The Changing World of Soviet Russia*. New Haven, Conn., Yale University Press, 1956.

DEAKIN, F. W., and STORRY, G. R., *The Case of Richard Sorge*. New York, Harper, 1966.

DERIABIN, PETER, *Watchdogs of Terror*. New Rochelle, N.Y., Arlington House, 1972.

DERIABIN, PETER, and GIBNEY, FRANK, *The Secret World*. New York, Doubleday, 1959.

DEWAR, HUGO, *Assassins At Large*. London, Wingate, 1951.

DJILAS, MILOVAN, *The New Class*. New York, Praeger, 1957.

———, *Conversations with Stalin*. New York, Harcourt, 1962.

DONOVAN, JAMES B., *Strangers on a Bridge*. New York, Atheneum, 1967.

DULLES, ALLEN, *The Craft of Intelligence*. New York, Harper, 1963.

DZYUBA, IVAN, *Internationalism or Russification?: A Study in the Soviet Nationalities Problem*, ed. by M. Davies. London, Camelot Press, 1968.

FLETCHER, WILLIAM C., *Nikolai*. New York, Macmillan, 1968.

———, *Religion and Soviet Foreign Policy 1945–1970*. London, Oxford University Press, 1973.

FOOTE, ALEXANDER, *Handbook for Spies*. Garden City, N.Y., Doubleday, 1969.

FRANKS, LORD, *Report on Official Secrets Act*. London, Her Majesty's Stationery Office, 1972.

GEHLEN, REINHARD, *The Service*, trans. by David Irving. New York, Popular Library, 1972.

GINZBURG, EVGENIA SEMYONOVNA, *Into the Whirlwind*. New York, Harcourt, 1967.

GORBATOV, GENERAL A. V., *Years Off My Life*, trans. by Gordon Clough and Anthony Cash. London, Constable, 1964.

GORKIN, JULIAN, *L'Assassinat de Trotsky*. Paris, Juilliard, 1970.

GOUZENKO, IGOR, *The Iron Curtain*. New York, Dutton, 1948.

HAGEN, LOUIS, *The Secret War for Europe*. New York, Stein & Day, 1969.

HARVEY, M. L., and PROKOFIEFF, V., *Science and Technology as an Instrument of Soviet Policy*. Miami, Fla., Center for International Studies, U. of Miami, 1972.

HENDERSON, ARCHIBALD, *George Bernard Shaw: Man of the Century*. New York, Appleton-Century-Crofts, 1932.

HINGLEY, RONALD, *The Russian Secret Police: Muscovite, Imperial Russian and Soviet Political Security Operations, 1556–1970*. New York, Simon and Schuster, 1970.

Historia Hors Serie, Histoire de L'Espionnage 1945–1971. Paris, Librairie Jules Tallandier, 1971.

JOHN, OTTO, *Twice Through the Lines*. New York, Harper, 1972.

JOSHUA, WYNFRED, *Soviet Penetration into the Middle East*. New York, National Strategy Information Center, 1970.

KAZNACHEEV, ALEKSANDR, *Inside a Soviet Embassy*. Philadelphia, Lippincott, 1962.

KHOKHLOV, NIKOLAI, *In the Name of Conscience*, trans. by Emily Kingsbery. New York, McKay, 1959.

KHRUSHCHEV, NIKITA, *Khrushchev Remembers*, trans. and ed. by Strove Talbott. Boston, Little, Brown, 1970.

KRAVCHENKO, VICTOR, *I Chose Freedom*. New York, Scribner, 1946.

KRIVITSKY, WALTER G., *I Was Stalin's Agent*. London, H. Hamilton, 1940.

KROTKOV, YURI, *I Am from Moscow*. New York, Dutton, 1967.

KUZNETSOV, ANATOLI (A. ANATOL), "Russian Writers and the Secret Police," *Daily Telegraph*, London, Aug. 10, 1969.

LATTIMORE, OWEN, "New Road to Asia." *National Geographic Magazine*, Dec. 1944.

LEDERER, WILLIAM, and BURDICK, EUGENE, *The Ugly American*. New York, Norton, 1958.

LENCZOWSKI, GEORGE, *Soviet Advances in the Middle East*. Washington, D.C., American Enterprise Institute for Public Policy Research, 1972.

LENIN, VLADIMIR ILYICH, *Collected Works*, 4th Russian Edition. U.S.S.R., 1950.

LEVINE, ISAAC DON, *The Mind of an Assassin*. New York, Farrar, Straus & Cudahy, 1959.

LIPPER, ELINOR, *Eleven Years in Soviet Prison Camps*. Chicago, Regnery, 1951.

LITVINOV, PAVEL, *The Demonstration in Pushkin Square*, trans. from the Russian by Manya Harari. Boston, Gambit, 1969.

MAANEN, GERT VAN, *The International Student Movement & Background*. The Hague, Interdoc, 1966.

MANDELSTAM, NADEZHDA, *Hope Against Hope: A Memoir*, trans. from the Russian by Max Hayward. New York, Atheneum, 1970.

MARCHENKO, ANATOLY, *My Testimony*, trans. by Michael Scannell. New York, Dutton, 1969.

MASSIE, ROBERT K., *Nicholas and Alexandra*. New York, Atheneum, 1967.

MAX, ALPHONSE, *Guerrillas in Latin America*. The Hague, Interdoc, 1967.

MEDVEDEV, ZHORES A., *The Rise and Fall of T. D. Lysenko*, trans. by I. Michael Lerner. New York, Columbia University Press, 1969.

————, *The Medvedev Papers: The Plight of Soviet Science Today*, trans. from the Russian by Vera Rich. London, Macmillan, 1971.

MEDVEDEV, ZHORES, and MEDVEDEV, ROY, *A Question of Madness*. New York, Knopf, 1971.

MOOREHEAD, ALAN, *The Traitors*. New York, Harper, 1952.

MOROZ, VALENTIN, "A Report from the Beria Reserve," Jan. 20, 1966.

MORROS, BORIS, *My Ten Years as a Counterspy*. New York, Viking, 1959.

NERUDA, PABLO, *Las Uvas y el Viento*. Santiago de Chile, Nascimento, 1954.

————, *Canción de Gesta*. Havana, Imprenta Nacional de Cuba, 1960.

NICOLAEVSKY, BORIS I., *Power and the Soviet Elite: "The Letter of an Old Bolshevik" and other Essays*. London, Pall Mall Press, 1966.

Nkrumah's Subversion in Africa, Documents Prepared by Government of Ghana, Accra-Terna, Ministry of Information, 1966.

ORLOV, ALEXANDER, *The Secret History of Stalin's Crimes*. New York, Random, 1953.

————, *Handbook of Intelligence and Guerrilla Warfare*. Ann Arbor, U. of Michigan Press, 1965.

PARES, BERNARD, *A History of Russia*, 5th Ed. Revised. New York, Knopf, 1951.

PARRY, ALBERT, *The New Class Divided*. New York, Macmillan, 1966.

PASEYRO, RICARDO, *Le Mythe Neruda*. Paris, L'Herne, 1965.

PENKOVSKY, OLEG, *The Penkovsky Papers*, trans. by P. Deriabin. Garden City, N.Y., Doubleday, 1965.

PETROV, VLADIMIR and EVDOKIA, *Empire of Fear*. New York, Praeger, 1956.

PHILBY, KIM, *My Silent War*. New York, Grove, 1968.

PIPES, RICHARD, *Some Operational Principles of Soviet Foreign Policy*. Washington, D.C., U.S. Government Printing Office, 1972.

PISTRAK, LAZAR, *The Grand Tactician: Khrushchev's Rise to Power*. New York, Praeger, 1961.

PORETSKY, ELIZABETH K., *Our Own People*. Ann Arbor, U. of Michigan Press, 1969.

Prominent Personalities in the USSR. [Compiled by the Institute for the Study of the USSR, Munich, Germany.] Metuchen, N.J., Scarecrow Press, 1968.

RAUCH, GEORG VON, *A History of Soviet Russia*, 5th ed. revised, trans. by Peter and Annette Jacobson. New York, Praeger, 1967.

REDDAWAY, PETER, *Uncensored Russia*. New York, American Heritage Press, 1972.

REITZ, JAMES T., *Soviet Defense-Associated Activities Outside the Ministry of Defense*. McLean, Va., Research Analysis Corp., 1969.

Report of the Royal Commission. Ottawa, Edmond Cloutier, 1946.

Report of the Royal Commission on Espionage, Commonwealth of Australia. Sydney, Government Printer for New South Wales, 1955.

ROMANOV, A. I., *Nights Are Longest There: Smersh from the Inside*, trans. by Gerald Brooke. London, Hutchinson, 1972.

SAKHAROV, ANDREI D., "Thoughts on Progress, Peaceful Coexistence and Intellectual Freedom," *New York Times*, July 22, 1968.

SALINGER, PIERRE, *With Kennedy*. New York, Doubleday, 1966.

SAREEN, C. I., *Bid for Freedom: USSR vs. Tarasov*. Englewood Cliffs, N.J., Prentice-Hall, 1966.

SAYILGAN, ACLAN, *Education of Foreign Revolutionaries in the USSR*. Ankara, Turkey, Baylan Press, 1973.

SCHWARTZ, HARRY, *Prague's 200 Days*. New York, Praeger, 1969.

SCOTT, E. J., *Soviet Affairs*, "The Cheka," St. Antony's Papers No. 1. London, Chatto and Windus, 1956.

SETH, RONALD, *Unmasked: The Story of Soviet Espionage*. New York, Hawthorn, 1965.

SHUB, DAVID, *Lenin*. New York, Doubleday, 1948. Rev. Ed.: New York, Pelican Books, 1966.

SOLZHENITSYN, ALEXANDER, *One Day in the Life of Ivan Denisovich*, trans. by Max Hayward and Ronald Hingley. New York, Praeger, 1963.

————, *The First Circle*, trans. from the Russian by Nicholas Bethell and David Burg. New York, Farrar, Straus, 1969.

————, *The First Circle*, trans. from the Russian by Thomas P. Whitney. New York, Harper, 1968.

Soviet Analyst (newsletter), ed. by Robert Conquest and Tibor Szamuely, London, July 20, 1972.

Soviet Spies in the Scientific and Technical Fields. Wavre, Belgium, Ligue de la Liberté, 1968.

Soviet Spies in the Shadow of the UN. Wavre, Belgium, Ligue de la Liberté, 1968.

Special Report: First U.S. Mission on Mental Health to USSR. Washington, D.C., U.S. Dept. of Health, Education and Welfare, 1969.

STRONG, SIR KENNETH, *Intelligence at the Top*. New York, Doubleday, 1969.

STRUVE, GLEB, *Russian Literature under Lenin and Stalin 1917–1953*. Stillwater, U. of Oklahoma Press, 1971.

STRUVE, NIKITA, *Christians in Contemporary Russia*. New York, Scribner, 1967.

SZAMUELY, TIBOR, "The New House of the Dead," *The Spectator*, London, Aug. 23, 1969.

TARSIS, VALERIY, *Ward 7*, trans. from the Russian by Katya Brown. London, Collins and Harvill Press, 1965.

TREVOR-ROPER, HUGH, "The Philby Affair," *Encounter*, London, April 1968.

TUCKER, ROBERT C., and COHEN, STEPHEN F., eds., *The Great Purge Trial*, the Verbatim Report of the 1938 Moscow Trial. New York, Grosset, 1965.

VLADIMIROV, LEONID, *The Russian Space Bluff*. New York, Dial, 1973.

WALLACE, HENRY A., *Soviet Asia Mission*. New York, Reynal, 1946.

WEST, REBECCA, *A Train of Powder*. New York, Viking, 1955.

———, *The New Meaning of Treason*. New York, Viking, 1964.

WHITESIDE, THOMAS, *An Agent in Place*. New York, Viking, 1966.

WISE, DAVID, and ROSS, THOMAS B., *The Espionage Establishment*. New York, Random, 1967.

WITTLIN, THADDEUS, *Commissar: The Life and Death of Lavrenty Pavlovitch Beria*. New York, Macmillan, 1973.

WOLFE, BERTRAM D., *Khrushchev and Stalin's Ghost*. New York, 1957.

———, *Three Who Made a Revolution*. Boston, 1957.

WOLIN, SIMON, and SLUSSER, ROBERT M., *The Soviet Secret Police*. New York, Praeger, 1957.

WRIGHT, JAMES R., *Industrialized Building in the USSR*. Washington, D.C. U.S. Dept. of Commerce, National Bureau of Standards, 1971.

UNITED STATES CONGRESSIONAL PUBLICATIONS

ABBREVIATIONS:

SSIS—Subcommittee to Investigate the Administration of the Internal Security Act and Other Internal Security Laws, Committee of *Judiciary, Senate*

HCIS—Committee on *Internal Security, House*

Senate GOVOP (Sub.NAT.)—Subcommittee on National Security and International Operations of Committee on *Government Operations, Senate*

A—Analysis prepared at committee or subcommittee request

H—Hearing or Hearings

M—Memorandum prepared at committee or subcommittee request

R—Report to or from committee or subcommittee

SS—Staff Study

SW—Selected Writings prepared for or by committee or subcommittee

Soviet Atomic Espionage, Joint Committee on Atomic Energy 1951

Testimony of N. E. Khokhlov, Former MGB Agent, *Activities of Soviet Secret Service,* H SSIS, 1954

The Episode of the Russian Seamen, R SSIS 1956

Scope of Soviet Activity in the U.S., SSIS 1956 (test. of Zborowski)

Speech of Nikita Khrushchev Before a Closed Session of the XXth Congress of the Communist Party of the Soviet Union on February 25, 1956, SSIS 1957

Exposé of Secret Espionage, R SSIS 1960 (prepared by the FBI)

Testimony of Richard Helms, Assistant Director, CIA, *Communist Forgeries,* H SSIS 1961

Testimony of Alexander Orlov, H Sept. 28, 1955, SSIS 1962

Communist Penetration and Exploitation of the Free Press, S SSIS 1962

State Department Security; The Case of William Wieland; The New Passport Regulations, R SSIS 1962

The Communist International Youth and Student Apparatus, R SSIS 1963

Testimony of Paul B. Anderson, *Recent Developments in the Soviet Bloc,* Subcom. on Europe, Comm. on Foreign Affairs, House of Rep., Part I, Jan. 27–30, 1964, pp. 100–101

The Wennerstroem Spy Case, SSIS 1964

Testimony of Peter Deriabin, *Murder International, Inc., Murder and Kidnapping as an Instrument of Soviet Policy,* H SSIS 1965

Testimony of Rev. Richard Wurmbrand, *Communist Exploitation of Religion,* H SSIS 1966

House Committee on Armed Services, CIA Subcommittee, March 17, 1966

The New Strategy of Communism in the Caribbean, R, Subcommittee on Inter-American Affairs of the Committee on Foreign Affairs, 1968, Hon. Armistead I. Selden, Jr.

Aspects of Intellectual Ferment and Dissent in the Soviet Union, R SSIS 1968

Aspects of Intellectual Ferment and Dissent in the Soviet Union, A SSIS 1969

The Soviet Approach to Negotiation, SW SSIS 1969

Industrialized Housing, Subcommittee on Urban Affairs of the Joint Economic Committee, 1969

International Negotiation, Exchanges of Scholars with the Soviet Union: Advantages and Dilemmas, M GOVOP, Senate, 1969 (Robert F. Byrnes)

Testimony of George Karlin, Parts I, II, III, H SSIS, Nov. 1969–Mar. 1970

Testimony of Col. Yevgeny Y. Runge, H SSIS, Feb. 5, 1970

Economic Performance and the Military Burden in the Soviet Union, A Compendium of Papers, Subcommittees on Foreign Economic Policy of the Joint Economic Committee, 1970

Robert Conquest, *The Human Cost of Soviet Communism,* M SSIS 1970

Departments of State, Justice, and Commerce, The Judiciary, and Related Agencies, Appropriations for 1972, H Subcommittees on Departments of State, Justice, and Commerce, the Judiciary and Related Agencies, Committee on Appropriations, House, Part I 1971

Testimony of Lawrence Britt (Ladislav Bittman), H SSIS 1971

Testimony of Francisco Antonio Teira Alfonso, *Communist Threat to the United States Through the Caribbean,* H SSIS, Parts 22 and 23, 1971

International Negotiation; The Impact of the Changing Power Balance, Senate GOVOP Sub. 1971

International Negotiation; Chinese Comment on Soviet Foreign Policy, Senate GOVOP Sub. 1972

Summary of Hearings in 1971, R SSIS 1972

Soviet Intelligence and Security Services, 1964–1970, A Selected Bibliography of Soviet Publications, R SSIS 1972

Richard Pipes, *International Negotiation: Some Operational Principles of Soviet Foreign Policy,* M Senate GOVOP Sub. 1972

Detente and the World Revolutionary Process; An Analysis of Current Soviet Revolutionary Aims, A SSIS 1972

Abuse of Psychiatry for Political Repression in the Soviet Union, H SSIS 1972

U.S.S.R. Labor Camps, H SSIS, *Parts I and II,* February 1 and 2, 1973

Negotiation and Statecraft, H, Permanent Subcommittee on Investigations of the Committee on Government Operations, Senate, Part I, with Walter Laqueur, April 17, 1973

INDEX

"Abel, Col. Rudolf" (William Fisher), Soviet spy exchanged for F. G. Powers, 106

Aeroflot, KGB agents on staffs abroad, 27, 28, 454

Afghanistan, 111; murder of publisher M. Gahiz, 24, 446–47

Africa, 111, 194, 196, 197, 323, 414; black guerrillas trained in Soviet camps, 34; Ghana while under KGB as continental threat, 342–45. See also respective countries

Afro-Asian Solidarity Committee, KGB front in U.S.S.R., 77, 78

Agayants, Gen. Ivan Ivanovich, former disinformation director, 225–26; conceived swastika operation, 234, 236, 431

"Agent Seven," presumed murderer of B. Lapusnyik, 195–96

Agents of Influence, 35–37, 112

Agriculture, Soviet, conditions on kolkhoz (collective farm) as revelation to V. N. Sakharov, 55–57; low living standards, 129; workers kept from cities, 135; chronic crisis, 450

Ahmad, Sheik Jaber el-, Kuwaiti Foreign Minister, 78

Ahram, Al, semiofficial Egyptian newspaper, 252

Air France. See Augros, Jean-Marie

Airplanes, hijacking by Arab terrorists, 77; Soviet plot to steal Lebanese Mirage, 245–53

Akhmerov, Robert Issakovich, directed KGB's Ghana operation, 343

Aksenov, Nikolai V., agent in Mexico, 316

Aksentyevich, Georgi, KGB Center officer, 424

Albania, 111

Aleksandrov, Yuri, KGB officer guarded B. Stashinsky, 428

"Alekseev, Aleksandr I." See Shitov, Aleksandr I.

"Alex." See Fomin, Aleksandr M.

Al Fatah. See Palestinian Guerrillas

Algeria, 298, 300

Alliluyeva, Svetlana, charged M. Sholokhov with plagiarism, 146; defamed by V. Louis, 242

Altunyan, Maj. Genrikh, imprisoned for possessing dissidents' writings, 20–21, 148

Amalrik, Andrei, imprisoned dissident writer on KGB's soundings of popular opinion, 14

Amtorg, Soviet trading company, 364

Anderson, Paul B., on religious adherents in U.S.S.R., 128

Andreyeva, Vera Ivanovina, KGB major and "wife" of "Gorbunov," 176, 177, 183, 187, 189–90

Andropov, Igor (son), friend of V. N. Sakharov, 39; favored treatment as student, 53, 54

Andropov, Yuri Vladimirovich, chairman of KGB and Politburo member, 14, 15, 97–99, 413; role in suppressing 1956 Hungarian revolt, 97; evaluates reports, 108

Antipov, Mikhail Mikhailovich ("Mike"), KGB agent formerly with Soviet U.N. delegation, 25, 414–15; supervised training of "Sabotka," 435–39

601

INDEX

ABOUT THE AUTHOR

JOHN BARRON is a Senior Editor of the *Reader's Digest*. He received bachelor and master degrees from the University of Missouri School of Journalism before serving in the U.S. Navy. Mr. Barron attended Naval Intelligence School, specializing in the Russian language, and was assigned to Berlin for two years as an intelligence officer. Upon release from the Navy in 1957, he went to work for the Washington *Star*, where his articles gained him national attention. Mr. Barron is the recipient of the Raymond Clapper Award; the George Polk Memorial Award for national reporting; the Washington Newspaper Guild Front Page Award for national reporting and the Newspaper Guild's grand award. He lives with his wife and two daughters in Falls Church, Virginia.